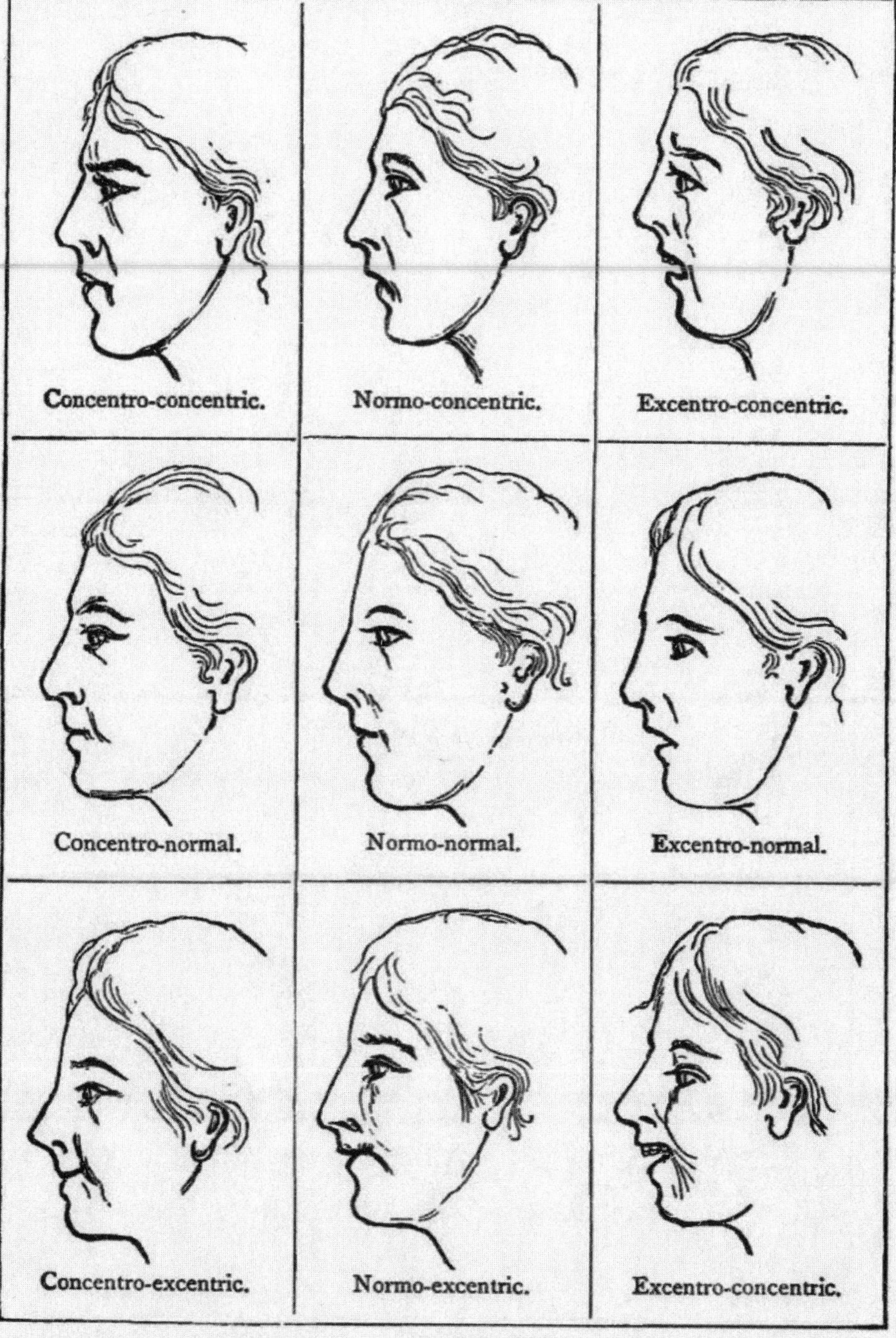
Concentro-concentric.
Normo-concentric.
Excentro-concentric.
Concentro-normal.
Normo-normal.
Excentro-normal.
Concentro-excentric.
Normo-excentric.
Excentro-concentric.

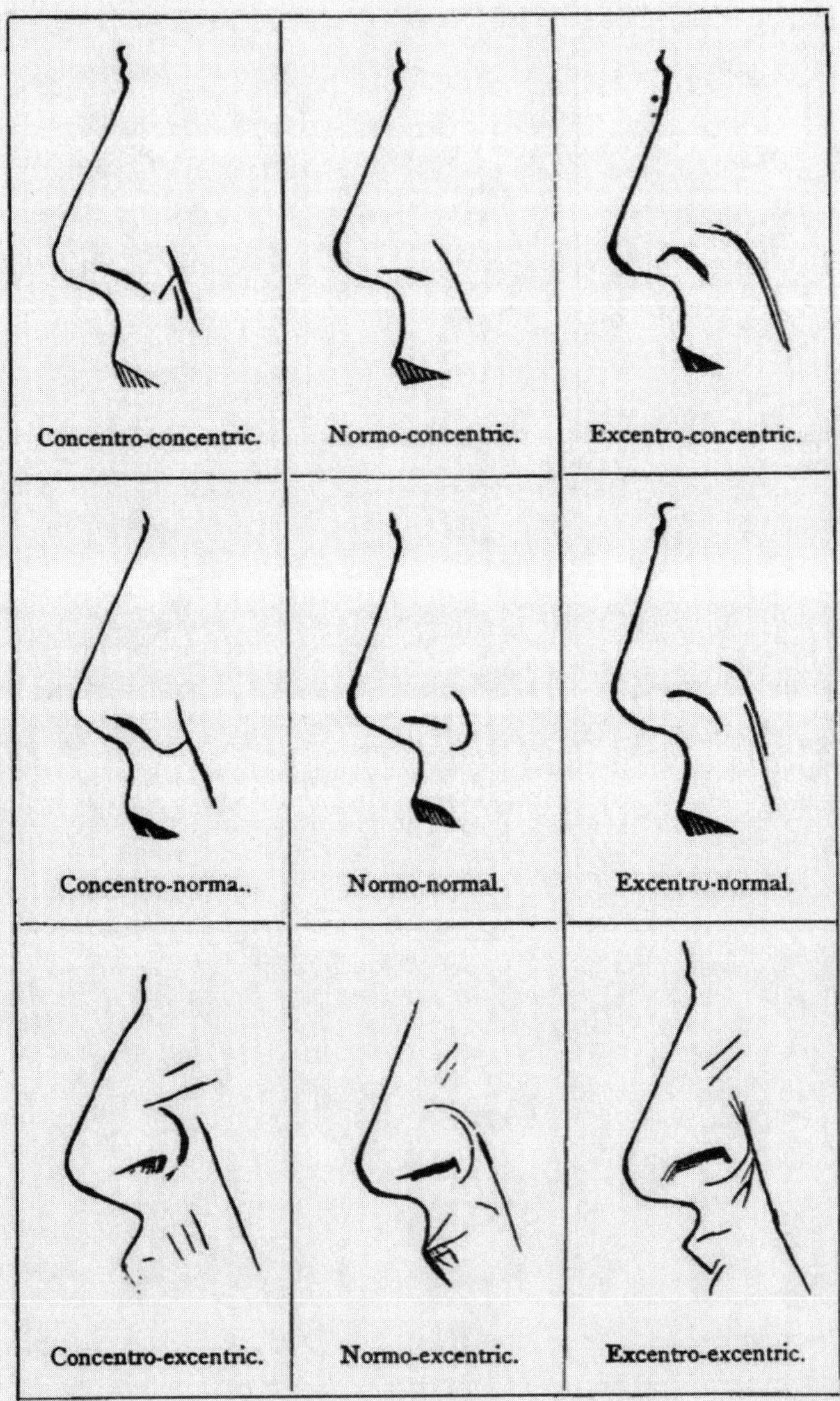
Concentro-concentric.
Normo-concentric.
Excentro-concentric.
Concentro-normal.
Normo-normal.
Excentro-normal.
Concentro-excentric.
Normo-excentric.
Excentro-excentric.

ALSO BY MARJORIE GARBER

The Muses on Their Lunch Hour

Loaded Words

The Use and Abuse of Literature

Shakespeare and Modern Culture

Patronizing the Arts

Profiling Shakespeare

Shakespeare After All

A Manifesto for Literary Studies

Quotation Marks

Academic Instincts

Sex and Real Estate: Why We Love Houses

Symptoms of Culture

Dog Love

Vice Versa: Bisexuality and the Eroticism of Everyday Life

Vested Interests: Cross-Dressing and Cultural Anxiety

Shakespeare's Ghost Writers: Literature as Uncanny Causality

Coming of Age in Shakespeare

Dream in Shakespeare

CHARACTER

CHARACTER

The History of a Cultural Obsession

MARJORIE GARBER

FARRAR, STRAUS AND GIROUX
New York

Farrar, Straus and Giroux
120 Broadway, New York 10271

Printed in the United States of America
First edition, 2020

Grateful acknowledgment is made for permission to reprint the following previously published material:
Excerpt from "'Richard Nixon,' Portrait of a Thin-Skinned, Media-Hating President," by Jennifer Senior, from *The New York Times*. © 2017 The New York Times. All rights reserved. Used under license.
Definition of "face book," from the *Oxford English Dictionary* (Oxford Publishing Limited, 1989), reproduced with permission of the Licensor through PLSclear.

Library of Congress Cataloging-in-Publication Data
Names: Garber, Marjorie, 1944– author.
Title: Character : the history of a cultural obsession / Marjorie Garber.
Description: First edition | New York : Farrar, Straus and Giroux, 2020. | Includes bibliographical references and index. | Summary: "An investigation into the concept of character, an enduring human obsession in literature, psychology, politics, and everyday life" —Provided by publisher.
Identifiers: LCCN 2020003433 | ISBN 9780374120856 (hardcover)
Subjects: LCSH: Character—History.
Classification: LCC BF818 .G31525 2020 | DDC 155.2—dc23
LC record available at https://lccn.loc.gov/2020003433

www.fsgbooks.com
www.twitter.com/fsgbooks • www.facebook.com/fsgbooks

10 9 8 7 6 5 4 3 2 1

Endpapers: Illustrations from *Delsarte System of Dramatic Expression*, 1886, by Genevieve Stebbins (Harvard University)

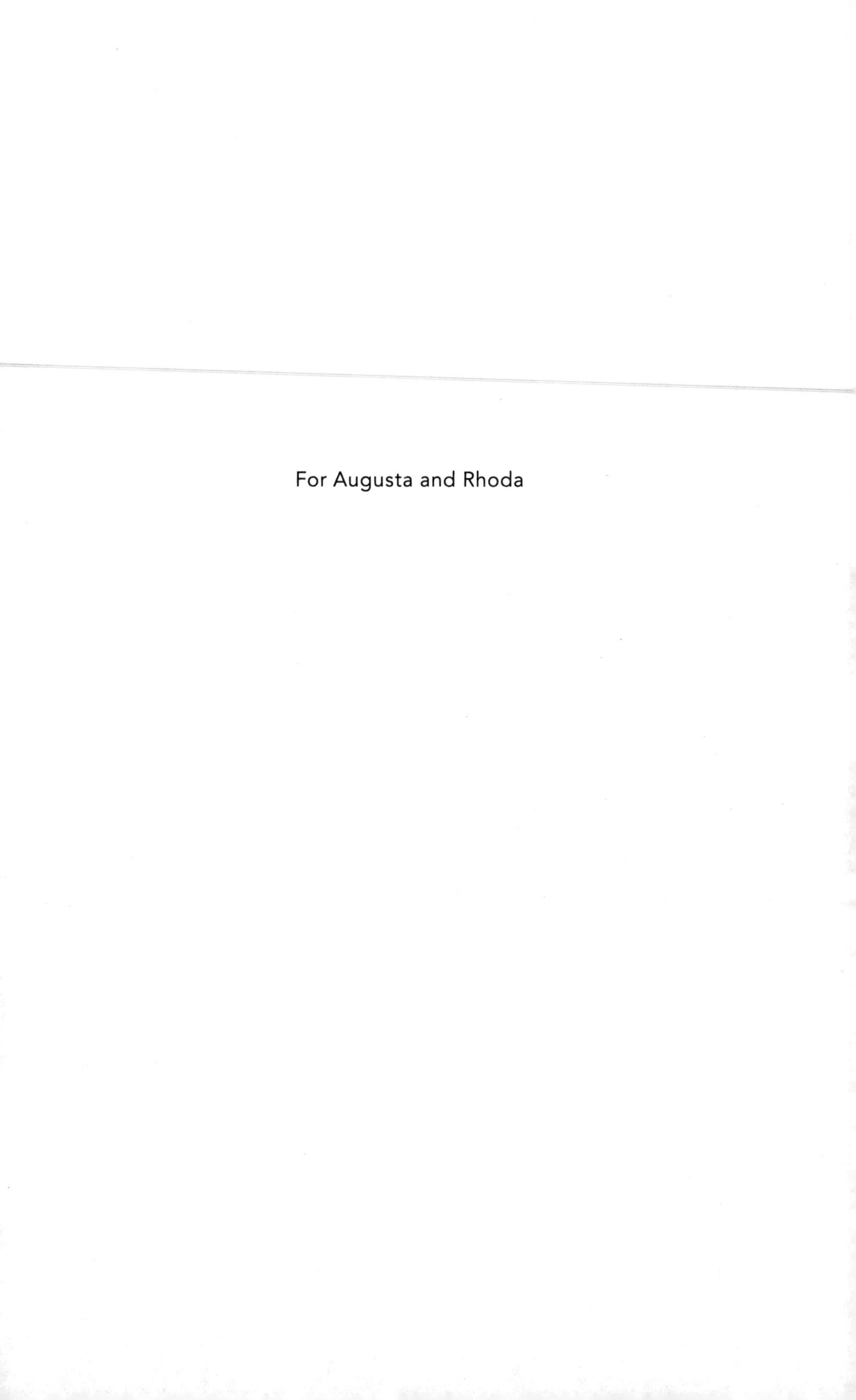

For Augusta and Rhoda

CONTENTS

INTRODUCTION: Character Witnesses 3

1. TESTING IT: Politics, Sports, Celebrity 23

2. TEACHING IT: Tales Out of School 57

3. CLAIMING IT: The Idea of National Character 131

4. READING IT: The Rise, Fall, and (Un)Surprising Return of Phrenology 195

5. NAMING IT: Psychoanalysis, Psychology, and the Emergence of "Personality" 240

6. SEEING IT: Art, Physiognomy, Photography, Gesture, Science 271

7. CHARACTER TYPES: Greeks, Geeks, Nerds—and Little Miss Hug 322

8. THE DIFFERENCE GENDER MAKES: Mettle, Spunk, and the Right Stuff 349

AFTERWORD: The Character Effect 375

Notes 385

Acknowledgments 425

Index 427

CHARACTER

INTRODUCTION

Character Witnesses

> A person whose desires and impulses are his own—are the expression of his own nature, as it has been developed and modified by his own culture—is said to have a character. One whose desires and impulses are not his own, has no character, no more than a steam-engine has a character.
>
> —J. S. MILL, "ON LIBERTY"

> He had clearly that—something—which is not this quality or that quality, but all sorts of qualities summed up into what one calls "character."
>
> —VIRGINIA WOOLF, "A SKETCH OF THE PAST"

> Most Women have no Characters at all.
>
> —ALEXANDER POPE, "EPISTLE TO A LADY"

"I have character." Thus did my handcrafted wooden desk announce its own desirable imperfection. A printed card enclosed at the time of delivery offered advice to the prospective owner:

> The irregularities of hand-planing and scraping will be clearly visible. These "features" include the "wavey" feel of the wood surfaces, as well as the occasional nick or

> ridge . . . There will be variations in the grain and color of the wood. Remember that tiger maple is an abnormal growth pattern of hard or soft maple. Therefore numerous defects are usually present in each board.[1]

By this account, "character," in the world of furniture, is a matter of nicks, ridges, and scrapes, as well as of variations and defects—in fact, "*numerous* defects," perhaps the more the better—caused by "abnormal" growth patterns. What is prized, and pricey, are the flaws. Too much homogeneity, too unblemished a surface, too normal an appearance would lessen the amount of character, and thus the value of the piece. It was the flaws, in fact, that conferred the "character."

We might pause for a moment to reflect on the intended reader of this printed card, with its own artfully antiqued blots and smears. Was the company's concern that a buyer, having chosen a piece with these specific "features" (the quotation marks are in the original), might, having brought the furniture home, begin to have second thoughts, focusing on the very qualities of handmade-ness, the very "irregularities," that make the object unique and interesting? Uniformity of surface, whether achieved in molded plastic or by expensive sanding and smoothing, would yield a very different look—and would in all likelihood have led the purchaser to shop in a very different store. I suppose it's possible to see this information, so kindly offered in such detail, as an act either of beneficial education or (alas) of inadvertent condescension. But I admired the desk. And I was intrigued by the way the manufacturer defined character.

The Character of "Character"

What is character? How can it be perceived, measured, assessed, developed, trained, or "built"? This question goes at least as far back as Aristotle. In every century, philosophers, moralists, artists, and scientists have engaged with the enigma of human character, its manifest expressiveness and its elusive essence. But it has never been more relevant, or more puzzling, than it is today.

Questions about the character of individuals in high places—often but not always politicians and jurists—have become flash points for public discussion. Yet, despite its periodic recurrence and persistent use, "character" remains one of the least understood of all modern terms.

Over its long history, the concept of character has been an incised mark, a moral idea, a type, a literary persona, a physical or physiological manifestation observable in works of art or in scientific experiments, an ingredient in drama, and the goal of various advocates of self-help. One of the most frequent issues still raised in all categories, national, personal, and fictional, is whether character is fixed or can change. Common phrases like "out of character" or "not in character" suggest that a person *has* an identifiable and readable character. Otherwise the observer could not—whether rightly or wrongly—detect an incompatibility between ideal and performance.

To "have" character (or to be a person "of character") is to be ethical and praiseworthy—or, as in the case of my desk, to show signs of experience and wear; to "be a character" is to be singular or eccentric; to have "character issues" is to fail to meet certain accepted standards for behavior; to be a "character type" is to cross boundaries across psychology, psychoanalysis, and literature. Neither too technical nor too colloquial, the word "character" has become a catchall term for a certain aspect of human—and sometimes, by projection, of animal—comportment. Whatever our definition, we often take both "character" and "characters" for granted, without thinking of the often contradictory uses to which this richly problematic and fascinating word is put.

Is character innate, learned, taught, or instilled? Are character traits fixed or changeable? Do they depend on heredity, on environment, on parents, teachers, mentors, or life experiences? Why do so many of our contemporary "character" phrases incline toward the negative (character flaw, character problem, character issue, character assassination)? Perhaps it's precisely because we accord a kind of numinous but empty value to "having character" that it has become so common to note its absence, or its quirky presence. And what is the relationship between "character" in the ethical or moral sense—a category that seems to have replaced "the soul" or "human nature" as something that we believe is within us—and "character" in the sense of the personae of fiction and drama, the "characters" of a novel or a play?

The word "character" in its oldest usage derives from a word for engraving or stamping, and came quickly to mean the *thing* engraved or stamped (for example, the characters of the alphabet) as well as the *process* by which these things came into being. A written "character reference" became over time shortened simply to a "character," so that an employer might say of a worker that he could give him or her a "good character," a testimonial to that person's probity and worth. The cemetery grave marker, with its inscription ("beloved mother"; "honored soldier") attested to the "character" of the dead person with "characters" incised in stone.

With the digital revolution, the old idea of a character as a distinctive mark or brand has reappeared (think Twitter's 140 or 280 "characters," or the "character recognition" capacities of some computer software). Over time, the notion of being engraved or "written" became associated with what we would now call character traits or dispositions, both on the stage and in social and political life. For a long time, this idea of character as something akin to persona or personality was the dominant one in common usage.

Fates and Flaws

But character also derives from another Greek word, later adapted into Latin, which meant moral principles, a word that survives in the modern "ethics," and was the title of two of Aristotle's treatises. The famous saying attributed to Heraclitus, *ēthos anthropos daimon*, is commonly translated as "Character for man is fate." "Fate," however complex a concept in ancient Greece, is no writing instructor's favorite idea, since it suggests an inevitability that is in application often merely tautologous ("it was fate" doesn't explain much, unless it explains Everything). But even if we bracket "fate" for a moment, what does the word "character" mean in this statement? In drama, and in literature generally, it seems to imply a kind of interior causality (Oedipus's tragedy was not that he married his mother and killed his father but, rather, like the relentlessly inquisitive detective he was, that he discovered that he had done so).

The tendency to hunt for, identify, and name the "tragic flaw" or "character flaw," as if there were a singular personality trait (hubris, ambition, jealousy, indecision, etc.) that somehow causes the downfall of the hero, carries over into journalism, biography, and politics. "[Politician A] says [Politician B's] extramarital affair showed a character flaw. But [A] says [B] had a good track record in terms of his actions as governor."[2] Or, "If [X, an actor] were a character from classical literature, his fidelity would be his tragic flaw."[3]

The "tragic flaw," as many recent translators of Aristotle's *Poetics* have noted, is an inexact translation of the Greek word *hamartia*, a word that is now taken to mean something closer to ignorance or error. The classical scholar and translator Stephen Halliwell suggests, "No particular English translation evidently recommends itself for this term," especially "in view of the fact that several of the possible candidates—error, fault, mistake, flaw—have been closely associated with various attempts to pin the word down to a restricted sense." Since a translator must, in practice, select among the options, Halliwell suggests that "the terms 'fallibility' and 'failing'" are "the least prejudicial ones available," but he notes that it is not possible to find a precise equivalent, and concludes that "there is much to be said, somewhat ironically, for avoiding a consistent translation for the term."[4]

Halliwell is also careful to point out that the modern idea of psychological inwardness, which we now often associate with character—especially in the novel or the dramatic soliloquy, which seem to allow the reader to enter the mind of the protagonist—would be at variance with Aristotle's definition of character in the *Poetics*, emphasizing as it does the element of "deliberate moral choice." Character "represents the ethical qualities of actions," and characters, in the sense of the persons of the drama, are not activated by "personality or individuality," but by the "manifestation of moral choice in word or action"—that is, what they *say* and what they *do*. This is the connection between "'character,' an attribute of persons, and 'characterisation,' a property of the work of art"—both encompassed by Aristotle's use of the word *ēthos*.[5]

The fact that "character flaw" is a flawed translation has not, of course, kept the phrase from use. In fact, it is fairly ubiquitous, and nowhere more so than in the self-help industry. A typical modern entry in the character-improvement category, *Flawless! The Ten Most Common Character Flaws and What You Can Do About Them* (1999) charts the bad stuff—raging indignation, the fixing of blame and nurturing of resentments, worry and fear, intolerance, addiction to being right, inadequacy, hypocrisy, martyr syndrome, and other, similarly alluring flaws—while advising the reader on how to develop "great strength of character" by overcoming them. "Every one of us has a fundamental flaw, an immaturity of character, a dark side or negative tendency. This character flaw, also known as a 'Chief Feature', tends to take control whenever we feel stressed, anxious or uncertain. To the extent that you can identify and handle yours, you are doing well in your personal growth."[6]

The author acknowledges at the outset that, at least among celebrities in politics and the arts, "the most flawed people seem to be among the most captivating," and this seeming contradiction, between the ordinary person's wish to get rid of character flaws and the celebrity whose fame is something dependent on them, is another major concern of his book.

Moral Character

What is sometimes called "moral character" is character for which the individual is, or is thought to be, responsible: qualities like those of judgment, fairness, financial and ethical probity, honor. Other terms, like "temperament," or phrases like "fitness for office," are sometimes used instead of "character," as we will see when we come to consider recent political campaigns.

Descriptions of "good" or "virtuous" moral character often also take their starting point from Aristotle, who describes virtue in book II of the *Nicomachean Ethics* as "a state of character concerned with choice, lying in a mean, i.e., the mean relative to us, this being determined by reason, and by that reason by which the man of practical wisdom would determine it."[7] The "mean" is "between two vices," one of which depends on "excess," and the other on "defect," or lack. But, he goes on to say, some actions and passions don't "admit of a mean"—feelings like spite, shamelessness, and envy, actions like adultery, theft, and murder. These are always bad—"however they are done they are wrong." On the other hand, temperance and courage are among his prized qualities, and here, too, there is no excess or deficiency—one can't be excessively temperate, or moderately courageous.

Aristotle goes on to describe some of the virtues he thinks most important. "With regard to giving and taking of money the mean is liberality, the excess and the defect prodigality and meanness." "With regard to honour and dishonour the mean is proper pride, the excess is known as a sort of 'empty vanity', and the deficiency is undue humility." With anger, too, there is a mean, though the names for these, he says, are harder to identify: "let us call the mean good-temper," and "the one who exceeds be called irascible." With truth, "the mean may be called truthfulness, while the pretence which exaggerates is called boastfulness, and the person characterized by it a boaster, and that which understates is mock modesty." As for pleasantness, there are two kinds. In "amusement," the mean is being "ready-witted," the extremes "buffoonery" and "boorishness"; in general pleasantness, the mean is "friendliness," the extremes "obsequiousness" and flattery on one side, quarrelsomeness and surliness on the other.[8]

Theophrastus, Aristotle's pupil and successor, drew on similar excesses and deficiencies in the writing of his famous "Characters," creating The Flatterer, The Surly Man, The Bore, and other enduring character types that would continue to be imitated, in prose and drama, through the Renaissance to the eighteenth and nineteenth centuries. As so often, "bad" characters had more literary appeal—and sometimes more political appeal—than "virtuous" ones.

One other key point from the *Nicomachean Ethics* is also worth a special note, since it, too, will recur in later discussions of character and "character building": Aristotle's stress on the importance of "habit." Moral virtue, he says at the beginning of his second chapter, "comes about as a result of habit, whence also its name (*êthikê*) is one that is formed by a slight variation from the word *ēthos* (habit)." The moral virtues do not arise directly from nature—rather, "we are adapted by nature to receive them, and are made perfect by habit."[9] Many self-described "character-training" programs—like the Boy Scouts and the Girl Guides—would later come to stress the importance of habit, or what we today would call "good habits," since "bad habits" (smoking, slouching, drinking, idleness) are also easy to develop with practice.

Commonplacing

For centuries, before there were published collections of quotations, readers, writers, and scholars assembled for themselves what were known as "commonplace books" to record important facts and sentiments. Hamlet gives us an early example of commonplacing, recording what he has learned about murder from his father's ghost: "My tables—meet it is I set it down / That one may smile and smile and be a villain" (*Hamlet* 1.5.108–109). "Tables" are tablets—Hamlet is taking notes (or rhetorically pretending to do so), later, presumably, to inscribe this bromide into his own collection of political verities. Polonius, in the same play, is demonstrably experienced in the same practice, as perhaps a politician in the period would have had to be. His advice to his son Laertes—"neither a borrower nor a lender be"; "give every man thine ear, but few thy voice"; "the apparel oft proclaims the man"; "this above all, to thine own self be true" (*Hamlet* 1.3.58–80)—was for many years one of the most quoted passages in the *Congressional Record.*

"These few precepts in thy memory / See thou character," Polonius tells Laertes, using the old word for "write down," one of the earliest meanings of "character." Laertes, if he wants a successful career, is urged to memorize, if not also to inscribe, the borrowed wisdom that his father has gleaned from a lifetime of public service. We may note that Polonius also cautions his son to be "familiar, but by no means vulgar," though the modern sense of vulgarity as "coarsely commonplace, lacking in good taste" had not yet fully developed. In brief—although Polonius is never brief—Laertes is to improve his *character* ("moral and mental constitution, personality")[10] by "charactering" ("writing down, inscribing")[11] the commonplaces assembled in what might fittingly be *characterized* as Polonius's Familiar (but not vulgar) Quotations.

The word "commonplace" is a translation from the Latin *locus communis*, defined as "a passage of general application," "a striking or notable passage."[12] Francis Bacon kept a commonplace book; so did John Milton, Samuel Taylor Coleridge, Ralph Waldo Emerson, and Henry David Thoreau. John Locke devised a system for indexing topics in his commonplace books under a general heading. "Unlike modern readers, who follow the flow of a narrative from beginning to end," notes the book historian Robert Darnton, "early modern Englishmen read in fits and starts and jumped from book to book. They broke texts into fragments and assembled them into new patterns by transcribing them in different sections of their notebooks."[13]

It took a couple of centuries for "commonplace" to deteriorate into what is virtually the opposite of its original meaning: trite, trivial, hackneyed, ordinary rather than extraordinary. By the nineteenth century, a commonplace was a platitude or truism: thus the historian Macaulay could write with deft scorn about "the commonplaces which all sects repeat so fluently when they are enduring oppression, and forget so easily when they are able to retaliate it,"[14] and Benjamin Jowett, the great translator of Plato, could suggest that "the paradoxes of one age often become the commonplaces of the next."[15] One of the favorite topics for collection and quotation, from the earliest times to the present, has been the description of human character.

Today it is easy to find commonplaces about character. Like all quotations, these excerpts are out of context, and since the compilers do not give any bibliographical information, it's unlikely that most quoters will check the source to see if the phrase in context is ironic. (Reading the whole of Polonius's speech, for example, might suggest some second thoughts about citing "Shakespeare's" views on borrowing and lending.) Still, one finds bromides that, secured between quotation marks and ascribed to great men (and the occasional woman), seem to declare certain truths about character. Here are just a few, selected from the abundance of Web sites dedicated to listing such things.

- "Character is the only secure foundation of the state." —Calvin Coolidge
- "Character is a by-product, and any man who devotes himself to its cultivation in his own case will become a selfish prig." —Woodrow Wilson
- "You must not give power to a man unless, above everything else, he has character. Character is the most important qualification the President of the United States can have." —Richard Nixon (from a 1964 TV ad for Barry Goldwater)
- "Politics ruins the character." —Otto von Bismarck

- "The politics of character tend to drive out the politics of substance." —Judith Lichtenberg
- "Character is power." —Booker T. Washington
- "Dreams are the touchstones of our character." —Henry David Thoreau
- "You cannot dream yourself into a character, you must hammer and forge yourself one." —James A. Froude
- "Between ourselves and our real natures we interpose that wax figure of idealizations and selections which we call our character." —Walter Lippmann

Even the most cursory glance will reveal that these high-sounding phrases, each of them—at least in the moment of reading—carrying conviction, are at odds with one another, and sometimes, as in the case of the future president Richard Nixon, at odds with the speaker's own "character" as revealed by subsequent events.

For this is the thing—or one of the things—about character. It inspires and provokes grand pronouncements. But if you push on the word itself, it often turns out to be enigmatic and elusive. Try replacing this word with another one in any of the quotations above. The list thus generated would, assuming one could manage it with a single word, be far from consistent in connotation—and probably no more susceptible to proof.

Character and "Moral Order"

Two popular books by the Scottish author Samuel Smiles, *Self-Help* (1859) and *Character* (1871), offered motivational advice and moral encouragement, praising the achievements of working-class and lower-middle-class people while extolling character as "the crown and glory of life," "the noblest possession of a man, constituting a rank in itself," "more powerful than wealth and less susceptible to envy."[16]

By the middle of the nineteenth century, character was fully established not only as a desirable but also as an achievable quality. It had two great advantages: it was seemingly secular, or at least not tied to any one religion. And it did not depend upon social station or on wealth.

"Character," declared Smiles, "is human nature in its best form. It is moral order embodied in the individual."[17] In this last observation, quoted from the chapter of *Self-Help* titled "Character—the True Gentleman," Smiles is borrowing freely from Ralph Waldo Emerson, whose 1844 essay on "Character" had said, "Character is this moral order seen through the medium of an individual nature"[18]—a phrase that reappears years later as an epigraph in Smiles's own book on character. As its title implies, "Character—the True Gentleman" argued that integrity, uprightness, honor, and self-respect, all defining aspects of character, were more important than noble birth. Words like "noble" and "gentle," long associated with social rank, were re-envisioned as personal qualities rather than hereditary entitlements. "Noble character" was achievable by anyone; "gentleness is indeed the best test of gentlemanliness."

The Smiles method combined inspiring maxims with brief biographies and historical examples: the subtitle of *Self-Help* announced that the book included *Illustrations of Character, Conduct, and Perseverance.* The same method, which had proved so successful, was used in *Character* (and in the subsequently published volumes on *Thrift* and *Duty*). Virtuous platitudes like "Although genius always commands admiration, character most secures respect," "A condition of comparative poverty is compatible with character in its highest form," "Intellectual culture has no necessary relation to purity or excellence of character," "Character is property," and "There are many persons of whom it may be said that they have no other possession in the world but their character, and yet they stand as firmly upon it as any crowned king"[19] all aimed at a readership for which character was both a desirable and an apparently achievable commodity.

Smiles wrote in 1871 that men of character "appear to act by means of some latent power, some reserved force, which acts secretly, by mere presence."[20] Emerson had written in 1844, "This is that which we call Character,—a reserved force which acts directly by presence, and without means."[21] Was Smiles working with Emerson's text before him, or had he taken notes from his previous reading? The correspondences are too close to be accidental, but although there are many footnotes and citations in Smiles's *Character*, Emerson's essay is not among them. Nor was Emerson his only unacknowledged model. As we've noted, Benjamin Disraeli wrote (in his 1835 *Vindication of the English Constitution*) that "nations have characters, as well as individuals"[22]; over thirty years later, Smiles declares in *Character*, without any indication that he is borrowing another's words, "Nations have their character to maintain as well as individuals."[23] We may think that this genial plagiarism reflects poorly on Samuel Smiles's own character. But his works often read like modern versions of the old "commonplace book." In any case, he had his subject, and his audience. The topic appealed to readers at all levels of education and sophistication. "Character" was a major preoccupation and a topic of almost endless interest.

"The man of character is conscientious," Smiles says. "The man of character is also reverential."[24] And what about a *woman* of character? She was, unsurprisingly, to be found in the home. "If we would have fine characters, we must necessarily present before them fine models. Now, the model most constantly before every child's eye is the Mother."[25]

> Woman, above all other educators, educates humanly. Man is the brain, but woman is the heart of humanity; he its judgment, she its feeling; he its strength, she its grace, ornament, and solace . . . Though man may direct the intellect, woman cultivates the feelings, which mainly determine the character.[26]

Smiles offers numerous examples of men whose characters were molded by their mothers, including Napoleon, George Herbert, Oliver Cromwell, Samuel Johnson, and Saint Augustine. Nothing is said directly about women molded by mothers. But women, like men, are encouraged to acquire skills in arithmetic and other "habits of business," since, "to direct the power of the home aright, women, as the nurses, trainers, and educators of children, need all the help and strength that mental culture can give them."[27] Smiles sets small store by the cultivation of "fleeting accomplishments" that "may enhance the charms of youth and beauty." Women influence "the morals, manners, and character of the people in all countries," so that "to instruct woman is to instruct man; to elevate her character is to raise his own."[28] But their spheres are different. Women, in effect, should know their (privileged) place.

> While it is certain that the character of a nation will be elevated by the enlightenment and refinement of women, it is much more than doubtful whether any advantage is to be derived from her entering into competition with man in the rough work of business and politics. Women can no more do men's special work in the world than men can do women's.[29]

When this has been tried, he reports, "the result has been socially disastrous," as, for example, in Paris: "The women there mainly attend to business," while the men "lounge about the Boulevards." Nor, thought Smiles, would it help to give women the vote. "To form the whole character of the human race" by their work in the home was surely more valuable than anything women could accomplish by voting for members of Parliament, "or even as lawmakers."[30] None of this should surprise us. Smiles does not present himself as either a social theorist or a reformer. The popularity of his work was based in part on its very predictability. Character had come of age as a social bromide.

Character, Self-Help, and Leadership

Today's self-help industry could hardly do without character and its discontents. From Smiles's *Self-Help* through works of "self-instruction" and "self-education" emerging from popular phrenology and the Boy Scout movement, character development has been linked to efforts at self-improvement and self-betterment.

Where there is self-help, there is also inspiration, aspiration, and also sometimes perspiration. Books with titles like *Character Matters* are written by missionaries, evangelists, and motivational speakers. Handbooks like *Character Makeover: 40 Days with a Life Coach to Create the Best You* stress what are identified as Christian aspects of character development, listing Humility, Confidence, Courage, Self-Control, Patience, Contentment, Generosity, and Perseverance as goals, and including, in an appendix, "scripture-rich" prayers for each character trait.[31]

These are works aimed at the consumer, the person, male or female, alone or in book clubs or church groups, who seeks to improve relationships, with others, with himself or herself, or with God. But at the high-net-worth end of this spectrum there has emerged a new industry aimed at business-school students and graduates, CEOs, presidents of companies and of universities, and others who seek not only to win friends but also to influence people.

"Leadership" is one of the contemporary buzzwords for what used to be called "character training" or "character building." Once aimed primarily at the young, the leadership industry has expanded over the years, but the goals of "success" remain consistent over time. Robert Baden-Powell, Dale Carnegie, and professors at modern schools of management and business all provide hints, tips, rules, and laws to guide future leaders through steps to develop character and capital. With the proliferation of leadership institutes and programs across the country and around the world, there has been a boom in business books on leadership and character aimed at popular audiences: *George Washington's Leadership Lessons: What the Father of Our Country Can Teach Us About Effective Leadership and Character*; *Robert E. Lee on Leadership: Executive Lessons in Character, Courage, and Vision*; *Questions of Character: Illuminating the Heart of Leadership Through Literature*.[32]

Leadership institutes for CEOs often focus on literary characters as imaginative triggers to explore choices in the world: what would Antigone or Portia or Henry V do when confronted with this or that situation? Somehow these fictional beings take on an imaginative reality that allows for identification and transference. If you were Falstaff, would you have your errant companions hanged, or would you pardon them? The method of the instructors is to use such characters to help develop character.

This practice raises a question that will recur regularly throughout this book. Call it the *back-formation of character*. Are our notions about fictional characters (Odysseus, Hecuba, Iago, Lady Macbeth, Jane Austen's heroines, the "antihero" of film noir, the lone cowboy, the Marvel superhero) in fact driving and helping to produce our ideas about "character"? Which comes first—literature or "life"? The answers are sometimes surprising. Scholars, theorists, scientists, and other investigators of human character have turned to literature to explain, describe, and label character types met with in life. Greek tragic heroes, Oedipus to Antigone, and fictionally enhanced biographies, from Alexander the Great to George Washington, have given both their names and their stories to the construction of character traits and character types.

For many years, though, and increasingly in the present, the go-to author for such inferences and proof-texts has been Shakespeare. Here are a few of my favorite titles: *Inspirational Leadership: Timeless Lessons for Leaders from Shakespeare's Henry V*; *Power Plays: Shakespeare's Lessons in Leadership and Management*; *Shakespeare in Charge: The Bard's Guide to Leading and Succeeding on the Business Stage*; *Shakespeare on Management: Leadership Lessons for Today's Managers.*[33] And there are more.

Shakespeare and Human Character

When early critics used the term "human nature" in describing the wisdom of Shakespeare's works, they often attributed both the knowledge and the essence of that "nature" not to human experience but to Shakespeare. Shakespeare was the author who provided, through his dramatic characters, not only powerful "imitations" of human conduct, emotion, and attitude, but the blueprint, the language, and the responses that taught us how to be us.

Not only was the study of Shakespeare's characters, from very early days, virtually equivalent to the study of Shakespeare, but it also seems as if the characters in effect preceded and then exceeded the plays, proving that Shakespeare knew human nature better than human nature knew itself. As the poet and Shakespeare editor Alexander Pope would write in the early eighteenth century, Shakespeare's characters were so true to "Nature" that "'tis a sort of injury to call them by so distant a name as Copies of her." Moreover, each character was unique in his or her own way, and exemplified that uniqueness in language: "Every single character in Shakespeare is as much an Individual, as those in Life itself; it is impossible to find any two alike . . . Had all the Speeches been printed without the very names of the Persons, I believe one might have apply'd them with certainty to every speaker."[34]

Consider, as just one telling example, the "lifelike" qualities of

Shakespeare's female characters. Juliet, Beatrice, Cordelia, Lady Macbeth, Volumnia, Constance, Miranda—each of these and many more have been singled out for their truth to nature, as young lovers, attentive and caring daughters, ambitious (or, in Constance's case, tender) wives and mothers. Yet there were no women players on the English stage in Shakespeare's lifetime. All these persuasive and incomparable roles were written for young men, for "boy players" whose voices had not yet broken.

It was not only women, of course, but also mankind in general and in particular that Shakespeare was thought to have nailed in his dramatic characterizations. Hamlet's truth to life was so compelling that virtually every major critic echoed or anticipated Coleridge's "I have a smack of Hamlet myself, if I may say so."[35] Names like Shylock and Romeo became familiar synonyms for "moneylender" and "lover," sometimes, especially in the case of Shylock, with unflattering associations ("shylocks" and "shylocker" appearing, sometimes, as lowercase nouns). Portia and Caliban are among other Shakespearean characters whose names have made it to a modern dictionary. In some cases the reader is expected to recognize the reference, but not in others; "Romeo," capitalized or lower case, is often used today to mean a philanderer or womanizer, rather than, as in Shakespeare's play, a lover so faithful that he kills himself for love.

Does Shakespeare create "character," or does character create "Shakespeare"? Both may be true. In the graceful formulation of the eighteenth-century Scottish historian William Guthrie, "It is not Shakespeare who speaks the language of nature, but nature rather speaks the language of Shakespeare."[36] Today that language still informs many of our convictions and beliefs. In psychological, sociological, and sometimes philosophical terms—as well as in literary studies—it is often Shakespeare who defines character and character types for the modern world.

Character Traits and Character Types

To psychoanalysts, traits of character have often been understood as "collections of defense mechanisms" mobilized by an individual. For that reason, broadly speaking, they can have a negative rather than a positive connotation. Two of Freud's earliest essays on character were "Psychopathic Characters on the Stage" (written in 1905 or 1906, though not published until 1942) and "Character and Anal Erotism" (1908); he had been thinking about Oedipus (and Hamlet) as early as his correspondence with Wilhelm Fleiss. Significantly, Freud tended to find examples of these problems in literary and dramatic characters (Richard III, the Macbeths, Ibsen's Rebecca West, as well as Oedipus and Hamlet); in his reading of these texts, the character problem generates the dramatic situation. Psychologists, following (and disputing with) Gordon Allport, have speculated about the concept of the "trait," a term that goes back to Freud, as well as to essay writers like Emerson. What is a "character trait," and—again—are such traits fixed or changeable?

And how does "character" differ from "personality"? The *Diagnostic and Statistical Manual of Mental Disorders*, published by the American Psychiatric Association, some time ago replaced the phrase "character disorders" with "personality disorders" in most familiar cases, and the *DSM-5*, which came out in 2013, sorts personality disorders into a range of categories, including odd or eccentric disorders (paranoid, schizoid); dramatic, emotional, or erratic disorders (antisocial, borderline, histrionic, narcissistic); anxious or fearful disorders (avoidant, dependent, obsessive-compulsive personality disorder); and personality changes caused by other medical conditions. To psychiatrists (as well as to psychologists and other theorists of social functioning), the distinction between "character" and "personality" is an important one. But pinning it down is not easy.

Some claim that character is related to ethics, values, and morals, whereas personality is connected to social interaction and behavior. "Character is what people make of themselves intentionally," says the psychiatrist Robert Cloninger, citing Kant.[37] But such distinctions sometimes break down when applied to specific cases, and in the varying uses of analysts and experts—and in public and political speech. Which "personality disorders" are treatable? Is a successful treatment one that changes the personality (or the "character"), or are these elements of the psyche fixed, even if they are not stable? Is character, as some analysts have claimed, a "style"? Is it (still) appropriate to talk about "character pathology"?

What does the word "character" mean in such circumstances? How is it different from the insistence that character is inborn, innate, heritable? Is character essence or performance? Inside or outside the "self"?

Performing Character

Actors and playwrights, experimenting with this question of character and interiority, have provided what is in effect a performance laboratory. In his famous *Paradox of the Actor*, Diderot claimed that, in order to move the audience, the actor himself must remain unmoved. Method acting claims the opposite: the actor should inhabit the emotions of his or her character, walk the walk, talk the talk. Is character the same as role? In modern and postmodern performance, Brecht's *Good Person of Szechwan* to TV's *The Good Wife*, the moral or ethical notion of character is sometimes the object of irony or silent commentary. Perhaps the most cited phrase about the actor's job in delineating character is Hamlet's "to hold as 'twere the mirror up to nature"—but it is worth considering that a mirror produces a *reversed* image. Is character intrinsic, or reflected?

Words like "reflection" are crucial here, because character, though we often regard it as intrinsic and essential to the individual, is in fact often produced by interactions *between* people, by perception and performance, whether in an ethical dilemma or in an act of perceived bravery or heroism. Character, though we claim it can be built, developed, assessed (and increasingly, in schools, graded on report cards), is an elusive entity.

Perhaps nowhere in modern life does the word "character" occur more insistently than in descriptions of athletes and sporting events, whether on television, in the morning paper, or at the breakfast table. The publisher's blurb for Frank Deford's *The Heart of a Champion: Celebrating the Spirit and Character of Great American Sports Heroes* says the book "presents the inspirational stories of great athletes and sports champions from the past seventy-five years who have been featured on Wheaties boxes."[38] But the world of sports is also where we sometimes find stories of character lapses. Books like *Sport and Character: Reclaiming the Principles of Sportsmanship*, by Craig Clifford and Randolph M. Feezell, both philosophy professors, urge that competitive sports can (still) teach character development. "In an era when our nightly news is filled with reports of athletes run amok on the field, on the court, and on the street, and when cheating by players and coaches has become part of the daily discourse," the Amazon write-up declares, "sportsmanship has never been a more timely topic." The timeliness is underscored by a change of title; an edition of the book was published twelve years previously as *Coaching for Character.*[39]

Meanwhile, the word "coach," now often in the context of "life coach," has gone even more mainstream. In this case, sports lingo crosses over to self-help, even in contexts where it might not be expected. Thus, for example, the back cover of *Jesus, Life Coach: Learn from the Best*, a business book aimed at CEOs, exhorts, "Don't be left in the stands just watching the game of life, when you could become the star pitcher, the starting quarterback, your team's most valuable player."[40]

If the athlete—or the actor—is seen as a model, what is the more general role of physicality in assessing character? Does a firm handshake indicate strength of character? Does someone who "looks you in the eye" demonstrate trustworthiness? (If so, does a person who looks away—whether out of shyness, deference, nervousness, or fear—"lack character"?) Can character be judged by appearance, by clothing and body style, by choices of ornament, by hairdos and tattoos? All of these have been used as markers in the past, whether loudly proclaimed or insistently whispered. From business deals to organized sports to the history of cultural, sexual, and racial prejudice, such questions, broadly and imprecisely linked to "character," have often made a palpable difference in individual lives.

The Character Issue

The phrase "character issue," as a euphemism for perceived moral or ethical failings, is often used in relation to public figures, whether they are politicians, sports heroes, or celebrities. An article called "Thomas

Jefferson and the Character Issue"[41] intimates by its title that it will be discussing Jefferson's liaison with the enslaved Sally Hemings—in this case noting that, "in effect, something that before the 1960s would have been universally considered a shameful blot on Jefferson's character has become almost an asset." "Character issues" might also appear on school report cards or less formal communications to parents, again as an umbrella term for a range of misbehaviors.

The chapters that follow address other "character issues," like "character education," psychology and psychoanalysis, character types, visual character, ethics and virtue, gender and character, and some once-reputable, now less respected and understood, modes of "character reading," such as phrenology and physiognomy.

The question of "character" arises in virtually every aspect of human life today. And in just about every one, there is the same fundamental tension, between something regarded as innate, inborn, or intrinsic to the individual, and something that can be taught, imitated, or copied. This book explores the stakes of these conflations, confusions, and heritages, from Aristotle, Theophrastus, and Plutarch to the present media preoccupation with "character issues," "character assassination," and the "character flaws" of celebrities, politicians, and other people in public life.

1 TESTING IT

Politics, Sports, Celebrity

> Let there be some more test made of my metal,
> Before so noble and so great a figure
> Be stamped upon it.
>
> —SHAKESPEARE, *MEASURE FOR MEASURE*

> The test of greatness is the page of history.
>
> —WILLIAM HAZLITT, *TABLE-TALK*

> It goes to character. You don't realize how important character is in the highest office in the land until you don't have it.
>
> —U.S. REPRESENTATIVE ADAM SCHIFF, IMPEACHMENT TRIAL OF DONALD JOHN TRUMP, JANUARY 24, 2020

Character Above All was the soaring title of a collection of essays on American presidents, by skilled observers including Doris Kearns Goodwin, Tom Wicker, David McCullough, and Peggy Noonan. The book was published in 1995. Viewed from the perspective of contemporary politics, it seems a lifetime ago. Noonan followed up her brief piece on Ronald Reagan—which, like the others, was initially delivered in a lecture series at the University of Texas at Austin—with a lengthier soft-focus panegyric called *When Character Was King*. These titles may seem at best nostalgic, and at worst deluded, to anyone observing political conduct today.

The idea of character in politics is hardly a new concern, of course, in this or any other century. But it was a recurrent issue in the post-Nixon and post-Watergate era, with more press, more media outlets, more competition for stories, more "-gates," and every man or woman his or her own Woodward or Bernstein. And from the Clinton years to the Trump presidency, the issue has ratcheted up, with the invaluable assistance of cable television and social media. In addition to the "character flaw" and the "character issue" and the "character question," there is the "character test," which must be "passed" (or "failed") by the aspiring candidate.

What exactly is a "character test"? Is it a defining moment, an ethical conundrum, a legal standard, a lifelong history, a crisis in publicity or in private life? Consider the following newspaper headlines, all of which appeared in *The New York Times* over the course of the last several decades:

- "'Heresy Hunt' Charged: Character Test for Teachers Is Assailed by Liberties Group" (July 24, 1935)
- "Bridge an Aid in Life: National Guard Chaplain Sees Characters Tested in Game" (August 30, 1937)
- "Second 'Character Test' Will Be Made Today at Maryland–West Virginia Football Game" (November 24, 1951)
- "Character Tests May Delay Bingo: City Licensing Aide Cites Fingerprinting as a Factor" (November 29, 1958)
- "U.S. Court Upholds State Law Requiring a Bar Character Test" (February 18, 1969)
- "Coping with Celebrity, the Red Carpet Character Test" (September 27, 2007)

Although none of these directly addresses the question of a "character test" for elected officials or candidates for high office, they are of interest, both individually and collectively, as illustrations of this modern-sounding term.

The National Guard chaplain at Camp Smith in Peekskill, New York, suggested at a regimental Sunday service in 1937 that playing bridge might be a good test of character. "There are such activities in life as bridge and dancing which strengthen our characters and improve our personalities," he told the assembled troops. "Bridge, for example, helps a person to acquire unselfish habits."

The football "character test" in 1951 was a literal one. The two competing teams were to be judged not only by the points they scored on the field, but also on eight different categories of "character": "Respect for [the judges'] authority; will to compete (win or lose); bench conduct (coach, players); player conduct (on and off field); mental poise (under pressure); alertness (makes own breaks); perfection (coached in details); and physical fitness (as game ends)." As the headline notes, this was the second game at which this system had been tried. Two categories from the first, played the previous week between Swarthmore and Haverford Colleges, had been eliminated: "fan conduct (booing, rowdyism)" and "appearance (spic and span)" were replaced by "courage" and "enthusiasm."

The "Heresy Hunt" headline of 1935 introduces a more ominous kind of character test, a loyalty oath asked of New York City teachers who sought probationary licenses. The requirement was opposed by a branch of the city's Civil Liberties Committee, which said forthrightly, in 1935, that the test gave school officials "a power over the education of the youth of New York City of which Hitler himself might well be envious." The 1969 "Bar Character Test" case, decided by a divided court, preserved requirements for "character and fitness" as standard for lawyers, over the objections of those who found these terms so "vague" as to be unconstitutional. And the "Bingo" article, also concerned with ethics and values, explains the issue in its first line: "The problem of how to certify 'the good moral character' of bingo operators under recently enacted legislation has posed difficulties that could delay the game's legal start, scheduled here on Jan. 1." As for 2007's "Red Carpet Character Test," it turns out to be a test of designers, not celebrities. How would they handle the presence of stars sitting in the audience? "Too much genuflecting or too obvious a focus on red carpet dressing and a designer loses credibility with the professionals, however good a show might be for the picture-hungry Internet."

When a "character test" is applied in politics, rather than law or popular culture, the resonances of these other associations remain.

Hard-to-define phrases like "character and fitness" and "good moral character," combined with notions of sportsmanship, loyalty, and style, inflect both public and private judgment. Does the "moral character" of a politician matter if his or her practice produces, say, a strong economy? Or a passionate fan base? Is "character" an ascertainable value in politics? In amateur and professional sports? In that broad spectrum of activities we now group under the general heading of "celebrity"?

In the past, at least, a perceived failure in character could lead to the politician's being disciplined or voted out of office. "Successful" character tests for politicians tend to be associated with bravery in fields other than politics, like the military. When "good" character is described, it often has to do with activities like charitable volunteering, church attendance, and devotion to parents and family. "Ethical" is heard less often as praise than is "unethical" as criticism.

For other people in the public eye, "character" is again often measured by the revelation of its absence, or of the shortcomings (or criminal behavior) of individuals. To "fail the character test" is often to be caught or exposed for long-standing activities or long-held sentiments that have only recently come to light.

In Chris Hegedus and D. A. Pennebaker's 1993 documentary film *The War Room*, the reporter Sam Donaldson asks George Stephanopoulos about Bill Clinton's "character problem." "Governor Clinton doesn't have a character problem," replies Stephanopoulos, indignantly. "Bill Clinton has passed his character test throughout his life and this campaign."

"Mitt Romney has failed the character test," declared Democratic senator Mark Udall, after Romney, then a candidate for president, told wealthy donors in a private meeting that 47 percent of Americans believed they were "entitled to health care, to food, to housing," but that his job was "not to worry about those people."[1] Romney lost the election. Six years later, after a successful run for senator, he sounded off on Donald Trump's character in an op-ed in *The Washington Post*. "With the nation so divided, resentful and angry," Romney wrote, "presidential leadership in qualities of character is indispensable. And it is in this province where the incumbent's shortfall has been most glaring."[2]

"Mark Sanford Strikes Out on Character Tests,"[3] announced a *Post* opinion piece in February 2013, noting that the former South Carolina governor had lied to his staff and used public money to conduct an extramarital affair. By May of that year, Sanford had won a special election for a seat in his state's congressional delegation, prompting the same columnist, Jennifer Rubin, to observe, "Gone for good, I think, is the sense that behavior in your personal life reflects character and therefore is relevant to one's political qualifications."[4] In 2019 Sanford announced his brief candidacy for the presidency.

"Character" words became unavoidable as the nation's interest turned toward the 2020 elections, and some expressed a nostalgia for the recent past. "Obama embodied nearly every character trait you'd want in a president," wrote one columnist. "His personal integrity was unimpeachable, and he conducted himself with grace and class every day he served, no matter how despicable the attacks he endured." Lest anyone miss the intended contrast, the same writer went on to describe his successor, "a walking collection of character flaws who is possessed of not a single identifiable human virtue."[5]

Why do so many of our "character" phrases incline toward the negative—character test, character flaw, character problem, character issue, character assassination? Perhaps it's precisely because we accord a kind of numinous but empty value to "having character" that it has become so common to note its absence, or its presence in a rather warped form. If we examine the language of character attached to some of these episodes, we will be able to see something of the term's range of meanings, its increasingly negative vibe, and its ubiquity.

Character-Gate

Before the presidency of Donald Trump, it was hard to imagine that things could be worse than in previous years, when the American public was witness to a presidential resignation under pressure of legal reprisal, and, later, an impeachment. But even in the run-up to Trump's election, things seemed more *generally* bad: the questionable character, the failure, once again, of the character test.

In April 2015, anticipating some of the issues surrounding public and private claims about "character," the *New York Times* columnist Paul Krugman offered a set of observations that applied to pundits as well as candidates: "Refusing to accept responsibility for past errors is a serious character flaw in one's private life," he said. "It rises to the level of real wrongdoing when policies that affect millions of lives are at stake."[6] A few days later, he tried to steer the public discussion away from the candidates' private lives and toward their "intellectual integrity," while acknowledging that this, "the character trait that matters most, isn't one the press likes to focus on. In fact it's actively discouraged."[7] It is the news media, he noted with concern, that often "try to make the campaign about personalities and character" instead of issues and policies. And this was before the campaigns had really gotten under way. When they did, of course, personalities and character were front and center.

Maureen Dowd reminded readers of the *Times* that character attacks are standard fare in high-stakes politics, even from those who claimed to be above the fray. Despite all the talk about civility, she wrote, "the Bushes threw out the red meat whenever they had to, from Lee Atwater and Willie Horton in '88 to W.'s supporters whispering in 2000 that John McCain came home from Hanoi with snakes in his head, to the W. 2004 campaign strategy of encouraging gay marriage ballot initiatives to rile up the evangelicals, to Jeb spending a fortune on ads this winter eviscerating the character of the man he deemed the disloyal protégé, Marco Rubio."[8]

"Obnoxiousness is the new charisma," Frank Bruni observed in the *Times* in January 2016, just prior to the earliest caucus and primary of the election season. "In a typical presidential campaign, the most successful candidates lay claim to leadership with their high-mindedness. They reach for poetry. They focus on lifting people up," wrote Bruni. But not the two Republican front-runners of that moment, Donald Trump and Ted Cruz. "They're unreservedly smug. They're unabashedly mean." Anger, as Bruni comments, "can have a noble dimension—as a response to injustice, as the grist for change." Neither of these candidates strove for nobility. "They're not so much angry as petulant, impudent," Bruni noted.[9] Nowhere in his column did the word "character" appear. It didn't have to. The specter of "character," and the so-called character issue in politics and public life, was implicit in the argument.

A month later, Bruni used the *c*-word explicitly, discussing a hypothetical candidate for whom he would be willing to "go to the barricades" if he or she had "talents I trust, positions I respect, and a character I admire."[10] In this case, "character" was a substantive, assumed to be as self-evident as "talent" and "positions"—a quality, presumptively ethical or moral or both, that distinguished one individual from another, and fit him or her for public office. Here the usage, a fairly common one in journalistic discourse, for better or worse, aligns itself with the kinds of arguments made by Bruni's *Times* colleague David Brooks. Brooks, who had written a book on the topic, chimed in on the election discussion to remark that, although he disagreed with Barack Obama on issues of policy, he admired his demeanor, especially in contrast with other, current candidates for president. "Many of the traits of character and leadership that Obama possesses, and that maybe we have taken too much for granted, have suddenly gone missing or are in short supply."[11]

The pairing of "character and leadership" is familiar from leadership institutes, which have arisen over the last few decades as a way of teaching, or reinforcing, "leadership" largely irrespective of what the "leader" will be leading—a corporation, a university, a government, a museum. So Brooks agreed with Bruni: something was badly wrong, something was acutely missing, in the campaigns of some of the most vivid contestants for high office, and that *something* was described, familiarly and conventionally, as "character." Brooks listed a few of its elements: "basic integrity," "basic humanity," "respect for the dignity of others," "soundness in [the] decision-making process," "grace under pressure," and "a resilient sense of optimism."

That this list of desirable qualities was not represented by the frontrunners in the Republican primaries was a point that other journalists, as well as politicians, audiences, and voters, had already noted. In a column called "The Brutalism of Ted Cruz," Brooks pointed out that during Cruz's time as solicitor general of Texas, he had enforced an extremely harsh sentence in defiance of state law. The case, Brooks said, revealed "something interesting about Cruz's character." Despite the fact that he had strong support among Christian evangelicals, "there is not a hint of compassion, gentleness and mercy" in his speeches. Instead, "he sows bitterness, influences his followers to lose all sense of proportion and teaches them to answer hate with hate."[12]

Interestingly, Brooks classed Cruz with other "inauthentic speakers" ("As is the wont of inauthentic speakers, everything is described as a maximum existential threat"). This implies that "authenticity," too, is an element of "character"—a view that Brooks had also expressed in his book.[13] And we might note as well a small but significant semantic detail, the way in which the word "character" in political speech can become shorthand for either merit or flaw. When Cruz later tried to establish his own integrity by firing an aide who had circulated a misleading video about Marco Rubio, a rival candidate, a news article reported that, according to Rubio's team, it was Cruz who had the "character problem."[14]

And the issues kept coming. Bridling at his rival Donald Trump's implied critique of his wife, Cruz spoke out forcefully in a morning interview with CNN: "If Donald wants to get in a character fight, he's better off sticking with me, because Heidi is way out of his league." The problem was, as various media reports quickly noted, that this ringing line was "lifted," or "borrowed," or "stolen," or "channeled," from a 1995 movie, *The American President*, written by Aaron Sorkin. In the film Michael Douglas, playing the part of the president, rebukes a journalist: "Do you want a character debate, Bob? You'd better stick with me, because Sydney Ellen Wade is way out of your league." A question about *Cruz*'s character inevitably arose: what should be said about the character of someone who appropriates, without attribution, a punch line about character? Trump had no hesitation in tweeting that Cruz was "just another dishonest politician," stealing "foreign policy from me, and lines from Michael Douglas."[15] This was, of course, many months before Trump's wife, as the new first lady, would be accused of stealing lines from Michelle Obama.

As Donald Trump's fortunes rose, media assessments of his character multiplied. Timothy Egan, summarizing Trump's apparent "hostile takeover of the Republican party," noted that "people have trotted out a host of character disorders," which he went on to list: "Narcissist. Racist.

Bully. Buffoon. Tyrant. Liar. Celebrity obsessive. Fact-denier." "You've heard them all," Egan said, "and they all apply, in varying degrees."[16]

"Character disorder" is a more clinical description and diagnosis than the less precise, freewheeling "character issue" or "character problem" or "character flaw," all of which are subjective, and the first two of which are euphemisms that have by now hardened into use. When Timothy Egan used "character disorder" rather than the more medically and technically correct "personality disorder," he was tapping into the reservoir of ideas people have about the importance of "character" (moral, ethical, supposedly enduring) in politics. A "personality" disorder, even though it may include what the *DSM* now calls narcissism ("emotional, erratic" personality) and bullying ("antisocial" personality), doesn't sound to the lay ear nearly so serious, or so clearly disqualifying for public office.

The Lady Macbeth of Chappaqua

Among the 2016 presidential candidates, however, no Republican, no matter how brutal, clownish, or disliked, was discussed in relation to "character flaws" and character problems with nearly as great frequency as Hillary Clinton. This was true even in articles and columns that aimed to be sympathetic or even admiring. Thus, for example, Gail Sheehy, who had written an appreciative book about Hillary Clinton in 1999, lamented her own "ambivalence" this time around, noting Clinton's "most consistent character flaw: the instinct to stonewall whenever she is confronted with a negative, but legitimate, criticism of her actions."[17] Charles Blow, a sympathetic observer, remarked, "She just can't seem to shake the email controversy and the idea that the issue raises—or raises *again*—some kind of character flaw." When a Quinnipiac University poll asked respondents to tell them the first word that came to mind when they thought of Hillary Clinton, the "top three responses," Blow reported, were "liar, dishonest, and untrustworthy. Ouch!"[18]

And these are comments over the period of just a few weeks, in one newspaper, *The New York Times*. Joe Klein, writing some months earlier in *Time* magazine, used the phrase "character issue" rather than the finger-pointing "character flaw," but Hillary Clinton was again the target, and, again, the tenor was criticism rather than unstinting admiration. "The ability to stand athwart your strongest supporters is a character issue, especially among the people who actually decide elections—the slowly evaporating middle," Klein said. "Clinton is on the rise because her debating and congressional-hearing personas are as tough as titanium, but her political persona remains vaguely vinyl. Americans tend not to like polyester Presidents, either."[19]

Hillary Clinton's connection with "character" issues in the public press goes back to her time as first lady (itself a "character role" of interest to both public and press), and in particular to Daniel Wattenberg's inflammatory 1992 article in *The American Spectator*, "The Lady Macbeth of Little Rock."[20] The title—reluctant kudos to the right-wingers at *The American Spectator*—was sheer genius, even if fundamentally misinformed about the history of portrayals of Shakespeare's character. As Wattenberg wrote, "The image of Mrs. Clinton that has crystallized in the public consciousness is, of course, that of Lady Macbeth: consuming ambition, inflexibility of purpose, domination of a pliable husband, and an unsettling lack of tender human feeling, along with the affluent feminist's contempt for traditional female roles."[21] "Of course" here is telltale bravado masking insufficient knowledge; over the years, as interpreted by actors like Sarah Siddons and Kate Fleetwood, Lady Macbeth has been played in a wide range of styles: Mrs. Siddons described her as "captivating to the other sex—fair, feminine, nay, perhaps even fragile."[22] And I am still waiting to hear more about Lady M's feminist "affluence."

Nonetheless, the notion, and the killer headline, took off. In the 1990s, I collected a stack of some hundred articles that linked Hillary Clinton to Lady Macbeth. This was a new and ingenious form of "character assassination"—critique and ridicule through an association with a literary/dramatic character. But the speeded-up news cycle, and the shift of generations, rendered this caricature dated or obsolete. Besides, at least for a while, fierce was back. During her campaign, Clinton appeared onstage with a range of female pop stars, including Lady Gaga, associating her fight with theirs. "They've racked up many 'firsts,'" she wrote in an appreciative essay in *Billboard*, "like first artist to get more than a billion views on YouTube (Lady Gaga) and first woman to chart more than 50 top hits ([Loretta] Lynn), and they're the best at what they do."[23]

Endorsing Clinton in the 2016 presidential election, *The New York Times* took the opportunity to praise her "character" while rejecting false or inappropriate criteria:

> Mrs. Clinton's occasional missteps, combined with attacks on her trustworthiness, have distorted perceptions of her character. She is one of the most tenacious politicians of her generation, whose willingness to study and correct course is rare in an age of unyielding partisanship. As first lady, she rebounded from professional setbacks and personal trials with astounding resilience. Over eight years in the Senate and four as secretary of state, she built a reputation for grit and bipartisan collaboration. She displayed a command of policy and diplomatic nuance and an ability to listen to constituents and colleagues that are all too exceptional in Washington.[24]

The editorial page went on to mention her "record of service to children, women and families," the "boldness" of her declaration in Beijing in 1995 that "women's rights are human rights," and a number of other positions and actions they deemed laudable. Whether or not you think it offers an accurate description of Hillary Clinton, this list of attributes provides a recognizable sketch of what is, or was, regarded as character in public life: tenacity, a willingness to study and to learn from past mistakes, resilience, "grit," ability to collaborate, moral boldness, public service, the ability to listen attentively and with respect. The editorial makes no mention of Donald Trump, but the list of qualities is all the more telling for this omission; rendered in the negative, each and all aptly describe Trump the candidate and Trump the president.

Others who commented on the "character issue" as it affected Clinton's candidacy noted that animadversions against her had "little to do with her character," and much more to do with old prejudices from the

1990s. As Susan Faludi noted in an opinion piece published just before the election, the setup was lose-lose: "if she denies the caricature, she's called a liar." At this point, of course, Faludi was among those who still envisaged a Democratic victory at the polls: "It would be a mistake to think that Mrs. Clinton, the imperfect politician, is not the right standard-bearer for this fight." As it turned out, she wasn't, for reasons Faludi had also foreseen—that the visceral dislike of Clinton would overbalance the personal flaws and dishonesty of Trump, even though, "compared with her opponent, she's George Washington." Character clearly *was* an issue here, even though (or perhaps *because*) the supposed character of Hillary Clinton was a calculated political fiction. "Her famous 'hiddenness,'" Faludi wrote, "is, at heart, her refusal to cop to the crime of purloined male authority."[25]

The slide from "character" to "caricature" is a familiar one, since the history of caricature has often seen it as a way of penetrating to the truth of character. One apparent piece of evidence supporting this was noted, eleven months later, by Tom Toles in *The Washington Post.* "Here's the latest update," he wrote:

> Clinton's so-called character weaknesses, the whole tar-bucket of them having done their work, are now being surgically removed from her, carried in a portable ice chest and grafted onto the next Democratic woman who happens to be standing in line, Sen. Elizabeth Warren.
>
> Yes, the woman who so recently was seen as the opposite of Clinton is now going to be portrayed as the exact SAME as Clinton. Untrustworthy. Hypocritical.

Toles's point was not about feminism per se—he also mentions the "swiftboating" of John Kerry and the attempted "de-citizening" of Barack Obama. "The main thing," he stressed, "isn't what the charge is; it's that it gets made. And that it is made early, is some form of character assassination, and is funded and repeated, repeated and repeated in a media atmosphere that needs a 'storyline' for it to understand a candidate."[26]

Character Traits and Character Traitors

After the 2016 election, "character" became nearly omnipresent in public discourse, with new scandals that surfaced around Donald Trump, the barely failed candidacy of Roy Moore, and the literal and figurative exposures of sexual predators like Harvey Weinstein and Anthony Weiner. Politicians, columnists, and correspondents in papers of record such as *The Washington Post* and *The New York Times* sought both to define the term and to document its absence.

Michael Gerson, who had been director of speechwriting for former president George W. Bush, explained the Trump doctrine of values: Trump, he wrote, is "fully responsible for creating and marketing an ethos in which victory matters more than character and real men write their own rules." Like others, Gerson at first found it "strange to hear religious conservatives claim that the character of leaders doesn't count," but the reason for changing his mind seemed clear: "the character of a president leaves an imprint on everyone around him." Thus, for Gerald Ford and George H. W. Bush, thought Gerson, there was a "general expectation of probity." And for Nixon or Trump, "scandal."[27]

In *The New York Times*, Thomas Friedman made a similar point, arguing against those in the media who had begun to feel that covering Trump's outbursts was doing the president a favor by keeping him in the public eye: "I want wall-to-wall coverage of Trump's every speech, rally, tweet and utterance, because they most reveal his character, and Trump's character is the ceiling on Trump's presidency—and he seems uninterested, and more likely unable, to change that."[28]

Reviewing John A. Farrell's prizewinning 2017 biography of Nixon, Jennifer Senior noted: "Farrell could not possibly have known who would be president on the day his fine book was published. That it happens to be Donald J. Trump is, for him, an extraordinary stroke of luck." Merely to compare the two men would be a disservice to Farrell's book, she said, but, nonetheless, "the similarities between Nixon and Trump leap off the page like crickets." For example, "there's the matter of their Old Testament fury at the news media. ('The press is the enemy,' Nixon told his aides. 'Write that on the blackboard 100 times and never forget it.')"

> What else? Their thin skin. Their skyscraping paranoia. Their cavernous memory for slights. It's hard to think of two modern presidents with a more dire case of political hemophilia. Once wounded, these men never stop bleeding.
>
> Like Trump, Nixon was a monomaniac on the stump, obsessed with the enemies lurking within. Nixon, too, had a penchant for sowing mayhem and a gourmand's appetite for revenge, especially in the wee hours of the morning. (Trump tweets. Nixon made phone calls.)
>
> These similarities in character lead to eerily similar behavioral consequences. In 1968, Nixon opened up a back channel to the president of South Vietnam, assuring him he'd get further support if he could just hold out for a Nixon presidency and resist Lyndon B. Johnson's offers to broker peace. Nearly 50 years later, Michael Flynn had private discussions with the Russians that seemed to promise them a friendlier American policy—if they could just sit tight until Trump was inaugurated.
>
> Both men went on to claim that their predecessors had wiretapped these discussions. Nixon said he'd been tipped off by J. Edgar Hoover.[29]

But some commentators felt Trump had in fact out-Nixoned Nixon. Paul Krugman described "Trump's character" as a "combination of petty vindictiveness with sheer laziness."[30] "The pervasiveness of lies" among his political appointees, he wrote, "reflects the character of the man at the top: No president, or for that matter major U.S. political figure of any kind, has ever lied as freely and frequently as Donald Trump."[31]

Longtime Trump observers had been frank and explicit about his character from the outset.

Charles Blow of *The New York Times*, perhaps Trump's most persistent and vehement critic, wrote months before the election, "This is the most frightening type of man, whose basic character is vile."[32] After the disclosure of a 2005 tape in which Trump boasted of predatory sexual behavior, Blow said: "This is not an issue that you can couch in policy or strategy. This is so very clearly about character. It is unambiguous and lecherous. It is repulsive and rapacious. And it appears to fit a pattern."[33] Addressing the candidate directly in his column, Blow wrote, "The coarseness of your character has been put on full display,"[34] and ten days later—still before the election—he returned to the necessity of focusing the public discussion "on character, or the lack thereof." Trump, asserted Blow, was "a shallow narcissist who is also a misogynist, bigot, nativist and xenophobe."[35] Then came the election.

"This is one of the worst possible people who could be elected president," Blow wrote in the immediate aftermath. "I remain convinced that Trump has a fundamentally flawed character and is literally dangerous for world stability and injurious to America's standing in the world."[36] "A staggering lack of character,"[37] he added in a later column, and then, after a few months of the Trump presidency, "If you were trying to create in a lab a person with character traits more unbecoming in a president, it would be hard to outdo the one we have."[38] Trump, Blow would suggest, "sees character as just another malleable thing that can be marketed and made saleable."[39]

Frank Bruni offered an equally critical assessment, both before and after Trump's election. "He's a repository of almost every character trait that we reprimand children for," Bruni observed in August 2016, after Trump's unbecoming feud with the parents of a soldier killed in Iraq. "Only a toddler could be so self-justifying and tone-deaf." Trump "isn't slouching toward gravitas, he's having a tantrum." But he was still convinced that Trump was "bound to lose the election."[40] Right before the election, in early November, Bruni noted the unpopularity of both candidates, and remarked, "No campaign in my adult lifetime has turned so little on policy and so much on character."[41] Months later, character was again on his mind: "Trump's quickness to deflect blame, readiness to designate scapegoats, unpredictable tirades and stinginess with the loyalty that he demands from others aren't just character flaws. They're serious and quite possibly insurmountable obstacles to governing."[42] The neo-Nazi rally in Charlottesville, Virginia, in August 2017—and Trump's ambivalent response to it—moved Bruni once again to raise the question of presidential character. "Atone? Adjust? Inspire?" he wrote. "These are outside of his character and beyond his ken." As for Trump's "fellow Republicans," they were "no doubt judging the politics of it all and looking to the numbers. How I wish," wrote Bruni, "they'd judge the morality of it all and look to their souls."[43]

The political theorist Danielle Allen raised the question of the "soul" as well, insisting that the only way to "deal with a problem like Donald Trump" was to resist the election of "tyrannical souls": "Character matters," she argued a month before the 2016 election, "because it is how we restrain the inner would-be tyrant in each one of us. It matters because it is how we limit the placement of great power in the hands of those with tyrannical instincts and appetites. If we've given up a commitment to character, we've already given up the game or, to speak more precisely, the work of protecting freedom, equality, and human flourishing."[44] It would not take many months to prove her right.

Both complaisant Republicans and colluding evangelicals were regularly reminded that they once cared about the character of elected officials. "You can't ignore moral character when you make decisions about whom to vote for or support," wrote the conservative columnist Ross Douthat in the *Times*. "This was something conservatives used to argue in the Clinton years; under Trump, many have conveniently forgotten it."[45] Before the 2016 election, Peter Wehner had made the same observation: "Republicans used to argue that character mattered in our political leaders. But apparently that applied only to Democrats like Bill Clinton. Today, we're told such considerations are irrelevant, inapposite, quaint. We're electing a president rather than a pope, after all, so there's no problem wrapping Republican arms around a moral wreck. At least he's our moral wreck."[46]

Writers in conservative publications like "*Breitbart*, *The Washington Times*, *The Federalist*, and the rest of the pro-Trump press," noted Bret Stephens, continued to support Trump because "he won and is therefore a winner." But "what about Trump's character? It doesn't matter [to them] so long as the Supreme Court remains conservative."[47]

In *The Washington Post*, Joe Scarborough, a former Republican lawmaker and the cohost of MSNBC's *Morning Joe*, quoted some words ascribed to "America's first Republican president," Abraham Lincoln: "Nearly all men can stand adversity. But if you want to test a man's character, give him power." Both "the current Republican president and his party," said Scarborough, were "spectacularly failing Abraham Lincoln's character exam."[48] The *Post*'s conservative columnist Jennifer Rubin, who contributes a regular opinion piece called Right Turn, described Trump's "loathsome character," his "total self-absorption," the "personality defects [that] make him unwilling to give up grudges," his inability "to control his anger," his failure to "show loyalty," and the fact that he "lies constantly"—all of this, she says, "evidence of his weak character and intellect, a sign of his abject unfitness for the job."[49] "I'm a big believer in the importance of character when it comes to any executive position, the presidency most of all," wrote Bret Stephens. "Trump's moral defects are a permanent stain on the presidency itself."[50]

The character issue came to a new crisis point with the candidacy of Roy Moore for Senate in Alabama and the accusations that he had approached, and molested, underaged girls. "Roy Moore is what Republicans get—and what they deserve," Stephens continued, "when they renounce the idea that good moral character is a requirement for high political office. It's also what happens when the only thing you care about, politically speaking, is to elect people you know will vote your way."

Other commentators made similar observations. One noted the increasing "denial of the importance of statesmen and their characters," observing that President Trump's counselor, Kellyanne Conway, had "suggested that it would be acceptable to elect a man credibly accused of molesting teenagers to the Senate because he would support the Republican tax plan." Trump himself upped the ante, tweeting, "We need his vote on stopping crime, illegal immigration, Border Wall, Military, Pro Life, V.A., Judges, 2nd Amendment and more."[51]

Perhaps inevitably, Roy Moore's supporters came to his defense by stressing his (good) character. A man who had served with him in the Vietnam War told a writer for *The Washington Post* that Roy Moore was a man of honor, character, and integrity, and that the allegations could not be true. "I know him better than that," he said.

Evangelicals were especially quick to find excuses or make distinctions. "Of course, moral character is still important," said Pastor David

Floyd of Marvyn Parkway Baptist Church in Opelika, Alabama. "But with Bill Clinton or Harvey Weinstein or Bill Cosby, we're talking about something completely different. You have to look at the totality of the man. That's why I support Judge Moore. I've prayed with him. I know his heart."[52] Terry Batton, the head of an organization called Christian Renewal and Development Ministries, said when interviewed for the same article that, although "the Bible definitely explains that people ought to choose men of upstanding character," if Roy Moore is "guilty of what they're talking about" but has "repented," then "it should be forgotten." Context, he said, is all-important: "with Bill Clinton, you had immorality in what he stood for, and with Roy Moore, you have a godly man whose positions live out his biblical precepts." In this view, "character" is an objectively meaningless label applied only when an individual's "positions," aka "the totality of the man," accord with those of the speaker. For these supporters, Moore's alleged criminal actions definitely did not speak louder than his "godly" words.

For Robert Jeffress, pastor of the First Baptist Church in Dallas, which has some thirteen thousand members, the Moore affair seemed to revisit the question of Donald Trump's fitness for office. When news first surfaced of the *Access Hollywood* tape in which Trump, then the Republican nominee for president, swapped lewd comments about women with television host Billy Bush as they traveled together en route to film an episode of the show, Jeffress told *The Washington Post* that, although he wouldn't "necessarily choose Donald Trump to be a Sunday School teacher," the "lewd, offensive, and indefensible" comments on the tape were "not enough to make me vote for Hillary Clinton." To say that Trump's remarks were disqualifying would assume, he wrote in a statement to the *Post*, "that Hillary Clinton is more moral than Donald Trump."[53] Although he remained an ardent Trump supporter, Jeffress was somewhat more equivocal in his remarks on Roy Moore a year later. For evangelical Christians, he told the *Post*, "leadership, experience, morality and faith are all important, and the rank of those changes according to circumstances." Morality, then, could drop to a trailing fourth place under the right—or wrong—circumstances. And if the allegations about Moore were true, he acknowledged, "that's disqualifying for public office."[54]

Discounting Character

"Character does count in America and in the United States Senate," declared majority leader Mitch McConnell in November 2017, recalling how, as a junior senator more than twenty years before, he had pushed to remove Republican senator Bob Packwood of Oregon from office after several women accused Packwood of harassment or abuse. (Packwood resigned in 1995.) However, as *The New York Times* reported, McConnell "sidestep[ped] a question about whether he would support" such an ouster if Roy Moore was elected to the Senate in 2018. In the event, since Moore lost, McConnell was not put to this character test himself.[55]

Meantime, in the previous month, President Trump had publicly commemorated National Character Counts Week, proclaiming, "Few things are more important than cultivating strong character in all our citizens, especially our young people."[56] This annual event, held in October, has been observed since 1993. But Alyssa Rosenberg of *The Washington Post*, citing Trump's pro-character proclamation as an example of the world turned upside down, noted that Trump had that year "apparently decided to mark [the occasion]" by "feuding with the National Football League, lying about his predecessors' treatment of Gold Star families to excuse his own lapses and making mockery of his already-enfeebled excuse for the most damaging act of his young presidency, his decision to fire FBI director James B. Comey." Rosenberg went on to insist that this was a time to "figure out what it means to be good. Though character has always been an essential quality, these days, we need it more than ever."[57]

I was struck by this earnest entreaty in connection with Trump's emphasis on cultivating "strong character . . . especially in our young people" and Rosenberg's phrase "young presidency." A perfectly accurate description of the short months between Trump's inauguration and his firing of Comey, "young presidency" also seemed to echo, with subdued irony, the many comments critics had made about the president's immaturity, lack of discipline and focus, impatience, restlessness, and unstoppable narcissism. "When the World Is Led by a Child" was the headline of a David Brooks column that called Trump an "infantilist" and pointed out that "immaturity is becoming the dominant note of his presidency, lack of self-control his leitmotif." The president, wrote Brooks, may have "betrayed an intelligence source and leaked secrets to his Russian visitors" not because of any "malevolent intent," but "because he is sloppy, because he lacks all impulse control, and above all because he is a 7-year-old boy desperate for the approval of those he admires."[58]

Like many other columnists and editorial writers, Brooks was offering these remarks as much in sorrow as in anger, but also in fear for the future. Drawing on the etymology of "character," he asserts that "our institutions depend on people who have enough engraved character traits to fulfill their assigned duties." "Engraved" here seems to imply permanence and stability, the very attributes Brooks—and so many others—were finding that Trump manifestly lacked.

The permanent engraving of character, in this view, develops through experience and maturity, and the metaphor of writing it suggests it is highly pertinent. "When we analyze a president's utterances we tend to assume that there is some substantive process behind the words, that it's part of some strategic intent," wrote Brooks, but Trump's statements don't "come from anywhere, lead anywhere or have a permanent reality beyond his wish to be liked at any given instant."[59]

If "character counts," or "character matters," as many columnists—and some politicians—have insisted, these testimonies to the "loathsome," "weak," "failing," and "narcissistic" character on the part of the nation's chief executive should have brought this familiar nineteenth-century standard for high office into sharp focus once again.

But through its frequent iteration, the word "character" may have lost some of its power.

The proud and faux-pious declaration that a revealed miscreant is "not a perfect man," or that one "never said" one was "perfect" is another instance of the rhetoric of hypocrisy. In its long history, character has never been equated with or mistaken for perfection; often, in fact, it has represented, or seemed to represent, a concerted effort of self-control as well as a sense of public and private duty. Perfection is nowhere on the character map; in fact, character might be said to be perfection's opposite, a quality, or set of qualities, earned and maintained by conscious effort and choice.

"A man of the utmost character, honor, and integrity" is how a Republican congressional representative described Congressman Jim Jordan, who was accused of ignoring athletes' claims of sexual abuse by the team doctor when he was an assistant wrestling coach at Ohio State University. Other supporters praised his "honesty" and "integrity" with what the editorial board of *The New York Times* called a "*Manchurian Candidate*–like ubiquity."[60] President Trump said Jordan was "an outstanding man," whom he believed "100 percent."

Political partisanship and a closing of the ranks accounted for the flood of instant praise—Jordan had been bruited as a leading candidate for Speaker of the House. But the use of "character" as a defense once again raised the question of whether, and how much, this time-honored concept had been devalued. Jordan couldn't be guilty of ignoring the welfare of athletes when he was in his twenties, because he was "a man of the utmost character."

The logic was tautological at best—no activities of conscience were cited in his defense, just the same old key words. The testimonies of at least eight of the former college wrestlers were, in the view of Jordan's supporters, not worth considering. The doctor said to have been the perpetrator of the abuses had committed suicide in 2005. But Jordan couldn't be guilty of failing the athletes' trust, because he was a man of character.

There are men of character in the U.S. Congress, both House and Senate. There are women of character, too. But the evidence for "character" needs to be something other than the iteration of the word itself.

Character Actors

The journalist Emma Roller offered a useful reading of the character debate: "Every presidential candidate plays a character, whether he or she admits it or not. We have the disheveled revolutionary, the pious doctor, the levelheaded statesman. The character Mr. Trump plays may be more honest than that of any of his rivals: He's the ambitious businessman who cares only about winning."[61] By injecting the notion of character as role rather than as "authenticity" into the discussion, her observation opens the question: what do we mean when we use a word like "character" to describe a public persona?

"The part he's been playing is evolving," said Donald Trump's newly installed campaign chief, Paul Manafort, to members of the Republican National Committee in late April 2016. The acknowledgment that Trump was acting, or performing a "part," was offered not as an excuse but as a description, a review of political theater in the round. "Fixing personality negatives is a lot easier than fixing character negatives," Manafort asserted, reflecting on what he regarded as Hillary Clinton's shortcomings. "You can't change somebody's character. But you can change the way somebody presents themselves."[62]

Manafort's distinction between character and personality, the one fixed and immutable, the other not only mutable but performative, does not necessarily accord with the way those words are used by psychiatrists and psychologists today.

"Personality" comes from "persona," a word for mask; "character" from handwriting, engraving, or stamping. It's arguable that in some sense the distinction between outer and inner, fleeting or lasting, might apply. Of the two terms, personality and character, it is the word "character" that often, and sometimes confusingly, crosses over from theater or fiction to "real life." But in the case of Donald Trump, who developed his public persona via a television "reality show," character, personality, and performance are sometimes hard to disentangle. Like Peer Gynt, whose self is described by Ibsen as like an onion with no center, Trump seems to have layers but no core. Unsurprisingly, the Trump critic Charles Blow responded with interest to the idea that, "up until now, the real estate developer's incendiary style was just an act." He speculated on how all Trump's supporters must feel on hearing that "maybe this has all been an act, a 'part he's been playing,' and you are the gullible audience who got played."[63]

What is the relationship—if any—between a dramatic or fictional character and the idea of "character" in the ethical or moral sense? Which comes first, *character* or *characters*?

What we call "literary characters" are very often presented, not only as *exemplars* of character and character types, but as *models* for them. No matter what the field, from philosophy to politics to the arts and sciences, it is not always easy—indeed, it is not always possible—to tell which came first. Over and over again, as we will see throughout these pages, what is often thought of as a secondary effect (literature copying life) turns out to have been a primary one (life copying literature).

Let's look at one more example from recent U.S. political history, the proud, and even perhaps defiant or defensive, assertion by then-President George W. Bush that he was the "decider," whatever his advisers—including many retired generals, appalled by the Abu Ghraib prison scandal—might propose. The decision in question was, initially, that of retaining Secretary of Defense Donald Rumsfeld. "I'm the decider, and I decide what's best," Bush declared in the White House Rose Garden. "And what's best is for Don Rumsfeld to remain as secretary of defense."[64] First rolled out on April 19, 2006, the word "decider" became an instant hit and an instant joke. *The New York Times*'s "quotation of the day" morphed into a comic-book character called "the Decider" on Jon Stewart's satirical *Daily Show*. "Decider" was, in itself, a slightly peculiar word, something a grade-schooler might say. Bush's rhetorical signature was this kind of awkward lexical choice (was it a response to his father's famously "patrician" convolutions of expression?), and "decider," rather than, say, "the person who makes the hard decisions," had a certain active—or action-hero—quality to it that stuck. (An earlier U.S. president, Harry Truman, had popularized a more colorful version, taken from the game of poker, and displayed on a sign on his desk: "The Buck Stops Here.")

Is "decision," or being a "decider," intrinsic to good character?

In 1804, a Baptist preacher, John Foster, published an essay called "On Decision of Character," which strongly influenced Romantic poets and painters as well as politicians, moralists, and phrenologists. The essay, in the form of a letter addressed to a friend, went through nine editions from 1804 to 1830. "Character," to Foster, meant exhibiting this "bold" and "commanding" quality, of which "courage" was a "chief constituent," and avoiding the troubles of "an irresolute mind." His examples of men of decision ("women in general have less inflexibility of character than men"[65]) come from the Bible (Daniel), ancient and modern history (Caesar, Luther, Cromwell, Christian missionaries), and literature—Milton's *Paradise Lost* (Satan, Abdiel) and, especially, Shakespeare's plays (Lady Macbeth—as usual, an exception that proves the supposed rule about women—as well as Macbeth, Richard III, and Prospero). Although Hamlet is not explicitly named, the long discussion of the man of "irresolute mind" is familiarly evocative, and when Foster comes to characterize the "first rank of decisive men," he contrasts it with those who, distracted by love or other personal concerns, are forgetful of all "enterprises of great pith and moment,"[66] clearly assuming that his readers will recognize this phrase from the "To be or not to be" soliloquy.

Foster is not indifferent to moral virtue, but he understands that "decision" does not always mean "ethical decision." In describing what his age called "a Ruling Passion," he notes, "When its object is noble, and an enlightened understanding regulates its movements, it appears to me a great felicity; but whether its object be noble or not, it infallibly creates where it exists in great force, that active ardent constancy, which I describe as a capital feature of the decisive character."[67] Although by "character" here he means to denote a constellation of personal qualities that he is recommending to his reader, the crossover between the fictional (Satan, Hamlet) and the historical or local in Foster's exemplars is untroubled and, in the main, untroubling.

For those who subscribe to a ruling-passion theory of human nature, literary characters not only *have* "character" in the sense of interiority and firmness of purpose, but they also *model* it for others. In "the poet's delineation," Foster wrote, Richard III "did not waver while he pursued his object, nor relent when he seized it."[68] Here, too, as in the case of Hamlet, the mention of a Shakespearean character is accompanied by a quotation, as Foster cites Richard of Gloucester's determination to "cut his way through with a bloody axe." This is a slight misquotation—the speech, from *Henry VI Part 3*, has Richard say he will "hew my way out with a bloody axe"—but the misquotation is itself indicative of how familiar these Shakespearean dramatic personages were to the writer and his presumed readership. Foster is recalling Richard's speech from memory, not looking it up in order to add gravitas to his essay. And, once again, the model for "character" is a *character*.

Character Parts

In his book *After Virtue*, the philosopher Alasdair MacIntyre uses the term "character" to describe special types of social roles. Characters, he writes, are "the masks worn by moral philosophies"; they "merge what is usually thought to belong to the individual man and woman and what is usually thought to belong to social roles."[69] He chose this term, he says, precisely because it crosses over between the dramatic and the moral. "A *character* is an object of regard by the members of the culture generally or by some significant segment of them. He furnishes them with a cultural and moral ideal. Hence the demand that in this type of case role and personality be fused. Social type and psychological type are required to coincide. The *character* morally legitimates a mode of social existence."[70]

MacIntyre says, for example, that "the culture of Victorian England was partially defined by the characters of the Public School Headmaster, the Explorer, and the Engineer," that of Wilhemine Germany by "such characters as the Prussian Officer, the Professor, and the Social Democrat."[71] For his "own time" (*After Virtue* was first published in 1981), he describes what he calls the "emotivism" of the period, "the specifically modern self,"[72] as embodied by the characters of the Rich Aesthete, the Manager, the Bureaucratic Expert, and the Therapist.

What might be the characters that embody *this* time? The "our own time" of *now*? I'd suggest that the answers include the Politician, the Athlete, and the Celebrity. (Other characters that "morally legitimate" contemporary modes of social existence might, of course, be proposed; for example, the Entrepreneur, the Donor, and the Philanthropist, three roles that often function as stages in a single individual's metamorphosis: the Very Hungry Caterpillar turns into a social butterfly—and sometimes into a Monarch.)

Out of Bounds

Rule 5 of the Baseball Hall of Fame stipulates, "Voting shall be based upon the player's record, playing ability, integrity, sportsmanship, character, and contributions to the team(s) on which the player played." The so-called character clause—drafted in 1939, when the Hall of Fame opened—has kept from election a number of players who might well, on playing ability alone, have been elected: Pete Rose (gambling), Steve Garvey (paternity suits; nonpayment of child support), Denny McLain (embezzlement), and many others excluded for drug use. Critics of the "character clause" have pointed toward the multiple misdeeds of earlier players inducted into the Hall, including racists, wife beaters, and a member of the Ku Klux Klan, and argue that players convicted of using performance-enhancing drugs should not be barred. Supporters point out that standards are standards, and that times have changed enough so that some of these early stars would today be barred from election.

Since the early nineteenth century, sports and sportsmanship have been linked as aspects of "character" in England and the United States, often with a reminder of the role athletics were thought to play in ancient Athenian culture. Sports were crucial to the development of a gentleman. Integrity, sportsmanship, and character are a familiar triad—and would have been applauded by Victorians who believed that the playing field was a moral force for good. But some twenty-first-century fans, including columnists, instead held the opinion neatly encapsulated in one sports column's headline: "Forget Character, Welcome Characters."[73]

The writer Jonathan Mahler noted that "two conservative, moralizing men were the prime movers behind Rule 5," and suggested that the "character clause" was a "single, smug sentence calling the Hall to some higher purpose than honoring the game's greatest players." Whether or not the relevant sentence can really be called "smug," the fact that it is routinely called a "character clause" lays bare some of the issues around both sports and character. Mahler objects to "turning ex-ballplayers into moral exemplars," something he regards as a category error deliberately developed for commercial purposes, "puffing up a sports museum into a holy American institution."[74] If "everybody does it," as is often said about behavior that comes under criticism (steroid use, in this case), why single out talented individuals for censure? Sometimes, though, it is behavior off the field rather than on it that comes under the character spotlight.

An online article called "Red Flags: 2015 NFL Draft Prospects with

Character Concerns" listed a group of highly successful college football players with comments like "was investigated in [a] domestic battery case"; "was ultimately dismissed from team over multiple run-ins with coaching staff"; "arrested twice for marijuana-related incidents"; "alleged role in an alleged burglary"; "perceived lack of work ethic and overall character"; "was indicted this week by a grand jury on two counts of aggravated rape." Each of these capsule descriptions was followed by a sentence by a football scout or director of athletic personnel indicating how high or low the player would probably go in the draft ("I wouldn't take him inside the first two rounds. He's good, but he's not that good that I would be willing to deal with his emotional issues." Or "He's tall and fast but he can't be trusted. Why would you take a guy like that before the third day?").[75]

Notice that there is no doubt that these players will be drafted. "The character stuff," as one director of scouting called it, was just another factor in the betting. A follow-up article by another journalist bore the headline "Why 'Character Concerns' Is a Meaningless Phrase in the NFL," a title that tells you all you need to know. "Character," "character issues," and "borderline character" (defined as "poor work habits and poor discipline on and off the field, but not law enforcement issues") are frequent phrases in the assessment of players as prospects, but, as one general manager of a professional team remarked, "Talent always trumps character." Or, as another general manager put it, "If you have a very, very talented individual who has a character issue, you're a lot more apt to accept them than someone who is more of a midline talent. That's just the way it is."[76]

But whereas character issues of a negative kind have plagued professional and college football, it is also the case that some athletes have emerged, in recent years, as exemplars of strong character on and off the field. The former San Francisco quarterback Colin Kaepernick began, and inspired, the silent kneeling protests in support of racial justice and Black Lives Matter. J. J. Watt of the Houston Texans founded a charitable organization to provide after-school opportunities for children. He raised over thirty-seven million dollars to help Houston-area victims of Hurricane Harvey; he offered to pay for the funerals of two adults and eight children killed in a school shooting in Santa Fe, Texas.

Malcolm Jenkins of the Philadelphia Eagles led a players' coalition that persuaded team owners to commit up to eighty-nine million dollars for grassroots organizations that combat injustice. Jenkins's teammate Chris Long, dismayed by white-nationalist protests in his hometown of Charlottesville, Virginia, donated his entire base salary for 2017—a million dollars—to charities that provide scholarships and promote educational equality.[77] And these are only a very few examples. The owner of the Eagles franchise, Jeffrey Lurie, said that he supported the players "as they take their courage, character and commitment into our communities to make them better or to call attention to injustice."[78] The New England Patriots employed a "character coach" for six seasons, charged with working on team development and being "better men on and off the field."[79]

Willfully misinterpreting the kneeling of football players during the playing of the national anthem as unpatriotic and disrespectful of the military, rather than as a moral protest in the best traditions of both patriotism and nonviolence, President Trump turned the "character issue" upside down. He was later joined by compliant NFL team owners, apparently fearful of both presidential wrath and fan disaffection.

Shortly afterward, with consistent inconsistency, the president who condemned moral protest at football games and suggested that protesting athletes should be "fired" or even deported, floated to the public and the press the idea of pardoning the boxer Muhammad Ali, who had been convicted of refusing to be drafted during the Vietnam War. Trump seemed not to know that Ali's conviction had been overturned by the Supreme Court in 1971.[80] "Look," he said of Ali, "he was not very popular then. Certainly his memory is very popular now." The moral protesters of the past are "popular"—especially if they are "winners." The moral protesters of the present are enemies of the state. "Character" is not a word frequently heard from this president. "Winning" and "losing" are the terms he prefers.[81]

Google "sports/character" and you will get the basketball coach John Wooden: "Sports do not build character, they reveal it." Wooden, who died in 2010, was an "inspirational" sports figure who turned his celebrity into a winning second career as a self-designated moral leader.

His famous "Pyramid of Success" looks a lot like a nineteenth-century diagram for character development: on the bottom level, Industriousness, Friendship, Loyalty, Cooperation, and Enthusiasm; above that, Self-Control, Alertness, Initiative, and Intentness; on the next level, Condition, Skill, and Team Spirit; then Poise and Confidence; and finally, on the top of the pyramid, Competitive Greatness. The sides of the equilateral triangle are labeled Faith and Patience.

Under the banner "Wooden on Leadership," this is, or was, pretty clearly an incentive to businesspeople as much as—or, indeed, more than—to actual present-day athletes. Terms like "slam dunk," "hail Mary," "full court press," "in your corner," and "(don't) drop the ball" are part of the daily language of people who work in offices, often on "teams."

We might also recall the vogue of the Promise Keepers, an organization of Christian men who gathered in football stadiums in the 1990s, founded by the head football coach at the University of Colorado, Boulder, and dedicated to strengthening character by, among other things, "practicing moral, ethical, and sexual purity," "building strong marriages," and "pursuing vital relationships with a few other men."[82] Even so tenuous a relationship to sports (the men were not gathered together as athletes; the coach may have been their "moral" or "religious" coach on this occasion, but he was not training them for the pros) could be mined, or sold, as character building.

That was one of many reasons why the Penn State scandal was so scandalous. Jerry Sandusky, a former assistant football coach, was convicted of forty-five counts of sexual abuse of young boys. "Character issue" and "character flaw" were profoundly insufficient terms in this case. But the question of "character" was everywhere in the narrative. A member of a profession that was supposed to instill character through sport was found to be egregiously violating and criminally betraying that trust.

Needless to say, character issues, in sports as elsewhere, can involve women as well as men, and individual as well as team sports. In 1994—about the time the Promise Keepers were raising their hands in mutual support in a stadium—the world of competitive ice skating was stunned when Nancy Kerrigan was attacked (and clubbed on the knee) by a man allegedly hired by associates of rival skater Tonya Harding. Even though Kerrigan recovered in time for the Olympic Games, the media, as well as the Olympic Committee, debated whether Harding—who was not yet charged with any crime—should be permitted to compete.

In the midst of the dispute, a psychiatrist wrote to the editor of *The New York Times* that he thought Harding should indeed skate in the Olympics, even though she embodied "values and qualities of character and style that I and others detest"; nonetheless, she had earned the right to compete. Furthermore, he was skeptical about any connection between sports and morality. "I believe," he wrote, "that the notion of Olympic athletes as exemplars of moral rectitude is a myth. I have never shared the view that competitive sports build character. I believe that they are inimical to the development of good character. Although this influence may be offset by the qualities and values of some coaches, parents, teachers, community leaders and peers, the idea that competing, winning and striving for excellence are important is more apt to vitiate than enhance development of the kind of character we profess to desire in our young people."[83]

Tonya did compete, and came in eighth; Nancy was second by a tiny margin, took it badly, was caught on camera saying some things she would regret, and headed right for Disney World, where they made her wear her silver medal to march with Mickey Mouse. Tonya was subsequently banned from skating for life and briefly took up boxing. Both women were subsequently contestants on the television show *Dancing with the Stars* (though they did not, this time, compete against each other).

Falling Stars

Celebrities are, by definition, public personalities, and sometimes their behavior or misbehavior is part of their celebrity. Alcoholism, drugs, drunk driving, extramarital affairs, fistfights, shouting matches, the public exchange of insults—all have been fodder for fan magazines and fan sites. "Character issues" for the well-known-for-being-well-known are therefore something of a moving target, depending upon how the public responds, and defined by the nature of the transgressions rather than by the articulation of any ideal. It is not obvious that we expect "good character" to be a selling point for this kind of fame. If we are to accept even provisionally Alasdair MacIntyre's idea that "the *character* morally legitimates a mode of social existence" for a historical and social time period, we would have to acknowledge that the celebrity does so precisely by stretching those boundaries.

Still, it turns out, there are limits. In part because of the vast increase in media and modes of personal communication, the characters of many in public life—long shielded by publicists and other enablers—have come into sharp and critical focus, and one result has been an attempt, by entertainment organizations on the one hand and ordinary people (aka fans, audiences, and ticket buyers) on the other, to rediscover a sense of character in a business that tends to thrive on bad actors.

Harvey Weinstein was ousted from the Academy of Motion Picture Arts and Sciences in 2017 because of "sexually predatory behavior and workplace harassment," and the academy's statement explicitly includes a message to anyone who may have looked the other way: "the era of willful ignorance and shameful complicity . . . is over."[84] But long before these actions, or the flood of public accusations by women that began the #MeToo movement, Weinstein's behavior was well known; the HBO Hollywood parody *Entourage* included a dramatic character named "Harvey Weingard," an influential and bullying producer. (Weinstein was reportedly not pleased, telling the show's star that the producers were "dead" if they mentioned him again.[85]) In the period of increased scrutiny and pent-up outrage that followed Weinstein's fall, others also lost jobs and power that had been achieved, or maintained, by the exploitation—often sexual—of their positions and influence.

The former NBC *Today* show host Matt Lauer was one of those who were fired after issues of sexual misconduct were raised. Sometime afterward, Lauer's purchase of a ranch in New Zealand was questioned in connection with New Zealand's "good-character test," which is required of foreign property-buyers. Did Lauer have a good enough character to retain his purchase, or would he be barred from ownership? What was "good character" in such a context, when a nation is trying to safeguard the moral probity of high-net-worth investors in buildings and land?

New Zealand's immigration rules are explicit about spelling out "good character" and the "serious character issues" that might lead to exclusion. For legal purposes, presumably, "character" in these stipulations is defined in the negative. Good character, that is to say, is the absence of bad character. Among the "serious character issues" are convictions for crimes that led to extended imprisonment, and risks to security, the public interest, or public order. Lesser "character issues," which require a "character waiver," include convictions for violence, drugs, dishonesty, dangerous driving, racist statements, and offenses "of a sexual nature."[86] When it was reported that Matt Lauer had been allowed to keep the ranch, *The New York Times* noted only that "New Zealand's definition of good character is broad," without specifying details.[87] Lauer had, apparently, passed the character test.

Entertainment celebrities, pretty much by definition, are not ordinarily associated with "character" in the Victorian moral sense, nor are they necessarily expected to be ethical role models; what passes for the "private" life of a celebrity is often given a pass. Nonetheless, since celebrities—again, by definition—transact a good deal of their business in public, and since whether or not they "have" character they are often called upon to promote it in others, their public remarks do occasionally trigger an equally public fall.

If a moralizing speaker is later found lacking in the very principle he extols, the results make for headlines, and sometimes for resignations or firings. A volubly anti-abortion congressman urges his mistress to have an abortion. A clergyman noted for preaching against sin is revealed to be on the take, or on the make. Or, in the case of the television journalist and interviewer Charlie Rose, his advice to university graduates turned out to be contrary to his own practice.

As the recipient of an honorary degree at Georgetown University in 2015, Rose offered the graduating class some advice on ethics and morals: "Think about what you would like to be remembered for at the end of your life," he urged the graduates and their families, as he stood before them in academic hood and gown. "It's not honor. It's not prestige.

It is character. It is integrity. It is truth."[88] No one paid much attention to these remarks at the time—they were de rigueur for a graduation ceremony. But two years later, after eight women accused him of sexual harassment, Rose was fired by CBS, and several of his honorary degrees were rescinded, as were professional honors like the Walter Cronkite Award for Excellence in Journalism and the National Citation Award he had received from the William Allen White School of Journalism and Mass Communications. At that point, reporters were quick to locate, and reprint, Rose's lofty phrases. The TV talk shows took notice—until the next instance of celebrity hypocrisy came along.

Perhaps the most dispiriting of celebrity unmaskings came in the trial and conviction of the actor-comedian Bill Cosby. For in this case Cosby had indeed stood for moral and ethical probity, at least in his fictional persona, and he had done so, crucially, as a role model for black middle-class family men. Cosby, reported *The New York Times* after his conviction for drugging and sexually assaulting a woman, had in recent years "admitted to decades of philandering, and to giving Quaaludes to women as part of an effort to have sex, smashing the image he had built as a moralizing public figure and the upstanding paterfamilias in the wildly popular 1980s and '90s sitcom *The Cosby Show*."[89] One of the prosecutors in the case took particular exception to the defense's attempted "character assassination"[90] of the woman who brought the suit against Cosby, who had been accused of seeking money and fame. As the critic Wesley Morris lamented, Cosby's television character, Cliff Huxtable, had been a role model for him, a fact that led to a profound sense of betrayal. Since Cliff "seemed inseparable from the man who portrayed him," the revelation of Cosby's actual behavior produced "cognitive dissonance" for those who—like Morris himself—had wanted to see the fictional "America's Dad" as real.[91]

Words like "irony" and "schadenfreude," though accurate, are insufficient to describe this kind of public downfall. For what is at stake is not only the behavior of a powerful individual who takes advantage of his power, but also the very language of character itself. Through incidents such as these and many others like them, from podium to pulpit, character talk has become increasingly debased currency. Flagrantly hypocritical examples like Donald Trump's proclamation of

National Character Counts Week, or Charlie Rose's clichés about character and integrity, or Bill Cosby's upended "role model," each offering the familiar double-speak of "Do as I say, not as I do," are part of what has made "character" in the twenty-first century a bland, sanctimonious, and increasingly empty term.

2
TEACHING IT
Tales Out of School

The most dangerous criminal may be the man gifted with reason, but no morals . . . Intelligence plus character, that is the goal of true education.

—MARTIN LUTHER KING, JR., "THE PURPOSE OF EDUCATION"

Like so many of his contemporaries Stephen worshipped "character" as a Kantian Thing-in-itself and failed to realize that character, unless instructed by the intelligence or informed by the emotions, is liable to be exerted on the side of injustice and intolerance.

—NOEL ANNAN, *LESLIE STEPHEN: THE GODLESS VICTORIAN*[1]

With lies, scams, and cover-ups so prominently in the news in recent years, it is natural to wonder whether lying is not escalating throughout society, and to look back to earlier periods in which honesty was more prevalent.

—SISSELA BOK, *LYING*

Throughout my life, my two greatest assets have been mental stability and being, like, really smart . . . a very stable genius.

—DONALD TRUMP

"I cannot tell a lie." So declared a future president of the United States. But that was many years ago—and the story is probably apocryphal. Mason L. Weems (better known as "Parson Weems") added the famous anecdote about George Washington and the cherry tree to the fifth edition of his popular biography of Washington in 1809. Subsequently reprinted in a standard American school text of the period, the *McGuffey's Reader*, it became a widely circulated model for "character." Children who aspired to be great as well as good, or good as well as great, were urged to follow the example of the truth-telling boy who would grow up to be the Father of His Country.

> As the story goes, George's father had a "beautiful young English cherry-tree," on which young George, then aged 6 and the proud possessor of his first hatchet, had "unluckily" tried the edge of his new toy. When Washington senior asked his son if he knew who had killed the tree, George, we are told, "staggered" for a moment under the weight of this question, and then "bravely cried out, 'I can't tell a lie, Pa; you know I can't tell a lie. I did cut it with my hatchet.'"[2]

We might note that in the Weems narrative little George speaks in contractions ("I can't tell a lie, Pa; you know I can't tell a lie"), whereas the more commonly cited version uses the formal and emphatic "I cannot." Like "doth" for "do" in faux-Shakespearese, this stylistic emendation may be chosen to impart a sense of old-style historical "authenticity" to a made-up tale. Scholars have in the main disputed its veracity. But even if little George couldn't tell a lie, his hagiographers presumably thought they could, in the service of what they regarded as a larger truth—what today might be called, in presidential narratives, either "alternative facts" or "truthful hyperbole." And it's also worth observing the specific term with which the overjoyed father greeted his son's moral confession: it was, he says, "an act of heroism." This early "act of heroism" would, Weems implied, prefigure the great man's later career.

Plutarch, Parson Weems, and the Uses of Heroism

The cherry-tree anecdote is told in a chapter on Washington's birth and education. A later chapter, on the "Character of Washington," commends his qualities as an adult. "To be truly great," Weems wrote, "a man must have not only great talents, but those talents must be constantly exerted," because, as the Greek military leader Epaminondas had said, "all of heroism depends on perseverance in great and good actions," which are only finally assessed when we are dead. In Washington's case, luckily for his country, religion and "her celestial daughters, the Virtues," had wrapped him in the "magic mantle of Character. And it was this that immortalized Washington."[3]

Weems's classical quotation—from Plutarch's "Life of Pelopidas"—was not unusual in this context. For centuries, Plutarch's *Lives of the Noble Greeks and Romans* (also called the *Parallel Lives*) had been—and would continue to be—models for human character, essential to the education of the young. Some ancient heroes were born great, some achieved greatness, and some had greatness thrust upon them, but all were taken as exemplary in the literal sense of that word. Plutarch, as the classical scholar C. J. Gianakaris would note, was "for centuries Europe's schoolmaster."[4] Authors and critics from the Renaissance to the nineteenth century quoted, translated, and borrowed from his *Lives*, and also from his *Moralia* or moral essays. Jacques Amyot's French translations of the *Lives* (1559) and *Moralia* (1572) were the basis for Thomas North's English version, published in 1579, which was, in turn, a crucial source for Shakespeare.

"Moral good," wrote Plutarch in his "Life of Pericles," "has a power to attract toward itself. It is no sooner seen than it rouses the spectator to action, and yet it does not form his character by mere imitation, but by promoting the understanding of virtuous deeds it provides him with a dominating purpose."[5] In undertaking the *Lives*, many of which were designed to parallel an account of a prominent Greek with that of an equally celebrated Roman (Alexander the Great with Julius Caesar; Demosthenes the Greek orator with the Roman Cicero), Plutarch set out deliberately to address the question of character. "I am writing Lives, not history," he famously declares in the prologue to his "Life of

Alexander," and "the truth is that the most brilliant exploits often tell us nothing of the virtues or vices of the men who performed them, while on the other hand a chance remark or a joke may reveal far more of a man's character than battles where thousands die." Like a portrait painter, then, who "relies above all on the face and the expression of the eyes," he focuses on "those details which illuminate the workings of the soul," and leaves to others the description of "great exploits and battles."[6] Likewise, introducing his "Life of Timoleon," he noted that, although he had begun the *Lives* for the sake of others, he now found that by using history as a mirror he could himself profit in moral improvement as well as in the pleasure of the imagined company of the great.

Plutarch's importance in what would much later be called "character education" was for a very long time both palpable and manifest. As Gianakaris notes, character has "a vital bearing on fate for Plutarch," which is one reason he "remains unimpressed by the renowned Antony whose faulted character led to a disappointing end."[7] Plutarch's essays, too, offered wise counsel on this most important of topics: a sign of genuine moral progress was "dearly to love the character of those whose conduct we desire to imitate, and always to accompany our wanting to be like them with goodwill which awards them respect and honour."[8] "The love which fills the character of a young man is, above all else, love of showing off before truly good people."[9]

The fact that Parson Weems could refer, in his chapter on Washington's character, to an occasion "when Epaminondas was asked which was the greatest man, himself or Pelopidas," without citing Plutarch by name, and expect his readers to recognize the allusion, gives some sense of the broad reach of Plutarchan examples in the early nineteenth century. Not only were the individuals Plutarch wrote about in the *Parallel Lives* models of character; his book itself became a model for other books, from Boswell's 1791 *Life of Samuel Johnson* (in which he cited Plutarch's "Life of Alexander") to two classics of the nineteenth century, Carlyle's *On Heroes, Hero-Worship, and the Heroic in History* (1841) and Emerson's *Representative Men* (1850)—and, indeed, to John F. Kennedy's *Profiles in Courage*. As early as 1832, Emerson had written in his *Journal*, "The British Plutarch and the modern Plutarch is yet to be written . . . I would draw characters, not write lives."[10]

"The History of the world is but the Biography of great men,"[11] declared Carlyle. A similar sentiment, coupled with an exhortation to action ("Be a hero in the strife!"), was voiced in a poem by Henry Wadsworth Longfellow:

> Lives of great men all remind us
> We can make our lives sublime,
> And, departing, leave behind us
> Footprints on the sands of time.[12]

Through the end of the nineteenth century and into the first years of the twentieth, the prestige of Plutarch and his observations on character remained high, thanks in part to the continued study of Greek and Latin in schools, and in part to the sense that education, no matter what a student's social status or professional aspirations, would naturally include both classical authors and moral precepts. As late as the middle of the twentieth century, both Irving Howe and Alfred Kazin could describe Edmund Wilson as "the American Plutarch"[13]—a phrase subsequently used for two book titles and a Web site (none of which focused on Wilson).

George Bernard Shaw described the self-help author Samuel Smiles as a "modern Plutarch,"[14] because of the way he wove biographical anecdotes into his books of advice. "The education of character is very much a question of models," Smiles had written in his bestselling *Self-Help.* "We model ourselves so unconsciously after the characters, manners, habits and opinions of those who are about us. Good rules may do much, but good models far more." Personal "contact with the good" was desirable whenever possible, but reading could supply what acquaintance did not. And here biography was an essential tool. "The chief use of biography consists in the noble models of character in which it abounds."[15]

Through the record of their lives, "our great forefathers still live among us," said Smiles, "still sit by us at table, and hold us by the hand." As is his habit, he offers copious examples of inspirational lives, from the autobiography of Benjamin Franklin to the *Discourses* of Sir Joshua Reynolds. He also recognizes the pervasive influence of Shakespeare, of whom he says, with satisfaction, that, however little is known of his life, "it is unquestionable that he sprang from a humble rank"—in short, a poor boy who made good. "For such is the accuracy of his sea phrases that a naval writer alleges that he must have been a sailor; whilst a clergyman infers, from internal evidence of his writings, that he was probably a parson's clerk; and a distinguished judge of horse-flesh insists that he must have been a horse-dealer." Whatever his background, Smiles concludes, Shakespeare "must have been a close student and a hard worker, and to this day his writings continue to exercise a powerful influence on the formation of English character."[16] Thus, with a rhetorical flourish, he is able to tie the playwright and his plays together: the indelible Shakespearean characters were produced by a hardworking man of character.

Today Plutarch, like so many other classics, ancient and modern, has become pretty much a "niche" author, beloved by those who know him, but virtually unknown to most schoolchildren and, indeed, even most college-educated adults.[17] Increasingly, the place his works once occupied as memorable and citable examples of "character" in general literary culture has been taken, as Samuel Smiles recognized, by Shakespeare, who has remained a powerful influence on the formation of American, as well as English, character. Had Parson Weems been writing now, he would probably have cited, on the question of character and posthumous reputation, not Epaminondas but Brutus, or Othello, or Hamlet, or perhaps Henry V.

Much "character education" today relies on books written for children or manuals written for teachers—which is, of course, also a way of describing many of the works we now call the classics. Current tell-all biographical practice—and current history—often provide few uncomplicated models for character emulation, nor has it gone unnoticed that the heroes and "representative men" of the past, like Plutarch's Greeks and Romans, tend, in fact, to be *men*. In the main, white men. But the idea of human "heroes" as cultural models for character is both recurrent and persistent. Books for children like *Good Night Stories for Rebel Girls* and *Women in Science: 50 Fearless Pioneers Who Changed the World* offer exemplary stories of women like Helen Keller, Rosa Parks, and Sally Ride. In an innovation aimed at older readers, *The New York Times* began an obituary series called "Overlooked No More," which has published belated biographical tributes to such women as the journalist Ida B. Wells, the photographer Diane Arbus, and the cookery innovator Fannie Farmer, none of whom were chronicled in its pages when they died. The American civil rights movement provided both heroes and role models, as have astronauts and space explorers, and the moral examples set by figures like Nelson Mandela and Mohandas K. Gandhi. The U.S. national holidays celebrating the births of Washington and Lincoln, now conflated into "Presidents' Day," have been joined by a day set aside to commemorate the birth of Martin Luther King, Jr. King's resonant wish, in his "I Have a Dream" speech on August 28, 1963, that his children "will one day live in a nation where they will not be judged by the color of their skin but by the content of their character," remains one of the most succinct and powerful statements about character in public discourse today.

Still, insofar as there are modern "cultural models" for character, such models are at least as likely to come from popular culture as from the study of history. In a way, this has, indeed, always been the case. We should remember that Plutarch's design was, as he said, to write lives rather than history—to shape his materials in an instructive as well as a pleasurable way. Shrewd Parson Weems knew that the cherry-tree story would grab his audience, as it did. The craze for chivalry in the Victorian period, which influenced everyone from the painters of the Royal Academy to the founder of the Boy Scouts, invented or tweaked "Arthurian" stories of knights, maidens, and dragons, making "history" (often "English history") out of myths and legends. Character, as Mary Poppins—and other nannies and governesses—would teach, often went down best with a spoonful of sugar.

Aristotle, Duty, and Will

Plutarch, of course, was only one of the ancient authors whose works were seen by educationists to model and uphold the standards of character. Another favorite classical text in the Victorian period was Aristotle's

Ethics, which was read, says the historian Frank Turner, by more Oxford students than any other single ancient treatise. "The *Ethics* particularly suited the education in character rather than scholarly accomplishment emphasized at nineteenth-century Oxford," Turner notes. "As a vehicle for training young men for careers in the church, politics, and the civil service, the *Ethics* possessed both charm and evident good sense and upheld the social elitism so much a part of Oxford life." The stress on forming good habits and on the strength of the will fit with prevailing beliefs, and, "in contrast to certain Platonic dialogues, the *Ethics* was a 'safe' book."[18]

The teaching of character development under headings like patriotism, morality, and good citizenship in the nineteenth century evolved, though sometimes in a rather imprecise or watered-down form, from *deontology*, literally "the study of duty," a concept associated with European philosophical thinkers like Kant and Comte. The theories of character formation, circumstance, and free will that animated thinkers like John Stuart Mill articulated tensions between "character" as indicative of moral and ethical duty and "character" as the developmental exercise of free will in response to economic, cultural, and personal circumstances.

The historian Stefan Collini set out the issues clearly when he distinguished between descriptive and evaluative accounts of character in the Victorian period, on the one hand, and voluntarism versus determinism, on the other.[19] In the first case, the issue was "scientific" objectivity versus moral judgment; in the second, the question of whether man—and, separately, woman—could change his or her character, and if so, how. A key word in these discussions was "will." As Collini observed, "It is particularly revealing that the feature of [Mill's] *On Liberty* to which contemporary critics took strongest exception was its perceived glorification of individual caprice and selfish indulgence at the expense of the stern demands of duty which were, it was indignantly affirmed, the true school of character."[20]

These debates framed and energized educational and philosophical schemes throughout that century and well into the following one. What was at stake was in part the very divergent, often intrinsically antithetical set of meanings that constellated around, and crystallized in, the concept of the word "character." Was it intrinsic or acquired? Could it be taught? Was a "strong character" one that acted, or one that withheld? And, above all, could it change? For, if human character could be changed—or could change itself—for the better, was it not the obligation of society and the individual, the schools and the home, to do what they could to "improve" it?

What twentieth- and twenty-first-century educators and politicians would rename "character education" was, for many of these thinkers, called "the formation of character." For some, including educational theorists and Victorian headmasters, it was the most fundamental, and most important, purpose of schooling.

Robert Owen and the Formation of Character

Robert Owen's Institute for the Formation of Character was opened in 1816 in what is sometimes called his "utopian" community of New Lanark, on the river Clyde, southeast of Glasgow. The new infant school, housed in a building that also supported evening classes and concerts for working-class adults, was, initially, an enormous success, attracting visitors from royalty to educational reformers who wanted to study and reproduce its innovations. The curriculum included music, dancing, games, and the use of maps, charts, and pictures to encourage enthusiasm among its young pupils, many of whom were the first in their families to attend a formal school. Owen's ideas influenced educational reform movements in both Britain and America, including the ideas of George Combe, one of the leading advocates of phrenology.

Like other social and educational reformers of his time, Owen was concerned with the state of the working class and of the child laborers who made up a good part of the workforce. Influenced by theorists like William Godwin and Erasmus Darwin, Owen insisted that character was a product of circumstance. It was training, environment, and education, not social rank or high birth, that produced good character and productive citizens. "Withdraw those circumstances which tend to create crime in the human character, and crime will not be created. Replace them with such as are calculated to form habits or order, regularity, temperance, industry; and those qualities will be formed."[21] His most often quoted assertion—one that John Stuart Mill and others would challenge—comes in his third essay on "The Principle of the Formation of Human Character":

> every day will make it more and more evident that the character of man is, without a single exception, always formed for him; that it may be, and is, chiefly created by his predecessors; that they give him, or may give him, his ideas and habits, which are the powers that govern and direct his conduct. Man, therefore, never did, nor is it possible he ever can, form his own character.[22]

The Institute for the Formation of Character was designed to improve "the *internal* as well as the *external* character of the whole village," and so it operated from the beginning like a modern day-care facility. "For this purpose," Owen told the inhabitants of New Lanark, "the Institution has been devised to afford the means of receiving your children at an early age, as soon almost as they can walk. By this means many of you, mothers and families, will be enabled to earn a better maintenance or support for your children; you will have less care and anxiety about them; while the children will be prevented from acquiring any bad habits, and gradually prepared to learn the best."[23]

Owen's institution had space for three hundred children, an orchestra (for singing and dancing), a playground, and educational exhibitions of animals and minerals. Girls learned to sew and knit, as well as to read, write, add, and subtract; boys were "instructed in military exercises," and those of them who had a taste for music were taught to play musical instruments—a skill not offered to girls, though children of both sexes, if they had "good voices," were taught to sing. Classes began at five-thirty in the morning, and after school those aged ten and older "were permitted to enter the works." Older children and "youth of both sexes," who had been working all day, could attend classes in the evening "to improve themselves in reading, writing, arithmetic, sewing, or knitting; or to learn any of the useful arts." Twice a week, in the evening, there was dancing and music, but "those who prefer to study" or to pursue any other occupation were assured that they would have a quiet place to do so. There was also adult education, which Owen described in his "Address to the Inhabitants of New Lanark" as "useful instruction to the older classes of the inhabitants," to include "the best modes of training your children," and "arranging your domestic concerns," and how to "direct your conduct towards each other" so as to "enable you to become greatly more happy than you have ever yet been."[24] Child care, homeschooling, household management, manners, and social (maybe even sex) education—the characters of adults were to be re-formed so as to help them to form the characters of their children.

The title of the Institute for the Formation of Character was an artifact of its time, like that of the Society for the Diffusion of Useful Knowledge, founded to provide reading materials on science and other elevated topics to working-class and middle-class readers, or to anyone who lacked the opportunity of or taste for formal education.[25] And, like that society, the institute had its critics; objectors found it insufficiently committed to religious education, and outlawed the singing, dancing, and marching that were at the center of many of the infant school's activities. Boys, who under Owen's supervision wore school uniforms that resembled kilts, were now "forced to wear pants,"[26] perhaps on the presumption that this intimation of traditional Scotland was contrary to a larger British sensibility.

Some critics were harsher still. The poet Robert Southey, who visited the Institute for the Formation of Character in 1819 and found himself disturbed by the "puppet-like motion" of the older children as they danced and marched, wrote in his *Journal*, "Owen in reality deceives himself. He is part-owner and sole Director of a large establishment, differing more in accidents than in essence from a plantation." Although "the persons under him happen to be white, and are at liberty to quit his service," they are while they reside there "as much under his absolute management as so many negro-slaves." As for the inhabitants of New Lanark, Southey reports that Owen called them "*human-machines*," and that "his humour, his vanity, [and] his kindliness of nature" made him want to "make a display of their happiness."[27]

Still, both the institution's example and its name stand out as signs of a preoccupation with character as something that could be "formed"—and, indeed, reformed—by collective social action. Remarking on the etiology of "what has been hitherto called wickedness in our fellow men," Owen set out the possible causes: (1) they were born with "faculties and propensities" that led them in that direction; (2) they were placed by circumstance—in particular countries, or with influence from parents and playmates from an early age—so that they were "gradually and necessarily trained" in "the habits and sentiments called wicked"; or (3) they became wicked as the result of some combination of these two factors.[28]

Any reader familiar with the ways of philosophical or theoretical argument will see immediately that the existence of option (3) makes it seem to be the "right" answer, though the initial binary division is essential to the program of character building that Owen proposes. But in fact Owen comes down largely on the side of circumstance and long-standing social prejudice against the poor, or what a later vocabulary would call the "underprivileged." In his new system, he says, there will not be

> any distinction made between the children of those parents who are deemed the worst, and of those who may be esteemed the best, members of society; rather, indeed, would I prefer to receive the offspring of the worst, if they shall be sent at an early age; because they really require more of our care and pity.

In fact, he explains,

> The system now preparing, and which will ultimately be brought into full practice, is to effect a complete change in all our sentiments and conduct toward those poor miserable creatures whom the errors of past times have denominated the bad, the worthless, and the wicked.

The real culprits are those who judge out of ignorance, "those who apply these terms to their fellow men," who are "themselves the immediate cause of more misery in the world than those they call the outcasts of society. *They* are, therefore, correctly speaking, the most wicked and worthless."[29]

This resounding accusation of hypocrisy in Owen's "Address to the Inhabitants of New Lanark" anticipates a similarly passionate reproach made a century and a half later, when the singer and political activist Paul Robeson was summoned to appear before the House Un-American Activities Committee: "You gentlemen," Robeson told the committee, "belong with the Alien and Sedition Acts, and you are the nonpatriots, and you are the un-Americans, and you ought to be ashamed of yourselves."[30] But the rhetoric of reform and revolution here is also more broadly familiar, and parts of Owen's "Address" look back to Gonzalo's ideal commonwealth in *The Tempest* (itself partly cribbed from Montaigne) and forward to Marx:

> A correct knowledge of human nature will be acquired; ignorance will be removed; the angry passions will be prevented from gaining any strength; charity and kindness will universally prevail; poverty will not be known; the interest of each individual will be in strict unison with the interest of every individual in the world. There will not be any counteraction of wishes and desires among men. Temperance and simplicity of manners will be the characteristics of every part of society. The natural defects of the few will be amply compensated by the increased attention and kindness toward them of the many.[31]

Owen's platform was radical for its time, although the degree to which this could be called "liberal" by a modern sensibility is limited in view of Owen's attitude (forgiving though skeptical) toward the adherents of any religion other than Christianity.

Mill's "Ethology," or the Science of Character

John Stuart Mill responded to Owen's expressed belief that "our characters are made for us, not *by* us," and that a system of education could produce "happiness," by rejecting what he saw as its fatalism or determinism in favor of the importance of the will. "Though our character is formed by circumstances, our own desires can do much to shape those circumstances," he declared in his *Autobiography*, and "what is really inspiriting and ennobling in the doctrine of free will, is the conviction that we have real power over the formation of our own character; that our will, by influencing some of our circumstances, can modify our future habits or capabilities of willing."[32]

In this way, Mill, using Owen's key words and phrases ("circumstances"; "formation of character"), offered a rebuttal of what he saw as a kind of passive capitulation to environment and social context. Education could indeed be beneficial to character, but it would do so most effectively if coupled with the force of individual will.

The push-back against the determinism of "circumstance" had, by mid-century, become familiar, and was frequently itself associated with the formation of character. "Instead of saying that man is the creature of Circumstance," wrote George Henry Lewes in 1855, "it would be nearer the mark to say that man is the architect of Circumstance. It is Character which builds an existence out of Circumstance."[33] And in the United States, Ralph Waldo Emerson, ruminating on the idea of "fate" in *The Conduct of Life* (1860), declared, "If we must accept Fate, we are not less compelled to affirm liberty, the significance of the individual, the grandeur of duty, the power of character."[34]

Mill's ringing statement about character, circumstance, and free will is frequently quoted. What is less often mentioned, however, is the *context* of his observations. The passage on free will occurs in a chapter of his *Autobiography* entitled "A Crisis in My Mental History," which records an emotional or nervous breakdown of sorts, a period of intense depression, for which the remedy was, at least in part, the reading of poetry. Mill quotes in particular from Coleridge, who had gone through a similar state of depression, but notes that he did not encounter works like Coleridge's "Dejection: An Ode," until sometime after his own crisis. The poet he did read was Wordsworth, whose poems were, he said, "a medicine for my state of mind," and exactly what suited his condition.[35]

"Poetry and the fine arts," including music, painting, and theater, wrote Mill, have "value in the formation of character."[36] It was "during the later returns of my dejection," as he explained, that the issue of free will as a mode of control over circumstances occurred to him. The result of this realization was "a relief to [his] spirits," both emotionally and intellectually, since he no longer saw an impasse between circumstance and free will, and was therefore no longer under the burden of "thinking one doctrine true, and the contrary doctrine morally beneficial."[37]

In his *System of Logic*, Mill would go on to try to codify the "laws of the formation of character," announcing a new "science" to which he proposes to give "the name of Ethology, or the Science of Character." Distinguishing ethology from psychology, which he defines as "the science of the elementary laws of mind," he says, "Ethology will serve for the ulterior science which determines the kind of character produced, in conformity to those general laws, by any set of circumstances, physical and moral." Thus, he argued, "Ethology is the science which corresponds to the art of education; in the widest sense of the term, including the formation of national and collective character as well as individual."[38]

The term "ethology" did not catch on quite as Mill hoped it might, although psychologists and philosophers like Alexander Bain praised it. By the late twentieth century, "ethology" had been adapted to describe not human character and character formation, but animal behavior.

Getting Up Steam

Of all Mill's memorable statements about character, though, perhaps the most intriguing—and certainly the most quoted by nonphilosophers—is the famous definition he provides in the essay *On Liberty*, first published in 1859:

> A person whose desires and impulses are his own—are the expression of his own nature, as it has been developed and modified by his own culture—is said to have a character. One whose desires and impulses are not his own, has no character, no more than a steam-engine has a character.

Mill continues his paragraph by expressing admiration for "persons who have much character," as if "character" were a cultural additive that could be increased or decreased:

> If, in addition to being his own, his impulses are strong, and are under the government of a strong will, he has an energetic character. Whoever thinks that individuality of desires and impulses should not be encouraged to unfold itself, must maintain that society has no need of strong natures—is not the better for containing persons who have much character—and that a high general average of energy is not desirable.[39]

But I always find myself distracted, as surely other readers do as well, by the arresting image of the steam engine that does not—or does it?—have a character.

First of all, this seems so much a "period" observation. The steam engine, invented by James Watt in 1781, was the driving force behind the Industrial Revolution, and by the early nineteenth century was used in factories, mills, and transportation on sea and land. Mill was not the only philosophic thinker to refer to it in his assessment of the new industrial world. Perhaps not surprisingly, in view of its importance, a connection can be found virtually everywhere in mid-Victorian culture between the steam engine and the proponents of "character."

Ralph Waldo Emerson, in the same essay in which he reflected on fate and character, personified steam power as—like fire—a Promethean gift to mankind:

> Steam was, till the other day, the devil which we dreaded. Every pot made by any human potter or brazier had a hole in its cover, to let off the enemy, lest he should lift pot and roof, and carry the house away. But the Marquis of Worcester, Watt, and Fulton bethought themselves, that, where was power, was not devil, but was God; that it must be availed of, and not by any means let off and wasted. Could he lift pots and roofs and houses so handily? he was the workman they were in search of. He could

> be used to lift away, chain, and compel other devils, far more reluctant and dangerous, namely, cubic miles of earth, mountains, weight or resistance of water, machinery, and the labors of all men in the world; and time he shall lengthen, and shorten space.[40]

Equally striking is the connection of these two topics, character and the steam engine, in the life and work of Samuel Smiles. Smiles is the celebrated author not only of *Self-Help* (1859)—which sold twenty thousand copies within a year of publication and over a quarter-million copies by the time of his death in 1904—but also of a series of other books on similar themes: *Character* (1871), *Thrift* (1875), and *Duty* (1880). But before he became famous, Smiles worked for over ten years as a secretary in the new railway industry, first for the Leeds & Thirsk Railway and after that for the South Eastern Railway, and he began his publishing career with an 1857 biography of George Stephenson, known as the "Father of Railways," who exemplified many of his ideas.[41] The steam-engine locomotive for railways—what we probably first think of today when we hear the term "steam engine"—was invented by Richard Trevithick and developed by Stephenson, who built his first locomotive in 1814.

Social Engines, Social Engineering

"One whose desires and impulses are not his own," Mill had written, "has no character, no more than a steam-engine has a character." But for us, in the present century, steam engines *do* have a character, whether in the form of the very popular Thomas the Tank Engine and his Friends, or of two earlier examples from children's literature: the doughty little blue engine in the 1930 children's classic *The Little Engine That Could* (puffing, "I think I can. I think I can. I think I can," as she pulls the train loaded with toys up the mountain, and then "I thought I could. I thought I could. I thought I could," as she descends triumphantly into the valley),[42] or the equally valiant steam shovel, Mary Anne, in *Mike Mulligan and His Steam Shovel*.[43]

Published in 1939, *Mike Mulligan* is unquestionably a story about character, grit, and empathy. Mike and his steam shovel have been replaced in the workforce by newer-model shovels, electric and gas and diesel. In order to prove their value, they volunteer to dig the foundation for a town hall in a single day, a job that it would normally take a hundred men a week to do. To the accompaniment of both cheers and skepticism from spectators, they accomplish this gargantuan task, only to find that they have forgotten to build an exit ramp from the deep foundation for Mary Anne. But a boy who has been observing the proceedings and cheering on the work suggests that Mary Anne might be converted to a steam boiler to heat the building, and that Mike might become the janitor, a proposal that meets everyone's approval.

The Little Engine That Could and *Mike Mulligan and His Steam Shovel*—both literary products of the Depression—are perpetual favorites on the U.S. National Education Association's "Teachers' Top 100 Books for Children" list. As fables of character, and indeed of "character education," they could hardly be bettered. And this is in part because they are well written. They are not only classics, they are literature.

The little blue engine is the smallest and least experienced of the engines in the story; larger and more sophisticated locomotives (a sleek passenger engine, a powerful freight engine) scorn the task of bringing a small load of toys and fruit to waiting children. And it takes a child (of course) to think of the answer to Mike's and Mary Anne's dilemma, whereas the town elders are clueless or, in one case, obstructive. Even this longtime resister is ultimately converted, however—the story has a genuinely happy, as well as an ingenious, ending, despite, or perhaps even because of, the shadow of hard economic times. And when we consider the fact that the one resister was a councilman who was hoping to get the work done on the cheap, assuming that Mike and Mary Anne would fail at their task (while digging part of the hole for no compensation), the issue of "character" becomes even more manifest.

Not only do the supposedly outmoded steam shovel and its operator succeed, they also act as moral agents to educate and change the character of a politically scheming adult. I'll add only that it's indicative, perhaps, that both of the Depression-era engines are female. For John Stuart Mill, the author of *The Subjection of Women*, who averred, "No other class of dependents have had their character so entirely distorted from its natural proportions by their relation to their masters,"[44] this is a point about the literary animation—and character—of steam engines that might retroactively have increased his interest. (What he would have made of the modern genre and fashion called steampunk is another question.)

"A Brave, Helpful, Truth-Telling Englishman"

Of course, *Mike Mulligan* and *The Little Engine That Could* were written almost a century after Mill's *On Liberty*, and in the United States, not in England. And their target audience was—and is—very small children. To get something of a sense of the "character ethos" of the nineteenth century, it will be useful to look at another classic work of literature for young people, one that speaks directly to the revolution going on in the emerging and influential Victorian public schools.

In this passage from Thomas Hughes's novel *Tom Brown's School Days*, published in 1857, Tom's father, Squire Brown, is pondering what useful advice to give his son as he sends him off for his first day at Rugby, the famous public school headed by Dr. Thomas Arnold:

> "Shall I tell him to mind his work, and say he's sent to school to make himself a good scholar? Well, he isn't sent to school for that—at any rate, not for that mainly. I don't care a straw for Greek particles, or the digamma: no more does his mother. What is he sent to school for? Well, partly because he wanted so to go. If he'll only turn out a brave, helpful, truth-telling Englishman, and a gentleman, and a Christian, that's all I want," thought the Squire, and upon this view of the case he framed his last words of advice to Tom.[45]

Tom is that mythical personage, the "well-rounded" boy, who grows up in his Rugby years to be popular with classmates, brave at fighting, good enough at lessons, captain of the cricket eleven, destined for Oxford. Literarily speaking he is sandwiched between, and contrasted with, the more devil-may-care Harry East (who, when he leaves Rugby, joins his regiment as a soldier in India) and the more bookish George Arthur, the son of a clergyman. At one point Dr. Arnold, always called "the Doctor" by the novel's narrator, inquires of his staff about East and Brown, who are "taking the lead" and are "very active, bold fellows," but seem to be on a potentially risky path: "I shan't let them stay if I don't see them gaining character and manliness," says the Doctor, using the two key words of his educational philosophy.[46]

The danger is averted in part through the quiet influence of Arthur, who encourages the boys to read the Bible together in the evenings, avoiding the overly intimate terrain of personal religious discussion, and opting instead to discuss the characters of the "men and women whose lives were there told," as if the Bible were "the most vivid and delightful history of real people." To Tom's initial surprise, "Arthur began talking about Joseph as if he were a living statesman—just as he might have talked about Lord Grey and the Reform Bill." From that moment, "the men and women, whom he had looked upon as something quite different from himself, became his friends and counselors." These readings and discussions continue "almost nightly for years afterwards," with Tom and Arthur occasionally joined by East or by other schoolmates.[47]

To a reader of the novel, there is a certain metafictional irony in Tom's realization that the characters in the Bible were for Arthur "real people, who might do right or wrong, just like any one who was walking about in Rugby—the Doctor, or the masters or the sixth-form boys"[48]—since Tom, East, and Arthur are for us literary characters no more or less real than those figures "walking about in Rugby" whom he goes out of his way to designate as really—that is to say nonfictionally—"real." Moreover—here the twist goes in the other direction—"the Doctor," Thomas Arnold, the headmaster of Rugby School and the father of Matthew Arnold, was "really real," as our inadequate language will put it; that is, he was a "real person" who lived, and died prematurely, a day before his forty-seventh birthday.

Inevitably, specific challenges test the character of the protagonists. The novel includes a spiritual crisis (East's tearful revelation that he has not been confirmed and thus does not take Communion, a problem instantly resolved when he gathers the courage to tell this to Dr. Arnold), an academic crisis, of sorts (Arthur convinces Tom to give up the use of a crib in reading Greek and Latin, and though East and others insist that in fact these cribs are part of school tradition, handed down from one generation to the next, Tom decides to persevere without them), and what might be called, I suppose, a behavioral crisis (when Arthur as a new boy kneels down by his bedside to pray he is teased and mocked by the other boys, but his unashamed public piety reminds Tom that he used to kneel this way as well, and before long the entire schoolhouse is doing so, reversing the "heathen" habits into which they had strayed through social cowardice).

Tom and East outwit the bully Flashman, who is forced to leave the school. Tom defends George Arthur by challenging a bigger boy, Slogger Williams, to a public fight, after which the two combatants shake hands and become friends—a transformation viewed benignly by the all-seeing, all-knowing Doctor Arnold. Character education—and this is surely one of the things *Tom Brown's School Days* is about—has more to do with the virtues Squire Brown instinctively values, from bravery and truth telling to Christianity, than it has to do with schoolwork.

Arnold's death in 1842, after Tom has left Rugby for Oxford, provides a coda for the story, an opportunity to demonstrate yet again how a schoolboy becomes a man. On a "fishing ramble" in the islands of Scotland with two college friends, Tom learns by accident, from a copy of an old newspaper, that the Doctor is dead. Immediately, and somewhat to the surprise and annoyance of his companions ("Yet they also were public-school men"[49]), Tom cancels his trip and makes a pilgrimage to his old public school. "His heart was still proud and high, and he walked up to the seat which he had last occupied as a sixth-form boy," but then, after reflection, he "rose and walked humbly down to the lowest bench, and sat down on the very seat which he had occupied on his first Sunday at Rugby."[50] The body of Doctor Arnold had been buried beneath the altar, and the novel leaves Tom kneeling there in tears. Altogether one feels that Squire Brown should feel satisfied in his expectations for his son's education.

"Play the Game": Character and the English Public Schools

"The Sixth Form were a group of older boys who were selected as having 'character' and were empowered to beat smaller boys," George Orwell reports in an essay on his school days in England from 1911 to 1916, the years just before the First World War. Later in the essay he extrapolates on this quality, describing it as "something called 'guts' or 'character', which in reality meant the power to impose your will on others." Orwell himself was "hopeless" at games, he says, and at his preparatory school "virtue consisted in winning." The "pattern of school life" was "a continuous triumph of the strong over the weak."[51] But not all of those who experienced—or observed—this mode of education were so critical of it.

"School as a place to train character—a totally new concept so far—was what came to distinguish the English public school from all other Western school systems," says Jonathan Gathorne-Hardy. "It was what amazed and impressed foreigners—and amazes them still."[52] As pupils became Old Boys and sometimes masters, as masters at one school became headmasters of other schools, the ideas of "character" and "tone" as important aspects of elite education flourished. J. H. Badley of Bedales, one of the most progressive of the public schools, brought with him from Dr. Arnold's Rugby a commitment to "character" and an expectation that his school would produce it, even though the two schools were in other ways greatly dissimilar.

The diplomat and writer Harold Nicolson would write that, having seen "so much of the foreign product," he believed that on balance the British school system (by which he meant the public schools) was probably "best adapted to our national temperament. It is true, of course," he continued, "that it standardises character and suppresses originality; that it somewhat ruthlessly subordinates the musical to the gymnastic. I am not convinced, however, that this is a bad thing."[53]

Even so atypical a schoolboy as Walter Pater, no hearty, could write reminiscently of his public school as a place that, like the culture of ancient Sparta, offered a special mode of training that brought out the "lights and shadows of human character." Pater compared the Spartan system directly to that of the English public school, for which a young boy "of the privileged classes left his home [and] his tender nurses." His schooling "involved, as with ourselves, the government of youth by itself; an implicit subordination of the younger to the older." Pater lists some key terms—"words, titles, which indicate an unflinching elaboration of youthful subordination and command with responsibility," which, he says, "remain as what we might call their 'public school slang.'"[54] The young Spartan man had "his friendships to solace him; and to encourage him, his sense of honour."[55] In short, "like some of our old English places of education, though we might not care to live always at school there, it is good to visit them on occasion." The analogies are persistent and telling: public schools; the government of youth by itself; subordination and command; friendships; honor; "the boys at school chanting";[56] all together engaged in "bringing out" (the literal meaning of "education") "the lights and shadows of human character."

But it was on the playing fields, above all, that "character" could be formed and tested.

One of the most essential elements of "character" for boys was "manliness," which could be developed at school in "games," from football to cricket to rugby. Games were more important than schoolwork, as well as more fun. They taught chivalry and team spirit, and the great character-building rules of fair play. As Robert Baden-Powell would later write, commending these activities to Boy Scouts and Rovers,

> You often see it said that the Public School education which the more well-to-do boys get is no good. It IS good, but not so much for what is taught in the class-room as for what is learnt on the playing field and out of school.
>
> A boy there learns that clean play and true sportsmanship, straight dealing and sense of honor, are expected of him by his comrades.[57]

A good try, a noble defeat, was said to be sometimes better than a victory. At the same time, the unquestioned school hero was the individual, the team captain, the boy who scored the winning goal. A

House Captain in *Tom Brown's School Days* rallies his troops by declaring, to "frantic cheers," that he would rather "win three School-house matches running than get the Balliol Scholarship any day!"[58] School subjects came a long way below games for all but the determined intellectual and the misfit. At his public school, Wellington College, Harold Nicolson later reflected, many boys came to believe "that intellectual prowess was in some way effeminate and that it was only by physical prowess that one could manifest, or even subscribe to, that aim of 'manliness' for which alone we had all, teleologically, been sent [to school]."[59] Games, unlike academic subjects, were believed—by both boys and many schoolmasters—to instill "character." The shared vocabulary of victory, defeat, and heroism was far from accidental.

That the Duke of Wellington did *not* say that the Battle of Waterloo was won on the playing fields at Eton is now more widely believed than that he *did* say it. But, like all cultural myths, this has something of a basis in fact. The terms of battle, fight, victory, defeat, and fair play moved easily between sport and war, and, to a certain extent, do so still.

The chorus of Henry Newbolt's popular poem "Vitaï Lampada" ("The Torch of Life," a phrase from Lucretius), often used independently as a rallying cry, was "Play up! play up! and play the game!" The poem moves from Newbolt's schooling at Clifton College in the first verse, to the heroic death (in defeat) of General Gordon in the Sudan in the second, and then to a third verse in which the "sons" of the school are exhorted to keep the flame alive. The second verse is the best known, since it marks the shift from the boy culture of sport to the man culture of war:

> The sand of the desert is sodden red,—
> Red with the wreck of a square that broke;—
> The Gatling's jammed and the Colonel dead,
> And the regiment blind with dust and smoke.
> The river of death has brimmed his banks
> And England's far, and Honour a name,
> But the voice of a schoolboy rallies the ranks:
> "Play up! play up! and play the game!"

Educators and leaders in the United States, some influenced by the British example and some by the Civil War and the rhetoric of chivalry it sometimes evoked, were likewise inclined to see sports as a good training ground for "men of character." College athletes became heroes, although there was some interesting push-back when codified rules and referees were added to intercollegiate sports, since it was felt that this took away from the individual player the responsibility for ethical decisions.[60] Charles W. Eliot, the president of Harvard, worried that in the way they played their games Americans were "morally inferior" to the English.[61]

But Theodore Roosevelt, who had fought in the Spanish-American War and was a strong proponent of the active life, enthusiastically endorsed the idea that college sports could test character. "Bodily vigour is good, and vigour of intellect even better, but far above both is character," he wrote in an essay called "Character and Success." "If between any two contestants, even in college sport or in college work, the difference in character on the right side is as different as the difference of intellect or strength the other way, it is the character side that will win."[62]

The next step, and perhaps one that was inevitable, was to widen the opportunities for organized character development beyond the exclusive public schools, while retaining, and sometimes enhancing, what were regarded as their most successful (nonacademic) elements. No one did this better, or with more energy and commitment, than Robert Baden-Powell.

The Boy Scouts and the "'Varsity of Life"

In 1933, looking back on his long career—first in the army and then as the founder of the Boy Scouts movement—Sir Robert Baden-Powell, the "hero of Mafeking," published an autobiography called *Lessons from the 'Varsity of Life*. The title page identified him as "Lord Baden-Powell of Gilwell, G.C.M.G., G.C.V.O., K.C.B., LL.D., D.C.L."

Gilwell Park was a country estate of over fifty acres of woodland that had been purchased by a Scottish benefactor as a training school for Scouters, the "boy men" who would lead scouting troops. Baden-Powell himself was officially the "Chief Scout." And "'Varsity," British slang for "university," was a deliberate choice. Baden-Powell himself had never attended university (he twice failed the entrance exam for Oxford), and he had still made a manifest success of his life.[63]

Under the heading "National Need for Character Training," Baden-Powell wrote that as an officer in the army he had seen hundreds of young men as recruits, "estimable young men, able to read and write, well-behaved and amenable to discipline," but "without individuality or strength of character, utterly without resourcefulness, initiative, or the guts for adventure." He acknowledged that he was "speaking, of course, of over twenty years ago," but although times had changed, the need for character training had not: "education has fresh difficulties to contend with to-day, in the shape of increased herd-instinct, undesirable teachings of a sensational Sunday press, immoral cinemas, and easy access to cheap, unhealthy pleasure, and gambling."[64]

B.-P. (whose initials, as he proudly noted in *Scouting for Boys*, were the source of the Boy Scout motto "Be Prepared") recalled: "In training our lads in the Army to be soldiers we had to remedy some of the shortcomings in their character . . . We had to inculcate a good many qualities not enunciated in school text-books, such as individual pluck, intelligence, initiative, and spirit of adventure." The skills of scouting in the army were taught "not through drill nor imposed instruction but by going back to nature and backwoodsmanship, by taking the men back as nearly as possible to the primitive, to learn tracking, eye for a country, observation by night as well as by day, to learn to stalk and to hide, to improvise shelter, and to feed and fend for themselves."[65] And since "the inculcation of character, health, and manliness" were "qualities as much needed in a citizen as in a soldier,"[66] he conceived his idea for training boys along these same lines.

The name of the organization, as he observed, had been central to its success.

> What to call it? There's a lot in a name. Had we called it what it was, viz., a "Society for the Propagation of Moral Attributes," the boy would not exactly have rushed for it. But to call it SCOUTING and give him the chance of becoming an embryo Scout, was quite another pair of shoes. His inherent "gang"

> instinct would be met by making him a member of a "Troop" and a "Patrol." Give him a uniform to wear, with Badges to be won and worn on it for proficiency in Scouting—and you got him.[67]

"Boy Scouts" was a term that would excitingly associate the training of boys with scouting, an activity practiced in dangerous situations or unfamiliar terrain by the manly men of the British forces—and also with "peace scouts," who explored and mastered the wilderness. The same point is clear from the title of the classic manual and manifesto of 1908, *Scouting for Boys.*

The Code of the Boy Scouts was a freely adapted version of the chivalric code of "the knights of the Middle Ages," including such character attributes as "Honour," "Self-discipline," "Courtesy," "Courage," "Selfless sense of Duty and Service," all under "the guidance of Religion." The Scout Law, as B.-P. himself emphasized, was not a list of "DON'TS," which "generally invites evasion since it challenges the spirit inherent in every red-blooded boy (or man)," but was devised "as a guide to his actions rather than repressive of his faults."[68]

Often, nonetheless, compared to the Ten Commandments, the Scout Law ultimately consisted of ten items stating "what is good form and expected of a Scout,"[69] although the tenth, "a scout is clean in thought, word and deed," was not included in the first edition of *Scouting for Boys,* but was added to the canon in 1911. (The phrase "morally straight" has been part of the Scout Oath of the Boy Scouts of America since 1911, but is not part of the British Scout Oath or Laws.) One of Baden-Powell's biographers attributes this delay in the inclusion of purity, which "would generally be considered a more urgent matter than cheerfulness, courtesy, or thrift," to the "strictly social character of the original laws," while acknowledging that Baden-Powell was "as hostile to all forms of sexual indulgence—and particularly the dread sin of self-abuse—as any moralist of the time."[70]

He may in fact have felt more strongly than some. The original typescript of *Scouting for Boys* had included an extensive and heartfelt warning that began: "The result of self-abuse is always—mind you, always—that the boy after a time becomes weak and nervous and shy . . . and if he carries on too far he very probably goes out of his mind and becomes an idiot. A very large number of the lunatics in our asylums have made themselves mad by indulging in this vice although at one time they were sensible cheery boys like any one of you."[71] The publisher of *Scouting for Boys*, Arthur Pearson, felt this would not be a likely way to attract scouts to the movement, and the printer, Horace Cox, found the material obscene, and stopped the presses. A much less explicit account of the dangers of self-abuse was finally printed only in the "Notes to Instructors," where the key word is "Continence." Nothing is said about homosexuality.

(In 2013, the National Council of the Boy Scouts of America lifted the ban on openly gay Scouts, and in 2015 ended the ban on gay adults in leadership positions. As of 2018, the restriction on gender had also been changed, so that girls were permitted to become Boy Scouts. The British Scouting Association removed the mention of God in the Scout Promise in 2013, to allow atheists to join. A few months earlier, the Girl Guides had made a similar change.)

The first nine Scout Laws offer a good template of "character" issues as Baden-Powell saw them: "A Scout's Honour is to be Trusted"; "A Scout is Loyal"; "A Scout's Duty is to be Useful"; "A Scout is a Friend to All"; "A Scout is Courteous"; "A Scout is a Friend to Animals"; "A Scout Obeys Orders"; "A Scout Smiles and Whistles Under All Difficulties"; "A Scout is Thrifty." Baden-Powell also drew up an "Analysis of the Scout Scheme of Training," which listed qualities under the headings of "Character and Intelligence" and "Health and Strength." "Intellectual qualities" did not mean schoolwork, but observation and deduction. The "Civic" qualities of character were fair play, discipline, leadership, responsibility, and respect for others, and the "Moral" qualities included honor, chivalry, and self-reliance, but also courage, the capacity for enjoyment, self-expression in art, "higher tone of thought," and religion.[72]

It's worth bearing in mind that many of these "character" categories were aimed at integrating working-class boys, often from urban backgrounds, into the spirit of scouting. Often there were parallels, some less exact than others, with the character expectations of the "public schools." An illustration drawn by Baden-Powell for *Lessons from the 'Varsity of Life*, titled "The Scoutmaster's conjuring trick," shows a magician, in formal clothes, in front of a cabinet marked "Scouting." An ill-dressed, slack-jawed, stooped young man, in ragged clothes and cap, smoking a cigarette, enters at one side of the cabinet; from the other side strides—in the approved Scout posture, shoulders back, head in the air—a classically handsome Boy Scout, in full uniform and hat.

On the Track of Character

Baden-Powell was an excellent draftsman, who could draw equally well with both hands. His sketches are found throughout *Scouting for Boys* and in many of his other publications, and have sometimes been called racially insensitive. The instructions under "Details of People" in the "Tracking" section use pictures to suggest how "character" can be read, a skill said to be useful for shop assistants and salesmen, and also for "detecting would-be swindlers": "It is said that you can tell a man's character from the way he wears his hat. If it is slightly on one side, the wearer is good-natured; if it is worn very much on one side, he is a swaggerer; if on the back of his head, he is bad at paying his debts; if worn straight on the top, he is probably honest but very dull."

This mode of observation seems to be concerned with a much less momentous kind of "character" than the spirit that built the Empire, but the implications are similar, and similarly class- and school-based. The accompanying illustrations, "How the wearing of a hat shows character," depict four men, one of whom is recognizably the "cheery" smiling Boy Scout in a bowler hat. The others are less admirable: the man with the hat on the back of his head ("bad at paying his debts") is long-nosed and chinless, the swaggerer (hat on side of head) has a cigarette in his mouth, and the honest but dull hat-wearer is an older man with pince-nez and a reproving look.[73]

Across the page is another illustration, this one of three heads in profile. Baden-Powell's comment reads, "Certainly the 'quiff' or lock of hair which some lads wear on their forehead is a sure sign of silliness. The shape of the face gives a good guide to the man's character." Then comes the invitation to the Scout-in-training: "Perhaps you can tell the character of these gentlemen?"[74]

"Gentlemen" may well be intended ironically. The man on the left, with the telltale "quiff" of hair, is chinless, with a mouth hanging open and a dull, unfocused eye; these "signs" would be recognizable in any contemporary chart of physiognomy, like those of Cesare Lombroso, as indicating lack of intelligence. The man on the right has close-cropped tightly curled hair, a deep frown that extends to his forehead, slitted eyes, and a pugnacious chin. It is not clear whether he is intended to be black, since the drawings are only in outline, but both of these images are in sharp contrast to the head in the middle, drawn to a slightly larger scale—a classic "Anglo-Saxon" boy-man with sculpted hair that resembles that of a Greek statue.[75] There is no explanatory commentary: the picture, which is intended to allow the aspiring Scout to "tell the character" of the three individuals from their profiled images, is expected to speak for itself.

Other physical clues to "character" that the aspiring tracker might notice include the description of various walks ("the fussy, swaggering little man paddling along with short steps with much arm action," the "slow slouch of the loafer," "the smooth-going and silent step of the scout"), shoes, and mustaches: Baden-Powell, whose own military mustache was one of his signatures, says he mistrusts "men with waxed moustaches," a sign of "vanity and sometimes drink." The mix of "sign" and prejudice throughout these examples is symptomatic. To deduce vanity from the waxing of a mustache, or dullness from a hat centered on the head, may be plausible; to extrapolate drunkenness from a mustache style or financial imprudence from the tilt of a hat suggests association rather than deduction. Two of the men whose heads are shown in profile are clearly related to Lombroso's criminal types or to Max Nordau's *Degeneration* (1893). In fact, the 1908 *Scouting for Boys* contains a "Hint to Instructors" on "How to Help in a Great National Work" that begins, "Recent reports on the deterioration of our race ought to act as a warning to be taken in time before it goes too far," and then lists two pages of statistics on army recruits with bad teeth, adenoids in the throat, pigeon breasts, curvature of the spine, defective sight, and low height and weight.[76] As Elleke Boehmer suggests, "Character observation in many ways meant reading for the signs of working-class poverty."[77]

Self-Instruction and the "Character Factory"

Scouting for Boys was first published in fortnightly parts, and was described as a "self-instructor," or what we might today call a self-help book. The same term, "self-instructor," had been used for popular handbooks in phrenology, such as Orson and Lorenzo Fowler's *Illustrated Self-Instructor in Phrenology and Physiology* (1849), which included "one hundred engravings, and a chart of the character." Both were related to Samuel Smiles's popular *Self-Help: With Illustrations of Character, Conduct, and Perseverance* (1859). Although phrenology is now largely regarded as a pseudoscience and an eccentric fad of the past, whereas scouting continues to be respected as a legitimate mode of "character training," the impulse and the occasion for these three "self-instructors" (or "self-educators") was similar. Self-improvement, the improvement of one's character, would pave the way to both personal and national success.

As Smiles had maintained, "The spirit of self-help, as exhibited in the energetic action of individuals, has at all times been a marked feature of the English character, and furnishes the true measure of our power as a nation."[78] Those who did not have access to higher education or the character training of the elite public schools and universities need not despair, for "schools, academies, and colleges, give but the merest beginnings of culture." Far more important were the activities of daily life, lessons of "action, conduct, self-culture, self-control—all that tends to discipline a man truly." These, said Smiles, offered "a kind of education not to be learned from books, or acquired by any amount of mere literary training."[79] This, too, then, was the "'varsity of life."

Baden-Powell shared this view of the relative values of experience and scholarship. But, unlike Smiles (or the Fowler brothers), he was already a "gentleman," in the social-hierarchical sense. When he failed to get into Oxford (where two of his brothers were already studying), he was immediately able to join an elite regiment in India, and went on to become a national war hero—in a war otherwise lamentably lacking in famous victories. The biography of the "Chief Scout" would continue to dominate the movement, and *Scouting for Boys* was strategically dotted with anecdotes about the "Mafeking Boy Scouts" as well as about King Arthur and the "Red Indians" of America.

"Character," that Victorian ideal, now became an Edwardian—and after that a Georgian—goal, stressed by many "youth specialists," clubs, and boys' brigades in the period. The objective was not just to provide the poor with access to the ideals of the public schools, but to serve the nation. The "greatest service" that "men of education and wealth" could provide, wrote the Reverend H. S. Pelham, was to "train the future citizen by bringing to bear upon him when he is young and unsettled the influence of a strong and healthy character."[80]

The "character factory," as the biographer Michael Rosenthal points out, was one of Baden-Powell's own descriptions of the Boy Scout movement. Like many others, he believed that character could be strengthened by exercise and habit—as, for example, in the daily "good turn" that *Scouting for Boys* enjoined as part of the Scout Laws. "Our business," he wrote in the *Headquarters Gazette* in 1911, "is not merely to keep up smart 'show' troops" but "to pass as many boys through our character factory as we possibly can: at the same time, the longer the grind that we can give them the better men they will be at the end."[81]

Tim Jeal's more psychologically inflected biography suggests that there may have also been more personal motivations. Baden-Powell, whose first career was that of a soldier, enjoyed the company of men and boys, and he met his closest male friend, with whom he shared living quarters for twenty years, while stationed in India. Whether or not his relationship with Kenneth McLaren, whom he called "Boy," or "the Boy," was physical—most biographers think not—it was clearly tender, passionate, and important. The two men continued to be friends after both married, though ultimately they grew apart, in part because Baden-Powell disapproved of his friend's second marriage, to a woman who had been the nurse of McLaren's first wife and then the governess of his daughter, and who, as a farmer's daughter with no money of her own, was not a "lady."[82]

It's perhaps worth noting that Baden-Powell had fewer concerns on this question of class mobility when it came to men. In a circular he distributed to the officers and men of the South African Constabulary in 1902, he "urged them to be 'gentlemen' not in the sense of having money or the right background, but as men 'who could be trusted on their honour to do a thing,'" assuring them that "by their personal self-respect and avoidance of bad habits" they would "give themselves a manliness and dignity which no humbug can attain to."[83]

Peter Pan

Robert Baden-Powell's favorite play was *Peter Pan*, the story of a boy who couldn't—or wouldn't—grow up. He first saw it in February 1905, shortly after it opened in London, and went back immediately to see it again, the following day, urging his mother to see it as soon as she could. When he met his future wife, he wrote to her to say that he wanted to take her to Barrie's play, and they went (for the first of many times) shortly after their wedding. Baden-Powell had written years before to a young girl—one of several with whom he corresponded—that he wanted her to be "a sort of Peter—(h'm that's odd, there is no feminine for Peter) a sort of girl Peter Pan, the boy who couldn't grow up. And long may you be so."[84]

When his son was born, he was named Arthur after his godfather, Robert after his father, and Peter—the name by which he was always known—for Peter Pan. (Lady Baden-Powell records happily in her autobiography that when she was pregnant with her first child "it had to be a boy, and, of course, it would have to be called 'Peter.'"[85])

Baden-Powell's wife, Olave, was much younger than he, and commendably athletic, much more so than other women he had known. She played tennis, hockey, and squash—more usually in the period a sport for public-school boys—and swam, bicycled, skated, and rode to hounds. Olave also enjoyed long walks, which she would continue to take with Baden-Powell.[86] After their marriage, she collaborated actively in her husband's work, and became the international head of the Girl Guides. Her title, "Chief Guide," was (deliberately) the pendant and equivalent of his title, "Chief Scout."

The mother of his three children, and sometimes a "mother" to Robert Baden-Powell as well,[87] Olave was also, as Jeal suggests, a version of the "girl Peter Pan" he had, much earlier, imagined. "She is a perfect wonder in camp," he told his mother, "and is as good as a backwoodsman."[88] But early in their courtship he had written to Olave, teasingly (and flirtatiously), having discovered that they had both played in Kensington Gardens, "Are you perhaps Wendy?"[89] In which case, presumably, *he* could be Peter Pan. (When Olave finally met James Barrie, however, she found him a "sad disappointment—a shy awkward uncouth little man."[90])

The "Epilogue" to Jeal's biography of Baden-Powell returns to Barrie's *Peter Pan* and links it with the lifelong and sometimes emotionally costly quest for "character."

> The reason for Imperial Britons dreading eclipse by other nations so intensely was their belief that national "greatness" depended upon "character" rather than upon technology, natural resources or size of population . . . Character was everything and yet it was threatened on every side—and nobody knew that better than [Baden-Powell], who had fought so long and hard to keep out the moral enemies which threatened him. "Be Prepared" was not just the perfect motto for an Edwardian youth movement but for an entire era in which so many different fears were linked.
>
> When calling to mind those cohorts of manly men filling the stalls night after night in performances of *Peter Pan*, and the eager "boy men" who became the first Scoutmasters, it is clear that aggression was very often not the only survivor of a highly disciplined upbringing. The child they had striven so hard to cast out, when bent on making men of themselves, was still lurking in the wings.[91]

Scouting and Manliness

Samuel Smiles's familiar list of the elements of character that "discipline" a man—"action, conduct, self-culture, self-control"—were still very much in force and in view half a century later. Of these, "self-control" was among the most persistent and the most difficult, since it meant the repression of feelings rather than their expression. (We can see some of the fervor behind this goal in the language Baden-Powell had drafted—and then had to "repress"—for his advice to Scouts on sexual "continence" and the avoidance of masturbation.) The key attribute of "manliness" seemed to demand both the resistance to emotion and its proper, even sometimes sentimental, display. At one point, reproving Baden-Powell's nephew Donald for kissing a housemaid, Olave wrote to him, "Try to develop yourself into what you ought to be—a fine manly man and a manly gentleman. Be a *Scout*!"[92]

But what did it mean to be "manly"? "Manliness," like "character," was in practice sometimes a conundrum. "The English concept of manliness changed dramatically in connotation over the Victorian period," writes J. A. Mangan in a study of the "games ethic" and British imperialism. "To the early Victorians it meant the successful transition from Christian immaturity to maturity demonstrated by earnestness, selflessness and integrity; to the late Victorians it represented neo-Spartan virility as exemplified by stoicism, hardness and endurance—the preeminent virtues of the late Victorian English public school."[93] When the boys were from another, "lower" class, the efforts to improve them took a similar path. "Since manliness was the necessary first step to gentlemanliness," says Mark Girouard, "boxing, cricket and football were considered essential elements of the boys' clubs which were the inevitable appendages to missions and settlements."[94]

Just as "character" could refer to nobility and self-sacrifice on the one hand, and to judgments based on social class and racial prejudice on the other, so "manliness" could mean at once self-restraint and aggression. It was not always obvious which occasions might call for which.

"Every boy ought to learn to shoot and to obey orders," Baden-Powell had insisted in his first "Campfire Yarn" in *Scouting for Boys*, "else he is no more good when war breaks out than an old woman."[95] The specter of this useless "old woman" haunts the text, and is periodically invoked in connection with manliness. Thus, in the "Notes for Instructors," having warned that in dangerous times "without manliness and good citizenship we are bound to fail," Baden-Powell declares, "Manliness can only be taught by men, and not by those who are half men, half old women."[96] (Note that Baden-Powell does not say "half men, half women"—such a hybrid would, presumably, be a slightly different thing.) Is being an "old woman" the inevitable alternative to being "manly"? And what about *young* women? How might they affect the manliness of a young man?

"Manliness" is the heading of a section in Baden-Powell's *Rovering to Success*, in the chapter on "Women," who are identified as one of the "Rocks to Success," around which the Rover is encouraged to steer. The subheads under "Manliness" are suggestive: "Chivalry" is followed by "Not My Job," which is in turn followed by "It Is Up to You to be Master of Yourself," "Auto-Suggestion," "The Parents' Influence" ("A large proportion of the men who have risen to eminence in the world admit that they have owed very much of their character and success to the influence of their mother"), and "Save Yourself and Help to Preserve the Race," before turning to a more general account of the healthy body and ending with a reminder to "fight the dragon of temptation" like Saint George. After "Manliness" comes "Marriage," but manliness is still an issue ("a young lad . . . likes to show [his girl] off as a sign of his manliness"), and aspiring Rovers are reminded that Girl Guides make especially good wives (they "can be better pals because they have got the same keenness on camping and the out of doors with all the necessary handiness and resourcefulness"). With a final warning about venereal disease—which can be contracted not only from prostitutes but also from "a girl who has been with men and who is not a real prostitute"—Baden-Powell signs off on the topic of "Women" with the reassuring advice that sex is "part of all living things and only requires proper management."[97]

"Character" itself is also, of course, a key topic for those who would Rover to Success, and is closely linked to "manly" behavior. One of its enemies was drink, since "to make a strong nation you must have men of character to form it." In some countries, Baden-Powell notes, there is a legal prohibition against liquor, but "prohibition will not be needed for a nation of character." In fact, such legal strictures are themselves unmanly. "Prohibition mainly offends the sense of free and manly people who would prefer to reform themselves from within, and who resent the remedy being pressed upon them by reformers, however well meaning, from without."[98] As we can see, this is entirely consistent with Baden-Powell's own ethic of self-repression and self-control. To be manly, to have character, is to play by your own, stricter rules.

Drinking is covered in a section called "Wine," which, like "Women," is a "Rock You Are Likely to Bump On." (The following section is not, however, called "Song," but is instead a caution against extremists in politics and "irreligion," here called "Cuckoos and Humbugs.") The best guard against all of these obstacles is "Character," represented periodically throughout the book by a variety of adages (called "What Other Fellows Have Said"): "Character has more value than any other attribute of life." "Self-control is three parts of Character." "You cannot dream yourself into Character. You must hammer and forge it for yourself (*Froude*)."[99] This last precept is attributed to James Anthony Froude, the English historian. The other "other fellows" are not identified.

In *The Quest of the Boy: A Study of the Psychology of Character Training*, F.W.W. Griffin, a medical doctor and the editor of *The Scouter*, sought to add "psychological teachings and definitions" to the Boy Scout truths about "the building of character."[100] He discusses "introverts" and "extroverts," and cites Robert Louis Stevenson's *Dr. Jekyll and Mr. Hyde* as a "psychologically accurate" assertion about the generality of mankind: "Broadly speaking, we may be said to be a kind of mixture of such personalities, some higher and some lower, all struggling to gain a larger share of our conscious attention."[101] Another of Griffin's literary models was "the well known message of Polonius: 'to thine own self be true,'" though he takes care to warn against the "error of Polonius," who did not live up to his own creed, but instead "by many words darkened council and failed to be convincing." The "own self," Griffin explains, is not the "imperfect self, with kinks in it," but "the ideal self."[102] He endorses the "triplicity of character"[103] embodied in the three categories of wisdom, power, and will, citing the *Journal of Neurology and Psychopathology* as well as the scouting movement.

Though he thinks it necessary to offer "a brief summary of the psychological content of adolescence," Griffin prefers to "avoid the ugly word 'adolescent,'" deciding instead to "use the word 'Rover.'"[104] He takes issue with those who inveigh constantly against masturbation ("self-interested gratification") as a sin. Speaking as a doctor, he insists, "The interest in morbidity is neither necessary in character training nor in healthy life, even though veiled in the specious excuses of a

'Purity crusade,'"[105] and lists as suggested reading several recent books on sexuality.

Character, not sin, is what is at issue. "Force of character" in the Rover years should naturally produce "widening vision and diminishing selfishness, involving the sublimation of the claims of the body with its emotions."[106]

"Selfishness," in a nod to Freud, is linked to the story of Narcissus, whose fate is described in an unforgettable way: having fallen in love with a reflection of himself "to the exclusion of his not unpleasing companions," he "fled from reality into introspection, and his subsequent life was purely vegetable!"[107] But Rovers are not yet grown men, nor are they overgrown boys; adults who understand this in-between phase, says Griffin, will avoid friction and misunderstanding.

Yet, when he comes to discuss the policy of organizing Rovers into parties larger than two at this impressionable stage of life, Griffin returns to the term "morbidity," which he had previously used as a medical euphemism: "The secondary grouping of individual comradeships into groups prevents morbidity, provides variety of outlook, and strengthens . . . the comradeship spirit." Here the unmentionable topic of homosexuality is glanced at, without speaking its name.

The cover of *The Quest of the Boy* shows an older man counseling a younger man; both of them, from their costumes, appear to be ancient Athenians, and, indeed, on a hilltop in the distance one can see the outline of the Acropolis. The stone bench on which the older man sits bears an inscription, "The Best Is Yet to Be"—a line of verse that Griffin elsewhere attributes, accurately, to a Victorian poem by Robert Browning about the twelfth-century poet and mathematician "Rabbi Ben Ezra" (Abraham ibn Ezra). This deliberate historical conflation is a vivid testimony to the way in which nineteenth-century character training drew, as it were ecumenically, from any and all sources that came its way and served its purposes.

Sparta or Camelot?

Scouting for Boys cites the legendary founder of Spartan education at the beginning of a section for Boy Scout instructors on "Self-Discipline."

"Lycurgus said that the wealth of a state lay not so much in money as in men who were sound in body and mind, with a body fit for toil and endurance, and with a mind well disciplined, and seeing things in their proper proportions."[108] The parallel was pursued and enlarged upon in *Rovering to Success*: "In the old days," wrote Baden-Powell, "the Spartans put their boys through a very rigorous training in hardness and endurance before they were allowed to count themselves as men." Likewise, the public schools required a "considerable hardening process," which was good for a boy at the end. But, "unfortunately," no such training was currently available for the "ordinary boy," and "we badly need some such training for our lads if we are to keep up manliness in our race instead of lapsing into a nation of soft, sloppy, cigarette suckers."[109]

In the same account, "the knights of old" were credited, in a rather strained process of logic, not only with "manliness" in general but specifically with one of the essential Scout virtues, "thrift." "Ordered by their rules to be thrifty," knights "were not allowed to beg," so that they needed to work to make money, so that they would "not be a burden to others" and have "more to give away to charity." It was a lesson that boys could learn, based not on modern commerce but on chivalric practice: "Thus money-making goes with manliness, hard work, and sobriety."[110]

The American *Boy Scouts Handbook*, first published in 1911 and based to a considerable extent on its British forerunner, offered advice on knightly conduct under the heading of "Character":

> If a scout is cheerful . . . and does a good turn to some one every day, he will come into possession of a strong character such as the Knights of the Round Table had; for, after all, character is the thing that distinguishes a good scout from a bad one. Character is not what men say about you . . . It was not the words of the knights of old that told what they were. It was their strong life and fine character.[111]

"Thrift," however, while still listed in the American handbook under chivalry, replaces the knights with a story about an enterprising boy who became a millionaire.[112]

The combination of Spartan or Greek history and Arthurian chivalry, of Lycurgus and Mallory, was powerful. Sometimes they were seen to be in conflict; Lord Acton had declared that "two great principles divide the world and contend for mastery, antiquity and the Middle Ages. These are the two civilisations that have preceded us, the two elements of which ours is composed . . . This is the great dualism that runs through our society."[113] But both favored an educational system in which adult men trained boys in physical and moral virtues, and thus in the development of character. Manliness was not inconsistent with mentorship or male-male friendship—quite the contrary. The progression in knightly training in the Middle Ages led from page to squire to knight. Spartan education downplayed academic subjects, reading and writing, in favor of soldierly training. From an early age, the young boy was removed from his family home and sent to live in a barracks with other boys until he completed his training at about the age of eighteen.

The analogies were recognized—and emphasized—by Victorians and Edwardians, and—as we have seen in the case of Walter Pater—not only by the Scouts. And it could carry over into adulthood, with some unlooked-for results. In the nineteenth-century cult of chivalry, "the doctrine that character was more important than intellect," writes Mark Girouard, was a "feature of the chivalrous gentleman. If carried to extremes, as it too often was, it could result in the belief that grit and pluck could deal with every problem." It also "led to a distrust of 'cleverness.'" As Girouard observes, "It is dangerous for a ruling class to be suspicious of intelligence."[114]

This has repeatedly proved to be a wise concern, whether in the nineteenth century or in the present day.

Character for Women

At the new girls' schools, which were founded in part to emulate the schools for boys, games quickly became popular—and in many cases compulsory. "By 1910 Godolphin and most other girls' public schools were playing compulsory cricket, hockey, and lacrosse, and being made to watch all of these when other schools were played."[115] Girls employed the same kind of slang that boys did—"ripping" was a favorite term—

sometimes had masculine nicknames, and at some schools wore Eton collars and ties. "Keenness" was a word used to describe the atmosphere at Cheltenham in 1907.[116] At Godolphin in 1919, the headmistress addressed the girls collectively to affirm, "School life *must* lead on to definite service in the larger life when school days are over," and to list the values that such a commitment required, including (in this order) "character," "self control," "good taste," "school before house," "the spirit of reverence," and "the school spirit."[117] Yet the expectation was that most of these wealthy middle- and upper-class girls would marry, have houses and children. In addition to academic subjects (and sometimes in lieu of them), they were taught needlework, dancing, and "domestic science."

"Haven't women got as much character as men?"[118] Robert Baden-Powell had written in the early years of the Boy Scout movement, arguing that girls were often overprotected, and therefore rendered less fit as true companions for men.

From the beginning of his plan for the Boy Scouts—and even earlier, as a regimental commander—Baden-Powell had urged that boys and men learn to sew, cook, make bread (mixing and kneading it on the inside lining of their uniform coats), and, in general, master the supposedly feminine skills, so that they could make themselves self-sufficient. This was also true of the Scouts' American forerunner, Ernest Thompson Seton's Woodcraft Indians. Seton, seeking to enhance the appreciation of nature and the arts, "blended stereotypical feminine virtues into his version of manliness."[119] His ideas would influence the Campfire Girls as well as the U.S. scouting movement. Baden-Powell's Boy Scouts were eligible for badges as Artists, Tailors, Cooks, and Florists. Girls, in turn, could surely learn Stalking, Signaling, Cycling, Swimming, and other physical skills.

But a concern for the niceties of gender difference worried some in the movement, especially those from high-placed families, and after a bold start Baden-Powell made sure to head off what Tim Jeal calls "Establishment fears that he would coarsen young ladies." He determined that girls should not be called "Scouts," and made sure to modify the activities in *Scouting for Boys* so that they would be suitable: "You do not want to make tomboys of refined girls."[120]

"Scouting for girls is not the same as for boys," wrote Baden-Powell and his sister, Agnes, in a document attached to *Pamphlet B: Baden-Powell Girl Guides, a Suggestion for Character Training for Girls*, and later included in the first edition of *The Handbook for Girl Guides*. "The chief difference in the training of the two courses of instruction is that scouting for boys makes for MANLINESS, but the training for Guides makes for WOMANLINESS, and enables girls the better to help in the battle of life."[121]

Agnes, to whom Baden-Powell initially entrusted the leadership of the Guides, attached to the pamphlet a fictional letter from a mother whose daughter's too-enthusiastic interest in "rough games and exposure" ran the risk of "rough and worn hands," unsuitable for nurses or pianists. "Vulgar slang" terms picked up from boys (like "topping," "ripping," and "what ho!") were likewise inappropriate for a young girl, not to mention that "violent jerks and jars" could damage her female organs ("a woman's interior economy").[122]

When the brother and sister published *The Handbook for Girl Guides, or How Girls Can Help to Build the Empire* in 1912 (the cover read, "By Miss Baden-Powell and Sir Robert Baden-Powell"), Agnes added sections on child care, nursing, invalid food, and housewifery, while retaining many passages and activities from *Scouting for Boys*. The "Details of People" to notice in tracking remained the same, though without the illustrations, and the section on a man's telltale walk inserted "(or a woman)" in parentheses, though the examples and the pronouns remained male.[123] Sexual matters are discussed only obliquely, though the message was clear: "Keep clear of girls who tell you nasty stories or talk to you of indecent things." "Don't read trashy books." And like the Scouts, the Guides were also to steer clear of masturbation: "All secret bad habits are evil and dangerous, lead to hysteria and lunatic asylums, and serious illness is the result." "Resisting temptation will make you more noble." "Evil practices . . . lead you on to blindness, paralysis, and loss of memory."[124]

The future for Guides seemed clearly to anticipate marriage, although Agnes Baden-Powell herself was an unmarried professional woman. "High principled women as wives can be of enormous assistance to their husbands, both as sympathetic advisers and in carrying out great works," begins the section on "Guides of the Future." "Thus in various ways women can be the guides of men if they try to Be Prepared for that duty."[125]

Agnes, less than two years younger than her brother, was interested in outdoor sports (principally ballooning and bicycle polo) and was an accomplished artist. The scaling back of the more athletic side of guiding had been a concession to Edwardian sensibility rather than a personal shrinking from adventure. Nonetheless, she was later replaced as the chief officer of the Girl Guides—greatly against her own wish—by her brother's young wife, Olave, who criticized the *Handbook* as if he had had nothing to do with it. Olave, as we have seen, exemplified the qualities Baden-Powell esteemed in a life companion. She was also clearly "prepared" to be a "guide" to her husband, and to assist him in "carrying out great works."

"There are women and there are dolls," Robert Baden-Powell would later counsel in *Rovering to Success*, subtitled *A Book of Life-Sport for Young Men*. Once you get over the "calf-love" stage, he assures his readers, "you will find a girl whose character you admire and respect, whose tastes are like your own, and whose comradeship you long for." And—as an additional point in favor of the Girl Guide as wife—should Baden-Powell himself happen "to visit you in your home later on," he was confident that he would find "not only a happy home but a clean one."[126] Character for girls was a selling point in marriage, likely to ensure future compatibility and happiness. As the Chief Scout felt was the case in his own life.

"Character Building" and "Character Training"

The idea of "character building"—a major theme in nineteenth-century self-help schemes, from Samuel Smiles to scouting—was that qualities like emotion, will, and conscience could be developed through habit and exercise, and established through a conscious choice of virtue over laxity and indulgence. The term itself appears in a book dated 1859, and by the end of the century newspapers could refer to "the paramount importance of character-building" and the rise of "character-building literature."[127]

But if "character building" was an invitation to personal initiative, "character training" was its organizational mode.

In 1909, when Robert Baden-Powell wrote two pamphlets on Girl Guides, precursors of *The Handbook for Girl Guides*, he gave each the same subtitle, *A Suggestion for Character-Training for Girls*. By this time, "character training" had become, it seems, a standard term. Earlier movements, from the Glasgow Boys' Brigade, the Jewish Lads' Brigade, the London Cadets, and the YMCA, had rallied young English youth to patriotism and service. The term lost some of its appeal after the rise of youth movements in Hitler's Germany and Mussolini's Italy. Baden-Powell, initially interested in the idea of government support for youth training as part of the educational system, later became concerned about what he called "mass suggestion"—though he continued, as late as 1937, and against the advice of colleagues on the Boy Scout International Committee, to consider (out of optimism rather than political conviction) establishing connections between the Boy Scouts and the Hitler Youth.[128] He was convinced that no British boy could ever become a Nazi.

"Character training" would also be the goal of Outward Bound, founded in 1941 to develop growth by offering participants challenging outdoor adventure programs through which to test their limits. The title of the organization comes from a nautical expression describing a ship leaving port—its initial impetus came from a desire to train young seamen whose ships had been torpedoed in wartime. The Outward Bound motto, "To Serve, To Strive, and Not to Yield," is an adaptation of the last line of Lord Alfred Tennyson's poem "Ulysses"—the line as Tennyson wrote it reads, "To strive, to seek, to find, and not to yield." "Find" may have sounded more like conquest, exploration, or even plunder than the organization wished, though it is odd to change a line of verse as famous as this one was at the time. (Another odd fit is the poem's plot, which presents Ulysses in old age, bored with government and nation, turning over home rule to his more placid son—who is described as "decent," "blameless," activated by "slow prudence" and "offices of tenderness"—while the restless father rallies his comrades to set off again in quest of new challenges:

> One equal temper of heroic hearts,
> Made weak by time and fate, but strong in will
> To strive, to seek, to find, and not to yield.

With its stay-at-home youth and its venturesome veteran—"He works his work, I mine"—this celebrated poem seems to set an imperfect example for young adventurers.)

The authors of a sociological study of "the character-training industry" in the late twentieth century note that Outward Bound, as the first and best known of these programs, is often used as both a model and a label, since "the phrase 'character-training'" may now "awaken memories of Hitler youth."[129] But from recreational adventure to vocational instruction to adult education, "character-development or training" is, they say, what such programs are all about. "Industry"—a term they defend, since attracting sponsors and enlisting participants both involve "a commercial approach"—sounds a good bit like Baden-Powell's "character factory," though in his case the word "factory" seems to have been designed as a provocative analogy or figure of speech. By 1974, when this study was published, the enterprises involved had diversified, though the goal was the same.

> Course organisers do not see themselves as engaged in a brainwashing exercise and everyone connected with the movement appreciates that each youngster will carry his own personal likes, dislikes, attitudes and beliefs through a course and into his subsequent life. Trainees are not expected to trade-in their existing characters in exchange for different models. However, the intention is to exert some influence upon each trainee as a person, in ways that will affect his reactions to situations subsequently encountered.[130]

The sense here, despite the "character-training" phrase, is more like behavioral modification. "Existing characters" are not to be exchanged for different or better ones; rather, new experiences will chart paths for future responses. Once again the word "character," which seems so essential to the description of such programs, is asked to do two contradictory things at once: to define both the intrinsic tendencies of the individual and the social changes to be gained from "training." Is "character" fixed or alterable? It was the old question yet again. In this case, the sociologists offer a guarded "yes"—or perhaps a prudent "maybe"—to both.

"Making a Good Impression"

From Robert Owen's plan for the formation of character through programs for character building and character training, ideas about the development of "character" flourished and proliferated in the nineteenth century and well into the twentieth. Some were designed to work through the agency of a school, an institution, or a program; others, though they proposed prescribed courses of training, were intended to take place apart from any formal institutional structure, and in some cases explicitly to reward independent initiative and adventure. Larger institutional frameworks—from the military to "life" and "success"—were often invoked as both models and goals, and many, even today, retain implicit or stated links with religion.

Nonetheless, and despite the connection of "character" with elite schools and certain privileged team sports, there hovered around the term a wistful hope of egalitarianism; for Baden-Powell's slouching and smoking "loafers" or the less athletically inclined boys at a public school, character could be "instilled" or "inculcated" through will, dedication, and practice. Most boys—and girls—could learn to "play the game."

Sometimes, however, the magic quality of "character," so hard to define, so essential to have, could also seem unreachable, in part because it was thought to belong to others.

In his memoir *A Walker in the City*, the critic Alfred Kazin describes the almost mystical, and certainly mysterious, meaning of "character" to a Brooklyn Jewish schoolboy in the 1920s. Instructed that it was important to "make a good impression" on his teachers, "who were to be respected as gods," the young Kazin came immediately to understand that the most essential, if ineffable, quality was *character*, "a word I could never hear without automatically seeing it raised before me in gold-plated letters."

> Satisfactory as my "character" was, on the whole, except when I stayed too long in the playground reading; outrageously satisfactory, as I can see now, the very sound of the word as our

> teachers coldly gave it out from the end of their teeth, with a solemn weight on each dark syllable, immediately struck my heart cold with fear—they could not believe I really had it. Character was never something you had; it had to be trained in you, like a technique. I was never very clear about it. On our side *character* meant demonstrative obedience; but teachers already had it—how else could they have become teachers? They had it; the aloof Anglo-Saxon principal whom we remotely saw only on ceremonial occasions in the assembly was positively encased in it; it glittered off his bald head in spokes of triumphant light; the President of the United States had the greatest conceivable amount of it. Character belonged to great adults. Yet we were constantly being driven on to it; it was the great threshold we had to cross. *Alfred Kazin, having shown proficiency in his course of studies and having displayed satisfactory marks of character . . .* Thus someday the hallowed diploma, passport to my further advancement in high school. But there—I could already feel it in my bones—they would put me through even more doubting tests of character; and after that, if I should be good enough and bright enough, there would be still more.[131]

That "the President of the United States" had "the greatest conceivable amount" of character might well have been a generalized statement about that august office, especially as seen from the perspective of a child of immigrants. Kazin, born in 1915, attended elementary school sometime in the 1920s. The U.S. presidents in that period were Woodrow Wilson (1913–1921), Warren G. Harding (1921–1923), Calvin Coolidge (1923–1929), and Herbert Hoover (1929–1933). From this list it is not easy to choose the paragon of character that would have struck a sentient schoolboy with such moral force.

By mid-century, firmly established among what he called the "ruling cultural pundits of American society," Kazin could congratulate himself on having exchanged places with his inquisitors: "I who stood so long outside the door wondering if I would ever get through it, am now one of the standard bearers of American opinion—a *judge* of young men."[132] This was from a 1963 entry in his private journal, which may be one reason Kazin does not envisage himself, or other cultural pundits, as necessarily judging the work of young—or not so young—women, many of whom were still standing outside that door.

But the young Kazin's perception that he would be judged by his teachers—and perhaps especially by that aloof Anglo-Saxon principal—in terms of the elusive and daunting thing called "character" was not an error. The cliché about "making a good impression," however over-familiar, was related to the etymology of character as an engraving, a stamp, or a brand—something that stayed. At the same time, Kazin—a child of his times—sees "character" as the result of training. "Character was never something you had; it had to be trained in you, like a technique." At a New York City public school, rather than an elite "public school" in England, he learned that "character belonged to great adults." The rhetoric of "greatness" was both Plutarchan and American. It would soon be attached, as well, to that most literate of twentieth-century self-help programs, the *Great Books of the Western World*.

The Rise of "Character Education"

If previous "character" labels or slogans had been directly or indirectly related to leadership training, games, and warfare—and thus, as many would proudly claim, to the spirit that built the British Empire, then "character education," a term that came to prominence in the 1980s, seems pre-eminently American.

What are we to make of this term, which has dominated a certain aspect of educational and political thought and writing? Is it a redundancy, or a contradiction in terms? A pleonasm, or an oxymoron?

Like the equally infelicitous "public intellectual," "character education" has over time come to put in question both of the terms that comprise it. "Public intellectual" seems to imply, retroactively and retrospectively, a critique of all those previously called "intellectuals" (aka "academics" or what George Wallace labeled "pointy-headed intellectuals"), since such persons now seem to be described implicitly as *not* "public"—whether "public" means "accessible to nonspecialists" or "frequently seen on talk shows and at TED conferences." Similarly, the term "character education" appears to suggest that other kinds of education are not good for, or are not sufficiently mindful of, "character"—that they need to be tweaked, adjusted, or replaced by practices that consciously develop a sense of morality, fairness, and justice (by, for example, reading novels for their moral and ethical lessons, rather than for their structure, language, and relationship to literary history). Or, contrariwise, that "character" and "education" are themselves mutually resistant if not exclusive terms, so that parents and students and teachers might have to choose *between* building character and studying complex scholarly fields such as history, philosophy, mathematics, biology, and literature.

There is something of a contradiction in bringing these two apparently anodyne terms into a forced alliance, or a collision course, with each other. If education is a way of teaching students (and teachers, and parents, and indeed everyone) to think and question and challenge ideas, it will sometimes come into conflict with bromides about morality and virtue. Intellectual life is about taking risks, thinking counterintuitively, imagining the unimaginable. Galileo is many people's favorite example of intellectual martyrdom. Thomas More is at least some people's idea of principled resistance to the tyranny of a closed mind. Rosa Parks refused to move to the back of the bus. Character education presumably has little difficulty in reincorporating such rebels into the history of (good) ideas. But it is less clear how it will or can deal with the apparently challenging ideas of the present and the future, including the very uncomfortable "freedom for the thought that we hate."[133] What looks like "morality" and "virtue" in the present or past cannot always be counted on to look that way in, or from, the future. Another name for this is "moral reasoning," and the "reasoning" part of this term is not an afterthought. Above all, the problem is smugness, self-satisfaction, "knowing." Education is knowing that we don't, and can't, and won't, always know.

The list of educators who have subscribed to some version of what is now called character education is long, and the educators are often distinguished and innovative: the list includes, in America, figures like Benjamin Franklin, Horace Mann, and William Holmes McGuffey, the developer of the bestselling series of textbooks that taught morals, hard work, and self-discipline through the use of poems, essays, stories, and the Bible. *McGuffey's Readers* were so important to the industrialist Henry Ford that he republished and distributed to schools across the country all six of the *Readers* in the 1867 edition, and later paid to have the log cabin where McGuffey was born moved to his personal museum of Americana in Dearborn, Michigan.[134] Whatever we might think today about the enforced morality and explicit Christianity of *McGuffey's Readers*, there is no question about their influence on American education in the nineteenth century and, indeed, up to the present. Some 120 million copies of the *Readers* were sold between 1836 and 1960, sales figures comparable in that period to the Bible and Webster's dictionary, and sold well through the 1990s. Once out of print, they have now been republished by Mott Media, a Christian publisher that sells books especially for homeschooling.

Making Believe

At the same time that *McGuffey's Readers* were to be found in classrooms across the nation, another "character narrative" caught the imagination of American children and adults. Its author shrewdly sought to distinguish his work from that of the moral stories so popular both in school texts and in European fairy tales like those of the brothers Grimm.

"Modern education includes morality; therefore the modern child seeks only entertainment in its wonder tales and gladly dispenses with all disagreeable incident,"[135] declared L. Frank Baum in his prefatory note to *The Wonderful Wizard of Oz*, first published in 1900. Whether the wicked Witch of the West, the Winged Monkeys, and the various apparitions of Oz, the Great and Terrible, constituted "disagreeable incident[s]" for the "modern child" of the early twentieth century is not entirely clear, but if they were disagreeable they must have been so in the most agreeable way, since Baum's "modernized fairy tale"[136] became one of the bestselling children's books of the century.

Nor did his book entirely eschew morality for entertainment, despite its author's declaration of purpose. The quest of the Scarecrow for a brain, the Tin Woodman for a heart, and the Cowardly Lion for courage offers one of the clearest examples of what might today be called "character education."

Oz, the Great and Terrible—who has appeared to them variously as a lovely lady, a terrible beast, and a ball of fire—promises them these attributes of character as a reward if they are able to kill the wicked Witch of the West. So, when Dorothy accidentally sprinkles the Witch with water, causing her to melt away, the travelers return to the Emerald City and seek out the Throne Room of the Great Oz to claim their rewards—there, of course, to find, not a Great Wizard but a "common man"—indeed, a "humbug."

> "I have been making believe," he tells them.
>
> "But this is terrible," said the Tin Woodman. "How shall I ever get my heart?"
>
> "Or I my courage?" asked the Lion.
>
> "Or I my brains?" wailed the Scarecrow.

Dorothy, who clearly lacks none of these qualities, is quick to judge their host. "I think you are a very bad man," she tells him. "Oh, no, my dear," he replies. "I'm really a very good man, but I'm a very bad Wizard."

We might pause for a moment to consider the Wizard's phrase "making believe," which has become so common a cliché that we almost never notice the craftwork involved in "making."[137] That "making believe" is a technique at once psychological, interpersonal, and rhetorical or aesthetic is clear from the way the Wizard goes about distributing his imaginary bounty.

Pressed to supply the Scarecrow with brains, he tells him: "You don't need them. You are learning something every day . . . Experience is the only thing that brings knowledge." To the Lion, he says: "You have plenty of courage . . . All you need is confidence in yourself." And he tells the Tin Woodman that he is wrong to want a heart: "It makes most people unhappy. If you only knew it, you are in luck not to have a heart." Predictably, none of the suitors is mollified, and Dr. Oz—in Baum's version of the story—therefore promises to give them what they want on the following day.

He stuffs the Scarecrow's head with a mixture of bran and pins and needles, telling him, "Hereafter you will be a great man, for I have given you a lot of bran-new brains" (the pun is Baum's). He cuts a hole in the Tin Woodman's chest and inserts a heart made of silk and stuffed with sawdust, "a heart that any man might be proud of." And he offers the Cowardly Lion a drink from a square green bottle, explaining, "You know, of course, that courage is always inside you, so that this really cannot be called courage until you have swallowed it." Indeed, once he has drunk it up, the Lion declares that he feels "full of courage." (Whether there is a gentle little joke here about "Dutch courage," or intoxication, it's not entirely possible to say.)

In any case, these much-desired character traits, however questionably bestowed, seem entirely successful when transplanted. The Scarecrow becomes the new ruler of the Emerald City, where his people are proud to believe that "there is not another city in all the world that is ruled by a stuffed man." The Tin Woodman is "well-pleased" with his new heart, and the Lion is "content knowing that I am as brave as any beast that ever lived, if not braver."

"How can I help being a humbug," Oz thinks to himself, "when all these people make me do things that everybody knows can't be done?"

Of the many changes made by the several screenwriters who were hired—and fired—in the making of MGM's 1939 film *The Wizard of Oz*, the most significant from the point of view of character may have been the scene in which the Wizard grants the wishes of these three earnest applicants. In Baum's original fairy tale, as we've seen, Oz performs what seem like rudimentary "medical" operations, taking off the Scarecrow's head to fill it with pins, needles, and bran; cutting a hole in the Tin Woodman's chest to insert the silk heart; and serving the Lion a liquid diet of courage. In most of the scripted versions submitted to the studio, the Scarecrow, Tin Woodman, and Lion realize that they have always had the brains, heart, and courage they thought they lacked. But in the final version, the lyricist E. Y. "Yip" Harburg contributed a scene in which the Wizard gives the Scarecrow a diploma, the Tin Woodman a testimonial, and the Cowardly Lion a medal.

"Back where I come from," the Wizard tells the Scarecrow,

> we have universities, seats of learning—where men go to become great thinkers, and when they come out, they think deep thoughts—and with no more brains than you have—*but!*—they have one thing you haven't got! A diploma! *(He picks up several diplomas, selects a parchment scroll with seal and ribbon, and presents it to the SCARECROW.)* Therefore, by virtue of the authority vested in me by the *Universitatus Committeeatum e pluribus unum* I hereby confer upon you the honorary degree of Th.D.[138]

This is an acronym that, he explains, stands for "Doctor of Thinkology."

He offers the Lion similar assurance, and a similar material sign of merit. "You are under the unfortunate delusion that simply because you run away from danger, you have no courage. You're confusing courage with wisdom."

> Back where I come from, we have men who are called heroes. Once a year they take their fortitude out of mothballs and parade it down the main street of the city. And they have no more courage than you have—*but!* they have one thing that you haven't got! A medal! *(He takes a big triple-cross medal out of his black bag and pins it on the LION's skin as he imitates a French Legion general.)* Therefore, for meritorious conduct, extraordinary valor, conspicuous bravery against wicked witches, I award you the Triple Cross. You are now a member of the Legion of Courage. *(He kisses LION on both cheeks.)*[139]

As in Frank Baum's original story, so also in the film script the Wizard initially tells the character now known as the Tin Man that he is lucky not to have a heart: "Hearts will never be practical until they can be made unbreakable." When the Tin Man persists in his wish, however, the Wizard once again recalls an example from his former life.

> Back where I come from, there are men who do nothing all day but good deeds. They are called phil . . . er . . . phil . . . er . . . yes . . . er . . . good-deed-doers, and their hearts are no

> bigger than yours—*but!* they have one thing you haven't got! A testimonial! *(He takes a huge heart-shaped watch and chain out of his black bag.)* Therefore, in consideration of your kindness, I take pleasure at this time in presenting you with a small token of our esteem and affection. *(Hands it to TIN MAN.)* And remember, my sentimental friend, that a heart is not judged by how much you love, but by how much you are loved by others.[140]

"Philanthropy" today, for better or worse, is a career path rather than a character trait. But the Wizard's gentle admonition to his sentimental friend has lost no pertinence in a business world increasingly peopled by "venture philanthropists," whose prizes and awards are often far more conspicuous than the Tin Man's watch and chain.

Remarking on the changed ending of the film, Yip Harburg told Aljean Harmetz that he "devised the satiric and cynical idea of the Wizard handing out symbols because I was so aware of our lives being the images of things rather than the things themselves."[141] The Scarecrow is immediately able to do a geometrical equation, the Tin Man's watch ticks like a heart, and the Lion, reading the word "Courage" on his medal, is instantly convinced: "Ain't it the truth!"[142]

As a phrase, "making believe" is meant to describe a creative act. But if we read "making" as compulsion rather than creativity, to "make [someone] believe" is to force a belief upon them. Here we have, in little, the ethical conundrum of "character education." Whose view of "character" will count?

Counting on Character

> We celebrate National Character Counts Week because few things are more important than cultivating strong character in all our citizens, especially our young people. The grit and integrity of our people, visible throughout our history, defines the soul of our Nation. This week, we reflect on the character

> of determination, resolve, and honor that makes us proud to be American.
>
> As President Reagan declared, "There is no institution more vital to our Nation's survival than the American family. Here the seeds of personal character are planted, the roots of public virtue first nourished." Character is built slowly. Our actions—often done first out of duty—become habits ingrained in the way we treat others and ourselves. As parents, educators, and civic and church leaders, we must always work to cultivate strength of character in our Nation's youth.
>
> Character can be hard to define, but we see it in everyday acts—raising and providing for a family with loving devotion, working hard to make the most of an education, and giving back to devastated communities. These and so many other acts big and small constitute the moral fiber of American culture. Character is forged around kitchen tables, built in civic organizations, and developed in houses of worship. It is refined by our choices, large and small, and manifested in what we do when we think no one is paying attention.
>
> As we strive every day to improve our character and that of our Nation, we pause and thank those individuals whose strength of character has inspired us and who have provided a supporting hand during times of need. In particular, we applaud families as they perform the often thankless task of raising men and women of character.
>
> NOW, THEREFORE, I, DONALD J. TRUMP, President of the United States of America, by virtue of the authority vested in me by the Constitution and the laws of the United States, do hereby proclaim October 15 through October 21, 2017, as National Character Counts Week. I call upon public officials, educators, parents, students, and all Americans to observe this week with appropriate ceremonies, activities, and programs.[143]

When Donald J. Trump followed the precedent set by three other U.S. presidents in proclaiming "National Character Counts Week," there was no lack of commentary on the ironies involved. From his "birther" days to his tangled finances, his ethical lapses, his disrespect for Gold Star families and prisoners of war, his coarse language and treatment of women, his record-setting daily fibs, his bullying tweets, and his penchant for personal (and often vulgar) insult, Trump was a classic example of "Do as I say, not as I do," except that it was surely not he who drafted the words to which he affixed his flourish of a signature. In particular, the sentiment that character "is refined by our choices, large and small, and manifested in what we do when we think no one is paying attention" may not have been drawn to his attention.

Yet in allying himself with this fine-sounding "week," like so many other honorific or celebratory "weeks" he would proclaim as part of his presidential duties, Trump was, in a way, following his own familiar practice of conflating patriotism, politics, and private enterprise. National Character Counts Week is an annual event, and when, in the midst of an impeachment investigation, Trump issued a proclamation urging his fellow Americans to "strive every day to improve our character and that of our Nation," and enjoining them to "set an example for others of the timeless values of respect, compassion, justice, tolerance, fairness, and integrity," some commentators were quick to note the irony.[144] "May we never forget," the proclamation declared, "that our Nation is only as strong as the virtue and character of our citizenry." The week passed, but the impeachment investigation continued, perhaps inadvertently fulfilling this pious wish signed in the president's name.

Character Counts! is a "coalition" organized by the nonprofit Josephson Institute of Ethics, which also sponsors programs in ethics for sports, business, public service, and policing. The coalition supports what it calls "consensus ethical values" for young people, in the form of the "Six Pillars of Character": trustworthiness, respect, responsibility, fairness, caring, and citizenship. Its description of purpose says it is "the most widely implemented ethics/character education program in the world, reaching 10% of school-age children (6 million) in the United States." Its goal is "to overcome the false but surprisingly powerful notion that no single value is intrinsically superior to another; that ethical values vary by race, class, gender and politics; that greed and fairness, cheating and honesty carry the same moral weight, simply depending on one's perspective and immediate needs."

I have to say that I was surprised to see this notion described as "surprisingly powerful," since I have never encountered it except in dystopian fiction.[145] My guess is that it is a somewhat caricatured view of the "Values Clarification" movement in the 1960s and 1970s, which has become a reliable if very much outdated punching bag for conservative proponents of "values."[146] But then I was also surprised to find that not one but four U.S. presidents had declared a National Character Counts Week since the program was founded in 1993, since Character Counts!, though its PR makes it sound like a government program, is in fact the product of a private, albeit "nonprofit," foundation, supported by donors and by fees charged for educational materials, training seminars, and in-service programs. The official materials describe CC! as closely approximating a "franchise operation" and boast, "The presidential declaration of a National Character Counts! Week is a triumph of marketing."[147]

On its Web site the organization displays its name in all capital letters, followed by an exclamation point: "CHARACTER COUNTS!" It's not clear whether the absence of capital letters and exclamation points in President Trump's proclamation—or in those of his predecessors—is deliberate, inadvertent, or due to the protocol of such official announcements. (All the caps in "CHARACTER COUNTS!" might be seen to distract from the solemnity of the caps in "I, DONALD TRUMP.") But there is considerable semantic difference, at least to me, between a National Character Counts Week and a National CHARACTER COUNTS! Week, especially when the executive proclamation urges only that participants observe the week with "appropriate ceremonies, activities, and programs" rather than with materials advertised by the Josephson Institute. The appeal of such grammatical imperatives may lend itself to ostensibly "nonpolitical" public statements, especially those that concern character. After First Lady Melania Trump announced a program called "Be Best" to promote the well-being of children, the president proclaimed May 7, 2018, as "the inaugural Be Best Day." With the Six Pillars of CHARACTER COUNTS! in mind, we might note that the official "Be Best" site describes "Three Pillars of Be Best": Well-Being, Online Safety, and (presumably Avoiding) Opioid Abuse.[148]

As the example of Donald Trump has already demonstrated, irony (and schadenfreude) may always lurk around the corner whenever character is too officially linked to presidential deportment. National Character Counts Week dates from 1994, when the U.S. Congress passed a joint resolution, sponsored by Senator Pete Domenici of New Mexico, to "proclaim the week of October 16 through October 22, 1994, as 'National Character Counts Week.'"[149] The first U.S. president to proclaim it was therefore Bill Clinton, who did so (like all his successors) annually every October.

In 1998, Clinton expanded on his announcement to explain the importance of the topic. "One of the greatest building blocks of character is citizen service," Clinton said.

> We must do more as individuals and as a society to encourage all Americans—especially our young people—to share their time, skills, enthusiasm and energy with their communities. Whether we teach children to read, mentor young people, work at a food bank or homeless shelter, or care for people living with AIDS, citizen service calls forth the best from each of us. It builds a sense of community, compassion, acceptance of others and a willingness to do the right thing—all hallmarks of character.[150]

This call to "citizen service," with its specific mention of social values like working at a homeless shelter or caring for people with AIDS, is manifestly more trained on "character" per se than on Character Counts!, which may explain why it is not mentioned in the coalition's talking points (much less described as a "triumph of marketing"). The presidential announcement ended with a call for "service": "During National Character Counts Week, let us reaffirm to our children that the future belongs to those who have the strength of character to live a life of service to others." Clinton had made much the same appeal, to a much larger audience, two years previously, when he said in his 1996 State of the Union Address, "I challenge all our schools to teach character education, to teach good values and good citizenship."[151] But in between January 1996 and 1998 came the news of his involvement with a White House intern, Monica Lewinsky. On October 8, 1998, a week before the proclamation of National Character Counts Week, the House of Representatives had initiated Clinton's impeachment; on December 19, the House formally adopted articles of impeachment and forwarded them to the Senate (which ultimately voted to acquit).

Clinton detractors predictably seized upon his statement as an attempt, not very successful, at personal rehabilitation:

> Character? Bill Clinton is a character, all right. The very fact that he can issue such a proclamation with a straight face and no sense of shame or embarrassment, after dragging this once great nation through scandal after scandal, crime after crime, shows he is a very unusual person. But character?
>
> Character has to do with moral constitution, strength, self-discipline. Are these traits that make you think of Bill Clinton? So why is Bill Clinton lecturing the nation on character?
>
> Because he's trying to redefine it. Since he doesn't have any character, Clinton seeks to change the definition in a way that suits him.[152]

Clinton's, the author declared, was "the most corrupt, unethical, law-breaking White House in the history of the American Republic."

It seems possible that the writer of this diatribe believed, wrongly, that the "week" was somehow Bill Clinton's idea, invented to clear his name, or, alternatively, appropriated to perform the same public-relations task. I cite this passage at length, though, largely because it rings the changes on the various conflicting meanings of "character," from being "a character" to "having character" (here defined as "moral constitution, strength, self-discipline") to the accusation that someone, in this case the president of the United States, "doesn't have any character." That the definition Clinton's proclamation offers, "citizen service," which "builds a sense of community, compassion, acceptance of others and a willingness to do the right thing—all hallmarks of character," strikes the author as eccentric or outlandish (Clinton "seeks to change the definition in a way that suits him") may tell as much about his political views (and his "character"?) as it does about Bill Clinton. But if we overlook for a moment the attempt at vitriol, we have here a pretty clear primer of the various aspects of "character," all seemingly self-evident, and yet somehow mutually contradictory or perceived as being in conflict.

When President Barack Obama endorsed National Character Counts Week, he acknowledged the role of "educators and mentors" as well as "parents and coaches and neighbors and colleagues," but put additional stress on "the brave men and women who serve and sacrifice to protect the freedoms we hold dear," and the "first responders who keep us safe." Above all, what the framing of his 2015 proclamation sought to underscore was the importance of "greater tolerance and empathy among all people":

> This week, as we hold true to the ideals that bind us together, let us remind our children of their important role in charting our journey forward and empower them with strength and conviction to pursue progress with hope and compassion. If they are able to draw on the inherent qualities of our Nation's character—our commitment to each other, our courage and optimism in the face of challenges, and our determination to make the world a better place—I am confident they will continue serving as stewards of kindness and charity and contributing to a fairer, more generous, more peaceful America.[153]

The actual proclamation ("NOW, THEREFORE, I, BARACK OBAMA . . .") followed the same text used by other presidents, enjoining "public officials, educators, parents, students, and all Americans to observe this week with appropriate ceremonies, activities, and programs." National Character Counts Week had become a regular "event" in the annual series of occasions that presidents proclaim, and schools and communities observe. But what's especially striking about Obama's take on the week is his specific connection of character traits to (American) *national* character: courage, optimism in the face of challenges, a determination to make the world a better place. Taken together with the obliquely religious but nondenominational phrase "stewards of kindness and charity," Obama's proclamation in effect enjoined the nation to spend National Character Counts Week becoming what George

H. W. Bush had once called (at a Republican National Convention, in a speech written by Peggy Noonan) a "kinder, gentler nation."[154]

Core Values

The Character Counts! program is noteworthy because of its aggressive marketing and the highly successful way its name has been adapted into an annual government observance, but there have been numerous other explicit "character education" programs across the United States, from the beginning of the twentieth century to the present day. In the early years of the last century, the Character Education League produced a curriculum for home and school that taught thirty-one virtues—assigned to specific grades—with the idea that these would culminate in the achievement of a thirty-second virtue, "character."[155]

Toward the end of the century, dozens of new organizations and programs sprang up, some of them in response to the perceived laxness and permissiveness of the decades of the sixties and seventies, others, like the Facing History and Ourselves program originated in Brookline, Massachusetts, which taught middle- and high-school students about the Holocaust, to redress what were thought of as crucial omissions to the curriculum in a world increasingly diverse and multicultural. As is only to be expected, not all the educational and cultural politics of these programs were, or are, the same. To suggest the range, we might mention, for example, character.org (formerly the Character Education Partnership, U.S.), the Heartwood Ethics Curriculum for Children, the Character Education Institute in San Antonio, Texas, and the For Character Program in Chicago. And this is just a sampling. Some of these programs are explicitly religion-based, often reflecting the Christian heritage of nineteenth-century education reformers, but others are not. Character.org, for example, an advocacy program based in Washington, D.C., has described itself as "a nonprofit, nonpartisan, nonsectarian" coalition, as does the Character Counts! Coalition. But some critics of the movement have argued that appeals to "the exercise of free will and character" are, in fact, merely expressions of "conservative ideology."[156]

In the 1990s, the heyday of such programs and debates, the progressive educational theorist Alfie Kohn drew attention to what he saw as a pervasive and dangerous confusion between two quite different notions of "character education."

> The phrase character education, [writes Kohn], has two meanings. In the broad sense, it refers to almost anything that schools might try to provide outside of academics, especially when the purpose is to help children grow into good people. In the narrow sense, it denotes a particular style of moral training, one that reflects particular values as well as particular assumptions about the nature of children and how they learn.
>
> Unfortunately, the two meanings of the term have become blurred, with the narrow version of character education dominating the field to the point that it is frequently mistaken for the broader concept.[157]

Kohn substantiated his critique with many citations from visits to specific programs and published articles on the subject. "The point," he maintains, "is that it is entirely appropriate to ask which values a character education program is attempting to foster, notwithstanding the ostensible lack of controversy about a list of core values."[158]

The idea of "core values," and the problematic mystique of the notion of a "core," seems to look forward, presciently, to the debate about the "Common Core" in U.S. education that has preoccupied teachers, politicians, and commentators in the second decade of the twenty-first century.

The Core Standards prescribe the reading of "myths and stories from around the world, America's founding documents, foundational American literature, and Shakespeare," as if that list were itself clear and incontrovertible evidence of "the importance of content knowledge" in the Common Core.[159] We might notice that, in a description of what the standards call "content coverage," Shakespeare alone is singled out. Are no other individual authors worthy of mentioning by name? Placing Shakespeare in a category by himself—although, as we have already noted, the study of Shakespeare has since the eighteenth century very often been made equivalent to the study of "character"—seems virtually to suggest that Shakespeare *is* British literature, or at least all of British literature that an American student absolutely needs to know. The Common Core's emphasis on "founding"/"foundational" is equally indicative, since "foundational" has itself become a sign word for a certain kind of conservative legal interpretation. More centrally, "core" has itself in certain contexts become virtually a synonym for the word to which it is so often linked in character education, and to which Kohn had linked it—namely, "values."

"Grit"

Donald Trump's praise of the "grit and integrity of our young people" in his National Character Counts Week proclamation invoked what was, for a brief time, a buzzword in character education: "grit." Popularized by the psychologist Angela Duckworth in a bestselling book (*Grit: The Power of Passion and Perseverance*) and a TED talk viewed more than eight million times, the term, and Duckworth's research, were praised by several other scholars in the education field, including Paul Tough (*How Children Succeed*) and Charles Duhigg (*The Power of Habit*). This was self-help in yet another guise, as the elements of social and emotional education were added to the instructional plans of schools throughout the country. "Grit," as the word suggests, meant "having stamina, sticking with your future . . . and working really hard to make that future a reality."[160] It bears a close resemblance, in fact, to the same traits celebrated in the elite British public schools of the nineteenth century, and in character-training schemes like the Boy Scouts, under the names of "character" and "manliness."

But critiques of the "grit" ethos quickly followed. The educational benefits when investigated were seen to be minimal, Duckworth was said to have misinterpreted her original data, and the capacity for "perseverance" was linked to opportunity and socioeconomic status.[161] "Grit" as an antidote to the luxuries of wealth was one thing, but focusing on grit rather than actual academic skills and knowledge was seen to place poor children at yet another disadvantage. "Grit" was part of their daily lives, critics argued; what they needed was not character education, but education.[162]

Term Limits

"Character education," writes John Doris in a book forthrightly called *Lack of Character*, "is naturally understood not simply as a method for teaching moral values or moral reasoning—no need for a grand name in that case—but as a method for inculcating desirable traits of character or virtues."[163] ("Inculcate," especially in a sentence followed by a reference to William J. Bennett's *Book of Virtues*, is a strong word; dictionary mavens might be interested to note that it comes from the Latin meaning "to stamp in with the heel.") For Doris, "a story might teach fairness, equality, or any number of other central moral ideals without proceeding in the discourse of character."[164] Moreover, he suggests that "one person's or culture's good character is often enough another's bad," so that it is "difficult to say what sort of character the character educator should cultivate," asking pointedly, "Is a 'more moral' child one who is respectful and obedient or curious and independent?"[165] And, furthermore, "what exactly are the reasons for thinking that character is central to moral education?"[166]

Terms like "character education," "moral education," "virtue ethics," and "character ethics" can be difficult for the nonphilosopher to disentangle.

No matter how it is spun, "character education" remains either a pleonasm or an oxymoron. All education should, and does, affect "character," whether we define that term as innate or emergent, absolute, situational, or contingent. But, on the other hand, tilting educational tasks in the direction of character building, either by lesson plans or via general educational "mission," may have the effect, intended or inadvertent, of neglecting the actual ideas, theories, details, questions, and intellectual and stylistic challenges of the work under consideration in favor of "moral lessons" (aka "morals," aka platitudes) they are thought to teach—or, indeed, to "inculcate."

Let's return to Alfie Kohn's trenchant critique of certain movements within character education.

> Rather than employ literature to indoctrinate or induce mere conformity, we can use it to spur reflection. Whether the students are 6-year-olds or 16-year-olds, the discussions of stories should be open-ended rather than relentlessly didactic . . . They may even invite students to reflect on the larger question of whether it is desirable to have heroes. (Consider the quality of discussion that might be generated by asking older students to respond to the declaration of playwright Bertolt Brecht: "Unhappy is the land that needs a hero.")[167]

Kohn is not against the central goals of what has come to be known as character education; nor am I. But I share his concern about what that movement has become, especially in some of its versions.

I am concerned when readings slide too quickly from the particular to the general, or from the pleasures of the text to the "moral" or the "message." The point of reading *Macbeth* cannot be to warn us against the moral or political dangers of regicide. The experience of reading the poetry of Wordsworth should not be equivalent to suggesting that we will be happier if we spend more time in nature. The principal accomplishment of a Jane Austen novel is not to advise young women about good and bad ways to seek husbands. This doesn't mean that such works can't be read in these ways—surely, they have been. One of the most gratifying things about works of literature is that they are Teflon tough: nothing, no adaptation, no weak movie version, no narrow or appropriative reading, can damage them, either immediately or over time. The problem is not that "character education" readings are wrong, or right—no one can really arbitrate such judgments, which need simply, but always, to be based on evidence from within the text (not just what the author claimed to intend). It's that such readings are thin or insufficient. They cheat the reader.

When literature becomes moral instruction or character education, it ceases to be literature, and I would hazard a guess that the same is true for history, political theory, and, indeed, for philosophy, even though Aristotle is so often cited as the authority for and forerunner of "virtue ethics." To use the word "character" as a way of controlling rather than opening up meanings is manipulative and meretricious, as well as unfair to the history of the word. If character education, dismal phrase though it may be, has any value at all in educational terms, it will be in teaching students—and adults—to think rigorously and read carefully, basing their opinions on evidence, argument, and a respect for alternative views. The poet Milton, William Blake wrote, was "of the devil's party without knowing it." This was literary criticism, not moralizing, based on Blake's attentive reading of *Paradise Lost*. It is disheartening to think what a frank statement of this kind might provoke in some quarters today.

Difficult Admissions

In the United States, as we've seen, character has been, in many minds, connected to the idea of education and upward mobility. From the middle of the nineteenth century to the beginning of the twentieth, American university presidents spoke out often about the importance and enduring nature of character as a democratic ideal.[168] In 1880, James Burrill Angell, the president of the University of Michigan, observed, "A society is always just what its members make it by their character; nothing more, nothing less."[169] In his autobiography, published in 1905, Andrew Dickson White, cofounder and president of Cornell, extolled the virtues of the university's military training program (ROTC) in transforming "slouchy, careless" farmers' boys and "pampered," "wayward" city boys into young men who could take commands and give them. "I doubt," he wrote, "whether any feature of instruction at Cornell University has produced more excellent results upon *character* than the training thus given."[170] And President Charles Eliot of Harvard, who served from 1869 to 1909, told the incoming class of 1906 that "growth of human character" was the paramount goal of education.[171]

"Character" in these cases was broadly understood to be a benefit of educational training, not—at least not explicitly—a prior qualification for it. But when assessments of "character" were added to the college admissions process by some of America's most prestigious private universities, the motivations were not always idealistic.

Who could possibly object to the idea of "character" as a criterion for the evaluation of college applicants? It seems the most anodyne of inquiries, just as character seems the most democratic of qualities. But, as inherited from the Victorian past, and from the kind of standard that Cecil Rhodes established for the prestigious Rhodes Scholarships, the concept of "character" in elite college admissions has a more complex, less innocent history—one that was in its design more parochial than egalitarian, and more exclusionary than inclusive.

Though the word "character" in its ordinary usage connoted a kind of moral excellence unconnected to class, gender, race, sexuality, or country of origin, it could sometimes, in its very ubiquity and obliquity, become a cover for other things. In the 1920s, "character" became for the first time a criterion for admission to elite colleges and universities.

As Jerome Karabel points out in a detailed and scrupulously researched study, the appearance of "character" as a category for admission to top Ivy League colleges in the 1920s was a genteel way of discriminating against "undesirable" candidates with high academic qualifications, most of them Jews. Writing in particular about Harvard, Yale, and Princeton in this period, Karabel notes that intangibles like "character" and "leadership" were in this period for the first time added as admissions criteria by concerned university presidents and their admissions officers. The "personal letter of recommendation" and the "personal interview," later augmented by passport-sized photographs, helped to screen out applicants whose academic achievements would otherwise have strongly qualified them for admission.

"The key code word here was 'character'—a quality thought to be frequently lacking among Jews but present almost congenitally among high-status Protestants,"[172] observes Karabel matter-of-factly, adding that one member of Harvard's Board of Overseers wrote to President

A. Lawrence Lowell, who was deeply concerned about finding a way to limit the number of Jewish students, that a model might be found in the criteria used to select Rhodes Scholars: adopting "a character standard somewhat in line with the Rhodes conditions" might help to prevent a "Jewish inundation."[173] The title of Karabel's book, *The Chosen*, reflects with irony on the phrase "the chosen people" (itself often used by bigots ironically and with anti-Semitic intent[174]); his subtitle, *The Hidden History of Admission and Exclusion at Harvard, Yale, and Princeton*, explains the term's relevance to the question of college admissions policies past and present. Throughout the first two hundred pages, which chronicle the rise of anti-Jewish sentiment in early-twentieth-century admissions decisions, the word "character" occurs over and over again, wielded as a euphemism by presidents, alumni, admissions chairs, and some faculty members.

Princeton University was the first of what were then called the "Big Three" to add "character" to its official admissions criteria: "In determining admission to the University," declared a report in 1922, "the primary considerations shall be scholarship and character." Stated like this, it seems completely harmless. But—as Karabel notes—adding "character" to "scholarship" builds "enormous discretion into the very heart of the admissions process."[175] Instead of ranking and admitting students on the basis of their academic achievement, the admissions committee could do whatever it chose, and put the decision down to "character."

Not to be outdone, President James Rowland Angell of Yale announced in 1923 that in future admissions "scholarship will be the prime consideration" for admission, but added quickly, "This does not mean that no attention will be paid to qualities of personality and character."[176] These two words, as we've seen, were taken in the last century—and the century before that—to stand for particular sets of attitudes or values. But for Angell's chairman of admissions, Robert Nelson Corwin, the objective was to exclude those "Jewish boys" who were—as Karabel quotes him from a memorandum in the Yale archives—"'alien in morals and manners' and lacking the 'ethical' code of their fellow students."[177]

Harvard President Lowell, writing in 1925 to the chair of the Special Committee on the Limitation of the Size of the Freshman Class, likewise suggested the implementation of the device successfully used by Princeton: "To prevent a dangerous increase in the proportion of Jews, I know at present only one way which is at the same time straightforward and effective, and that is a selection by a personal estimate of character on the part of the Admission authorities, based upon the probable value to the candidate, to the college, and to the community."[178] "Character" in this context becomes a conveniently empty space, to be filled in by the "Admission authorities" so as to obtain the desired result: the admission of the desired, and the exclusion of the "undesirable." The probable value to "the college" and "the community" were particularly open and flexible assessments.

These sections of Karabel's book offer a very clear illustration of the dangers posed by the word "character" when it passes, in these cases quite deliberately, into the realm of vague and subjective opinion—or even into the realm of the calculated ruse. For who indeed could object to "character" as a quality deserving of reward? Somewhere in the background, as all three of the "Big Three" acknowledged, were the Rhodes Scholarship criteria of "leadership," athleticism, and "manly Christian character." Manliness and Christianity were Victorian categories of value, linked throughout the nineteenth century to character. And Jewish applicants, so self-evidently not "Christian," were also often deemed unmanly, regarded as the "bookworms" that Cecil Rhodes had so firmly said he did not want.[179]

Over the course of the ensuing century, the incidences of overt discrimination in college admissions toward Jews, African Americans, or any other previously disfavored group gradually became less evident, if they did not, in some quarters, entirely disappear. The word "character" and other intangible qualities ("personality," "energy," "leadership," etc.) remained, and could—still—be interpreted as the admissions officers wished, sometimes in the effort of what was now called "diversifying" the class, but often continuing to include, in the service of diversification, athletes and legacies (sons and daughters of alumni).

Inevitably, and beneficially, "character" lost, over time, some of the specific associations with Victorian imperial values and "manly" Christianity, but its fraught history is not without lessons for the future—and the present.

For this is not merely an old story from another world a hundred years ago. A case filed against Harvard in 2014 by a group representing Asian Americans claims that Harvard's admissions practices unlawfully discriminate against Asians. Asian Americans, like Jews in the early part of the twentieth century, are sometimes regarded as scoring so highly in grades and tests that they threaten to "unbalance" the college population. Writing in *The New Yorker*, Harvard Law Professor Jeannie Suk Gersen cites phrases like "holistic review" and "intangible characteristics," the latter of which, she says, "echoes the sort of language that often describes the individualizing or leadership qualities that many Asian American applicants, perceived as grinds with high test scores, are deemed to lack." Suk Gersen cites the "history of using similar language to describe Jewish students nearly a century ago."[180] Her careful analysis notes that "admissions offices cannot admit to efforts at racial balancing or anything that sounds remotely like quotas," so "Harvard's litigation position must attribute the resulting race composition and the percentage of Asians in its class *solely* to the holistic method." And this in turn would be "plausible if, in fact, despite disproportionately strong academic credentials, Asian applicants are severely less likely than white ones to have the special personal qualities that colleges seek."[181]

Suk Gersen describes occasions on which, as a young Asian student herself, she was told that Asian students were too much alike. Returning, with the Harvard case in view, to the "longstanding perceptions of Asians as indistinguishable from one another," she observes that "the lawsuit may well entail an inquiry into whether Asian applicants' non-academic qualifications were disproportionately un-special compared to those of white applicants." The impartial legal tone here does not fully conceal the comedy of "disproportionately un-special." It is also worth noting the phrase "non-academic qualifications," itself so oddly familiar by now that we may not think to question it. "Special personal qualities," "non-academic qualifications," "individualizing or leadership qualities"—these are the "intangible characteristics" that tip the balance in the "holistic review." And just as "character" was code for that je ne sais quoi that WASPs were thought to have and Jews to lack, words like "special" and "personal" and "individualizing" and especially "leadership" are twenty-first-century code for what was once called character.

When details of Harvard's admissions process were unsealed in June 2018, against the university's strong resistance, President Drew Faust, a passionate proponent of intellectual freedom, wrote to alumni and friends of Harvard to assert strongly that diversity was "the source of our strength and our excellence," and to affirm the integrity of the process. "Year after year," Faust said, "Harvard brings together a community that is the most diverse that any of us is likely to encounter. Harvard students benefit from working and living alongside people of different backgrounds, experiences, and perspectives as they prepare for the complex world that awaits them and their considerable talents." And, again, "A diverse student body enables us to enrich, to educate, and to challenge one another. As a university community, we are bound across differences by a shared commitment to learning, to pursuing truth, and to embracing the rigor and respect of argument and evidence."[182]

Faust's repeated use of the word "diverse" was strategic and pointed. Several commentators noted that those bringing the suit were longtime opponents of affirmative action, and that their real target was not the rate of admission of Asian Americans but, rather, diversity policies as they affected African American and Hispanic students. Their goal was the elimination of diversity, not the downgrading of "character." But the euphemistic dodges of the early part of the century perversely came to the assistance of the modern-day opponents of social and cultural inclusiveness.

Because the magic name of "Harvard" was in the headlines, there was a good deal of publicity, with historical references to the university's policies toward Jewish applicants in the 1920s and 1930s. Subjective words denoting personal traits, like "'positive personality,' likability, courage, kindliness, and being 'widely respected,'"[183] were cited as vague criteria invoked to give admissions officers latitude in making their decisions.

The problem, almost inescapably, was "character," that troublesome key word that had seemed such a happy thought to the guardians of the gates in the 1920s, and which had become deeply ingrained in college admissions policies over the ensuing century. But perhaps the very ambiguity of the word might now be rethought in the service of progressive action. For what Drew Faust seemed to be describing was the collective character of a community, one of the manifold definitions of that curiously ample word: "The sum of the moral and mental qualities which distinguish an individual or a people, viewed as a homogeneous whole; a person's or group's individuality deriving from environment, culture, experience, etc.; mental or moral constitution, personality."[184] The character of such a group—which is not a people or a nation, but a community, in this case a college or university's annual incoming class—will consist of many individuals with distinctive traits or characteristics, together forming what Faust in her letter termed "a community that is the most diverse that any of us is likely to encounter."

The ruling in the case by Judge Allison D. Burroughs on September 30, 2019, found in favor of Harvard. In a 130-page "finding of fact and conclusion of law," the judge rejected the argument of the plaintiffs, and said that the university had, in its admissions process, met the strict constitutional standard for considering race.[185] The concept of "character" appears explicitly in the ruling three times, twice in citations of Harvard documents and a third time in a summary of a study supporting Harvard's position. All three mentions are suggestive, and show the university seeking to describe this elusive concept and its importance to a college community.

"The personal rating criteria," Judge Burroughs wrote, "perhaps in response to this lawsuit, were overhauled for the class of 2023," and the reading procedures now explicitly state that "an applicant's race or ethnicity should not be considered in assigning the personal rating" and encourage admissions officers to consider "qualities of character" such as "courage in the face of seemingly insurmountable obstacles," "leadership," "maturity," "genuineness, selflessness, humility," "resiliency," "judgment," "citizenship," and "spirit and camaraderie with peers."[186] A quotation from the Harvard *Interviewer Handbook* advises: "Attempts to define and to identify precise elements of character, and to determine how much weight they should be given in the admissions process, requires discretion and judiciousness. But the Committee believes that the 'best' freshman class is more likely to result if we bring evaluation of character and personality into decisions than if we do not."[187]

Summarizing the argument of Professor David Card, an economics professor at the University of California at Berkeley, about the importance of including the "personal rating" in assessing an applicant for admission, the ruling says (paraphrasing Professor Card), "the personal rating captures other relevant characteristics unrelated to race that will not be taken into account at all by the modeling if the personal rating is excluded, such as the extent to which an applicant demonstrates character, leadership ability, self-confidence, grit, or other distinctive qualities that might benefit the Harvard community."[188]

Many, perhaps most, of these qualities— leadership and citizenship, selflessness and humility, grit and resiliency, judgment and maturity— are familiar terms from the history of character. The difference, if there is one, comes from the fact that college admissions officers are trying to predict or encourage future performance. But this is also what happens in an election contest, or a job hire, or a political appointment. "Evaluation of character," however imprecise, is a constant—as well as a crucial—aspect of social, professional, and personal life.

The consideration of "character" as a criterion in the college admissions process may be said to have migrated, over the course of the intervening century, from querying the moral standing of applicants deemed suspect for reasons of religion or race, to noting and valuing the particular traits, skills, backgrounds, and gifts of applicants who are diverse— which is to say *different* from one another. If the word "character" itself does not appear in any of these contemporary conversations, no matter which political or institutional side is speaking (or suing), it may be because the term has become so frayed or so loaded that it is best omitted, lest it stir up more controversy. Should that be the case, it would represent at least one clear achievement in the murky field of character education.

3

CLAIMING IT

The Idea of National Character

There is no end to the illusions of patriotism. In the first century of our era, Plutarch mocked those who declared that the Athenian moon is better than the Corinthian moon; Milton, in the seventeenth, observed that God is in the habit of revealing Himself first to His Englishmen; Fichte, at the beginning of the nineteenth, declared that to have character and to be German are obviously one and the same thing.

—JORGE LUIS BORGES, "OUR POOR INDIVIDUALISM"

The Prince, in a word, was un-English. What that word precisely meant it was difficult to say; but the fact was patent to every eye . . . But Lord Palmerston was English through and through, there was something in him that expressed, with extraordinary vigour, the fundamental qualities of the English race.

—LYTTON STRACHEY, *QUEEN VICTORIA*

If we do not make a stand we shall in a few weeks be asked to call Leghorn "Livorno," and the BBC will be pronouncing Paris "Paree." Foreign names were made for Englishmen, not Englishmen for foreign names.

—WINSTON CHURCHILL, *THE SECOND WORLD WAR*

Is there such a thing as "national character"? And if so, how is it reflected in the behavior, politics, and leadership of a nation? Buzzwords across the political spectrum attest to the allure, and danger, of the idea; words like "heritage," and "identity," and "tradition." What about "nationalism," the most visible of these contestatory terms? How—if at all—is nationalism related to ideas of national character? In the nineteenth century, a "nationalism" meant a way of speaking, in idiom or phrase, associated with the people of a particular nation.[1] Although this use is now obsolete, vestiges of such an us/them divide still remain. Political debates about immigration, emigration, and the status of refugees tacitly engage this question, when they do not explicitly raise it.

The issue has been front and center during the presidency of Donald Trump. Trump's campaign slogan, "Make America Great Again," suggests that something specifically "American" has been lost, and needs to be recaptured or restored. Opponents have contended that, to the contrary, it is Trump who is endangering the character of the nation. Trump "has done real damage to the American character," said Senate Minority Leader Charles Schumer, sparking immediate protests from conservative media outlets.[2] "The character of a nation is not the character of its president," declared Senator Elizabeth Warren. "The character of a nation is the character of its people."[3]

National character is a very old topic. It goes back (at least) to classical times, when authors like Herodotus in Greece, and Tacitus in Rome, discussed the "character" of various nations and peoples. Such descriptions—of the Scythians, the Egyptians, the Spartans, the inhabitants of Britain and Germany—constitute a kind of "comparative ethnography"[4] long before the term was invented. European philosophers of the eighteenth century, often citing these early commentaries, took an interest in the question, debating whether the causes of difference in national character were "moral" or "physical"—a debate that has continued, under other and purportedly more scientific reasoning, virtually to the present day.

In the England of the 1830s, there was a surge of new attention to the idea of "national character." Interest spiked again during each of the European world wars, and yet again in the nationalist-postnationalist-terrorist political climate of the twenty-first century. Over the years, opinions have varied, with impassioned statements on all sides of the question. "Nations have characters, as well as individuals," Benjamin Disraeli had contended, early in his long career, well before he became Queen Victoria's prime minister.[5] On the other hand, Max Weber, the sociologist and economic theorist, completely dismissed the idea: "The appeal to national character," he said, "is generally a mere confession of ignorance."[6]

But what *is* a "national character"? Is it a set of beliefs, a racial or cultural inheritance, an instance of wartime grit, a wishful fantasy, a political slogan, an anthropological category, or a gossipy social reputation? A boast or a slur? How can "character," often regarded as an individual trait or set of traits, become nationalized? And what happens if a citizen, or a group of citizens, doesn't conform to, or perhaps even aspire to, the "national character"?

Questions like these can help to unpack the ways in which national character has been asserted, projected, and internalized in connection with the modern nation-state. Precisely because this seductive, sometimes complacent, and occasionally dangerous concept has resurfaced recently, spread by viral media and (sometimes virulent) politicians at a time when its alternatives include "multinational," "multicultural," "cosmopolitan," "international," and "global," it is worth focusing attention on the term itself, and its vicissitudes. How does the troublesome modifier "national" affect the meaning and use of "character"? Many of the examples here will be drawn from England and from the United States, although we will also consider the work of cultural anthropologists and others who have engaged with the "national characters" of lands they have visited or studied.

Plus Ça Change

It may be helpful at the outset to consider some key terms from Raymond Williams, one of the most acute modern analysts of linguistic and cultural change. For national character is one of those phrases that lie in wait for an occasion, often sitting dormant until stirred by events. Observations about national character tend to be *residual*, developed over decades and centuries, from both within the "nation" (itself a late concept in political terms) and from outside. But attention to these ideas becomes acute, or what Williams calls *emergent*, at times of political or cultural pressure, change, or concern. "National character" is a concept often invoked at times of stress, as a marker not so much of social progress as of social and cultural anxiety.

Thus, as we will see, truths or truisms about what is "American," or "English," or "British," or "French," or "Japanese," can come to the fore in public debates when provoked by perceived crises large and small: hot- or cold-war tensions, immigration, language, economics, race. Whatever its shortcomings, or perhaps indeed *because* of its inherent ambiguity and instability, "national character" has endured as a concept, migrating across research protocols and disciplines. A glance at the daily paper or at social media will illustrate all too well that things have not changed much, in this respect at least, over the years. Sometimes it is a regressive move, and sometimes a call to remember our better selves.

"Not American" was the opinion voiced by a prominent Republican senator in June 2018, speaking out against the Trump administration's policy of separating immigrant children from their parents if they cross the border illegally into the United States.[7] "Cruel and contrary to American values," said the top official of the Business Roundtable. "This is not who we are."[8] The columnist Frank Bruni offered a similar critique: "In a country of immigrants that has proudly held itself up as an exemplar, it's about morality. It's about values. Few aspects of American policy define us in the world as sharply as our treatment of immigrants does. Few define us as sharply, period."[9] Paul Krugman saw the issue of separating families—and other recent Trump activities, like "insulting democratic allies while praising murderous dictators," and "demanding that law enforcement stop investigating his associates and go after his political enemies"—as directly linked both to the character of the president and to the looming end of "American goodness."

> What do these stories have in common? Obviously they're all tied to the character of the man occupying the White House, surely the worst human being ever to hold his position. But

> there's also a larger context, and it's not just about Donald Trump. What we're witnessing is a systematic rejection of longstanding American values—the values that actually made America great.[10]

But before Americans congratulate themselves on these defining characteristics, we might take a moment to recall other historical moments, like the McCarthy era and the Red Scare, in which "America" and "values" were used to defame, incarcerate, and even to execute individuals suspected of not conforming to those values.

Character and Identity

Any cultural observer who believed that notions of "national character" were either out of date or out of synch with the times might have been moved to think again during the tumultuous political years of the early twenty-first century in the United States, Britain, or France.

"Brexit will be good for the British national character," wrote the historian Andrew Roberts a few days before the country's historic vote to leave the European Union. "It will reintroduce risk-taking, self-reliance and a sense of being in control of our national destiny, elements that have been severely weakened during the 43 years of our EU membership." Invoking a term perhaps more frequently heard in American politics, he stressed "Britain's historical exceptionalism," arguing that to "deny" or to "refuse to recognize" it "is as absurd as to be embarrassed or ashamed of it." His essay closed with an extended quotation from Sir Walter Scott's "Lay of the Last Minstrel" ("Breathes there the man, with soul so dead, / Who never to himself hath said, / This is my own, my native land!"), with a final exhortation derived from its ringing patriotic lines: "Don't be unwept, unhonour'd, and unsung: vote 'leave' on June 23."[11]

No hint of irony is voiced here in the citation of a poem about the Scottish border as exemplar of British exceptionalism. ("This is my own, my native land" is inscribed on Walter Scott's stone slab outside the Writers' Museum in Edinburgh; the Scots, notably, voted in significant numbers to "remain" rather than to "leave" the EU.) Both before and after the referendum, in fact, it was "resurgent Englishness," rather than British identity, that seemed to have inspired many of those who voted for "Brexit" (the catchy portmanteau phrase that stood for "British exit"). The campaign, said Robert Tombs, the author of *The English and Their History*, is "all about us and the English identity,"[12] and a former speechwriter for David Cameron told a reporter, "There is a strong element in the Tory character that . . . thinks to the strains of Elgar and stirs at the words 'destiny,' 'democracy' and 'nation.'"[13]

Sir Edward Elgar (1857–1934) was the composer of "Land of Hope and Glory" and the "Pomp and Circumstance Marches," the latter taking their collective title from a particularly despairing speech in *Othello*, when the heroic soldier, convinced of his wife's infidelity, bids "farewell" to his career and to all the "pride, pomp and circumstance of glorious war." Elgar wrote many successful orchestral works in his lifetime, but his name is invoked by Cameron, with implicit reference to these popular tunes, as shorthand for a certain kind of nostalgic patriotism and national pride. (Despite Elgar's iconic "Englishness," the most famous of the "Pomp and Circumstance" marches is regularly played at U.S. graduation ceremonies, both high school and university, and is sometimes known there simply as "The Graduation March," thereby shedding both its history and its national character.)

"Raw nationalism has a characteristic turn of mind," wrote a thoughtful Irish commentator on the dilemmas faced by Britain after the Brexit vote. "It defines itself by what it is not. The Irish nationalism of my youth did this by defining Ireland as the anti-England. Likewise, the English nationalism that emerged with the demand for Brexit defines Englishness by what it is against: immigrants and the European Union. We Irish had to learn by our mistakes that this way of thinking is worse than useless. But English nationalism is hardly inclined to heed the Irish experience. It wants to make all the old mistakes before learning anything."[14] This description of "raw nationalism" as a force that "defines itself by what it is not" names one of the most consistent lessons of modern history—one that has had a powerful, and powerfully negative, effect upon both the concept and the deployment of the idea of national character.

In France, the rise of the nationalist party of Marine Le Pen was accompanied by a concern about the loss of "Frenchness" in towns and cities across the country.[15] The burkini, a body-covering swimsuit, was banned by several French mayors on the grounds that they were un-French: in the words of an official of the city of Cannes, "clothing that conveys an allegiance to the terrorist movements that are waging war against us."[16] In the midst of the political campaign for president—which she ultimately lost, although she gained an unprecedented portion of the vote—Le Pen described the issue as a clash of civilizations. "We are being submerged by a flood of immigrants that are sweeping all before them. There are prayers in the street, cafés that ban women and young women who get threatening looks if they wear a skirt. I will say when I become president that this is not the French way."[17]

And again, in her appearance on the television show *60 Minutes*: "I'm opposed to wearing head scarves in public places. That's not France. There's something I just don't understand: The people who come to France, why would they want to change France, to live in France the same way they lived back home?"[18]

This was not a new story in France, either. Frantz Fanon, brought up in French-speaking, French-allegiant Martinique, was disconcerted—and then politically inspired—when, after moving to metropolitan France to continue his education, he found that he was regarded as black rather than as French. ("The fact is that the European has a set idea of the black man, and there is nothing more exasperating than to hear: 'How long have you lived in France? You speak such good French.'"[19])

In the event, Le Pen did not come to power, and France found itself instead under the leadership of Emmanuel Macron, whose preferred venues for public events were grand palaces and châteaux, and one of whose sobriquets was "president of the rich." After Macron ordered a new presidential dinner service from the famous porcelain factory at Sèvres, there was a wave of criticism in the press, because Macron had just complained about the cost of French welfare spending. The factory's director general justified the purchase of the plates, each of which contains an individualized image of the Élysée Palace, as a matter of national pride and character: "He represents France and the French. At dinners of state he must be in a position to represent France, and the French tradition of art de vivre. And since the 18th century, Sèvres has been its incarnation."[20]

"Acting Like an American"

When a man at a political rally for the then–Republican candidate Donald Trump was arrested for having allegedly sucker-punched a protester, he explained that the protester was "not acting like an American," adding, "The next time we see him, we might have to kill him."[21] Trump's immediate response was to support his supporter—"he obviously loves his country, and maybe he doesn't like seeing what's happening to the country"—and he briefly considered paying the man's court costs, while at the same time decrying "violence."[22]

What does "not acting like an American" mean here? Perhaps the accused attacker thought the protester was trying to stifle free speech rather than express it. But the right to peaceful protest is, one might have thought, one of the most "American" of rights. Whatever he might have meant, this clearly was an "us versus them" declaration, an epithet meant to "other" the opposition. In his own view, the assailant was, presumably, "acting like an American" in punching someone with whose views and actions he took issue. The accused man, seventy-eight-year-old John Franklin McGraw, nicknamed "Quick Draw," was white. The man he allegedly sucker-punched and shoved, Rakeem Jones, twenty-six, was African American. Jones was initially placed in custody, and McGraw was not, until a video of the event went viral. Ultimately, Jones, who said his life had been changed forever by the attack and the threat of future violence, forgave his attacker and shook his hand. (Acting, we might say, very much "like an American" of the kind our nation likes to think we are.)

"Not American" is an accusation often leveled at individuals and groups with whom the speaker disagrees. At a rally in September 1941, the aviator Charles Lindbergh, spokesman for the (first) America First Committee, declared, "The leaders of both the British and the Jewish races . . . for reasons which are not American, wish to involve us in the war."[23]

Acting—or not acting—"like an American" will also, for any American of a certain age, invoke HUAC, the House Un-American Activities Committee, which interrogated, and blacklisted, hundreds of American citizens who were alleged to have had ties with the Communist Party.

Established in 1938 as a special investigative committee by the U.S. House of Representatives, it became a standing committee in 1945, and targeted supposed communist "sympathizers" and subversives, many of them Jewish, and many connected to the motion-picture industry.[24] At that time, as Garry Wills observes:

> It was not enough to be American in citizenship or residence—one must be American in one's thoughts. There was such a thing as Americanism. And lack of right thinking could make an American citizen un-American. The test was ideological. That is why we had such a thing as an Un-American Activities Committee in the first place. Other countries do not think in terms of, say, Un-British Activities as a political category. But ours was the first of the modern ideological countries, born of revolutionary doctrine, and it has maintained a belief that a return to doctrinal purity is the secret of national strength for us.[25]

Many who were summoned before the committee strove to point out that those fingered as "un-American" were often more "American" in their defense of the nation's heritage of rights and ideals than the interrogators who accused, interrupted, and vilified them. Here we might recall Paul Robeson's powerful riposte at the end of his testimony: "You are the nonpatriots, and you are the un-Americans, and you ought to be ashamed of yourselves."[26]

How unusual is "un-American"? The *Oxford English Dictionary* gives definitions for "un-French," "un-English," "un-German," "un-Greek," and "un-Roman." "Un-English" has its own political resonances ("the un-English practice of secret voting"; "a false patriotism that thought it un-English to wear foreign fabrics"), and "un-Greek" is defined as "not Greek in character; not in accordance with Greek ideas or habits," where "Greek" implicitly but clearly means "ancient Greek," with references to the Thebans and to Plato's *Republic*. The Gallic institution set up to combat un-Frenchness is the Académie Française, whose forty "immortals" guard the purity of the French language. But the self-appointed foes of un-Americanism were not authors, linguists, or philosophers but partisan politicians and demagogues.

The writer Lillian Hellman twice pointedly cited the "American tradition" in her letter to the chairman of HUAC, explaining why she would not give the names of others when she testified before the committee:

> I was raised in an old-fashioned American tradition and there were certain homely things that were taught to me: to try to tell the truth, not to bear false witness, not to harm my neighbor, to be loyal to my country, and so on. In general, I respected these ideals of Christian honor and did as well with them as I knew how. It is my belief that you will agree with these simple rules of human decency and will not expect me to violate the good American tradition from which they come.[27]

It's characteristic of Hellman's verve and style that the phrase "I cannot and will not cut my conscience to fit this year's fashions," which made her letter so memorable and quotable, is coupled with the fact, also reported in *Scoundrel Time*, that she went out and bought "a beautiful, expensive Balmain," a "very expensive hat," and "a fine pair of white kid gloves" to wear in her appearance before the committee.[28] But another phrase in her letter is also worth noting: the mention of "ideals of Christian honor." Hellman herself, like so many of the committee's targets, was Jewish. The ideals she here cites are not restricted to Christian belief, and several of them might be said to be violated by the existence and methods of HUAC itself. But her citation of "Christian honor," whether or not ironically pointed, underscores the degree to which Jews were disproportionately identified as potential subversives. Were Jews—even those raised in a "good American tradition"—"good Americans"?

Consider the statement in November 1947 of Congressman John Rankin of Mississippi, acting chair of HUAC, about the "real names" of some Hollywood actors and entertainers. The names were those of members of the Committee for the First Amendment who had signed a petition protesting the activities of HUAC.

> One of the names is June Havoc. We found out from the motion-picture almanac that her real name is June Hovick.

> Another one was Danny Kaye, and we found out that his real name was David Daniel Kaminsky.
>
> Another one here is John Beal, whose real name is J. Alexander Bliedung.
>
> Another one is Cy Bartlett, whose real name is Sacha Baraniev.
>
> Another one is Eddie Cantor, whose real name is Edward Iskowitz.
>
> There is one who calls himself Edward Robinson. His real name is Emmanuel Goldenberg.
>
> There is another one here who calls himself Melvyn Douglas, whose real name is Melvyn Hesselberg.[29]

This would be purely comic if it were not so close to tragic. Rankin's iteration of "we found out" on the one hand and "who calls himself" on the other implies both detection and secrecy. But the source that revealed the supposed deceptions is "the motion-picture almanac," an annual volume published in New York by the Quigley Publishing Company and readily available to any interested purchaser. Stage and professional names here are said to hide "real names," with the implication that there is something bogus and suspect about those whose birth names are listed in an industry publication.

Beal was born in Joplin, Missouri; Douglas in Macon, Georgia; Cantor in New York City; Kaye in Brooklyn; Havoc in Vancouver, British Columbia. Sy Bartlett, a screenwriter born in a part of Russia that is now Ukraine, was never known as "Cy."

Garry Wills notes soberly, in connection with HUAC and the Hollywood blacklist:

> If it is not enough to possess citizenship and obey the laws, if one must also subscribe to the propositions of Americanism, then we create two classes of citizens—those loyal and pure in doctrine, and those who, without actually breaking any law, are considered un-American, insufficient in their Americanism. These latter can be harassed, spied on, forced to register, deprived of governmental jobs and other kinds of work.[30]

These observations, although first published in 1976, have a telling pertinence to the "America First" and "Make America Great Again" ideologies of the Trump years. And as Eric Hobsbawn has pointed out, such ideological underpinnings derive from a long and systematic tradition that defines "American" against its supposed other, "un-American":

> The concept of Americanism as an act of *choice*—the decision to learn English, to apply for citizenship—and a choice of specific beliefs, acts and modes of behaviour implied the corresponding concept of 'un-Americanism'. In countries defining nationality existentially there could be unpatriotic Englishmen or Frenchmen, but their status as Englishmen and Frenchmen could not be in doubt, unless they could also be defined as strangers (*metèques*). Yet in the U.S.A., as in Germany, the 'un-American' or 'vaterlandslose' person threw doubt on his or her actual status as a member of the nation . . .
>
> Whether the concept of 'un-Americanism', which can be traced back to at least the 1870s, was more of a reaction of the native-born against the strangers or of Anglo-Saxon Protestant middle-classes against foreign-born workers is unclear. At all events it provided an internal enemy against whom the good American could assert his or her Americanism, not least by the punctilious performance of all the formal and informal rituals, the assertion of all the beliefs conventionally and institutionally established as characteristic of good Americans.[31]

"Good Americans." Here is that phrase again, implying, by its very presence, the possibility that some Americans were not "good." It's possible to hear, as Hobsbawn may be hinting, an unwelcome echo of "good Germans." And to recall Robeson's sharp comment on true patriotism. Congressman Rankin of HUAC was an unapologetic racist who proudly used the *n*-word on the floor of the House,[32] labeled Albert Einstein a "foreign-born agitator," called the journalist Walter Winchell a "slime-mongering kike,"[33] advocated for Japanese internment during World War II, and complained that "the white Christian people of America, the ones who created this nation," were the victims of prejudice.[34] Even in hindsight, it is worth asking whether it was Rankin or his targets who really represented "American values."

Nor, as we have already seen, was HUAC by any means the end of the story of "un-Americanism" and its discontents. But, as was the case with Paul Robeson, the epithet could be turned on the accusers, questioning their character and upholding that of the nation.

When President Donald Trump tweeted in July 2019 that four congresswomen of color should "go home" to the countries they came from—although three were in fact native-born Americans, and the fourth a naturalized Somali refugee who had lived in the United States since she was ten—cries of "un-American" were heard on all sides. The "love it or leave it" rhetoric of Trump's supporters, some of whom chanted, "Send her back," as the president basked in the roar of the crowd,[35] was balanced by the lawmakers' own swift and forthright replies ("the only country we swear an oath to is the United States"[36]) as well as by the dignified statement of Representative Ted Lieu (Democrat of California), himself both an immigrant and an air force veteran, who wrote in *The Washington Post* that to regard immigrants as untrustworthy and unpatriotic is "not just wrong: it is un-American."[37]

Exceptionalism and Its Discontents

The belief in what has become known as "American exceptionalism" has been espoused, at various times in U.S. history, by progressive, liberal, and conservative thinkers; in recent years it has become an insistent mantra of the American right. It is said to be a very old idea, virtually coterminous with the founding of the republic, linked on the one hand with the Puritan idea that America was a nation chosen by God as an example to the world (John Winthrop's "City Upon a Hill") and on the other to sentiments like Thomas Jefferson's vision of "this solitary republic of the world, the only monument of human rights, sole depository of the sacred fire of freedom and self-government"—a sentiment he expressed on leaving the presidency in 1809.

Alexis de Tocqueville's *Democracy in America* (1835) is sometimes credited with the origin of "American exceptionalism," although

Tocqueville does not quite use the term, and what he says about the "exceptional" situation of Americans is a decidedly mixed bag. The passage appears in a section of his second volume under the heading "How the Example of the Americans Does Not Prove That a Democratic People Could Have Neither the Aptitude nor the Taste for the Sciences, Literature, and the Arts." Unscrambling this double negative, what we get is American exceptionalism, all right, but as gentle critique rather than celebratory praise.

Tocqueville is discussing the dependence of America on European, and specifically English, science, learning, and culture, and the fact that "in few of the civilized nations of our day have the higher sciences made less progress than in the United States and that in few have great artists, distinguished poets, or famous writers been more rarely found." Is this lack of culture and intellectual distinction a failure of American "national character"? Tocqueville, it seems, thinks not. He believes the issue is what we might call "situational" rather than "intrinsic," a matter of history, contiguity, and convenience. "I cannot agree to separate America from Europe," he writes, "despite the ocean that divides them. I consider the people of the United States as a sample of the English people responsible for developing the forests of the New World while the rest of the nation [i.e., England], enjoying more leisure time and less taken up with the material cares of life, can devote itself to thought and to the enlargement in every direction of the human mind." There then follows, immediately, the passage so often, if imprecisely, recalled:

> The American position is, therefore, entirely exceptional and it is quite possible that no democratic nation will ever be similarly placed. Their strictly Puritan origin, their exclusively commercial habits, the country they inhabit, which appears to divert their minds from the study of science, literature, and the arts, the nearness of Europe which allows them to neglect such study without relapsing into barbarism, a thousand such reasons of which I have been able to signal only the main ones, must have focused the American mind, in this unusual manner, upon purely practical concerns. Everything—his passions, needs, ed-

> ucation, circumstances—seems to unite in inclining the native of the United States earthward. Only religion persuades him to raise an occasional and absent-minded glance toward heaven.
>
> Let us, therefore, stop viewing all democratic nations under the example of the American people and let us try to view them with their own characteristics.[38]

Thus the "exceptional position" of the Americans among "civilized nations" is that they not only lack interest in the higher sciences and the arts but also that they can get away with it, at least in the short term, by depending upon the cultural and theoretical achievements of England and the other countries of Europe. (If this devaluation of science and the arts seems to accord with recent U.S. government proposals to strip the NSF, the NIH, the NEH, the NEA, and the PBS of funding, the reader may credit that fact to coincidence, prescience, or "national character.")

Elsewhere, Tocqueville directly mentions the "American national character," but his opinion is again less than wholly complimentary: the "ever-increasing despotism of the American majority" is, he thinks, the reason that "already some vexing effects are evident in the American national character," including the relative absence from political life of "remarkable men."[39] American politicians behave more like courtiers than like men of distinction, he observes, flattering the powerful and seeking their favor, and this he regards as an unintended consequence of democracy. "Democratic republics place the spirit of a court within the reach of a great number of citizens and allow it to spread through all social classes at once. That is one of the most serious criticisms that can be made against them."[40]

As for the source of the specific phrase "American exceptionalism," it seems, ironically enough, to be traceable to a dispute between the American Communist Party and Joseph Stalin. American communists in the 1920s spoke of "American exceptionalism" in areas like natural resources and industrial capacity as elements that might, for some time at least, help the nation "avoid the crisis that must eventually befall every capitalist society."[41] Stalin forcefully objected to this idea, and his 1929 remarks, in translation, decried "the heresy of American exceptionalism."[42] The following year, in the wake of the stock-market crash, an article appeared in the monthly English-language magazine *The Communist* in which "a faith in American 'exceptionalism'" was described as the false belief of those who had not seen the inevitability of the class struggle in the United States and the strong prospect of revolution.[43]

It's not wholly unusual to have catchphrases coined from one political viewpoint taken up by the proponents of an opposing viewpoint; this has been the case, for example, with "political correctness," a term invented, in a spirit of ironic self-critique, by the modern left, and wielded like a bludgeon by the right. But the passionate defenders of "American exceptionalism" as a mark of national destiny (and, in some cases, superiority) might pause for a moment on this particular piece of linguistic history. "Yes, we are exceptional," trumpets the prologue of Dick Cheney and Liz Cheney's *Exceptional: Why the World Needs a Powerful America*.[44] "We," as always, is a dangerous word.

When then-President Barack Obama was asked on a political visit to Europe about his belief in American exceptionalism, he replied, "I believe in American exceptionalism, just as I suspect that the Brits believe in British exceptionalism and the Greeks believe in Greek exceptionalism"; he was derided by the Fox broadcaster, minister, and former Arkansas governor, Mike Huckabee. "He grew up more as a globalist than an American," said Huckabee. "To deny American exceptionalism is in essence to deny the heart and soul of this nation."[45] Note that Obama did not say he did not believe in American exceptionalism. He merely acknowledged, gracefully, that other people might believe their own countries to be exceptional as well. But to Huckabee this was denying "the heart and soul" of America. Could an "American" also be a "globalist"? In 2010, when Huckabee made these remarks, "globalist" was already, apparently, approaching un-Americanism, joining words like "transnational," "multinational," and "international" as somehow the vaguely suspect, if not fully treasonous, opposite of "American." The Cheneys, too, took exception to Obama's remarks on exceptionalism.[46] Only one truly "exceptional" nation existed, apparently, for patriotic Americans.

But try telling that to the British. Or, indeed, the French.

National Caricature (1)

The tendency to type and characterize nationalities is, as we've noted, an old story in history, politics, and culture. And when used to describe another people, and not one's own, this issue of "national character" often comes uncomfortably close to stereotyping, and sometimes to prejudice and racism. This has been demonstrably true in political rhetoric and in pseudoscience over the centuries. But it also happens, and sometimes most disconcertingly, in literature, drama, and other arts.

It's easy to see how some of these national types could segue or morph into theatrical or "stage" types: the "stage Irishman" or "stage Welshman" were standard comic turns in the nineteenth-century English theater, and the stage Jew, it is perhaps needless to say, long before. Two plays by Shakespeare, written and performed just a few years apart, give striking evidence of this interest in *national* character. Each produces memorable and enduring *dramatic* characters, some of whom speak for, and others against, the idea of a national stereotype. One of these plays is a history play; the other, nominally, a comedy.

In Shakespeare's *Henry V*, regional types play a large role, but their characterizations are part of a pattern of what might be called "national-character building": the image of a unified nation ruled by a brave and soldierly English king. The battlefield conversations among Captains Jamy (the Scot), MacMorris (the Irishman), Gower (the Englishman), and Fluellen (the Welshman) are written in dialect; Fluellen, like all stage Welshmen after him, says "look you" a lot, and pronounces his *b*'s as *p*'s so that he is heard to boast proudly that all the water in the Welsh river Wye could not wash the Prince of Wales's Welsh "plod" out of his "pody." He is also, as we will learn, something of a classicist and a military historian.

When his language is mocked by the braggart soldier Pistol, Fluellen has his revenge in the memorable scene in which he forces Pistol to eat a leek—the large onionlike vegetable that is the national emblem of the Welsh. ("Must I bite? . . . I eat and eat," says the cowardly Pistol as he does so.) The English Captain Gower, an interested onlooker, sums up this event in words that speak directly to "national character" at a moment of political transition: "You thought, because he could not speak

English in the native garb, he could not therefore handle an English cudgel: you find it otherwise; and henceforth let a Welsh correction teach you a good English condition" (*Henry V* 5.1.67–70). For good measure, and good contrast, the play also features some effete and ineffectual French royals and nobles, including one who writes a sonnet to his horse, and a pair of lively Frenchwomen who, in a language-learning scene written in French, find themselves pronouncing English words ("foot" and "gown") that sound to them, and to the audience, very much like vulgarities. National character, and national characters, could be said to be at issue in virtually every scene.

Shortly before *Henry V*, Shakespeare wrote another play that also addressed the question of national character in ways that seem problematic today. The play was *The Merchant of Venice*, and its characters included not only Shylock and his fellow Jews but also a host of other national stereotypes, some merely spoken of, some present—and wittily mocked—on the stage. And although Gratiano and other Venetians make merciless fun of the Jews, the chief mocker of other supposed national traits is the play's much-admired heroine, Portia, who delivers the famous "quality of mercy" speech in the courtroom scene—and then declines to show Shylock much in the way of mercy at the end. The "dark" elements of this comedy, which are often so powerful that the play seems more like a tragedy, are in fact not wholly unexpected. They are prefigured, as we'll see, by the earlier scenes with Portia's suitors—scenes that may at first seem to be part of quite a different play.

Ruing the lottery her father has ordained as a test for her suitors, Portia engages, with her friend Nerissa, in a bantering dialogue of dismissal on the basis of the national clichés they are said to embody and represent. The Scot is quarrelsome; the German is drunk. The "Neapolitan Prince" does nothing but talk about his horse; the Count Palatine is "full of unmannerly sadness" and "doth nothing but frown"; the French lord is vain and competitive: "he hath a horse better than the Neapolitans, a better bad habit of frowning than the Count Palatine. He is every man in no man . . . He will fence with his own shadow"; Falconbridge, the young baron of England, knows no language but his own ("he hath neither Latin, French, nor Italian" at a time when an educated person might well speak all of them) and his costume, as was

The Scoutmaster's Conjuring Trick; Lord Robert Baden-Powell, drawing, 1933 *(H. Cox)*

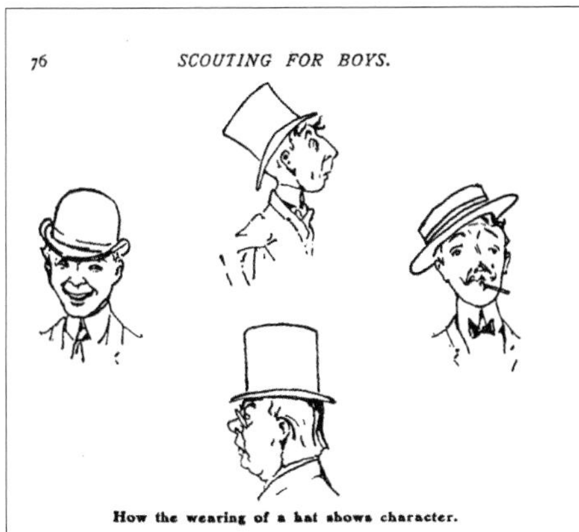

How the Wearing of a Hat Shows Character; Lord Robert Baden-Powell, drawing, 1908 *(C. Arthur Pearson Ltd.)*

A virtuous Boy Scout leaping over man's shortcomings; Lord Robert Baden-Powell, drawing *(Scout Association)*

Samuel Smiles; George Reid, painting, 1877 *(Wikimedia Commons)*

Robert Baden-Powell *(Library of Congress)*

Agnes Baden-Powell in her Girl Guide uniform; photograph *(Girl Guides of Canada, BC Program Committee)*

Olave Baden-Powell *(Bassano Ltd., half-plate negative, November 27, 1958, National Portrait Gallery, London)*

Patience in Adversity; Pont (Graham Laidler), color lithograph, 1937 (Punch *magazine)*

Love of Travelling Alone; Pont (Graham Laidler), color lithograph, 1937 (Punch *magazine)*

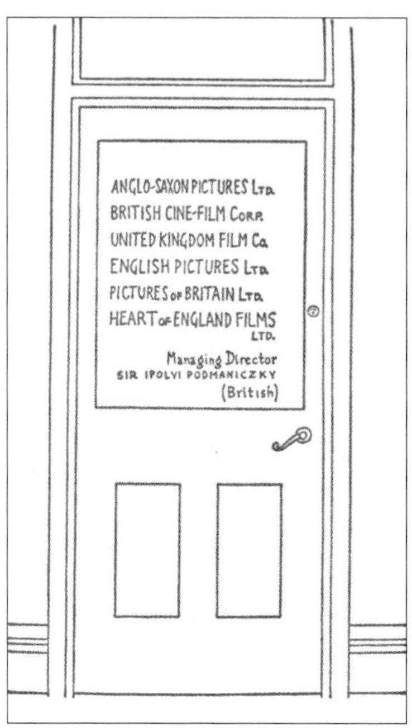

How to Be a Film Producer; George Mikes and Nicholas Bentley, drawing, 1946

The Two-Party System

The Two-Party System; George Mikes and Nicholas Bentley, drawing, 1946

'Can't you understand plain English?'

Can't You Understand Plain English?; George Mikes and Nicholas Bentley, drawing, 1946

"Makes you kind of proud to be an American, doesn't it?"

Makes You Kind of Proud to Be an American, Doesn't It?;
Peter Arno, drawing, 1960 *(Condé Nast)*

Donald Trump with Miss USA contestants at Trump Tower;
Cindy Ord, photograph, 2017 *(Getty)*

Franz Joseph Gall; Zéphirin Félix Jean Marius Belliard, engraving
(Wikimedia Commons)

Gall examines the head of Louis-Philippe and finds bumps that indicate various virtuous qualities; wood engraving, 1832
(Wellcome Collection)

Gall examines the head of a pretty young girl; Edward Hull, lithograph with watercolor, 1825 *(Wellcome Collection)*

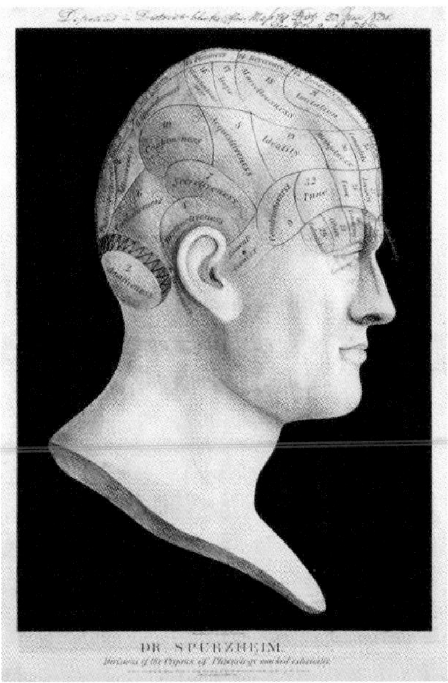

Spurzheim, with divisions of the organs of phrenology marked externally; Pendleton's Lithography, lithograph, c. 1834 *(Library of Congress)*

Johann Gaspar Spurzheim; J. Egan, mezzotint, 1838 *(Wellcome Collection)*

Spurzheim in his consulting room measuring the head of a peculiar-looking patient; J. Kennerly, colored aquatint, 1816 *(Wellcome Collection)*

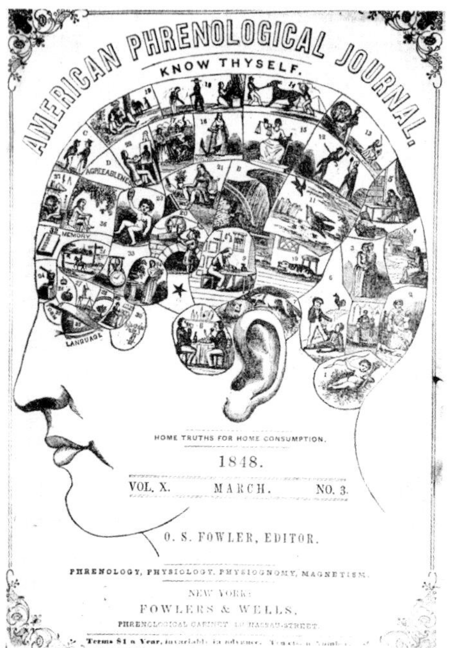

American Phrenological Journal, cover; Fowler & Wells, print, 1848
(Wikipedia)

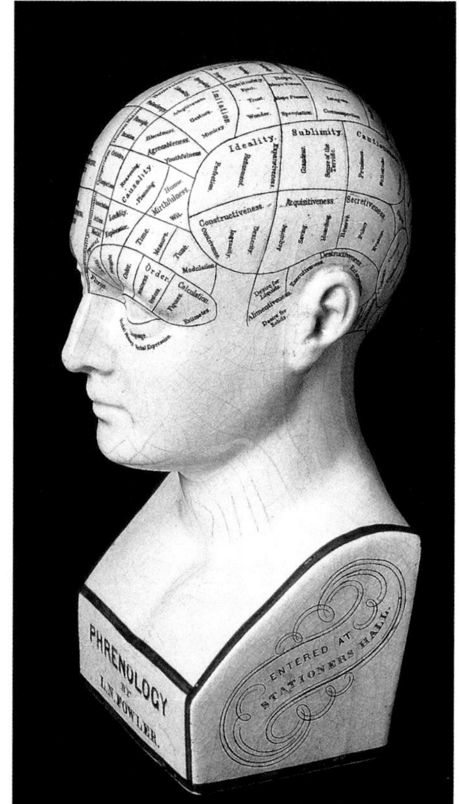

Phrenological head; L. N. Fowler, porcelain
(Wellcome Historical Medical Museum and Library)

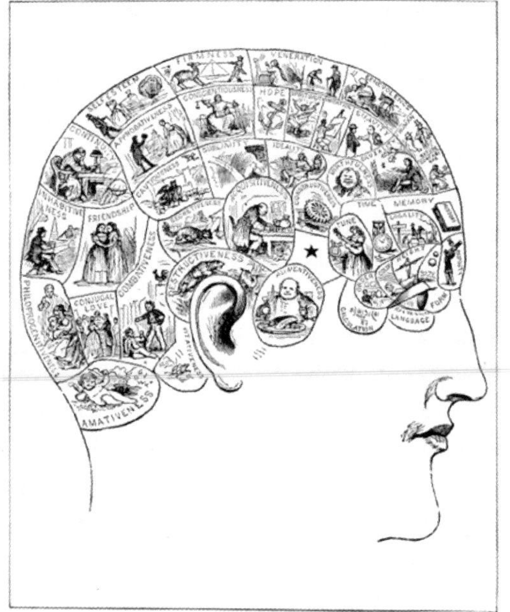
FIRMNESS
VENERATION
HOPE
FRIENDSHIP
CONJUGAL LOVE
COMBATIVENESS
DESTRUCTIVENESS
AMATIVENESS
TIME
MEMORY
LANGUAGE
Phrenological Chart of the Faculties.

Phrenological Chart of the Faculties, from *The People's Cyclopedia of Universal Knowledge*; W. H. De Puy, print, 1883 *(Wikimedia Commons)*

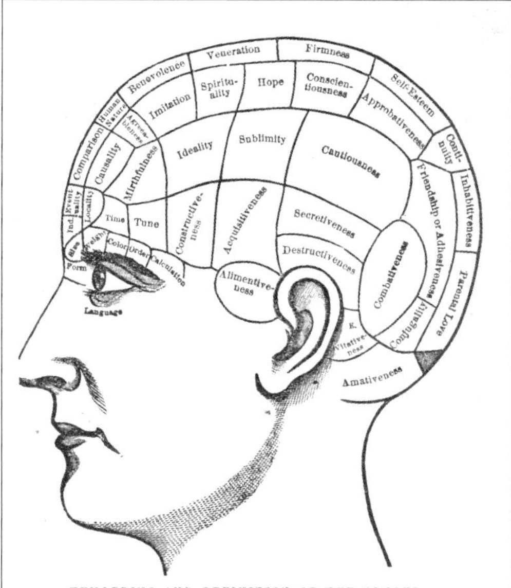
Veneration
Firmness
Benevolence
Self-Esteem
Spiritu-ality
Hope
Conscien-tiousness
Imitation
Approbativeness
Conti-nuity
Comparison
Causality
Ideality
Sublimity
Cautiousness
Inhabitiveness
Mirthfulness
Friendship or Adhesiveness
Locality
Time
Tune
Constructive-ness
Acquisitiveness
Secretiveness
Destructiveness
Combativeness
Parental Love
Color
Order
Calculation
Form
Alimentive-ness
Conjugality
Language
Amativeness
NUMBERING AND DEFINITION OF THE ORGANS.
Amativeness, Love between the sexes.
Conjugality, Matrimony—love of one. [etc.
2. Parental Love, Regard for offspring, pets,
3. Friendship, Adhesiveness—sociability.
4. Inhabitiveness, Love of home
5. Continuity One thing at a time.
Vitativeness, Love of life.
6 Combativeness, Resistance—defense.
7. Destructiveness, Executiveness—force.
8. Alimentiveness, Appetite—hunger.
9. Acquisitiveness, Accumulation.
0. Secretiveness, Policy—management.
1. Cautiousness, Prudence—provision.
2. Approbativeness, Ambition—display.
3. Self-Esteem, Self-respect—dignity.
4. Firmness, Decision—perseverance.
5 Conscientiousness, Justice. equity.
6 Hope, Expectation—enterprise.
7 Spirituality, Intuition—faith—credulity.
8 Veneration, Devotion—respect.
Benevolence, Kindness—goodness
20. Constructiveness, Mechanical ingenuity
21. Ideality, Refinement—taste—purity.
B. Sublimity, Love of grandeur—infinitude
22. Imitation, Copying—patterning.
23. Mirthfulness, Jocoseness—wit—fun.
24. Individuality, Observation.
25. Form, Recollection of shape.
26. Size, Measuring by the eye.
27. Weight, Balancing—climbing.
28. Color, Judgment of colors.
29. Order, Method—system—arrangement.
30. Calculation, Mental arithmetic.
31. Locality, Recollection of places.
32. Eventuality, Memory of facts.
33. Time, Cognizance of duration.
34. Tune, Sense of harmony and melody.
35. Language, Expression of ideas.
36. Causality, Applying causes to effect. [tion
37. Comparison, Inductive reasoning—illustra
C. Human Nature, Perception of motives.
D. Agreeableness. Pleasantness—suavity

Character chart; O. S. and L. N. Fowler, engraving, 1875 *(Library of Congress)*

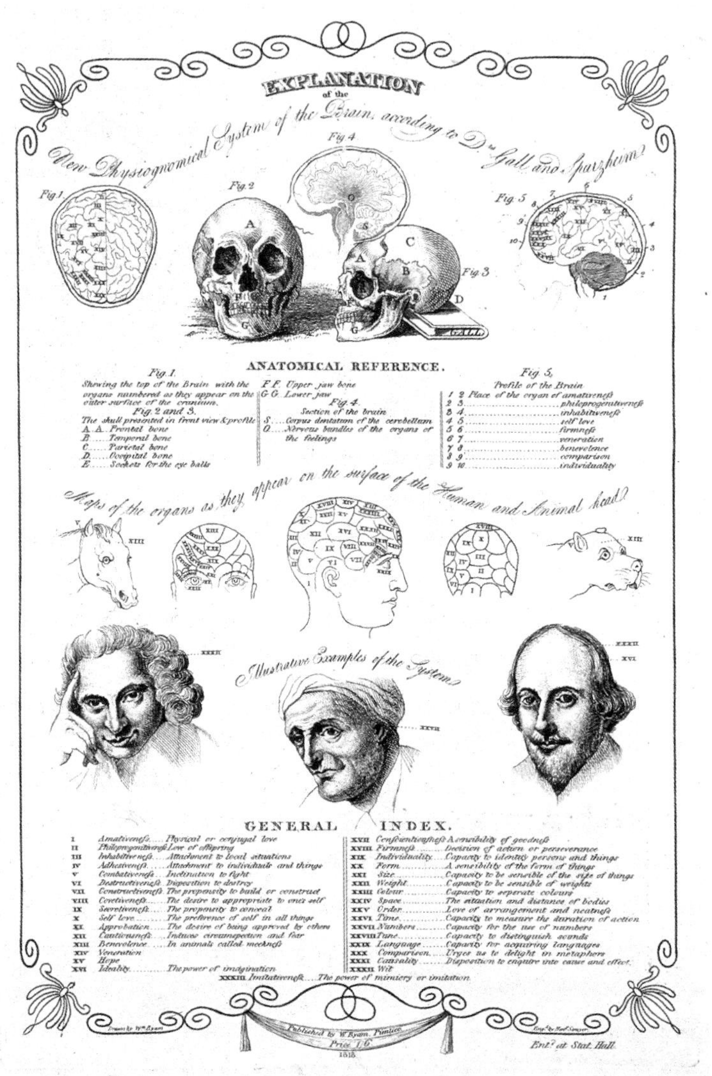

Phrenological diagrams of the skull and brain, with three portraits: Laurence Sterne, a mathematician, and Shakespeare, exemplifying the faculties of wit, number, and appearance, respectively; H. Sawyer after W. Byam, engraving, 1818 *(Wellcome Collection)*

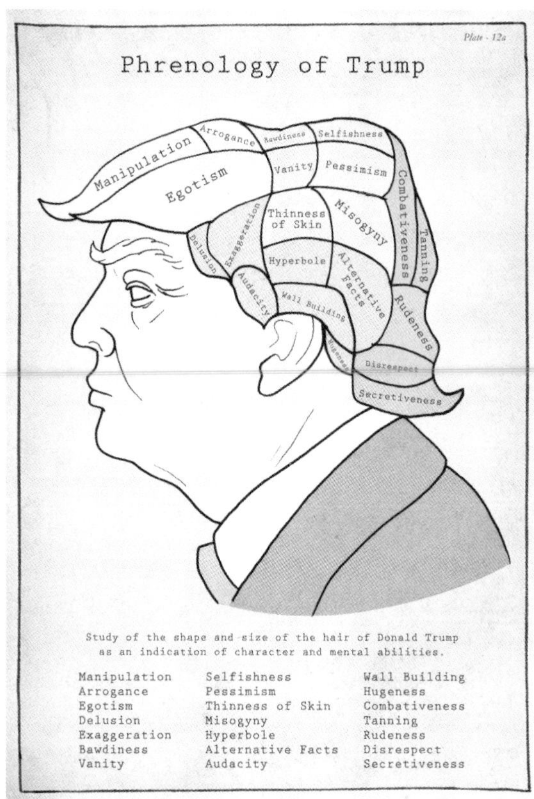

Phrenology of Trump; Benjamin Atmore, print

An Old Maid's Skull Phrenologised; E. F. Lamber, print, c. 1830 *(Center for the History of Medicine, Harvard Medical Library)*

Portrait of Whitman taken at Mathew Brady's studio in Washington, D.C.; photograph, 1865–1867 *(National Archives)*

* *Phrenological Notes on W. Whitman*, by L. N. Fowler, *July*, 1849.—Size of head large, 23 inches. Leading traits appear to be Friendship, Sympathy, Sublimity, and Self-Esteem, and markedly among his combinations the dangerous faults of Indolence, a tendency to the pleasures of Voluptuousness and Alimentiveness, and a certain reckless swing of animal will.

Amativeness large, *6; Philoprogenitiveness, 6; Adhesiveness, 6; Inhabitiveness, 6; Concentrativeness, 4; Combativeness, 6; Destructiveness, 5 to 6; Alimentiveness, 6; Acquisitiveness, 4; Secretiveness, 3; Cautiousness, 6; Approbativeness, 4; Self-Esteem, 6 to 7; Firmness, 6 to 7; Conscientiousness, 6; Hope, 4; Marvellousness, 3; Veneration, 4; Benevolence, 6 to 7; Constructiveness, 5; Ideality, 5 to 6; Sublimity, 6 to 7; Imitation, 5; Mirthfulness, 5; Individuality, 6; Form, 6; Size, 6; Weight, 6; Color, 3; Order, 5; Calculation, 5; Locality, 6; Eventuality, 6; Time, 3; Tune, 4; Language, 5; Causality, 5 to 6; Comparison, 6; Suavitiveness, 4; Intuitiveness, or Human Nature, 6.

* The organs are marked by figures from 1 to 7, indicating their degrees of development, 1 meaning very small, 2 small, 3 moderate, 4 average, 5 full, 6 large, and 7 very large.

Phrenological Notes on W. Whitman; L. N. Fowler, print, 1856 *(Fowler and Wells)*

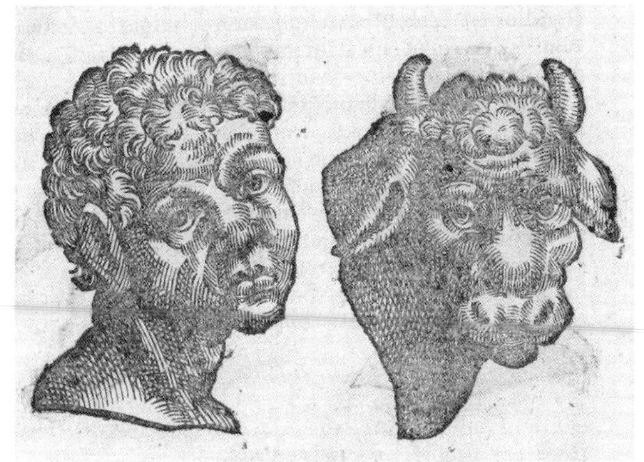

Man and Ox; Giambattista della Porta, engraving, 1586 *(Houghton Library, Harvard University)*

Man and Owl; Giambattista della Porta, engraving, 1586 *(Houghton Library, Harvard University)*

Man and the Head of Ram; Giambattista della Porta, engraving, 1586 *(Houghton Library, Harvard University)*

Le Desespoir [Despair]; Jean Audran, after Charles Le Brun, engraving, 1727 *(The Warburg Institute Library)*

L'Effroy [Dread]; Jean Audran, after Charles Le Brun, engraving, 1727 *(The Warburg Institute Library)*

L'Horreur [Horror]; Jean Audran, after Charles Le Brun, engraving, 1727 *(The Warburg Institute Library)*

From left: *Colere mélée de rage* [Anger mixed with rage]; *Colere mélée de crainte* [Anger mixed with fear]; *Extreme desespoir* [Extreme despair]; Jean Audran, after Charles Le Brun, engraving, 1721 *(The Warburg Institute Library)*

Six physiognomy heads in profile; Johann Caspar Lavater, engraving, 1789 *(Readex, Harvard University)*

Physiognomy head in three angles; Johann Caspar Lavater, engraving, 1789 *(Readex, Harvard University)*

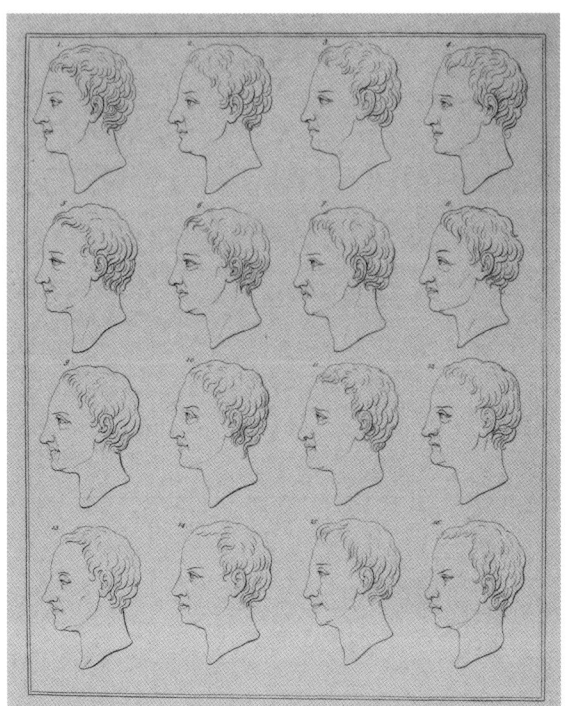

Sixteen physiognomy heads in profile; Johann Caspar Lavater, engraving, 1789 *(Courtesy of Harvard Fine Arts Library, Digital Images & Slides Collection d2009.12344)*

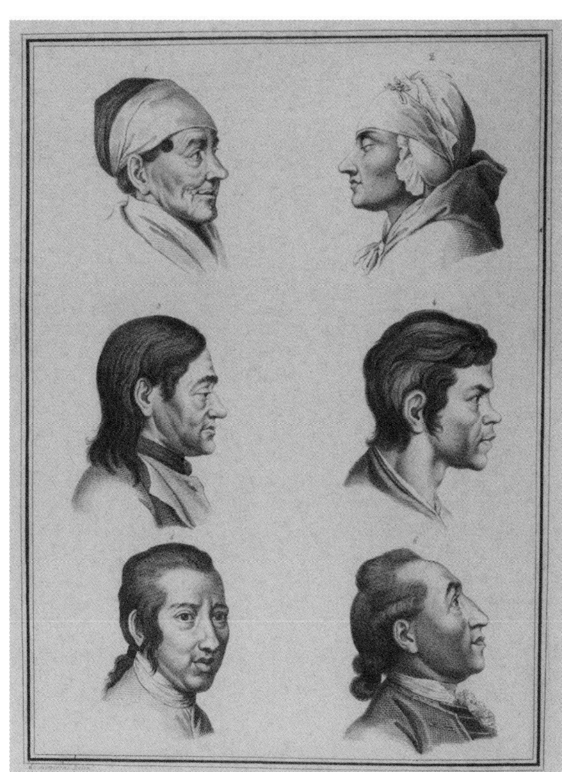

Six physiognomy heads; Johann Caspar Lavater, engraving, 1789 *(Readex, Harvard University)*

proverbial of the English, was a hodgepodge of styles: "How oddly he is suited! I think he bought his doublet in Italy, his round hose in France, his bonnet in Germany, and his behaviour everywhere" (*Merch.* 1.2).

These unsuitable suitors, who have fled before they have risked a chance at the lottery, do not appear as characters in the play, so the audience is unable to judge them. They are offstage national types, instantly recognizable to the audience *as* types through the comic caricatures that Portia shares with her friend: good for a laugh, a reliable source of amusement. But to a certain extent, the same is the case with those outsiders who do arrive in Belmont.

When the first of the remaining suitors, the Prince of Morocco, presents himself to her, his opening line is "Mislike me not for my complexion" (2.1.1), and he goes on to insist that his blood is as red as that of "the fairest creature northward born." Of course he chooses the wrong casket, to his astonishment and discomfiture. And as soon as he leaves the stage we hear Portia, reputedly so honorable and fair-minded, comment to herself and to the audience, "Let all of his complexion choose me so."[47] Footnotes in a modern edited text sometimes suggest that "complexion" here means "temperament," exculpating the beloved Portia from any hint of race prejudice, but the effort is doomed by the frequency and consistency of her remarks, offered, again, as clever asides to Nerissa.

The same fate befalls the second candidate, the Prince of Aragon, often played in modern productions as an old man, his silver hair matching the silver casket. The black man and the old man; the Moor and the Spaniard. The winner of the lottery, the only suitor who suits her, is a Venetian, Bassanio, a man she has in fact met before, in her father's time. An insider rather than an outsider. Never mind that he, too, is initially focused on the money she has inherited: "In Belmont is a lady richly left."

Portia herself is a charmer, and a longtime favorite with audiences and actors, as well as with literary critics. This, of course, is what "naturalizes" her social views and makes them seem, if not acceptable to modern judgment, at least less virulent (and therefore, we might note, a little more insidious). The casket-choice scene, with the discomfiture of the two outsiders, is often played as comedy, and the courtroom scene, these days, as tragedy or tragicomedy, with the audience sympathy split between Portia and Shylock, depending upon the portrayals and the casting.

Yet some critics have noted with misgivings her narrowness and xenophobia. Her harsh treatment of Shylock, so inconsistent with "the quality of mercy," follows directly upon her "othering" of Morocco and Aragon. If the Jew and the Moor had been among the thumbnail sketches in her conversation with Nerissa, rather than brought to life on the stage, the element of caricature would have been more evident. Shakespeare, of course, is writing a play, not a tract. But it is often the inadvertent elements that signify most strongly. It's apparently sufficient, and indeed amusing, for Portia to offer her witty dismissals of national types, with the expectation that the audience will respond, if not with agreement, at least with the kind of perverse pleasure that sometimes today greets the cruder remarks of stand-up comics and talk-show hosts.

National Caricature (2)

"The vulgar are apt to carry all *national characters* to extremes," noted the eighteenth-century Scottish philosopher David Hume. "Having once established it as a principle, that any people are knavish, or cowardly, or ignorant, they will admit of no exception, but comprehend every individual under the same censure." Hume made it clear from the outset that the concept of national character was itself already a kind of caricature, but as he warmed to his subject he granted that there might be something in the idea, at least as it touched on other nations.

> Men of sense condemn these undistinguishing judgments: Though at the same time, they allow, that each nation has a peculiar set of manners, and that some particular qualities are more frequently to be met with among one people than among their neighbours. The common people in SWITZERLAND have probably more honesty than those of the same rank in IRELAND; and every prudent man will, from that circumstance alone, make a difference in the trust which he reposes in each. We

> have reason to expect greater wit and gaiety in a FRENCHMAN than in a SPANIARD; though Cervantes was born in SPAIN. An ENGLISHMAN will naturally be supposed to have more knowledge than a DANE; though TYCHO BRAHE was a native of DENMARK.[48]

Hume stresses *moral* causes over *physical* ones in the determination of national character, "since a nation is nothing but a collection of individuals," and the manners of individuals are frequently determined by things like "the nature of the government, the revolutions of public affairs, the plenty or penury in which the people live, the situation of the nation with regard to its neighbours, and such like circumstances."[49] Unlike some later ethnographers, he discounts climate, air, and food, ostensible physical causes, as irrelevant. Yet since "the human mind is of a very imitative nature," and "the propensity to company and society is strong in all rational creatures," it makes sense to him that

> causes like passions and inclinations . . . run, as it were, by contagion, through the whole club or knot of companions. Where a number of men are united into one political body, the occasions of their intercourse must be so frequent for defence, commerce, and government that, together with the same speech or language, they must acquire a resemblance in their manners, and have a common or national character, as well as a personal one, peculiar to each individual.[50]

So far so good, we might think—but prematurely, as it turns out. For, when Hume begins to direct his attention, hitherto focused on abstractions and rationales, on individual groups or "nations," we find ourselves back in the world of caricature and indeed of prejudice and slander, no more agreeable for being so "rationally" set forth. Thus, on the question of what today we might call cosmopolitan or international groups, he tells his reader:

> Where any set of men, scattered over distant nations, maintain a close society or communication together, they acquire

> a similitude of manners, and have but little in common with the nations amongst whom they live. Thus the JEWS in EUROPE, and the ARMENIANS in the east, have a peculiar character; and the former are as much noted for fraud, as the latter for probity.[51]

We will return later to this question of what might be called "international" character, and the particular role, or roles, played in such characterizations by the Jews and others. It is worth noting now Hume's iteration ("scattered over distant nations"; "hav[ing] but little in common with the nations amongst whom they live"), as if these dislocations were themselves character traits, rather than literally alienating conditions imposed upon them by other nations.

As for the Ancients and the Moderns, Hume laments that the modern Greeks and Italians are a sad falling off from their noble forebears, whereas the French have greatly improved over time. Once more the tone is matter-of-fact, not deliberately tendentious—simply setting out the way it is.

> The manners of a people change very considerably from one age to another; either by great alterations in their government, by the mixtures of new people, or by that inconstancy, to which all human affairs are subject. The ingenuity, industry, and activity of the ancient GREEKS have nothing in common with the stupidity and indolence of the present inhabitants of those regions. Candour, bravery, and love of liberty formed the character of the ancient ROMANS; as subtilty [*sic*], cowardice, and a slavish disposition do that of the modern . . . Though some few strokes of the FRENCH character be the same with that which CAESAR has ascribed to the GAULS; yet what comparison between the civility, humanity, and knowledge of the modern inhabitants of that country, and the ignorance, barbarity, and grossness of the ancient?[52]

Hume, a Scot, thought the English were oddly difficult to stereotype:

> The ENGLISH government is a mixture of monarchy, aristocracy, and democracy. The people in authority are composed of

> gentry and merchants. All sects of religion are to be found among them. And the great liberty and independency, which every man enjoys, allows him to display the manners peculiar to him. Hence the ENGLISH, of any people in the universe, have the least of a national character; unless this very singularity may pass for it.[53]

This view of English "singularity," variously translated by non-English observers as English "humor" or "eccentricity," could either be an asset or a detriment, depending upon the context, the politics—and sometimes the nationality—of the observer.

Over the years, the English national character has been often discussed and debated, both from within and outside of England and Britain. The historian Peter Mandler notes the emergence of "national character" as a term of art in England in the early nineteenth century, citing in particular a set of works published in the 1830s: Thomas Arnold's "On the Social Progress of States" (1830), Richard Chenevix's *Essay upon National Character* (1832), Sir Francis Palgrave's *The Rise and Progress of the English Commonwealth* (1832), Edward Bulwer-Lytton's *England and the English* (1833), John Stuart Mill's essay "The English National Character" (1834), and Benjamin Disraeli's *Vindication of the English Constitution* (1835).[54]

"The laws of national (or collective) character," Mill would declare in describing his theory of ethology, "are by far the most important class of sociological laws." Why? Because the past was a determinant of the future: "the character, that is, the opinions, feelings, and habits, of the people, though greatly the results of the state of society which precedes them, are also greatly the causes of the state of society which follows them."[55]

In the 1830s, travelers between Europe and the United States began to single out the "national character" of the countries they visited as a topic of fascinated interest, both to themselves and to the reading public. Three celebrated texts, Ralph Waldo Emerson's *English Traits* (published in 1856, but begun during his first trip to England, in

1833), Fanny Trollope's *Domestic Manners of the Americans* (1832), and Alexis de Tocqueville's *Democracy in America* reflect their authors' conviction that something called national character could be identified and described. Partly autobiographical and partly ethnographic, these books report the observations and experiences of interested investigators (what modern anthropology might call "informants"). What they have in common, beyond a shrewd eye for detail and a keen attention to tone and nuance, is a talent for description. Travelers' tales by skilled writers and cultural analysts, each has become, in its own way, a classic.

Bottom, Mettle, and Pluck: Emerson's Englishmen

As we saw with Hume, it is often easier to type, and to stereotype, from outside a group than from within it. Some of the most vivid descriptions of "English traits," and also some of the most admiring ones, can be found in the witty little book by that title by Ralph Waldo Emerson. Emerson visited England twice, once as a young man, later as a celebrity. Both times he jotted notes, made cultural observations, and—implicitly or explicitly—compared the citizens of his own, emergent nation with the more venerable and established classes and types of England.

Emerson invokes the central notions of "bottom," "mettle," and "pluck," all synonyms for a kind of moral character, as essential aspects of Englishness.

> I find the Englishman to be him of all men who stands firmest in his shoes. They have in themselves what they value in their horses, mettle and bottom. On the day of my arrival in Liverpool, a gentleman, in describing to me the Lord Lieutenant of Ireland, happened to say, "Lord Clarendon has pluck like a cock, and will fight till he dies;" and what I hear first I heard last, and the one thing the English value, is pluck. The cabmen have it; the merchants have it; the bishops have it; the women have it; the journals have it; the *Times* newspaper, they say, is the pluckiest thing in England, and Sydney Smith had made it a proverb, that

> little Lord John Russell, the minister, would take command of the Channel fleet tomorrow.[56] [Russell—the grandfather of the philosopher Bertrand Russell—was five feet four and three-quarters inches tall.]

The English, he thinks, are intensely practical.

> They are impious in their skepticism of a theory, but kiss the dust before a fact. Is it a machine, is it a charter, is it a boxer in the ring, is it a candidate on the hustings—the universe of Englishmen will suspend their judgment, until the trial can be had. They are not to be led by a phrase, they want a working plan, a working machine, a working constitution.[57]

They have a "passion for utility."

> They love the lever, the screw, and pulley, the Flanders draught horse, the waterfall, wind-mills, tide-mills; the sea and the wind to bear their freight ships . . . Now, their toys are steam and galvanism.[58]

They have a strong "dislike of change," and "hate innovation."

> They keep their old customs, costumes, and pomps, their wig and mace, sceptre and crown. The middle ages still lurks in the streets of London.[59]

Eccentricity, that key word for Englishmen through the ages, is grist for Emerson's mill:

> I know not where any personal eccentricity is so freely allowed, and no man gives himself any concern with it. An Englishman walks in a pouring rain, swinging his closed umbrella like a walking-stick; wears a wig, or a shawl, or a saddle, or stands on his head, and no remark is made. And as he has been doing this for several generations, it is now in the blood . . . In short,

every one of these islanders is an island himself, safe, tranquil, incommunicable.[60]

Moreover, the English have their own views of national character:

> The ruling passion of Englishmen, in these days, is, a terror of humbug. In the same proportion, they value honesty, stoutness, and adherence to your own. They like a man committed to his objects. They hate the French, as frivolous; they hate the Irish, as aimless; they hate the Germans, as professors.[61]

Having been well entertained on his visits, Emerson admits to an occasional sense of social inadequacy—or, at least, of competition:

> The dress-dinner generates a talent of table-talk, which reaches great perfection: the stories are so good, that one is sure they must have been often told before, to have got such happy turns. Hither come all manner of clever projects, bits of popular science, of practical invention, of miscellaneous humor; political, literary, and personal news; railroads, horses, diamonds, agriculture, horticulture, pisciculture, and wine.[62]

By contrast, he had to acknowledge, "In America, we are apt scholars, but have not yet attained the same perfection." It was practice that made perfect. "The usage of a dress-dinner every day at dark, has a tendency to hive and produce to advantage everything good. Much attrition has worn every sentence into a bullet."[63]

These were discursive skills that Emerson would himself shortly have the opportunity to practice at home in Boston, encouraged by English fluency and flair. The year of the book's publication, 1856, was also the official year of the founding of the Saturday Club, a table-talk organization, meeting over dinner in the Parker House hotel, of which he was an early member, together with such other luminaries as Oliver Wendell Holmes, Sr., Louis Agassiz, James Russell Lowell, and Henry Wadsworth Longfellow.[64] The group led to the founding of *The Atlantic Monthly*, of which another Saturday Club member, William Dean Howells, became the editor. In a nostalgic poem about the club written almost thirty years later, the poet and physician Oliver Wendell Holmes commemorated his friend Emerson with affectionate wit: "If lost at times in vague aerial flights / None treads with firmer footsteps when he lights."[65]

Freedom and Hypocrisy: Trollope's Americans

Emerson coveted, and adopted, some English "traits" and qualities. Fanny Trollope, who traveled to the United States in a spirit of egalitarian energy, hoping to join a utopian community of freed slaves, returned to England far more conservative than she had left.

In her bestselling travel book, *Domestic Manners of the Americans*, first published (on both sides of the Atlantic) in 1832, Mrs. Trollope was acerbic about what she regarded as American hypocrisy:

> Had I, during my residence in the United States, observed any single feature in their national character that could justify their eternal boast of liberality and the love of freedom, I might have respected them, however much my taste might have been offended by what was peculiar in their manners and customs. But it is impossible for any mind of common honesty not to be revolted by the contradictions in their principles and practice. They inveigh against the governments of Europe, because, as they say, they favour the powerful and oppress the weak. You may hear this declaimed upon in Congress, roared out in taverns, discussed in every drawing-room, satirized upon the stage, nay, even anathematised from the pulpit: listen to it, and then look at them at home; you will see them with one hand hoisting the cap of liberty, and with the other flogging their slaves. You will see them one hour lecturing their mob on the indefeasible rights of man, and the next driving from their homes the children of the soil, whom they have bound themselves to protect by the most solemn treaties.[66]

By "the children of the soil" Trollope meant indigenous Native Americans, or, as she put it, the "last of several tribes of Indians" who were "chas[ed] . . . from their forest homes" by Congress and the president, in violation of previous legal agreements. "If the American character may be judged by their conduct in this matter," she wrote, "they are most lamentably deficient in every feeling of honour and integrity."[67] And she quoted, "In justice to those who approve not this treacherous policy," a New York newspaper editorial that made a similar point: "We know of no subject, at the present moment, of more importance to the character of our country for justice and integrity than that which related to the Indian tribes in Georgia and Alabama, and particularly the Cherokees."[68]

"National character" and "American character" are assumed, in these observations, to be meaningful categories, constructed partly of theory and partly of (divergent) practice. What Americans said about themselves and their country's adherence to shared goals and principles—that they stood, above all, for equality, justice, and freedom—is tested, and controverted, by the shameful way in which they violated those principles.

Mrs. Trollope objected to a number of other American "domestic manners," like spitting, whiskey drinking, "the frightful manner of feeding with their knives . . . and the still more frightful manner of cleaning the teeth afterward with a pocket knife,"[69] and the way husbands treated their wives, as well as the practice in the city of Cincinnati of loosing pigs in the streets to deal with the accumulated garbage.[70] Her book sold out quickly, running through four English and four American editions in the first year, and then being translated into French, Spanish, German, and Dutch.[71] Some readers and reviewers reviled her for her opinions: John Quincy Adams quipped in his diary that she had "done much to justify her name."[72] A reviewer made the same inevitable joke, declaring in print that her surname expressed "with the greatest brevity possible, the precise idea that was entertained of her character."[73] Another, noting her disenchantment with her traveling companion, the abolitionist and feminist Frances (Fanny) Wright, asked rhetorically how, if she was so "deceived in the character of her bosom friend," she could possibly "venture on the character of a people."[74] But her book continued to sell.

As for Trollope's description of "the character of a people," a modern editor of *Domestic Manners*, surveying it more than a century and a half later, found it remained convincing. "Reading her comments on the Americans' love of electioneering, the prevalence of religious fanaticism, social conformity and prudery," wrote Trollope's biographer Pamela Neville-Sington in 1997, "it is difficult not to conclude that her portrait of America—and the Americans—still rings true today."[75]

The Character of Democracy: Tocqueville's Masterwork

It's sometimes forgotten that Alexis de Tocqueville, a hereditary aristocrat from the minor nobility, lived through the French Revolution, the Terror, the monarchies of Charles X (abdicated) and Louis-Philippe (abdicated), the revolutionary upheavals of 1848, the short-lived republic, and the revived empire under Louis Napoleon, a modern dictator who declared himself Napoleon III. The apparently benign title of his book, *Democracy in America*, so appealing to the spirit of United States culture after World War II, should be understood as describing both a work of social anthropology and a political experiment.

It was also, for Tocqueville, both lucrative and prestigious, an unexpected and hugely successful "masterpiece," as his French publisher described it. After the publication of volume II, in 1840, Tocqueville was made an *immortel*, or a member of the Académie Française, France's highest honor for intellectuals. Yet, for many decades after Tocqueville's death in 1859, the book was obscure and almost forgotten. Used as a school text for a while after the Civil War, it was out of print by World War I. The hundredth anniversary of the publication of volume I in 1935 was the occasion for a revival of interest, and when new, popularly priced translations were published, first in 1945, and then, to critical fanfare, in 1966, *Democracy in America* became once again a central, and indeed a defining, part of American political and historical culture.[76]

Two developments in particular were hospitable to the new importance of Tocqueville's book at mid-century: the rise of the academic field known as American studies, and the Cold War. Each sought, in a quite different way, to define "American" as a way of thinking, as well as a way of writing and being. As Vernon Parrington outlined the task in the introduction to his three-volume work, *Main Currents in American Thought*, scholars now began to trace the history of "certain germinal ideas that have come to be reckoned traditionally American—how they came into being here, how they were opposed, and what influence they have exerted in determining the form and scope of our characteristic ideals and institutions."[77]

Over the next century, historians, political scientists, sociologists, and literary critics parsed "American" and "character" with Tocqueville in mind and in view. High-school and college syllabuses were studded with passages from *Democracy in America* from the fifties onward. The title fit perfectly into the postwar and Cold War moments, and Tocqueville's book became a cliché in political oratory and writing in mid-century America, quoted by politicians from Dwight Eisenhower to Bill Clinton, Hillary Clinton, Eugene McCarthy, and Joseph Lieberman, as well as by reporters and scholars across the political spectrum.

As the introduction to a recent translation notes, "*Democracy in America* is a protean text, capable of being stretched and adapted to serve just about everyone."[78] Although the initial impetus for the Tocqueville revival came from the left, from writers like Max Lerner and David Riesman in the United States and Harold Laski in England, from the 1980s onward the book has been a bible to the American right wing, praised by scholars at conservative think tanks like the Heritage Foundation, the Claremont Institute, and the American Enterprise Institute. To these groups the aristocratic Alexis de Tocqueville, it has been claimed, developed into a "neoconservative superhero."[79] But, whether viewed from the right, the left, or somewhere in between, Tocqueville's book, a compendium of opinions, analyses, reports, and anecdotes, remains a startlingly perceptive, often surprising, and frequently prescient assessment of its topic.

Tocqueville's ideas about national character in America are spread across the two volumes of *Democracy in America*. Sometimes, of course, his observations are out of date (American literature, art, and science have not only caught up with Europe but in some cases surpassed it), but at other times they seem still right on the mark. The two volumes focus on different aspects of American culture. The first is a study of government and political economy, the second a mixture of anthropology and sociology.

Over and over again in the first volume—and, indeed, throughout the book—Tocqueville emphasizes the American preoccupation with wealth. "I am not," he writes, "even aware of a country where the love of money has a larger place in men's hearts or where they express a deeper scorn for the theory of a permanent equality of possessions."[80] Words like "selfish," "mercenary," and "practical" appear with striking regularity, as, for example, when Tocqueville explains the lack, in most Americans, of a "disinterested passion" for scientific knowledge, as contrasted with the use of scientific advances to make a profit.[81] Tocqueville, writes Isaac Kramnick, "returns repeatedly to the acquisitive and materialistic core of American individualism, suggesting, in fact, that Americans' distinctive national trait is a love of money."[82]

As we've seen, the phrase "national character" appears in Tocqueville's first volume, but it does so in a rather foreboding spirit: "Already some vexing effects are evident in the national character." It's hard to decide whether the "vexing effects" are more, or less, disturbing than the word "already," which indicates not only that trouble has been anticipated, but that more is probably on the way.

"American courtiers," as Tocqueville describes the flatterers who attach themselves to a man in high office, are dangerously obsequious: unlike courtiers to monarchs, "they do not give him their wives and daughters for him to raise them to the position of his mistresses but, in sacrificing their opinions to him, they prostitute themselves."[83] These problems are clear to a few observant Americans, he says, but although they may confide their concerns in him, they tell another story in public: "They often go so far as noting the defects which are changing the national character, and outline the means for correcting them. But you are the only one to listen to them and you, the confidant of these secret thoughts, are nothing more than a foreigner passing through. They are quite ready to release useless truths to you and use quite another language once down in the market square."[84] These accounts of politics and politicians almost two centuries ago have, as so often in Tocqueville's pages, a disquietingly modern relevance. They could be found in a newspaper or an online commentary today.

There are also in volume I occasional observations about what might be described as the psychology of democracy, as Tocqueville saw it. For example: "Anyone living in the United States learns from birth that he must rely upon himself to combat the ills and obstacles of life; he looks across at the authority of society with mistrust and anxiety, calling upon such authority only when he cannot do without it."[85] Or this: "There is nothing more irksome in the conduct of life than the irritable patriotism Americans have."[86] Or this shrewd assessment of the consequences of a renewable presidential term: "The wish to be re-elected dominates the President's thoughts, and . . . all the policies of his administration are geared to this objective," with the result that "the principle of re-election makes the corrupting influence of elective governments still more widespread and more dangerous, while leading to a decline in the political morality of the nation and the substitution of craft for patriotism."[87] Again the contemporary pertinence of these comments is startling.

But it is in volume II of *Democracy in America* that the question of a national character begins most forcefully to emerge. Here are found major sections on "The Influence of Democracy Upon the Intellectual Movement in the United States," "The Influence of Democracy on the Opinions of Americans," and "The Influence of Democracy on Customs as Such."

Covering topics as diverse as religion, poetry, "the literature industry," the theater, (the absence of) "parliamentary eloquence in the United States," and the "particular effects of the love of physical pleasures in democratic times," Tocqueville comments on the manners, morals, and mores of American men and (to a considerably lesser extent) American women. On theater: "People who spend every day of the week making money and Sundays praying to God give no scope to the comic muse."[88] On parliamentary eloquence: "Hardly a single member of Congress will agree to return home without dispatching at least one speech back to his electorate, nor will he tolerate any interruption before he has succeeded in including within the scope of his harangue all the useful things he can say about the twenty-four states of the Union and especially about the district he represents. He, therefore, presents to the minds of his listeners a succession of great generalizations (which often he alone comprehends and expresses but confusedly) as well as very minor subtleties which he does not find easy to reveal clearly."[89] On "the literature industry": "In democratic times, the public often treats its authors the way kings usually do their courtiers: it enriches and despises them."[90] On physical pleasures: "The wealthy living in democracies . . . sink into self-indulgence rather than outright debauchery."[91]

Under the heading of "Honor in the United States," Tocqueville explains to his readers why bankruptcy does not entail any loss of honor for the businessman, whereas vices that "damage the marriage bond" are taken so seriously: "American public opinion only gently checks the love of money which promotes great industrial progress and national prosperity; but it is particularly hard on bad morals which divert men's minds from their search for material success and disturb the family harmony which is so vital for business success."[92] On American national pride and defensiveness: "The American leaves his country with a heart swollen with pride. He arrives in Europe and observes at once that we are not as concerned with the United States and the great people living there as he had supposed. This begins to annoy him."[93] And on what he carefully does not call American gaucheness: "I have noticed many times that it is not an easy matter in the United States to convey to someone that his presence is unwelcome. To make that point, roundabout methods are not always enough."[94]

Personal mini-vignettes of this kind (the story of how to extricate oneself from the conversational clutches of an American bore goes on for two more paragraphs) are akin to the "Characters" of writers like Theophrastus and La Bruyère, producing a vivid picture of an individual acting in a way that is "characteristic" of his station and setting. There is more of this concise style of national portraiture in volume II than in the more didactic volume I, so that the reader is offered—in a volume the author explicitly describes as chronicling "a multitude of feelings and opinions unknown in the old aristocratic societies of Europe"[95]—not only a sense of presumed American values but also a telling glimpse of particular American behaviors.

Early in his project, Tocqueville had written to his friend Ernest de Chabrol that he expected to find in America a people "without a national character":

> Imagine, my dear friend, if you can, a society formed of all the nations of the world: English, French, Germans. People having different languages, beliefs, opinions: in a word, a society without roots, without memories, without prejudices, without routines, without common ideas, without a national character, yet a hundred times happier than our own; more virtuous? I doubt it. That is the starting point: What serves as the link among such diverse elements? What makes all of this into one people? Interest. That is the secret. The private interest that breaks through at each moment, the interest that, moreover, appears openly and even proclaims itself as a social theory.[96]

In fact, he told de Chabrol, "as one digs deeper into the national character of the Americans, one sees that they have sought the value of everything in this world only in the answer to this single question: how much money will it bring in?"

This may not be the answer that mid-century America, or twenty-first-century think tanks, expected or wanted from the ordained sage and seer of American democracy. Tocqueville's travels over the ensuing decade complicated his assessment, and time has added cultural and intellectual achievements to the nation he saw as obsessed with material gain. The issue is not whether Tocqueville was right or wrong about American national character. In many ways, he was both. And, writing near the beginning of the American experiment, he could hardly be charged with seeing with 20/20 sight into the distant future. What is at stake here is not Tocqueville's conclusions, but the use that has been made of them. As the political or scholarly equivalent of "I told you so," *Democracy in America* has been cited and taught as if it were a visionary master plan for American exceptionalism and the American character. To the degree that this has been a self-fulfilling prophecy, it has mirrored the beliefs of those who consulted it. A long book, it contains something for almost everyone, including (in a section on "The Present-Day State and the Probable Future of the Three Races Which Live in the Territory of the United States") many passionate and eloquent pages on the situation of slaves and American Indians. What it does prove is that Tocqueville himself thought the concept of national character worth addressing and exploring, and that he found evidence for his conclusions in both the written texts and the cultural contexts of American life.

Native Informants

However different their views, one thing Emerson, Trollope, and Tocqueville had in common was that they were visitors to a land not their own. Whether we call their work ethnography, social research, autobiography, or anecdote (or a mixture of these), each set out to write about the "traits" or "national character" of another country and its people. This was, of course, also true of an early writer like Herodotus, and, indeed, of New World adventurers like Columbus and Walter Raleigh. But "national character" is as often described from the inside as from the outside. The tone in which such descriptions are undertaken often reveals as much about national character as the descriptions themselves.

Not surprisingly, national characteristics, observed or imagined, were most frequently cited when they seemed to underlie related issues, like tourism, transnational travel, or war. In England and the United States in the early twentieth century, what had been an occasional subject for commentary became a recurrent theme. With typical panache, Virginia Woolf provides an example of the "insider" and "outsider" views at once. Reviewing Henry James's *English Hours* (1905), Woolf wrote genially—for James was an old family acquaintance—

> It is a little surprising, it must be owned, to find from Mr. James's pages how spectacular we are; and were it not for the grace and urbanity with which the show is exhibited, we might fairly resent the position in which we are placed. We are, according to him, enormously old; we are full of ancient manner-

> isms and antiquated phrases; we have accumulated such a deposit of tradition and inheritance on top of us that the original substance is scarcely to be discovered.

In fact, she continues, "the commonest handful of English earth, like the most ordinary young man or woman at a country tea-party, is something venerable and subtle, and probably more than a little quaint." At the end of her review she turns the tables on the eminent author, noting that his observations are typically American ("we see a good deal of America reflected in our own face"), while acknowledging that James's portrait of England and the English is "after all, so charming and so true."[97]

Starting in the 1930s, the *Punch* cartoonist known as Pont,[98] a childhood nickname acquired after a visit to Rome—published several collections, the most popular of which was *The British Character.* From 1934 to 1938, he drew illustrations of traits like "a disinclination ever to go anywhere," "a tendency to be hearty," "absence of the gift for cooking," "failure to appreciate good music," "love of arriving late at theatrical productions," "refusal to admit defeat," "keen interest in the weather," "tendency to be embarrassed by foreign currencies," and "the importance of tea," each caption accompanied by a droll cartoon depicting British national types at work and play. This was, of course, just before the war.

After the war, a book of short, witty essays in a similar spirit was published by the author George Mikes. Mikes, born in Hungary, called his 1946 book—which became a bestseller—*How to Be an Alien.* It included sections on "How Not to Be Clever," "How to Be Rude," "How to Compromise," "How to Be a Hypocrite," "How to Plan a Town" ("Street names should be painted clearly and distinctly on large boards. Then hide these boards carefully"), and "The National Passion" (queuing). Two further volumes, *How to Be Inimitable* and *How to Be Decadent,* followed in 1960 and 1977, and the three were published together as *How to Be a Brit* (1984).

It may be one of the differences between British and American national character that it is hard to imagine a bestselling book called *How to Be an American* with similarly deflating comic headings, although awkward American travelers were certainly tweaked in Mark Twain's *Innocents Abroad*. *The Ugly American*, the title of a 1958 novel and a 1963 film, became an unwelcome description of boorish, arrogant, and demeaning behavior by Americans both abroad and at home, but American citizens were unlikely to celebrate these as endearing traits of national character. The historian Richard Hofstadter probably had it right when he attributed much of this behavior to feelings of inadequacy: "For all their bragging and their hypersensitivity, Americans are, if not the most self-critical, at least the most anxiously self-conscious people in the world, forever concerned about the inadequacy of something or other—their national morality, their national culture, their national purpose."[99] As a definition of national character (without mentioning the term), this is compelling. Whether it is as true now as when Hofstadter wrote it half a century ago I will leave to the reader to decide. Hofstadter was responsible for two of the most arresting book titles in American studies: *Anti-Intellectualism in American Life* and *The Paranoid Style in American Politics*. Again, it's possible to imagine these key words as part of a witty self-critique in Britain; in the United States, despite Hofstadter's clear explanation that he was "not speaking in a clinical sense" about national paranoia but "borrowing a clinical term for other purposes,"[100] the titles were taken very seriously by both the left and the right.

Although some modern American cartoon artists, such as Garry Trudeau, have certainly been countercultural, they tend not to satirize "Americans" as such, perhaps because it is so large a country, and regional jokes and boasts work better. My uncle, a proud Galvestonian, bought me when I was a child a copy of a pamphlet called *Texas Brags*, a profusely illustrated account of that state's "firsts," "more thans," lingo, and legends. (Example: "The fabulous King Ranch, between Houston and San Antonio and Brownsville, is so big that there is a month's difference in seasons between the northern and southern parts."[101] Second example, in the same spirit: "It is farther from El Paso to Texarkana than it is from Chicago to New York." Third example, in case the reader hasn't yet gotten the point: Texas is "larger by 144,000 square miles than the United Kingdom."[102])

Peter Arno, the longtime cartoonist for *The New Yorker*, made a specialty of images of elderly plutocrats ogling buxom showgirls, often in nightclub settings. The spirit of his wit is largely urban or cosmopolitan. But I found at least three "American" cartoons in his collected work. In one, a pair of middle-aged men with ribbons in their lapels stand onstage next to a long row of women in bathing suits, each one draped in a state banner ("Miss Nevada," "Miss New Jersey," "Miss Utah" . . .). One man—they are apparently contest judges—remarks to the other, "Makes you kind of proud to be an American, doesn't it?" A second Arno cartoon takes place in his favored locale, a nightclub, where two balding businessmen are at a table with two much younger women. They are eating oysters and drinking champagne. One man says to the other, "I love this country of ours, Summers. It's been good to me." A third cartoon is set on a rocky mountaintop, where a man in snow boots and earflaps is peering with a magnifying glass at a nest containing four large eggs. Over him, alarmed, hovers a bald eagle. The caption, spoken by the man to the agitated eagle, declares, in defensive explanation, "I'm an American citizen!" Whether any narrative of "American national character" can be derived from these three examples is unlikely, yet there is a certain family resemblance among them.

The Home Front

National eccentricities can be comic or endearing, especially when described from within the home culture, but they take on a certain edge of pride during wartime, or at other moments of historical and political change or challenge. Two of the most striking visions of the English national character in the 1940s were offered by celebrated writers. Each, in its way, was a traveler's tale. And each provided not only a description, but also a list.

In the early years of World War II, George Orwell published *The Lion and the Unicorn* (1941), subtitled *Socialism and the English Genius*. As Arthur Koestler observed about this engaging and powerful book, "Its opening section, 'England Your England,' is one of the most moving and yet incisive portraits of the English character, and a minor classic in itself."[103] Orwell's essay, which begins, arrestingly, "As I write, highly civilized human beings are flying overhead, trying to kill me," includes the following extended description:

> When you come back to England from any foreign country, you have immediately the sensation of breathing a different air. Even in the first few minutes dozens of small things conspire to give you this feeling. The beer is bitterer, the coins are heavier, the grass is greener, the advertisements are more blatant. The crowds in the big towns, with their mild knobby faces, their bad teeth and gentle manners, are different from a European crowd. Then the vastness of England swallows you up, and you lose for a while your feeling that the whole nation has a single identifiable character. Are there really such things as nations? Are we not forty-six million individuals, all different? And the diversity of it, the chaos! The clatter of clogs in the Lancashire mill towns, the to-and-fro of the lorries on the Great Northern Road, the queues outside the Labour Exchanges, the rattle of pintables in the Soho pubs, the old maids biking to Holy Communion through the mists of the autumn morning—all these are not only fragments, but *characteristic* fragments, of the English scene. How can one make a pattern out of this muddle?
>
> But talk to foreigners, read foreign books or newspapers, and you are brought back to the same thought. Yes, there *is* something distinctive and recognizable in English civilization. It is a culture as individual as that of Spain. It is somehow bound up with solid breakfasts and gloomy Sundays, smoky towns and winding roads, green fields and red pillar-boxes. It has a flavour of its own. Moreover, it is continuous, it stretches into the future and the past, there is something in it that persists, as in a living creature. What can the England of 1940 have to do with the England of 1840? But then, what have you in common with the child of five whose photograph your mother keeps on the mantelpiece? Nothing, except that you happen to be the same person.

> And above all, it is *your* civilization, it is *you*. However much you hate it or laugh at it you will never be happy away from it for any length of time. The suet puddings and the red pillar-boxes have entered into your soul.[104]

Orwell's method here is an effective combination of the personal memoir and the travel narrative, as he pictures himself "com[ing] back to England from any foreign country" and seeing it with new eyes, while buttressing his observations with the commentary, implied rather than quoted, of "foreigners," "foreign books," and newspapers. He is not uncritical or adulatory. Among the "generalizations about England that would be accepted by almost all observers" he includes, "The English are not gifted artistically," and "The English are not intellectual."[105] But "in moments of supreme crisis the whole nation can suddenly draw together and act upon a species of instinct, really a code of conduct which is understood by almost everyone, though never formulated."[106]

Acknowledging that "national characteristics are not easy to pin down, and when pinned down they often turn out to be trivialities,"[107] Orwell embraces this description, noting the "addiction to hobbies and spare-time occupations, the *privateness* of English life." Thus he offers the reader his list:

> We are a nation of flower-lovers, but also a nation of stamp-collectors, pigeon-fanciers, amateur carpenters, coupon-snippers, darts-players, crossword-puzzle fans. All the culture that is most truly native centres round things which even when they are communal are not official—the pub, the football match, the back garden, the fireside and the "nice cup of tea."[108]

Various considerations, personal and political, had convinced him, in short, that there was something like a national character, or what he calls "our national way of life":

> One must admit that the differences between nation and nation are founded on real differences of outlook. Till recently, it was

> thought proper to pretend that all human beings are very much alike, but in fact anyone able to use his eyes knows that the average of human behaviour differs enormously from country to country. Things that could happen in one country could not happen in another. Hitler's June purge, for example, could not have happened in England. And, as western peoples go, the English are very highly differentiated. There is a sort of back-handed admission of this in the dislike which nearly all foreigners feel for our national way of life. Few Europeans can endure living in England, and even Americans often feel more at home in Europe.[109]

The sly pride of his phrase "the dislike which nearly all foreigners feel for our national way of life" is perhaps the most "English" element of this paean to the national character of the English. (Note that Orwell—born in British India, educated at Eton, early posted to Burma as an imperial policeman, later resident in Paris and London—does not say "British" but "English.")

One famous American of Orwell's time, of course, did feel at home in England, enough so that he renounced his American citizenship and became a British subject. With what might almost be described as the zeal of a convert, T. S. Eliot's *Notes Towards the Definition of Culture*, published in 1948, contains a succinct and memorable enumeration of what Eliot calls "the characteristic activities and interests of a people":

> Derby Day, Henley Regatta, Cowes, the twelfth of August, a cup final, the dog races, the pin table, the dart board, Wensleydale cheese, boiled cabbage cut into sections, beetroot in vinegar, nineteenth-century Gothic churches and the music of Elgar. The reader can make his own list.[110]

The "people" here—and the "culture"—are, of course, those of Eliot's adopted nation, not his natal land. His list, or some elements of it, may mystify a modern reader. August 12, sometimes known as the Glorious Twelfth, is the start of the shooting season for red grouse. Cowes, an English seaport town on the Isle of Wight, has been a home of international yachting races since 1815, and is the site of the world's oldest regular regatta, Cowes Week, which is held in August. A "pin table" is a pinball machine. The rest of these terms are, I am guessing, more or less decipherable. Whether "characteristic activities and interests" are the same as "national character" can certainly be debated, and the disarmingly open (or irritatingly condescending) Eliotic loophole, "the reader can make his own list," allows for some variation both in class and in nationality, although not, perhaps, in gender. But the invitation to make one's own list also gestured toward a method, if not a methodology, for asserting and describing "national character."

Despite the mention of the "pin table" (one word in Orwell, two words in Eliot), there seems at first as if there is not much crossover between Eliot's list of the "characteristic activities and interests of a people," and Orwell's. Henley regatta versus coupon snipping. Shooting grouse versus raising pigeons. The class differences make the two lists seem more dissimilar than they are, despite the pin table and the darts. But the very fact that these writers thought in terms of *lists*—and of their "own" lists rather than some abstract catalogue—is telling, as are the dates. In the 1940s, perhaps under the pressure of first the hot and then the Cold War, there seemed a certain urgency, political as well as cultural, aesthetic as well as behavioral, in defining—however impressionistically—certain perceived qualities of national character.

The personal nature of these lists was not, needless to say, replicable. No "science" of national character could be based upon them. But was there a need for such a "science"? What, if anything, might the study of national character, if systematized and regularized, contribute to the war effort, or to postwar politics and security?

The same world-changing events that led Orwell and Eliot to write about characteristic attitudes and interests among the English led, in the United States, to the development of academic research protocols for the study of "national character" by scholars in a range of social-science fields: anthropology, sociology, psychology, and, sometimes, psychoanalysis. These research areas became influential at mid-century, during the postwar period and the Cold War, and in some cases continued to be so until the end of the twentieth century. But after a decade or two of intense scholarly activity, the attention to "national character" in most social-science fields was superseded by other disciplinary directions and priorities. It had become an "unscientific" category.

"The term 'national character' is a metaphor, which should not be taken literally," wrote the social anthropologist and popular author Kate Fox, in *Watching the English: The Hidden Rules of English Behaviour*, first published in 2004. "A few personality psychologists have wasted a lot of time 'proving' that national character stereotypes are 'untrue' on the grounds that they do not correlate with aggregate scores on five personality factors. The supposedly 'reserved' English, for example, score high on 'extraversion' in personality questionnaires."[111] Fox's book was praised by the tabloid *Daily Mail* in a phrase that was itself an assertion of national character: "She doesn't write like an anthropologist," declared the *Mail* approvingly, in a quotation featured on the book's back cover, "but like an English woman."

The analysis of "national character," once largely the province of popular culture, political rhetoric, historical study, and elite journalism, would in the twenty-first century return to those genres, although now armed with new language and new tools. How this came about, and the criteria that twentieth-century social scientists evolved for assessing their elusive quarry, is worth our attention.

The Social Science(s) of National Character

In June 1944, the cultural anthropologist Ruth Benedict was commissioned by the United States government to produce an analysis of the Japanese national character. The United States was then at war with Japan. How would the Japanese conduct themselves as the war continued, or when it ended? What role did their family structure, their codes of honor, and their obeisance to the emperor play in the Japanese view of life and death?

Benedict, a professor at Columbia University, a former student of

Franz Boas, and a friend of the linguist Edward Sapir, was a leader in what would become known as the "culture-and-personality" approach to anthropology. She had suggested in her earlier book *Patterns of Culture*, "A culture, like an individual, is a more or less consistent pattern of thought and action," so that even the most apparently "ill-assorted acts" become "characteristic of its peculiar goals."[112] As her friend and colleague Margaret Mead described this idea, human culture was for Benedict "personality writ large."[113] But for the Japan project, a standard anthropological method like fieldwork was obviously out of the question under the circumstances. Benedict, who had never been to Japan, therefore studied books and articles, interviewed Japanese Americans, read Japanese novels in translation, watched Japanese films, and in general practiced, for this government assignment, what became known as "anthropology [or "culture"] at a distance." The result was *The Chrysanthemum and the Sword: Patterns of Japanese Culture* (1946), a book that became a bestseller. Widely regarded as a successful study of "national character," the book was translated into Japanese, became the topic of fruitful exchanges between Japanese and Western scholars, and met with respectful critical responses—if not always with agreement.[114]

As early as 1940, with the support of the U.S. Office of Naval Research, Benedict had begun to develop institutions dedicated to improved cultural understanding during the difficult years of World War II. She herself had undertaken several studies of "cultures made inaccessible by wartime conditions," including Romania, Germany, the Netherlands, and Thailand as well as Japan.[115] An Institute for Intercultural Studies was founded in 1944 to provide an academic home for scholars like Mead, Gregory Bateson, Rhoda Métraux, and Geoffrey Gorer, as well as socially oriented clinical psychiatrists like Erik Erikson. A larger research group involving over 120 scholars, Columbia University Research in Contemporary Culture, was in formal existence from 1947 to 1952.[116] Their methods for studying culture at a distance included group research, work with informants, and the study of films, written and oral literature, imagery, and, with some reservations, the use of projective tests like the Rorschach. When Ruth Benedict died in 1948, the administration and leadership of the Columbia program was assumed by Margaret Mead.

Mead had written highly regarded studies of the Samoans and the British. Moved, like Benedict, to respond to the changed circumstances imposed by wartime conditions, she wrote a book published in the United States as *And Keep Your Powder Dry* (1942) and in England as *The American Character* (1943), in which she described American character as a "peculiar drive toward efficiency and success,"[117] a mind-set that provided "the psychological equipment with which we can win the war."[118]

Their colleague, the English anthropologist Geoffrey Gorer, who had published a highly praised book on Africa, hypothesized in *The People of Great Russia: A Psychological Study* (1949) that Russians were cold and distant because they were tightly swaddled as children. Gorer was strongly influenced by psychoanalysis, and had written a study of the marquis de Sade. (He would go on to write books about the Americans and the English.) Not surprisingly, "national character" became an increasingly used, and increasingly contested, term.

Acknowledging its "ambiguity and imprecision," Gorer later explained, "The initial studies that were labeled studies in national character were made under the stress of World War II, when practical aims (e.g., a framework for psychological warfare) were more urgent than theoretical precision."[119] But what did this term mean to anthropologists? And how could it aid in the war effort?

"In wartime," Mead had suggested in her book on American character, "people begin to think again in terms which had fallen into disrepute in the last quarter of a century, in terms of national character. What is an American, a German, an Englishman, or an Australian? What are his strengths and his weaknesses, what is his peculiar pattern of strength and weakness, invincible under one set of conditions, infinitely vulnerable under another?"[120] Her argument was based on "the premise that, in total war, national character, what Americans are now, today, in the 1940's, is one of our principal assets, and may nevertheless become, not wisely handled, one of our principal liabilities. We are the stuff with which this war is being fought. If we had been born somewhere else and reared somewhere else, we would be different kinds of people."[121]

Mead's anthropological view, as this argument suggests, was that character was developmental and situational, a matter of culture, not of heredity, except insofar as one generation passed stories and expectations down to another. Among the qualities and social practices that she identified as characteristically American, all of which she felt would help in the war effort, were: boasting; a tendency to exhibitionism; a desire both to please one's parents and to outdo them; "playing fair"; a moral conscience; technical problem solving; a drive for success. Americans, she said (echoing Alexis de Tocqueville), were proud of their "home towns," attracted to voluntary associations like clubs and lodges, eager to seek out other Americans when traveling abroad. They were reared more by mothers than by fathers. (In a preface written in 1943, she reports that one or two of her American friends thought it "unwise" to publish, in England, a book "which discusses us so frankly."[122])

"Culture and personality," later renamed by some of its proponents "psychological anthropology," remained an important strand of anthropological and social thought until the 1950s. Geoffrey Gorer published *The Americans: A Study in National Character* in 1948 and *Exploring English Character* in 1955. But the field of anthropology was shifting its emphasis away from patterns, forms, and personal development toward what some regarded as a more rigorous model of analysis: as one critic of Benedict's *The Chrysanthemum and the Sword* commented in 1955—in a book pointedly titled *Without the Chrysanthemum and the Sword*—"in complex societies with a history and a past," what is needed are "many-faceted models," since "the problem of the research worker is not so much to hit on the more or less poetical formula which will explain the whole as to say with a certain degree of precision who does what."[123]

When *The Chrysanthemum and the Sword* was reissued in 2005, almost sixty years after its initial publication, Ian Buruma, the author of several books on modern Japan, praised it as a "great book," while at the same time offering tempered thoughts on "the premise of classical cultural anthropology, which is that such a thing as 'national character' exists." As Buruma notes, "it is not a fashionable idea nowadays," having been tainted by pseudoscientific theories of race and nation. "Theorists now prefer to stress 'hybridity' or the multicultural aspects of nations," he said, even though books about national heroes and national "values" remain popular with the reading public.[124]

Yet, as the anthropologist William Beeman points out, there is considerable commonality between what Ruth Benedict, Margaret Mead, and others were doing in their research and a postmodern intellectual movement like cultural studies, with its interest in evidence drawn from psychoanalysis, popular culture, film, and literature.[125] Intellectual movements and styles are often cyclical rather than one-directional; what has been rejected as old-fashioned or out of date by one generation of scholars is often rediscovered, or reinvented, by the next generation, whether or not they are conscious of the fact. This disciplinary amnesia is part of how ideas evolve over time. And as Mead, Gorer, and others pointed out in the 1940s and '50s, cultural changes and social and political pressures may return a previously disfavored term to use and favor.

Shortly after cultural anthropologists began to investigate "national character," another group of social scientists set out to do the same from their own disciplinary perspective. In an essay in the *Handbook for Social Psychology*, first published in 1954, the sociologist Alex Inkeles and his colleague the psychologist Daniel Levinson offered a definition: "National character refers to relatively enduring personality characteristics and patterns that are modal among the adult members of a society."[126] (A "modal personality structure," as Inkeles explains, is "one that appears with considerable frequency.")[127] To avoid "impressionistic, introspective, and loosely evaluative" results, Inkeles, whose papers were later collected in a volume called *National Character: A Psycho-Social Perspective*, recommended the use of the tools of social science—surveys, clinical interviews, projective techniques, the Thematic Apperception Test, the Rorschach test, and others.[128] His focus, and that of several other scholars who took this approach, was largely on questions of politics and public policy.

Inkeles noted some other possible definitions that had, to one extent or another, attracted both scholarly and popular interest: "National Character as Institutional Pattern" (commonly used by political scientists and economists), "National Character as Culture Theme" (focusing on family, friendship, the local community, religion, and values), "National Character as Action" (the belief that there is a predisposition on the part of certain peoples or societies to certain kinds of behavior: warlike or peaceful, pragmatic or idealistic, etc.; the case in point in many of these postwar studies was Germany), and "National Character as Racial Psychology" ("one of the oldest and most common approaches, and in modern social science the one most severely criticized if not actively abhorred"; here Inkeles inserts, as an illustration of this resistance to prejudice, a footnote citing Benedict's *The Chrysanthemum and the Sword*).[129]

"The field of 'national character' has risen and fallen over the years," wrote the sociologist Daniel Bell, who had known Inkeles at Harvard, "as writers and social scientists have grappled with the concept. We all sense that 'something of the sort' exists, but any definitions have lacked precision." Bell called Inkeles's book *National Character: A Psycho-Social Perspective* the "benchmark" on the subject, one that not only showed "the existence of such a concept in various countries," but also related "'national character' to sociocultural systems."[130] An example of the methods, conclusions, and possible pitfalls of such an inquiry may show something of both the scope and the limitations of this kind of analysis.

A study of "the American Creed," on which Inkeles reported in 1990 but which was drawn from surveys conducted in the early 1980s, charted the percentage of respondents who answered such questions as "Private ownership of property is as important to a good society as freedom" (78 percent), "People who hate our way of life should still have a chance to be heard" (82 percent), "There is something wrong with a person who is not willing to work hard" (75 percent), "I sometimes feel that laziness is almost like a sin" (77 percent), and "Everyone should try to amount to more than his parents did" (74 percent).[131] Inkeles draws from these responses and others the conclusion that "Americans hold a very positive view of themselves," that they "see themselves as religious, hardworking, energetic, moral, and family oriented," and that, "summing it all up, they resoundingly affirm that they are proud to be Americans, whereas the same kind of pride," he suggests, citing a 1986 study by two other scholars, "is manifested by only some 20 percent of West Germans and 30 to 40 percent of the Danes and the Dutch."[132]

What about the pitfalls and limitations? Inkeles himself admitted, in describing this project, "It may be claimed that Americans who so regularly tell the survey interviewers how much they support the American creed are merely mouthing slogans which they know they are expected to subscribe to publicly," and also that the elements of this "creed" might be described as so "general, vague, and innocuous" that all people everywhere might support them, "in which case they lose all utility for distinguishing one national character from another." But this would be an "empirical question," and to test it, he says, would involve asking the same questions of national samples in other countries, which he had not done. Nonetheless, based on the comparative survey data available in 1990–1991, when this chapter was first published, his guess was that using such questions "would yield quite diverse responses."[133]

Inkeles does not, of course, say "guess." He says that it is "likely": "What is more likely is that each national population would show a distinctive profile," and "It is likely that each national population will affirm some creedal principles special and even unique to it." The exceptions, he thinks, might be "Great Britain and its English-speaking offshoots," whose views could perhaps more closely resemble those of the "American creed."[134]

We might pause for a moment on this term, before exploring how it relates to the concept of national character. The phrase "American creed" dates from a resolution passed by the U.S. House of Representatives on April 3, 1918. The original statement of national fidelity, written by William Tyler Page as an entry into a patriotic contest, was called "The American's Creed," and the House resolution bears that title, but the term was widely taken up by political commentators such as Seymour Martin Lipset as a national, rather than a personal, quality. "The American Creed," wrote Lipset, "can be described in five terms: liberty, egalitarianism, individualism, populism, and laissez-faire."[135] The subtle but important shift from "American's" to "American," from the individual to the nation, is itself a marker of ideology, the sign of a belief in something like national character.

The adoption of the word "creed" by mid-twentieth-century American intellectuals was a sign of the times. Lipset, who was Jewish and active in Jewish causes, used it without comment. Yet "creed," though it has developed over time to mean something like a system of belief, has its roots in specifically Christian worship. "America is the only nation in the world that is founded on a creed,"[136] declared the English author and journalist G. K. Chesterton, a devout Catholic, in a phrase often favorably quoted by American scholars. What was the special appeal of the term? For some, it might have indicated the religion of the Founders; for others, a wished-for inclusiveness that made patriotism itself a kind of secular religion crossing over, and even (temporarily?) obliterating, religious differences. This, too, we might say, is—or was—an element of "national character," for better or for worse. In any case, what Inkeles called the "creedal principles" of other nations—or, rather, of the modal personalities of other nations—might arguably (or even "likely") number among them some resistance to the idea of a national "creed."

One does not hear "creed" so often these days when reflexively coupled with "American." It has become either a generalized name for all belief ("We are not made from a land or tribe or particular race or creed"[137]) or a slightly suspect term for foreign ideas that may or may not be instigated by religion ("Ms. Le Pen's anti-euro creed"[138]; "an intolerant creed that fuels terrorism"[139]). A word-association test seeking an upbeat partner for "American" would be more likely (perhaps) to link it with "Dream."

Yet even this aspirational term has come in for some real-world deflating, from many points on the political spectrum. For many non-U.S. commentators—and, indeed, for many within the United States—the axiomatic American Dream is associated with nationalism rather than with international cooperation. After a terrorist attack in Brussels in March 2016, the political editor of *Die Zeit* commented on one of the ancillary effects of the European Union: "Official Europe has worked hard to move past nationalism, so that there is no German or French Dream. But there's no European Dream, either, not yet. So new migrants have no spirit to tap into, as they do in the United States. Instead, some Muslims find it more attractive to give their loyalty to Allah, their fellow believers or the Islamic State."[140] Meantime, the pressure on so-called Dreamers (illegal immigrants who came to the United States as small children) and the increased difficulty of home purchase and other traditional components of the American Dream have put its fulfillment, for many, out of reach.

Riesman's "Social Character": Directedness, Conformity, and Style

Perhaps the most influential approach to national character offered by a social scientist in the mid-twentieth century was that of David Riesman in *The Lonely Crowd*, subtitled *A Study of the Changing American Character*. First published in 1961, *The Lonely Crowd* became the bestselling book ever written by an American sociologist, according to a 1997 study.[141] Riesman firmly grasped the nettle of "character," defining it as "the more or less permanent socially and historically conditioned organization of an individual's drives and satisfactions—the kind of 'set' with which he approaches the world and people."[142] This definition allowed him to introduce a key term of his own, "social character": "that part of character which is shared among significant social groups and which . . . is the product of the experience of these groups."

Riesman set aside questions like heredity versus environment, and "whether there is an empirical proof that it really exists," citing recent work by Benedict, Mead, Gorer, Erich Fromm, Abram Kardiner, and others to support his idea that social character "is becoming today a more or less visible premise of the social sciences." He wanted to find "the relation between social character and society," and he undertook to do so by coining three other terms, "tradition-directed," "inner-directed," and "outer-directed"—terms that would have a significant influence not only on the field of sociology but also on popular culture.[143] To these key terms for his research he added one more that would likewise become a buzzword for the early sixties and a point of resistance by the end of that turbulent decade: "conformity." To what principles and beliefs did societies, and individuals, seek to conform?

The tradition-directed person, Riesman explained, was principally influenced by culture, and by membership in a particular age group, clan, or caste; the sanction for failure to conform to social norms for such a person was *shame.* The inner-directed person, strongly influenced by elders, authority figures, and parents, was regulated by feelings of *guilt.* And the other-directed person, described by Riesman as "cosmopolitan," influenced by a "far wider circle than is constituted by his parents," was psychically controlled not so much by shame or guilt as by *anxiety.* As American society shifted in the 1950s from "an age of production to an age of consumption," changes in social character followed.

Riesman's thesis was, as can be seen, much inflected by the work of Freud, Benedict, and Veblen, among others. His terminology, and his timely analysis of American character and society, appealed to a wide range of readers, scholarly and popular, making his key words themselves elements of the culture, even for those who had not read—or perhaps even heard of—his book. The scope of the book was extensive, engaging topics of morality, morale, media, and politics. When considering the last of these, he insisted that the relationship of American politics to character depended upon "the impressionistic term 'style.'" His contention, buttressed by examples, was that "a political realism that ignores the dimension of character, that ignores how people interpret configurations of power on the basis of their psychic needs," would have only short-term value, if indeed it had any value at all.[144]

A brief catalogue of what Riesman described as the personality types in American politics may help to explain the relation of style to his notion of character. (It will also be useful as a point of comparison with the various "character types" discussed by psychoanalysts from Freud onward.) Among Riesman's types were the "indifferents," the "moralizers" (further divided into "moralizers-in-power" and "moralizers-in-retreat"), and what he called, in the jargon of the 1950s, the "inside-dopesters." Among the "moralizers" was Woodrow Wilson, represented by a pertinent epigraph: "Sometimes people call me an idealist. Well, that is the way I know I am an American. America is the only idealist nation in the world."[145]

Wilson's Peace

Wilson's claim of American exceptionalism links the character of the person (in this case, Woodrow Wilson himself) with the character of the nation (America). It announces a backward derivation, from "America" to "American"—people call him an idealist, and that is how he knows he is an American. But such idealism, whether characteristically "American" or not, did not always prove effective, as one interested observer would suggest, in describing Wilson's participation at the Paris Peace Conference in 1919.

> His thought and his temperament were essentially theological and not intellectual . . . The President had thought out nothing; when it came to practice his ideas were nebulous and incomplete. He had no plan, no scheme, no constructive ideas whatever for clothing with the flesh of life the commandments which he had thundered from the White House . . .
>
> Not only was he ill-informed . . . but his mind was slow and unadaptable . . .
>
> The President's attitude toward his colleagues had now become: I want to meet you so far as I can; I see your difficulties and I should like to be able to agree with what you propose; but I can do nothing that is not just and right . . . Thus began the weaving of that web of sophistry . . . that was finally to clothe with insincerity the language and substance of the Treaty . . .
>
> I believe that his temperament allowed him to leave Paris a really sincere man; and it is probable that to this day he is genuinely convinced that the Treaty contains practically nothing inconsistent with his former professions . . .
>
> In the language of medical psychology, to suggest to the President that the Treaty was an abandonment of his professions was to touch on the raw a Freudian complex. It was a subject intolerable to discuss, and every subconscious instinct plotted to defeat its further exploration.[146]

This shrewd report is that of John Maynard Keynes in *The Economic Consequences of the Peace* (1919), a book written in response to what Keynes viewed as a ruinously punitive treaty that would, as it did, lead to another war. Wilson, Keynes saw, had been outthought, outplayed, and outfoxed by Clemenceau and Lloyd George. His failings and failure were a matter of what Keynes called "temperament," what Riesman would call "social character." The boast—for it was a boast—that "America is the only idealist country in the world" was disastrously ill-suited for the task of crafting a workable political settlement to the European war.

In many of these cases, as we've seen, questions of "national character" arose for social scientists in connection with war: its inception, prevention, or successful conclusion; the nature of the opposition; the emotional and temperamental fitness of a populace, or an individual, for conflict or combat. Of course, part of the motivation here came as well from the availability of funding; such issues were not merely "academic," they were matters of survival and of vital national interest. As happens so often, though, the terms and techniques developed for one purpose were also applied and appropriated for others, some benign or beneficial, others arguably not. When "national character" was understood to be a matter of uniformity and to be regarded as a synonym for loyalty, the search for exceptions to an "exceptionalist" doctrine could take on a much darker tone.

International Character

One of the most acute of Sigmund Freud's political observations was his assessment of what he called "the narcissism of minor differences." He first describes it, with disarming symmetry, in *Group Psychology and the Analysis of the Ego* (1921):

> Of two neighboring towns each is the other's most jealous rival; every little canton looks down upon the others with contempt. Closely related races keep one another at arm's length; the South German cannot endure the North German, the Englishman casts every kind of aspersion upon the Scot, the Spaniard despises the Portuguese.[147]

In the context of "group psychology," this local enmity is a kind of mechanism, a structure. Only as a sort of aside does Freud add, "We are no longer astonished that greater differences should lead to an almost insuperable repugnance, such as the Gallic people feel for the German, the Aryan for the Semite, and the white races for the colored."

Less than a decade later, the situation of the Aryan and the Semite, or the Christian and the Jew, clearly called for a more direct and extensive accounting. When Freud returned to the narcissism of minor differences in *Civilization and Its Discontents* (1930), it was with an ironic pointedness that stopped just short of resignation. His ostensible topic is aggression, and how it binds people together "in love, so long as there are other people left over to receive the manifestations of their aggressiveness." We have noticed similar sentiments in the discussions, by Orwell and others, of the unifying effect of war.

Here is Freud's passage, which I will quote in full, not only because it ends with so elegant a period, but also because its middle section, which addresses the role of the Jews in history and what Freud chose, in 1930, to call their "most useful services to the civilizations of the countries that have been their hosts"—that is, as the unifying targets of aggression. He begins, however, not with the Jews, but with the nations and nationalities of Western Europe.

> I once discussed the phenomenon that it is precisely communities with adjoining territories, and related to one another in other ways as well, who are engaged in constant feuds and in ridiculing each other—like the Spaniards and Portuguese, for instance, the North Germans and South Germans, the English and Scotch, and so on. I gave this phenomenon the name of "the narcissism of minor differences," a name that does not do much to explain it. We can see now that it is a convenient and relatively harmless satisfaction of the inclination to aggression, by means of which cohesion between the members of the community is made easier. In this respect the Jewish people, scattered everywhere, have rendered most useful services to the civilizations of the countries that have been their hosts; but unfortunately all the massacres of the Jews in the Middle Ages did not suffice to make that period more peaceful and secure for their Christian fellows. When once the Apostle Paul had posited universal love between men as the foundation of his

> Christian community, extreme intolerance on the part of Christendom toward those who remained outside it became the inevitable consequence. To the Romans, who had not founded their communal life as a State upon love, religious intolerance was something foreign, although with them religion was a concern of the State and the State was permeated by religion. Neither was it an unaccountable chance that the dream of a Germanic world-dominion called for anti-semitism as its complement; and it is intelligible that the attempt to establish a new, communist civilization in Russia should find its psychological support in the persecution of the bourgeois. One only wonders, with concern, what the Soviets will do after they have wiped out their bourgeois.[148]

Freud, who once described himself as a "Godless Jew," became in his last years, as Hitler and the "dream of a Germanic world-dominion" murdered and exiled so many, increasingly interested in Jewish history and culture. In *Moses and Monotheism*, a book begun in Vienna in 1934 but completed after his forced migration to England in the spring of 1938, Freud asked himself why there had been so much "hatred of the Jew" over the course of human history.

"A phenomenon of such intensity and permanence," he thought, "must of course have more than one ground." Briefly, he mentions the claim that Jews are "aliens," though, as he notes, it is often the case that they have been, to the contrary, among a region's oldest inhabitants.

He suggests two kinds of "grounds"—from "reality" and from underlying psychological sources—and of these the first addresses fairly directly the "national" question: "Of the former [i.e, "the ground clearly derived from reality"], the reproach of being aliens is perhaps the weakest, since in many places dominated by anti-semitism to-day the Jews were among the oldest portions of the population or had even been there before the present inhabitants."

But "other grounds for hating the Jews are stronger," Freud continues, with his usual serene tone of rational discourse, even as he is discussing the abdication of reason. Like the fact that "they live for the most part as minorities among other peoples," and "the communal feeling of groups requires, in order to complete it, hostility toward some extraneous minority, and the numerical weakness of this excluded minority encourages its suppression." The phrases "extraneous minority" and "excluded minority" indicate, again without undue heat, the fact that Jews were often not permitted to be citizens. It is at this point that Freud's irony, up to now held in check, comes briefly but perceptibly to the surface. "There are," he writes, "two other characteristics of the Jews which are quite unforgivable."

> First is the fact that in some respects they are different from their "host" nations. They are not fundamentally different, for they are not Asiatics of foreign race, as their enemies maintain, but composed for the most part of remnants of the Mediterranean peoples and heirs of the Mediterranean civilization. But they are none the less different, often in an indefinable way different, especially from the Nordic peoples, and the intolerance of groups is often, strangely enough, exhibited more strongly against small differences than against fundamental ones. The other point has a still greater effect: namely, that they defy all oppression, that the most cruel persecutions have not succeeded in exterminating them, and, indeed, that on the contrary they show a capacity for holding their own in commercial life and, where they are admitted, for making valuable contributions to every form of cultural activity.[149]

The stylistic technique here might be called either projection or free indirect discourse. The Jews are, throughout the passage, called "they," not "we." But the word "unforgivable" (with its own undertone of "revenge," now attributed to those who hate the Jews) leaps out and accosts the reader. After which the calm tone of the man of reason and science returns, though not without a final defiant note of quiet satisfaction.

Often described as "cosmopolitan" and sometimes, by necessity, as "wandering" or stateless, Jews have been taken to exemplify not national character but *international* character—a portrait that slides, all too predictably, into the dark fantasy world of the "international conspiracy." In his essay "Of National Characters," David Hume referred glancingly, as we noted, to the reputation of the Jews for fraud, an observation he apparently found so incontestable that he did not bother to expand upon it. Ralph Waldo Emerson, writing about the pervasive effects of what he called "race" as a social and behavioral determinant ("It is race, is it not?"), declared, "Race is a controlling influence in the Jew, who, for two milleniums, under every climate, has preserved the same character and employments."[150] This one sentence is full of flash points: "under every climate" is the "wandering" (or, often, exiled) Jew. "Employments," without mentioning the gritty details, is a cover for "money lending," "banking," and other mercantile (and implicitly lucrative) activities—"employments" in the plural suggests business and busyness rather than a regular job, career, or profession. "The Jew" rather than "Jews," or "the Jewish people," in a paragraph that otherwise describes "Celts," "Saxons," "the French," and "the Germans," is an allegorization and personification: one busy Jew controls everything. What does "character" mean in Emerson's sentence about "the Jew"—does it mean "nature," or "ethics," or "values," or "personality type," or some combination of all of these?

At least one more time in *English Traits*, Emerson returns to the situation of the Jews in England—in this case, as one might expect, in a chapter on religion. Here, too, the topic is approached via a discussion of the English national character—and here, too, the question of money seems to come up as soon as there is a mention of the Jews.

> The doctrine of the Old Testament is the religion of England. The first leaf of the New Testament it does not open. It believes in a Providence that does not treat with levity a pound sterling. They put up no Socratic prayer, much less any saintly prayer for the queen's mind; ask neither for light nor right, but say bluntly, "grant her in health and wealth long to live." And one traces this Jewish prayer in all English private history . . . The bill for the naturalization of the Jews (in 1753) was resisted by petitions from all parts of the kingdom, and by petition from the city of

> London, reprobating this bill, as "tending extremely to the dishonor of the Christian religion, and extremely injurious to the interests and commerce of the kingdom in general, and of the city of London in particular."[151]

Though Emerson himself turns a new page with the next paragraph ("they have not been able to congeal humanity by act of Parliament . . . The new age has new desires, new enemies, new trades, new charities, and reads the Scriptures with new eyes"[152]), the negative trifecta of Jews, money, and questionable citizenship is established as somehow related to the English prayer, now called a "Jewish prayer," for Queen Victoria's health and wealth. The "commerce" the city of London had sought to protect in the middle of the eighteenth century was a national—or in this case civic—commerce that must not be disrupted, or usurped, by foreign "interests," which were only foreign because a previous monarch, centuries earlier, had confiscated the wealth of English Jews and deprived them of the right to be English.

The "international Jew" is a bogeyman, a tired but often reworked cliché. But sometimes in the context of national character the word "international" itself becomes an epithet or a scare word. Even among nations that purported to be liberal or enlightened, the accusation that Jews were "foreign," rather than a legitimate part of a nation's culture or character, was a consistent, or at least a persistent claim.

As Americans should know, *The International Jew* is the title of a four-volume set of pamphlets published and distributed in the early 1920s by Henry Ford. Three of the volumes addressed supposed Jewish power and influence in the United States; volume 1, *The International Jew: The World's Foremost Problem*, led off the series with an opening section on "The Jew in Character and Business."

In England during the same years, G. K. Chesterton, beloved as a journalist and a mystery writer, suggested that there was a "Jewish problem" in Europe because Jews were of a different nationality from other Europeans. Chesterton wrote frequently, in both his fiction and his journalism, about differences he perceived between Christian Europeans and Jews. Patriotism required a sense of nationality, which Chesterton felt "the Jew" lacked: "Moving in a crowd of his own kindred from country to country, and even from continent to continent, all equally remote and unreal to his own mind, he may well feel the events of European war as meaningless energies of evil. He must find it as unintelligible as we find Chinese tortures."[153] Perhaps the most significant element in this passage, beyond the tone of the whole, is the word "we," sharply separating Jews from Englishmen and from the "European" First World War. If a Jew were to be chosen as prime minister or lord chancellor, Chesterton suggested, he should, as a condition of taking office, be "dressed like an Arab"—a matter on which Chesterton insisted that he was entirely serious. "The point is that we should know where we are; and he would know where he is, which is in a foreign land."[154]

Anti-Semites in the United States, taking aim at the Jewish influence in Hollywood in the 1940s, claimed that foreign-born Jews could not be good American citizens. "Those primarily responsible for the propaganda pictures are born abroad," declared Senator Gerald Nye of North Dakota, a favored speaker at America First rallies, where he opposed American entrance into the Second World War. "They came to our land and took citizenship here, entertaining violent animosities towards certain causes abroad." As for the specific individuals to blame, said Nye, he would "confine himself to four names, each that of one of the Jewish faith, each except only one foreign-born."[155]

It was a short step from Senator Nye's animadversions about "foreign" Jews, under the impetus of HUAC and the Red Scare, to the implication that even Jews born in the United States were susceptible to treasonous or disloyal activities. The idea of an international Jewish conspiracy, itself almost as old as history, was re-enlivened by the claim that many Jews were communists, and thus members of another (or was it the same?) international conspiracy. "International" in such a phrase essentially *meant* "conspiracy" to those who hurled it at others as an accusation, conspiracy against nations and nationhood, conspiracy against patriotism, conspiracy against "national character."

At moments of heightened hypernationalism, like the rise of Hitler in Germany or the Cold War (and the Red Scare) in the United States, "extreme intolerance on the part of Christendom" (to quote Freud's phrase on page 186) set not only nationalism against internationalism but also national character against international character. It's symptomatic that the most famous anthem of the left is "The Internationale," with its refrain, "*Groupons-nous et demain / L'Internationale / Sera le genre humain*" ("Let us work together and tomorrow / The Internationale / Will be the human race"). Named after the "First International," a workers' congress in 1864, the song has been adopted by socialists, communists, anarchists, democratic socialists, and social democrats. Originally written in French, it has been translated into numerous languages. Terms like "humankind" and "the human race" seem designed to be inclusive, uniting all nations and races. But once it became the official song of the Communist Party of the Soviet Union and was played at the end of radio broadcasts during the Cultural Revolution in China, the "Internationale" (if not also the "international") was often, in the West, identified as the enemy.

In recent years, other terms—"multinational," "transnational," "postnational," "global"—have often augmented or replaced "international," especially when the topic is race or trade (not incidentally, two of Tocqueville's preoccupations). We have seen how "global" itself can be used as an epithet when offered, in an American politician's description of Barack Obama, as an alternative to "American"—or, indeed, in the phrase "global elites." The backlash against globalism has been part of the impetus for a new, or renewed, kind of nationalism, seizing on a concept of "national character" that excludes rather than includes. The inclusive spirit of Shakespeare's Agincourt battlefield or the optimism of the mid-century American "melting pot" is hard to locate in incidents where U.S.-born citizens of Asian and Latin American descent are told to "go back" to countries they have never visited. "Melting pot" itself has become a dead metaphor, its origins forgotten, along with the idea that *all* Americans would be beneficially transformed by the addition of new residents to their nation.

Cultural Nostalgia and Modern Politics: The Character of National Character

Is the claim of "national character" a defense mechanism or a sign of national maturity? A stage or an end? A political fiction or a political reality? The only functional answer is *both.*

Over and over again, the concept of "national character" emerges at times of stress and change. Deeply unfashionable just before the turn of the century, displaced by nuanced critical attention to identity, postnationalism, and the effects of decolonization, national character soon returned in books both popular and scholarly. "What is the national character of the multinational nation?" the scholar Emily Apter asked, in a book published in 1999.[156] What she could not have foreseen then was the way resurgent populism and angry nationalism would thrust "the problem of national character" back into the headlines, and the ballot boxes, of the twenty-first century.

As memories of the British Empire morphed into EU immigration, books on "the English" began to proliferate: the journalist Jeremy Paxman's popular, and bestselling, *The English* (1998); Antony Easthope's *Englishness and National Culture* (1999), Krishan Kumar's scholarly *The Making of English National Identity* (2003), the anthropologist Kate Fox's *Watching the English* (2004, revised in 2014 with "new research, observations & over 100 updates"), and Peter Mandler's *The English National Character* (2006). Then came Brexit, and a fresh set of concerns about identity and belonging.

Meantime, in the United States, "character" considerations took a more personal turn, first with Bill Clinton, later with the election of Donald Trump. Was the character of the president emblematic of the character of the nation? Noting President Donald Trump's insistence on displaying armored vehicles near the Lincoln Memorial to celebrate the Fourth of July in 2019, the *New York Times* columnist Gail Collins observed dryly, "He thought watching a bunch of tanks roll through Washington, D.C., would be a great way of celebrating our national character." However—as Collins went on to report—since the city streets would have been seriously damaged by such a rolling display, the military instead trucked in tanks and "other tanklike vehicles" for temporary stationary installation, "in a very expensive show totally unrelated to their actual function."[157] It is hard not to see this episode as itself a commentary on the relationship between Trump's presidency and his idea of national character.

Representative book titles in this period ranged from *American Sphinx: The Character of Thomas Jefferson* (Joseph Ellis, 1996) to *American Betrayal: The Secret Assault on Our Nation's Character* (Diane West, 2013) to *American Character: A History of the Epic Struggle Between Individual Liberty and the Common Good* (Colin Woodard, 2016)—and these are just some of the titles beginning with *A*. A handbook called *Keywords for American Cultural Studies*, its second edition published in 2014, included dozens of entries, from "Abolition" and "Aesthetics" to "White" and "Youth," but nothing under "Character."[158] But the term, seemingly so old-fashioned, impressionistic, and imprecise, re-emerged in the second half of the decade with renewed force and point. Responding to a Washington, D.C., conference on "national conservatism" in the summer of 2019, the contributing opinion writer Will Wilkinson wrote in *The New York Times*: "The molten core of right-wing nationalism is the furious denial of America's multiracial, multicultural national character. This denialism is the crux of the new nationalism's disloyal contempt for the United States of America. The struggle to make good on the founding promise of equal freedom is the dark but hopeful thread that runs through our national story and defines our national character."[159]

As it goes in and out of fashion, "national character" remains a strong belief that is older than many nations. It will not go away anytime soon. Understanding both its history and its psychology, especially at a time of high tension and high anxiety, is both difficult and essential. Part cultural myth, part autosuggestion, part pop-history heritage, part shared narrative and lore, national character is, however described and defined, nonetheless a "real thing," in the ways that ideas are real, whether or not they are true. It shares with literary character a narrative arc; it shares with ethical character a set of beliefs and standards; it shares with theatrical character a tendency to comic—or tragic—exaggeration. That it is not necessarily true of all inhabitants—or, indeed, perhaps of any—does not make it less real in the minds of those, from fiction writers to politicians, who depend upon its archetypes.

As with so many other complex uses of the concept of "character," this one cannot be wished away because it sometimes has malign effects. One question we ask of personal character is also one we ask of national character: can it change? Much in the world of politics and diplomacy, not to mention warfare, has been predicated, one way or another, on the answer.

4

READING IT

The Rise, Fall, and (Un)Surprising Return of Phrenology

> There seems no doubt that Phrenology, however little it satisfy our scientific curiosity about the functions of different portions of the brain, may still be, in the hands of intelligent practitioners, a useful help in the art of reading character.
>
> —WILLIAM JAMES, *THE PRINCIPLES OF PSYCHOLOGY*

> Let's visualize those phrenology skulls mapping distinct faculties in the brain, the ones that spur chastity, sympathy, philanthropy, philoprogenitiveness, mirthfulness, sincerity, grace, morality, generosity, kindness, benevolence.
>
> Then think of the president's skull, which is stuffed with other humours: insecurity, insincerity, victimhood, paranoia, mockery, self-delusion, suspicion, calculation, illogic, vindictiveness, risk, bullying, alimentiveness, approbativeness, vitativeness. Gall, divided into three parts.
>
> —MAUREEN DOWD, "TRAPPED IN TRUMP'S BRAIN," *THE NEW YORK TIMES*, FEBRUARY 18, 2017

At a news conference in September 2018, President Donald Trump declared that China had "total respect" for him and for his "very, very large brain." His source was apparently Michael Pillsbury, director for Chinese Strategy at the Hudson Institute, a conservative think tank. Pillsbury had been interviewed the previous month by the Fox News commentator Tucker Carlson, although Trump's remark, which referred to himself in the third person, is not close to a direct quotation. (Pillsbury had told Carlson the Chinese viewed Trump as a "master tactician.")[1]

The idea of brain size, the bigger the better, was the artifact of a fallacious nineteenth-century scientific belief, "craniometry," or the measurement of brains. The French physician and anthropologist Paul Broca claimed that the brain is larger "in men than in women, in eminent men than in men of mediocre talent, in superior races than in inferior races."[2] As Stephen Jay Gould notes, in a book pointedly titled *The Mismeasure of Man*, craniometry became a popular obsession: "Conclusions flooded the popular press. Once entrenched, they often embarked on a life of their own, endlessly copied from secondary source to secondary source."[3] In fact "the obsession with brain size," the authors of *Not in Our Genes* report, "continued well into the twentieth century."[4]

Responses to Trump's anatomical claim included one from a scientist who pointed out that over the centuries the human brain has become smaller, rather than larger (Neanderthals and early *Homo sapiens* had larger brains than modern humans), suggesting that evolution had made smaller brains more efficient, like computers.[5] Decades earlier, the cognitive psychologist Howard Gardner had observed that brain size was not an indicator of either intelligence or achievement: "Individuals with very small brains, such as Walt Whitman and Anatole France, have achieved great success, even as individuals with massive brains are sometimes idiots and all too often decidedly unremarkable."[6] But to a president who had defended his small hands by saying that "something else" was definitely not small ("I guarantee there's no problem"), size seemed to matter.

Gould's book, which vigorously exposed the errors and prejudicial effects of weighing and measuring brains, had far more forgiving and even complimentary things to say about a concurrent development, phrenology. Phrenologists, Gould suggested, were "philosophically on the right track," since they "celebrated the theory of richly multiple and independent intelligences,"[7] leading to the work of such modern psychologists and educational theorists as Gardner and Daniel Goleman.

In fact, although the word "phrenology" today more often provokes associations with quackery than with insight, at its beginnings—and, indeed, for quite a long time—it was a highly honored theory, espoused not only by scientists and physicians but also by scholars, college presidents, and imaginative writers. And its object, explicitly stated, was the determination and assessment of human character.

The Science of Character

Figures like Freud, Darwin, and Marx are often regarded today as initiators of new and compelling modes of thought about human nature, cultural innovators who changed the way we understand who we are. No one today would suggest that the names of Franz Joseph Gall or Johann Gaspar Spurzheim would belong in this company—in fact, it might be difficult to find many people who recognize those names at all. But in the nineteenth century, Gall and Spurzheim were familiar names in Britain, the United States, and much of Europe. The "science of mind" they invented, phrenology, had thousands of adherents and practitioners; inspired the founding of phrenological journals, societies, and publishing houses; and led to a wave of "practical phrenology" that remained popular in America for decades.

As a way of reading character, whether in philosophy, in the cultural marketplace, or in the public fairground, phrenology was one of the nineteenth century's Big Ideas. Hundreds of thousands of copies of phrenological books were cheaply published and often given away to those who eagerly submitted to an examination of the head and skull.[8] Imaginative writers from Edgar Allan Poe and Herman Melville to Charlotte Brontë and George Eliot were intrigued enough to include "phrenological" readings in their tales and novels. Walt Whitman would publish his own phrenological reading in an edition of *Leaves of Grass*. "Phrenology was the 'new psychology' of the second quarter of the nineteenth century,"[9] explains Charles Rosenberg, a historian of science.

Throughout the Victorian period, phrenology continued to be favored by the good and the great. Charles Baudelaire, Honoré de Balzac, and Karl Marx all submitted to phrenological examination, as did the children of Queen Victoria. An Edinburgh phrenologist consulted by Lewis Carroll deduced "emulousness" as well as "mathematical ability, and love of children," and the biographer of Julia Margaret Cameron speculates that her penchant for photographing eminent men in profile "had the advantage of bringing out clearly the precise shape of heads for those who believed, like the inventor of phrenology, that the profile was 'the truest representation that can be given to a man.'"[10]

The Scottish philosopher and educationalist Alexander Bain hoped in 1861 to "reanimate the interest in the analytical study of human character, which was considerably awakened by the attention drawn to phrenology, and which seems to have declined with the comparative neglect of that study at the present time." In phrenology, he believed, the world had its first "SCIENCE OF CHARACTER."[11] The science of character was also John Stuart Mill's translation of his term "ethology," which Bain would cite and praise. Even at the end of the century, when it had become common to express skepticism about phrenologists and their theories, the naturalist and social thinker Alfred Russel Wallace predicted: "In the coming century phrenology will assuredly gain general acceptance. It will prove itself to be the true science of mind. Its practical uses in education, in self-discipline, in the reformatory treatment of criminals, and in the remedial treatment of the insane, will give it one of the highest places in the hierarchy of the sciences."[12]

The goal of phrenology was to unlock the secrets of character, the age's central preoccupation. Character was believed to be the key to human nature, and thus to education, vocation, economic success, social relations, and happiness. Was it—as phrenologists suggested—located in, or defined by, the brain, and if so how could it be analyzed, developed, improved?

As the century turned, and phrenology gave way to behavioral psychology, psychoanalysis, educational and penal reform, it was easy, perhaps too easy, to forget—or parody, or trivialize—the questions asked by the early phrenologists, researchers trained in disciplines like philosophy, anatomy, and physiognomy.

The Craniologists: Phrenology at Yale and Harvard

Franz Joseph Gall, the originator of the theory he called "craniology," was a German physician born in Tiefenbrunn in Baden in 1758 and educated at Strasbourg and Vienna. He was offered the position of court physician in Vienna in the 1790s, but elected to remain in private practice, continuing to serve his fashionable clientele. Later, he embarked on a speaking tour throughout Europe, and ultimately moved to Paris, where he numbered ten ambassadors among his patients, and wrote a foundational text on the anatomy and physiology of the brain and nervous system. He was broadly admired as a scientist, theorist, and medical experimentalist. Metternich declared him "the greatest observer and thinker he had ever known, a most indefatigable investigator, and true philosophic mind."[13]

Gall's early collaborator—and eventual successor—Johann Gaspar Spurzheim became a highly successful writer and lecturer in London and Paris. Spurzheim demonstrated brain dissection, did battle with the initial skeptics at *The Edinburgh Review*, and brought the good news to America in a brief but stunningly effective visit that ended, dramatically and unforgettably, in his death a few months later from overwork.

In a few short months, Spurzheim lectured at Yale, demonstrated brain dissection at its medical school, visited various institutions in Hartford, and offered a series of public lectures at the Boston Athenaeum (transferred to the Masonic Temple because of the number of interested attendees), at Harvard College, and at the Boston Medical Society, as well as making visits to "prisons and institutions of beneficence" and "returning the calls of his friends."[14] At the invitation of the president of Harvard, Josiah Quincy, he attended the university's commencement exercises and those of the Phi Beta Kappa Society. Exhausted from this schedule, which he had insisted upon pursuing, he died on November 10, 1832.

Spurzheim's funeral in Boston was overseen by a blue-ribbon committee that was chaired by Josiah Quincy, and included the mathematician Nathaniel Bowditch, Supreme Court Justice Joseph Story, and Harrison Gray Otis, a former senator from Massachusetts and mayor of

Boston. At the funeral, a professor of German at Harvard, Charles Follen, delivered an oration to a congregation of some three thousand persons, including the entire membership of the Boston Medical Society, who gathered at the Old South Church. "Several hundred came and went away disappointed," wrote Spurzheim's biographer, Nahum Capen. "An Ode to Spurzheim," written by the poet and minister John Pierpont, was sung on this occasion by the Handel and Haydn Society.[15]

Spurzheim was buried with appropriate ceremony in Mount Auburn Cemetery in Cambridge, Massachusetts, only the second person there interred. The cemetery is the resting place of many of the great and good from the region and elsewhere, including Louis Agassiz, Felix Frankfurter, Isabella Stewart Gardner, Oliver Wendell Holmes, and dozens of other writers, politicians, artists, and scholars. Spurzheim's burial in this newly founded and prestigious location is another indication of the high regard in which he was held. Nor was Harvard the only university that honored him during his brief visit to the East Coast of the United States. After his ship landed in New York, Spurzheim had traveled to New Haven, attending the Yale commencement exercises with his host, Benjamin Silliman, a professor of chemistry. "Indeed, the professors were in love with him," Silliman told Nahum Capen.[16]

Loving Phrenology

"Love" for Spurzheim was also expressed by one of his chief adherents, the man who would do more than anyone else to disseminate the theories of the new science after Spurzheim's death. A hostile notice about phrenology had appeared in the prestigious *Edinburgh Review* in 1815 ("Such is the trash, the despicable trumpery, which two men, calling themselves scientific inquirers, have the impudence gravely to present to the physiologists of the nineteenth century as specimens of reasoning and induction"[17]), and Spurzheim rushed to Edinburgh to reply to his accusers, performing a brain dissection before an audience of doctors and scholars, then remaining to offer a series of lectures. There he inspired a young lawyer, George Combe, who became a committed author and lecturer on phrenology, founding, with his brother Andrew, a doctor, the Edinburgh Phrenological Society and the *Phrenological Journal*, which influenced the field for the next forty years.

"I love you," Combe wrote to Spurzheim in 1824, and "love phrenology."[18] Edinburgh, despite—or perhaps because of—the initial opposition of *The Edinburgh Review*, became thenceforth the European center of phrenology. "Combe's *Essay on the Constitution of Man and Its Relation to External Objects* first appeared in Edinburgh in 1827 and was reprinted many times in pre-bellum America," writes Charles Rosenberg. "In terms of its impact on popular social thought in ante-bellum America, Combe can—with only minor exaggeration—be compared to Darwin in the decades after the Civil War."[19]

The Constitution of Man became a longtime bestseller, available in cheap editions underwritten by a bequest by an adherent of phrenology who had left his entire estate to the cause. Combe embarked on his own highly successful series of lectures in Britain and the United States, where he was regarded as Spurzheim's natural successor. His lecture materials—like those of his mentor—included skulls, casts, charts, and other illustrative materials. "Phrenology," as the *Albany Evening Journal* commented approvingly when Combe spoke in that American city in 1840, is "a demonstrative science, and is therefore much more understandingly taught by Lecture than by written work."[20]

One of those Combe impressed and befriended was the American educator Horace Mann, who became a passionate advocate of the new system: "I look upon Phrenology as the guide of Philosophy and the handmaiden of Christianity. Whoever disseminates Phrenology is a public benefactor,"[21] he wrote, a statement that Samuel Wells would place on the title page of his handbook, *How to Read Character.* Mann admired Combe so much that he named one of his sons after him.

Another prominent American convert and reformer whom Combe strongly influenced was Samuel Gridley Howe, the abolitionist and advocate of education for the blind, who had known Spurzheim and was active in the Boston Phrenological Society. His wife, Julia Ward Howe (later to be the author of "The Battle Hymn of the Republic"), reported that on their wedding journey they traveled to Italy, where "the presence of the celebrated phrenologist, George Combe, in Rome at this time added much to Dr. Howe's enjoyment of the winter, and to mine. His wife was the daughter of the great actress, Mrs. Siddons, and was a person of excellent mind and manners."[22]

> Dr. Howe and Mr. Combe sometimes visited the galleries in company, viewing the works therein contained in the light of their favorite theory. I remember having gone with them through the great sculpture hall of the Vatican, listening with edification to their instructive conversation. They stood for some time before the well-known head of Zeus, the contour and features of which appeared to them quite orthodox, according to the standard of phrenology.
>
> In this last my husband was rather an enthusiastic believer. He was apt, in judging new acquaintances, to note closely the shape of the head, and at one time was unwilling even to allow a woman servant to be engaged until, at his request, she had removed her bonnet, giving him an opportunity to form his estimate of her character or, at least, of her natural proclivities. In common with Horace Mann, he held Mr. Combe to be one of the first intelligences of the age, and esteemed his work on "The Constitution of Man" as one of the greatest of human productions.[23]

The scene has a certain compelling, if inadvertently comic, appeal: the two learned men observing the shape of the head of a classical statue in the Vatican, and thereby confirming (for themselves, each other, and the attentive young Julia Ward Howe) the wisdom of the ancient Greeks in intuiting the wisdom of phrenology. But the account also describes a somewhat disconcertingly practical (and intrusive) side to Samuel Howe's phrenological belief, his use of the job interview to inspect the shape of a woman servant's head, in order to determine her suitability for employment—or, as Mrs. Howe puts it, her "character" and "natural proclivities." It was a strategy George Combe would commend in his *System of Phrenology*: "A lady who is in the habit of examining the heads of servants before hiring them, told me, that she has found, by experience, that those in whom Veneration is large, are the most deferential and obedient."[24] Apparently, male job applicants could also be vetted in this way. The American newspaper editor and politician Horace Greeley, another phrenology enthusiast, proposed that railroad employees should be hired based on the shapes of their heads, so as to ensure that they were suited for their work ("But how? *By the aid of phrenology*, and not otherwise").[25]

Mr. Rochester's Forehead

Testimony to the respectability of phrenology, and perhaps to its prestige, can be found in some of the major novels of the period. Charlotte Brontë's *Jane Eyre*, published in 1847, provides clear evidence for the wide acceptance of phrenological terms. Not only do characters in the novel refer to these terms, they also use them in the expectation that they will be generally understood.

"I suppose I have a considerable organ of veneration,"[26] Jane confides to the reader, noting that she still recalls the sense of awe with which she first regarded Miss Temple, the superintendent of the charity school in which she was placed as a girl. Later in the novel, when Jane meets Mr. Rochester, he invites her to examine his forehead for telltale phrenological signs. "He lifted up the sable waves of hair which lay horizontally over his brow, and showed a solid enough mass of intellectual organs, but an abrupt deficiency where the suave sign of benevolence should have risen." To Jane's disconcertingly direct query about whether he was a philanthropist (which conspicuous organs of benevolence might have indicated) Rochester replies with force—and pleasure at her frankness:

> "No, young lady, I am not a general philanthropist, but I bear a conscience"; and he pointed to the prominences which are said to indicate that faculty, and which, fortunately for him, were sufficiently conspicuous; giving, indeed, a marked breadth to the upper part of his head.[27]

In direct contrast, Brontë will show us a group of society ladies gushing over a man with a "sweet-tempered forehead," with "none of those frowning irregularities" they "dislike so much."[28] When a Gypsy fortune-teller arrives on the scene, one of these ladies—the one to whom Jane imagines Rochester to be engaged—notes that the others must have "organs of wonder and credulity" that are "easily excited" if they believe that the old "hag" is a genuine witch. She is right, and wrong, and her own organ of credulity has been at work, for, as Jane soon perceives, the "hag" is Mr. Rochester in disguise.

These references, and the slightly flirtatious conversation between Jane and Mr. Rochester that turns on them, suggest not only that such terms from phrenology are familiar but that they are worthy of consideration and respect. That the society ladies use them, too, does not discredit the topic; imagine a modern dinner party in which terms like "ego" and "narcissism" and "inferiority complex" are bandied about. (Despite some determined naysayers, this kind of loose reference does not undermine the legitimacy of psychoanalysis.)

Brontë was apparently curious enough about the practice to try it herself. When, in 1851, she visited a phrenologist in the Strand together with her young publisher, George Smith, they pretended to be brother and sister. Dr. Browne found the pseudonymous "Miss Fraser" to have a "very remarkable" head, deducing, "Her attachments are strong and enduring," and "Her sense of truth and justice would be offended by any dereliction of duty." His reading of her character concluded: "She is sensitive and is very anxious to succeed in her undertakings, but is not so sanguine as to the probability of success . . . Her sense of her own importance is moderate and not strong enough to steel her heart against disappointment."[29]

This visit, which took place several years after the publication of *Jane Eyre*, was clearly not "research" but professional consultation, whatever the motivation that led to it. (Had she sought an appointment under her own name, her fame would presumably have influenced the reading; it's assumed that Dr. Browne's examination of "Miss Fraser" was not colored by previous knowledge of her identity.) Sometime after she received the report, officially titled "A Phrenological Estimate of the Talents and Dispositions of a Lady," Brontë sent it on to Smith, though there is no record of what he thought of it.[30]

George Eliot Visits the Phrenologist

Nor was Charlotte Brontë the only significant Victorian novelist to visit the studio, as such places were called, of a phrenologist. George Eliot, then still known as Mary Ann (or Marian) Evans, went to London in 1844 with the philanthropist and reformer Charles Bray to have a cast made of her head. "Miss Evans's head is a very large one," Bray wrote in his autobiography. "George Combe, on first seeing the cast, took it for a man's."[31] The two friends "afterward took lessons of Mr. Donovan, on Organology, when he was staying at Coventry and converting all the leading men of the city to the truth of the science by the correctness of his diagnosis of character."[32] Mr. Donovan's diagnosis of Eliot, which Bray faithfully reports, includes the information that "in her brain-development the Intellect greatly predominates," and that "in the Feelings, the Animal and Moral regions are about equal; the moral being quite sufficient to keep the animal in order and in due subservience." Her "adhesiveness" (friendship and love of society) was among her most active social feelings. Still, he felt,

> Her sense of Character—of men and things—is a predominatingly intellectual one, with which the Feelings have little to do, and the exceeding fairness, for which she is noted, towards all parties, towards all sects and denominations, is probably owing to her little feeling on the subject,—at least not enough to interfere with her judgment.[33]

Eliot's interest in phrenology, fostered by her connection with Bray, had begun as early as the 1830s. She met George Combe, "the foremost apostle of phrenology," in 1851, and they became close friends and frequent correspondents, sharing interests in philosophy, criminality, "genius," and mesmerism, among other topics. Combe, writing in his *Journal*, had immediately noted her "very large brain," and identified the organ of Destructiveness as prominently developed, though he also thought—contrary to what would turn out to be the fact—that her Amativeness and Philoprogenitiveness were small.[34] The friendship ended, however, when Evans eloped with George Henry Lewes, a married man—and, apparently more to the point, not an admirer of Combe. After some initial interest in the subject, Lewes's belief in phrenology had waned, and in 1857 he added a chapter to his *History of Philosophy* in which he was critical both of Gall's system of craniology and of phrenologists, singling out Combe by name.[35]

A critic in *The Westminster Review*—a periodical for which Evans, at Combe's urging, had briefly served as editor—would note that, in works like *Scenes of Clerical Life* (1858) and *Romola* (1863), George Eliot's "profound penetration and insight into the most intrinsic workings of the human character" was "largely indebted to the phrenological philosophy of George Combe."[36] But in *Felix Holt: The Radical* (1866), phrenology appears only as a topic of rather playful conversation between two men who are just making each other's acquaintance.

> "A phrenologist at Glasgow told me I had a large veneration; another man there, who knew me, laughed out loud and said I was the most blasphemous iconoclast living. 'That,' says my phrenologist, 'is because of his large Ideality, which prevents him from finding anything perfect enough to be venerated.' Of course I put my ears down and wagged my tail at that stroking."
>
> "Yes, yes; I have had my own head explored with somewhat similar results. It is, I fear, but a vain show of fulfilling the heathen precept, 'Know thyself,' and too often leads to a self-estimate which will subsist in the absence of that fruit by which alone the quality of the tree is made evident. Nevertheless—Esther, my dear, this is Mr. Holt, whose acquaintance I have even now been making with more than ordinary interest. He will take tea with us."[37]

Felix, indeed, seems like a textbook example of small rather than large Veneration: he is not blindly deferential and obedient, nor does he manifest particular "respect for titles, rank, and power; for a long line of ancestry, or mere wealth," as specified in Combe's 1834 *System of Phrenology*.[38] But it is the shared reference to phrenology, not the accuracy or inaccuracy of the Glasgow phrenologist, that delineates character in this little scene. This is the kind of experience that social conversation between men like these might well touch on, even at a first meeting. If they turn the deprecating joke onto themselves, it is in part because they lent enough credence to phrenology to participate in its character analysis in the first place. Even the pious and godly minister Mr. Lyon has "had [his] own head explored." In short, although some readers might have agreed that, in George Henry Lewes's unrelenting phrase, "the basis of Phrenology is laid on shifting sand,"[39] its terms and practices, both for the reader and for the residents of Eliot's fictional town of Treby Magna, were familiar enough then to be used in a novel without any need for further explanation.

These examples are worth noting not only because they are interesting in and of themselves, but also because they underscore the high regard with which phrenology and its founders and early disseminators were held at the intellectual or speculative level. Eliot's friend Charles Bray, a lifelong believer in phrenology, was converted to it, he says, by purest accident. He had sent to London for a copy of Andrew Combe's *Physiology*, but was sent, by mistake, George Combe's *Phrenology*, a book on the topic of which he then held "a most supreme contempt . . . such contempt being based, as it usually was, on ignorance." When he read Combe's *Phrenology*, though, he was first "intensely interested" and then "wildly excited."[40] He had his own head shaved and a cast taken, he purchased one hundred other casts from the phrenologist, and he soon held phrenological views about such luminaries as Thomas Carlyle (based on a photograph he bought for the purpose: "Carlyle had a small organ of Benevolence. He had infinite Pity, but this came from his Self-esteem"),[41] Charles Dickens ("no Phrenologist would have been surprised" at the sad end of Dickens's career; "his strongest feelings were Love of Approbation and Acquisitiveness, and he literally killed himself in their gratification"),[42] and the author of Shakespeare's plays ("All I can say is that Bacon's head, as given us in the well known bust by Roubiliac, is the only one that I have seen out of which Shakespeare's plays could have come").[43]

In his autobiography, first published in 1884, Bray is at pains to point out that, when Combe was a candidate for the chair of Logic at Edinburgh in 1836, "a host of the leading literary and scientific men of the day" testified to the value of phrenology as "superior to any system of mental philosophy which has preceded it," and he predicts that "it will not be long before we must be brought back to the only practical Science of Mind."[44] But, "unfortunately," he laments, "the science has now fallen into disrepute," partly because of the opposition of clergymen, and also because "it has been followed for gain by incompetent 'Professors,' who profess to reveal a great deal more than phrenology in its present state is able to tell even were such men its competent exponents."[45]

From the perspective of today, it is not easy to distinguish between the respectable phrenological expertise of the specialists Bray consulted in the Strand, and the exploitative practice of the "incompetent 'Professors'" who made a mockery of the science of mind. But that such a distinction existed at the time seems clearly indicated both by the schism of reputation between "high" and "low" practitioners, and by the rise and equally precipitous fall of phrenology during the course of the century. Perhaps because it was both appealing and superficially "practical," there was almost from the first a popular version, one that is far more likely to be the common—and somewhat misleading—understanding of the term today. The easy dismissal of phrenology as something between a confidence game and a pseudoscience is largely based on its popularized versions, and on its connection with the growing interest in self-development and self-help.

Practical Phrenology

The American branch of phrenology in the nineteenth century was not "theoretical" or philosophical, like the work of the European phrenologists, but rather prided itself on being, precisely, "practical phrenology"—a program for character reading that emphasized capacities, propensities, capabilities, and the opportunity for "cultivation" of the organs, or self-improvement. In both avatars, however, phrenology was a social-reformist doctrine. You could increase your good propensities and decrease your negative ones by practice and experience (following the helpful examples given in handbooks)—so that your character was, in theory and in practice, available for improvement. Hence the perceived relevance of phrenology to education, penal reform, bodily and mental health, and other social concerns of the age.

When he visited America in the late 1830s, George Combe initially resisted the entertainment aspect of what he regarded as both a science and a "new philosophy," writing to his brother Andrew that he was not willing to "downgrade phrenology & myself by getting up three flashy lectures."[46] Many of his competitors for the American market were self-taught opportunists armed with magic lanterns, and, moreover, often charged little or nothing for their presentations, tempting even competent phrenologists to "turn quack."[47] He worried that the predilection for what was widely called "practical phrenology," and the popularity of practitioners who, he said, "examine heads and predicate characters for fees," was giving his philosophical reform movement a bad name. "This practice, which in the eyes of the uninitiated, resembles palmistry and fortune-telling, is said to have created a strong feeling of disgust against phrenology itself in the minds of men of science and education."[48]

His own audiences, though considerably smaller than the crowds he had become accustomed to in Edinburgh, were notably "intelligent and respectable,"[49] and often "connected with the world of letters,"[50] according to the approving reports of American newspapers. When he spoke in New York, one paper gushed, "Seldom have we seen so great a number of intelligent persons assembled on such an occasion."[51]

The doyens of American phrenology, though, were the enterprising Fowler brothers, Lorenzo Niles Fowler and Orson Squire Fowler, phrenological lecturers, publishers, and social reformers, interested in issues of health, women's and children's rights, and moral uplift. They opposed the consumption of coffee and tea and the use of tobacco. Their brother-in-law and publishing partner in the firm of Fowler & Wells, Samuel R. Wells (the author of *How to Read Character*), was a founder of the American Vegetarian Society. His wife, their sister Charlotte, also wrote and lectured, and was known as the Mother of Phrenology.

The Fowlers and Wells were also the proprietors of an exhibition called the Phrenological Cabinet in downtown New York, which attracted hundreds of thousands of visitors, who paid to see the collection of skulls, casts, artifacts, and paintings, and also to have their characters read. The firm supplied roll-up charts and other paraphernalia to traveling phrenologists, and capitalized on the burgeoning interest to begin training programs, first under the banner of their own Institute of Instruction, later at a Phrenological College founded in 1849 by a new American Phrenological Society, and ultimately at an American Institute of Phrenology.

Among the numerous prominent Americans who had phrenological examinations were future President James A. Garfield, the psychologist G. Stanley Hall, the poet Walt Whitman, and the "Siamese twins" Chang and Eng. The nurse and educator Clara Barton, the founder of the American Red Cross, is said to have chosen her vocation after such an examination, as did the financier and philanthropist Bernard Baruch, who was taken to see Lorenzo Fowler by his mother soon after the family moved from South Carolina to New York City.[52]

Orson and Lorenzo Fowler's first book, *Phrenology Proved, Illustrated and Applied* (1836), was reprinted sixty-two times in twenty years. Orson also wrote *Self-Culture and Perfection of Character*, *Love and Parentage*, *Matrimony*, *Amativeness*, and *Hereditary Descent*, among others. Lorenzo Fowler, who, like his brother, wrote, taught, and performed "examinations" or "readings" of heads, was the "L. N. Fowler" whose ceramic phrenology head, first sold at the Fowlers' London outpost in Ludgate Circus, can still be purchased at curio shops. "For thirty years," Fowler proclaimed—on the base of the bust labeled "Phrenology by L. N. Fowler"—"I have studied Crania and living heads from all parts of the world, and have found in every instance that there is a perfect correspondence between the conformation of the healthy skull of an individual and his known characteristics. To make my observations available I have prepared a bust of superior form and marked the divisions of the Organs in accordance with my research and varied experience."

Initially, as John Davies notes, the Fowlers had "designed a chart which was given away with examinations"; later, "this was increased to sixty pages, with the examinee's name, that of the examiner, and the date being written on the flyleaf."[53] The cost of the examination was a dollar, including that sixty-page book. A longer handwritten analysis cost more: three dollars. And for four dollars you could even have your character read by mail, "from a good daguerreotype, the ¾ pose preferred."[54] Proximity to a phrenologist's studio was no longer a necessity. Just as medical diagnoses today can be undertaken, if necessary, via Internet or Skype, a phrenological analysis of character could be done long-distance, allowing rural and heartland dwellers access to this exciting new technology of the self.

Phrenology on the Fourth of July

To get the full flavor of American practical phrenology of the "entertainment" variety, we might turn to its depiction in Ross Lockridge, Jr.'s *Raintree County*. Published in 1948, but set in the previous century, the novel describes the encounter of its protagonist, Johnny Shawnessy, with an itinerant phrenologist whose reading changes Johnny's way of thinking about his character and his life. The key scene takes place in the Court House Square on the Fourth of July, 1854. To give the reader a clear sense of the social context, the phrenologist's booth is right next door to that of the miracle hair restorer, and the phrenologist buys hair tonic from his neighbor before he commences his spiel.

> "Friends, it is my happy good fortune to have it within my power to open up to each and every one of you all the marvelous secrets of a great new science, by which you can achieve, like thousands before you, complete self-knowledge and self-control. That science, Ladies and Gentlemen, is the great new science of Phrenology.
>
> "Now, we all know that the brain is the instrument of every mental act, just as every movement of the body has to be performed by a muscle. Certain areas of the brain control certain human faculties and are large or small in proportion to the development of the faculties they control. Thanks to the great experiments and studies of Professors Gall, Spurzheim, and Fowler, it is now possible to say with the strictest accuracy which part of the brain controls which faculty. These facts are

> now available to all. Nothing is simpler, once these principles are known, than to apply them.
>
> "I have myself become a specialist in the science of Phrenology. I have examined the heads of three Presidents and many other great and distinguished heads here and abroad, not excepting the crowned heads of Europe. By helping people to become better acquainted with their strong and weak points, I have been able to direct them to a fuller exercise or restraint of certain faculties."[55]

Displaying for the crowd both his phrenological chart and the "little book" that will tell them all they need to know—the "*Phrenological Self-Instructor*," with "one hundred and fifty-four illustrations," on sale for a dollar a copy—he offers to give a demonstration of Phrenological Analysis, and Johnny Shawnessy is pushed by his older brother to volunteer. This accident will prove for him, at least in his own estimation, a turning point in his understanding of his character and destiny.

"Ladies and Gentlemen," declares the Professor, "we have an interesting head here, a very interesting head. To you this may be only another head, more or less, but to the practical eye of the phrenologist, this boy's character and potentialities—nay, his whole past, present, and future are legible in the geography of his skull."[56]

With his pointer he locates on the "glazed, segmented head" the area below the eye, labeled LANGUAGE, and declares his subject to be skilled at memorization, a quality obligingly corroborated, from the audience, by his friend. Running his hands over Johnny's head, and referring periodically to a chart in his book, he locates "Mirthfulness . . . very large," suggesting that "this boy ought to be the fiddle of the company," and at the base of the skull, "unusual" and "extree-ordinary" for a boy of his age, "the lump of AMATIVENESS is remarkably distended," indicating that "this young gentleman is going to be an extra-special catch for the ladies."[57]

This forecast of erotic prowess has predictable appeal, and leads, indeed, to various audience members' presenting their own "lumps" for expert vetting, until the Professor changes the subject and begins to sell his stack of books. "Know thyself! Know thyself! One dollar, while they last." Soon the pile is gone. Johnny Shawnessy, availing himself of the cut-rate price offered to the volunteer subject ("Unusual development of the bumps of Calculation and Eventuality," jokes the Professor, reluctantly acceding to the bargain), feels that his life has been changed by this encounter.

> In the presence of the people he had become a child of prophecy; his consecration had been sanctified by the majestic adjective "scientific" and the formidable epithet "phrenological." Here, suddenly and by accident on the Court House Square, there had been a confirmation of something Johnny Shawnessy had always secretly believed—that he was destined to be a great man and to find one day the key to all knowledge. For a while, he felt jealous of all the other people who had purchased the same cheap ticket to intellectual beatitude, but when he saw the innocent, shy joy on their faces, as they wandered somewhat confusedly like himself in the Court House Square, clutching their *Self-Instructors*, he was thrilled to think that he was to be one of a whole community of Americans working together toward the creation of a perfect republic.[58]

Johnny's own copy of the handbook differed in one crucial respect from that purchased by others that afternoon, since it bore the autograph of the Professor. "On the title page where it said THE CHART AND CHARACTER OF" the Professor wrote, "on blank lines provided for the purpose,

> John Wickliff Shawnessy
> As Marked By
> Professor Horace Gladstone
> July 4, 1854[59]

Self-Instruction

The book to which Johnny Shawnessy's examiner so regularly and confidently referred was *The Illustrated Self-Instructor in Phrenology and*

Physiology, by O. S. and L. N. Fowler, emblazoned with the defining phrase "Practical Phrenologists" on the first page, followed by the declaration: "Your head is the type of your mentality. Self-knowledge is the essence of all knowledge." The *Self-Instructor* made it clear from the outset that its topic was character—the word appears again and again. In the preface and explanation, the reader was informed that its first object was "to teach learners those organic conditions which indicate character," and its second object "to record character," using the "accompanying tables," the "SEVEN degrees of power—large, very large, full, average, moderate, small, and very small," as well as the paragraphs that describe the organs and "contain specific directions how to PERFECT THEIR characters."[60] Aspiring self-instructors are told, for example, that "The Laugh Corresponds with the Character": thus, "those who ha, ha, right out, unreservedly, have no cunning, and are open hearted, . . . those who suppress laughter, and try to control their countenance in it, are more or less secretive." The Fowlers also list the "intellectual laugh," the "love laugh," the "horse laugh," the "Philoprogenitive laugh," the "friendly laugh," and many other kinds of laugh, each one indicative of character. "The Walk" was likewise revealing, as were "Dancing" and "the Mode of Shaking Hands." "The Mouth and Eyes" were "Peculiarly Expressive of Character," as were "Intonations." The self-instructor, it seems, needed to be constantly vigilant in order to strive for characterological perfection.

The extended descriptions of the individual faculties, or organs, are so lengthy as perhaps to tax the reader, but it may be a necessary tax to pay in order to get the full flavor of these character analyses and how the combination of organs produce particular, almost novelistic, effects.

Consider, for example, the Fowlers' account of faculty number one, "Amativeness," described as "Conjugal love, attachment to the opposite sex; desire to love, be loved, and marry; adapted to perpetuate the race." (This was the faculty, it will be recalled, that elicited a titter from the crowd during the examination of fifteen-year-old John Shawnessy.) A person with large Amativeness, the *Self-Instructor* advises,

> is strongly attracted toward the opposite sex; admires and loves their beauty and excellencies; easily wins their affectionate re-

gards, or kindles their love; has many warm friends, if not admirers, among them; loves young and powerfully, and wields a powerful influence for good or evil over the destinies of its subject, according as it is well or ill placed; with Adhesiveness and Union for Life large, will mingle pure friendship with devoted love; cannot flourish alone, but must have its matrimonial mate, with whom it will be capable of being perfectly identified, and whom it will invest with almost superhuman perfections, by magnifying their charms and overlooking their defects; in the sunshine of whose love it will be perfectly happy, but proportionately miserable without it; with Ideality and the mental temperament large, will experience a fervor and intensity of first love, amounting almost to ecstasy or romance, can marry those only who combine refinement of manners with correspondingly strong attachments; with Philoprogenitiveness and Benevolence also large, will be eminently qualified to enjoy the domestic relations; to be happy in home, and render home happy; with Inhabitiveness also large, will set a high value on house and place, long to return home when absent, and consider family and children as the greatest treasures of its being; with large Conscientiousness, will keep the marriage relations inviolate, and regard unfaithfulness as the greatest of sins; with Combativeness large, will defend the objects of its love with great spirit, and resent powerfully any indignity offered to them; with Alimentiveness large, will enjoy eating with the family dearly; with Approbativeness large, cannot endure to be blamed by those it loves; with Cautiousness and Secretiveness large, will express love guardedly, and much less than it experiences; but with Secretiveness small, will show, in every look and action, the full, unveiled feeling of the mind; with Firmness and Self-Esteem large, will sustain interrupted love with fortitude, yet suffer much damage of mind and health therefrom; but with Self-Esteem moderate, will feel crushed and broken down by disappointment; with the moral faculties predominant, can love those only whose moral tone is pure and elevated; with predominant Ideality, and only average intellectual

> faculties, will prefer those who are showy and gay, to those who are sensible yet less beautiful; but with Ideality less than the intellectual and moral organs, will prefer those who are substantial and valuable more than showy; with Mirthfulness, Time, and Tune, will love dancing, lively society, etc.[61]

Any novelists active in the same years that copies of the *Self-Instructor* circulated—and the 1850s was a great decade for novels—might have taken heed of, if not inspiration from, this varied account of the vicissitudes of love and loving. Indeed, a writers' workshop today might find any of these categories or subcategories intriguing as the basis for exercises or plots. And this is only "Amativeness large." Similar paragraphs described the characters of those who possessed Amativeness very large, full, small, or very small, and so on to the next of the thirty-seven organs, Philoprogenitiveness (parental love), which, perhaps predictably, offers its own treasure trove of character. Thus an individual with Philoprogenitiveness large

> loves its own children, devotedly . . . with Continuity large, mourns long and incessantly over their loss; with Combativeness, Destructiveness, and Self-Esteem large, is kind, yet insists on being obeyed; with Self-Esteem and Destructiveness moderate, is familiar with, and liable to be ruled by, them; with Firmness only average, fails to manage them with a steady hand; with Cautiousness large, suffers extreme anxiety if they are sick or in danger; . . . with large excitability, Combativeness, and Destructiveness, and only average Firmness, will be, by turns, too indulgent, and over-provoked—will pet them one minute, and punish them the next; with larger Approbativeness and Ideality than intellect, will educate them more for show than usefulness—more fashionably than substantially—and dress them off in the extreme of fashion.[62]

Victorian parents from Jane Austen's fictional Mrs. Bennet to the real-life Edward Barrett Moulton-Barrett, the father of Elizabeth Barrett Browning, might well be encompassed by this list. Indeed, despite some distinctive period markers (e.g., mourning for the loss of children in an era of high infant mortality), such characterizations, though they sound comically ponderous, are not completely inappropriate for a modern-day society of helicopter parents, children's high fashion, and competitive applications to nursery school.

Walt Whitman's Phrenology Chart

One feature of Ross Lockridge's novel is that many of its turning points take place on July 4, which is also Johnny's birthday. The date, 1854, places this event in the heyday of American popular phrenology. One year later, Walt Whitman would have his own phrenology chart—which had been personally produced by Lorenzo Fowler after an examination of the poet's head in 1849—bound into the 1855 edition of *Leaves of Grass*.

> This man has a grand physical construction, and power to live to a good old age. He is undoubtedly descended from the soundest and hardiest stock. Size of head large. Leading traits of character appear to be Friendship, Sympathy, Sublimity and Self-Esteem, and markedly among his combinations the dangerous faults of Indolence, a tendency to the pleasure of Voluptuousness and Alimentiveness, and a certain reckless swing of animal will, too unmindful, probably, of the conviction of others.

Whitman elected to omit the last phrase when he reprinted the chart, so that it ended with "a tendency to the pleasure of Voluptuousness and Alimentiveness, and a certain swing of animal will"[63]—all terms that one might conceivably find in one of his poems.

"Voluptuousness and Alimentiveness" sounds so much more comprehensive and scientific than "desire and appetite." The vocabulary of phrenology, with its Latinate roots and Teutonic sonority, was, and remains, part of its appeal.

Who could resist the idea that he, or she, might have "Constructiveness very large," or "Veneration large," or "Inhabitiveness," the "love of home and country, a desire to have a permanent abode, an attachment to any place where one was born or has lived." "The feeling," notes Samuel R. Wells in *How to Read Character: A New Illustrated Hand-Book of Phrenology and Physiognomy for Students and Examiners*, "is particularly strong in the Swiss, and in the inhabitants of mountainous countries generally."[64] Never fear, though: if you lack sufficient Inhabitiveness you can cultivate this character trait by "planting trees, vines, and shrubs," or by reading the history of your country "and cherishing a just pride in its greatness and glory." If, on the other hand, you have an excess of Inhabitiveness, you may suffer from "a terrible feeling of home-sickness" when you are absent from your home or country. But here, too, a remedy is at hand. It is possible to ameliorate this "excessive local attachment" by "going frequently abroad, reading books of travel, and becoming interested in foreign countries."

Inhabitiveness, as it may not surprise the modern reader to learn, was a trait especially to be found in women, as are Adhesiveness, Philoprogenitiveness (love of offspring), Benevolence, and Veneration, whereas men had the advantage in Combativeness, Firmness, and Self-Esteem. Amativeness "nearly doubles in size" for males between the ages of ten and twenty. It could be cultivated by trying "to be as agreeable as possible to those persons of the other sex with whom he or she is brought into contact." Excessive Amativeness was a problem, and one often caused by "a too stimulating diet; liquors, wines, tea, coffee, and tobacco." It was not to be attributed, necessarily, to the size of the organ (and by "organ" here is meant the specific region of the brain and skull, in the cerebellum, at the "base of the back-head," not the genitals). As for Alimentiveness, that element of character so prominent in Walt Whitman's phrenological chart, it indicated (just as it seems it should) an interest in food. Alimentiveness very large meant gormandizing, living to eat rather than eating to live. Bibativeness, located right nearby (just over the ear), was a fondness for drinking not only liquor but also water, and for bathing and swimming; someone with average or moderate Bibativeness might be "rather averse to bathing; dislike swimming, sailing, etc., and shrink from a sea voyage as something fearful."[65]

One more point on these "organs," or aspects of character, is worth underscoring, and that is that even traits that might sound negative to modern ears were regarded, in the right proportions and in the right social context, as potentially beneficial. Thus Acquisitiveness, Secretiveness, and Destruction all had their strong positive valences (the first could indicate industriousness; the second, discretion; the third, a manifestation of "great energy and executive power," as well as a nonsqueamishness appropriate to a surgeon; excesses in any could be restrained or counterbalanced by one or more other organs).[66] Phrenology was, or became, a reformist movement determined to bring about social improvement.

It is not an accident that many of the most prominent phrenological practitioners, from Spurzheim to the Fowlers to George Combe, paid visits to prisons, insane asylums, and schools, often astounding the wardens with their insights about the characters of various inmates, frequently by merely looking at them, sometimes by examining their heads. Like the (more optimistic) reading of Johnny Shawnessy's head in *Raintree County*, these institutional readings seemed infallibly to identify thieves, forgers, clever calculators—and the occasional ringer, a warden or wardress dressed as a prisoner to test the powers of the investigator. Thus the biographer of Johann Gaspar Spurzheim reported on the "magical" and "instantaneous" way in which Spurzheim "seized the peculiarity of [the] characters" of inmates in the town jail at Hull in 1827. Here is only one of several examples given:

> [an] individual, whom a worthy magistrate, that accompanied us, spoke of as one whose look and manner would deceive any body, but that he was a notorious thief! Dr. S. found him very large in imitation, secretiveness, firmness and self-esteem. The latter combination induced him to make the remark, that this person would always be a leader, such individuals would never be subordinate; and this proved to be the fact. He had always been the *head* man in all schemes of plunder; and as a sheep-stealer he was notorious.[67]

In the same town's Charity Hall, he encountered a man with "the organ of 'marvelousness' very large," who, he learned, was constantly reading his Bible, and two young boys with very large organs of combativeness, firmness, and destructiveness, who turned out, when asked, to aspire to the profession of butcher.[68]

Speaking in Tongues: The Languages of Phrenology

Phrenologists believed that human beings had one or a combination of two of the three temperaments—Mental, Motive, or Vital—which were clearly related to the classical four humors. Gall's theory further held that human character and intellect were the result of physiological and anatomical factors, specific areas of the brain that he called "organs." He identified twenty-seven of them, and gave each a number and a name: Number 1, *Zengunstrieb*, the instinct of generation; Number 2, *Jungenliebe*, *Kinderliebe*, the love of offspring; Number 3, *Anhänglichkeit*, friendship, attachment; Number 4, *Muth*, *Raufsinn*, courage, self-defense; Number 5, *Würgsinn*, murder, the wish to destroy. And twenty-two more, equally sonorous in German and in English.[69]

Perhaps understandably, commentators have been particularly intrigued by the organ called "murder," a designation that later theorists and practitioners were at pains to disavow. Gall, it is said, accepted the possibility of evil, and thought that most men needed to be governed. A less ominous-sounding counterpart from the *American Phrenological Journal*, though titled "Destructiveness," was described more generally as an organ of self-preservation: "It imparts the energy and executiveness necessary to enable us to overcome obstacles and remove or crush whatever is inimical to our welfare; to tunnel mountains, fell trees, blast out rocks, and face the storm. It impels us to destroy in order not to be ourselves destroyed; to endure and to inflict pain, when necessary, as in a surgical operation; to kill the animals necessary for our subsistence, and even to take human life in defense of our own lives, our liberties, or our country's safety."[70]

Gall was an Austrian, and the names he gave to the organs were, as we've seen, German names. His early collaborator and eventual successor, Spurzheim, was also a native German speaker, who was born in Germany and then came to study with Gall in Vienna. Gall settled in Paris after lecturing for five years in Germany, Switzerland, and the Netherlands, but Spurzheim, who collaborated with Gall on a multivolume study of the anatomy and physiology of the nervous system, ultimately went his own way, altering some of Gall's concepts. He taught himself English in six months, and immediately departed for a lecture tour of Great Britain. It was Spurzheim who invented the word "phrenology," literally the "science" [or "knowledge"] of "mind," a term Gall never accepted, preferring his own, more localized term, "craniology." And it was Spurzheim who gave the organs, which he now numbered thirty-seven, the deliciously multisyllabic and "Teutonic" names by which they became known to practitioners and popular audiences in Scotland, England, and the United States.

I emphasize this point because I think that it is not only the idea of phrenological practice that appealed to people but also the specific names of the "organs": Alimentiveness, Philoprogenitiveness, Approbativeness, Marvelousness, Adhesiveness. Who would not like to be told that they had Amativeness very large, or that a neighbor had very large Secretiveness with large Acquisitiveness and only small Benevolence? And if "Alimentiveness" today does not sound fully medical, it certainly sounds, and surely would have sounded, more formidable and authoritative, more like a "faculty" or an "organ" or a "propensity," than the more biblical "gluttony" or the more ordinary "taste [or appetite] for food."

Before we dismiss these phrenological terms and categories as comical or forced, it might be useful to look at some of the current psychological classifications and subclassifications in the *DSM*, the Big Five Factor Personality model, or other commonly used personality concepts, such as "need for achievement, internal locus of control, innovativeness and self-efficacy,"[71] which might be compared to phrenology's overarching categories of "Propensities" and "Moral Sentiments," or at handbooks of literary, aesthetic, or philosophical terms, which might be compared to its list of "Intellectual Faculties." Allowing for some differences in style between the nineteenth century and the twenty-first, there are a number of odd similarities.

Some of Wells's terminology may strike modern readers as familiar from more recent classifications. For example, "selfish," in what he calls the "Selfish Group," refers to the preservation of life, the "animal wants," personal defense and the accumulation and protection of property, and may remind modern readers of the evolutionary biologist Richard Dawkins's 1976 coinage "the selfish gene."[72] (The selfish propensities—Vitativeness, Combativeness, Destructiveness, Alimentiveness, Acquisitiveness, and Secretiveness—all sound vaguely sinister, but might better be regarded as the obverse of E. O. Wilson's "interested altruism":[73] self-preservational traits that can, when not abused, be turned to productive use. In the case of the list above, the positive versions of these apparently negative organs would be love of life, courage, executive force, appetite, accumulation, and discretion.)

The so-called Literary Group involved memory and the ability to communicate ideas and feelings through written or spoken words. The "Semi-Intellectual Group" (one of my favorite of these designations) encompassed self-improvement and the love and production of what is beautiful. Its components included "Ideality" (refinement; love of beauty, taste, and purity), Imitation (copying; mimicry; the propensity for acting), Sublimity, Mirthfulness, and "Human Nature," glossed by Wells as "perception of character and motives."

Phrenological practitioners tied their categories both to literature and to the zeitgeist. Persons who had "large Secretiveness," for example, buttoned up their coats to the chin, or wore tight cravats, or, if they were women, wore dresses fitting high up on the neck, "admirably exemplified in our likeness of Constance Emily Kent, the murderess." A quotation from Sir Walter Scott reinforced this impression ("For evil seemed that old man's eye / Dark and designing, fierce yet shy. / Still he avoided forward look"). On the other hand, those who are deficient in Secretiveness are "characterized by a lack of tact, great bluntness of manner," and a tendency to blurt out their thoughts. They "seldom suspect any hidden purpose," and here the author cites Iago on Othello: "The Moor is of a free and open nature, / That thinks men honest that but seem to be so."[74]

Likewise, the organ of Approbativeness "gives regard for character, desire to excel and be esteemed, love of praise, ambition, affability and politeness," but "no faculty is more prone to excess." To restrain it, one must "Have less fear of 'Mrs. Grundy,'" the conventional figure of priggish social disapproval. "The French are remarkable for large development of this organ," says Wells's *Handbook* briskly, "while the English are more noted for Self-Esteem."[75]

Citing illustrative examples of persons deficient in Benevolence, such as Caligula, Nero, Catherine de' Medici, Danton, Robespierre, and various "tribes of men remarkable for cruelty," Wells informs the reader that "murderers generally have the forehead 'villainously low'" (such quotations, or near quotations, of Shakespeare and other English literary classics are frequently deployed). Lofty foreheads, indicating persons distinguished for their benevolent feelings, were observable on Trajan, Marcus Aurelius, Henri IV, Oberlin, and Henry Ward Beecher.[76] (Beecher, a passionate proponent of phrenology, declared that it was central to his understanding of his ministry, and once said that the best preparation for Christian conduct was "a practical knowledge of the human mind as is given by phrenology."[77]) Those with large organs of Individuality (the facility for observation) included the writers Shakespeare, Sheridan, and Walter Scott. "It is not so large in the Germans as Causality; it is larger in the English, and still larger in the French and Americans," and could be cultivated by the study of "natural history" or (it was almost needless to say) of "Phrenology and Physiology."[78]

Individuals with large Constructiveness (mechanical ingenuity) who were insufficiently guided by the intellectual faculties were prone to "great waste of time and labor in attempts to invent perpetual motions or other impossible machines." Moreover, if they happened to have "deficient Conscientiousness," they might employ themselves in "making counterfeit money, false keys, and other dishonest contrivances."[79]

The language of phrenology is part of its own distinctive character. When a proponent of a rival (and derivative) American system called "characterology" sought a century later to distinguish his theory from that of its predecessor, he zeroed in on the matter of terminology. "The titles of the phrenological organs of the Gallian System form a strange vocabulary, difficult to remember and requiring much time to comprehend. Polysyllabic terms, such as philoprogenitiveness, alimentiveness, individuality, vitativeness, gregariousness, and the like, are a hindrance rather than an assistance to a science which should be simply worded and clearly stated in order to be of practical utility."[80] But he was wrong. It was in part the exoticism and strangeness of the terms that helped enhance the popular belief that phrenology was a kind of science. And at the same time, their very oddity appealed to imaginative writers.

Poe and Melville

Edgar Allan Poe became a fan of the new science in the 1830s, reviewing enthusiastically Mrs. L. Miles's *Phrenology and the Moral Influence of Phrenology: Arranged for General Study and the Purposes of Education* (1835). "Phrenology is no longer to be laughed at. It is no longer laughed at by men of common understanding. It has assumed the majesty of a science, and, as a science ranks among the most important which can engage the attention of thinking beings."[81] Throughout his life, he remained intrigued by phrenology, using its terms to analyze poetry and to mark individual characters.

Sometimes the references read today as wry, though they are, in context, deeply knowledgeable. Thus, for example, the narrator of "The Imp of the Perverse" remarks, "The phrenologists have failed to make room for a propensity which . . . has been equally overlooked by all the moralists who have preceded them." This propensity, neglected by "the Spurzheimites," is *perverseness*, a faculty that, he insists, is not to be confused with "the *combativeness* of phrenology." Combativeness is a "safeguard against injury," related to self-defense. But *perverseness* is willful: its manifestations might include "tantalis[ing] a listener by circumlocution"; deliberately delaying the performance of a task until it is too late; standing on the edge of a precipice and meditating a plunge. "We perpetrate them because we feel that we should *not*."[82] As a plausible addition to the phrenological repertoire, *perverseness* has its distinct appeal, even though—or because—the speaker ultimately reveals himself to be a murderer.

Though he was not a zealous convert like Poe, Herman Melville, too, saw the possibilities raised by phrenology's curious, popular, and sometimes risible terms. When Ishmael undertakes a phrenological reading of the head of the whale in *Moby-Dick*, we can hear something of Melville's delight in both deploying and sending up a professional and vocational vocabulary. The size of the sperm whale's skull is delusive, being as it is filled with sperm, says Ishmael, so that, if it were scaled down and placed among the skulls of human beings, "remarking the depressions on one side of its summit, in phrenological phrase you would say—This man had no self-esteem, and no veneration." But if instead, convinced by Ishmael's newly minted "spinal branch of phrenology," you were to consider the spine as an extension of the cerebellum ("For I believe that much of a man's character will be found betokened in his backbone"), then the whale's hump, rising over one of the larger vertebrae, would "from its relative situation" be identifiable as "the organ of firmness or indomitableness in the sperm whale."[83]

Melville was speaking to, and writing for, a readership captivated by terms and terminology (as his "Cetology" section makes clear). Ishmael's self-instruction in phrenology was the perhaps inevitable consequence of a belief in character that could be deduced from observation and from physical signs; the "character" of the whale is a crucial element in the novel. But none of the character language about the hump of the whale as an organ of "indomitableness" would make sense—or be funny—if contemporary readers had not been immersed in the neologisms of Gall, Spurzheim, and their followers.

The Theater of Phrenology

So influential had phrenology become by the second half of the nineteenth century that major figures of the past were assessed by phrenological readings of their images. Thus, the journalist and phrenologist E. T. Craig, the author of *Shakespeare's Portraits Phrenologically Considered*, deplored the appearance of the bust of Shakespeare that marks the poet's burial place in Holy Trinity Church, Stratford-upon-Avon. Craig, who claimed to have examined "many thousands of heads," was not convinced that this "stout unintellectual figure" could be a true likeness. The head was broadest at its base, evidence of "destructiveness, secretiveness, alimentiveness, and acquisitiveness," while "ideality and wit are scarcely indicated." Much more appealing was the familiar Droeshout engraving in the First Folio, in which "his large benevolence, veneration, and ideality, and his small destructiveness and acquisitiveness," suggested Shakespeare's "control over his feelings and generous sympathy with others."[84] Other portrait images offered yet more phrenological clues, some consistent, some contradictory.

Whatever the measure of Shakespeare's head, however, there was no question about the popularity of his dramatic characters with phrenological interpreters.

George Combe was a passionate theatergoer who knew and admired the great eighteenth-century actress Sarah Siddons, and, after her death, married her youngest daughter, Cecilia. In his view, as David Stack notes, the theater and phrenology were analogous and related in the ways in which they depicted human nature.[85] Manifestly, the study of "character," both dramatic and moral, was at the center of this happy connection.

In his *System of Phrenology*, Combe comments under the heading of "Imitation": "This organ contributes to render a poet or author dramatic, such as Shakespeare, Corneille, Moliere, Voltaire, &c. It is large in the portraits of Shakespeare, and also in the bust of Sir Walter Scott, whose productions are strongly characterized by their dramatic scenes."[86]

Actors succeed or fail, says Combe, depending upon which of their organs are fully or imperfectly developed in the brain. But: "It does not follow, however, from these principles that an actor, in his personal conduct, must necessarily resemble most closely those characters which he represents to the best advantage. To enable an individual to succeed eminently in acting *Shylock*, for example, *Firmness*, *Acquisitiveness* and *Destructiveness* are reckoned indispensable; but it is not necessary, merely because *Shylock* is represented as deficient in Benevolence, Justice, Veneration, and Love of Approbation, that the actor also should be so."[87] On the other hand, "an individual possessing little *Combativeness* and *Destructiveness*" could not "represent with just effect the fiery *Coriolanus*."[88]

Perhaps because of Combe's interest, or perhaps because others in the world of phrenology were interested in the connection between dramatic character and human character, *The Phrenological Journal and Miscellany* announced in an early issue its "intention occasionally to give examples of this mode of applying the science, by analyzing a few of the characters which occur in the writings of some of our best dramatists and novelists; and we trust we shall be able to shew, that these writers who, in their delineation of character, have shewn the deepest and most accurate knowledge of human nature, are throughout the most strictly phrenological."[89] Inevitably, perhaps, the first nod went to Shakespeare.

The phrenological accounts of Othello and Macbeth are about what you might expect—"Self-esteem is the prevailing feature of [Othello's] character; being combined, however, with large Conscientiousness and Love of Approbation," together with "large Combativeness and Destructiveness." But his love for Desdemona also demonstrates "the power of his Amativeness and Adhesiveness."[90] Macbeth, assessed phrenologically, seems to share some of these same characteristics, especially Self-Esteem, Love of Approbation, and Conscientiousness,[91] raising the question whether such characteristics are fairly standard for (a) men of action, and/or (b) Shakespeare's tragic protagonists.

These are competent and effective readings of the plays, full of quotations from the text followed by analyses of them. (Lady Macbeth's phrase "the milk of human kindness" is described as "a most expressive term for *benevolence*."[92]) The analyses make use of terms from phrenology but not to the exclusion of other language. Their goal is to show that phrenology is a system that accurately describes human nature, and Shakespeare's characters are selected as test cases for two reasons: "First, Because the characters of that incomparable master are invariably drawn with such a force and breadth, that it is impossible to mistake the lines by which they are pourtrayed; and, secondly, Because it is admitted, on all hands, that he possessed a knowledge of human nature the most profound and accurate of any man who ever write, insomuch that it has been often observed, that studying Shakespeare is studying nature."[93]

However, when *The Phrenological Journal* turns its attention to the character of Iago, a proven minefield for psychological assessment, the author uses a more inventive mode, which might be described as an experiment, a test, or a dirty trick, depending upon one's point of view. In any case, it makes for rather delicious reading. "A phrenologist of this city, on the suggestion of a friend, studied and analyzed the character of Iago as drawn by Shakespeare, and reduced it to what he conceived to be its phrenological elements." The undertaking was made possible by the skill with which the playwright has delineated him. Thus "Secretiveness is so powerfully manifested, that the organ, if the individual had existed, must have been large; Conscientiousness is so feebly shewn, that its organ must, on such a supposition, have been small, and so on with others." Notice "if the individual had existed"—to this point the clear distinction is maintained between a fictional dramatic character and an actual living person. The phrenologist produced the standard chart of (in this case) thirty-two organs, from number 1, "Amativeness, large," through 31 and 32, "Causality, very large," and "Wit, full." He then handed it to a second phrenologist, who had no idea that the individual there described was fictitious, and asked him to "write out his opinion of the talents and dispositions" that the chart indicated. At this point, the article becomes a dramatic dialogue:

> *2d Phren.* This is a fearful combination; but you have not told me in what sphere of life he moves.
> *1st Phren.* He is an officer in the army, of inferior rank . . .
> *2d Phren.* Is he educated?
> *1st Phren.* Not much.
> *2d Phren.* What is his age?
> *1st Phren.* About 40.
> *2d Phren.* What is the size of his head? The force of his character depends on this.
> *1st Phren.* It is an average size.

A third phrenologist, in on the joke, is then consulted by phrenologist number 2:

> *2d Phren.* Do you know any thing about the individual? Shall I be safe to write what I think of such a wretch?
> *3d Phren.* I know him as well as Mr.—— (the 1st Phren.); you are perfectly safe, and may freely write your ideas without fear of his resentment.

On the next day, the second phrenologist called on the first, and delivered in writing a long account, which began with a kind of prologue:

> I can hardly imagine a case, where a firm belief in the truths of phrenology would be productive of more beneficial consequences than in the present; for this is, without exception, the most unfavourable development I ever saw. Phrenology is eminently *practical*, and the present sketch is attempted not so much with a view to the illustration of the science, as from a real desire that it may be useful to the individual who is the subject of it, by laying open to him the hidden springs of his actions and conduct. He must, therefore, be prepared to hear the TRUTH, and with "all plainness of speech."

Among the highlights of his report on the unknown subject (Iago) were:

- "Selfishness will here reign with a predominating sway.—Totally indifferent to the rights and feelings of others, he will pursue his own selfish ends and gratifications without once being turned aside by the calls of benevolence, justice, or friendship.
- "He will utterly despise and condemn those who act from noble and disinterested motives. It will indeed be extremely difficult for him to conceive that this is possible, and hence he will be prone to regard them as hypocrites; but if satisfied that this is not the case, he will assuredly turn round and esteem them fools and blockheads. He is not one of those who will seek reputation at the cannon's mouth . . .
- "He would take intense delight in witnessing the destruction of his foes . . .
- "He will be remarkably distinguished by a talent for humour, or, I should rather say, satire, which will be characterized by its being biting, severe, and sarcastic.
- "He will be an attentive observer of every thing that is passing around him. He will have an excellent memory for facts and occurrences . . .
- "The large endowment of Cautiousness and of the Intellect are invaluable in such a character."

The phrenologist further notes that the subject's "*Self-Esteem*, *Combativeness*, and *Destructiveness*" will "be powerfully aided by *Language*, *Wit*, and *Secretiveness*."

Concluding his report, the article's author, noting that "every reader may find amusement" in the correspondence between the phrenologist's assessment of the unknown (and unmet) subject and Shakespeare's Iago, uses the anecdote to affirm the validity of "this application of the science."

> There is first an analysis of the character into its elements by one phrenologist; then these are handed to another, quite uninformed as to their source, and he, by synthesis, produces a portrait which turns out to be a fac simile of the original. To a reflecting mind, this constitutes striking proof that we do not juggle with the combinations, but that phrenologists have made decided progress in ascertaining philosophically their effects in nature.[94]

As a "blind" experiment, this—if it's a true story—has its merits. As a story, whether true or not, it has its distinct charms, not the least of which is the invention of the characters of the three phrenologists and their delightfully distraught dialogue. I wouldn't call it a shaggy-phrenologist joke, exactly ("Three phrenologists went to the theater . . ."), but as a combined tribute to phrenology and to Shakespeare, it's very appealing. At least to me.

"Good at Scheming": An Inventor's Take on Practical Character

The American inventor Hamilton McCormick's *Characterology* of 1920, pointedly subtitled *An Exact Science*, is a late entry into the character sweepstakes, appearing after Freud, who is nowhere mentioned in McCormick's text. Instead, he positions his "exact science" in a chart that traces it from anthropology and ethnology through what he calls "reconstructed phrenology," with ancillary contributions from "revised physiognomy" and "amplified pathognomy" (the study of the passions or emotions, especially from facial expressions).

Characterology is full of detailed assertions about the nose, the cheeks, the jaws, the chin, and various types of heads (the "cogitative nose . . . broad throughout and blunt at the tip, [is] also known as 'the philosopher's nose' and is exemplified in Socrates, Darwin and Alfred Russel Wallace"[95]; black hair "suggests Southern descent, the phlegmatic temperament, passive affection, memorizing power and musical ability; it also signifies religious tendencies, love of brilliant colours, judgment of flavours, lethargy, lack of initiative, a tendency to follow rather than to lead, and to accept the views of others but not to originate"[96]).

It's tempting to think of these assertions as prejudices (literally, prejudgments), which, indeed, they are, and also as hopelessly old-fashioned, which they are not. The universalism of some of these claims has resurfaced in the late twentieth and twenty-first centuries as part of some systems of evolutionary psychology. McCormick's two-page discussion of the special qualities of "full lips," for example ("full lips are affectionate, benevolent, trusting and appreciative. They also imply love of poetry, music and art . . . good nature, a kindly disposition, generosity, appreciation of high living," etc.[97]), might be compared to the evolutionary psychologist David Buss's claim that "full lips" are one of a set of universal criteria of what are called "mate preferences" or "strategies of human mating."[98]

Potentially of more interest in McCormick's scheme is his explicit linkage of character traits to practical matters, such as the education of children, the use of agents and salesmen in judging their customers, the hiring of domestic servants, the casting of parts by theatrical managers, the selection of officers for military and naval institutions, the pursuit of criminals by detectives, and the choice of a marriage partner.[99] In general, the supposed beneficiaries of these principles—who also include teachers, businessmen, physicians, and "alienists" (i.e., psychiatrists)—are a cross section of middle- and upper-middle-class life.

In his critique of phrenology, McCormick had called out not only its "polysyllabic vocabulary" and "the unsatisfactory use of the term 'organ'" but also "the manipulation of the cranium by the hands," a process he considered "impracticable and doomed to failure," since "a delineator cannot handle the heads of more than one percent of the individuals whom he wishes to diagnose." (As we've seen, the Fowlers and Samuel Wells dealt with this problem directly—and lucratively—by both arranging for long-distance readings via daguerreotype, and marketing, at an attractively low price, the handbooks for "phrenological self-instructors.")

McCormick also thought the manipulation of the head was "a disagreeable process for both analyst and subject."[100] That this was certainly not universally the case is attested to, not only by the hundreds of clients who thronged to the Fowlers' place of business on Nassau Street but also by the anecdote, related by Franz Joseph Gall and cited by Combe, of how Gall manipulated the seat of amativeness in a young widow "of irreproachable character" so as to bring her to orgasm.[101]

McCormick's concluding essay on "Character" crosses over from the descriptive to the evaluative, asserting that "Character is based upon principle," that "a man of character pursues the right, the just and the true," and that "men of character associate with men of character."[102] In these declarations—recall that the book was published in 1920—we can hear some echoes, however popularized, of the voices of Galton and Darwin, especially since the next of McCormick's "characterological essays" is on "Genius." But it is one other observation, deliberately but briefly set out, that points toward the next set of debates about the elusive thing called "character." "Character," declares McCormick, "should not be confounded with personality. The former refers to the disposition of an individual and to the traits which he possesses, while the latter embraces the entire man both physically and mentally."[103]

This question of character and personality would be taken up again by Gordon Allport in his classic work of 1937, *Personality: A Psychological Interpretation.* For Allport, "characterology," which had been for Hamilton McCormick the name of a highly complicated system, was merely a "convenient" general term for "the science of the characteristics of men,"[104] or for "all the diverse schemes advanced in the past to account for, or to depict, forms of human individuality."[105] Character in Allport's view was an ethical concept, and therefore of no use to the psychologist. "*Character is personality evaluated, and personality is character devaluated*," he wrote, emphasizing his rhetorical flourish with italics, and continuing directly, "Since character is an unnecessary concept for psychology, the term will not appear again in this volume, excepting in quotations from other writers, or in a clear historical context."[106] *Sic transit gloria verborum.*

Requiem for a System

What happened to phrenology? Did it, like other so-called pseudosciences, disappear without a trace?

For a long time, George Combe's *Constitution of Man* was enormously popular. Its ready availability and inexpensive price were made possible in part by a bequest from W. R. Henderson, who left the following instruction in his will: "The whole residue of my means and estate shall . . . be applied for the advancement and diffusion of the science of Phrenology."[107]

Henderson's bequest underwrote several cheap editions, as well as a more elegant version for a higher-paying clientele, through the time of George Combe's death in 1858. But by 1893, when another edition was published, the intellectual climate had changed. Both Henderson and Combe had regarded *The Constitution of Man*'s focus on phrenology to be central to an understanding of human nature, and therefore essential to its argument. At the end of the century, though, this phrenological argument had become a liability.

"The system of Phrenology which the author incorporated with his ethical teaching," wrote the editor of the 1893 volume, "has been to many readers a hindrance rather than a help." Accordingly, "in this popular version of the Work," the editor "retained only so much of that system, and of its terminology, as seemed to be warranted by the estimate of its scope and utility now adopted by men of science."[108] The book was much abbreviated. The conclusion, which in the sixth edition had promised to answer the question "What is the practical use of

Phrenology, even supposing it to be true?" and went on to discuss its use with reference to politics, legislation, education, morals and religion, now began with politics and legislation, removing all reference to phrenology. And whereas, on the last page of the sixth edition, the "animal propensities" of mankind were seen to be exacerbated by social institutions, so that Acquisitiveness was "fostered by our arrangements for accumulating wealth," and "Combativeness and Destructiveness by our warlike professions,"[109] these sentences are excised from the edition of 1893. Essentially, and despite the fervor of both Combe and the "Henderson Bequest," phrenology, which Combe had called in earlier prefaces "the basis of this work,"[110] had been made to disappear. Although it lingered on in some forms into the twentieth century, it was increasingly reclassified as a pseudoscience, the term "phrenology" itself often linked with astrology, palmistry, and other fairground traps for the unwary.

Phrenology's fall had been exacerbated by its popularity. What had once earned the admiration of eminent scholars, politicians, and a Supreme Court justice was now a DIY system of feeling "bumps" on the head. And its demise was hastened by racial comments, which, though common to too many emergent "sciences" at the end of the century, were sometimes singled out as phrenology's besetting sin.

Off the Menu

In 2017, the chef Tom Colicchio, who had named a New York City restaurant Fowler & Wells after the publishing company and scientific institute that had once occupied the same site, changed his restaurant's name when his attention was called to phrenological comments by Orson Fowler about people of African descent.[111]

That such racial opinions were shared by some prominent scientists and eugenicists of the time does not make them less offensive, and Colicchio's decision to change the restaurant's name was widely commended. He told a reporter that he knew little about phrenology prior to choosing the restaurant's name; the article explained to readers that phrenology was "a popular 19th-century belief that the shape of one's skull revealed characteristics like mental aptitude and personality."

Though this is true, or true enough, it ignores the huge self-help side of popular phrenology, the hope—shared by its founders, popularizers, and proponents—that character could be developed and improved through self-instruction. In their preface, Fowler and his coauthors had written ardently of "this land of plenty and equal rights, conscious of its liberty to exercise any and all of its powers," in which "the human mind marches unfettered and free."[112] If these words, written in 1836, read to us ironically today in view of the history and legacy of slavery, it's nonetheless worth noting that the American phrenologists thought of themselves as liberals, whose work would enable their countrymen, regardless of income or education, to discover and develop their "own character and talents" for the betterment of themselves and the nation.

The philosophical and self-improvement aspects of the term, once well respected, have been obscured and occluded by subsequent popularization. The use of "phrenology" as if it were the simple equivalent of quackery ignores important aspects of its history, and its complicated connection with the nineteenth century's obsession with character. Phrenology today may be critically, contemptuously, or humorously regarded in some quarters, but several of its practices remain in use—and indeed, in vogue—under other names. Dozens of Web sites feature lists of "character traits" for the edification of browsers. What also remains in the popular imagination is the deliciously Latinate language of phrenology's key terms—and, above all, the familiar image of the phrenology bust, readily available in ceramic reproduction, marked with "the division of the Organs," from the Literary, Observing, and Knowing faculties in the forehead to Love of Sex, Amativeness, and Reproductive Love at the base of the skull.

"A Scientific Game-Changer"

What goes around comes around, in science as in philosophy and politics. Already, in fact, the reputation of phrenology—if not the practice—is, in a way, on the rebound. Having been the go-to target for know-nothing popular science for a hundred years, it is now being cautiously cited and methodologically explored.

Howard Gardner began his 1983 book, *Frames of Mind: The Theory of Multiple Intelligences*, with a generous rehabilitation of some of phrenology's key ideas, pushing back on its wholesale dismissal. Gall, he said, was "among the first modern scientists to stress that different parts of the brain mediate different functions." Even more germane to Gardner's own argument, Gall proposed "this fascinating claim: there do not exist general mental powers, such as perception, memory, and attention; but, rather, there exist different forms of perception, memory, and the like for *each* of the several different intellectual faculties, such as language, music, or vision."

For Gardner, the idea, "though seldom taken seriously throughout most of the history of psychology," was "highly suggestive," and, he thought, "may well be correct."[113] His theory of multiple intelligences proposed that there were at least eight, and perhaps a ninth, kind of intelligence: visual-spatial, linguistic-verbal, interpersonal, intrapersonal, logical-mathematical, musical, bodily-kinesthetic, naturalistic, and perhaps also existential intelligence. Each had specific strengths, characteristics, and career aptitudes. A person with visual-spatial intelligence might head for a career as an artist, an engineer, or an architect. Someone with linguistic-verbal intelligence could aim to be a writer, journalist, or lawyer. And so on. Critics of Gardner's theory have argued that these categories are closer to talents and personality traits than varieties of "intelligence," but the theory was and remains popular in the field of education, and is often adapted for classroom teaching.

The potential contributions of phrenology to modern neuroscience have also attracted attention. Stephen Jay Gould had written in *The Mismeasure of Man* that even if the "cranial bumps" were "nonsense," the idea of "cortical localization of highly specific mental processing is a reality of ever-increasing fascination in modern neurological research."[114] Twenty-first-century researchers have perceived the connection, and been willing to say so (a sign in itself of the surprising revival of interest in this long-maligned subject). The development of functional magnetic resonance imaging had provided a new way of looking at the operations of the brain. "Imagine that fMRI had been invented in the 1860s rather than the 1990s," proposed the psychologist and neuroscientist Russell Poldrack in a useful counterfactual:

> Instead of being based on modern cognitive psychology, neuroimaging would instead be based on the faculty psychology of Thomas Reid and Dugald Stewart, which provided the mental "faculties" that Gall and the phrenologists attempted to map onto the brain. Researchers would have presumably have jumped from phrenology to fMRI . . . [and] they almost certainly would have found regions in which activity was correlated with the strength of each faculty across subjects.[115]

Poldrack included a chart mapping some of Gall's phrenological (or craniological) categories onto the brain. The faculty Gall called the "impulse to propagation" was paired with its modern neuroimaging equivalent, the "viewing of romantic lover vs. other individuals," and tied to the associated brain region of the basal ganglia. Gall's "friendly attachment or fidelity" became the modern "viewing friend vs. stranger," and was associated with the right temporoparietal cortex. "Poetic talent," translated, rather unpoetically, into the "generation of creative vs. uncreative narrative," was linked to the "right medial frontal cortex"; "ambition and vanity," modernized into "activation for judgment about self vs. others," to the "medial prefrontal cortex"; and the famous "sense of locality," often called in lay terms a "bump of locality," found its neuroimaging equivalent in "scenes vs. nonscenes," and its associated region in the "parahippocampal cortex."[116]

"When you start to think about it, phrenology wasn't such a bad idea," wrote Michael Anderson in *After Phrenology: Neural Reuse and the Interactive Brain* (2014), though he cautioned against "any specific functional attribution to a particular structure of the brain," suggesting instead a dynamic, interactive theory of brain networking. Nonetheless, Anderson maintained that "contemporary neuroscience must be seen as deeply continuous with phrenology." An earlier study by William Uttal, *The New Phrenology* (2001), invoked the comparison in order to critique it; the book's subtitle was *The Limits of Localizing Cognitive Processes in the Brain*.[117] The analogy was almost inevitable, whatever the ultimate decision on its relevance. In 2018, a group of Oxford researchers, who had begun their inquiry into phrenology in "a spirit of scientific fun," nevertheless noted that it was "among one of the earlier disciplines to recognize that different parts of the brain have different functions." When they checked, they found that current brain-imaging databases corresponded, in some instances "very closely," to phrenology's list of personality factors: "Phrenology's 'eventuality' (aptness to receive an education)" mapped with "the modern version, 'age completed full time education,'" while "'tune' (sense for sounds, musical talent) in phrenology matched with 'musical profession.'" In fact, these initially skeptical researchers discovered, these days "phrenology is largely considered as a scientific game-changer, with the roots of many modern scientific, but also pseudoscientific disciplines, following in its wake."[118]

In 1890, at the end of the long nineteenth-century boom in phrenology, William James had offered a retrospective assessment. "There seems no doubt," he wrote, "that Phrenology, however little it satisfy our scientific curiosity about the functions of different portions of the brain, may still be, in the hands of intelligent practitioners, a useful help in the art of reading character."[119] As sensible as this opinion may have seemed at the time, current researchers (appropriately enough for phrenology) have turned it on its head.

Scientists curious about the functions of the brain now cite William James as an intuitive forerunner to their investigations. As we will see when we come to the question of "seeing" character, the use of fMRIs, PET scans, and other photographic techniques to find out more about language, thought, emotion, and perception is among the most highly regarded and well-funded scientific inquiries. But the word "character" itself, so central to the interests of nineteenth-century psychologists, has quietly disappeared from scientific view.

Why is it that "character" does not appear in recent scientific assessments of the brain? Perhaps it is seen as either too fuzzy or too judgmental to function in a discipline that aims at objective analysis. Other, preferred terms, such as "personality" and "personality factors," having been quantified and enumerated, are regularly acknowledged. "Do Brain Regions Have Personalities of Their Own?" is the title of one of the chapters in Anderson's *After Phrenology*. At the same time, "character," once the most significant goal of phrenological inquiry, goes conspicuously unmentioned by neuroscientists and psychologists today.

5

NAMING IT

Psychoanalysis, Psychology, and the Emergence of "Personality"

What we describe as our "character" is based on the memory-traces of our impressions; and, moreover, the impressions which have had the greatest effect on us—those of our earliest youth—are precisely the ones which scarcely ever become conscious.

—SIGMUND FREUD, *THE INTERPRETATION OF DREAMS*

A personality may create circumstances, as Lindbergh created good will between the United States and Mexico. Events may create a personality, as the Cuban War created the political figure of Roosevelt. It is often difficult to say which creates the other. Once a public figure has decided which ends he wishes to achieve, he must regard himself objectively and present an outward picture of himself which is consistent with his real character and his aims.

—EDWARD L. BERNAYS, *PROPAGANDA*

Character is personality evaluated, and personality is character devaluated.

—GORDON W. ALLPORT, *PERSONALITY: A PSYCHOLOGICAL INTERPRETATION*

The typical Hollywood film, says Jim Cullen, a historian of popular culture, exemplifies the contrast between "an older American Dream rooted in character, and its replacement, a Dream rooted in personality."[1] Character, in this account, means ethics, values, and hard work: virtue, industry, and ambition. Personality means almost the opposite: celebrity, fame, likability, a talent for publicity and conspicuous consumption. Character is enduring; personality is superficial. But it was not always thus. Nor, indeed, is it so for some personality psychologists and medical professionals today, for whom personality, not character, marks out the boundaries and the fluctuations of human behavior.

In the early years of the twentieth century—about the same time that Douglas Fairbanks and Mary Pickford were creating the Hollywood version of the American Dream—a certain dissatisfaction with "character" had set in among psychologists and others who regarded it as too closely tied to moral and ethical judgment. "Personality" became the preferred term in psychology departments, though the ethical sense of "character" never entirely lost its popular appeal, especially in the wake of various political scandals and personal downfalls. And, in the meantime, psychoanalysts, following Freud, used words like "character," "character traits," and "character types," as well as "personality," in ways that were descriptive and diagnostic, medical rather than aspirational. Both "character" and "personality" would be appropriated by popular culture, further skewing any attempt to pin down precise or "scientific" meanings.

The story of their fluctuations, and of the psychologists and psychiatrists who sought in different ways to define and limit these terms, begins as a reaction to the success of a certain understanding of character for a previous generation of thinkers and practitioners, both learned and popular.

The Rise of Personality

One of the many useful aspects of "character" as a term in the nineteenth century, as we've noted, was that it was aspirational without being explicitly religious. The doctrine of character could extend across sectarian boundaries, and was, strictly speaking, secular, although it was often in individual cases related to faith or belief. But popular usage classified character as either good or bad, noble or base, high or low, "and," as the psychologist A. A. Roback observed, "all these predicates are appraisals rather than statements of fact."[2] As a result, the study of "character" began to be viewed with some skepticism by psychologists, even as it flourished in the maxims, books, and sermons of moralists. Gradually, "personality" became the preferred term.

Initially, theorists and researchers sometimes conflated the terms, or even reversed their connotations. The neurologist Morton Prince, who would pioneer work in America on dissociative disorders, defined character as the perceived outer self, whereas personality was "the sum total of all the biological innate dispositions" of the individual and "all the acquired dispositions and tendencies." Roback, the author of *The Psychology of Character*, reversed these inner and outer descriptions: personality was equivalent to "charm, bearing, carriage and presence," and character was "deeper or inner," reflecting will and inhibition.[3] But as a psychologist Roback lamented the fact that "character," as a term, had been "spoilt by [the] ethical atmosphere."[4] Spoilt, that is to say, for purposes of a more rigorous social-scientific use. The rise of "personality" had begun.

In the 1920s, Richard Clarke Cabot, a physician and the chair of the Department of Social Ethics at Harvard, taught a course called The Study of Character in Difficulties, which followed the usual path of "character" discussions inherited from the previous century. Cabot's course was moral and inspirational in design, based to a considerable extent on the study of exemplary lives (among them Saint Augustine, Abraham Lincoln, Leo Tolstoy, Phillips Brooks, and Jesus Christ).[5] In 1924, Gordon Allport, then a beginning instructor in social ethics, added to the department's offerings a course called Personality and Social Amelioration—the title suggested by Cabot to distinguish Allport's course from his own. The introduction of the term "personality" rather than "character" was significant, and accorded with Allport's own beliefs that the distinction between personality and character was important for psychologists to maintain. Character was ethical. Personality was psychological.

For the architects of the psychology of personality, their chosen term, unencumbered by the baggage that "character" had acquired, allowed for a more scientific approach to the human person. As Roback noted dryly in 1928, "The announcement of courses on personality, which at one time would have been greeted not without a perceptibly amused expression," had been by that date "rather welcomed by educators, at least in the United States."[6] A little more than a decade later, as Ian Nicholson reports, the shift was even more pronounced. "Universities across the United States were offering courses on personality, while courses on character quietly disappeared."[7]

"Character" and "Personality" in Psychoanalysis

Concurrently with these developments, however, another set of meanings for "character" was emerging from the theory and practice of psychoanalysis. To Sigmund Freud and his colleagues and interlocutors, "character" was the result of dispositions, memories, and experiences dating from earliest infancy. The word "character" was likely to be mentioned in tandem with "defect" or "problem," concerned not with morality but with social functioning. And for Freud, psychoanalysis itself was a science, nonjudgmental, intent upon understanding the structure of the mind.

Twenty-first-century psychologists tend to treat the works of Freud and his followers as largely irrelevant to their own work. Part of the dismissal—or resistance—derives from his use of dynamic or humanistic methods, rather than surveys or laboratory observations. Another reason for rejecting Freud's contributions is based on a judgment of the time period in which he lived and wrote, with the assumption that the science he practiced is no longer real science. Yet another derives from his insistence that "character-formation" begins in earliest infancy, and that traits of character develop from infantile desires and responses. The celebrity of Freud himself may also be a factor.

It's difficult for today's readers and scholars to recall how much of a sensation Freud was a hundred years ago. The psychologist William McDougall observed in 1926, "In addition to [his] professional followers, a host of laymen, educators, artists and dilettanti have been fascinated by the Freudian speculations and given them an immense popular vogue, so that some of the technical terms used by Freud have become embodied in the popular slang of both America and England."[8] One of

Freud's supporters wrote that psychoanalysis had been greeted, both by adherents and by detractors, as if it were "a new religion" rather than "a new area for research." Popularization inevitably meant distortion and oversimplification. The label of "scientist," which Freud prized above all others, would be put into question by these fashionable appropriations, and misuse, of his carefully chosen terms.

In addition to specialized terms like "id," "ego," and "superego," "reaction formation," "transference," and others that are distinctively "Freudian," Freud uses both "personality" and "character" in his writings, and the way he uses them is important for later interpretations of these concepts. An examination of the contexts in which his observations appear will be helpful in understanding his reasoning and the evidence that he finds to support his conclusions.

Character Types

When Freud uses a term like "character-type" to describe a distinct kind of mental quality and behavior, he very often takes his examples from literature, and specifically from drama. Partly, as he explains, this is a result of his respect for analytic confidentiality, although some of his most famous case studies describe individuals he has treated. As both writer and psychoanalyst, Freud appeared to get not only considerable pleasure but also a good measure of enlightenment and diagnostic confirmation from comparing literary examples with patients encountered in his practice. In "Some Character-Types Met with in Psycho-Analytic Work" (1916) he discusses "The Exceptions," where his chief example is Shakespeare's Richard III, as well as "Those Wrecked by Success," for which the models are Macbeth, Lady Macbeth, and Ibsen's Rebecca West.

Along the way, he compares the pleasurable act of detection and discovery on the part of the analyst and the audience, to the psychological skill of the gifted playwright in offering subtle clues to secret motives. Here is a telling passage from the section on "The Exceptions":

> Now we feel that we ourselves might become like Richard, that on a small scale, indeed, we are already like him. Richard is

> an enormous magnification of something we find in ourselves as well. We all think we have reason to reproach Nature and our destiny for congenital and infantile disadvantages; we all demand reparation for early wounds to our narcissism, our self-love. Why did not Nature give us the golden curls of Balder or the strength of Siegfried or the lofty brow of genius or the noble profile of aristocracy? Why were we born in a middle-class home instead of in a royal palace? We could carry off beauty and distinction quite as well as any of those whom we are now obliged to envy for those qualities.
>
> It is, however, a subtle economy of art in the poet that he does not permit his hero to give open and complete expression to all his secret motives. By this means he obliges us to supplement them; he engages our intellectual activity, diverts it from critical reflection and keeps us firmly identified with his hero.[9]

According to this interpretation, the poet-playwright skillfully elicits engagement and identification from readers and audience members; readers and audience in turn "supplement" the hero's motives with their own private feelings, desires, and longings. In effect, they project their own feelings onto, and into, him. Freud here describes a dynamic of character that comes close to the heart of theater—and also of psychoanalysis.

Freud's dramatic examples tend to come from tragedies, from *Macbeth* and *Hamlet* and *King Lear*; as far as I can tell, he never uses the term "tragic flaw,"[10] or its more general literary equivalent, the "character flaw," in the singular, as if one trait could be the entire object of professional scrutiny or explanation. But he does write of "character disorders"—"phobias, hysteria, obsessional neurosis"—and of "abnormalities of character which have been developed in place of those illnesses."[11] (These are the only cases, he says, for which analytic therapy is suitable; other conditions, such as narcissism and psychosis, are "unsuitable" for analysis to a greater or lesser degree.) "Character" in this case consists of clusters or patterns developed, once again, through (1) instincts, or (2) sublimations of those instincts, or (3) reaction formations against them. Thus, as Freud says cheerfully in another context, "a number of our virtues" come from reaction formations against "perverse impulses which have been recognized as unutilizable" and are therefore held in check.[12]

In an early paper, never published in his lifetime, he examines "Psychopathic Characters on the Stage" (1905/1906), arguing, after Aristotle, that "Suffering is . . . the subject-matter of drama, and from this suffering it promises to give the audience pleasure."[13] The audience member's enjoyment, though, is "based on an illusion," and his suffering alleviated by his knowledge that, "firstly, it is someone other than himself who is acting and suffering on the stage, and secondly, that it is after all only a game, which can threaten no damage to his personal security."[14] Among the categories of drama that he mentions in this connection are *religious* tragedies, in which the hero struggles against divinity, as in ancient Greek plays; *social* tragedies, where the hero struggles against human society, as in Ibsen (these examples are Freud's); tragedies of *character*, in which two heroes struggle against each other; *psychological* drama, in which the hero is conflicted, as between love and duty, or love and social convention; and *psychopathological* drama, "when the source of the suffering in which we take part and from which we are meant to derive pleasure" is a conflict between a conscious impulse and a repressed one.[15]

This last category is really the point of his paper. "The precondition of enjoyment," Freud goes on to suggest, "is that the spectator should himself be a neurotic, for it is only such people who can derive pleasure instead of simple aversion from the revelation and the more or less conscious recognition of a repressed impulse."[16] His chief example of psychopathological drama, it is almost needless to say, is *Hamlet*, here described as a "modern drama,"[17] since it is part of Freud's contention—in this piece, in his other comments on *Hamlet*, and in the later *Civilization and Its Discontents*—that modern people are necessarily repressed and therefore necessarily neurotic. Some conditions attach to this sort of drama in order that it be successful: the hero does not begin by being psychopathic but only becomes so in the course of the play; "the repressed impulse is one of those which are similarly repressed in all of us"; and the impulse "is never given a definite name," so that "in the spectator too the process is carried through with his attention averted, and he is in the grip of his emotions instead of taking stock of what is happening."[18]

Characters onstage thus perform therapeutic functions, allowing the spectator, who "longs to feel and to act and to arrange things according to his desires—in short, to be a hero"—to "*identify himself* with a hero," while sparing him the ultimate pains and sufferings that may well come with heroism in the world. Attending a dramatic performance "does for adults what play does for children," a point, as James Strachey, the general editor of the *Standard Edition* of Freud's work, has noted, that Freud emphasizes by hyphenating the ordinary German word for dramatic performance, *Schauspiel*, into *Schau-spiel*, spectacle-play.[19]

Character Traits

If "character" in the works of moralists and educationalists was ethical and inspirational, "character" in Freud's work might be said, by contrast, to indicate the presence of, or a tendency toward, some kind of psychological problem. "Character traits" for Freud are "permanent"[20] and "unalterable,"[21] in part because their origins in earlier personal development have been forgotten or repressed. As early as 1900, Freud had written, "What we describe as our 'character' is based on the memory-traces of our impressions; and, moreover, the impressions which have had the greatest effect on us—those of our earliest youth—are precisely the ones which scarcely ever become conscious."[22]

Later in his career, Freud explained how what he called "fixations" and "avoidances," positive and negative responses to trauma, could make "powerful contributions to the stamping of character" by either generating a compulsion to repeat, on the one hand, or producing inhibitions and phobias, on the other. In both cases, the positive and the negative, the result might lead to "unalterable character traits," although, or, as he notes, "precisely because" their historical origins in personal experience are forgotten.[23]

This description is purposefully abstract; it does not single out any one particular character type, but instead summarizes the general process as Freud has come to understand it. But in an earlier, more clinical account, he is far more specific. "Among those whom we try to help by our psycho-analytic efforts," he wrote in 1908, "we often come across a type of person who is marked by a certain set of character-traits, while at the same time our attention is drawn to the behavior in his childhood of one of his bodily functions and the organ concerned with it."

The "character-traits" Freud had in mind in this case were orderliness, parsimony, and obstinacy, and he explains that each of the words actually refers to a "series of interrelated character-traits":

> "Orderly" covers the notion of bodily cleanliness, as well as of conscientiousness in carrying out small duties and trustworthiness. Its opposite would be "untidy" and "neglectful." Parsimony may appear in the exaggerated form of avarice; and obstinacy can go over into defiance, to which rage and revengefulness are easily joined.[24]

The essay in which he described these linked character traits and his theory of their origin was "Character and Anal Erotism."

As James Strachey observes, "The theme of this paper has now become so familiar that it is difficult to realize the astonishment and indignation which it aroused on its first publication." Strachey notes that orderliness, parsimony, and obstinacy and their connection with anal erotism had been mentioned by Freud in a letter to Jung in 1906, and that he had "associated money and miserliness with faeces" in another letter, written in December 1897.[25]

In a later essay, "On Transformations of Instinct as Exemplified in Anal Erotism," Freud, recalling his earlier discussion of the "three character-traits of *orderliness*, *parsimony*, and *obstinacy*" (also here called "avarice, pedantry, and obstinacy"), again alludes to the etymology of "character": "The cases in which these defects of character were combined," he writes, "in consequence bore a special stamp (the 'anal character')."[26] "Defects of character," in this sentence, might conceivably be taken to imply that there was a theoretically or hypothetically ideal character from which these traits diverged.

I will make two brief points here, in relation to the essay on "Character and Anal Erotism." The first concerns the title: the association of "anal erotism" with the word "character," though entirely consistent with Freud's understanding of character formation in early childhood and convincing to his psychoanalytic colleagues, may have made some readers resistant to "character" as a descriptive term. As illogical as it may be to endow a piece of scholarly analysis with the qualities that it itself is describing, the notion that this was somehow a "dirty" topic to be avoided (or repressed?) gained some adherents among the interpretatively squeamish.

My second point is that the ideas expressed in this essay have now become part of the common culture. In 1964, Senator Barry Goldwater had been puzzled by the term "anal character" when it was applied to him by psychiatrists in a survey published by *Fact* magazine. "I don't know what an anal character would be," he testified in his successful libel suit against the magazine. "I tried to look it up in the dictionary, but couldn't find it."[27] But things have changed a great deal in the intervening years. "I am so anal about everything," cheerfully admits one of the twin brothers who host the popular *Property Brothers* series on HGTV. (Perhaps in unconscious compensation, the author of a feature article on the brothers begins by describing them as "squeaky-clean," and then describes one of them, on-camera, yanking a toilet from a house under renovation.[28]) "Anal" as verbal shorthand for the three character traits Freud describes has become part of ordinary speech, and ordinary thinking.

Freud on Personality

The theoretical conclusion of the "Anal Erotism" essay generalizes about how "character in its final shape" is developed from the instincts. This is a point that Freud will make repeatedly, most strikingly in *The Ego and the Id* (1923) and again in the *New Introductory Lectures on Psycho-Analysis* (1933), where he explicitly links it to personality.

Discussing structures under the general heading of "The Dissection of the Psychical Personality,"[29] Freud describes the id as the "dark, inaccessible part of our personality,"[30] and sums up his argument by returning explicitly to "this division of the personality into an ego, a super-ego, and an id."[31]

Not only does he discuss these entities, he wittily personifies them: "The poor ego," he says sympathetically,

> serves three severe masters and does what it can to bring their claims and demands into harmony with one another . . . No wonder the ego so often fails in its task. Its three tyrannical masters are the external world, the super-ego, and the id. When we follow the ego's efforts to satisfy them simultaneously—or rather, to obey them simultaneously—we cannot feel any regret at having personified the ego and set it up as a separate organism. It feels hemmed in on three sides, threatened by three kinds of danger, to which, if it is hard pressed, it reacts by generating anxiety.

The ego "strives . . . to be a loyal servant of the id, to remain on good terms with it." It is often "obliged" to "profess, with diplomatic disingenuousness, to be taking note of reality even when the id has remained rigid and unyielding." Thus "the ego, driven by the id, confined by the super-ego, repulsed by reality, struggles to master its economic task of bringing about harmony among the forces and influences working in and upon it."[32] The "poor ego" is thus not only anxious in itself, but a cause of anxiety in others.

So "the personality" for Freud is "psychical"—i.e., mental, an aspect of the mind. The internal struggles of this "personality," including repression, identification, idealization, resistance, and displacement, all contribute to what Freud calls, in this same lecture, the "formation of character."[33]

Character is the outward sign, so to speak, of an inward personality. In extreme cases, where the aspects of the personality are too incompatible, they may appear as separate entities—the equivalent of what we mean when we say that someone has, or manifests, "multiple personalities." In the "Rat Man" case, he writes that his patient "had, as it were, disintegrated into three personalities": one, the unconscious one, consisted of "passionate and evil impulses"; in a second, his "normal state," he was "kind, cheerful, and sensible—an enlightened and superior kind of person"; and "in his third psychological organization he paid homage to superstition and asceticism."[34] In dreams, and also in hallucinatory paranoia, he notes, "the personality may be split."[35]

Jung and Reich

Two other contemporary contributions to the question of "character" and "personality" in psychoanalysis are worth noting briefly in the context of Freud's ideas—those of Carl Gustav Jung, in his book *Psychological Types*, originally published in German in 1921, and Wilhelm Reich, in *Character Analysis*, published in German in 1933.

Jung would seem at first to have relatively little to contribute to the discussion of "character" per se. *Psychological Types* may be chiefly memorable for his two enduring coinages, the "extravert" and the "introvert," terms later also used by the British personality psychologist Hans Eysenck. Jung's short chapter called "The Type Problem in Human Character" is essentially a set of quotations from, and equivocal comments on, a book called *Character as Seen in Body and Parentage*, by Furneaux Jordan,[36] which had been sent to him by an "esteemed colleague" in London.

Published in 1896, Jordan's book is a fairly typical product of the period, written by a surgeon and professor of anatomy, full of familiar historical examples (Thomas à Becket, Napoleon, the Duke of Wellington, Gladstone) and physiological arguments about the skeletal structure and body carriage of poets and statesmen. Jung's main interest in it, other than to debate or refute various of its arguments, is to align his own terms "extravert" and "introvert" with Jordan's "less impassioned" and "more impassioned" man and woman.[37] Jung will comment, for example, that he "cannot subscribe to Jordan's view that the very worst characters are to be found among passionate introverted natures. Among extraverts there is just as much inveterate wickedness. But whereas introverted passion expresses itself in brutal actions, the vulgarity of the extravert's unconscious thoughts and feelings commits crimes against the soul of the victim. I do not know which is worse."[38]

The word "character" is not one of the terms Jung lists among the "Definitions" in *Psychological Types*, but under the heading of "Soul" he describes what he calls "character-splitting in normal individuals."

His example is a man "from the educated classes" who participates in both "the domestic circle and the world of affairs." Since, in Jung's view, these two spheres require two different "characters," it often comes about that "men who in public life are extremely energetic, spirited, obstinate, willful and ruthless appear good-natured, mild, compliant, even weak, when at home and in the bosom of the family."[39] So "which is the true character, the real personality?" Rather than choosing the one or the other, Jung concludes: "Such a man has no character at all: he is not *individual* but *collective*, the plaything of circumstance and general expectations. Were he individual, he would have the same character despite the variation in attitude." Instead, "he deceives others, and often himself, as to his real character. He puts on a *mask*, which he knows is in keeping with his conscious intentions." This mask, Jung explains, is "the *persona*, which was the name for the masks worn by actors in antiquity."[40]

What does "character" mean in this discussion? It is apparently at least in some cases the same as "personality," which is described in the section on "Soul" as "a clearly demarcated functional complex." Both character and personality are imagined to have the capacity to be "real," or "true." "Such a man" as is described here "deceives others, and often himself, as to his real character." He instead opts for a persona, described, like "personality," as "a functional complex," but in this case one that "comes into existence for reasons of adaptation or personal convenience."

We are entering the thicket of Jungian terminology here, for it is at this point that Jung introduces the word "anima" as the converse of "persona": the anima is "the inner personality," the face "turned toward the unconscious," whereas the persona is "the outer personality," "the outward face."[41] If we stick resolutely with "character," though, we may then want to ask what it might mean to have, as Jung asserts of the man split between social and domestic concerns, "no character at all." Does character in this sense revert to the "evaluative" mode, so that "no character" means "a poor or weak character"?

"No character" (or "no characters") seems in these contexts to mean something different from "no personality." To have "no personality" would be to be dull, lifeless, unsparkling; to have "no character" would presumably revert to the older idea of ethical character, and thus to suggest that the person discussed lacks good morals or values, and perhaps also may lack "backbone," "spine," or whatever the current jargon for resoluteness of purpose might be. So Jung's hypothetical man split between the "social character" and the "domestic character" is said to deceive others, and sometimes even himself, as to his "real character," and this vacillation, or indecision, or indeterminacy, is then equated by Jung with having "no character at all."

The other terminological contribution to the psychoanalytic lexicon of character we might note here comes from Wilhelm Reich. For Reich, the term "character analysis," the title of his book, meant the clinical analysis of what he came to call, in a vivid phrase, "character armor"—the individual's "neurotic character traits as a whole," which function as a defense mechanism against "our therapeutic efforts."[42] This "character resistance" can be found both within the analytic framework of transference and outside it: "In given situations, the patient's character becomes a resistance. In everyday life, in other words, the character plays a role similar to the one it plays as a resistance in the treatment: that of a psychic defense apparatus."[43]

"Character armor" has not survived as a major term in psychoanalytic discussions, although its metaphorical possibilities are intriguing. The styles of medieval and Renaissance armor, from heroic plated assemblages that make the wearer look large, powerful, and sometimes anonymous, to sculpted armor that mimics the look of the muscled naked body, are worth comparing to the varying modes of psychological defense. But character resistance, as a concept, has had a more substantial afterlife.

Resistance can turn, over time, into a series of permanent character traits, like bodily stiffness, or a fixed smile, or contemptuous or arrogant behavior—all examples given by Anna Freud in her account of Reich's theory of the "armor-plating of character."[44] She describes the process of "character analysis" clearly: "Whenever the interpretation touches on the unknown elements of the ego, its activities in the past, that ego is wholly opposed to the work of analysis. Here evidently we have the situation which we commonly describe by the not very felicitous term 'character analysis.'"[45] For Anna Freud, then, "character analysis" is a psychoanalytic process through which the analyst tries to break down the ego's resistances. In other words, it is a kind of therapeutic "analysis" that works on, and with, the "character."

But the term "character analysis" had also been used, in the previous century, to describe some popular scams. Roback chose to leave them out of his comprehensive bibliography of character and personality in 1927: "Books on character-analysis, so-called, and other fads and quackeries have been deliberately omitted except in a few instances, where it was difficult to decide or where the brazen employment of scientific terms required a note of warning."[46] (Roback had no such ethical qualms about "occult approaches to characterology," which he did include in his volume, observing, "We must distinguish between an honest, though perhaps misguided belief and a money-making scheme to delude the helpless well-to-do masses."[47])

Both of these meanings of "character analysis" are, of course, different from the academic literary activity called "character analysis." The identical terminology is not likely to mislead many, but it is indicative of the problems we encounter when trying to disentangle "character" from its various specialized or historical meanings.

Freud and Personality Psychology

Sigmund Freud's career was long and consistently productive. He began publishing at the end of the nineteenth century, and some of his major work was written in the last years of his life; he died in 1939. So the development of personality psychology, in the twenties and thirties, took place in the same decades during which Freud was producing psychoanalytic work like *The Ego and the Id*, *Civilization and Its Discontents*, and *New Introductory Lectures on Psycho-Analysis*. Though some of his critics may have regarded him as a figure of the past, he was not only alive and writing but still revered in 1937, when Gordon Allport published *Personality: A Psychological Interpretation*. By the time Allport revised his book a quarter of a century later, times had changed.

In 1937, it was possible to think of jettisoning "character" altogether from the lexicon of academic psychology. Allport summed up the problem and the proposed solution. Character, he wrote, though "frequently used as a synonym of personality," was evaluative and ethical, often connected (by "the church," "educators," and "common speech") with will and volition. But Allport thought it unwise to separate volition from personality. It was "sounder" to "admit frankly" that character was an ethical concept, concerned with evaluating moral behavior. In fact, "the psychologist does not need the term at all; personality alone will serve." He therefore—as we've seen—proposed to avoid "character" completely in his book on personality, except when compelled to do so in citations to other authors, or when using the term historically. His elegantly chiastic declaration ("Character is personality evaluated, and personality is character devaluated") seemed to clear the decks, once and for all. "Character" was obsolete, from the point of view of psychology. "Personality" would be the word of the future.[48]

What, then, precisely, was "personality," apart from its relationship with character? Allport offered a definition: "Personality is the dynamic organization within the individual of those psychophysical systems that determine his unique adjustments to his environment."[49]

Many years afterward, when the field of personality had been fully established in psychology departments, Allport undertook to revise his by then classic text. The new version, retitled *Pattern and Growth in Personality*, now included chapters on "cultural factors," "cognition," and "the self." *Pattern and Growth* still contained summary accounts of physiognomy, phrenology, literary characterology, and the four temperaments, all of these now grouped collectively under the heading of "Insights from the Past." In the revised text, Allport retained his useful etymology of the terms "personality" and "character," noting, as many have done before and since, that "persona" is Latin for mask, and "character" comes from a Greek word for "engraving." "The former term suggests appearance, visible behavior, surface quality; the latter suggests deep (perhaps inborn), fixed, and basic structure."

And what about Freud? In 1937, Allport had written of the "tremendous vogue of psychoanalytic interpretations of personality," explaining that Freud had insisted that "the neglected facts of emotion are the most important facts of all for psychology," and that the "promise of such a new dynamic doctrine attracted doctors, laymen, and psychologists themselves." Allport explicates psychoanalytic concepts such as the pleasure principle, the reality principle, the unconscious, ambivalence, repression, sublimation, and identification, many of which he finds "serviceable." A footnote at the beginning of the relatively brief section on Freud explains Allport's brevity and critical tone: psychoanalysis, he writes, deals with neurotic and pathological cases, not with "normal personality," and its applicability to the latter is "in many respects questionable." In addition, the story of psychoanalysis was "too familiar to require another detailed exposition."[50]

By 1961, though, the footnote about Freud's fame and ubiquity has been altered to a more informative description in the text. Freud's ideas are no longer too familiar to require explanation. Allport explains: "Freud was more successful than any other writer in history in calling our attention to the hidden formative processes that often shape our personalities without our knowing that they do so. Thanks to Freud, even the man in the street now knows that we often act for reasons we do not understand, and that we harbor unconscious sentiments that would surprise us if we knew we had them."[51] Even though "the man in the street" may have absorbed some version of the general drift, several pages of further explication follow. Allport is generous in his overall assessment of Freud's thought, but maintains that Freudian theory still "seems best to fit certain types of neurotic disorder, but falls short as a formula for the healthy personality."[52]

"My own point of view is considerably different," he added. "The normal processes of growth and becoming are, in the main, neglected in Freud's theories of personality. Although traces of neurotic traits and mechanisms may be found in many healthy people, these threads are minor compared with the sturdier weave of wholesome growth."[53]

The banishment of "character" as a term was in this new account replaced by an acknowledgment that "the ancient difference in flavor of the two terms seems to account for present-day regional preferences." European psychologists, Allport noted, "seem to have a preference for *character*, while American psychologists favor *personality*." Freud "speaks often of character-structure but seldom of personality." Europeans use the term "characterology," but it is seldom—he says—used by Americans. Allport noted as well that the denotations of words change over time, and that "personality" and "character" were "often used interchangeably,"[54] a point that would also be made by psychoanalysts.

Despite all attempts to distinguish between them, each of the two words was used in ordinary life quite frequently to assist in defining the other. "Personality" meant "the distinctive personal or individual character of a person" in both literary and technical writings throughout this period. "To have personality" was defined by the *Oxford English Dictionary* as "to have particular qualities or traits of character, especially to an unusual or noteworthy degree,"[55] with illustrative quotations from 1710 to 1994, including one from William Dean Howells, in 1902, that explicitly equates the two words: "How many houses now have character—personality?"[56] (This sense of a house or property with "character" is still to be found in real-estate descriptions, and often goes along with a hefty price. But shelter magazines and Pinterest also direct the twenty-first-century reader to "Houses with Personality.")

Allport strongly preferred "personality," in part, as he said, because of the moral and judgmental associations that attach to "character." But he was alert to the conflations and confusions that persisted, and even his definition of personality had undergone a quiet revision from 1937 to 1961. It now read: "Personality is the dynamic organization within the individual of those psychophysical systems that determine his characteristic behavior and thought."[57] The individual was still, for the moment, normatively male. But instead of "unique adjustments to his environment," as in 1937, he now exhibited "characteristic behavior and thought."

An attentive stylist, Allport is slightly troubled by "characteristic." "In a sense," he concedes, "it is redundant to employ the term *characteristic* in our definition. Yet redundancy is not necessarily a bad thing; it helps to drive a point home."[58] This ignores, for the moment, the fact that "characteristic" contains the disfavored word "character." But a few pages later, the worrisome issue resurfaces, and what had been an etymological distinction between the approaches of European and American psychologists is now frankly appropriated to the American side. "It is a curious fact that 'characteristic' should have kept its primitive meaning," Allport observes, "whereas its root-form [i.e., "character"] has gathered much ethical moss."[59] Thus, while retaining his earlier rejection, he offered an etymological loophole: "*Character* is a term we can largely dispense with since it refers (by our definition) to the evaluation of personality. *Characteristic*, on the other hand, keeps its original meaning of engraving (a uniquely etched feature) and is therefore useful for our purposes."[60]

The initial zeal of reform is here, arguably, tempered by time and success. In the 1930s, American theorists of personality had set aside what they regarded as mistaken or confusing terminology. "Character" was for them too vague, too broad, too closely associated with moralism and evaluation, and linked with dubious "sciences" like physiognomy. "Personality" seemed like a better word, offering a fresh start. A generation later, however, "character," while still encumbered with evaluative associations, had endured as a technical and medical term in the work of many important analysts. Although psychologists of personality might feel they could "largely dispense" with it, it would not entirely go away. In fact, as Allport acknowledged, in the language of psychoanalysis, a language of "character-structure," "character-formation," and "character defects," it had never been displaced.

Moreover, "personality," however advantageous it might seem to social scientists, was not without some baggage of its own. If "character" had, in Allport's curious phrase, gathered "ethical moss" (by not being a rolling stone?), "personality" had gained associations of a different kind—with, for example, groups like the Rolling Stones. Popular culture, like some strains of politics, could generate a "cult of personality," or "personality cult"—the phrase goes back to 1927, but picked up traction mid-century. When "personality" is used as a substantive today, the difference is clear: someone who is described as "a personality," sometimes with a capital *P*, is quite different from someone described as "a character." The former is likely to show up on Page Six, the latter to feature in affectionate family reminiscences ("Uncle Arnold was a real character"). In the twenty-first century, an individual can be described as a "personality" as if that constitutes not a set of qualities, but an occupation or a role. Rush Limbaugh is a "radio personality"; Kim Kardashian is a "reality-TV personality"; the golfer Tiger Woods is a "sports personality."

But the gradual shift of "personality" from an indication of true distinction to famous-for-being-famous took some time. In Virginia Woolf's novel *Night and Day* (1919), the term is a kind of magnet, emboldening one young woman to make the acquaintance of another: "Mary, feeling, as she had said, that Katharine was a 'personality,' wished so much to speak to her that, in a few minutes, she did."[61] And in an essay on "Libidinal Types" (1931), Sigmund Freud notes that individuals of the narcissistic type "impress others as being 'personalities'; they are especially suited to act as a support for others, to take on the role of leaders."[62] The internal definitions and quotation marks in these examples draw attention to the specific use of the word in this sense. As a term, it is still emergent.

Furthermore, these citations imply that the "personality" in question possesses some special quality or merit (a woman of originality; a leader). The world of the "reality-show personality" and "YouTube personality," for whom celebrity was itself a goal, lay in the future. The now common confusion between fame and notoriety would be a secondary by-product of that development. By the end of the twentieth century, this new use of "personality" had been assured by the media transformation of formerly staid genres like the academic lecture, now restyled as viewer-friendly, "personality"-focused events like TED talks, Aspen Institute lectures, and open-to-the-public conferences and fundraisers headlined by public "personalities" with media credentials (Arianna Huffington, "author, columnist, TV personality"[63]).

Meanwhile, Freud's "id," "ego," and "superego" survive hardily in journalistic articles, headlines, and pronouncements about public figures and celebrities. "Ego Clashes Exposed in Leaked Emails from Democratic National Committee."[64] "Trumpism is the GOP's id triumphing over its weak superego."[65] That these pop-Freudian references come from descriptions of contemporary politicians should not be much of a surprise. Recent political campaigns have renewed the usefulness of Freud's terms, despite—or, rather, because of—objections, like Allport's, that Freud accentuates the negative.

Furthermore, as "personality" was evolving into a stand-alone term for a celebrity, the word also took on a different, but not completely unrelated connotation of lively sociability (or, as a more modern parlance might describe it, "good 'people skills'"). This kind of "personality," too, has had its ups and downs in popular usage. A person described as having "a great personality" is all too often being tacitly compared with someone of exceptional physical or sexual appeal, as if "personality" were a last resort or a consolation prize—especially for women. (Johnny Burke's risqué lyrics for a 1945 song, "Personality," teased this idea by using "personality" as a comic euphemism not for character but for voluptuousness: Madame du Barry was the toast of Paris because of her "well-developed personality"; Salome "danced and had the boys entranced" because she "knew how to use her personality." A beat that drops before "personality," like an elbow in the ribs, underscored its deliberate inappropriateness.)[66] But these associations were far from what American theorists of personality had in mind in the early part of the century. To them, as we've noted, "character" was an outworn word, seen as evaluative and judgmental. "Personality" seemed, by contrast, fresh, morally neutral, and scientific.

The "Big Five"

The evolution of the Five Factor Model,[67] sometimes called the "Big Five," began in 1936 when Gordon Allport asked one of his graduate students to identify all the trait-descriptive adjectives—"ambitious," "brave," "calm"—in the second edition of *Webster's New International Dictionary.*[68] There were, it turned out, approximately eighteen thousand such words.

Other researchers refined the terms, combining synonyms, and decided that these words could be grouped under five "factors." Twenty years later, another psychologist "began again with the dictionary" and "again found five factors" that closely resembled the previous five. From the end of the 1980s onward, psychologists tested out these five factors, and their research, it is said, "led to the widespread adoption of the FFM as an adequate taxonomy of personality traits." The concept was refined and put into general use by 1990, garnering praise for its "robustness"—a social-science term of art which meant that it seemed to work. Thereafter, "personality research flourished."[69]

The five traits decided upon by psychologists were: Openness to Experience, Conscientiousness, Extraversion, Agreeableness, and Neuroticism. Although these sound judgmental—"Agreeableness" sounds good, "Neuroticism" bad—the underlying idea is that each term reflects a range: "Neuroticism" is thought to cover the territory from extreme sensitivity on the one side to security and confidence on the other: an individual who was wholly unneurotic could be calm but also flat and dull, whereas a touch of the neurotic might move his or her personality in the direction of dynamism and high energy. Likewise, too much Agreeableness might make a person undiscriminating or submissive, too much Conscientiousness might verge upon obsession, and too much Openness to Experience might result in lack of focus. *DSM-5*, since it is concerned with diagnosing disorders, gives a list of what it calls "maladaptive variants" of the "Big Five," naming as the five broad domains of personality-trait variation Negative Affectivity (versus Emotional Stability), Detachment (versus Extraversion), Antagonism (versus Agreeableness), Disinhibition (versus Conscientiousness), and Psychoticism (versus Lucidity).

The modern "factors" may not appear, to a lay observer, so different from the terminology of the previous century's phrenologists (Concentrativeness, Conscientiousness, Ideality, Love of Approbation, Secretiveness, etc.). But whereas those "propensities" and "sentiments" were said to correlate to explicit parts of the brain or mental functioning, the "five factors" are explicitly called "personality traits," and refer to the whole personality. They are sometimes taken as predictors of success—academic, professional, personal, romantic, etc. In their "maladaptive" variants, they can predict, or indicate, serious problems that may require medical intervention. Deficits of "Agreeableness," listed in *DSM-5* under "Antagonism," might include grandiosity, deceitfulness, manipulative behavior, attention seeking, and callousness. Similar deficits in "Extraversion," listed under "Detachment," range from withdrawal and the avoidance of intimacy to depressivity, anhedonia (the absence of feelings of pleasure), and suspiciousness.

What does FFM have to do with character? As we've seen, a major objection to the concept of "character" was that it was evaluative and tied to moral considerations. But when FFM is used for testing and prediction, even of a social rather than a narrowly "moral" kind, can it be genuinely said to avoid values and evaluation? Psychologists who use self-descriptive questionnaires to determine personality are depending in part on how the individuals who answer these questionnaires respond to statements that, even if not overtly "ethical," are hardly devoid of affect: "I feel others' emotions"; "I am the life of the party"; "I worry about things"; "I am not interested in other people's problems."

If we take this—or any—selection of FFM survey questions out of the context of personality testing for a moment, and imagine them as part of a novel or a play, we can see how the line between "personality" and "character" might again seem to blur. We don't usually talk of Emma Bovary or Captain Ahab as having "personalities," although it would be possible to do so. But a recent study by personality psychologists, "The Five-Factor Model in Fact and Fiction," undertook to "define the conditions under which an examination of fictional characters can usefully contribute to scientific psychology,"[70] and ended by urging the reverse as well, the adoption of FFM trait analysis by literary scholars.

"Facts" and "Fictions"

"Shakespeare was a keen observer of human nature, but he never had the opportunity to read the *Journal of Personality*,"[71] the authors of "Fact and Fiction" say, and they are only half joking. As this sentence suggests, they are believers in "human nature" (never rendered in quotation marks) who view personality both as evolutionary and as relatively unchanging over the history of literature: "Research on other species shows that personality traits evolved before human beings, and there is every reason to think that the FFM characterized people in Homer's day as much as today."[72] Falstaff is said by the article's authors to be low in Conscientiousness but high in Extraversion. Milton's Satan, on the other hand, is high in Conscientiousness. An Internet study of 519 people interested in nineteenth-century English literature found Catherine Earnshaw in *Wuthering Heights* "low on Agreeableness and high on Neuroticism," a result the authors thought "sensible."[73] By contrast, they are dismissive of Freud as a model for literary interpretation. "To interpret, say, the plays of Ibsen or stories of Poe in classic Freudian terms is to write fiction about fiction. Real scholarship requires a more current conception of psychology."[74]

It is not clear whether, in singling out Ibsen and Poe, the psychologists are thinking specifically of Freud's work on those authors, although he wrote two important essays that deal with Ibsen and a foreword to his friend Marie Bonaparte's influential psychoanalytic study of Edgar Allan Poe.[75] But sometimes the blanket condemnation of "Freud" derives from a consideration only of his writings on sexuality and on the theory of the Oedipus complex (what the authors appear to mean by "classic Freudian terms"). "Real scholarship" might be said to require a fuller consideration of his work.

"The Five-Factor Model in Fact and Fiction" (a title that nods to Eysenck's *Fact and Fiction in Psychology*, but is perhaps more double-sided than the authors intended) concludes with a quasi-evangelical call for "literary scholars" to "join this conversation" about FFM, which has provided a "natural link between readers, writers, and psychologists."[76] The real topic, it seems—other than the advancement of the FFM theory—is "human nature," addressed not only in the article itself but also in the abstract that introduces its online version. Such abstracts are standard for academic articles, but this one contains a terminological surprise. Composed apparently by the authors ("We argue that . . ."), it explains, in straightforward language, the value of the study of personality: "For the writer and reader, an understanding of current knowledge about personality can contribute to a keener perception of human character and a deeper appreciation of its depiction."[77]

The purpose of the study of "personality," then, is the understanding of "human character." Here is that pesky word again, so often banished, so often resurgent. The article's abstract doesn't conflate "human character" with literary characters—it is at pains to say that the "methods and findings of contemporary trait psychology" can be applied to "broad questions about genres, literary periods, and individual authors, as well as to the interpretation of individual characters." The "perception" and "appreciation" of "human character" is the goal of all these proposed literary investigations. So personality, which was in Allport's vision to encompass character, is in the second decade of the twenty-first century itself encompassed by character.

It may indeed be time, as the authors of this study suggest, for a bit of an entente, or at least a détente, between psychologists of personality and psychoanalytic theorists. It's tempting to adduce another piece of Freudian theory here, his idea about the "narcissism of minor differences." Although the differences between these two fields are far from minor, in terms of training, archive, bibliography, rhetoric, and method, they share an abiding interest in the questions of human character and personality, and, indeed, in "human nature."

Where the developers of the Five-Factor Model in psychology came to explicate the range of behaviors that could develop from a "personality trait" like Openness to Experience ("contrasts such traits as imagination, curiosity, and creativity with traits such as shallowness or imperceptiveness"), Agreeableness ("contrasts traits such as kindness, trust, and warmth with such traits as hostility, selfishness, and distrust"), or, closest to Freud's "anal erotism," Conscientiousness ("contrasts such traits as organization, thoroughness, and reliability with traits such as carelessness, negligence, and unreliability"[78]), it is possible to see the same three options of continuity, sublimation, and resistance that were outlined by Freud long ago, although without the claim that these traits derive from "the original instincts" of infancy.

Freud's description of the "obsessional neurotic" in the *Introductory Lectures on Psychoanalysis* (1917)—a book that had a wider circulation in his lifetime than any of his others, with the possible exception of *The Psychopathology of Everyday Life*—sounds a great deal like the personality afflicted with too much Conscientiousness in the Five-Factor Model, or like the obsessive-compulsive personality disorder of *DSM-5*. Such a person, says Freud, "starts off with a very energetic disposition, he is often extra-ordinarily self-willed and as a rule he has intellectual gifts above the average. He has usually reached a satisfactorily high level of ethical development; he exhibits over-conscientiousness, and is more than ordinarily correct in his behavior."[79] These ideas are not identical, but they are closely related. Strong protestations of important differences should not obscure the similarities between what Freud chose to call "character-traits" and the "personality traits" of the Five-Factor Model, which has been claimed to be near-universal, not merely situational or culture-specific.

One inevitable result of the disciplinary rejection of Freud and Freudians in the late twentieth and early twenty-first centuries is that psychologists (and others) no longer read his work carefully, if at all. He is often remanded to the distinctly unscientific category of "literature," and sometimes his ideas themselves are described, not admiringly, as fiction. As with almost any theoretical concept or method that swings from high endorsement to dismissal, this is both right and wrong, but it is right for the wrong reasons and wrong for the right ones.

It is right methodologically, in that literary analysis, close reading, and comparisons to literary examples may be revealing in connection with Freud's theories. And it is wrong in the assumption that quantitative methods and paper-and-pencil surveys are more accurate, and more "objective," than the combination of skilled personal observation and wide cultural knowledge.

As we have seen, many of Freud's examples derive from literature and myth as much as they do from the interpersonal dynamics of the consulting room. His deliberate connection between "characters" on the stage and "character-traits" in the individual, a connection that dates at least as far back as Aristotle, suggests a reciprocal development, anticipating later writings on social dramas (Victor Turner and other anthropologists) and the presentation of the self in everyday life (Erving Goffman and other sociologists). When psychologists insist that his work is not relevant to their own, they may be ignoring the extensive work on culture and behavior that marked the second half of Freud's remarkable career.

Personality Disorders and Character Pathology

One place where "personality" has seemed definitively to replace "character" in modern parlance is in the language of mental disorders. The fifth edition of the *Diagnostic and Statistical Manual of Mental Disorders* (*DSM-5*) describes a personality disorder as an "enduring" and "inflexible" pattern of "long duration" that leads to significant distress or impairment and is not due to use of substances or another medical condition. "Personality disorders are linked to a range of behaviors that may impede normal functioning in social, personal, or professional settings, and that often lead to feelings of anxiety or depression."[80] *DSM-5* lists ten personality disorders: schizoid, paranoid, histrionic, borderline, obsessive-compulsive, dependent, negativistic, avoidant, narcissistic, and antisocial. There is no index entry in *DSM-5* under "character," nor does the word appear in the "Glossary of Technical Terms."

Freud had used the phrase "character disorders" in describing the value of analytic therapy: "The analysis of character disorders," he wrote, "calls for long periods of treatment; but it is often successful." Among the "disorders" for which such treatment was recommended were "phobias, hysteria, obsessional neurosis," and "abnormalities of character which have been developed in place of these illnesses."[81]

The key word here is arguably neither "character" nor "personality" but "disorder," a term that indicates a seriousness of dysfunction requiring professional attention. "Classifying personality disorders is problematic for several reasons," wrote the psychoanalyst Otto Kernberg in 1984. "One is quantitative: How intense must the disturbance be to warrant calling it a disorder? Another is semantic: A variety of terms—character neuroses, neurotic characters, character disorders, personality trait disturbances, personality pattern disturbances, personality disorders (the term used in the *Diagnostic and Statistical Manual–III*)—have been applied to the same clinical syndromes." The choice of terms depends on the "theoretical assumptions regarding the determinants of personality organization."[82] Here Kernberg adds, succinctly, "In clinical psychiatric practice the terms *character* and *personality* have been used interchangeably."[83]

Kernberg's definition of "personality disorders," in a book intended largely for the use of mental-health practitioners, was "constellations of abnormal or pathological character traits of sufficient intensity to imply significant disturbance in intrapsychic and/or interpersonal functioning."[84] His "classification of character pathology" categorizes *DSM* personality types by the severity of their problems, beginning with the least severe or "better functioning" and progressing to the most functionally impaired.[85] This is more technical information than most lay readers will need, but the general point should be clear: "character" in the context of "character pathology" will include all the various "personalities" that are included in a manual of mental disorders.

The Medicalization of Modern Speech

As much as professionals would like to restrict and control the crucial terms of art of their various fields, popular usage will often pre-empt, exploit, and sometimes misuse them. This is nowhere more evident than in the popular appropriation of the phrase "personality disorder," once only used as a precise psychological or medical term, now a ubiquitous description in print and television journalism, blogs, and other lay discourses. "Personality disorder" has entered popular discourse in the same way as other psychological terms—as "psychotic" did some time ago. Once these terms have migrated from clinical to popular use, or misuse, there is little that can be done to limit them. The perverse triumph of "personality" in the twenty-first century is that, although it was initially chosen in part for its neutrality and lack of affect, it has now taken on specialized popular meanings, both as a noun ("television personality") and as an adjective ("personality disorder").

The advertising executive and "television personality" Donny Deutsch commented on MSNBC's *Morning Joe* that President Donald Trump "clearly has a personality disorder," adding, "And when you have a personality disorder you need to create drama to feel alive."[86] Peter Wehner, a senior fellow at the Ethics and Public Policy Center, who served in three Republican administrations, wrote in *The New York Times* that Trump's "disordered personality thrives on mayhem and upheaval, on vicious personal attacks and ceaseless conflict."[87] So many columns, articles, and letters to the editor speculated on Trump's mental state that a psychiatrist felt called upon to correct the record.

"Most amateur diagnosticians have mislabeled President Trump with the diagnosis of narcissistic personality disorder," said Dr. Allen Frances in a letter to the editor of *The New York Times*. "I wrote the criteria that define this disorder, and Mr. Trump doesn't meet them." His reason: Trump "may be a world-class narcissist, but that doesn't make him mentally ill, because he does not suffer from the distress and impairment required to diagnose mental disorder."[88]

Others have expressed a different view. In *The Dangerous Case of Donald Trump: 27 Psychiatrists and Mental Health Experts Assess a President* (2017), Dr. Bandy Lee and her coauthors address what they see as the core issue, which is not the actual medical diagnosis but the dangers that Trump's psychological and mental states pose to the nation. As Lee explained in a follow-up article in *The Guardian*, the authors kept "within the letter of the Goldwater rule—which prohibits psychiatrists from diagnosing public figures without a personal examination and without consent." Nonetheless, she said, mental health professionals can tell a lot from "observations of a person's patterns of responses, of media appearances over time, and from reports of those close to him." And while "a diagnosis in itself, as much as it helps define the course, prognosis, and treatment, is Trump's private business," it is the public's right to know "whether the president and commander-in-chief has the capacity to function in his office."[89]

Many terms that were once the proper province of medical specialists have now moved into a gray area where they seem to be acceptable as memes or metaphors. The op-ed columnist Roger Cohen can write in *The New York Times* about Donald Trump's "manic personality"[90] without being charged with practicing medicine without a license, and the same, presumably, could be said for the financier Weijian Shan when he described China's economy as having a "split personality."[91]

As for "character," its older moral or ethical meaning, once seen as disqualifying it for modern use, has now returned to apparent pertinence and favor, at least in political speech. Before his election, Donald Trump—everyone's favorite pop political analysand—was criticized from the right (Mona Charen, "Donald Trump Doesn't Have the Character to Be President"), the left (Rick Ungar, "Donald Trump and the Decline of American Character—A Cautionary Tale"), and by a best-selling novelist channeling Heraclitus (Richard North Patterson, "Trump's Character Is His Fate").[92] The former deputy director of the Central Intelligence Agency wrote an op-ed column in *The New York Times* in which he said that "the character traits" Trump had exhibited suggested that he would be a "dangerous" commander in chief; among these were "his obvious need for self-aggrandizement," "his overreaction to perceived slights," and "his routine carelessness with the facts."[93]

The use of popularized medical and psychological terms in the 2016 presidential campaign also went in the other direction. When Donald Trump became the Republican candidate for president, he launched renewed attacks on Hillary Clinton's character: "Unstable Hillary Clinton lacks the judgment, temperament and moral character to lead this country," he said at a rally in Des Moines, Iowa, and repeated this assessment later, in Green Bay, Wisconsin: "She's a weak person. She's actually not strong enough to be president." Clinton, he wrote on Facebook, "is a pathological liar."[94] "Liar" is an accusation; "pathological" is a diagnosis. But the medicalization of popular discourse and common speech—together with the memelike tendency to think of phrases like "pathological liar" as indissoluble units rather than as particular, and specialized, psychological assessments—has made such labels commonplace, and has emptied them of both clarity and accuracy.

"Temperament," yet another "psychological" term, with a pedigree as old as "character," also returned as a political term of art during the 2016 campaign. Based on the ancient idea of the four temperaments (melancholic, choleric, sanguine, phlegmatic), each originally linked to a bodily fluid or "humor" (black bile, yellow bile, blood, phlegm), "temperament" in the work of modern psychologists addresses emotional response, and is often regarded as at least partly hereditary. The original idea was that all humans are influenced by these four elements in the body, and that one of them often predominates. But though the word has survived in modern usage—and some commentators have not hesitated to describe Donald Trump as "choleric"[95]—politicians tend to employ it without any reference to the four temperaments (or the four humors).

With the exception of Trump's boasting about his own "greatest" temperament and his singular "stability," the uses of terms like "character," "personality," and "temperament" in political discourse have increasingly tended to be negative rather than positive. We hear that a candidate "lacks" or "doesn't have" the character (or temperament) to serve in public office. When "character traits" are mentioned, they are as likely to be taken from a lexicon of "character defects" as from the upbeat self-improvement qualities endorsed by Victorians like Samuel Smiles. Some politicians continue to evoke "character" in the moral/ethical/backbone sense, as in Massachusetts Senator Elizabeth Warren's assertion: "The character of a nation is not the character of its president. The character of a nation is the character of its people."[96] (Had Warren said "the personality of a nation is the personality of a people" she might have been understood to mean something quite different.) Likewise, in his campaign for the Democratic presidential nomination, Joe Biden declared that "character is on the ballot." But if "character" remains the ideal, "personality," both in its psychological and in its modern lay sense, is often the means.

There is a certain cultural logic to the fact that the man who became known as the "father of public relations," Edward Bernays, was a double nephew of Sigmund Freud: his mother was Freud's sister; his father's sister, Martha Bernays, was Freud's wife.[97] In a book called *Propaganda* (1928), Bernays wrote:

> A personality may create circumstances, as Lindbergh created good will between the United States and Mexico. Events may create a personality, as the Cuban War created the political figure of Roosevelt. It is often difficult to say which creates the other. Once a public figure has decided which ends he wishes to achieve, he must regard himself objectively and present an outward picture of himself which is consistent with his real character and his aims.[98]

For many years now the "making" of a president has been understood to be an advertising campaign as much as, or more than, an education. Increasingly, the language of politics tends to be performative rather than essential: "looking presidential," "sounding presidential," "acting presidential." The task, and the goal, became to make character visible.

6
SEEING IT
Art, Physiognomy, Photography, Gesture, Science

I saw Othello's visage in his mind,
And to his honours and his valiant parts
Did I my soul and fortunes consecrate.

—SHAKESPEARE, *OTHELLO*

face book, n. A directory containing photographs and biographical details of students (esp. incoming freshmen) at a university or college, published at the start of the academic year to facilitate contact between students. Also: a similar publication produced by another type of institution or organization.

—*OXFORD ENGLISH DICTIONARY*

Faception uses machine learning to score facial images using personality types like "academic researcher, "brand promoter," "terrorist" and "pedophile."

—*THE NEW YORK TIMES*, JULY 10, 2019

What does character look like? Can it be read, or recognized, from a visual image? From the face, or the expression, or the pose? From measurements, charts, or scans?

"Look at that face!" exclaimed the then-candidate Donald Trump when a television camera focused on a fellow candidate for president, Carly Fiorina. "Would anyone vote for that? Can you imagine that, the face of our next president?" When his comment was reported in *Rolling Stone*, Trump defended himself to a TV anchor by saying he was "not talking about looks, but about persona."[1]

The goal of making character both visible and legible has long compelled image makers, whether painters, sculptors, caricaturists, photographers, criminologists, or, most recently, scientific researchers who read, study, and map the brain through functional magnetic resonance imaging, or fMRI. But as one mode of depiction joins with or succeeds another, issues of interpretation, detection, and representation have persisted, together with claims of bias (the flattery of patronage; the discriminatory attitudes of race and class; the persona and psychology of the artist).

"There's no art / To find the mind's construction in the face," observes Shakespeare's King Duncan, reflecting on the unsuspected treason of the Thane of Cawdor. "He was a gentleman on whom I built / An absolute trust" (*Macbeth* 1.4.11–14). Yet no sooner has the traitor been exposed and condemned to death than the title is immediately bestowed on Macbeth, whom Duncan, praising his faithful service and loyalty, will address as "my worthy Cawdor." Duncan, in fact, makes the same mistake twice. This new thane of Cawdor will be a traitor, too, and one of his first acts will be the killing of the king.

"Art" in Shakespeare's time meant technical ability, the result of knowledge or practice; in the course of the seventeenth century, the word would increasingly take on the modern meaning of creative or imaginative skill. But in both senses, the quest for an "art / To find the mind's construction in the face" continues, despite Duncan's—and Shakespeare's—cautious doubts. (Macbeth, we might recall, adopts a deliberately deceptive contravening strategy: "False face must hide what the false heart doth know.") A century and a half later, Duncan's countryman Henry Home, Lord Kames, a leading spirit of the Scottish Enlightenment, would claim, "The character of a man may be read in his face."[2]

Della Porta's Animals and Le Brun's Passions

Aristotle, it is said, declared that "to read the character of a man one only had to trace in his physiognomy the features of the animal which he resembled most."[3] Giambattista della Porta, a sixteenth-century Italian scientist, playwright, and polymath, expanded on this idea and published his conclusions in 1586. His suggestion that there was a physiological relationship between the expressions of animals and human beings was demonstrated by an accompanying series of beautifully detailed woodcuts: man and owl, man and ox, man and bird, man and greyhound, man and monkey, man and pig. An especially engaging example is *The Man and the Ram*, in which the two curly-headed subjects, pictured in profile, gaze equably and incuriously in the same direction. In each case, the human being is seen in profile, the eyes, hair, ears, and particularly the nose resembling, wittily and convincingly, the corresponding feature of his animal other. The underlying idea was that the resemblance extended beyond appearance to character—that some men were wise, noble, piggish, etc. (There are no images of women.)

Over time, della Porta's book would influence the ideas of Johann Caspar Lavater in the eighteenth century and of both Cesare Lombroso and Charles Darwin in the nineteenth.[4] Della Porta's work was also adapted by painters, such as Charles Le Brun, the First Painter to Louis XIV and the director of the Académie Royale de Peinture et de Sculpture. Le Brun's treatise on the expression of the "passions" in painting[5] was to influence artists and theorists of art for more than two centuries.

The question of the "passions," and their relationship to the ancient humors or temperaments, had long engaged the interest of physicians and philosophers. (The word "emotion," which we are more likely today to use than "passion" in this sense, did not appear in English until the mid-sixteenth century, and seems to have derived from a French term that originally meant something like commotion, uprising, or civil unrest. Thus an "emotion" in our more modern sense was, in effect, an uprising within the self.[6])

The passions were seen as essential components of character. When one emerged as the "ruling passion," it could define or dominate the character of an individual. Cicero said there were only four passions: fear, desire, distress, and pleasure. Thomas Aquinas thought there were eleven, divided into two groups, the concupiscible passions (love, hate, desire, aversion, pleasure, and sadness) and the irascible passions (hope, despair, fear, courage, and anger).[7] Early modern writers added more.

As an artist, and one who trained other artists, Le Brun was concerned with how to *represent* such states of mind. His theory of physiognomy was indebted to that of Descartes, who postulated a relationship between the facial features and the pineal gland, which he believed to be the seat of the soul. Following della Porta, Le Brun matched each human passion with the face of an animal thought to typify that passion or emotion, each meticulously sketched and proportionally set out for the novice, and even for the expert, to copy. Terror and Horror, drawn both frontally and in profile. Depictions of Extreme Despair, Anger Mixed with Fear, and Anger Mixed with Rage, meticulously sketched, all three on a single page. Le Brun's drawings are idealized images of "the passions," not the particular or immediate passions of the painter. Like Diderot's paradox of the actor, they show how to *indicate* feeling, not how to feel.

Physiognomy and Pathognomy

Of these two terms, the former is certainly more familiar than the latter. Yet it is "pathognomy," the study of the "passions" or emotions, that still enjoys some current repute, generating interest among scholars and artists, while "physiognomy," the study of facial features and other bodily attributes as indications of character, is often associated, when attributed to individuals or groups, with social and racial biases. Studies of character sometimes combined, or claimed to combine, these two supposed sciences with phrenology, as in the title of Leander McCormick's handbook published in 1920, *Characterology: An Exact Science, Embracing Physiognomy, Phrenology, and Pathognomy.* The "science" of physiognomy, as we will see, very quickly evolved, or deteriorated, into highly unscientific statements about race, national heritage, and character. But bad theories of character are part of the history of character, and are therefore worth both our notice and our symptomatic analysis.

The vogue for physiognomy that began in the late eighteenth century was due in large part to the work of Johann Caspar Lavater, a Swiss minister, poet, and writer. Lavater's *Essays on Physiognomy*, published between 1775 and 1778, became enormously popular, and were translated into French and English. The illustrations, 360 outline portraits and engravings, provided visual "proof" of such observations as "The outline of the forehead is most extraordinary, and highly characteristic of great and bold enterprise," and "Unbounded avarice, unfeeling wickedness, knavery unequalled, in the eye and mouth, eradicate every pleasing expression."[8]

"Physiognomy teaches the knowledge of character at rest," wrote Lavater, "and pathognomy of character in motion."[9] Intrinsic to his argument was that habitual states of mind impress themselves upon the "soft and flexible parts of the face."[10] Thus he proposed what he called his "theorem": "The beauty and deformity of the countenance is in a just and determinate proportion to the moral beauty and deformity of the man. The morally best, the most beautiful. The morally worst, the most deformed."[11] Character, he insisted, "was not the result of education" but, rather, of heredity; just as "features and forms were inherited, so were moral propensities."[12]

> Let us suppose men of the most beautiful and noblest form, and that they, and their children, become morally degenerate; abandon themselves to their passions, and progressively, become more and more vicious. How will these men, or their countenances at least, be, from generation to generation, deformed! What bloated, depressed, turgid, stupid, disfigured and haggard features! What variety of more or less gross, vulgar, caricatures, will rise in succession, from father to son![13]

This unhappy process was, however, reversible, with proper foresight, by removing children from their families and encouraging eugenic policies:

> Take the children of the most ordinary persons, let them be the exact image of their parents; let them be removed, and educated in some public, well-regulated seminary; their progress from deformity towards beauty will be visible. Arrived at the state of puberty, let them be placed in circumstances that shall not render the practice of virtue difficult, and under which they shall have no temptations to vice; let them intermarry; let an active impulse to improvement be supposed . . . What a handsome race of men will the fifth or sixth generation produce, if no extraordinary accidents intervene! Handsome, not only in the features of the countenance, but in the solid parts of the head, in the whole man, accompanied by contentment, and other virtues.[14]

Lavater's list of "One Hundred Physiognomonical Rules" included eight instructions for reading the forehead, six on wrinkles of the forehead, thirteen on the eyes, three on the eyebrows, eight on the nose, ten on the mouth, and two on the lineaments of the cheeks. Here are two examples:

- Foreheads inclining to be long, with a close-drawn wrinkleless skin, which exhibit no lively cheerful wrinkles even in their few moments of joy, are cold, malign, suspicious, severe, censorious, conceited, mean, and seldom forgive.
- Noses which are much turned downward are never truly good, truly cheerful, or noble, or great. Their thoughts and inclinations always tend to earth. They are close, cold, heartless, incommunicative; often maliciously sarcastic, ill humoured, or extremely hypochondriac, or melancholic. When arched in the upper part, they are fearful and voluptuous.[15]

A few of the "physiognomonical rules" are reserved for the discussion of women, of whom Lavater declares that "vanity or pride is the general characteristic," prefacing this statement with a claim of prudent discretion: "Not the thousandth part of what is to be observed may be

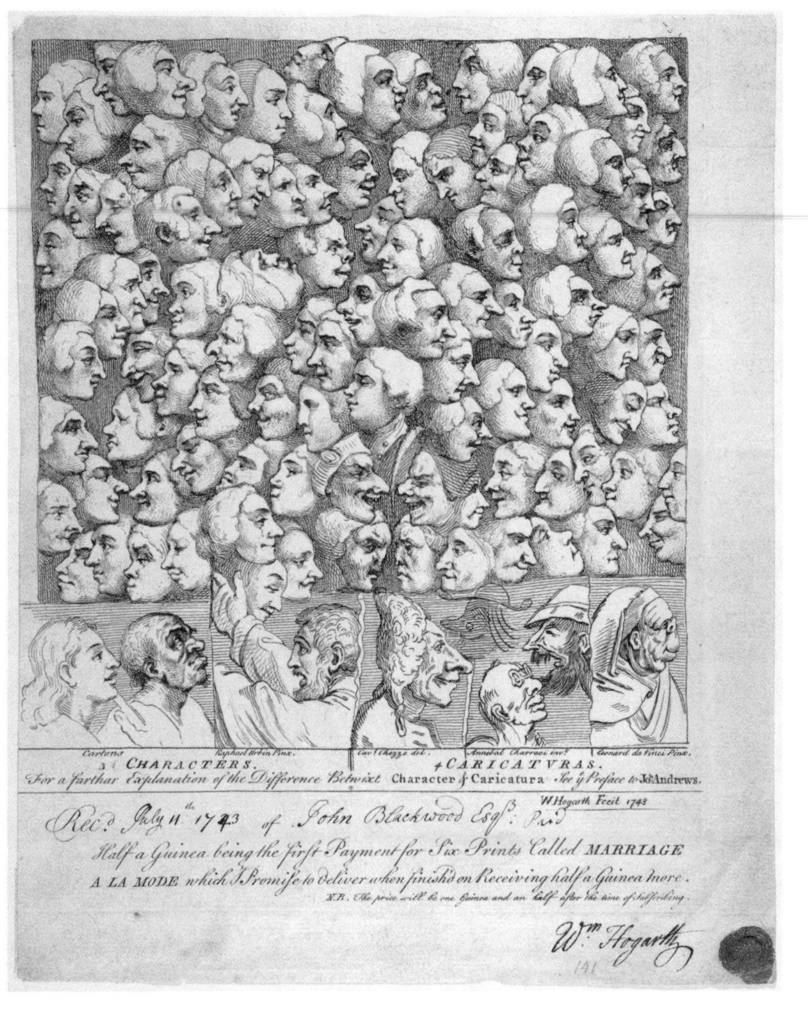

Characters and Caricaturas; William Hogarth, print, 1743
(The Metropolitan Museum of Art)

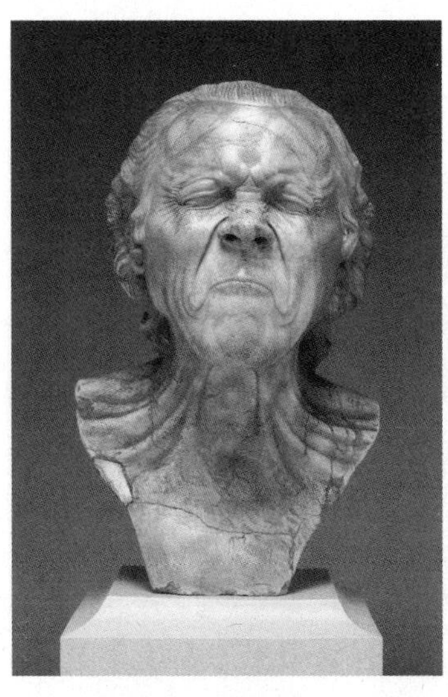

The Vexed Man; Franz Xaver Messerschmidt, alabaster, 1771–1783 *(The J. Paul Getty Museum)*

A Strong Man; Franz Xaver Messerschmidt, tin-lead alloy, 1771–1783 *(The J. Paul Getty Museum)*

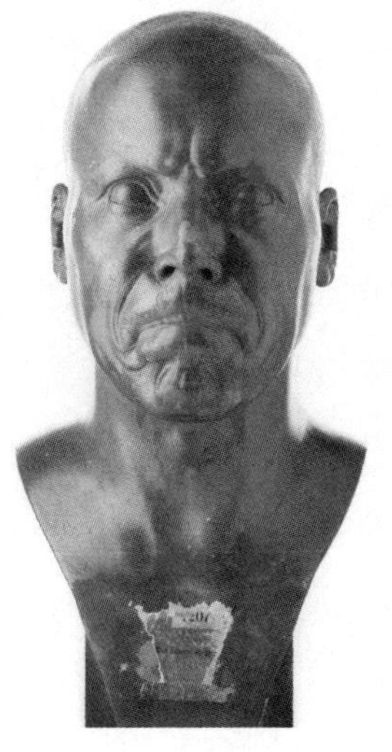

The Difficult Secret; Franz Xaver Messerschmidt, tin cast, 1771–1783 *(Photography by Hulya Kolabas)*

Just Rescued from Drowning; Franz Xaver Messerschmidt, alabaster, 1771–1783 *(The J. Paul Getty Museum)*

Grief Locked Up Inside; Franz Xaver Messerschmidt, tin-lead cast, 1771–1783 *(Belvedere, Vienna)*

The Simpleton; Franz Xaver Messerschmidt, alabaster, 1771–1783 *(Wien Museum, Karlsplaz, Austria)*

Strong Smell; Franz Xaver Messerschmidt, metal cast, 1771–1783 *(ArtResource)*

A Cheeky Nitpicky Mocker; Franz Xaver Messerschmidt, alabaster, 1771–1783 *(The J. Paul Getty Museum)*

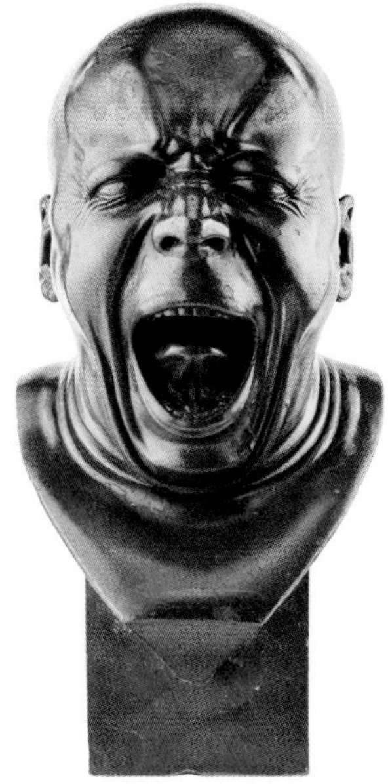

The Yawner; Franz Xaver Messerschmidt, tin cast, 1771–1783 *(Museum of Fine Arts, Budapest)*

Messerschmidt's "Character Heads"; Matthias Rudolph Tom, lithograph on paper, 1839 *(Österreichische Nationalbibliothek, Vienna)*

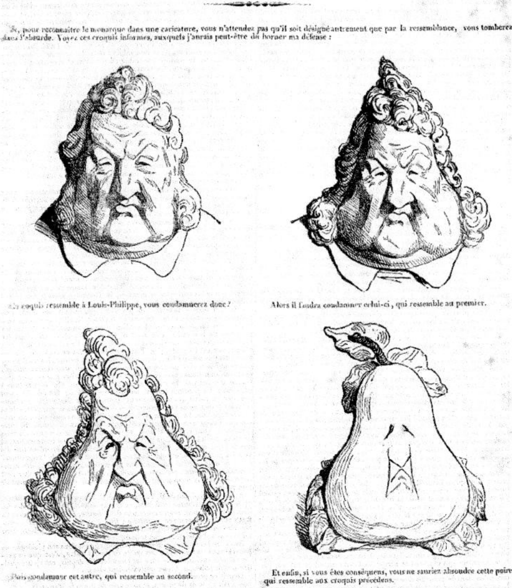

LES POIRES,

Faites à la cour d'assises de Paris par le directeur de la CARICATURE.

Vendues pour payer les 6,000 fr. d'amende du journal le *Charivari*.

Si, pour reconnaître le monarque dans une caricature, vous n'attendez pas qu'il soit désigné autrement que par la ressemblance, vous tomberez dans l'absurde. Voyez ces croquis informes, auxquels j'aurais peut-être dû borner ma défense :

Ce croquis ressemble à Louis-Philippe, vous condamnerez donc ?

Alors il faudra condamner celui-ci, qui ressemble au premier.

Puis condamner cet autre, qui ressemble au second.

Et enfin, si vous êtes conséquens, vous ne sauriez absoudre cette poire, qui ressemble aux croquis précédens.

Ainsi, pour une poire, pour une brioche, et pour toutes les têtes grotesques dans lesquelles le hasard ou la malice aura placé cette triste ressemblance, vous pourrez infliger à l'auteur cinq ans de prison et cinq mille francs d'amende ! !

Avouez, Messieurs, que c'est là une singulière liberté de la presse ! !

Les poires; Honoré Daumier, drawing, 1839 *(Gallica Digital Library)*

Essai d'autographie [Autographic test]; Rodolphe Töpffer, lithograph, 1842/1845 *(The Elisha Whittelsey Collection)*

Panthéon Nadar [The Nadar Pantheon]; Nadar, lithograph, 1854 *(The Metropolitan Museum of Art)*

Self-portrait; Nadar, photograph, c. 1860 *(Bibliotheque Nationale de France, Paris)*

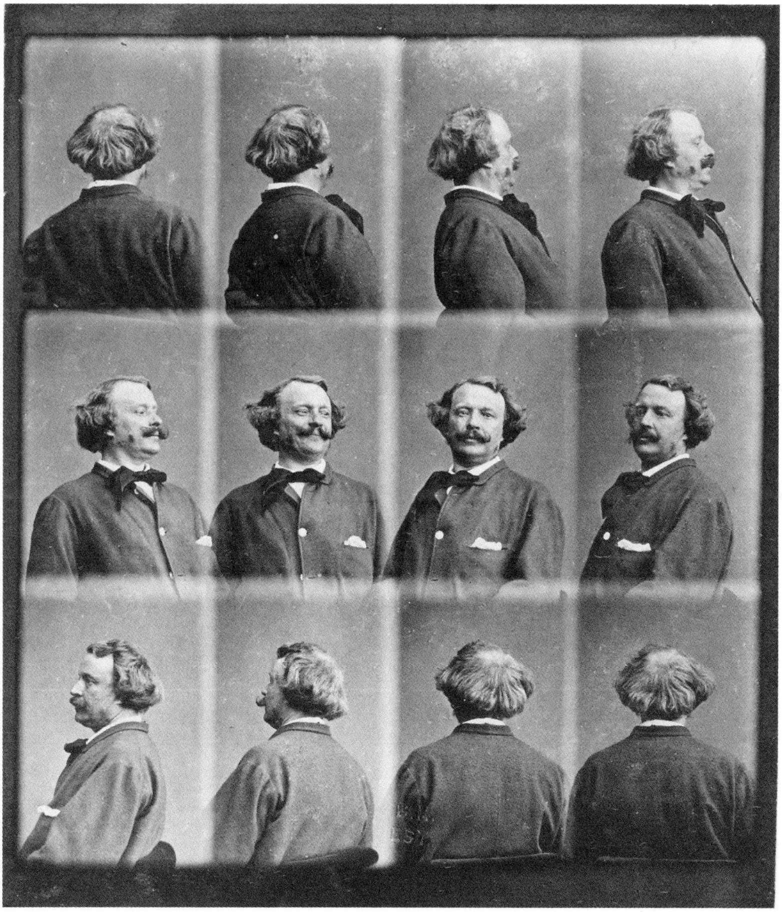

Revolving self-portrait; Nadar, photograph, c. 1865 *(Gallica Digital Library)*

George Sand; Nadar, photograph, 1864 *(Museum of Fine Arts, Houston)*

Sarah Bernhardt; Nadar, photograph, 1864 *(Wikimedia Commons)*

Hector Berlioz; Nadar, photograph, 1860 *(Monir Tayeb and Michel Austin, www.hberlioz.com)*

Victor Hugo; Nadar, photograph, 1880 *(The J. Paul Getty Museum)*

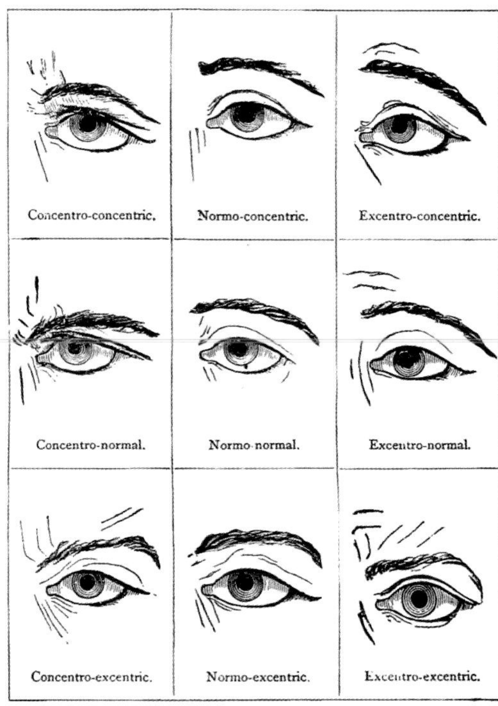

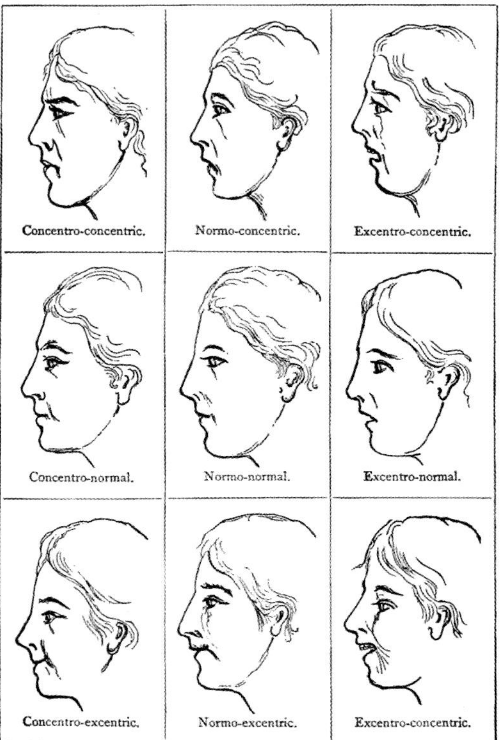

Chart XII: *Expressions of the Eyebrow* and Chart XIV: *Expressions of the Mouth*; Genevieve Stebbins, *Delsarte System of Dramatic Expression*, drawing, 1886 *(Harvard University)*

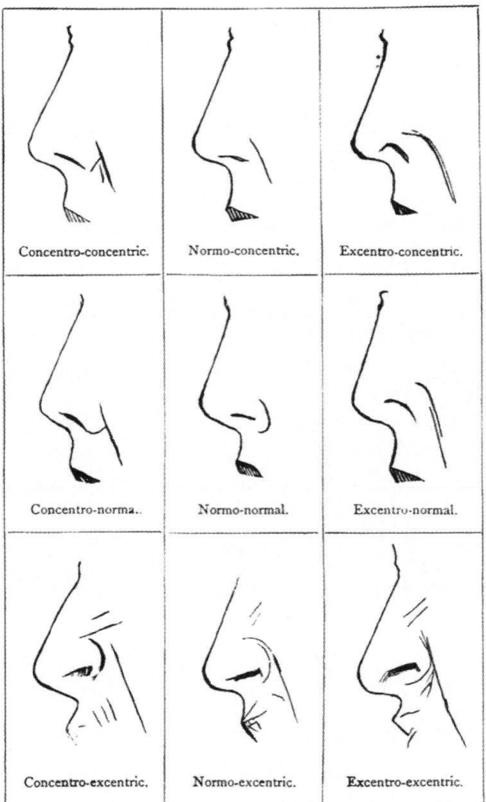

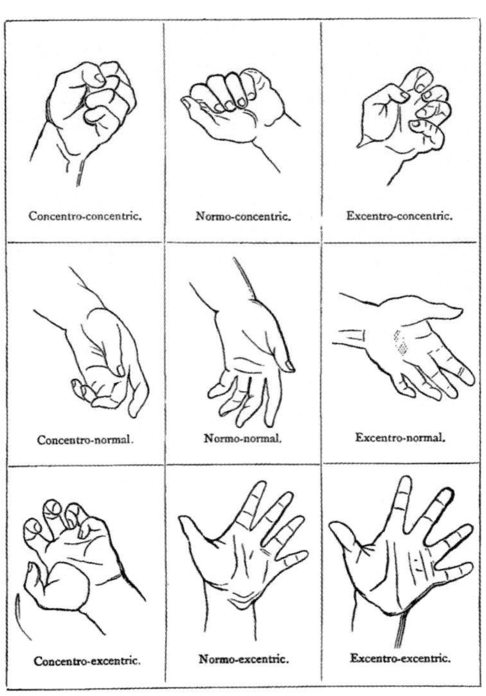

Chart XIII: *Expressions of the Nose* and Chart III: *Expressions of the Hand*; Genevieve Stebbins, *Delsarte System of Dramatic Expression*, drawing, 1886 *(Harvard University)*

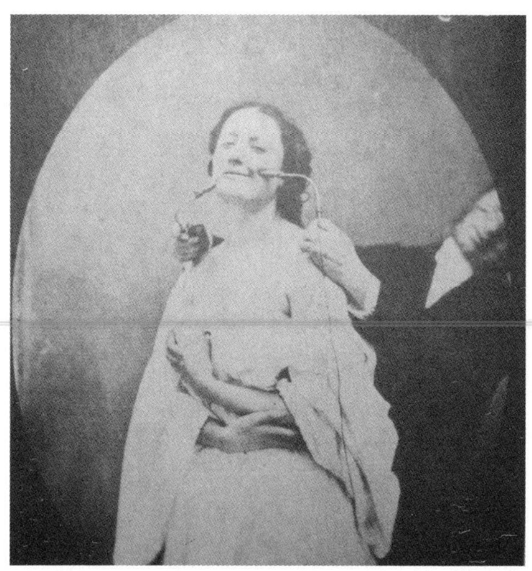

Plate 78: Scene of coquetry, full and detail;
Guillaume-Benjamin-Amand Duchenne, albumen silver print from glass negative, 1854–1856, printed 1862 *(The Metropolitan Museum of Art)*

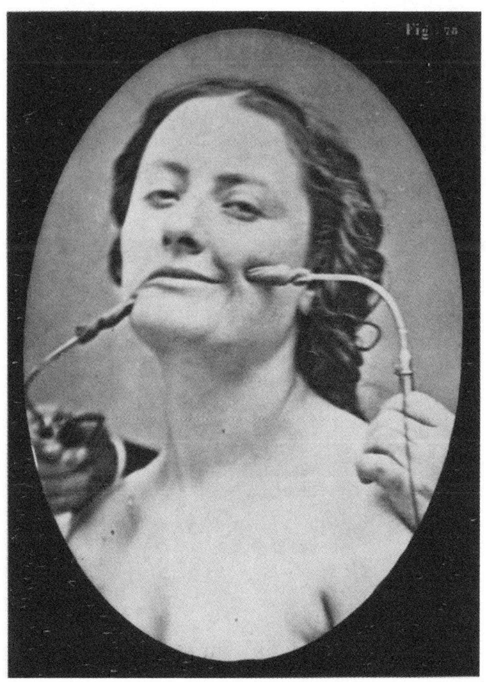

Expressions of grief; Oscar Gustave Rejlander, heliotype, 1871–1872, printed 1872 *(Wellcome Collection)*

Pl. 4

1

Heliotype 2

Hatred and anger; Oscar Gustave Rejlander, heliotype, 1871–1872, printed 1872 *(Wellcome Collection)*

Charles Darwin; Herbert Rose Barraud, photograph, 1881 *(Huntington Library, San Marino, CA)*

Surprised Man; Oscar Gustave Rejlander, heliotype, 1871–1872, printed 1872 *(The J. Paul Getty Museum)*

Self-portrait: *Laughing/Crying*; Oscar Gustave Rejlander, heliotype, 1871–1872, printed 1872 *(Wikimedia Commons)*

Pride and shrugging; Oscar Gustave Rejlander, heliotype, 1871–1872, printed 1872 *(Wellcome Collection)*

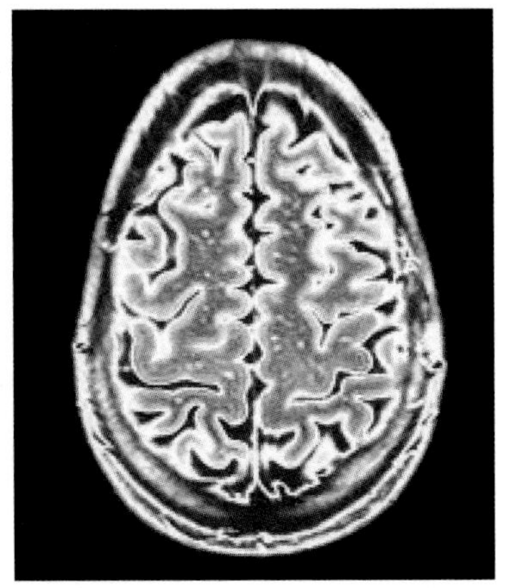

Functional MRI image
(Getty Images)

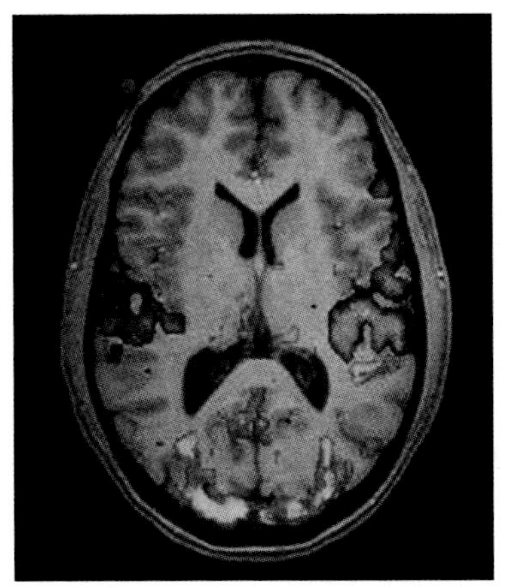

Functional MRI image
(Open University)

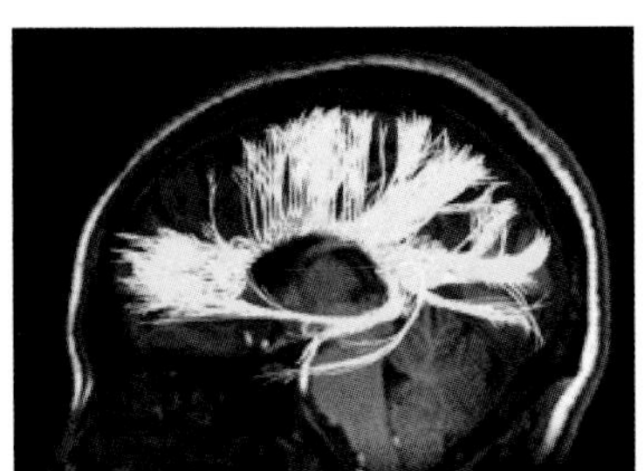

Functional MRI image
(Center for Functional MRI in the Department of Radiology, UC San Diego School of Medicine)

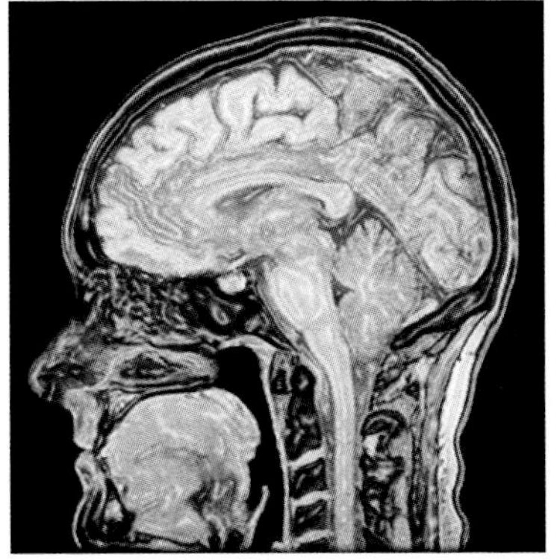

Functional MRI image
(Human Brain Mapping)

committed to writing." His roster of women does not include many physical traits he finds attractive—most of his paragraphs are dismissive ("if the manner of walking of a woman be disgusting, decidedly disgusting, not only disagreeable but impetuous . . ."; "Women with rolling eyes, tenderly-moveable, wrinkly, relaxed, almost hanging skin, arched nose, ruddy cheeks, seldom motionless mouth . . . are not only of persuasive speech, prolific in imagination, ambitious, and distinguished for capacious memory—but also by nature extremely inclined to gallantry [i.e., to amorous intrigue or immorality]").[16]

It's easy to see how this kind of physiognomic checklist might provoke amateur analyses and generate the nineteenth-century enthusiasm for "pocket physiognomy," one of whose principal handbooks was *The Pocket Lavater*,[17] which distilled Lavater's massive tome (originally published in English in three volumes) to a trim 116 pages of print.

Lavater had devoted a section of *Essays on Physiognomy* to the discussion of individual artists and their skill—or lack of skill—in physiognomy. Rubens is said to excel in depicting "the lineaments of all that is cruel, powerful, benign—and hellish," and Rembrandt displayed "all the most tasteless passions of the vulgar." The heads of van Dyck's portraits "contain too few of the small lines" that indicate character; "the best pictures of Erasmus, by Holbein, greatly exceed all the portraits of Vandyke, in truth and simplicity." Lavater singles out the caricatures of Annibale Carracci for special praise: "He had the gift, so necessary to the physiognomist, of portraying much character in a few strokes." Likewise William Hogarth, the English painter and pictorial satirist, who is said to find "little of the noble" and "little of the beauteous expression" in his subjects, but offers "an immense treasury of features of meanness in excess, vulgarity the most disgusting, humour the most irresistible, and vice the most unmanly." Both Charles Le Brun and Lavater's friend the English painter Henry Fuseli are honored for their skill in pathognomy.[18] Indeed, Lavater laments that the study of most painters will produce only "pathognomonical knowledge"—the seeker after "physiognomical acquisitions" is likely to be disappointed.

Lavater also believed in the truth of "national physiognomy," which in his sense of the term included race: "Compare a Negro and an Englishman, a native of Lapland and an Italian, a Frenchman and an inhabitant of Terra del Fuego. Examine their forms, countenances, characters, and minds. Their difference will easily be seen."[19] He adds to his description quotations from like-minded thinkers such as Fuseli and the art historian J. J. Winckelmann, who offered specific descriptions of Negroes, Jews, American Indians, Russians, and Turks, together with assertions of the value of physiogmony. "Our eyes convince us," wrote Winckelmann, "with respect to the form of man, that the character of nation, as well as of mind, is visible in the countenance."[20]

A proud citizen of Zürich, Lavater described one of the many comparative images in his book as "a sketch of a countenance such as will scarcely be found in any other nation. No Englishman looks thus, no Frenchman, no Italian, and certainly, no citizen of Basel, or Berne. The love of labour, innocent benevolence, tender irritability, and strength of imagination, are some of the ideas read in this short-sighted, and, apparently, inquiring eye, which seems to speak what all eyes understand."[21]

The image bears a striking resemblance to portraits of Lavater himself.

Messerschmidt's "Character Heads"

While Lavater was outlining his theories in Switzerland, a remarkable collection of what came to be called "character heads" was produced in Austria by the Bavarian-born sculptor Franz Xaver Messerschmidt. Messerschmidt (1736–1783) was in his early years a highly successful court sculptor, metalsmith, and architect, and a professor at the Vienna Academy of Arts. Around 1771, however, he seems to have undergone a severe personality change, becoming suspicious and paranoid. He was passed over for promotion at the academy, reacted strongly against this new slight, and ultimately moved to an isolated location near Bratislava, where he began to craft a series of sculpted heads.

Friedrich Nicolai, a writer who visited the artist at work, describes Messerschmidt pinching himself repeatedly below the ribs on the right side, peering at himself in a mirror, going back and forth between mirror and sculpture in his attempt to convey, as accurately as possible, the full range of human expressions. "In his opinion," wrote Nicolai, "there were sixty-four variations on the grimaces."

> He already had, by the time I was at his house, completed sixty different heads, some of marble, some of a composition of pewter and lead, most of them life-sized; and he had occupied himself unceasingly with this wretched labor full eleven years with an enduring patience which must astonish one. All those heads were his own likeness. I saw him working on the sixty-first head. He glanced into the looking glass every half minute and made the face he needed with the utmost precision. As works of art, especially those heads that have natural poses, they are masterpieces.[22]

The sixty-nine heads Messerschmidt made between 1770 and 1783, cast in lead or tin alloy, or in some cases carved in alabaster, depict what has been called "the furthest limits of human expression."[23] These were not commissioned pieces, nor were they intended to be sold. Two and a half centuries later, they strike a modern viewer with their immediacy and power.

The term "character heads" was not given to these works by the artist—he called them *Kopfstücke* ("head pieces")—and the picturesque names by which they have come to be known were also bestowed after Messerschmidt's death. He left behind a large number of these heads, forty-nine of which were brought to Vienna ten years later and exhibited, for the first time, in 1793. An anonymous author who published a small brochure to accompany the exhibition called these works "character heads," and gave to them a series of individual names. It is by these names or titles that the heads have since been known.

The titles have become part of the appeal of the character heads and also of their mystery, since they do not always seem to correspond to the works in question, and in some cases seem deliberately provocative: *The Vexed Man*, *A Haggard Old Man with Aching Eyes*, *The Difficult Secret*, *Just Rescued from Drowning*, *The Strong Odor*, *A Cheeky Nitpicky*

Mocker, The Incapable Bassoonist, A Hypocrite and Slanderer, Afflicted with Constipation.

Do these heads reflect the biography and mental state of the artist, or the contemporary fascination with theories of affect and with physiognomy and pathognomy, the measurement of facial proportion and expression? The psychoanalyst Ernst Kris, who trained as an art historian, suggested in an influential essay that Messerschmidt suffered from a psychotic condition, and that many of the grimaces represented in the character heads were attempts at warding off—or yielding to—the demons that threatened to possess him.[24] Other critics have addressed these works in the context of eighteenth-century science or as prescient works of modern art.

Critics have gone out of their way to disavow the legitimacy of the post-facto titles. But when Ronald S. Lauder brought an exhibition of Messerschmidt's work to the Neue Galerie in New York in the fall of 2010, the character heads were exhibited with their descriptive titles, and one of the manifest pleasures of some museum patrons was to try to interpret the sculptures in light of the label each one bore. Some mimicked the facial expressions, turning to their companions to have them "read" the character or emotion displayed.

Which comes first, the concept of "character" or its visualization in stone, metal, or paint? As is the case with literary and stage characters, these remarkable sculptures raise questions of priority, authenticity, and back-formation. Do we originate our expressions, or borrow and recognize them from models, imitating the enigmatic smile of the *Mona Lisa*, or the suffering of Laocoön, just as a child patterns facial expressions upon those of a parent?

The philosopher Ludwig Wittgenstein, it is said, kept a copy of Messerschmitt's *The Simpleton* on his desk.[25] From Egon Schiele to Oskar Kokoschka, Francis Bacon, Arnulf Rainer, Bruce Nauman, Tony Cragg, and Tony Bevan, the character heads have, often explicitly, influenced modern art and contemporary artists. Bevan, who produced some *Self-Portraits After Messerschmidt*, wrote an undergraduate thesis on his work and later noted that he had always held "aspects of Messerschmidt . . . in my subconscious somewhere."[26] Cragg, who has exhibited some of his sculptures in a "dialogue" with Messerschmidt's, observed, "The work is not just representational but also has become a test for psychological responses and for unusual physical states of the face or for unusual facial expressions."[27]

What might the character heads tell us about "character"? Ernst Kris is right, I think, to link these sculptures to a certain mode of caricature. "The successful caricature," he wrote, "distorts appearances but only for the sake of a deeper truth" that "penetrates to the essence of a person's character."[28] If we leave aside the question of the artist's own mental state, Messerschmidt's works, regarded today, are eloquent and effective. His *Yawner* has been persuasively compared to painter Francis Bacon's *Head VI*, and even to Edvard Munch's famous *Scream*. Whether *The Yawner* is indicating sleepiness or terror, the powerful dramatic effect comes through.

Like the thirty "Characters" of the ancient writer Theophrastus, Messerschmidt's character heads offer a lexicon of character types that would be quoted and augmented by later practitioners. Messerschmidt has his *Hypocrite and Slanderer*, Theophrastus his "Grumbler" and "Bore." In neither the character heads nor the Theophrastan characters is the set definitive; further types can and would be added by others. Rather, the selection constitutes an artistic narrative, a set of vivid, often visceral, sometimes comical portraits that tell a story, both about humankind and about society.

We might also compare the heads to the masks of the commedia dell'arte, with its stock theatrical types of the Capitano, the Dottore, the Zanni, Pierrot, and Pierrette. Messerschmidt's character heads are the *dramatis personae* of a powerful, personal vision, whether psychotic, neurotic, scientific, or merely inspired. If they are all, or almost all, portraits of the artist, this does not keep them from being generalizable as social mirrors, investigations of how we "read" human character, in terms both of immediate emotion and of underlying structure and expression.

"Loaded Portraits": Character and Caricature

"The portrait painter's task," wrote Ernst Kris and E. H. Gombrich, "was to reveal the character, the essence of the man in an heroic sense; that of the caricaturist provided the natural counterpart—to reveal the true man behind the mask of pretense, and to show up his 'essential' littleness and ugliness."[29]

The Italian term for caricature in the seventeenth century was *ritratti carichi*, "loaded portraits," and, like our modern phrase "loaded words," this suggests something of the supercharge that the artist can provide. "The successful caricaturist distorts appearances but only for the sake of a deeper truth," say Kris and Gombrich, and in doing so, "the artist penetrates to the essence of a person's character."[30] In other words, "the caricaturist seeks for the perfect deformity, he shows how the soul of the man would express itself in his body if only matter were sufficiently pliable to Nature's intentions."[31] Their contention is that caricature is serious art.

It's fitting that a psychoanalyst with art-historical training and an eminent art historian should team up on the topic of caricature, since, as they note, a caricature is something like a dream, in which two words can become one, or two figures merge into one. "This double meaning, this transformation, ambiguity, and condensation," are aspects, they suggest, of "the primary process used in caricatures in the same way that Freud has demonstrated it to be used in 'wit.'"[32]

One of the best-known examples of caricature as loaded wit is Charles Philipon's famous image of Louis-Philippe as a pear, or, rather, of King Louis *turning*, slowly and inexorably, *into* a pear in the course of four images. (The most familiar version of this caricature is that of Daumier, but the original was drawn by Charles Philipon, the editor of the journal *La Caricature*, who was promptly convicted of "contempt for the king's person.") "*Poire*" was slang, suggest Kris and Gombrich, for "fathead," but this translation is an instance of their own wit, since Louis did indeed have a fat head; slang-dictionary equivalents for *poire* are more likely to be "mug" or "fall guy" or "sucker." Nonetheless, let us enjoy "fathead"—a term not used in English till the nineteenth century—as the *mot juste* here, a verbal equivalent of the visual caricature, a genre the authors themselves liken to a pun.

Gombrich returned to the topic of caricature again some years later, reminding his readers that the brothers Carracci in the sixteenth century had "invented the joke of transforming a victim's face into that of an animal, or even a lifeless implement,"[33] and that William Hogarth, in the eighteenth century, "gave pride of place to schemata for 'character' and 'expression.'"[34] "Caricature shows the artist as a creator of convincing types," Gombrich declared, "and here, Hogarth hints, comic art is no less supreme than the much-admired grand manner of Raphael who also did no more—but no less—than create character."[35]

Hogarth preferred to describe his work as "comic history painting," a term he took from his friend Henry Fielding, who had praised him directly in the preface to *Joseph Andrews* as "the Ingenious *Hogarth*," adding that it was far easier "to paint a man with a Nose, or any other Feature of a preposterous Size, or to expose him in some absurd or monstrous Attitude, than to express the Affections of Men on Canvas."[36] Although he is now celebrated as a master of the form, Hogarth was "deeply insulted, to the end of his life, when people called his work 'caricatures,'"[37] writes Jenny Uglow.

His famous engraving of 1743, *Characters and Caricaturas*, is designed to show the difference between the two modes: a collection of a hundred heads in profile—"long-nosed and snub-nosed, toothless and heavy-jawed, bewigged and bald, round and skinny, pensive and scowling"[38]—occupies three-quarters of the picture space. Below these are a row of three heads from Raphael's cartoons, clearly marked "Characters," and four grotesques, marked "Caricaturas." The image, originally untitled, was the subscription ticket for Hogarth's popular series *Marriage à-la-mode*. The juxtaposition of the Hogarthian profiles with the examples of "characters" and "caricatures" was clearly intended to show the affinity of Hogarth's art with Raphael's; one of the figures drawn from Raphael points toward a Hogarth head, as if to place it among the others—or to bring it toward himself.

"The face is the index of the mind," Hogarth would assert in his book *The Analysis of Beauty*.[39] In fact, he liked the phrase enough so that he repeated and enlarged upon it a few years later: "It has ever been allow'd that, when a Character is strongly mark'd in the living face, it may be consider'd as an Index of the mind to express which with any degree of justness in painting, requires the utmost Efforts of a great Master."[40] In a chapter of his *Analysis* titled "Of the Face," he offered some observation on face reading of a kind that, centuries later, would interest scientists and criminologists:

> How often is it said, on the slightest view, that such a one looks like a good-natur'd man, that hath an open honest countenance, or looks like a cunning rogue, a man of sense, or a fool, &c. . . . It is reasonable to believe that aspect to be a true and legible representation of the mind, which gives every one the same idea at first sight.

Lest this seem to place too much stress on outward appearance, "like a physiognomist," Hogarth hastens to say that many different causes can produce facial expressions, so that appearances can deceive: "The bad man, if he be an hypocrite, may so manage his muscles, by teaching them to contradict his heart, that little of his mind can be gather'd from his countenance."[41]

"Like a physiognomist." This was precisely the topic that would lead Gombrich to Rodolphe Töpffer's 1845 "Essay on Physiognomy." Töpffer, a Swiss artist and writer, "invented and propagated" what Gombrich calls "the picture story, the comic strip."[42] Troubled with weakened eyesight, he turned to lithography and simplified line drawings, and in his essay he describes his technique. "A little experimentation with noses or mouths," as Gombrich explains it, "will teach us the elementary symptoms, and from here we can proceed simply by doodling, to create characters."[43]

Töpffer distinguished between "permanent traits" that signified character and "impermanent ones" that indicated emotion. For example, he drew a page of twelve profiles, all with "the same forehead, that of the Apollo Belvedere,"[44] but conspicuously different in every other feature from eyes to chin. One looks wise, another merry, yet another foolish, and still others calculating or glum. All are drawn with a few deft strokes, and no attempt at portraiture. Gombrich points out that the immediate source of Töpffer's theories was a 1788 pamphlet called *Rules for Drawing Caricatures* by an English antiquarian named Francis Grose, just as the source of Töpffer's types was the art of Thomas Rowlandson. But Gombrich's focus is on one of the great caricaturists of all time, and on the role of caricature in the invention of modern art. "Artistically the English tradition of humorous art had an heir much greater than the Swiss inventor of the comic strip. Without Hogarth and Rowlandson there could have been no Daumier."[45] One of the many great achievements of Daumier was that, "in and with" his art, "the tradition of physiognomic experiment began to be emancipated from that of humor."[46] This emancipation would lead to Munch's *Scream* and the expressionism of Ensor. And in France, the example of Honoré Daumier, printmaker, caricaturist, painter, and sculptor, would inspire not only a powerful tradition of caricature in journals and feuilletons, but also a new art form that intriguingly combined physiognomy and pathognomy to reveal "character": the photographic portrait.

Nadar: From Caricature to Photography

The celebrated French photographer Nadar, born Gaspard-Félix Tournachon, made his name as a caricaturist before he ever touched a camera. His early caricatures, as represented in his *Galerie des gens de lettres*, pictured writers, famous and less famous, with big heads on little bodies, a technique also used by Daumier.[47] A second series, developed for the new *Petit Journal pour rire*, was a "Magic Lantern" ("*Lanterne magique*") of Paris's authors and arts celebrities, accompanied by clever commentary, five or six caricatures per oblong panel, like a modern newspaper comic strip. The initial panel in the series showed Victor Hugo on the road to Mount Parnassus, with "friends and family clinging to his coattails."[48]

Nadar's debut piece for the *Petit Journal*, in May 1849, had been a switchback line of sixty delegates to the Constituent Assembly. In a later, more grandiose project, he conceived of what he called the

Panthéon Nadar, four lithographs containing caricatures of writers, playwrights, artists, and magicians, each organized, like the Constituent Assembly, in a snaking line, queuing for fame. Only one was completed: a group of 250 writers and journalists, each recognizable, from Hugo and the bust of George Sand at the head of the procession, to, and beyond, Charles Baudelaire at number 200. Hugo and Baudelaire are instantly recognizable, as are all those who remain in the literary pantheon—indeed, it is through images like these that they have been preserved in the visual imagination. Nadar himself is pictured, not in line for posterity but seated beside a large sign that is addressed to a thirty-first-century gentleman frantically seeking a copy of the *Panthéon Nadar*. His name—"Nadar"—written in larger and darker letters than the message to the future collector, is both a witty signature and a tour de force. It is clear whose work posterity will seek to honor.

In subsequent years, Nadar became a photographer, leaving the art of caricature behind. But as Adam Begley notes, he was in a sense carrying on with the *Panthéon Nadar* project in his new medium, "amassing portrait by portrait a vast gallery of notable Parisians."[49] A contemporary reviewer observed that "the whole constellation, literary, artistic, dramatic, political—intelligent, in a word—of our era, has filed through his studio . . . The series of portraits he's exhibiting is the Pantheon, serious this time, of our generation."[50] Nadar himself wrote in 1856 about the "psychological aspect of photography," which he described as sensing "the moral intelligence of your subject—the rapid tact that puts you in communion with your model," enabling the photographer to produce "a more familiar and favorable resemblance, the intimate resemblance."[51] The word "psychological," he insisted, "seems to me not too ambitious" to describe this process. But perhaps the most striking phrase he uses in this description is "moral intelligence." It's not possible to know whether for Nadar this was equivalent to what we now call "character," but it's a telling and effective concision—and a better description than most.

Two brief stories that Nadar tells in his memoir, *When I Was a Photographer*, speak amusingly to this question of an "intimate resemblance."

One day, in the hall of his lavish studio, which was also his home, Nadar saw a client reviewing the proofs of his photographs. He paused to address the client:

> —And you, sir, would you like me to help you to be critical? First of all, how do you find yourself?
>
> —Not bad, sir. I'm satisfied.
>
> —Let me see . . .
>
> I look at the two proofs—I raise my eyes to the model . . .
>
> It was the proof of someone else that he was holding in his hand—and with which he was "satisfied."[52]

The second anecdote is prefaced by some sage professional commentary on the endemic vanity of successful men:

> I have found in men considered serious by everyone, in the most eminent personages, an anxiety, an extreme agitation, almost an agony in regard to the most insignificant details of their appearance or to a "nuance of their expression." It has been depressing, sometimes even repugnant.
>
> One of them came back one time, early in the morning the day after his visit to see the proofs, all thrown off by a hair—I say *one hair*—which was sticking out past the part and which he wanted to see return to the line. "But wouldn't there be a way, Mr. Nadar? And wouldn't it be better to redo it? . . ." And this is what this solemn man had come to ask me at dawn, dropping everything.
>
> The whole night he had been unable to sleep a wink—and in full candor he confessed it to me.[53]

"So good is everyone's opinion of his or her physical qualities," Nadar says with the wisdom born of experience, "that the first impression of every model in front of the proofs of his or her portrait is almost inevitably disappointment and recoil (it goes without saying that we are talking here of perfect proofs). Some people have the hypocritical modesty to conceal their shock under an appearance of indifference, but do not believe them. They had entered through the door defiant, aggressive, and many will come out furious."[54]

The character of the sitter is such that he does not perceive the portrait to be *in* character; it is instead a disappointment, perhaps even an affront. Such, presumably, are the travails of the celebrity portrait photographer, whose clients are often famous, powerful, vain, and used to having their own way.

Needless to say, things are quite different when the "clients" are poor, patients in asylums, or willing subjects for photographic experiments, as in the case of Nadar's contemporary, Guillaume-Benjamin Duchenne de Boulogne.

Duchenne and "the Orthography of Facial Expression"

Duchenne, a neurologist, published *The Mechanism of Human Facial Expression* in 1862. Only a few copies were produced, because each contained some one hundred original photographic prints, which were individually pasted into the volumes. The photographs have become famous, often independent of Duchenne's text. Viewers recognize the image, but not always the source.

Duchenne used electrical impulses to stimulate the muscles of the face, generating, or mimicking, looks of surprise, horror, terror, fear, and delight. His chief experimental subject was, in Duchenne's own description, "an old toothless man, with a thin face, whose features, without being absolutely ugly, approached ordinary triviality, and whose facial expression was in perfect agreement with his inoffensive character and his restricted intelligence." Furthermore, "the subject had reduced sensation. He was suffering from a complicated anaesthetic condition of the face," so that, Duchenne wrote, "I was able to experiment on his face without causing him pain." This was opportune, for, as he admits, "there are few people who are willing to submit to this kind of experiment, because, without being extremely painful, electrization of the facial muscles often provokes involuntary movements resulting in contortion of the facial features."[55] Unsurprisingly, although disturbing to modern ideas about human experimentation, he found this ideal subject in a hospital for "incurables," the Salpêtrière in Paris, the same hospital where his most famous pupil, Jean-Martin Charcot, would later study (and photograph) hysteria—a study that would be of great interest to one of Charcot's famous pupils, Sigmund Freud.

In a phrase he would use several times, Duchenne described his findings as "the orthography of facial expression in movement."[56] Orthography, or spelling, was the "literary" image of his choice: the muscles spelled out the emotions. The "Scientific Section" of his book, published independently of the later "Aesthetic Section," named the muscles according to the emotions they produced, with the Latin names for those muscles in parentheses: "the muscle of attention (*m. frontalis*)"; "the muscle of pain (*m. corrugator supercilii*)," etc. Included in the list were the muscles of reflection, aggression, joy and benevolence, lasciviousness, sadness, weeping and whimpering, surprise, fright and terror, as well as a set of analyses (some subsequently disputed) of the facial expressions and underlying musculature of classical statues, such as the *Laocoön*.

His written explanations of some of the best-known images of the old man, in conjunction with the accompanying photographs, seem to describe not an electrical simulation but, rather, the actual emotion: "This man is frozen and stupefied by terror; his face shows a dreadful mixture of horror and fear, at the news of a danger that puts this life in peril or of inevitable torture."[57] After the dramatic report comes the scientific explanation: "In all these figures, which portray terror so clearly, dropping the lower jaw is combined with other movements which . . . represented fear. The expression of terror only comes perfectly by associating *mm. platysma* and *m. frontalis* with the muscles lowering the mandible." It's as if we have gone behind the scenes, no longer an Aristotelian audience experiencing pity and terror by seeing terror performed onstage, but instead watching from backstage as a puppeteer, armed with an electrophysiological device, pulls the strings.

Nor is this the end of the event, for there are two more photographic plates to come in this series. The passage describing them begins with the voice of the scientist, shifts to that of the observer convinced that he is watching a real emotional response, and ends with a comment in yet another key.

By the conclusion of this account, which is also the conclusion of the photographic series featuring the old man, the narrative has returned, so to speak, to the front of the house, watching the expressions of the experimental subject as if they did indeed represent the feelings of terror and fright that have been electrically manipulated: "a man terrified by the idea of near death"; "the horrible pain of torture." We are told that the old man in fact felt no pain, and had no other physiological signs of distress, but is this really reassuring?

Some of the photographs show the old man alone; others show us Duchenne attaching the electrical devices as his assistant holds the subject steady. These latter are in a way even more horrifying, because of the difference between the expression on the scientist's face (focused, attentive, unemotional) and the gaping mouth and staring eyes of his subject. "His face," wrote Duchenne, "was insensitive, which allowed me to study the individual action of the muscles with as much effectiveness as on a corpse." The old man's "worn, insensitive skin was a perfect experimental surface on which to explore the movements of human facial expression."[58]

The title of Duchenne's book is *The Mechanism of Human Facial Expression*, but it is the manipulation rather than the mechanism that holds our gaze. Duchenne tells us that he photographed most of the seventy-three plates himself, or "presided over their execution" with the help of the photographer Adrien Tournachon, Nadar's younger brother. None of the photographs, according to Duchenne, were retouched. But the lighting employed is deliberately managed so as to emphasize the emotion. "Thus the plates that portray the somber passions, the sinister ones—*aggression*, *wickedness*, *suffering*, *pain*, *fright*, *torture mingled with dread*—gain singularly in energy under the influence of chiaroscuro; they resemble the style of Rembrandt," while the photographs that portray "*astonishment*, *amazement*, *admiration*, *gaiety*" are "very brightly and evenly illuminated."[59]

In short, this *is* art, or fiction, or theater. The emotions are accurately performed, but are not experienced or felt by the actor/subject.

Nor is the "old man"—described by Duchenne as of "too low intelligence or too poorly motivated"[60]—able to understand or himself reproduce the emotion being depicted, which is why Duchenne also hired a professional actor to perform for the camera, without electrical prompting, the same set of emotions, as a kind of scientific "control."

A modern sensibility, opposed to the idea of human subjects conscripted for such experimental purposes, is likely to feel pity and indignation at the process, especially when confronted with emotions like "torture mingled with dread."[61]

Where is "character" in such an experiment, in such a portrayal? Duchenne the neurologist is charting "facial expression in movement," which, he insists, should precede, or should have preceded, such inquiries as Lavater's on facial expressions at rest.[62] His experiments are building blocks, elements that can produce, when combined, "*complex* expressions," and as they so often do, his chosen examples come from literature (in this case, the Bible) and the history of art. The attention produced by the contraction of one muscle, and the joy caused by the contraction of another, he says, are "primordial expressions. Altogether, the face announces that the soul is alive to new happiness, to an unexpected pleasure." But "if to these two primordial expressions one adds *lasciviousness* or lust, by making *m. nausalis* contract synergistically with the previous muscles, the sensual traits belonging to this last emotion will show the special character of *attention* brought on by something that excites lubricity. It will portray perfectly, for example, the faces of the lewd old men spying on the chaste Susanna."[63]

So "lust," too, can be scientifically simulated and modeled, for the use of painters and actors as well as scientists. And only photography, Duchenne claimed, could catch, and fix, these fleeting expressions accurately. His chosen phrase, "the grammar and orthography of facial expression,"[64] is itself an indication of his goal. He wanted to investigate "the semiotic meaning of individual and groups of facial muscles as they portrayed particular emotions."[65] Words like "orthography" and "semiotics," both taken from the practice of writing and reading, suggest that Duchenne was investigating and recording something that might be called a *visual emotional style*. A language of facial expression, with its own syntax and vocabulary.

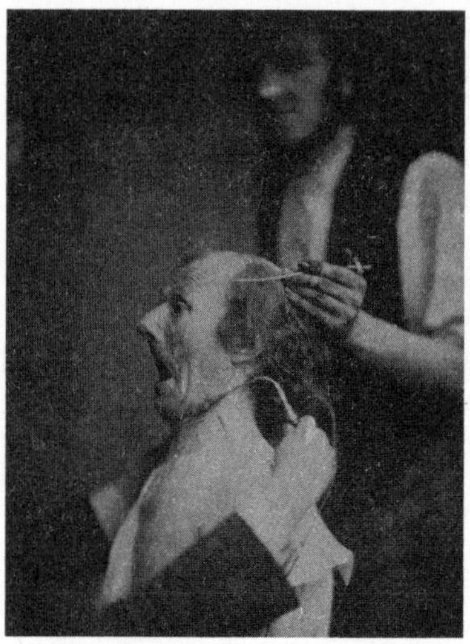

Untitled électro-physiologie photographique, fig. 62; Guillaume-Benjamin-Amand Duchenne, albumen silver print from glass negative, 1854–1856, printed 1862 *(The Museum of Fine Arts, Houston)*

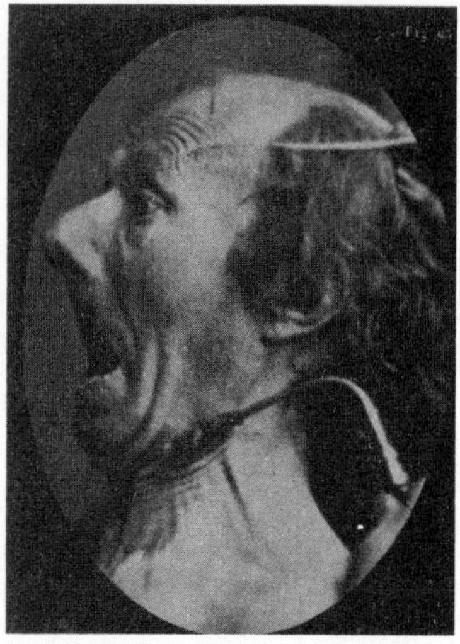

Expression of terror; Guillaume-Benjamin-Amand Duchenne, albumen silver print from glass negative, 1854-1856, printed 1862 *(The Metropolitan Museum of Art)*

Untitled électro-physiologie photographique, fig. 65; Guillaume-Benjamin-Amand Duchenne, albumen silver print from glass negative, 1854–1856, printed 1862 *(The Museum of Fine Arts, Houston)*

Man smiling; Guillaume-Benjamin-Amand Duchenne, albumen silver print from glass negative, 1854-1856, printed 1862 *(The J. Paul Getty Museum)*

Lady Macbeth, moderate expression of cruelty, detail; Guillaume-Benjamin-Amand Duchenne, albumen silver print from glass negative, 1854–1856, printed 1862 *(Houghton Library, Harvard University)*

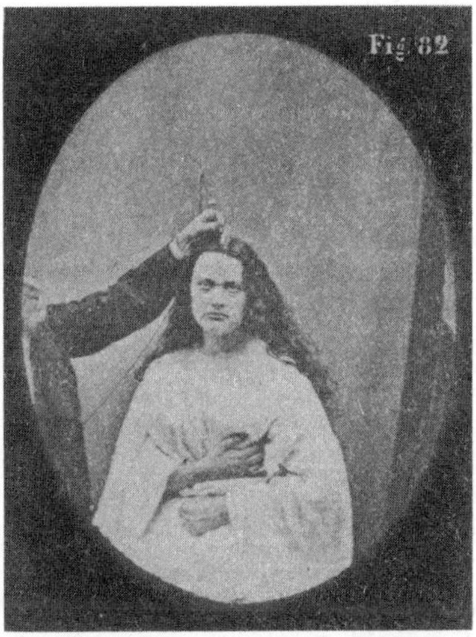

In describing the purpose of his research, Duchenne wrote that actors can sometimes imitate emotion, but that even they sometimes fall short:

> It is very true that certain people, comedians [i.e., actors] above all, possess the art of marvelously feigning emotions that exist only on their faces or lips . . . But it will be simple for me to show that there are some emotions a man cannot simulate or portray artificially on the face; the attentive observer is always able to recognize a false smile.[66]

What is still today known as the "Duchenne smile," a smile that involves both the muscles that raise the corners of the mouth and the muscles that raise the cheeks and make crow's-feet around the eyes, is interpreted as real or genuine. A smile that only raises the corners of the mouth is read as false. (This latter is sometimes called the "PanAm smile," after the now defunct airline and its professionally smiling flight attendants; it is often also the effect produced when we are instructed to say "cheese.") But both of Duchenne's smiles, the "sincere" and the "insincere," were produced by electrical stimulation on the faces of his subjects, not by happy news or the glad recognition of a friend. The "sincere" smile may be "in character" for the one who smiles, yet it, too, can be mechanically (or artistically) generated. There is no "inner" character here but, rather, an artificial image of character: the experimental subject cast as a "character actor."

Some readers of an early edition of Duchenne's book had taken exception to his choice of model, an "old man" with "common, ugly features." For a subsequently added Aesthetic Section, he therefore included, "in an attempt to placate those who have a 'sense of beauty,'" a set of new studies in which, he wrote, "I hope the principal aesthetic conditions are fulfilled: beauty of form, associated with exactness of the facial expression, pose, and gesture"[67]—all photographed by Duchenne himself. As his "aesthetic" model for this new section, he chose a young woman, "neither pretty nor ugly but [with] regular features," who was almost blind, and whom Duchenne was treating for her medical condition, an atrophy of the optic nerve, so that she had become accustomed to the discomfort of the electrization and was therefore "well suited to my electrophysiological experiments." She was "large, fairly well built, suitable for the external study of the shape of the body," he wrote, "but she cannot understand the gestures or the poses that I show her, so that I am obliged to position her and dress her as if she were a mannequin."[68] This model he used for his photographic portrayal of women, from the statue of Saint Theresa to Guido Cagnacci's painting of Cleopatra to a scene from the *Iliad* (Andromache smiling through her tears) to, most notably, in a set of four photographic plates, Shakespeare's Lady Macbeth.

> Plate 81: Lady Macbeth: Had he not resembled
> My father as he slept, I had done't. (*Macbeth*, act II, scene II)
> *Moderate expression of cruelty*. Feeble electrical contraction of *m. procerus*.
>
> Plate 82: Lady Macbeth: Come, you spirits
> That tend on mortal thoughts, unsex me here,
> And fill me, from the crown to the toe, top-full
> Of direst cruelty. (*Macbeth*, act I, scene V)
> *Strong expression of cruelty*. Electrical contraction of *m. procerus*.
>
> Plate 83: Lady Macbeth, about to assassinate King Duncan.
> Expression of *ferocious cruelty*. Maximal electrical contraction of *m. procerus*.
>
> Plate 84: Lady Macbeth—receiving King Duncan with a perfidious smile. (*Macbeth*, act I, scene V)
> False smile on the left, by covering the right side of the mouth; frigid air of discontent on the right, by covering the left side of the mouth. Feeble electrical contraction of the left *m. zygomaticus major* at the time when the face expressed malcontentment.[69]

Several pages of literary interpretation explain Duchenne's choices for illustrations, and describe the poses of the subject. In one image, "the resemblance of her royal victim to her sleeping father has caused her such emotion that her strength has abandoned her. So I have represented her falling onto a seat and restraining the violent beating of her heart. But her heart is made of bronze, we know from the hard gaze and the wicked attitude that she still retains. She wants to be queen, even at the price of her king's life!"[70] In a note to Plate 83, "Lady Macbeth, about to assassinate King Duncan," Duchenne says, "I have imagined that Lady Macbeth, in recognizing a resemblance between King Duncan and her sleeping father, lost her courage to strike and collapsed onto a seat. (This scene is not in Shakespeare.)"[71]

Remember that this subject was, according to Duchenne, unable to understand any of the gestures or poses, so that he was obliged to "position her like a mannequin"—by which he means not a living model but a life-sized image made of wood or wax for the use of artists in the studio.

And as the visual story unfolds, he offers details on his experimental process. In order to show that the "terrible Lady Macbeth" has "not lost any of her beauty, . . . *m. procerus* has been very lightly stimulated." But in the next photograph, although the muscle has been "only moderately stimulated," it is enough to have "altered the beauty of my model," and in a third, "the facial expression of this young girl was made more terrible and more disfigured . . . by the maximal contraction of this little muscle, and we need to consider it as the principal and true agent of the aggressive and wicked passions, of hatred, of jealousy, of cruel instincts."[72] Duchenne produces and then photographs these passions on the face of his uncomprehending subject, who has almost surely never read or seen Shakespeare's play, or perhaps even heard of Lady Macbeth.

At least one critic, reviewing Duchenne's book in 1862, declared that he found "the combination of artist, scientist, and worst of all, photographer, abhorrent!"[73] The ethics of manipulating a young woman—or an old man—in these ways, to make an "aesthetic" point or even a "scientific" one, might certainly be declared abhorrent today. These are emotions devoid of emotion, facial expressions devoid of ordinary expressiveness, signifying nothing from the subject, expressing instead the will of the experimenter. A literary character as full of "character" as Lady Macbeth, whose passionate speeches are faithfully quoted and knowledgeably discussed by the book's author-photographer-scientist, is presented in photographic plates as an empty visual artifact, her smiles, frowns, glares, and sneers generated by electricity applied to the facial muscles.

Categories like "fake" and "real," "false" and "true," "genuine" and "artificial"—traditional elements in assessments of personal character—are in these experiments vacated, or conflated, so as to produce a "scientific" and "aesthetic" template for future readings of character: orthographic, syntactical, a grammar of facial sincerity and insincerity.

And yet the photographs continue to fascinate. They are frequently reproduced, with and without explanation or attribution. Charles Darwin obtained the right to use some of them in *The Expression of the Emotions in Man and Animals.* Duchenne gave them to him free of charge, since "questions of money should not arise between men of science,"[74] and Darwin's reprinting greatly increased their visibility.

It's intriguing to compare these studies, done by a highly regarded nineteenth-century neurologist, with Messerschmidt's character heads of a century before. Both Duchenne's photographs, prized by scientists and increasingly by artists, and Messerschmidt's heads, once regarded as symptoms of the sculptor's inner demons, now widely admired and imitated, are documents in the history of expression, using experimentation and the idea of a vocabulary of forms to designate and encompass visual character.

Both sets of images were produced by specific acts of physical stimulation. Duchenne produced emotional expressions on the faces of his experimental subjects, distinguishing between "real" and "false" not by the actual emotions experienced but by their orthography or legibility. Messerschmidt was his own model, and the grimaces shown in his character heads were "real," in that they were produced by his pinches and also by his interpretation of the reflection in the glass. But the "characters" or characterizations of them conveyed by their expressive titles are not those of the sculptor, and their specificity in the representation of emotions, sentiments, or mental states has been imposed—or intuited—by others. Though in some cases the titles seem merely descriptive

(*The Vexed Man*, *The Simpleton*), in others they seem clearly novelistic or dramatic (*The Difficult Secret*, *Just Rescued from Drowning*). The impulse to tell a story—or to allude to one—becomes part of the aesthetic and cultural response to the image.

In both cases, then, character was increasingly tied to performance and interpretation. During the same period, in the performing arts, which included theater and rhetoric, the long-standing connection between character and gesture was being codified and taught.

Strike the Pose: Acting and the Delsarte System

At about the same time that Nadar was presenting his celebrity clients for posterity, and Duchenne posing his mentally challenged subjects, another French pioneer of the arts, François Delsarte, was devising what came to be known as the Delsarte method, or Delsarte System, of acting.

Designed to coordinate the interior emotions with the physical gestures of the body, Delsarte's language of gesture was translated into what he called "The Science of Applied Aesthetics." Neither Delsarte nor his American protégé, Steele MacKaye, wrote books about his practice, but MacKaye's student, the American actress and teacher Genevieve Stebbins, published the *Delsarte System of Expression* in 1885. The book was an enormous commercial success.

A few examples will show both the organic nature of the system and its perhaps inevitable capacity to become stylized and misunderstood, captive to empty gestures that had lost their physical connection with meaning.

"The hand," Stebbins writes, "indicates the intention or attention of the being; this is shown by the inflections of the hand in gesture." To indicate "indifference, prostration, imbecility, insensibility, or death," the thumb should be "attracted inward." To signify "approbation, tenderness," the performer should hold "the thumb abducted; the fingers curved gently." And so on to "exasperation," displayed by the "hand as in convulsion, only more spread from palm; hand expanded, fingers crooked," and "exaltation of passion," performed with the "hand spread to its greatest extent, fingers and thumb wide apart."[75]

"The shoulder raised indicates sensibility, passion; the shoulder dropped indicates prostration, insensibility, death," Stebbins observes, quoting Delsarte, who had said that "the shoulder . . . may be fitly called the *thermometer of sensibility*," the elbow a "thermometer of the affections," and the wrist a "thermometer of vital energy."[76] The torso, which is said to represent the "moral element or love of the being," has three "relative" attitudes: "leaning *to* the object," "leaning *from* the object," and "leaning *before* the object."[77] The first signifies attraction, the second repulsion, and the third, depending upon the circumstance, humility, shame, obsequiousness, or reverence. Attitudes of the head, the eye, the eyeball, the eyebrow, the lips, and the jaw are equally meticulously distinguished and described.

(As a test of the current effectiveness of the system, readers of this book are invited to take a moment to follow these careful directions, preferably with an observer to interpret the results.)

Each Delsarte attitude or pose is accompanied by what are called "Aesthetic Gymnastics," exercises for a specific body part: thus, for example, to exercise the nose, "Dilate and contract the nostrils as rapidly as possible; move no other part of the face."[78] Both the "attitudes" and the "Aesthetic Gymnastics" resemble features found in other kinds of handbooks for visualizing or performing expressiveness, from Charles Le Brun in the seventeenth century to the recent work of the psychologist Paul Ekman. Stebbins's illustrations include a profile drawing of the Zones of the Head, labeled Vital, Mental, and Moral,[79] reminiscent of the familiar phrenology head with its similarly marked zones. Charts showing "expressions of the nose," "expressions of the eyebrow," and "expressions of the mouth" and "attitudes of the head,"[80] though intended to indicate options for stage performance, are not unlike the later criminal comparison charts of Cesare Lombroso or the posed photographs used by some modern-day psychologists of facial expression.

As befits a method designed for the training and use of actors, the Delsarte System also includes some direct observations about character. A person's walk "is temperamental, as much an indication of the habit, character, and emotions, as the voice."[81] But the primary sense of *character*, as we might expect, is theatrical. "I cannot too strongly recommend the following method of utilizing the Delsarte System of Dramatic Expression, in the creation of character," Stebbins asserts to the "dear pupil" to whom she addresses many of her remarks, while citing the "master's" caution against too mechanical an adherence to the rules once one has learned them.[82]

That this was all too present a danger is made clear even in Stebbins's opening remarks, in which she cautions her "dear invisible one" that there is no substitute for hard work: "for there is but one step from the sublime to the ridiculous; and if, at the end of these lessons, you have not freed the channels for expression, you will simply be ridiculous, and will merit all the fun which is leveled at the mechanical mugging of so-called Delsarteans."[83] By 1885, when her book was published, the enormous success of the Delsarte System—a system that had been crucial to the development of modern dancers like Isadora Duncan, Ruth St. Denis, and Ted Shawn—had spread so widely, and been copied so freely (in Australia and the United States, among other places) that its original insights about the face and the body had turned, despite themselves, into stereotypical gestures and poses. Melodrama, rather than drama, was now read in its moves, while the connection to the emotions, central to Delsarte's own ideas, was gradually forgotten or lost. To discern character in the Delsartean turned wrists, arched eyebrows, inclined torso, and tight disapproving lips became, all too often, a comical rather than an affecting experience. The Delsarte System, once vital, was now often regarded—and sometimes performed—as a set of rigid clichés.

It was against this parody and travesty of a once-rigorous training that new theater artists like Constantin Stanislavski developed their own systems. Both *An Actor Prepares* and *Building a Character* focused attention on the physical construction of character onstage through the use of movement, expression, and speech. These were the same elements that Delsarte had emphasized, but the imaginative innovator of the mid-nineteenth century was now regarded as the arbiter of an out-of-date practice that was anything but true to life.

Stanislavski would also have a "system," which he preferred to spell with a small *s*, lest it sound too dogmatic.[84] And that system, too—codified and capitalized as "the Method"—would in turn become parodied, misinterpreted, and subject to both envious and rebellious critique.

Darwin's Emotions

While these explorations and developments in the visual expression of character were taking place in France, Charles Darwin was pursuing his own investigations in England. As befit the times, and the crossover between science and the arts, Darwin's researches came to include all three of the "character" practices we have observed in mid-century France: photography, scientific experiment, and theater.

The Expression of the Emotions in Man and Animals (1872) was the fourth, and last, in the sequence of Darwin's major publications, following *Voyage of the Beagle* (1839), *On the Origin of Species by Means of Natural Selection* (1859), and *The Descent of Man* (1871). It addressed some key questions he had left out of earlier books, reserving them for a moment when he could give them his focused attention. In his introduction, he notes that his own interest in this topic began in 1838 and continued up to the time when the book was published.

Among the comparison groups Darwin observed were animals (both wild and domestic), children (including his own, closely followed from infancy), the insane (in consultation with Sir James Crichton-Browne, a physician and psychiatrist working at the West Riding Asylum), and classical painting and sculpture. He sent out a questionnaire asking for cross-cultural observations, hoping to learn whether human emotions were, in the main, universal or culture-specific. Impressed with the work of Duchenne on the muscles of the face and the emotions they portrayed, he obtained from him permission to use as many of his photographs as he wished, but the cost of photographic reproduction led the publisher to limit the number of plates. As a result, some of Duchenne's images are represented by drawings rather than actual photographs. Other images were created especially for *The Expression of the Emotions* by the photographers Oscar Gustave Rejlander, in London, and Adolf Kindermann, in Hamburg.

One of Darwin's goals was to refute the view—maintained by such contemporaries as Sir Charles Bell, Sir Charles Lyell, and Alfred Russel Wallace—that some kind of divine intervention or "power" had enabled the development of human beings with higher faculties than those of animals. Darwin regarded the question as one of science: scientists should seek evidence and universal laws, and in his observations over many species and many places, what was clearly demonstrated was the continuity between man and the other animals, not human exceptionalism. His book set out to demonstrate that point. "With mankind some expressions, such as the bristling of the hair under the influence of extreme terror, or the uncovering of the teeth under that of furious rage, can hardly be understood, except on the belief that man once existed in a much lower and animal-like condition," he wrote in his introduction. "He who admits on general grounds that the structure and habits of all animals have been gradually evolved, will look at the subject of expression in a new and interesting light."[85]

Thus, for example, in explaining how "a half-playful sneer graduates into one of great ferocity when, together with a heavily frowning brow and fierce eye, the canine tooth is exposed," he cites Bell's description of an actor who could express hatred by drawing up the outer part of the upper lip and revealing "a sharp angular tooth." This is the same action, says Darwin, as that of a snarling dog, and "a dog when pretending to fight often draws up the lip on one side alone, namely that facing his antagonist." He completes the comparison by offering evidence from etymology: "Our word sneer is in fact the same as snarl, the l 'being merely an element implying continuance of action.'"[86]

We might note that both of these examples are those of performance: the actor and the dog "pretending to fight." The expression of emotion here—as has also sometimes been the case in the work of other researchers, like Duchenne—is a sign or gesture of feeling rather than the feeling itself. "I suspect that we see a trace of this expression in what is called a derisive or sardonic smile," adds Darwin. "One corner of the mouth is retracted on the side towards the derided person."[87]

Darwin's biographer Janet Browne considers *The Expression of the Emotions in Man and Animals* to be a sequel to the *Descent*, a supplementary volume that argues the case for anticipatory vestiges of "memory, imagination, attention, and reason"[88] in animals. "Darwin tried to reduce every expressive gesture to the stark outlines of neuro-muscular physiology," she writes. "The wide staring eyes of astonishment were, he thought, the natural result of attempting to see more of the thing that caused surprise, the curled lips of a sneer a side effect of originally wrinkling the nose at unpleasant odors."[89]

But when displayed without captions, the expressions in the photographs Darwin included with his text—whether commissioned from Rejlander and Kindermann, or borrowed from Duchenne or Crichton-Browne—were not always self-evident to viewers. Some were misread—a possibility that Darwin himself acknowledged:

> When I first looked at Dr. Duchenne's photographs, reading at the same time the text, and thus learning what was intended, I was struck with admiration at the truthfulness of all, with only a few exceptions. Nevertheless, if I had examined them without any explanation, no doubt I would have been as much perplexed, in some cases, as other persons have been.[90]

The same was the case with Dr. Crichton-Browne's portrait photographs of inmates in the asylum. When he saw their faces Darwin "fell into the trap of 'seeing' insanity,"[91] assisted by the provenance of the photographs and Browne's explanatory notes. Frequently, readings of what we would call "character" were imposed upon the images: Duchenne's photograph of the old man with an electrically induced "false smile" was interpreted by those to whom Darwin showed it as an indication of malice or surprise.[92]

Many of the photographs in the book were staged and posed rather than spontaneous; body language, of the kind long used by painters and actors, could increase the "legibility" of human emotions. The genial Oscar Rejlander participated not only as a photographer but also as a model—a role that he seems, from his expressions and the brio of his performance, to have thoroughly enjoyed. In describing the sensation of disgust, which "primarily arises in connection with the act of eating or tasting," Darwin observes that "Mr. Rejlander has simulated this expression with some success," and directs his reader to two photographs in which Rejlander mimes annoyance and "gestures as if to push away or to guard oneself against the offensive object," while opening his mouth as if to say "*ach* or *ugh*."[93]

Sometimes Rejlander took the photographs on a time-lapse device; at other times he had his wife assist him. The images in which he appears tend to be highly theatrical, enhanced by the costumes Rejlander is wearing; they look staged rather than "real." The same is true of the photographs intended to demonstrate helplessness or impotence, about which, Darwin says, "Mr. Rejlander has successfully acted the gesture of shrugging the shoulders."[94] To a modern observer, the bearded, shrugging Rejlander, dressed in a dark velvet long-sleeved costume, his hands held out before him in a gesture of (not entirely convincing) supplication, may resemble an actor playing Shylock.

Darwin's Shakespeare

Shylock is, in fact, one of the few Shakespeare characters *not* invoked or quoted in *The Expression of the Emotions in Man and Animals.* Throughout the book, passages from the plays are offered as evidence of human emotional response, serving, in their regular occurrence and in the relative absence of other documented evidence, as a kind of control. In the section on "Disdain, Contempt, and Disgust," a footnote points to the phrase "Do you bite your thumb at us, sir," from *Romeo and Juliet* (1.1).[95] In the section on "Hatred and Anger," Darwin writes, "Shakespeare sums up the chief characteristics of rage as follows," and quotes a famous passage from *Henry V*:

> When the blast of war blows in our ears
> Then imitate the action of the tiger:
> Stiffen the sinews, conjure up the blood,
> Disguise fair nature with hard-favoured rage,
> Then lend the eye a terrible aspect;
> . . .
> Now set the teeth, and stretch the nostril wide,
> Hold hard the breath, and bend up every spirit
> To his full height. On, on, you noblest English.
>
> HENRY V 3.1[96]

A passage from *Titus Andronicus* exemplifies the instinctive practice of turning away the face out of shame; two Shakespearean remarks—by Falstaff and the Duke of Norfolk—are offered as evidence of spitting as a sign of contempt or disgust.[97] Three quotations from the plays personify envy.[98] The climactic and important section on blushing cites (and misinterprets, correcting the error in a footnote added later) Juliet's remark to Romeo in the balcony scene (2.2):

> Thou know'st the mask of night is on my face;
> Else would a maiden blush bepaint my cheek,
> For that which thou hast heard me speak tonight.

(Darwin's text says that Shakespeare "erred" here, since he reads the passage as implying that Juliet did not blush, since it was dark, whereas "several ladies, who are great blushers," have told him they "believe they have blushed in the dark." A letter from a reader, cited in the corrective footnote, suggested to him, "Shakespeare meant that the blush was unseen, not that it was absent."[99])

The last page of the book quotes Hamlet's soliloquy on the First Player, as evidence that "even the simulation of an emotion tends to arouse it in our minds. Shakespeare, who from his wonderful knowledge of the human mind ought to be an excellent judge, says:—

> Is it not monstrous that this player here,
> But in a fiction, in a dream of passion,
> Could force his soul so to his own conceit,
> That, from her working, all his visage wann'd;
> Tears in his eyes, distraction in 's aspect,
> A broken voice, and his whole function suiting
> With forms to his conceit? And all for nothing!
>
> *HAMLET* 2.2[100]

Other literary authors—Homer, Chaucer, Spenser, Lady Mary Wortley Montagu—are occasionally cited in Darwin's book, as is the Bible, but the overwhelming number of comparisons between literary descriptions and observed behavior are drawn from Shakespeare. "The language he knew best was the language of Milton and Shakespeare," as Janet Browne notes, "not the objective, value-free terminology sought (although rarely found) by science."[101]

In this radically important and influential study from 1872, there are no social-science survey numbers. Darwin's human evidence comes from his study of his children as infants, from his own responses to stimuli, from ladies who blush, from "a small wager with a dozen young men that they would not sneeze if they took snuff" (they tried so hard to win that they defeated their own instincts, and had to pay him the wager),[102] from Dr. James Crichton-Browne's reports on patients in the insane asylum, from other medical specialists on the mind and on "mental physiology," from various anthropological accounts, each scrupulously credited, of the expression of emotions in other cultures around the world—and from literature. Time after time, the conclusive "proof" is offered in the form of a literary quotation. Human nature is a literary artifact, and the experts in it are the poets.

Darwin's principal interest was not in "the way human beings learned to read and recognize expressions" but, rather, in "the way man's body actually worked." And the "core" of his argument was a "discussion of the origins of the higher—more 'human'—emotions,"[103] of which the most salient was the blush. The section of *The Expression of the Emotions in Man and Animals* most frequently cited as evidence of the power of "self-attention" (what we might call self-consciousness) is his extensive discussion of blushing.

"Whenever we believe that others are depreciating or even considering our personal appearance," writes Darwin,

> our attention is vividly directed to the outer and visible parts of our bodies; and of all such parts we are most sensitive about our faces, as no doubt has been the case during many past generations. Therefore, assuming for the moment that the capillary vessels can be acted on for close attention, those of the face will have become eminently susceptible. Through the force of association, the same effects will tend to follow whenever we

> think that others are considering or censuring our actions or character.[104]

This is one of Darwin's most direct references to "character," here clearly understood as moral or ethical. Blushing, he says, "whether due to shyness—to shame for a real crime—to shame for a breach of the laws of etiquette—to modesty from humility—to modesty from an indelicacy—depends in all cases on the same principle," the "sensitive regard for the opinion . . . of others."[105] As Christopher Ricks notes in *Keats and Embarrassment*, "The point is not, of course, that nobody previously blushed, but that blushing and embarrassment came to be thought of as crucial to a great many social and moral matters."[106]

The medical source for many of Darwin's observations about blushing is Dr. Thomas Henry Burgess's *The Physiology or Mechanism of Blushing* (1839), which provides him with clinical examples and also with some key phrases. The "beauty" of female blushing will provide many of his literary examples (the first chapter, "The Natural History of Blushing," begins with a section on "The Poetry of Blushing"); the book will go on to discuss the physiology of male and female, young and old, joyful and sorrowful, describing the characteristics of the True Blush, the Blush of Feeling, and the False (or Deceptive) Blush, the Hectic Flush, the Flush of Rage, and the Blush of Shame—the besetting and indicative illnesses of civilization.[107]

For Darwin, blushing was "the most peculiar and the most human of expressions," which may be why he devoted so much of his book to it. A blush, he says, cannot be caused by any action on the body, like tickling (which can cause laughter) or a blow (which can cause pain). "It is the mind that must be affected. Blushing is not only involuntary; but the wish to restrain it, by leading to self-attention, actually increases the tendency."[108]

The Body Thinking: Freud's Darwin

One classic passage from English poetry, highly germane to Darwin's argument, is not quoted in his text: John Donne's description of a young woman's blush, in his "Elegy on Mistress Elizabeth Drury":

> . . . her pure and eloquent blood
> Spoke in her cheeks, and so distinctly wrought,
> That one might almost say, her body thought.

It was the work of Donne and other metaphysical poets that led T. S. Eliot to articulate his argument about the "direct sensuous apprehension of thought" in early modern poetry and the subsequent "dissociation of sensibility" that developed in the later seventeenth century and continued, he believed, through the English poets of the Victorian period. "Tennyson and Browning are poets, and they think; but they do not feel their thought as immediately as the odour of a rose. A thought to Donne was an experience; it modified his sensibility."[109]

It's not usual to couple the names of T. S. Eliot and Charles Darwin. Certainly Darwin, much more than Eliot, admired the Victorian poets of his time. But the "principle of the direct action of the excited nervous system on the body, independently of the will,"[110] was one of Darwin's three general principles of expression. His own lifelong struggles with digestive ailments also made him acutely aware of the body's effect upon the mind.

In this context, it is also germane to note that one of the most profound and wide-ranging effects of Darwin's book on the expression of the emotions was its influence on Sigmund Freud. In the early *Studies on Hysteria*, discussing phrases like "stabbed in the heart" and "swallowing" an insult, Freud wrote, "These sensations and innervations belong to the field of 'The Expression of the Emotions', which, as Darwin has taught us, consist of actions which originally had a meaning and served a purpose." Such phrases, he says, have become mere figures of speech, but in all probability they were once literal, and "hysteria is right in restoring the original meaning of the words in depicting its unusually strong innervations."[111] Writing about phobias more than twenty years later, Freud mentions Darwin's instinctive recoil from "a snake that struck at him, even though he knew he was protected from it by a thick sheet of glass."[112]

"Freud's views on the expression of the emotions in general," writes his editor and translator James Strachey, "seem certainly to have been derived from Darwin."[113] As early as the *Studies on Hysteria*, Freud cited and interpreted Darwin's arguments to develop his own theories about emotion, affect, and what he memorably described as "the secular advance of repression in the emotional life of mankind."[114] His claim that the inhibition of emotion leads to repression—which in turn leads to neurosis—is very similar to Darwin's set of basic principles regarding emotional expression,[115] and closely anticipates his own later argument in *Civilization and Its Discontents* (1930).[116] "The price we pay for our advance in civilization," Freud argues there, "is a loss of happiness through the heightening of the sense of guilt."[117] And to this statement he appends a simple, unattributed footnote: "Thus conscience does make cowards of us all . . ." There is no need, he implies, to cite the source, Hamlet's "To be or not to be" soliloquy. He assumes that his readers will recognize it. Furthermore, "if the development of civilization has such a far-reaching similarity to the development of the individual," might it not be justifiable to suggest that, "under the influence of cultural urges, some civilizations, or some epochs of civilization—possibly the whole of mankind—have become 'neurotic'?"[118] This question, too, has its roots in his much earlier discussion of Shakespeare's play, where Hamlet's "self-reproaches" and "scruples of conscience" led Freud to describe him there as "a hysteric."[119]

From the self-reflective "hysteric" of 1900 to the more generally "neurotic" civilization of 1930, the road—Freud's "royal road to a knowledge of the unconscious activities of the mind"[120]—passes through Shakespeare's *Hamlet* and Darwin's *Expression of the Emotions in Man and Animals*, a book that ends, as we have noted, with another of Hamlet's anguished soliloquies.

For Freud, as for Darwin and others, *human* character is here interpreted with the help of *dramatic* character. The apparently indirect route is the most direct. The soliloquy, that great innovation of the Renaissance stage, provides a window into the unconscious.

Science and Caricature: Visualizing the Criminal

It is tempting to view these investigations of "visual character" with some optimism, coupling the visual and performing arts and what Darwin described, in the last paragraph of his book, as "expression itself, or the language of the emotions."[121] But, as some aspects of Lavater's work on physiognomy—and its dissemination in popular forms—have already made clear, finding the mind's construction in the face could sometimes produce misreadings and misconstructions, even in the apparent pursuit of "disinterested" science. A case in point is that of Cesare Lombroso.

Lombroso, the Italian physician and criminologist, is regarded by some as the visionary founder of a modern field of study, and by others as an example of prejudicial thinking about racial and physical types. Both are correct, and neither tells the whole story. Cesare Lombroso's work on the "born criminal" made him famous, and his comparative discussion of the physical attributes of criminals—the shapes of their heads and their noses, the thickness or sparseness of hair and beard, the "virile" voices of women criminals—was indebted, or so he argued, to Darwin's work on evolution, highly influential at the time. *Criminal Man*, first published in Italian in 1876, went through five editions in twenty years, in the course of which Lombroso's ideas changed somewhat, as did the evidence he provided as "proof" of his assertions.

The "slippage from likeness to stereotype," note Lombroso's modern editors and English translators, demonstrates that in many cases "his preconceptions about how criminals should look influenced his preparation of images for publication."[122] "There is an unconscious element of caricature" even in the source material for his images, said one of the successors to Lombroso's chair in criminology at the University of Turin.[123] Another scholar has suggested that in the transition from photograph to drawing to engraving there can be seen "a gradual process of deformation—and the formation of a monster."[124]

"Nearly all criminals have jug ears, thick hair, thin beards, pronounced sinuses, protruding chins, and broad cheekbones,"[125] Lombroso wrote in 1876. And in their "emotional intensity, criminals closely resemble not the insane, but savages."[126] "Savages," to him, were members of any race other than European whites. The left-handed, the colorblind, and those insensitive to pain were also, in his view, more likely to be criminals. By the fourth edition of *Criminal Man*, perhaps responding to critics who said he neglected environmental factors in favor of biology, Lombroso had added the "occasional criminal" to his lexicon, though his insistence on what he called a "positivist" approach still centered on the "born criminal." Born criminals could be identified, and recognized, by physical anomalies and insensitivities. They were biologically destined to commit crimes. Their characteristics summed up, and indicated, their character.

When criticized for his methods, Lombroso defended his position, describing it as a modern scientific development: "As a psychiatrist rather than a natural scientist, I simply replaced the abstract approach of the past with clinical and anthropological methods," he wrote, explaining that he relied on "clues from physiognomy and craniometry."[127] He excoriated those critics who misinterpreted his new science: "I am suggesting the use of these methods only on individuals already suspected of crime," he wrote. "I would not dream of detaining for life anyone with abnormal features until he is accused and convicted by the courts. On the other hand, absence of those features can save an innocent person from a libelous charge . . . My methods simply add evidence to that gained from witnesses and confessions. To claim that criminal anthropology threatens individual liberty is . . . absurd."[128]

By the fifth and final edition of *Criminal Man* (1896–1897), Lombroso had expanded the number of "criminal craniums" he had examined from the original 66 skulls to 689, and the number of live subjects whom he measured for his data on anthropometry and physiognomy from the 832 in the first edition to 6,608. (Although Lombroso did not endorse the earlier "science" of phrenology, he was very familiar with the work of Franz Joseph Gall, and his modern editors remark, "Phrenological assumptions about the relationship of brain formation to behavior often lay behind his criminal anthropological claims."[129]) As developed by Lombroso, criminal anthropology became, at least up until the turn of the century, the authoritative approach to criminal behavior, and the forerunner to what would become criminology, the study of the causes and prevention of crime.

Female criminals, as described in a companion volume, *Criminal Woman, the Prostitute, and the Normal Woman*, shared the general "deficiency" of all women. "Women have no particular talent for any art, science, or profession," Lombroso declares. Compared with men, they are notably lacking in "genius," and even in the few cases of female genius they are anomalous: "One need only look at pictures of women of genius of our day to realize that they seem to be men in disguise."[130] Even in the number and degree of criminal attributes women were inferior to men, a fact he attributed in part to the necessity for women to be attractive if they wanted men to be their criminal accomplices. But some women were "born criminals," and these could be identified by the same kinds of examinations of the face and skull as could men.

Big jaws, swollen lips, and a "virile" look are among the signs of female criminality he detects, though some of these are temporarily obscured by youth, only to emerge unmistakably as the woman ages. Often animated by "the worst qualities of women," including cruelty, lust, and a desire for revenge, the female born criminal can, he asserted, exhibit "extraordinary wickedness," and, "when a full type, is more terrible than the male."[131] His examples were often taken from recent history, like that of "Bell-Star, the female outlaw who several years ago terrorized all of Texas," or Madame Lafarge, who "stole her friend's diamonds, not to sell them, but only to possess them."[132]

In addition to the features of the face, hair growth and pattern, and head size and shape, there was for Lombroso another visual sign of the criminal, this one acquired rather than innate: the tattoo. *Criminal Man* includes detailed sketches of the tattoos on the bodies of his subjects, including not only the face, chest, and back but also, in some cases, the genitals. Lombroso regards the practice of getting tattooed as a "disadvantageous custom" that caused "discomfort and damage," and offers some "anthropological" hypotheses for its persistence, including religion, imitation, boredom, a sense of camaraderie, love or eroticism, and, at least occasionally, "noble human passions" like those for the paternal village, the patron saint, scenes of infancy, and depictions of distant friends—"naturally one does not want to forget these things."[133] He associates tattoos with gangs and organized crime and suggests that judges and practitioners of forensic medicine might come to understand that "tattoos can signify a previous incarceration." Tattoos, like scars, were "professional characteristics" for the criminal man.[134]

As for the criminal woman, whose tattoos he also discusses and illustrates, once again she is found to be inferior to her male counterpart: "the absence of epigrams, obscene signs, and cries of vengeance, and the presence of only ordinary symbols and initials" are to be taken as "another indication of women's lesser ingenuity and weaker imagination."[135] (Despite this dispiriting account, he does mention—and illustrate—one clever tattoo he found in a book on French prostitutes—an arrow on the woman's thigh pointing toward her genitals, with the inscription *Excelsior*. "This is the only simultaneously pornographic and witty tattoo that I have found among women," he writes, rather grudgingly.[136])

Criminals—and here again Lombroso means his "born criminals"—often choose, he says, to express themselves in pictures rather than words: hieroglyphics, pictographs, and gestures. He attributes all of these—like so much else in his work—to "atavism," a regression to a more primitive stage of development. As an experiment, he once hypnotized "a young person of honest habits" and convinced him that he was a famous brigand: "His handwriting—normally civilized, cultivated, and almost feminine—became rough and malformed, resembling that of [some] criminals, who cross their *t*s with flourishes." When the subject was told that he was a little boy, "he conserved some of the brigand's energy in his infantile script," and when told that he was again the brigand, he "returned to a rough script" that somehow carried some elements of the child's handwriting. All of which, Lombroso concludes, goes to prove "the wonderful discovery by [the physical anthropologist Giuseppe] Sergi that each individual's character has many layers."[137]

The word "character" here is both indirectly quoted from another speaker, and translated from Italian to English, so it is difficult to know exactly what is meant. But in Lombroso's anecdote, hypnosis functions as a kind of temporarily induced personal atavism, peeling back the layers of "civilization" to reveal the primitive "criminal" and the "child." The "individual's character" would then be the aggregate constituted by such layers, with the perceived present-day reality ("a young person of honest habits") at the top, or—more accurately—on the surface. (One of the meanings of the word "character"—in Italian as well as in English—is "a particular person's style of handwriting," though it's unclear whether Lombroso had this historical definition in mind in his chapter on "Handwriting of Criminals.")[138]

Lombroso is not always a strict biological determinist. When he is more familiar with a particular group, he can modify both his absolute views and his style of writing and reasoning to encompass social and environmental factors. For example, when writing about Jews in the second edition of *Criminal Man*, Lombroso, himself a Jew, notes in a chapter called "Etiology of Crime: Weather and Race," that "according to statistics, in some countries the level of Jewish criminality is lower than that of their fellow citizens," and that "even more distinctive" are the types of crimes they commit, largely forgery, swindling, and receiving stolen goods, rather than, for example, murder. The reasons behind the involvement of Jews in some of these crimes, he says, include poverty, exclusion from jobs and public assistance, and "a need for protection against persecution," which may have led them "to become accomplices to feudal lords." Under the circumstances, "it is surprising that Jewish crime rates are not higher. Instead, they began to decrease as soon as political life was opened to Jews." No sooner has Lombroso struck this humane and historical note, however, than in the next paragraph he turns all his immoderate vituperation on "Gypsies, who epitomize a thoroughly criminal race, with all its passions and vices." His style as well as the content of his assertions changes, from the social context, national specificity, and statistical reasoning with which he addresses the problem of crime among Jews, to flat statements about "Gypsies" in the present tense: "they are deceitful with one another"; "they are extremely vengeful"; "they kill for money without remorse."[139] He endows the entire race with a single set of negative characteristics that purport to sum up its character.

At stake here is not only his own level of information and personal involvement but, more broadly, his discursive methodology: the historian and the criminal anthropologist in him are at odds with each other. In order to make racial or other generalizations, he needs a certain distance from his subjects; the closer he gets, the more exceptions and historical and social conditions get in the way. This was also, to a certain extent, the problem for Lavater: generalization, which might have seemed nonprejudicial because it was impersonal, became, in practice, the source of (or refuge for) cultural and racial opinions that sounded "scientific" and were in fact anything but. The exception, when acknowledged, often disproved the rule.

Nor is this a quest with a foreseeable end. In the summer of 2019 Americans learned that the U.S. Immigration and Customs Enforcement agency had used techniques of "facial recognition" on driver's license photographs without the owners' knowledge. It became clear that the theories of late-nineteenth-century figures like Francis Galton and Cesare Lombroso could be allied to artificial intelligence and computing in ways that revived old notions of visible character. Algorithms based on mug shots and old photographs (what one researcher called "haunted data") have been employed to assess people without their knowledge and consent. As with many of the earlier "eugenic" and "criminological" studies, these calculations were particularly ill-suited to judge individuals from a diversity of racial and social backgrounds. "When will we finally learn we cannot predict people's character from their appearance?"[140] asked a subheadline in *The New York Times*. The answer is far from clear.

Modern Face-Reading

Despite recurring concerns about the way it might be affected by issues like race, ethnicity, and nationality, the study of physiognomy—the prospect of understanding character through face-reading—has continued to intrigue observers. In the eighteenth century, Lavater made it the basis of his work. In the nineteenth century, Ralph Waldo Emerson declared that "each religious sect has its physiognomy. The Methodists have acquired a face; the Quakers, a face; the nuns, a face."[141] In the twentieth and twenty-first centuries, this interest has continued, and has in recent years been abetted by technology.

Reading the Face: Understanding a Person's Character Through Physiognomy was published in Germany in 1935 by the Austria-born physician Norbert Glas, an admirer of the philosopher and social reformer Rudolf Steiner. In 1961 the book was reprinted, and an English translation was published in 2008, more than twenty years after Glas's death. Illustrated with numerous photographs and line drawings, the book is full of such information as "people with a well-shaped curve at the back of their heads" are "liberated people who want to have the freedom to develop themselves," whereas a "bull neck" is "usually an expression of a person with a will largely directed to the material world."[142] An easily recognizable profile image of Johann Caspar Lavater goes unidentified in the text, labeled only as an example of "the protruding noses of musicians, artists, or priests"[143] (although Lavater's name is given in the list of illustrations at the back). Eyebrows that point sharply downward, a characteristic shared by "Mephistopheles" and "Holbein's portrait of Henry VIII," suggest "underhandedness and spite."[144] By contrast, brows in a "beautifully shaped arch" indicate "a certain openness and willingness to make sacrifices," and are often found on pictures of the Madonna.[145] The physiognomy of Napoleon's nose reveals "almost all the characteristics . . . that belong to the choleric temperament," and his "wide nostrils" are compared to "old pictures of fire-spewing dragons."[146] The publisher's blurb on the back cover suggests, "This book will be valuable to doctors, teachers, or anyone wishing to better understand—and hence tolerate and love—their fellow human beings."

A similar description can be found in the introductory pages of a 2003 book by the American psychologists Paul Ekman and Wallace V. Friesen, *Unmasking the Face: A Guide to Recognizing Emotions from Facial Clues*: "This book is for psychotherapists, ministers, physicians and nurses, trial lawyers, personnel managers, salesmen, teachers, actors."[147] The authors then add, in immediately subsequent pages, the suggestion that their book will also be useful "for job applicants, loan seekers, customers, voters, jurymen . . ." and "for friends, spouses, parents, lovers, relatives" as well as (perhaps inevitably) "for you alone."[148]

Ekman had previously published several studies of the human face intended for researchers in the field. *Unmasking the Face*, with its frequent address to "you," was a more popular handbook, offering what it described as "blueprints of facial expressions."[149] How were these "blueprints" produced? First the authors developed what they called an "Atlas of the face," drawing on the previous work of Darwin, Duchenne, and two American scholars, the anatomist Ernst Huber and the psychologist Robert Plutchik. For each of what they called the six "primary emotions" (surprise, fear, disgust, anger, happiness, sadness), they photographed models instructed to move particular facial muscles, taking separate photographs of the upper, middle, and lower face. The authors' description of the photographic process reads uncannily like an updated version of Duchenne:

> We specially made the pictures for this book, photographing faces under controlled laboratory conditions. Our two models followed detailed instructions based on the Facial Atlas. They were not told to feel an emotion, but rather were given instructions such as "lower your brow so that it looks like this," or "raise the outer corner of your upper lip," or "tighten your lower eyelid." The models recreated the faces we had seen and studied when people were really experiencing emotions. We were in a sense drawing with a camera—not relying on imagination, as an artist might, or on the models' possible dramatic skill in trying to feel an emotion, but tracing photographically the muscular movements shown in the Facial Atlas.[150]

In the 1860s, Duchenne had used electrical impulses to stimulate the muscles of his subjects; Ekman and Friesen gave verbal instructions. But in both cases the "mechanism" of emotion was what was on display. Following the experimenters' cues, the modern models were not "really experiencing" emotions any more than were their nineteenth-century predecessors, but were, instead, mechanically reproducing them. The creators—"drawing with a camera"—were scientists. And their models were not "sad" or "angry" or "happy," but compliant. The readers of the book, whether salesmen, job seekers, ministers, or physicians, were being taught to recognize *simulations* of emotion.[151] The question of character does not arise.

Ekman is a prolific author on his chosen subject. In *Emotions Revealed: Understanding Faces and Feelings*, published in the same year, he cited the famous "Duchenne smile," comparing it to some twentieth-century "nonenjoyment smiles": Ronald Reagan's "miserable smile" or "grin-and-bear-it smile" after a speech to the NAACP, Richard Nixon's "trace of a smile" at the time of his forced resignation from the presidency.[152] In the last pages of *Emotions Revealed*, Ekman says that, although he has "no doubt" that there are other emotions beyond his basic six, such as embarrassment, guilt, shame, and envy, he does not include them, "because I have not done research on them myself."[153]

As in *Unmasking*, there is no direct mention of "character." The word, and perhaps the felt need, has been replaced by "affect," with citations from Silvan Tomkins (the "affect program," described by Ekman as an "inherited central mechanism that directs emotional behavior"[154]) and evolutionary psychology. Nonetheless, the intended use of popular books of this kind, much like that of the phrenology and physiognomy handbooks of a previous age, is self-education: "You will find that this powerful information can be applied to your friendships, your workplace, and your family life."[155] In service of that goal, presumably, both books conclude by directing their readers to Web sites where they can purchase copies of the Facial Atlas photographs as well as CDs for practicing the recognition of "all the subtle expressions" revealed in *Emotions Revealed*. Once again, a self-taught system for detection of inner thoughts and feelings was being offered—at a price—to the interested consumer.

Six years after the publication of these two books, Paul Ekman was named one of *Time* magazine's one hundred most influential people in the world. In the same year, 2009, Fox aired what became a hit TV show, *Lie to Me*, based on Ekman's research, especially that presented in his book *Telling Lies*.

Perhaps significantly, none of these books use "character" (or, indeed, "morality" or "ethics") as relevant categories. Neither in the indexes nor in the pages of the text are these terms used, although "empathy" appears a few times in *Emotions Revealed*. It's not that such values are necessarily unimportant to the authors. In *Telling Lies*, after assessing the roles of lying and political deception in the public careers of Richard Nixon, Lyndon Johnson, Ted Kennedy, Oliver North, Clarence Thomas, and Anita Hill, Ekman wrote—in a chapter first published in 1992—that "lying by public officials is still newsworthy, condemned not admired."[156] But his primary interest is in detecting deception, not in counseling against it. A section on "emblems" (deliberate nonverbal signs, like the headshake for "no" or the "come-here" beckon) suggests that these social "tells" can function much like Delsarte's signaling hands, elbows, and eyebrows in expressing felt emotion; what Ekman calls "leakage emblems" reveal, inadvertently, something the social performer is trying to conceal.[157] (In 2019, a reporter for CNN identified what he called a "tell" in President Donald Trump's public pronouncements. "I've fact-checked every word Trump has uttered since his inauguration," wrote Daniel Dale. "I can tell you that if this President relays an anecdote in which he has someone referring to him as 'sir,' then some major component of the anecdote is very likely to be wrong."[158])

Something had changed in the realm of investigatory and evolutionary social science. Had "character" become an old-fashioned term, too unscientifically tinged with moral judgment or with ethics? Or was it merely not clinically useful? If "tells" for character could be induced, trained, simulated, and staged, it might be that the long run of this problematic but persistent concept was, medically speaking, over.

But not so fast. For perhaps, as another group of cutting-edge scientists speculated, the problem was, rather, that the wrong tools were being used.

Seeing Character in the Brain

The quest to isolate "character" as a defined and discernible object by scientific means, whatever its difficulties and shortcomings, remains both seductive and tantalizing. Photography had appeared, for at least a brief while, to indicate a way to "see" character. Technology continued to advance, even as the quarry remained maddeningly elusive.

The turn of the twenty-first century suggested a more sophisticated option, one that, not content with reading the "countenance" or the "expressions," would peer directly into the human brain: functional magnetic resonance imaging, or fMRI.

Could there be there a neural basis of morality? Some researchers have sought not only to demonstrate the existence of such a basis but also to visualize it through the techniques of fMRI. During experiments on volunteers concerning social and moral violations, active brain regions—the ventromedial prefrontal cortex, the superior temporal sulcus—seemed to suggest what has been called a "brain signature for viewing moral scenarios and making moral judgments."[159]

But medical specialists stress that it is a misconception to think that cognitive processes can be located in specific and delimited areas of the brain. Whenever an individual responds to a stimulus, a network of interconnected brain areas—not specific locales for morality, self-control, or any other emotional or social aspects of cognition—is at work. One recent study insists, "fMRI is far from phrenology,"[160] but another view derides or dismisses it as "the new phrenology," with many of the shortcomings of its predecessor.[161]

There was more than one kind of phrenology, however, and the philosophical and self-improvement aspects of that term, well respected in the nineteenth century, have been obscured and occluded by subsequent popularization. The use of "phrenology" as if it were the simple equivalent of quackery ignores important aspects of its history, and its complicated connection with the nineteenth-century obsession with "character." But it is true that fMRI is not phrenology.

"Semantic maps," produced through neuroimaging, are used to reveal significant information about brain function, behavior, and cognition. The spectacular beauty of these images can be distracting, but it is not clear whether aspects of human character, innate or developed, can really be "seen" in them. In one semantic map, "green areas are mostly related to physical and perceptual categories," says the caption, while "red and purple areas represent human-related categories."[162] The decision to depict these areas in color is a scientific and also an aesthetic one. But what are the "human-related categories," and why are they marked as they are? The key word here is "represent": the colors are arbitrary; what we see is an "image," an artifact. If the brain itself were to be magically (or surgically) opened, its color would not be at all like the "map," any more than the old British colonies, colored red on the imperial map, had red grass or red sand or red trees. As a child I was disappointed to find that when you crossed from Connecticut to Massachusetts there was no corresponding change in color, and no visible line of demarcation. I wanted to believe the map, and not my eyes.

Although some have tried, researchers have thus far not succeeded in locating any "single brain area of morality that is not also active during other processes."[163] The brain region associated with the perception of speech, motion, faces, and the theory of mind, among other processes—the superior temporal sulcus—has been called "the chameleon of the human brain,"[164] a figure of speech that suggests not only change but coloration, and, indeed, protective coloration. Skilled physicians and neurologists understand how to read the details on their maps, just as skilled cartographers do. The maps they design are a starting point, something to facilitate further exploration. But a lay viewer is likely to imagine sites as definitive rather than suggestive. Even if we were to equate character with morality, it would not be easy to see it on a brain scan. And if character is some mixture of morality, ethics, social attitudes, cultural conditioning, education, intelligence, and belief—a more-than-random list, which nonetheless seems far from definitive—the goal of "seeing it," whether in a face, a caricature, a photograph, a stage gesture, an expression of emotion, or even an fMRI, seems still as much a projection as it is an observation. The eye-catching colors in which the various brain functions are indicated on fMRIs hold out the traditional promise of the rainbow, but as yet, in the quest to visualize character, there is no pot of gold.

7

CHARACTER TYPES

Greeks, Geeks, Nerds—and Little Miss Hug

Fielding's Allworthy is not a character, but a type of a simple English gentleman; and Squire Western is not a character, but a type of the rude English squire. But Sir Roger de Coverley is a character, as well as a type; there is no one else like him.

—JOHN RUSKIN, *FORS CLAVIGERA: LETTERS TO THE WORKMEN AND LABOURERS OF GREAT BRITAIN*

"Low types," said the old Etonion, "very low types."

—GEORGE ORWELL, *DOWN AND OUT IN PARIS AND LONDON*

"Number one, she's not my type. Number two, it never happened. It never happened, okay?"

—DONALD TRUMP, JUNE 24, 2019

The "Theophrastan character" is not often mentioned today, perhaps because it is so little known as a genre. Yet for centuries this was what "character" meant in literature.[1] A list of familiar social types compiled in the fourth century BCE that chronicled human traits and foibles—from bore to boaster, cynic to coward—influenced the development of later fiction and drama, and remains sharply pertinent in psychology, journalism, cartoon art, and popular culture.

Theophrastan character sketches deliberately describe a recognizable model of behavior rather than a mocked or skewered individual. Dickens's ever-hopeful Mr. Micawber, clinging to the thought that "something will turn up," is a descendant of the Theophrastan character, as are Molière's miser and hypochondriac. Psychologists and psychoanalysts have created character types on what could be called the Theophrastan model, like the obsessive-compulsive, the hysteric, the impulsive man, and the paranoid (whom Theophrastus, lacking the resources of the *DSM*, might have called "The Suspicious Man"). The "white working-class voter" is a Theophrastan type, as is the equally hypothetical "soccer mom," not to mention generational "types" like the baby boomer and the millennial. By the twenty-first century, the "character sketch" (or "character portrait") had become the frequent province of editorial journalism, both print and electronic, as well as of social media and stand-up comedy. "Any kid with a passionate interest in science was a wonk, a square, a dweeb, a doofus, or a geek," wrote the scientist Stephen Jay Gould, a self-confessed geek.[2] (Within a year or two, however, this "depreciative" term—"an overly diligent, unsociable student," according to the *Oxford English Dictionary*—would morph into the glamorous style called "geek chic.")

Why has this ancient mode survived so long? "The *Characters* suggested an adaptable form and a set of basic techniques, according to which human types of any century or country could be depicted," observes J. W. Smeed. "The book seemed to offer an invitation to later writers to borrow the method and use it to describe their own contemporaries." He adds, "I cannot think of a smaller book with a greater influence."[3]

A consideration of that influence, beyond the "character collections" of the seventeenth and eighteenth centuries, which were enormously popular in their own time but much less so today, will speak directly to the fascination with character that still dominates intellectual and public life.

Theophrastus

Theophrastus (c. 370–285 BCE), born Tyrtamus, was a student and colleague of Aristotle, chosen by him as his successor to direct the Peripatetic school in Athens. His name, which translates to "the divine speaker," is an honorific said to have been given him by Aristotle in acknowledgment of his eloquence.

Called by some "the father of botany," a topic on which he wrote two large and important early treatises,[4] Theophrastus produced a wide range of scholarly work, very little of which has survived, in areas as diverse as physics, biology, law, ethics, rhetoric, mathematics, music, and poetics. He is best known today for the thirty fictional sketches that are known collectively as the *Characters*, each of which illustrates a dominant attribute, or fault, or "vice."

As Jeffrey Rusten points out in his edition and translation of the *Characters*, "If it were not firmly established, Theophrastus' title might better be rendered 'traits,'" since it is part of his conception that "individual good or bad traits of character may be isolated and studied separately"—a point also made by Aristotle in the *Nicomachean Ethics*.[5] Aristotle himself had produced in that work a striking description of magnificence, or "the magnificent man,"[6] situated at the mean between stinginess and vulgarity, but the virtuous mean is not the substance with which Theophrastus will work in the *Characters*. His thirty memorable "characters" are all extremes, whether deficient or excessive.

Whether his goal in writing them was ethical, rhetorical, satiric, comic, or to enliven his classroom lectures—scholars have suggested all of these, sometimes in combination[7]—the result was remarkable: his imitators and stylistic heirs included some of the most notable writers of the seventeenth, eighteenth, and nineteenth centuries, as well as a surprising number and variety of modern practitioners. The psychologist Gordon Allport quoted the whole of "The Penurious Man" in his *Pattern and Growth in Personality*, observing, "Though written over two thousand years ago it is applicable to some of our acquaintances today."[8]

Theophrastus's most immediate literary influence, however, was on the comic playwright Menander, who may have been one of his students.[9] "You will find," the British scholar G. S. Gordon told an Oxford audience,

> that whenever Characters are written there is this same conjunction, of Character-Writing and Comedy; to every Theo-

> phrastus, his Menander. To Hall, Overbury, and Earle, the accepted imitators of Theophrastus in England, corresponds Ben Jonson with his Comedy of Humours, an earlier, harsher, and profounder version of the later Comedy of Manners. To La Bruyère, his professed disciple in France, corresponds the comedy of Molière, the French Menander. To the *Tatler* and the *Spectator*, the New Testament, as I may call them, of Character-writing in England, corresponds the comedy of Congreve, our English Molière.[10]

Gordon added that such a conjunction always implies or reflects some philosophy of conduct. "Virtue once admitted to be the mean," as Aristotle had established, "it became necessary to define all the extremes, the too little and too much of the social appearances of man."[11] This "too little and too much" would furnish the basic materials of comic types, from the miser to the libertine, the fashionable peacock, and the glutton.

Comedy, as is often observed, is an essentially conservative genre, as is satire. Both point toward the foibles and follies—and sometimes the delusions and sheer wickedness—of human beings. Here ethical "character" and two different but related modes of literary "character," the Theophrastan prose sketch and the theatrical role, come together.

The Characters in the *Characters*

Since they would exercise so great an influence upon his imitators and (witting or unwitting) literary heirs, it may be useful here to list the thirty "characters" as we have them from Theophrastus. Richard Aldington's titles for them, derived from scholarly work of the early twentieth century and generally adopted by commentators, describe the person ("The Flatterer," "The Arrogant Man," etc.), whereas Benjamin Boyce, and Jeffrey Rusten in his recent Loeb translation, names the characteristic, or foible ("Flattery," "Arrogance"). In Aldington's version, the original Theophrastan characters are:

The Dissimulator
The Flatterer
The Chatterer (or "The Bore")
The Rustic
The Complaisant Man
The Reckless Cynic
The Loquacious Man
The Newsmonger
The Unscrupulous Man
The Penurious Man
The Gross Man
The Unseasonable Man
The Officious Man
The Stupid Man
The Surly Man
The Superstitious Man
The Grumbler
The Distrustful Man
The Offensive Man
The Unpleasant Man
The Vain Man
The Mean Man
The Boaster
The Arrogant Man
The Coward
The Oligarch
The Late-Learner
The Slanderer
The Friend of the Rabble
The Avaricious Man[12]

From this list, even without looking at the individual descriptions, it is easy to understand Allport's sense that these two-thousand-year-old types are readily recognizable in the modern world.

"Theophrastus' characters remain fixed," notes the philosopher Amélie Rorty. "They are not transformed by the unfolding of events. On the contrary, their dispositional characteristics allow them to be used to develop a narrative or to stabilize the structure of a society."[13] In other words, as events unfold, the "character" becomes even more like himself or herself—sometimes to the point of comedy or parody. "At a time when bad behavior flourishes, even among our leaders," says the novelist and critic Francine Prose, Theophrastus's "portraits of boors, braggarts, and blowhards have never felt more current." The classicist Mary Beard agrees: "These *Characters* are people we know—they're our quirky neighbors, our creepy bosses, our blind dates from hell."[14]

The format of the *Characters* is fairly uniform. Each begins with a definition of a quality ("Chattering is the mania of talking hugely without thinking"; "Grumbling is complaining too much of one's lot"; "Penuriousness is economy carried beyond all measure"), although not all scholars agree that Theophrastus himself wrote these opening sentences. Then the chosen trait is illustrated by a series of descriptions of actions or words. The Chatterer (in some translations, "The Bore") "sits down beside someone he never saw before and begins by praising his wife; then describes a dream he had the night before; then passes to his dinner and relates it in detail." When the Grumbler is told of the birth of a son, he retorts, "You should add . . . that my property is now halved, and you would be telling the truth." Of the Penurious Man (or "The Pennypincher") we are told, "At a dinner where expenses are shared, he counts the number of cups each person drinks," and "When his servant breaks a pot or a plate, he deducts the value from his food. If his wife drops a copper, he moves furniture, beds, chests and hunts in the curtains."[15] "The inner man emerges from this description of externals," observes Smeed. "There is no abstract analysis."[16] The form is perfect in and of itself.

Here is one of Theophrastus's "characters" quoted in full, to give you a sense of how the shape of the whole small form coheres. "The Gross Man" (or "The Obnoxious Man," or "Obnoxiousness") is one of the briefer "characters," but every sentence is telling.

> Grossness is not hard to define; it is obtrusive and objectionable jesting. The Gross Man is the sort of person who, meeting free-born women, pulls up his clothes and exposes his genitals. At the theatre he goes on clapping when others cease, and hisses the actors whom the public like. In the midst of a general silence he leans back and belches to make everybody turn round. When the market-place is crowded he goes up to the stalls where they sell nuts or myrtle-berries and pilfers from the pile as he talks to the stall-keeper. Somebody he does not know comes by in a hurry—he tells him to stop. Another comes out of court where he has lost an important case—he accosts him and offers congratulations. He goes personally to do his marketing and hire flute-players; he shows his provisions to everybody and invites them to the feast. He stops in front of the barber's or perfumer's and tells the customers he is going to get drunk.[17]

The "sort of person who" structure allows for a list of distinguishing actions and behaviors that describe not a specific individual (what later practitioners and scholars would call a "portrait") but, rather, a recognizable "type." The obnoxious man does things *like* the ones here mentioned. The reader can be relied upon to think up some additional examples to fit the pattern. The generality of the form, and the present tense ("he goes on clapping"; "he stops in front of the barber's or perfumer's"), underscores both the typicality of the behavior and the way it might translate into another place or time. (Think "frat party" or "#MeToo.")

Theophrastus and the Drama: Ben Jonson

Theophrastus's editors all point out that he was the teacher of Menander and therefore in some sense the godfather of ancient Greek comedy; some have suggested that the *Characters* were written as part of a treatise on comic writing, "meant as models for contemporary playwrights."[18]

In this context, the Renaissance playwright Ben Jonson was his natural English heir. The titles of two of Jonson's plays, *Every Man in His Humour* and *Every Man Out of His Humour*, will attest to their connection to the classical theory of the four humors; a comedy of humors was one in which a prevailing trait or obsession—what was often called a "ruling passion"—dominated a character's behavior to a comical, and often self-defeating, extent. Jonson included in the prefatory material to the printed text of *Every Man Out* a set of brief satirical sketches called "Characters," describing the persons of the drama.[19] For example:

> ASPER, his Character
>
> He is of an ingenious and free spirit, eager and constant in reproof, without fear controlling the world's abuses; one whom no servile hope of gain or frosty apprehension of danger can make to be a parasite either to time, place, or opinion.
>
> MACILENTE
>
> A man well parted, a sufficient scholar, and travelled; who (wanting that place in the world's account which he thinks

> his merit capable of) falls into such an envious apoplexy, with his judgement is so dazzled and distasted that he grows violently impatient of any opposite happiness in another.
>
> FUNGOSO
>
> The son of Sordido, and a student; one that has revelled in his time, and follows the fashion far off like a spy. He makes it the whole bent of his endeavours to wring sufficient means from his wretched father to put him in the courtier's cut, at which he earnestly aims, but so unluckily that he still lights short a suit.

We might note the nicely cartoony way in which names function here: Asper's name comes from the same root as "aspersion," a sharp critique; "macilent" means lean, shriveled, or thin; "fungoso" is a mushroom (fungus), or, in modern parlance, a sponge. Other equally wonderful names adorn Jonson's satirical play—Fastidius Brisk, for a fashionable gallant; Deliro, for a man besotted with his wife; Sordido, for an unscrupulous miser; Clove and Orange for an inseparable pair of fops. Of a minor character, Mitis (the "mild-mannered" one; cf. our word "mitigate"), Jonson adds, at the very end of his list,

> MITIS
>
> Is a person of no action, and therefore we have reason to afford him no character.[20]

Jonson's play *Cynthia's Revels* contains a list of characters with similar prose descriptions, most satirical, one admiring. The character of "A Gallant Wholly Consecrated to his Pleasures" begins, "These are his graces. He doth (besides me) keep a barber and a monkey; he has a rich wrought waistcoat to entertain his visitants in, with a cap almost suitable. His curtains and bedding are thought to be his own; his bathing tub is not suspected. He loves to have a fencer, a pedant, and a musician seen in his lodgings a-mornings. Himself is a rhymer and that's thought better than a poet."[21] The "Nymph," of a "most wandering and giddy disposition," runs "from gallant to gallant," willing at last to be "your procurer or pander"; the "Traveller" walks about with a (then fashionable) toothpick in his mouth, dominates table conversation, is willing to fight, but only "out at a window" (in other words, vicariously rather than in person), and changes his clothes at least once a year.[22]

The one nonsatirical character sketch in *Cynthia's Revels*, that of "The True Critic," invokes the four humors directly. Some of Jonson's rivals claimed this was a wishful self-portrait; in any case, its opening lines are certainly complimentary.

> A creature of a most perfect and divine temper: one in whom the humours and elements are peaceably met, without emulation of precedency. He is neither too fantastically melancholy, too slowly phlegmatic, too lightly sanguine, nor too rashly choleric; but in all so composed and ordered, as it is clear nature went about some full work, she did more than make a man when she made him.[23]

The perfectly balanced "humours," none jostling for domination ("without emulation of precedency"), allow for an ideal temperamental balance. Whether the very perfection of this mix is also an evidence of Jonson's dry wit is a judgment left to the reader.

Commedia Types

At the same time that Ben Jonson was developing his comedy of humors, the commedia dell'arte, the traditional Italian comedy of types, became popular across Europe—a popularity that continued from the sixteenth to the eighteenth century and has been resurgent in recent years. The stock types in commedia include the cunning Zanni, the swaggering Capitano, the pompous Dottore, the ingénue lovers, the old Magnifico, Pantalone (the miser), and other familiar figures like Arlecchino and Pulchinella. All of these "types," like those of Theophrastus, have long histories, and—like many Theophrastan types—can at the same time seem uncannily current.

When the actor Simon Callow sat in on some commedia classes taught by the Italian director and mask maker Antonio Fava, he observed that once the students put on their masks they were immediately transformed: "A short stumpy actor was suddenly lean, elegant, lyrical; a tall one, dwarflike. Moreover these sudden transformations were not mere adjustments of shape: a whole character with an entire repertory of movements arrived onstage. Everything he or she did was in character, was in fact of the essence of the character; another principle of being had taken over the actor." As Callow points out, in commedia "each of the characters is driven along by strong impulses in the grip of which they find themselves pushed to the extreme of their temperaments. There is no attempt in Commedia to explain why anyone is the way they are: character is a given fact."[24]

The list of commedia stock roles can be put to a myriad of uses. When the *New York Times* columnist Roger Cohen looked up the name of the quickly ousted White House communications director, Anthony Scaramucci, he found that it matched that of a commedia character, known in English as the Scaramouch. (Jokes about names might sometimes be seen as inappropriate, but Scaramucci had gladly spread the word that his personal nickname was "The Mooch.") The Italian stock character's name, Scaramuccia, means "little fighter" or "skirmisher," and a handbook of commedia types says that he is "often employed as a go-between," that among his "characteristics" is that "he boasts not so much of his physical prowess as that he is a marquis or a prince of several countries which exist, however, only in his imagination," and that his plot function is to be "a stirrer."[25]

Cohen identified Scaramouch as a "braggart and a poltroon" in the old Italian comedy, and he then took the opportunity to match up other occupants of the White House with the stock characters of commedia: President Trump as "the miserly Venetian known as Pantalone wandering around in red breeches with the oversized codpiece of the womanizer"; Steve Bannon, "Trump's chief strategist," as the Dottore; Sebastian Gorka as the "belligerent, windy Capitano"; Ivanka Trump and Jared Kushner as the young lovers.[26] The piece was wickedly funny and devastatingly persuasive to anyone who knew the commedia types, though I am sure there are those whom it did not amuse.

The point, though, is that these *are* types, comic, satiric, oddly moving human "characters," whose ensemble embodies and embraces a society that looks (always) a lot like the present. Here is Simon Callow again: "Psychology is by no means absent—in fact the psychology of each of the types is absolutely watertight and organically consistent—it is simply that the emphasis is on what it is to be human rather than what it is to be this particular human. There is a Zanni in all of us, a Dottore, a Brighella, waiting to be released, and that is what the Commedia is concerned with, rather than Zanni X, Dottore Y, Brighella Z."[27]

"More Fashionable Than Sonnets"

The *Characters* of Theophrastus were all clearly comic or satirical, leading to some speculation that a parallel list of virtuous characters must once have existed and been lost. Some of his English imitators remedied the absence, as is clear from their titles: Joseph Hall's *Characters of Virtues and Vices* (1608) or Nicholas Breton's *The Good and the Bad, or Descriptions of the Worthies and Unworthies of This Age, Where the Best May See Their Graces, and the Worst Discern Their Baseness* (1616). In the early years of the seventeenth century, the "vogue, almost the craze, for character-writing" in the style of Theophrastus flourished. It became a literary fad, even, it is said, "more fashionable than sonnets."[28]

There are no women among Theophrastus's characters, but character writers would quickly supply them, both on the virtuous and on the less virtuous sides of the mean. The extremely popular *Characters, or Witty Descriptions of the Properties of Sundry Persons* by "Sir Thomas Overbury and other learned gentlemen, his friends," included "A Good Woman," "A Very Woman," "A Whore," and "A Very Whore" among other "characters" of women in their collection. ("Very" in this sense was an emphatic word, used frequently in the period to qualify something bad or undesirable—we might compare it to the emphatic modern sense of "real" when coupled with disparagement: "he was a real bastard.") The year after Overbury's sensational murder in 1613, his *Characters* appeared, and quickly went through five editions.

The art of the "character" in England continued to be practiced in the seventeenth century by noblemen and by clerics—as well as by the occasional woman.[29] Many continued to be satiric, but a few were not only admiring but also lyrical in their praise of the "character" in question.

John Earle's *Microcosmography, or, A Piece of the World Characterized*, was also already in its fifth edition a year after its initial publication in 1628.[30] Earle, a man known to his friends as learned, witty, innocent, and "facetious"[31] (i.e., "amusing"; the word was a compliment at the time), later became tutor to the future Charles II, and ultimately, after the Restoration of the monarchy, dean of Westminster and bishop of Salisbury.

Earle's characters are exceptionally well drawn, elegantly observed, and often moving. In his collection (as sometimes in Overbury's), the title phrase becomes the grammatical subject of the first sentence, so that Earle can write "*A discontented man* Is one that is faln out with the world, and will be revenged on himself," or "*A mere great man* Is so much heraldry without honour, himself less real than his title," or "*A partial man* Is the opposite extreme to a defamer, for the one speaks ill falsely, and the other well, and both slander the truth . . . His friend always shall do best, and you shall rarely hear well of his enemy."[32] All of these and many more remain applicable today.

Characters About the "Character"

So popular a literary mode inevitably produced reflections on it as a form of art. The appeal and mystique of the "character" concept was such that the Overbury collection ended with a character of the genre of the "character":

> What a Character Is
>
> If I must speak the schoolmaster's language, I will confess that character comes from this infinite mood χαραξω that signifyeth to engrave, or make a deep impression. And for that cause, a letter (as A. B.) is called a character.
>
> Those elements which we learn first, leaving a strong seal on our memories.
>
> Character is also taken from an Egyptian hieroglyphic, for an impress, or short emblem; in little comprehending much.
>
> To square out a character by our English level, it is a picture (real or personal) quaintly drawn, in various colours, all of them heightened by one shadowing.

> It is a quick and soft touch of many strings, all shutting up in one musical close; it is wit's descant on any plain song.[33]

The title of the collection, *Characters, or Witty Descriptions of the Properties of Sundry Persons*, had offered one definition of "character." But this elegant tailpiece goes further, commenting on the etymology of the word, and offering two epigrammatic phrases that have become effective characterizations: "in little comprehending much" (from the Latin *multum in parvo*), and "wit's descant on any plain song," where a "plain song" is a simple melody and a "descant" is a musical accompaniment, written in parts, like a counterpoint ("a quick and soft touch of many strings, all shutting up in one musical close," a good description of the economy and brevity of the character form). "Descant" also carried, by this time, the metaphorical sense of a commentary, criticism, or remark, as does our "counterpoint" today. Having paid due diligence to etymology ("If I must speak the schoolmaster's language . . ."), the author turns, with happy chauvinism, to a home-grown definition from "our English," using a figure from carpentry ("to square out," using a "level"), which then metamorphoses into "a picture . . . quaintly drawn, in various colours." Significantly, the various colors are to be "heightened by one shadowing," the dominant trait or ruling passion. Without such "heightening," the character is not really a "character," but merely a description.

One further sentence from the character of "a Character" is also worth underscoring here, although it has attracted less attention than the quotable "wit's descant"—that is, the sentence in which the author notes that "those elements which we learn first" leave a "strong seal on our memories." "Seal" is again an allusion to the language of stamping, engraving, and impression, which is the etymology of the word "character"—but "those elements which we learn first" leaps ahead three hundred years to psychoanalysis and to Freud. Whoever the author was, whether Overbury or one of his unnamed gentlemen friends,[34] he feels confident in asserting that the earliest impressions are the deepest and most lasting—the ones that impress the individual with what we, in modern terms and modern times, call "character."

The classicist and clergyman Henry Gally would attach a longer essay on "Characteristic-Writings" to his 1725 translation of Theophrastus. Part of Gally's objective was to return the character to a form more like that used by its originator. The focus and organizing principle of the form should be the ruling passion ("'tis the Master Passion which must determine the Character"[35]), and the task of the writer is to make sure the reader understands this coherence. On the other hand, an author "must not dwell too long upon one Idea; as soon as the masterly Stroke is given, he must immediately pass on to another Idea," for if he insists, "in a paraphrastical manner," on making the same point over and over again, "the Work will immediately flag, the Character grow languid, and the Person characteris'd will insensibly vanish from the Eyes of the Reader."[36] If it is done correctly, however, "the Character is then genuine and compleat, the Thing or Person design'd is drawn to the Life, and the Reader is left uncertain, whether the Character, that lies before him, is an Effect of Art, or a real Appearance of Nature."[37]

In short (and here is where Gally most closely resembles the epigrammatic and quotable Sir Thomas Overbury), "Much must be contained in a little Compass," and "Matters shou'd be so order'd, that every perfect Sentence may contain a perfect Thought, and every perfect Thought may represent one Feature."[38]

Latecomers

The editor of the English satirist Samuel Butler's *Characters*, published in 1759, long after Butler's death, remarked in the preface to that work, "The writing of Characters was a Kind of Wit much in Fashion in the Beginning of the last Century"—adding that "how agreeable these Sort of Essays were to the public Taste" could be seen by the number of editions of Overbury ("fourteen Editions before 1632") and Earle ("six between 1628 and 1633").[39] Butler's characters included two that were explicitly drawn from the theory of humors, the Melancholy Man and the Choleric Man, and a third merely described as a "Humourist," what we might today call an enthusiast or even a zealot: "He knows no mean;

for that is inconsistent with all Humour, which is never found but in some extreme or other."[40]

Butler offered as well the usual gallery of political and social types—a Politician, a Degenerate Noble, a Wooer, a Cutpurse, and so on. Some of Theophrastus's original characters are reprised, like the Newsmonger, who in both ancient Athens and seventeenth-century London is said to try to pass off false events as true ones.[41] Even "fake news," it seems, has a history.

But some of the freshness has, over time, gone from the form. If Butler's characters were each half as long as they are, they might be more effective, and perhaps seem less dated. The sheer number of characters has also grown exponentially—Butler's edition has 185, to Theophrastus's thirty—and the Theophrastan originals seem by contrast pleasingly compact, both in number and in length. "By the end of the seventeenth century," wrote J. W. Smeed, "the 'character' had reached something of a dead end in England."[42]

Character writers in the following years, notes Deidre Lynch, would wrestle with the question of "how many characters it might take to anthologize and to sum up human nature," and "how many traits, or characteristics, must be set down for a portrait to be complete."[43] The eighteenth century would have its own adept practitioners of this literary form: Richard Steele's "Tom Courtly" and the "Character of Lord No-where" are gems, as is his "Character of an Affectionate Couple" (called "Matrimonial Quarrels" in *The Tatler*), in which a couple argue constantly about trivial matters while their dinner guest looks helplessly on, seeking to escape at the first opportunity. Joseph Addison's "A Devotee" ("one of those who disparage religion by their indiscreet and unseasonable introduction of the mention of virtue on all occasions"), first published in *The Spectator*, describes a figure as recognizable today as she was three hundred years ago. Versions of this kind of "character-writing" made their way into the novel, the forerunners, in many cases, of the so-called flat character of fiction. The "inset 'character'" can be found in novels by Fielding, Trollope, Dickens, Thackeray, and many others.[44] Dickens's early *Sketches by Boz* included a section on "Characters," including "The Parlour Orator," "The Hospital Patient," "The

Mistaken Milliner," and "The Dancing Academy." Although these are short stories in format, and originally published separately, the word *Sketches* indicates something of their lineage. Mr. Podsnap in *Our Mutual Friend* is a good example of a later figure derived from the same genre, his name now the root of a term—"Podsnappery"—defined as "insular complacency and blinkered self-satisfaction."[45] Those novelists for whom the "sketch" was less congenial, like Jane Austen, are those for whom character *development* was of more interest than character *type*.

The *Caractères* of La Bruyère

In France, however, the "character" achieved its most significant and canonical standing in the seventeenth century, with the publication and celebrity of Jean de La Bruyère's *Les Caractères*. The book became an instant bestseller in 1688, went through nine editions in less than ten years, and remains a classic of French literature.

La Bruyère lived first as a tutor, and then a librarian, at the Versailles-like court of Condé, where he had the opportunity to observe the good, the bad, and the great of France at work and play. His collection of *remarques*—maxims, observations, and "characters"—originally bore the title *The Characters of Theophrastus Translated from the Greek, with the Characters or the Customs of This Century*, and was published with the passages from Theophrastus printed in large type. By the sixth edition, in 1691, the fame of La Bruyère's satirical portraits had eclipsed that of his classical prototype, and the size of the type was reversed. Everyone at court tried to guess the "real" identities of the character portraits; various "keys" to the characters were circulated and debated.

Over the years, La Bruyère's translation of Theophrastus dropped out of the book altogether,[46] but its presence in the first editions is a sign of the name recognition and prestige of the Theophrastan characters at that place and time. We may have forgotten them, but La Bruyère's age held them in high regard.

Some of the *remarques* are epigrammatic, others more extended; all have a definitive voice. But it is the character portraits, or "characters," of the book's title that made the volume a sensation in its time. They were recognizable enough to fascinate contemporary readers, while retaining enough elements of satire and caricature to protect the author. Even without the temptation to identify the individuals depicted, they are vivid, and recognizable across the ages.

A close look at a pair of La Bruyère's most famous "characters" makes clear the brilliance of his observation and craftsmanship. This is a long quotation, but rewarding reading, since the contrast between the two figures is so artfully—and wittily—drawn.

> *Giton* is fresh-complexioned, with a full face and heavy jowls, a self-confident stare, square shoulders and a high stomach, and a firm deliberate gait. He speaks with assurance; he makes his interlocutors repeat his words, and then is but ill pleased with what he hears; he unfolds a huge handkerchief and blows his nose noisily; he spits a long way and sneezes very loud; he sleeps by day, he sleeps by night, and soundly too; he snores in company. At table and out with his fellows, he is the centre of the group, if he stops they all stop, if he goes on walking they all go on, all follow his example; he interrupts and corrects whoever is speaking; nobody interrupts him, all listen to him for as long as he chooses to go on talking, they agree with him, they believe all his stories. When he sits down he sinks into an armchair, flings one leg across the other, pulls his hat over his eyes so as to see nobody and then pushes it back, baring his brow with a proud, defiant gesture. He is jovial, much given to laughter, impatient, presumptuous, hot-tempered, independent, knowledgeable about politics, given to mysterious hints about the affairs of the day; he fancies himself talented and witty. He is rich.
>
> *Phédon* is hollow-eyed, with flushed cheeks, a lean body and a gaunt face; he sleeps little, and that lightly; he is dreamy and absent-minded, and though intelligent seems stupid; he forgets to say what he knows, or to speak of events about which he is well informed; if he sometimes does so he acquits himself badly; afraid of boring those to whom he is talking, he tells his story briefly but lifelessly, so that nobody listens and nobody laughs;

> he smiles approval of what others tell him, agrees with them, hastens, nay flies, to do them some small service; he is obliging, obsequious, over-zealous, secretive about his own affairs, sometimes untruthful; he is superstitious, scrupulous, timid; he walks quietly and lightly, seeming afraid to tread the ground; he walks with downcast eyes, which he dare not raise to look at passers-by; he is never one of those who gather in a group to talk; he stands behind whoever is speaking, takes furtive note of what is said and shrinks back if anyone looks at him; he has no place, he takes up no room, he goes about with his shoulders hunched up and his hat pulled over his eyes so as to be unnoticed, he withdraws and hides behind his cloak; no streets and galleries are so crowded and congested that he cannot pass through them with ease, and slip by without being seen; if he is asked to sit down, he perches on the edge of his chair; in conversation he mumbles and dare not raise his voice; yet he speaks freely about public affairs, grumbles about the way of the world and has a poor opinion of the government and its ministers. He opens his mouth only to answer you; he coughs and blows his nose under cover of his hat, he spits practically over himself; he waits until he is alone to sneeze, or if it should happen to him in company, nobody notices, nobody has to say God bless you. He is poor.[47]

From the parallel but contrasting descriptions of faces and bodies in the first sentences, to the sting in the tail of the last, these portraits are clearly pendants. Both men—but how differently—blow their noses, take seats, pull their hats down, talk with acquaintances, spit, sneeze, and walk down the street. The resulting diptych is a small masterpiece that invites immediate rereading. Each time you do so, you catch more correspondences between the character of the rich man and the character of the poor man, and yet the style is so unforced that one sentence seems to flow from the next without any ulterior motive of design.

The psychologist Gordon Allport, giving Giton as his single example from *Les Caractères*, notes that, in "shifting from types to portraits," La Bruyère "depicts an individual style of life, a consistent pattern of traits, and not merely a single cardinal disposition." The larger point for Allport is that Theophrastus, in locating a "dominant trait" in his characters, was a forerunner of personality psychology, while later imitators diverged from this "important theory of personality" in the direction of literature.[48]

Lytton Strachey's La Bruyère: The Bloomsbury Portrait

Both the titles and the execution of Lytton Strachey's brilliant little essay collections, *Books and Characters* (1922) and *Portraits in Miniature* (1931), show the influence of La Bruyère on one of twentieth-century England's most psychologically acute and stylistically pointed character writers. (A third collection of Strachey's essays, *Characters and Commentaries* [1933], was edited and published after his death by his brother James.) Strachey's initial opinion of the *Caractères* was expressed in his early book *Landmarks in French Literature*: "Psychologically, these studies are perhaps less valuable than has sometimes been supposed: they are caricatures of humanity rather than portraits—records of the idiosyncrasies of humanity rather than humanity itself."[49] He singles out, "as one instance out of a multitude," La Bruyère's description of "the crank who devotes his existence to the production of tulips."[50]

This is the young Strachey speaking, though, a Strachey who had not yet written his own smash bestsellers, *Eminent Victorians*, *Queen Victoria*, and *Elizabeth and Essex*, in which "the idiosyncrasies of humanity" are tellingly described and identified as the clearest signs of "humanity itself." The besotted tulip-lover is exactly the kind of "crank" who would show up, periodically and effectively, in Lytton Strachey's own later books.

Books and Characters includes "characters" of both French and English figures from Sir Thomas Browne and Madame du Deffand to the gossipy diarist Mr. Creevey and the trouser-wearing Lady Hester Stanhope. (The "character" of this last-named begins, with typical Strachey brio, "The Pitt nose has a curious history. One can watch its transmigrations through three lives."[51]) *Portraits in Miniature* contains, among other pleasures, memorable accounts of Sir John Harington (Queen Elizabeth's godson, and the inventor of the water closet), and of John

Aubrey, the idiosyncratic seventeenth-century author of *Short (or Brief) Lives*, of whom Strachey, a biographer, would write, "a biography should either be as long as Boswell's or as short as Aubrey's."[52] It was a style that Strachey's friend John Maynard Keynes would adopt in his own "characters" of figures like Isaac Newton, Carl Melchior, and Woodrow Wilson. Virginia Woolf would describe *Portraits* as a "compressed yet glossy account which requires logic, reasoning, learning, taste, wit order & infinite skill"[53]—the perfect form for Strachey's vision and style, and a description that could justly also be applied to the *Caractères* of La Bruyère.

Roland Barthes's La Bruyère: The "Character" as Metaphor

Perhaps the best of all modern commentators on La Bruyère is the French literary theorist Roland Barthes, who observes, succinctly and acutely, that "the 'character' is a metaphor; it is the development of an adjective."[54] A more extended description captures the idea of the "single disposition" or "ruling passion" fundamental to the Theophrastan form. "A portrait by La Bruyère," writes Barthes, "has an eminently metaphorical structure; La Bruyère chooses features which have the same signified, and he accumulates them in a continuous metaphor, whose unique signified is given at the end." His chief example is, once again, "the portrait of the rich man and the poor man":

> In *Giton* are enumerated, one right after another, all the signs that make him a rich man; in *Phédon*, all the signs of the poor man; we thus see that everything that happens to Giton and to Phédon, although apparently recounted, does not derive, strictly speaking, from the order of narrative; it is entirely a matter of an extended metaphor.[55]

Thus, Barthes says, "the 'character' is a false narrative, it is a metaphor which assumes the quality of narrative without truly achieving it." This is for him the definition of La Bruyère's art.

Let us return for a moment to that most Barthesian claim, "The 'character' is a metaphor; it is the development of an adjective." How is the development of a metaphor different from the development of a trait? Is it the same as the difference between literature and psychology? Between semantics and enumeration? La Bruyère's characters may be drawn "from life," but they come to us as written statements, as "literature." Giton is far more alive to us than the rich Frenchman on whom he may have been modeled, just as Theophrastus's Bore has eclipsed any possible Athenian original, if there ever was one. But modern psychology, too, has developed its categories of disorders from adjectives: antisocial, histrionic, narcissistic, obsessive-compulsive. What if we were to delete the quotation marks that indicate that the "character" is a literary form, and adapt Barthes's statement to say, "Character is a metaphor; it is the development of an adjective"?

To do so is to risk the umbrage of those who respond to similar statements about literary character as if this meant that they were somehow not "real." But the experience of "real life" is almost always mediated, whether by language, conventions of speech or thought, models of character (a "great man"; a "Napoleon" or "Joan of Arc"; a "Hamlet"), or by reference. To say that character is a metaphor is not to deny its reality, but to understand how we encounter and apprehend it, and how we fix upon the words that describe it as true.

Barthes wants to distinguish, in his own account, between La Bruyère's time and the present—although the "present," like "here" and "now," is what linguistics calls a shifter, which alters according to the speaker and the circumstance.

> La Bruyère's man is always *here*; ours is always elsewhere; if it occurs to think of someone's character, we do so either in terms of its insignificant universality (the desire for social advancement, for instance), or of its ineffable complexity (of whom would we dare say quite simply that he is a *dolt*?). In short, what has changed from La Bruyère's world to ours, is what is notable.[56]

This change Barthes attributes in part to the rise of the "human sciences," including psychology and psychoanalysis, giving as his example this *remarque* from La Bruyère: "A father-in-law likes his son-in-law and his daughter-in-law. A mother-in-law likes her son-in-law and dislikes her daughter-in-law. These feelings are all mutual."[57] Barthes's paraphrase is deliberately selective and provocative: "La Bruyère notes that a father-in-law loves his daughter-in-law and that a mother-in-law loves her son-in-law; this is a notation which would concern us more today if it came from a psychoanalyst, just as it is Freud's Oedipus who sets us thinking now, not Sophocles."[58] "Loves" for "likes," and the omission of the other named relations—the father's liking for the son-in-law, the rivalry between mother-in-law and daughter-in-law—turn a sociological observation into a psychoanalytic one. So whose "characters" are these? La Bruyère's, or Freud's, or Barthes's? Or, as he claims, those of the modern world?

"For us, characters exist only marginally," Barthes insists. "It is no longer La Bruyère who gives a name to men now, it is the psychopathologist or the psychosociologist, those specialists who are called upon to define not essences but (quite the contrary) divergences."[59] And all this, he says, is in service of a change from character to "personality" in the sense of celebrity, role, and reflecting mirror.

"There ensues a complete reversal in the interest we can take in characters," says Barthes.

> In the past, the character referred to a "key," the (general) *person* to a (particular) *personality*; today, it is the opposite; our world certainly creates, for its spectacle, a closed and personalized society: that of the stars and celebrities which we might group under the name of modern Olympians; but this society does not yield characters, only functions or roles (the love goddess, the mother, the queen enslaved by her duty, the vixen princess, the model husband, etc.); and contrary to the classical circuit, these "personalities" are treated as persons in order that the greatest number of human beings can recognize themselves in them . . . We no longer seek out the typical but the identical; La Bruyère condensed a character in the fashion of a metaphor; we develop a star like a narrative.[60]

Not only La Bruyère but also Theophrastus can be encompassed by this argument: "we no longer seek out the typical but the identical."

Theophrastus's characters, however different they are from La Bruyère's, are tinged with the moral, the ethical, the ironic and satiric: we laugh at them, we recognize them, but we don't want to *be* them. If they are mirrors, it is as fun-house mirrors that we encounter them; no one wants to be (seen as a) Giton, however successful he may be with his toadying friends, much less as Theophrastus's Grumbler or his Flatterer, Chatterer, or Surly Man.

Post-It Notes

The American equivalent of La Bruyère, as Edmund Wilson once noted, was probably the imperturbable Emily Post, whose *Etiquette*, expanded and revised (like the earlier English and French characterbooks) as time and popularity demanded, offered "models which can never deviate, and thoroughly priggish figures which would lend themselves to satirical comedy."[61] In the pages of *Etiquette* the reader encounters figures like the Worldlys of Great Estates, the Gildings of Golden Hall, Mr. and Mrs. Kindhart, old Colonel Bluffington, the Toploftys, Grace Smalltalk, Mr. and Mrs. Spendeasy Western, Mr. Richan Vulgar (dropped from later editions), and the unhappy and socially disregarded Miss Nobackground. But the "real hero and heroine"[62] of *Etiquette*, in Wilson's opinion, are Mr. and Mrs. Oldname, whose name, like so many of these, says it all.

A few examples from Mrs. Post's chapter on "The Fundamentals of Good Behavior" will make the link to the genre of the "character" even clearer, since—as one might expect—most of her statements about good behavior are actually statements about bad behavior: "A gentleman does not"; "A gentleman never"; "One who is not well off does not"; "One who is rich does not"; "A man of breeding does not slap strangers on the back"; etc. Likewise with women: "Nothing so blatantly proclaims a woman climber as the repetition of prominent names, the owners of which she must have struggled to know. Otherwise, why so eagerly boast of the achievement?" And "When you see a woman in silks and sables and diamonds speak to a little errand girl or a footman or a scullery maid as though they were the dirt under her feet, you may be sure of one thing; she hasn't come a very long way from the ground herself."[63]

Wilson seems rather pleased to detect "something like sadism" in the whole approach of the book ("She likes to humiliate"), and accurately, I think, attributes Mrs. Post's popularity in part to this tendency. Even if we are unlikely to need advice on "children, left-handed, setting table for," or "lobsters, eating," or "regrets, due to White House invitation" (just a few of the many irresistible index entries in the 1950 edition), *Etiquette* is a treasure trove of twentieth-century characters, clued in or clueless. Whether you are avoiding the overly friendly "Mrs. Nextdoor" or introducing yourself to a total stranger ("My name is Mrs. John Jones. That's my husband sitting opposite you. We live in the country and raise prize poultry and dahlias, but we come to town very often in the winter to hear music"[64]), when you are immersed in Emily Post World you encounter brief but unforgettable "characters" at every turn of the page.

The names of her characters have about them a certain flair more typical of the eighteenth century, when a revival of the vogue for character writing filled periodicals like *The Spectator* and *The Tatler*. Witty short essays like Richard Steele's "Character of Lord-No-where," "Character of Tim Dapper," and "Characters of an Affectionate Couple" (who "make no scruple to let those who are by know they are quarreling with one another"[65]). Steele's Tom Courtly and Joseph Addison's Sir Timothy Tittle are ancestors of Post's Jim Smartlington and Bobo Gilding. But Post has embedded them in a larger narrative about social conduct, in effect a moral or at least a behavioral guide. The French word "etiquette" derives originally from a word meaning a label or a note attached to something listing its contents—the same word from which we get "ticket." It meant the prescribed rules of ceremony and behavior at court; at the Spanish court in the sixteenth century, these strict rules were enumerated in an official list. So "etiquette," like "character," is itself derived from a certain specialized practice of writing. To call *Etiquette* a moral treatise is not really so much of a stretch.

We could say the same of satirical galleries like *Modern Types*, written by anthropologist Geoffrey Gorer and illustrated by Ronald Searle. Here we find Lady Something, Mr. Callow, Mrs. McGhoul, Flinching McWhoolie, M.P., and Professor Blank, among others. Meticulously observed and wickedly drawn, these twenty-two characters ring the changes on postwar England (the book was published in 1955). The scientific Professor Blank joined the Communist Party during the war ("Here at last, he felt, were the scientific laws he had been searching for; dialectical materialism showed that human behavior was as explicable and predictable as that of the sub-microscopic physical world which, was, for him, the model of the universe"), shares scientific information with the Russians ("our Glorious Allies"), and is disconcerted when, "after the Soviets repealed the Mendelian law," he is kept from withdrawing by evidence of his collusion.[66] For Miss Rowbotham, a perfect Theophrastan obsessive, "the word 'experiment' is the most alluring in the English language"; her cooking ("all proteins one meal, all carbohydrates the next, and so on"), her enthusiasm for "experimental unions" between men and women ("Physically, Miss Rowbotham is a virgin"), and her political zeal to take part in the "Chinese experiment" and the "Russian experiment" are all perfectly attuned.[67]

Most of Gorer's characters are executed in two or three pages of blithely scathing prose (again the "disinterestedness" of the Theophrastan model is perceptible). But here is the complete "character" of Mr. Lloyd Carter, in three sentences: "In Parliamentary elections, Mr. Lloyd Carter frequently stands as a Liberal candidate. He always loses his deposit. Luckily he can afford to do so."[68]

The rest of the page is eloquently empty. The Searle illustration, on the facing page, shows a graying, balding man in a tweed suit, leaning on a makeshift podium, adorned by a homburg hat and furled umbrella, and smiling vapidly above a poster of himself, perceptibly younger, with a full head of dark hair and dark mustache. A resentful boy and an interested dog are the only visible audience, other than a lady canvasser (the loyal Mrs. Carter?) offering handbills. "Frequently" has clearly been going on for quite a long time.

From "The Chatterer" to "Little Miss Chatterbox"

As unusual as it may seem to compare Theophrastus to Emily Post, it might seem even more unusual to compare the Theophrastan characters to those of the children's book writer Roger Hargreaves, Britain's third-bestselling author of all time, with over a hundred million books sold.

Hargreaves wrote and illustrated the highly successful *Mr. Men* and *Little Miss* series, which his son Adam continued after Roger's death in 1988, each of which contains dozens of titles: *Little Miss Hug. Little Miss Sunshine. Little Miss Stubborn. Little Miss Chatterbox. Little Miss Naughty. Little Miss Busy. Little Miss Bad. Mr. Greedy. Mr. Nosey. Mr. Clever. Mr. Nobody. Mr. Brave. Mr. Tickle.* You get the idea. In most cases, the dominant trait or action is under some challenge: Little Miss Hug, whose hugs have always been welcome, finds a resistant recipient in the person of Mr. Grumpy, but ultimately receives at least a half-hug in return. If these are "moral tales," they wear their morals very lightly—there is no enforced sense that we should all hug our grumpy acquaintances. More to the point, Mr. Grumpy will remain Mr. Grumpy, just as Mr. Bump will remain Mr. Bump, and Mr. Nosey will remain Mr. Nosey, in any further encounters. They may be taken "out of themselves" by a chance meeting, but they will "revert to type," as we have learned to say, or return to character.

Since these are children's books, and presumably meant to instruct as well as to delight, the implication is not that you are stuck permanently with one or another of these dispositions, like Theophrastus's Grumbler, or Overbury's Ignorant Glory-Hunter, or La Bruyère's poor man, but, rather, that they represent moods or options that a child—or, indeed, an adult—might assume or inhabit from time to time. Still, the notion of a dominant trait, or, to use the old but useful phrase, a ruling passion, is important: these are recognizable types, or avatars—familiar social and psychological roles. Who does not know a Mr. Bump, cheerfully accident-prone, or a Little Miss Splendid, too good, in her own mind, for ordinary things?

Scholarly accounts of the Theophrastan character have focused, with good reason, on those writers whose work hews most closely to the original, or who cite Theophrastus in their adaptations of the form—as in the novelist George Eliot's *Impressions of Theophrastus Such*, with its incidental mentions of such characters as the tedious Semper, "who often responds at public dinners and proposes resolutions on platforms" (mentioned in a chapter called "How We Come to Give Ourselves False

Testimonials, and Believe in Them") or the unscrupulous financier Sir Gavial Mantrap (in the chapter on "Moral Swindlers").[69]

But, as Benjamin Boyce noted in his 1947 book on the Theophrastan character, modern "conversation would come to a stop if we could never employ such absolute concepts as 'cheerful extrovert,' 'G. I. Joe,' 'Hollywood blonde,' and 'Hearst journalism.'" E. M. Forster's description of "flat" characters in the novel, and the reliance of theater on what are often called "stock characters," are part of the same heritage of recognizable and unchanging character types.[70]

Character types, in other words, are both *characters* and *theories of character*, recognizable, risible, plausible, and compellingly human. The "profile," the "feature," the "cameo," the "character sketch," the stand-up comedy routine, and the satiric political cartoon in the style of David Levine and his successors—all of these prolific and popular forms are indebted to the Grumbler, the Boaster, the Flatterer, and the Friend of the Rabble who populate the *Characters* of Theophrastus, and flourish in the works of his imitators and admirers in the seventeenth and eighteenth centuries. If Theophrastus did indeed conceive of these characters as a way of enlivening his lectures—or influencing comic theater—he would seem to have succeeded beyond what he might have imagined.

And one last thought: If we are looking for dominant traits or ruling passions, it is less of a leap than you might think from Little Miss Busy to Jane Austen's Emma, or from Mr. Daydream to Hamlet. Although some literary characters may seem to escape typing—like Emma and Hamlet and Falstaff and that other Emma, Madame Bovary—they often, by the strength of their characterization, themselves become types, the subject of analysis (and even psychoanalysis), and of cultural as well as literary imitation. It has become a truism rather than a witticism to say that life imitates art.

8

THE DIFFERENCE GENDER MAKES

Mettle, Spunk, and the Right Stuff

> O God that I were a man! I would eat his heart in the market place.
>
> —SHAKESPEARE, *MUCH ADO ABOUT NOTHING*

> HIGGINS: You know, Pickering, that woman has the most extraordinary ideas about me. Here I am, a shy, diffident sort of man. I've never been able to feel really grown-up and tremendous, like other chaps. And yet she's firmly persuaded that I'm an arbitrary overbearing bossing kind of person. I can't account for it.
>
> —GEORGE BERNARD SHAW, *PYGMALION*

A "bold" man is ambitious and brave; a "bold" woman is what used to be called a "hussy"—itself originally a word for "housewife" or "thrifty woman," but transformed by the eighteenth century into "a disreputable woman of improper behaviour, or of light or worthless character."[1] Although the word "hussy" is out of fashion, boldness for women still often connotes sexual rather than political or martial forwardness. It's not an accident that among the most highly touted female candidates for political office—and for popular heroism—are women who are, or have been, airplane pilots trained in the military, a place where women's "boldness" is not out of place.[2]

A woman with "nerves of steel" is invaluable—and possessed of strong character—when she is steering a damaged plane to safety.[3] On the ground, in ordinary life, a woman with "nerve" may be presumptuous rather than admirable. If she shows signs of "nerves," on the other hand, she may be weak, if gender-appropriate. "Nerve" is a sign of strong character; "nerves," of the opposite. "My nerves are bad tonight," complains a voice in T. S. Eliot's *The Waste Land*, and we have no doubt that it is a woman speaking. "Neurotic" means nervy, and not in a good way. A medical reference handbook from the 1880s explains, "The neurotic woman is sensitive, zealous, managing."[4]

Does "Character" Have a Gender?

Terms like "character assassination" and "character witness" were front and center during the September 2018 Senate Judiciary Committee hearing on Judge Brett M. Kavanaugh, whose nomination for the Supreme Court had been put into question by Professor Christine Blasey Ford's allegation that he had sexually assaulted her when they were both in high school. The assertions of some of Kavanaugh's Yale classmates that he had misrepresented his history of hard drinking and partying, as well as challenges to the truth of his previous Senate testimony and reactions to his emotional outburst and comportment in his widely viewed televised appearance, led to claims by both supporters and detractors that his was a test case of character.

After Blasey Ford's allegation became known, sixty-five women who had known Kavanaugh when they were in high school signed a document attesting to his good character and asserting that "he always treated women with respect."[5] But the "character witness" most often cited in the media—a witness who declined to appear at the hearing—was his friend Mark Judge, who had written a memoir about his own blackout drinking. "Brett Kavanaugh's Awful Character Witness" was the headline in the *Washington Monthly*, and many other media outlets used the same phrase—"character witness"—to describe Mark Judge. *Slate* called Kavanaugh's high-school yearbook, with its celebration of drinking and its apparent sexual slur on a young woman described and named there, a "character witness" against him.

"Candor speaks to a person's character," said Senator Patrick Leahy in a radio address. "Only nominees of unquestioned character and forthright candor should sit on the Supreme Court, and Judge Kavanaugh threw both into question."[6] That was a week *before* Christine Blasey Ford's testimony and Kavanaugh's angry response. But things really broke loose, of course, after the televised appearances on September 27—Blasey Ford in the morning, composed and determined, Kavanaugh, alternately shouting and weeping, in the afternoon.

In his opening statement, Kavanaugh accused Democrats of "grotesque and obvious character assassination," a phrase picked up in headlines by Fox News, Breitbart, the *National Review*, the *Chicago Tribune*, and other supporters.[7] And Kavanaugh deliberately carried the "assassination" image further when he described the second hearing, in the same statement, as "a calculated and orchestrated political hit."

"Character assassin" and "character assassination" were coinages of the early twentieth century, and became especially prominent in the McCarthy era. Ordinarily, the victims of "character assassination" in that period—and later—were far less powerful than their accusers. In describing himself this way, Kavanaugh reversed the casting: the woman who—at some considerable cost to her own privacy and safety—accused him of sexual violation had become the "assassin," rather than the victim.

More than twenty-four hundred law professors signed a letter, presented to the U.S. Senate on October 4, declaring that the Senate should not confirm Kavanaugh to the Supreme Court because of his comportment at the hearing: "Instead of trying to sort out with reason and care the allegations that were raised, Judge Kavanaugh responded in an intemperate, inflammatory and partial manner, as he interrupted and, at times, was discourteous to senators." Although they had "differing views" about Kavanaugh's other qualifications, the signators were, they wrote, "united, as professors of law and scholars of judicial institutions, in believing that he did not display the impartiality and judicial temperament requisite to sit on the highest court of our land."[8] Retired Supreme Court Justice John Paul Stevens, in a public statement, said that he had changed his mind about Kavanaugh's nomination after his second hearing, suggesting that he had displayed "potential bias" strong enough to keep him from performing "his full responsibilities" were he to sit on the court.[9] Nonetheless, the Senate voted fifty to forty-eight, just days after the hearing, to confirm Kavanaugh's nomination; he was sworn into office a few hours later. That evening, President Donald Trump addressed a cheering rally in Topeka, Kansas. "Brett Kavanaugh is a man of great character and intellect,"[10] Trump declared. What did "character" mean to President Trump when he made this declaration? Or, to phrase the question more precisely in Trump's case, what effect did he seek to produce in using this term? "Great character," proclaimed rather than demonstrated, seemed to be designed to obliterate all criticism. A "man of great character" could not be culpable. Could he?

Trump had mocked Christine Blasey Ford at a campaign-style rally in Mississippi on October 2, behavior that Republican Senator Jeff Flake called "appalling" and that Michael Bromwich, one of Blasey Ford's lawyers, called "a vicious, vile, and soulless attack." Blasey Ford, he wrote on Twitter, was a "remarkable profile in courage," and Trump, in his attack on her, "a profile in cowardice."[11]

The "radical" Democrats and their "disgraceful" campaign were, by Trump's claim and Kavanaugh's, character assassins.[12] But, as many commentators observed at the time, had it been a *woman* who wept, shouted, and treated senators with disrespect on national television, she would have been very unlikely to be confirmed for the Supreme Court—"or any office," tweeted Joanna Robinson, a senior writer for *Vanity Fair*.[13]

Displaying emotion used to be a sign of character weakness for men (see "Senator Edmund Muskie, weeping," for an example that derailed a candidacy). Now it can be a sign of righteous passion or of "empathy." But a show of emotion by women in similar public contexts is still frequently read as an indication of emotional instability or frailty, sometimes even of the dread exhibition of "hormones," as if only one gender had them.[14]

"Hormonal," like "neurotic," makes an adjective out of a common bodily component and pins it on women whose "characters" are in need of strengthening. "Hysterical," of course, goes further, since its root is in the word for "womb"; a hysterical man is never a good thing, unless his name is Hamlet. But the occasional woman in public life may be described, not entirely without admiration, as having "balls." When

Madeleine Albright, then the American delegate to the United Nations, excoriated Cuba for downing two unarmed civilian airplanes by using the vernacular Spanish word—"Frankly, this is not cojones, this is cowardice"—she was met with outrage. "She tried to say a man's word, and it was uncalled for," said a former Venezuelan representative. But President Bill Clinton called it "the most effective one-liner in the whole Administration's foreign policy," and Cuban Americans made it into a bumper sticker.[15]

Or, for a quality of a different sort, how about "likability"? Barack Obama, as a candidate, seemed to undercut Hillary Clinton by telling her in a televised debate that she was "likable enough," just before the New Hampshire primary, but the state's Democratic voters supported Hillary. Is "likable" a gender-based character trait? Consider Sally Field's famous Oscar acceptance speech: "You like me, right now, you like me," in context, a sly reference to a line of dialogue from her earlier role in *Norma Rae*; it is often misquoted as "you like me, you *really* like me!"—a version Field later delivered as part of a Charles Schwab commercial. Both the actual event and its persistent media revision speak to the question of personal character as well as of dramatic characters. What comparable male star would worry—or profess to worry—about whether the academy members, or the general public, liked him (except now, of course, in the thumbs-up, social-media sense)?

A Woman of Valor—or a Diligent Wife?

Consider the case of a well-known biblical proverb (Proverbs 31:10). This verse of praise for a woman is a favorite of both Christian and Jewish clergy. In recent years it has been added to many Jewish Shabbat observances, and is often recited at funerals. But a glance at some of the many translations of this verse shows a surprisingly wide range of interpretations. The *King James Bible* reads, "Who can find a virtuous woman? For her price is far above rubies." The *New International Version* declares, "A wife of noble character who can find? She is worth far more than rubies." Chabad.org and other sources give "pearls" rather than rubies: "For her value is far above pearls."[16] And that's just the beginning. Here are some other current versions of the same proverb.

- "Who can find a virtuous and capable wife? She is more precious than rubies." (New Living Translation)
- "An excellent wife who can find? She is far more precious than jewels." (English Standard Version)
- "What a rare find is a capable wife! Her worth is far beyond that of rubies." (Jewish Publication Society)
- "Who can find a wife of noble character? She is far more precious than rubies." (*Berean Study Bible*)
- "An excellent wife, who can find? For her worth is far above jewels." (*New American Standard Bible*)
- "A truly good wife is the most precious treasure a man can find!" (*Contemporary English Version*)
- "How hard it is to find a capable wife! She is worth far more than jewels!" (*Good News Translation*)

My goal here is not to identify the most accurate scholarly translation of this ancient statement but, rather, to illustrate the surprising range of meanings imputed to it, and to the woman, or wife, whose praises are being sung. Is the female subject of Proverbs 31:10 "virtuous," "valiant," "capable," "excellent," "worthy," "diligent," "truly good," "of valour," "of worth," "of noble character," or "of strong character"? Is she, indeed, a *woman* or a *wife* (or *the most precious treasure a man can find*)? These words are far from synonyms: to be "capable" or "diligent" is not at all the same thing as to be "valiant"; "noble" character may or may not be the same as "strong" character; "virtue" is not the same as "valor." The adjectives are not in themselves gendered: men, too, can be capable, diligent, or valiant. But the kind of woman being described—let us call it her "character," especially since that word is used in a few of the biblical translations—will differ greatly depending upon the word choice and, perhaps, the reader's own notions of what makes for a praiseworthy woman (or wife).

The same could be said of men, of course: a diligent man is not—or not necessarily—a man of noble character, and the person valuing or praising him, whether an obituary writer or a spouse, would perhaps have different expectations in using these terms. But most of Proverbs chapter 31 is a description of a good wife, and the support (material, spiritual, and familial) that she can provide for her husband.

Who is speaking these words, we might ask? The answer is not always supplied when this praise of a virtuous/valiant/diligent woman (or wife) is cited. The speaker cited at the beginning of Proverbs 31 is the mother of King Lemuel, and her advice to him begins not with the praise of a good woman, but with some words of caution for kings and princes. Do not chase after women; do not drink wine or strong drink (a drunken king is a bad ruler); judge righteously; plead the cause of the poor and needy. This is what a man ("the son of my womb . . . the son of my vows") should do. And a woman? She gives food to her household, buys and plants vineyards, spins flax, makes cloaks and sells them, speaks words of wisdom and kindness, cares for her children and her husband. Charm and beauty are false and vain. These are not the qualities a man should admire in a woman.

Some commentators have preferred to separate the two parts of Proverbs 31, regarding the maternal advice as covering only the deportment of a king, and leaving the description of the capable/valiant/virtuous woman uncredited, though of course not unauthorized. We might pause for a moment on the last—and seldom heeded—piece of advice, or wisdom, about what a man should admire in a woman. The *King James Bible* (1611) says, "Favor is deceitful, and beauty is vain" (Proverbs 31:30). Chabad.org translates the same words as "charm is false and beauty is futile."[17]

Whether or not these are the cautionary words of a mother to her son, it is not clear that the long list of selfless female virtues that precedes them (verses 6–29) is enough to outweigh these two seductive traits, then or now. Which may be why they are tucked into a half-verse at the end of the chapter, bracketed by renewed invitations to prayer and praise.

Fitness

Even today—and certainly in the novels, biographies, and epistles of previous centuries—a woman "of character" or "of strong character" is often either a woman not notable for beauty or charm, or an older woman. There is a sense in which some of these terms verge on euphemism or social code, a type of linguistic signaling still very much in vogue today, even though the meanings of some of these terms have shifted. "For our euphemistic era," writes the columnist Bari Weiss about the language with which women are described, "'strong' is the code word for skinny, and 'healthy' for beautiful."[18] That "strong" and "healthy" are character words—which in this context they are—shows us the degree to which character language is itself subject to cultural modulation. ("Skinny" women, no matter what code was used, would not have been an aesthetic ideal in an earlier age, and "health," in eras marred by tuberculosis and smallpox, might only be mentioned if the results of a woman's illness were disfiguring.)

A quick attempt at gender substitution will demonstrate that these equivalences are not at all the same for men. "Skinny" as a word is not a male cultural ideal, though the more ambiguous "fit" is used for both genders. But fit for *what*? "Fit" historically meant suitable or appropriate, and when used of persons would ordinarily be followed by "for . . ." It was only in the 1980s that British slang started using "fit" to mean sexually attractive; all the *Oxford English Dictionary*'s examples are descriptions of women. In these cases, what women are deemed "fit" *for* is sex. More generally, though, since etymology is increasingly a lost art, women today described as "fit" are thought—and think of themselves—as "fit," period. But body shape and character have, of course, a long and complex history, both within and across cultures. As we can see by moving from "fit" to "fat."

"Let me have men about me that are fat," Shakespeare's Julius Caesar says to Antony,

> Sleek-headed men and such as sleep a-nights.
> Yond Cassius has a lean and hungry look.
> He thinks too much. Such men are dangerous.
>
> *JULIUS CAESAR* 1.2.193–96

"Fat" in this case means "well-fed," satisfied with life. In Caesar's view, ambitious men, "hungry" for power and influence, do not fulfill themselves merely by filling themselves, by eating and sleeping well. Those familiar with the play, or with Roman history, will know that Caesar is right to fear Cassius. His remark, though it echoes Plutarch, has an important dramatic role in Shakespeare's play. For like other clues to the impending assassination, it is a reading of "character" that Caesar ignores at his peril.

The phrase "lean and hungry look" has persisted into modern culture as a title for television episodes and books as well as for mottos printed on T-shirts, tank tops, and hoodies. Such is the power of Shakespeare. But in all of these cases, "lean and hungry" means "slim and fit," and when it is not the object of envy or irony, it is a positive description. Despite the visible corpulence of some public figures, having "men about me that are fat" is not a present-day desideratum for political counselors or high office.

Nonetheless, it is far more often women than men who are "fat-shamed" in public, or otherwise criticized for being women: as a candidate, Donald Trump implied that Megyn Kelly's aggressive questioning during a presidential debate was triggered by her menstrual cycle.[19] Two years later, President Donald Trump described Mika Brzezinski, another female television journalist who had subjected him to harsh on-air critique, as "bleeding badly from a face-lift"[20] when he saw her at a social gathering. Not only were these attacks personal, they were also gendered: "bleeding" in both cases was a sign of female difference and deficiency (as if men did not also have face-lifts, or use Propecia to stop hair loss[21]). Again, my point is not (just) to deplore these personal comments about mood and appearance, but to emphasize that they are also implicitly—and sometimes explicitly—assessments of character, as the contemporary world understands that concept. A woman having her period would (says the argument from "character") be emotional rather than rational; a woman who wanted—or needed—a face-lift would displace her dissatisfactions onto an external target. These are what are known as *ad hominem* (or *ad feminam*, or *ad personam*) arguments, a term used to describe "arguments which impugn the character or question the abilities or motivations of the person involved."[22]

Comments about Trump's hairstyle, weight, and food choices have also been complexly gendered. That he worries about his looks, and spends a lot of time "styling" his hair, is a vanity more usually, these days, attributed to women. That his doctor seems to have added an inch to Trump's official height in order to avoid classifying him as "obese" speaks again to personal vanity, but was not mocked as much in the press as it might have been in the case of a woman on the cusp of obesity. And that his favorite edibles are fast-food items makes him seem typically male and even "American"; a woman who spent a lot of time watching television in bed and preferred cheeseburgers to kale shakes would not so readily be given a character pass.

Testing Your Mettle

"Mettle" is a good old-fashioned word for character, dating from the early sixteenth century. Originally a variant of "metal," and sometimes, in early uses, spelled that way, it survives today in phrases like "to show (one's) mettle." A clear example of the early use can be found in Shakespeare's *Henry V*, where the Constable of France wonders aloud where the English fighting forces have gotten their "mettle" (surely not, he thinks, from their climate, which is "foggy, raw and dull" [*Henry V* 3.5.15–16]).[23] In this very pro-English scene, the French Dauphin is then moved to contrast the mettle of the English with that of his countrymen:

> Our madams mock at us and plainly say
> Our mettle is bred out, and they will give
> Their bodies to the lust of English youth,
> To new-store France with bastard warriors.
>
> *HENRY V* 3.5.28–31

This is the same Dauphin who, as we saw in our discussion of national character, will boast—two short scenes later—that he has written a sonnet to his horse. Horses, indeed, were directly associated with "mettle," a word which, in animals, meant friskiness, liveliness, and eagerness, and writers from Shakespeare through Pope and Mary Wollstonecraft used it as a praise of equine spirit.[24] *Male* horses, that is; female horses, if possessed of it, were to be restrained, at least according to John Dryden's translation of Virgil: "As for the Females . . . Take down their Mettle, keep 'em lean and bare."[25]

There was an etymological reason for this, too. One of the concurrent meanings of "mettle," from the early seventeenth century through to the very end of the nineteenth century, was "semen." This is the sense of the dauphin's complaint that "our mettle is bred out" so that Frenchwomen would have to have sex with lusty "English youth" to produce a new crop of stronger "bastard warriors." Grose's *Classical Dictionary of the Vulgar Tongue* (1785) defines "mettle" as "the semen," and the phrase "to fetch mettle" as "the act of self pollution." The educator Bronson Alcott, father of Louisa May Alcott, wrote of the procreative function of "mettle" in his journal: "Fluids form solids. Mettle is the Godhead proceeding into the matrix of Nature to organize Man. Behold the creative jet!"[26]

A similar doubleness attaches to the word "spunk," which means "spirit, mettle; courage, pluck," but also has had, since the late nineteenth century, the "coarse slang" meaning of "seminal fluid."[27] Although "spunk" seems initially to have been used to describe spirited men, women today are often described as having spunk, or being "spunky." Kelli O'Hara, "a radiant, wholesome singing actress from Oklahoma," was praised in a review headed "Oodles of Spunk";[28] an actress playing Queen Victoria in a television series was said to have made that formidable queen seem "spunky, sharp-edged, thoroughly modern."[29] "Feisty" or "lively" women could have "mettle," too. A woman, girl, or "lass" with "mettle" was someone to be reckoned with. No surprise, perhaps, that D. H. Lawrence's Lady Chatterley has it: "Her mettle was roused, she would not be defeated."[30] Indeed, in the very next paragraph, Lady Chatterley, who is looking for the gamekeeper's cottage, comes upon her future lover washing himself, "naked to the hips, his velveteen breeches slipping down over his slender loins." An online Amazon description of *Lady Chatterley's Lover* calls it, apparently without any attempt at conscious wit, "Lawrence's seminal novel of illicit passion and forbidden desire." And let us not forget Macbeth's fervent praise of his wife when she revives his flagging courage: "Bring forth men-children only, / For thy undaunted mettle should compose / Nothing but males" (*Mac.* 1.7.72–74).

The sexual/metaphorical sense of "mettle" is no longer operative, and the metal/mettle variants are lost, too, though they may have initially reinforced the sense that to have "mettle" was to be strong. The *Oxford English Dictionary*'s first definition for "mettle" is "A person's character, disposition, temperament; the 'stuff' of which one is made, regarded as an indication of one's character." Whether the "stuff" of "mettle" was metal, semen, or simply "the right stuff" (described by Tom Wolfe as "the same vital force of manhood that had made millions vibrate and resonate thirty-five years ago to Lindbergh"[31]), to have mettle was to exhibit spirit, courage, and skill—all essential signs of character.

The Characters of Women

"Most women have no characters at all," the poet Alexander Pope is said to have said in 1743. This oft-quoted pronouncement, found in the opening lines of Pope's "Epistle to a Lady," is itself a quotation, ascribed there to the poet's lifelong friend Martha Blount—though Pope has no difficulty in filling in the details.

> Nothing so true as what you once let fall,
> "Most Women have no Characters at all."
> Matter too soft a lasting mark to bear,
> And best distinguished by black, brown, or fair.
>
> 1–4

The exception, needless to say, is Martha Blount herself, to whom the "Epistle" is a loving tribute.

Pope's satiric poem is both a general indictment of malleable, self-absorbed society women and a specific compliment to one who escapes these faults and flaws. (The phrase "lasting mark," in the third line, is a familiar reference to "character" as an impression or stamp.) The poem's extended subtitle reads "Of the Characters of Women, treating of this sex only as contradistinguished from the other. That their particular characters are not so strongly marked as those of men, seldom so fixed, and still more inconsistent with themselves."

The word "honor," which attaches to moral character in men, is in women, Pope suggests, reduced to a term that describes not even their sexual virtue but, rather, their *reputation* for sexual virtue: "Still round and round the Ghosts of Beauty glide / And haunt the places where their Honour dy'd" (241–42). This is a point Pope had already made in an earlier poem, *The Rape of the Lock*, offering a mock-equivalence in imminent social disasters: "Or stain her honor, or her new brocade." The "Epistle to a Lady" goes one step further, seeking to define the difference between men and women in relation both to the public/private divide and to the idea of the "ruling passions," a favorite phrase of the period:

> But grant, in Public, Men sometimes are shown,
> A Woman's seen in Private Life alone:
> Our bolder Talents in full light displayed;
> Your Virtues open fairest in the shade.
> Bred to disguise, in Public 'tis you hide;
> There, none distinguish 'twixt your Shame or Pride,
> Weakness or Delicacy; all so nice,
> That each may seem a Virtue, or a Vice.
>
> In Men, we various Ruling Passions find;
> In Women, two almost divide the kind;
> Those, only fix'd, they first or last obey,
> The Love of Pleasure, and the Love of Sway.
>
> 199–210

Men have *talents*, which can be seen in the "full light" of public view. Women have *virtues*, but these can only be truly known in private—and Pope here allows as well for a bawdier implication in the suggestion that "your virtues open fairest in the shade." In any case, since society women are trained to dissimulate, it is impossible to tell in public whether they are virtuous or vicious. Likewise, men have a variety of "ruling passions." (Pope's contemporary Lord Chesterfield would suggest in his character of Pitt that "his ruling passion was an unbounded ambition," and of the Duke of Newcastle he wrote that "his ruling, or rather his only, passion, was, the agitation, the bustle, and the hurry of business."[32]) Women, by contrast, are divided simply into those who love pleasure and those who love power (both of these "passions," of course, directly contrary to the supposed ideals for women: chastity and obedience). Furthermore, since the only form of "sway" that the eighteenth century recognized in women was sexual, the one ruling passion would often collapse into the other.[33]

> Men, some to Bus'ness, some to Pleasure take;
> But ev'ry Woman is at heart a Rake:
> Men, some to Quiet, some to public Strife,
> But ev'ry Lady would be Queen for life.
>
> Yet mark the fate of a whole Sex of Queens!
> Pow'r all their end, but Beauty all the means . . .
> Beauties, like Tyrants, old and friendless grown,
> Yet hate Repose, and dread to be alone,
> Worn out in public, weary ev'ry eye,
> Nor leave one sigh behind them when they die.
>
> 215–20, 227–30

The belief that men have "bolder talents" and "ruling passions" in the public world, whereas women have "virtues" (and ruly or unruly desires), would continue to influence the discussion of personal character from the eighteenth century to—at least—the beginning of the twentieth, both for the supporters of this idea and for its critics.

Here, for example, is John Stuart Mill, writing, in *The Subjection of Women* (1869), about the question of gender and character:

> All women are brought up from the very earliest years in the belief that their ideal of character is the very opposite to that of men; not self-will, and government by self-control, but submission, and yielding to the control of others . . . It would be a miracle if the object of being attractive to men had not become the polar star of feminine education and formation of character.[34]

And:

> What is now called the nature of women is an eminently artificial thing—the result of forced repression in some directions, unnatural stimulation in others. It may be asserted without scruple, that no other class of dependents have had their character so entirely distorted from its natural proportions by their relation with their masters.

The inevitable result of this "unnatural" treatment, Mill believed, was a further distortion, with deleterious effects on male as well as female character development:

> Think what it is to be a boy, to grow up to manhood in the belief that without any merit or exertion of his own, though he may be the most frivolous and empty or the most ignorant and stolid of mankind, by the mere fact of being born a male he is by right the superior of all and every one of an entire half of the human race . . . What must be the effect on his character of this lesson?[35]

A century and a half later, Mill sees what Pope saw, though Pope's description of women's "love of sway" describes a (class-limited) rebellion against Mill's more general, and more overtly political, discussion of "subjection."

The Persistence of Manliness

"Manly," which long ago meant merely "human," became over time "having those qualities or characteristics traditionally associated with men as distinguished from women or children; courageous, strong, independent in spirit, frank, upright."[36] Chaucer's robust monk, who took more pleasure in hunting than in prayer, was praised by the admiring narrator of *The Canterbury Tales* as "a manly man, to been an abbot able"—his "manliness" in the field apparently marking him out for preferment in the church. Nineteenth-century preachers and politicians associated character with "manliness," and "manly character" became a watchword for probity and social comportment.

Other definitions of "manly," some markedly obsolete but still indicative of the word's history, include "humane, charitable; generous"; "courteous"; and "adult, mature." The poet Robert Lowell might call Queen Elizabeth I "England's manly queen" and intend a compliment, but "manly" (or "mannish") for women was not always intended as praise, unless used to describe Amazons or women warriors. A female friend of the novelist Samuel Richardson wrote to him disapproving of certain modes of education for girls: "I hate to hear Latin out of a woman's mouth. There is something in it, to me, masculine."[37]

"Manliness" was a desirable—if sometimes slightly elusive—ideal for the boys at Victorian public schools as well as for Robert Baden-Powell's Boy Scouts. At the beginning of the twentieth century, both "success in manly outdoor sports" and "qualities of manhood" became integral to the description of a new and prestigious international fellowship for (male) college graduates. A codicil to Cecil Rhodes's will, dated 1901, set up what would become the Rhodes Scholarships, with the following instructions:

> My desire being that the students who shall be elected to the Scholarships shall not be merely bookworms I direct that in the election of a student to a Scholarship regard shall be had to (i) his literary and scholastic attainments (ii) his fondness and success in manly outdoor sports such as cricket football and the like (iii) his qualities of manhood truth courage devotion to duty sympathy for the protection of the weak kindliness unselfishness and fellowship and (iv) his exhibition during school days of moral force of character and of instincts to lead and to take an interest in his schoolmates for those latter attributes will be likely in afterlife to guide him to esteem the performance of public duties as his highest aim.[38]

The phrases—as well as the punctuation—are Rhodes's own, and they have from time to time produced problems of interpretation for

Scholarship selectors. What was "moral force of character"? As Philip Ziegler notes, "One committee in the United States chose their Scholar on the ground that he was the only one who did not smoke." A group of American Rhodes Scholars sailing to England in 1904, "cowed by this ruling," briefly "abstained from drinks, cigarettes or gambling," but their resolve lasted only two days, and by the time the ship landed they had "relapsed."[39] And what was meant by "success" in "manly outdoor sports such as cricket football and the like"? Was "success" winning, or playing the game like a gentleman? One early "Oxford Secretary" for the Rhodes Trust contended that when Cecil Rhodes specified "success" he meant "the training in fair play, the absence of all trickery, the chivalrous yielding of advantage to an opponent, the acceptance of defeat with cheerfulness."[40] Some years later, Sir Henry Newbolt would concur in the denigration of "bookworms" in his comparison of the English public-school system to the "old method of training young squires to knighthood." The "great merit" of the public school "was that it made men, and not sneaks or bookworms, and that its direct objects were character and efficiency."[41]

Rhodes himself was apparently an engaging amalgam of power, ambition, personal charm, and the oddly ruthless innocence of that era. William Plomer notes that he "would utter clumsy platitudes in the belief that they were epigrams, but somehow when 'the rapid sentences poured out of the broad chest in curiously high notes that occasionally rose to a falsetto,'"[42] his listeners were enchanted. One of the young men, who was to become his private secretary, reported that he "would lie awake half the night, working myself up into a state of delirious excitement, speculating on the joy and pleasure which would be mine when I should be his secretary."[43] Another observed that, "whether Rhodes liked women or not, he preferred the society of men."[44]

The ideal recipient of the scholarship that would carry Cecil Rhodes's name exemplified many of the qualities that the nineteenth-century Englishman would have called "character." "This successful footballer and kind *litterateur*, this dutiful hero and moral exhibitionist, this cricketing paragon of muscular Christianity," wrote Plomer, bears "a close relationship to some common types of upper-middle-class

Victorian manhood."[45] As Lytton Strachey observed at the end of his portrait of Dr. Arnold in *Eminent Victorians*:

> Teachers and prophets have strange after-histories; and that of Dr. Arnold has been no exception. The earnest enthusiast who strove to make his pupils Christian gentlemen and who governed his school according to the principles of the Old Testament has proved to be the founder of the worship of athletics and the worship of good form. Upon those two poles our public schools have turned for so long that we have almost come to believe that such is their essential nature, and that an English public schoolboy who wears the wrong clothes and takes no interest in football is a contradiction in terms.[46]

"It would be hard to conceive any set of characteristics more remote from Rhodes's own practices in politics or in business," says Philip Ziegler about the Scholarship standards, though he adds, "Rhodes did not envisage his Scholars as being moulded in his own image."[47] In any event, success in "manly" sports has tended, over the years, to be interpreted by Rhodes selectors far more by the measure of victories and championships than by the cheerful acceptance of defeat.

In 1961, the Warden of Rhodes House, Edgar Williams, rewrote the terms of selection, attempting to phrase Rhodes's conditions in words to suit a new era. "Quality of both character and intellect is the most important requirement for a Rhodes Scholarship and this is what the Selection committee will seek," read the revised document.

> The Rhodes Scholar should not be a one-sided man; or a selfish man. Intellectual ability should be founded upon sound character and integrity of character upon sound intellect. Success in being elected to office in student organisations may or may not be evidence of leadership in the true sense of the word. Cecil Rhodes evidently regarded leadership as consisting of moral courage and interest in one's fellow men quite as much as in the more aggressive qualities . . . Physical vigour is an essential qualification for a Rhodes Scholar, but athletic prowess is less

important than the moral qualities which can be developed in sports.[48]

Williams might have particularly prided himself on the chiastic statement "intellectual ability should be founded upon sound character and integrity of character upon sound intellect." But what actually did it mean? Like many a chiasmus, this is more a rhetorical feat than a definition or description, closer to a tautology or a riddle than to a clarification. "Character," "sound character," "integrity of character" all remain blanks to be filled in, as do the still-elusive "moral qualities which can be developed in sports." As for "leadership," now a popular topic in business schools and Leadership Institutes, it remains questionable whether, either in 1961 or half a century later, its practice in fact consists of "moral courage and interest in one's fellow men quite as much as in the more aggressive qualities." More specifically, it is not clear that those qualities are the ones that voters (or shareholders) look to when choosing their own leaders in what Rhodes had termed "afterlife"—by which he meant the years after Oxford.

Although phrases like "manly outdoor sports" and "qualities of manhood" had been dropped from the revised memorandum, the Rhodes Scholarships remained closed to women until 1976, a year after the Equal Opportunities Bill became law in the United Kingdom. Oddly, it took even longer for Rhodes's specific proscription against marriage for Scholars to be overturned. "No one," as Ziegler observes, "could doubt what Rhodes himself would have thought on either issue. Women, whether as students or as appendages, had no place at Oxford; they would distract the men from the serious business of sport, examinations and societal bonding and might well pick up unsuitable ideas about the role they should play in later life."[49] The ban on marriage for the second and third year of the Scholarship was nonetheless changed in the sixties, after a number of promising candidates declined to apply (and a few Scholars dropped out sometime after arriving in Oxford), but the regulation against first-year marriages was still in place until the end of 1994. It was presumably with unintended irony that Edgar Williams had written in a memo for a trustees' meeting in 1968, "We are seeking in our Rhodes Scholars outstanding ability married to unselfishness."[50]

Feminists, Bookworms, and the Manly Man

An American professor of government, Harvey C. Mansfield, argued that, after the incursions of feminism, postmodernism, and several other cultural developments that he considered bad actors, "manliness" was a topic in need of revival in the twenty-first century.

"A manly man is nothing if not an individual," wrote Mansfield, "one who sets himself apart, who is concerned with the honor rather than survival of his individual being. Or, better to say, he finds his survival only in his honor."[51] Mansfield's heroes include Theodore Roosevelt, Tarzan, John Wayne, Hemingway, Plato, and Aristotle. Roosevelt, he reports, "spoke frequently of 'character,' but by this he meant just one character, the energetic character, forgetting other forms of determination to set one's own course in life."[52] "Assert" is his "favorite word,"[53] he reminds the reader, and Mansfield's *Manliness* is, not unexpectedly, full of assertions about assertiveness, such as "Asserting is the business of manliness (= courage),"[54] and "It should be expected that men will be manly and sometimes a bit bossy and that women will be impressed with them or skeptical."[55]

Mansfield opposes affirmative action, which is "manly if you do it for yourself, otherwise not."[56] Feminism, he suggests, is responsible for the idea of the "*sensitive male*, the man whose manliness demands that he abandon manliness."[57] This is clever—Mansfield is a good stylist—but blinkered, at least in terms of the word's history. Of the *Oxford English Dictionary*'s ten examples of "sensitive," meaning "very susceptible to, or readily affected by, emotional or aesthetic impressions; possessing delicate or tender feelings; having sensibility," dating from 1735 to 2002, all but one refer to men rather than to women, and most are modes of praise. Sensitivity, it appears, has only fairly recently become an insensitive way of describing a man.

Ultimately, as is perhaps inevitable given his book's title, the argument of *Manliness* rests on tautology: women "should be free to enter on careers—yet they should also be expected to be women"; men "should be expected, not merely to be free, but to be manly."[58]

Womanliness

And what about "womanliness"?

If "manly" could only in certain exalted circumstances be an admiring word for a woman, "womanly" had, as its historically first use in English, the description of an "effeminate" man.[59] "Womanly" also meant "befitting a woman," but was not always meant as praise: John Knox's *First Blast of the Trumpet Against the Monstrous Regiment of Women* (1558) cautions, "Lest that again she slide and fall by womanly facility"; George Sandys describes "burning with a womanly spleen" (1615); and Lady Mary Wortley Montagu writes, in a letter from 1716, of "the womanly spirit of contradiction that works in me."[60] In fact, the entire first heading under "womanly" in the *Oxford English Dictionary* is prefaced by the statement, "Frequently *depreciative*." Another definition of the same word, which seems at first to echo the "adult, mature" status of "manly," winds up tipping in a familiar direction: "resembling an adult woman in appearance or behavior, esp. with regard to sexuality." To be manly was to behave in a certain way. To be womanly was to look a certain way: curvy; full-figured; (sexually) mature.

At the time of the founding of Girton, the first women's college in Britain, the feminist and suffragette Emily Davis wrote of the importance of a "certain amount of solitude, so necessary in the formation of character." Davis thus proposed, in her outline for the college, that each student would have "a small sitting room to herself"—the prototype, in 1868, of Virginia Woolf's "room of one's own."[61] But to others at the time a college-educated woman was by definition unwomanly. Montagu Burrows, a historian at Oxford, wrote in an article on "Female Education" in the *Quarterly Review* in 1869:

> The one thing men do not like is the man-woman, and they will never believe the College or University woman is not of that type. Sensible men will always like sensible and cultivated women; but they will always prefer that their good sense and cultivation should have come through channels which they recognize as suitable for the womanly character.

Burrows reminded his readers, "We have to consider the whole complete phenomena of life, the relations between the sexes, the formation of the *whole* character of woman, the difference between men and women."[62] These were established entities, based upon a necessary "difference between men and women." The formation of character could also, Burrows implies, lead to its deformation, the production of that undesirable (and undesired) academic hybrid, the "man-woman."

We might also recall that half a century later *The Handbook for Girl Guides*, written by Agnes Baden-Powell in collaboration with her brother Robert, would declare that "Scouting for girls is not the same as for boys. The chief difference in the training of the two courses of instruction is that scouting for boys makes for MANLINESS, but the training for Guides makes for WOMANLINESS, and enables girls the better to help in the battle of life."

This pronouncement appears in an early subsection of the *Handbook* headed "Be Womanly," which begins, "One doesn't want women to be soldiers; we none of us like women who ape men," and goes on to counsel: "Girls will do no good by imitating boys. Do not be a bad imitation. It is far finer to be a real girl, such as no boy can be. One loves a girl who is sweet and tender, and who can gently soothe when wearied with pain."[63] At the end of the list of injunctions for girls to "Be" ("Be Womanly," "Be Brave," "Be Strong," "Be Useful," "Be Handy," expanding on the "Be Prepared" motto that the Guides shared with the Boy Scouts) comes the final section, titled "Be Good Mothers." One of the benefits of joining the Guides is that girls will "BE PREPARED for doing what is your greatest duty in life—to bring up good citizens for your country." The paragraph that follows, if not written by Robert Baden-Powell, clearly captures his sentiments: "Almost every man who rose to be a great man in history was helped largely by his mother and what she taught him. Britain has been made great by her great men, and these great men were made great by their mothers."[64]

It perhaps goes without saying that *Scouting for Boys* says nothing about preparing boys for fatherhood, even in the "hints to instructors" section on "Continence," which is aimed at avoiding masturbation ("not even a manly vice, but . . . everywhere looked down upon with contempt"[65]) rather than pregnancy. The description of "Chivalry" does say that the knights of old were "particularly courteous and polite to all women and children," but there is no advice about marriage. The scouts were being prepared to be "great men," not great parents.

For the period in which they are written, of course, these gendered character traits are fairly typical. "Womanliness" is not "Manliness for Women," but something quite different. Agnes Baden-Powell wrote in the foreword to her *Handbook* that the training offered by the Girl Guides, while useful to "all classes," would be especially so for "those for whom it is so vitally needed—the girls of the factories and of the alleys of our great cities, who, after they leave school, get no kind of restraining influence, and who, nevertheless, may be the mothers, and should be the character trainers of the future men of our nation." She adds that Guiding can also be beneficial to "young women who have had a better upbringing, but whose lives are at present largely wasted in doing nothing that 'counts.'"[66] If the *Handbook*'s description of great men who owe everything to their mothers may be read as Robert Baden-Powell's autobiography in little, there is a sense in which this short passage in the foreword, signed by "Agnes Baden-Powell, *President*," seems like at least a brief reflection on his sister's life experience.

"Womanly," to Agnes Baden-Powell, had meant behaving like "a real girl." In an essay pointedly titled "Womanliness as a Masquerade" (1929), the psychoanalyst Joan Riviere would raise the question of "womanly" behavior as a strategy rather than a sign of authenticity. Riviere describes in detail the ways in which certain intellectual and professional women use flirtation, claims of incapacity or indecisiveness, and "particularly feminine clothes," to cover their ability and guard against criticism. "What is the essential nature of fully developed femininity?" Riviere asks. "The conception of womanliness as a mask, behind which man suspects some hidden danger, throws a little light on the enigma."[67] What was once thought of as an aspect of gender-appropriate comportment (behavior "in character") is in Riviere's essay analyzed and reinterpreted as display. In the essay's most often quoted paragraph, she returns to her key word: "The reader may now ask how I define womanliness or where I draw the line between genuine womanliness and the 'masquerade.' My suggestion is not, however, that there is any such difference; whether radical or superficial, they are the same thing."[68] Stephen Heath's paraphrase, underscoring the question of genuineness or authenticity so deftly upended by Riviere, reads, "Authentic womanliness is such a mimicry, is the masquerade."[69]

It's of some interest that Riviere should choose the word "womanliness" at all. Even in 1929, the word must have had something of an old-fashioned ring to it, conjuring bodily maturity rather than, or as well as, gender identity. (In Riviere's 1932 translation of Freud's essay on "Female Sexuality" it does not appear, although "femininity" appears several times, and "womanhood" once.)[70] But "womanliness" had something else going for it in the "Masquerade" essay. The long history of "manliness" connected to character—"character building," "character training," "moral character"—raised the question of whether "womanliness" was, or should be, a character word.

Riviere, a practicing psychoanalyst as well as a translator of Freud, was in her own essay centrally concerned with psychological defenses and projections on the part of her patients and others whose social performance she had occasion to observe. "Womanliness" for her is a description of a set of behaviors, not an "essence" or a "trait." If we ask our initial question, "Does 'character' have a gender?," we may in her case need to reverse the terms: "Does gender have a character?" In doing so, though, we have again substituted one sense of "character" for another, in a variant of the same shell game that constantly keeps the spectator guessing. Is "character" under this cover—or this one—or this one?

Early editions of the *DSM* saw "gender dysphoria" as a character disorder. Under President Donald Trump, the Defense Department in 2019 issued a policy that transgender troops could only enlist and serve if they "adhere to the standards of their biological sex," describing "gender dysphoria" as a "medical condition" like asthma or heel spurs.[71] They were—and are—subject to other forms of legal and social discrimination, as are many trans boys and trans girls. The old punitive idea was that a man wearing women's clothes was acting "unmanly" and therefore had a "bad character," and that the same was true for a woman who dressed or acted "like a man." Gendered behavior was tracked or identified with sexuality. "Hyper-manliness" became itself suspect. The "man-woman" that the nineteenth-century *Quarterly Review* regarded as the negative outcome of serious women's education still shadows descriptions of powerful and intellectual women.

"Manliness" and "womanliness," whether they go by those or other names, remain categories susceptible to cultural evaluation and character analysis. Often confused with or conflated with gender identity, these dated terms still haunt with their expectations, in which notions of "virtue" followed custom, and custom served socially conservative ends. Even if we have moved legally and societally beyond these prejudices—and I am far from sure that we have—the idea of "character" is often still entangled in moral judgments based upon custom and stereotype. Individuals who act "out of character"—whatever "character" society has assigned to them—are subject to bullying and liable to critique.

Conventional expectations about manliness and womanliness also continue to influence the language of character when it comes to another hot-button topic, money. A 2018 report from the U.S. Census Bureau offered evidence that in households where the woman earns more than the man, both women and men, on average, falsify the numbers to make it seem as if the woman earns less than she does, and the man earns more. In other words, respondents lie to preserve (1) their partners' self-esteem, (2) their own self-esteem, (3) their sense of the gendered norm of the "family breadwinner." The census researchers called this "manning up and womaning down."[72] As they were, of course, fully aware, "manning up" has its own specific meaning. In fact, it has two, and they are, in this case, in contradiction to each other. "To demonstrate manliness, toughness, or courage when faced with a difficult situation. Also: to take responsibility; to own up."[73]

Again, then, the question: does "character" have a gender? Or more than one? At a time when "nonbinary," "gender neutral," and "trans" are all categories of increasing significance and vitality, the past and present gender-typing of character may seem hopelessly out of step. But we would have to be blinkered to suggest that it has disappeared, or indeed shows many signs of disappearance.

Associations of character with gender have shaped our cultures and our languages as well as a range of strongly held beliefs, laws, and privileges. If "character" has a future as well as a past, it will need to take account of gendered language, both implicit and explicit, and to encompass both "bold" women and those unicorns of the 1970s, "sensitive" men. This does not mean calling out troops of (retired and semi-retired) language police, but, rather, acknowledging that "character," despite its apparent abstraction, is not only a philosophical but also a historical—and sometimes a political—term.

AFTERWORD

The Character Effect

A strange thing has happened to the idea of character on its way to the twenty-first century.

What once was an object of conviction, the belief in human character, has become more like a label, or an evaluation, or a good (or bad) grade. It's almost as if this qualitative term is better left unspoken—except in headlines, Senate hearings, job references, and obituaries.

Scientists tend not to use it. Nor do social scientists—psychologists, sociologists, anthropologists. Philosophers prefer "ethical" or "moral." Biographers may write warmly of the "character" of figures from the past, like Abraham Lincoln, Frederick Douglass, or Eleanor Roosevelt. But when "character" appears in the biographies of present-day figures, especially those of politicians and celebrities, the assessment is usually not so positive. Character flaws and character failings sell books. But in the process of this evolution, something of the term's complexity and history has been neglected, or forgotten.

Is bad presidential behavior bad "character," or just locker-room talk? Is a gross violation of decency, or a glaring instance of financial impropriety, "not in character" for a person whom we would like to praise, or hire, or vote for? "Out of character" implies a sense of what would be "in character" for the individual in question. But how do we know what is "in" his or her character?

In recent years, there seems to have developed something of a gulf between the ideal of character and its practice. "Preachers say, 'Do as I say, not as I do,'" noted the seventeenth-century English jurist and scholar John Selden, adding dryly that he would not take such advice from a doctor. Abbreviated as "Do as I say, not as I do," this compact description of hypocrisy has entered mainstream social quotation.[1] The familiar negative phrases—"character flaw," "character assassination," "out of character," etc.—are all too often the way we look at character: we may not agree on what it is, but we know when it is lacking.

References to the character of individuals in the public eye can range from a general chorus of praise—with one notable presidential dissenter—for Senator (and former POW) John McCain, to a heated debate about the "character, credibility and candor"[2] of the Supreme Court nominee (now Supreme Court justice) Brett Kavanaugh. When President Trump praised Kavanaugh after the Senate vote, saying that he was "a man of great character and intellect," a "totally brilliant scholar who has devoted his life to the law," "a loving husband, a devoted father, and a faithful public servant,"[3] a skeptical listener might have asked how many of these qualities were personally valued by the speaker, and how many offered in a scripted speech for public consumption. If "great character" can be measured by this checklist (omitting intellect and brilliance, which belong to a different category of assessment), does it matter that the credentials praised may not be those of the person who offers the panegyric? Sometimes it seems as if those who use the word most frequently are those who have the sketchiest understanding of its meaning and history.

I've been struck by the recurrence of a certain phrase, sometimes uttered by a person who has previously "misspoken" or acted badly, and sometimes by his or her friends, family, or supporters, as a kind of non-apology apology. The phrase is "That is not who I am"—or "That is not who he (or she) is." The out-of-body—or psychotic—meaning of such a phrase is pretty clearly not what the speaker intends. Still, "That is not who I am" is a disassociation from, or a disavowal of, the remark or action that has occasioned criticism or rebuke. "I" could not—or should not—have done such a thing. The implication, not always made explicit, has to do with character: the mistake was "out of character" for me. The phrase "That is not who I am" becomes a feedback loop, in which the speaker becomes his own character witness.

"That is not who he is," said Mark Judge, Brett Kavanaugh's childhood friend, after Christine Blasey Ford suggested that Kavanaugh had sexually harassed her. Kavanaugh then echoed the phrase in his testimony before the Senate: "That is not who I am, and that is not who I was." These statements, which are predicated on a pre-existing idea about the "character" of the individual involved, are offered as if they either constitute, or contain, a kind of *proof.* Either the allegation is false, or a brief or even unspoken apology is sufficient, since the action or statement is not "in character." The widespread currency of the phrase can be demonstrated by its use, to take another example, by a professional football player arrested for drunk driving. "This is not who I am," said the player, when asked by a reporter a few days later whether there was anything he wanted his team's fans to know. He declined to say more, since the matter was still legally pending.[4] But "This is not who I am" has now become a standard comment that purports to be somehow exculpatory. It is in its way the opposite of a mea culpa.

Shakespeare, it is perhaps needless to say, provides many variations on this arresting turn of phrase, from Richard III's "Is there a murderer here? No. Yes. I am," to Iago's "I am not what I am." And it's no accident that these speakers are strong dramatic characters as well as examples of bad (ethical, moral, human) "character." Does their amorality contribute to their strength? In literature? In life? Richard, Iago, and Edmund in *King Lear* are good liars, who can also sometimes lie to themselves. They speak to the audience in soliloquy, so as to let us know what they are really up to; in doing so, they make us not only their confidants but also their co-conspirators, their abettors. Unwillingly, and sometimes willingly—for these are great dramatic characters—we collude with them. But then we leave the theater. We return to the ongoing world of social action. And even if we are charmed and seduced by these characters, we are not deluded by them.

In offstage life, when the remark is intended to erase or obscure a previous faux pas, "This is not who I am" can become a weasel phrase. Since "I" am not that kind of person, "I" didn't do it. Or, "I couldn't help doing it, under the circumstances." Or if I did do it, it was not the "real me." Each of these explanations might translate into something like "I acted out of character." An earlier era might have considered this a version of demonic "possession": something else took over and spoke in my voice.

Now let's look at a variant of this phrase: "This is not who *we* are." Here the implication is recuperative rather than exculpatory: "we" do not commit mass shootings, or chant racial epithets, or display the Confederate flag as a sign of white supremacy. "We" in this case seems to mean "Americans," or "good Americans," or "good people," or "people I know," or "well-behaved student bodies," or others who are considered to have, and to value, what might be called good character. But, of course, some of "us" did do these heinous things, otherwise others would not need to speak out, or carry signs, to differentiate themselves. "This is not who we are" is spoken both from without and within; the "we" is some imagined collectivity of which the speaker is a part, and to which the perpetrators nominally belong, but are now marked as not belonging because of their actions.

"This is not who we are" is a hortatory statement as well as a resistant one; it invites "us" to behave well in the face of, and as a rebuke to, those who did "this." It is, to use a favored modern term, "aspirational." Alas, it is also a statement that, however brave, is false in the current era. Whether inflamed by over-the-top political rhetoric, provoked by system-fed messages of hate, or (and/or) enabled by lenient gun laws and the imitable provocation of previous gun massacres, these perpetrators are not so easily separated from "us." Indeed, the anguished protesters holding signs that bear this message are often the neighbors of the perpetrators as well as the friends and family of the victims. If the "we" in "This is not who we are" means, let us say, Americans (rather than, say, "progressive Democrats" or "members of the Federalist Society"), "we" *are* "this" today. And even if "This is not who we are" means "This is not who we ought to be," then the question reverts, or returns, to the vexed issue of "national character." Are "we" people who shoot up schools and nightclubs and synagogues? Certainly not. Then how is it that recurrent patterns, rather than just isolated individual instances, display, over and over again, this abhorrent behavior?

The unspoken word implied in these statements is "character." The term reverberates in its ghostly absence, and peers out from behind the curtain of empty words. Who I am. Who he is. Who we are. "Character" here becomes a label, a smoke screen, or a defense. Not a quality but an essence. Not a result of self-inquiry and social awareness but an a priori object of belief.

Here is a brief thought experiment: Imagine what might be called a phlogiston theory of character, modeled on the hypothetical substance once believed by eighteenth-century chemists to be released in the process of combustion. Phlogiston, they claimed, was "the cause of that light and heat which accompany burning." But what exactly was it? It couldn't be isolated; it was never actually located: it was an idea invented to explain an effect. The existence of phlogiston was denied by the chemist Antoine Lavoisier, though it was maintained for a longer time by Joseph Priestley, a theologian and a writer as well as a chemist. But by the middle of the nineteenth century, scholars could write about "the last dying echoes of the battle between the partisans of the phlogiston and the antiphlogiston camp."[5]

As often occurs, the idea of phlogiston found a place in literature and culture even as it was losing its relevance to science. The poet and critic Samuel Taylor Coleridge would write, "There exists undeniably a poetic phlogiston which adds by being abstracted and diminishes by its presence," and in the writings of the agricultural reformer Arthur Young we find this description of a Frenchman met in the course of his travels: he "pleases me much; the liveliness, vivacity, *phlogiston* of his character, do not run into pertness, foppery, or affectation."[6] The "*phlogiston* of his character" seems to me even today both a happy and a useful phrase. We might use a similarly "scientific" term today, like "electricity," or "magnetism," to describe the engaging aspect of a person who clearly, as we say, "makes a connection" with another.

Might character be what theorists call an "effect"—as phlogiston turned out to be? A concept generated by other things of which it was believed to be a cause or a catalyst? This is what the sociologist Erving Goffman argued in his landmark study, *The Presentation of Self in Everyday Life*, using the metaphor of social or cultural performance.

"In our society," wrote Goffman, "the character one performs and one's self are somewhat equated, and this self-as-character is usually seen as something housed within the body of its possessor." But

Goffman thought this was far from the whole story. Although one popular idea of human character is that of personal agency and control—"a correctly staged and performed scene leads the audience to impute a self to a performed character," and usually an appealing or "creditable" self—what actually happens, he wrote, is importantly different: "this imputation—this self—is a *product* of a scene that comes off, and is not a *cause* of it. The self, then, as a performed character . . . is a dramatic effect arising diffusely from a scene that is presented, and the characteristic issue, the crucial concern, is whether it will be credited or discredited."[7]

The "self," the "performed character," said Goffman, is an *effect*, not a cause: a "dramatic effect" that is the "*product* of a scene that comes off." And what is at stake is whether that performed character will be believed or disbelieved, "credited or discredited." "Discredited" here carries a vital double meaning, since it means "disbelieved" but also "dishonored." These words are powerful and persuasive, as they regard the "self" and the "character" in its dual sense as a presumed essence and a social or theatrical role.

Goffman's book was published in 1956, long before the heyday of social media and the "selfie"—before Senate hearings were televised, before CSPAN and televised press conferences, before it was conceivable that a U.S. president would communicate his thoughts to the nation and the world on something called Twitter. But the idea of human character as an effect of social performance rather than a pre-existing entity is at least as persuasive now as it was then.

What character is, who has it, whether it is malleable, detectable, inherited, or invented—these are all questions that have worried and fascinated thinkers across the centuries. As I have suggested throughout these pages, the word "character" itself, so apparently (and differently) clear to so many observers, may in fact be part of the problem.

Consider, in this light, the following observation:

> The tendency has always been strong to believe that whatever received a name must be an entity or being, having an independent existence of its own. And if no real entity answering to the name could be found, men did not for that reason suppose that

> none existed, but imagined that it was something peculiarly abstruse and mysterious.[8]

The author of these words is John Stuart Mill.

Mill had taken on the task of editing and annotating his father's book on the emotions and moral sentiments, *Analysis of the Phenomena of the Human Mind*, one of the Scottish Enlightenment's pioneering works on psychology. In this note to a chapter on "Classification," the younger Mill pays special attention to some overarching terms, or "names," that we might today associate with science, like "genus" and "species"—which may be one reason why the passage appealed to the biologist Stephen Jay Gould, who quotes it approvingly twice in *The Mismeasure of Man*.[9] But another problematic "entity" toward which Mill's comment might direct us, a term that is also presumed to "have an independent existence of its own," is "character."

Like "genus" and "species," "character" has been over the years understood to subsume a set of more specific "entities," whether they are those enumerated by Aristotle, or Theophrastus, or Gall and Spurzheim, or the group of psychologists who proposed the Five Factors of Personality.

But just because these entities, or factors, have been identified and specified—and each, though quite different from the next, has seemed in its own time persuasive—does that mean that the umbrella term, in this case "character," arguably "abstruse and mysterious," also has "an independent existence of its own"?

The passage from Mill, as Gould quotes it and as it is usually cited, ends in the middle of a sentence: men "imagined that it was something particularly abstruse and mysterious." The rest of the sentence, and the sentence that follows, are, however, equally illuminating. I supply them on page 382, in italics:

> The tendency has always been strong to believe that whatever received a name must be an entity or being, having an independent existence of its own. And if no real entity answering to the name could be found, men did not for that reason suppose that none existed, but imagined that it was something peculiarly

> abstruse and mysterious, *too high to be an object of sense. The meaning of all general, and especially of all abstract terms, became in this way enveloped in a mystical haze; and none of these have been more generally misunderstood, or have been a more copious source of futile and bewildering speculation, than some of the words which are names of names.*

By "names of names," Mill means those broad overarching categories that include other concepts, as "species" might include horses and cows, or "character," concepts like virtue, kindness, or leadership. The "mystical haze" that envelops abstract terms obscures their meanings, leading to misunderstanding as well as "futile and bewildering speculation."

To dispel just such a mystical haze around abstractions, or at least to call attention to it, the German philosopher Martin Heidegger developed a practice of putting problematic words *sous rature* ("under erasure"), a practice that was later employed by Jacques Derrida. The underlying idea was that the word itself was inadequate but also marked an important topic; as the critic and translator Gayatri Spivak explains, "Since the word is inaccurate, it is crossed out. Since it is necessary, it remains legible."[10] Heidegger's chief example is "Being," which he expressed in print as ~~Being~~. Other words that might appear "under erasure" for similar, or related, reasons today might—for example—be ~~Man~~ (or in Mill's paragraph, "~~men~~"), ~~democracy~~, or, if one were inclined to be partisan and critical, ~~President~~. Each marks a space of necessary meaning, but is for one or another reason inadequate or inappropriate.

Should we do the same with "character"? Printing the word as ~~character~~ throughout this book would have been both precious and cumbersome, as well as itself inaccurate, since for all of those many people who wrote, thought, worried, and argued about it, character was, in their contexts, a very real thing. Nonetheless, it is possible to say that, having looked at so many versions of this key word, we may reasonably remain in doubt as to whether it specifically names "an entity . . . having an independent existence of its own," to cite Mill's phrase once more. This is no reason to say that such a concept does not exist, much less that it cannot be discussed, debated, longed for, or mourned in its absence; it is only to say that the term itself is sometimes wrapped in a "mystical haze" that may accidentally—or even on occasion deliberately—mislead or confound. And that is in part because how we often discuss character suffers from a kind of category error. It is not an essence, but a mode of behavior, or a habit of being; a verb or a gerundive rather than a noun or a string of adjectives; an effect, not an image; a lifelong process, not a merit badge. And it is often most noticeable when it is absent. As U.S. Representative Adam Schiff said to the Senate in the impeachment trial of Donald John Trump, "You don't realize how important character is in the highest office of the land until you don't have it."

At a time when political corruption, sexual harassment, and renewed attacks upon blacks, Jews, Latinx, LGBTQ people, and immigrants are reported daily in the news, the idea of "character" may seem a quaint survival from a more naïve, more ethical, or at least less brazen past. Will we one day—and perhaps not too far from now—wonder about the longevity of this now antiquated notion, a preoccupation of statesmen, philosophers, psychologists, writers, and artists? Might "character" become a word that, like "phrenology" in some quarters today, seems to evoke quackery and gullibility, rather than a serious inquiry into human nature, human behavior, and human culture? Is it possible to imagine a moment when people will ask, not pointedly but with open curiosity, "What was character?"

This book is written in the expectation, and the hope, that such a moment will not soon come to pass. Like other key words that mark the difference between the human and the humane, "character" is a complex, sometimes self-contradictory, and often elusive concept, the meaning of which has itself grown and changed over time. Despite—or perhaps because of—its multiple uses, it remains both suggestive and generative. It may not be perfect, or perfectible, but it is at present the best we've got.

NOTES

Introduction: Character Witnesses

1. Eldred Wheeler, "Affordable Investment Furniture in the New England Tradition."
2. "The Latest: Parsons: Greitens' Resignation Will Heal State," *The New York Times*, May 29, 2018.
3. Kate Kelly, "James Staley's Series of Unfortunate Events," *The New York Times*, Aug. 26, 2017.
4. Stephen Halliwell, *Aristotle's Poetics* (Chicago: University of Chicago Press, 1998), p. 222.
5. Ibid., pp. 150–51.
6. Lewis A. Tartaglia, *Flawless! The Ten Most Common Character Flaws and What You Can Do About Them* (New York: Eagle Brook, 1999), quoted in "Character Flaws: The Seven Chief Features of Ego," The Michael Teachings, n.d., personalityspirituality.net.
7. Aristotle, *The Nicomachean Ethics*, trans. David Ross (Oxford, U.K.: Oxford World's Classics, 2009), 2.6, pp. 32, 33.
8. Ibid., 2.7, pp. 30–32.
9. Ibid., 2.1, p. 23.
10. "Character" entry, *Oxford English Dictionary*, n. 9a.
11. Ibid., v. 3.
12. "Commonplace" entry, *Oxford English Dictionary*, A.1, 3.
13. Robert Darnton, "Extraordinary Commonplaces," *The New York Review of Books* 47, no. 20 (Dec. 21, 2000), pp. 82, 86.
14. Thomas Babington Macaulay, *The History of England from the Accession of James II* (London: Longmans, 1849), vol. 1, p. 497, quoted in "Commonplace" entry, *Oxford English Dictionary*, n. 5a.
15. Benjamin Jowett, trans., *The Dialogues of Plato* (Oxford, U.K.: Clarendon Press, 1871), vol. 2, p. 140, quoted in "Commonplace" entry, *Oxford English Dictionary*, n. 5a.
16. Samuel Smiles, *Self-Help: With Illustrations of Character, Conduct, and Perseverance* (1859; rev. ed., 1866; Oxford, U.K.: Oxford University Press, 2002), p. 314.
17. Ibid.
18. Ralph Waldo Emerson, "Character," in *Essays: Second Series*, 1844, in *Emerson: Essays and Lectures*, ed. Joel Porte (New York: Library of America, 1983), p. 498.

19. Samuel Smiles, *Character* (1871; Rockville, MD: Serenity Publishers, 2009), pp. 7–10 passim.
20. Ibid., p. 11.
21. Emerson, "Character," p. 495.
22. Benjamin Disraeli, *The Vindication of the English Constitution in a Letter to a Noble and Learned Lord* (London: Saunders and Otley, 1835), p. 16.
23. Smiles, *Character*, p. 22.
24. Ibid., pp. 15, 16.
25. Ibid., p. 29.
26. Ibid., p. 30.
27. Ibid., p. 41.
28. Ibid., p. 44.
29. Ibid., pp. 44–45.
30. Ibid., p. 46.
31. Bruce Eamon Brown, *Teaching Character Through Sport: Developing a Positive Coaching Legacy* (Monterey, CA: Coaches Choice, 2003); Thomas Likona, *Character Matters: How to Help Our Children Develop Good Judgment, Integrity, and Other Essential Virtues* (New York: Touchstone, 2004); Mike Huckabee, *Character IS the Issue: How People with Integrity Can Revolutionize America* (Nashville, TN: Broadman and Holman, 1997); Katherine Brazelton and Shelley Leith, *Character Makeover: 40 Days with a Life Coach to Create the Best You* (Grand Rapids, MI: Zondervan, 2008).
32. James Rees and Stephen J. Spignesi, *George Washington's Leadership Lessons: What the Father of Our Country Can Teach Us About Effective Leadership and Character* (Hoboken, NJ: John Wiley, 2007); H. W. Crocker III, *Robert E. Lee on Leadership: Executive Lessons in Character, Courage, and Vision* (New York: Three Rivers, 2000); Joseph L. Badaracco, Jr., *Questions of Character: Illuminating the Heart of Leadership Through Literature* (Boston: Harvard Business School Press, 2006).
33. Richard Olivier, *Inspirational Leadership: Timeless Lessons for Leaders from Shakespeare's Henry V* (Boston: Nicholas Brealey, 2013); John O. Whitney and Tina Packer, *Power Plays: Shakespeare's Lessons in Leadership and Management* (New York: Touchstone, 2002); Norman Augustine and Kenneth Adelman, *Shakespeare in Charge: The Bard's Guide to Leading and Succeeding on the Business Stage* (New York: Hyperion, 1999); Paul Corrigan, *Shakespeare on Management: Leadership Lessons for Today's Managers* (London: Kogan Page, 1999).
34. Alexander Pope, preface, *Shakespeare Criticism: A Selection*, ed. D. Nichol Smith (London: Oxford University Press, 1946), p. 43.
35. Samuel Taylor Coleridge, *Table Talk*, Jun. 24, 1827, in *Shakespeare Criticism*, p. 262.
36. William Guthrie, *An Essay upon English Tragedy* (London: T. Waller, 1757), p. 11.
37. C. Robert Cloninger, *Feeling Good: The Science of Well-Being* (Oxford, U.K.: Oxford University Press, 2004), p. 44.
38. Frank Deford, *The Heart of a Champion: Celebrating the Spirit and Character of Great American Sports Heroes* (Minoqua, WI: NorthWord Press, 2002).
39. Craig Clifford and Randolph M. Feezell, *Sport and Character: Reclaiming the Principles of Sportsmanship* (Champaign, IL: Human Kinetics, 2009).
40. Laurie Beth Jones, *Jesus, Life Coach: Learn from the Best* (Nashville, TN: Thomas Nelson, 2004).
41. Douglas L. Wilson, "Thomas Jefferson and the Character Issue," *The Atlantic*, Nov. 1992.

1. Testing It

1. "Sen. Mark Udall on Romney's 47 Percent Remarks: 'Mitt Romney Has Failed the Character Test,'" *Huffington Post*, Sept. 19, 2012.
2. Mitt Romney, "The President Shapes the Public Character of the Nation: Trump's Character Falls Short," *The Washington Post*, Jan. 1, 2019.
3. Jennifer Rubin, "Mark Sanford Strikes Out on Character Tests," *The Washington Post*, Feb. 19, 2013.
4. Jennifer Rubin, "Sanford Wins," *The Washington Post*, May 8, 2013.
5. Paul Waldman, "Yes, Democrats Should Criticize Barack Obama: Here's Why," *The Washington Post*, Aug. 1, 2019.
6. Paul Krugman, "Nobody Said That," *The New York Times*, Apr. 27, 2015.
7. Paul Krugman, "Ideology and Integrity," *The New York Times*, May 1, 2015.
8. Maureen Dowd, "Escape from Bushworld," *The New York Times*, Feb. 21, 2016.
9. Frank Bruni, "Obnoxiousness Is the New Charisma," *The New York Times*, Jan. 9, 2016.
10. Frank Bruni, "Feminism, Hell, and Hillary Clinton," *The New York Times*, Feb. 9, 2016.
11. David Brooks, "I Miss Barack Obama," *The New York Times*, Feb. 9, 2016.
12. David Brooks, "The Brutalism of Ted Cruz," *The New York Times*, Jan. 12, 2016.
13. David Brooks, *The Road to Character* (New York: Penguin, 2015), pp. 61, 67, 249–50.
14. Alexander Burns, "At Nevada Caucuses, Donald Trump's Rivals Hope to Break His Streak," *The New York Times*, Feb. 23, 2016.
15. Karen Mizoguchi, "Ted Cruz Channels Michael Douglas," *People*, Mar. 2, 2016.
16. Timothy Egan, "A Unified Theory of Trump," *The New York Times*, Feb. 26, 2016.
17. Gail Sheehy, "The Women Who Should Love Hillary Clinton," *The New York Times*, Jan. 29, 2016.
18. Charles M. Blow, "Hillary Is Hobbling, for Now," *The New York Times*, Sept. 10, 2015.
19. Joe Klein, "A GOP Identity Crisis Eases the Path for Hillary Clinton," *Time*, Nov. 9, 2015, p. 28.
20. Daniel Wattenberg, "The Lady Macbeth of Little Rock," *The American Spectator*, Aug. 1992, pp. 25–32.
21. Ibid., p. 26.
22. Sarah Siddons, "Remarks on the Character of Lady Macbeth," in Thomas Campbell, *Life of Mrs. Siddons* (New York: Harper & Brothers, 1834).
23. Hillary Clinton, "Hillary Clinton Pens Billboard Essay for Women in Music Issue, Pays Tribute to Lady Gaga and Honorees," *Billboard*, Dec. 12, 2015.
24. "Hillary Clinton for President," editorial, *The New York Times*, Sept. 24, 2016.
25. Susan Faludi, "How Hillary Clinton Met Satan," *The New York Times*, Oct. 29, 2016.
26. Tom Toles, "The Three Kinds of Lies Are Now: Lies, Damned Lies and Political Money," *The Washington Post*, Sept. 29, 2017.
27. Michael Gerson, "An Administration Without a Conscience," *The Washington Post*, Jul. 13, 2017.
28. Thomas L. Friedman, "Keep Up the Blanket Coverage of Trump: It Hurts Him," *The New York Times*, Aug 8, 2018.
29. Jennifer Senior, "'Richard Nixon,' Portrait of a Thin-Skinned, Media-Hating President," *The New York Times*, Apr. 19, 2018. Farrell's book, *Richard Nixon:*

The Life (New York: Doubleday, 2017), won the New-York Historical Society's Barbara and David Zalaznick Book Prize, awarded annually to the best work in the field of American history or biography.

30. Paul Krugman, "Wrecking the Ship of State," *The New York Times*, Jun. 9, 2017.
31. Paul Krugman, "Goodbye Spin, Hello Raw Dishonesty," *The New York Times*, Mar. 3, 2017.
32. Charles M. Blow, "The Duplicity of Donald Trump," *The New York Times*, Aug. 31, 2016.
33. Charles M. Blow, "Donald Trump, Unshackled and Unhinged," *The New York Times*, Oct. 13, 2016.
34. Charles M. Blow, "Donald Trump, the Worst of America," *The New York Times*, Oct.17, 2017.
35. Charles M. Blow, "Donald Trump's Lack of Discipline and Discernment," *The New York Times*, Oct. 27, 2016.
36. Charles M. Blow, "America Elects a Bigot," *The New York Times*, Nov. 10, 2016.
37. Charles M. Blow, "No, Trump, We Can't Just Get Along," *The New York Times*, Nov. 23, 2016.
38. Charles M. Blow, "Trump and the Parasitic Presidency," *The New York Times*, Mar. 13, 2017.
39. Charles M. Blow, "Trump, Chieftain of Spite," *The New York Times*, Oct. 15, 2017.
40. Frank Bruni, "Stop Indulging Trump," *The New York Times*, Aug. 2, 2016.
41. Frank Bruni, "Why This Election Terrifies Me," *The New York Times*, Nov. 5, 2016.
42. Frank Bruni, "Donald Trump Is Never to Blame," *The New York Times*, Jun. 7, 2017.
43. Frank Bruni, "President Trump Cannot Redeem Himself," *The New York Times*, Aug. 14, 2017.
44. Danielle Allen, "Donald Trump Is a Walking, Talking Example of the Tyrannical Soul," *The Washington Post*, Oct. 8, 2016.
45. Ross Douthat, "The Pigs of Liberalism," *The New York Times*, Oct. 7, 2017.
46. Peter Wehner, "The Indelible Stain of Donald Trump," *The New York Times*, Jun. 10, 2016.
47. Bret Stephens, "The Happy Hooker Conservatives," *The New York Times*, Oct. 26, 2017.
48. Joe Scarborough, "Trump Is Killing the Republican Party," *The Washington Post*, Jul. 16, 2017.
49. Jennifer Rubin, "The Pathetic Neediness of Trump," *The Washington Post*, Nov. 27, 2017.
50. Gail Collins and Bret Stephens, "Thirteen Ways of Looking at a Sex Scandal," *The New York Times*, Nov. 21, 2017.
51. Greg Weiner, "The Scoundrel Theory of American Politics," *The New York Times*, Dec. 8, 2017.
52. Marc Fisher, "For Some Evangelicals, a Choice Between Moore and Morality," *The Washington Post*, Nov. 16, 2017.
53. Sarah Pulliam Bailey, "'Still the Best Candidate': Some Evangelicals Still Back Trump Despite Lewd Video," *The Washington Post*, Oct. 8, 2016.
54. Fisher, "For Some Evangelicals, a Choice Between Moore and Morality."
55. Jonathan Martin and Alexander Burns, "Republicans Try to Block Moore's Path as Candidate Denies Sexual Misconduct," *The New York Times*, Nov. 10, 2017.

56. William Cummings, "Trump Proclaims 'National Character Counts' Week," *USA Today*, Oct. 14, 2017.
57. Alyssa Rosenberg, "It's Absurd for Trump to Promote Good Character. But Character Counts Now More Than Ever," *The Washington Post*, Oct. 19, 2017.
58. David Brooks, "When the World Is Led by a Child," *The New York Times*, May 15, 2017.
59. Ibid.
60. "Is the G.O.P. Following Jim Jordan over a Cliff?," editorial, *The New York Times*, Jul. 12, 2018.
61. Emma Roller, "The Trump Brand, Win or Lose," *The New York Times*, Feb. 9, 2016.
62. Jonathan Martin and Jeremy W. Peters, "Donald Trump to Reshape Image, New Campaign Chief Tells G.O.P.," *The New York Times*, Apr. 21, 2016.
63. Charles M. Blow, "Clash of the Injured Titans," *The New York Times*, Apr. 25, 2016.
64. David S. Cloud, "Here's Donny! In His Defense, a Show Is Born," *The New York Times*, Apr. 19, 2006.
65. John Foster, "On Decision of Character," in *Essays in a Series of Letters* (1804; London: G. Bell, 1912), p. 79.
66. Ibid., p. 108.
67. Ibid., p. 89.
68. Ibid., p. 102.
69. Alasdair MacIntyre, *After Virtue: A Study in Moral Theory* (1981; London: Bloomsbury, 2011), p. 33.
70. Ibid., p. 34.
71. Ibid., p. 32.
72. Ibid., p. 35.
73. Jonathan Mahler, "Hall of Fame: Forget Character, Welcome Characters," *Bloomberg View*, Jan. 9, 2013.
74. Ibid. Kenesaw Mountain Landis, the baseball commissioner who banned eight members of the 1919 Chicago White Sox from playing even after they had been exonerated of criminal charges, and Stephen Clark, who founded the Hall as a boon to Cooperstown, New York.
75. Lawrence Zierlein, "Red Flags: 2015 NFL Draft Prospects with Character Concerns," NFL.com, Feb. 9, 2015.
76. Andrew Carroll, "Why 'Character Concerns' Is a Meaningless Phrase in the NFL," Arrowheadpride.com, May 9, 2015.
77. Glen Macnow, "Philly Doesn't Care What Trump Says About the Eagles," *The New York Times*, Jun. 6, 2018.
78. Jeffrey Lurie, quoted in Benjamin Hoffman, Victor Mather, and Jacey Fortin, "After Trump Blasts N.F.L., Players Kneel and Lock Arms in Solidarity," *The New York Times*, Sept. 24, 2017.
79. "Report: Patriots Character Coach Jack Easterby Will Leave Team," *Patriots Wire*, Feb. 28, 2019.
80. Eileen Sullivan, "Trump Says He's Considering a Pardon for Muhammad Ali," *The New York Times*, Jun. 8, 2018.
81. Trump was even willing to bash John McCain for being a prisoner of war rather than a victorious conqueror. "He's not a war hero," said Trump. "I like people who weren't captured" (Ben Schrekinger, "Trump Attacks McCain," *Politico*, Jul. 18, 2015). McCain spent five years in a North Vietnamese prison, including two years in solitary confinement, and was repeatedly tortured. He declined an

early release that was offered to him, insisting that, according to the POW code, all those taken prisoner before him would need to be released as well.

82. promisekeepers.org.
83. Allan Fay, letter to the editor, *The New York Times*, Feb. 4, 1994.
84. Brooks Barnes, "Harvey Weinstein Ousted from Motion Picture Academy," *The New York Times*, Oct. 14, 2017.
85. *The Hollywood Reporter*, quoted in Emily Yahr, "Harvey Weinstein's Behavior Was a Dark Inside Joke," *The Washington Post*, Oct. 10, 2017.
86. New Zealand Immigration, "Good Character," Immigration.govt.nz/new-zealand-visas.
87. Charlotte Graham-McLay, "Matt Lauer Can Keep New Zealand Ranch, Despite Inquiry into Conduct," *The New York Times*, Jun. 8, 2018. The New Zealand Overseas Investment Office, charged with assessing applications from foreigners who want to invest in sensitive land or business assets worth over $100 million, said it would continue to monitor Lauer's situation.
88. Kyle Swenson and Samantha Schmidt, "Charlie Rose: The Rise and Plummet of a Man Who Preached 'Character' and 'Integrity,'" *The Washington Post*, Nov. 21, 2017.
89. Graham Bowley and Jon Hurdle, "Bill Cosby Is Found Guilty of Sexual Assault," *The New York Times*, Apr. 26, 2018.
90. Jennifer Schuessler, "The Prosecutor Who Stared Down Bill Cosby," *The New York Times*, Apr. 29, 2018.
91. Wesley Morris, "Cliff Huxtable Was Bill Cosby's Sickest Joke," *The New York Times*, Apr. 26, 2018.

2. Teaching It

1. Noel Annan, *Leslie Stephen: The Godless Victorian* (New York: Random House, 1984), p. 38.
2. Mason Locke Weems, *A History of the Life and Death, Virtues and Exploits of General George Washington*, quoted in *The Life of Washington*, ed. Marcus Cunliffe (Cambridge, MA: Harvard University Press, 1999), p. 12.
3. Weems, *George Washington*, chap. 13, "Character of Washington."
4. C. J. Gianakaris, *Plutarch* (New York: Twayne, 1970), p. 131.
5. Plutarch, "Pericles," in *The Rise and Fall of Athens: Nine Greek Lives*, trans. Ian Scott-Kilvert (London: Penguin, 1960), p. 166.
6. Plutarch, "Prologue to the Lives of Alexander and Julius Caesar," in *The Age of Alexander: Ten Greek Lives*, trans. Ian Scott-Kilvert and Timothy E. Duff (London: Penguin, 2011), p. 279.
7. Gianakaris, *Plutarch*, p. 146.
8. Plutarch, "On Being Aware of Moral Progress," in *Essays*, trans. Robin Waterfield (London: Penguin, 1992), p. 143.
9. Ibid., p. 145.
10. Emerson, *Journal*, quoted in Edmund G. Berry, *Emerson's Plutarch* (Cambridge, MA: Harvard University Press, 1961), p. 256.
11. Thomas Carlyle, *On Heroes, Hero-Worship, and the Heroic in History*, ed. David R. Sorensen and Brent E. Kinser (New Haven, CT: Yale University Press, 2013), p. 30.
12. Henry Wadsworth Longfellow, "A Psalm of Life," originally published in *Knickerbocker Magazine*, Oct. 1838.

13. David Blight, "'Patriotic Gore' Is Not Really Much Like Any Other Book by Anyone," *Slate*, Mar. 22, 2012.
14. George Bernard Shaw, *Fabian Essays in Socialism* (London: Walter Scott, 1908), p. 10.
15. Samuel Smiles, *Self-Help: With Illustrations of Character, Conduct, and Perseverance* (1859; rev. ed., 1866; Oxford, U.K.: Oxford University Press, 2002), p. 303.
16. Ibid., p. 22.
17. See, for example, Roger Kimball, "Plutarch and the Issue of Character," *New Criterion*, Dec. 2000.
18. Frank M. Turner, *The Greek Heritage in Victorian Britain* (New Haven, CT: Yale University Press, 1981), p. 324.
19. Stefan Collini, "The Idea of 'Character' in Victorian Political Thought," *Transactions of the Royal Historical Society*, 35 (1985), pp. 29–50.
20. Ibid., p. 38.
21. Robert Owen, "A New View of Society; or Essays on the Principle of the Formation of the Human Character, and the Application of the Principle to Practice," in *A New View of Society and Other Writings*, ed. Gregory Claeys (London: Penguin, 1991), p. 32.
22. Ibid., p. 43.
23. Robert Owen, "Address Delivered to the Inhabitants of New Lanark," in *A New View of Society and Other Writings*, pp. 110–11.
24. Ibid., p. 112.
25. We might note the existence in the same period of at least two important groups, both of which influenced Robert Owen, that proudly included the word "literary" in their titles: the Manchester Literary and Philosophical Society and the Glasgow Literary and Commercial Society. It is difficult to imagine, today, any similarly powerful political, economic, or educational societies that would think to use "literary" as an honorable or prestigious honorific.
26. Stephen Tomlinson, *Head Masters: Phrenology, Secular Education, and Nineteenth-Century Social Thought* (Tuscaloosa: University of Alabama Press, 2005), p. 132.
27. Robert Southey, *Journal of a Tour in Scotland in 1819*, ed. C. H. Herford (London: Murray, 1929), pp. 263–64.
28. Owen, "Address," p. 115.
29. Ibid., pp. 114–15.
30. U.S. Congress, House Committee on Un-American Activities, "Investigation of the Unauthorized Use of U.S. Passports," 84th Cong., pt. 3, Jun. 12, 1956, quoted in *Thirty Years of Treason: Excerpts from Hearings Before the House Committee on Un-American Activities, 1938–1968*, ed. Eric Bentley (New York: Viking, 1971), p. 770.
31. Owen, "Address," p. 127.
32. John Stuart Mill, *Autobiography* (1873; London: Penguin, 1989), p. 135.
33. George Henry Lewes, *The Life of Goethe*, 2nd ed. (London: George Routledge, 1864), pp. 18–19.
34. Ralph Waldo Emerson, "Fate," in *The Conduct of Life* (1860), in *Essays and Lectures* (New York: Library of America, 1983), p. 943.
35. Mill, *Autobiography*, pp. 120–21.
36. Ibid., p. 123.
37. Ibid., p. 135.

38. John Stuart Mill, *A System of Logic, Ratiocinative and Inductive*, in Mill, *Collected Works*, vol. 8, ed. J. M. Robson (Indianapolis: Liberty Fund, 2006), pp. 869–74.
39. John Stuart Mill, "On Liberty," in *On Liberty, with The Subjection of Women and Chapters on Socialism*, ed. Stefan Collini (Cambridge, U.K.: Cambridge University Press, 1989, 2012), pp. 60–61.
40. Emerson, "Fate," in *Essays and Lectures*, p. 959.
41. Samuel Smiles, *The Life of George Stephenson, Railway Engineer* (London: John Murray, 1857).
42. Watty Piper [pseudonym of Arnold Munk], *The Little Engine That Could* (New York: Platt & Munk, 1954).
43. Virginia Lee Burton, *Mike Mulligan and His Steam Shovel* (1939; Torrance, CA: Sandpiper Books, 1977).
44. John Stuart Mill, "The Subjection of Women," in *On Liberty*, ed. Collini, p. 138.
45. Thomas Hughes, *Tom Brown's School Days*, ed. Andrew Sanders (1857; Oxford, U.K.: Oxford University Press, 2008), pp. 73–74.
46. Ibid., p. 211.
47. Ibid., p. 242.
48. Ibid.
49. Ibid., p. 371.
50. Ibid., pp. 374–75.
51. George Orwell, "Such, Such Were the Joys," in *Essays* (London: Penguin, 1994), pp. 417, 443. Originally published in *Partisan Review*, 1952.
52. Jonathan Gathorne-Hardy, *The Public School Phenomenon* (Harmondsworth, U.K.: Penguin, 1979), p. 85.
53. Harold Nicolson, *Some People* (1927; London: Constable, 1999), p. 21.
54. Walter Pater, "Lacedaemon," in *Plato and Platonism* (Middlesex, U.K.: Echo, 2006), p. 103.
55. Ibid., p. 108.
56. Ibid., p. 104.
57. Robert Baden-Powell, *Rovering to Success: A Book of Life-Sport for Young Men* (1922; rev. ed., London: Herbert Jenkins, 1930), p. 24.
58. Quoted in Gathorne-Hardy, *Public School Phenomenon*, p. 167.
59. Harold Nicolson, quoted in ibid., p. 169.
60. See Roberta J. Park, "Biological Thought, Athletics, and the Formation of a 'Man of Character': 1830–1900," in *Manliness and Morality: Middle-Class Masculinity in Britain and America 1800–1940*, ed. J. A. Mangan and James Malvin (Manchester, U.K.: Manchester University Press, 1987), p. 10.
61. Charles William Eliot, letter to the president of the University of California, 1906, quoted in Roberta J. Park, "From Football to Rugby—and Back, 1900–1919," *Journal of Sports History*, XI (1984), p. 25. Also in Park, "Biological Thought," p. 24.
62. Theodore Roosevelt, "Character and Success," in *The Strenuous Life* (New York: Century, 1904), pp. 212–13. Originally published in *The Outlook*, Mar. 31, 1900.
63. In the United States, "varsity" is the term for a university or college's top sports teams, though Baden-Powell is unlikely to have had this in mind.
64. Robert Baden-Powell, *Lessons from the 'Varsity of Life* (London: C. Arthur Pearson, 1933), pp. 272–73.
65. Ibid., p. 273.
66. Ibid., p. 275.

67. Ibid., p. 278.
68. Ibid., pp. 278–79.
69. Ibid., p. 278.
70. Michael Rosenthal, *The Character Factory: Baden-Powell and the Origins of the Boy Scout Movement* (London: Collins, 1986), p. 111.
71. Quoted in Tim Jeal, *Baden-Powell* (London: Hutchinson, 1989), p. 107.
72. Baden-Powell, *Lessons from the 'Varsity of Life*, pp. 281–82.
73. Lieut.-General R.S.S. Baden-Powell, *Scouting for Boys* (London: Horace Cox, 1908), p. 68.
74. Ibid., p. 69.
75. Michael Rosenthal, in a similar analysis of these drawings, identifies the classic profile of the boy in the center as clearly that of the "public school lad" (Rosenthal, *Character Factory*, pp. 180–81).
76. Baden-Powell, *Scouting for Boys*, p. 185.
77. Elleke Boehmer, introduction, *Scouting for Boys* (Oxford, U.K.: Oxford University Press, 2004), p. xxii.
78. Smiles, *Self-Help*, p. 20.
79. Ibid., pp. 20–21.
80. H. S. Pelham, *The Training of a Working Boy* (London: Macmillan, 1914), p. 9, quoted in Rosenthal, *Character Factory*, p. 8.
81. Robert Baden-Powell, in *Headquarters Gazette*, 9 (Feb. 1915), p. 9, quoted in Rosenthal, *Character Factory*, pp. 6, 284 n. 2. Rosenthal notes that factories produce "uniform products under detailed specifications for particular uses," and argues that the "emphasis on submission and discipline, on curbing the impulses of the self in the service of the community," was "an ideology firmly rooted in the self-interest of the upper classes." However genuine Baden-Powell's commitment to scouting as character training might have been, he says, bringing "public school ideals to the poor" should not be seen as disembodied altruism but, rather, as "a thoroughly political act with significant social consequences."
82. Jeal, *Baden-Powell*, p. 77.
83. Quoted in ibid., p. 366.
84. Letter to Dulce Wroughton, in ibid., pp. 86, 353.
85. Olave, Lady Baden-Powell, *Window on My Heart: The Autobiography of Olave, Lady Baden-Powell, as Told to Mary Drewery* (1973; London: Hodder and Stoughton, 1977), p. 109.
86. Jeal, *Baden-Powell*, p. 429.
87. As Jeal notes (ibid., p. 444), he included this observation "rather tactlessly" in a letter to his mother.
88. Ibid., p. 445.
89. Robert Baden-Powell, letter to Olave Soames, Jul. 9, 1919, quoted in *Window on My Heart*, p. 90.
90. Baden-Powell, *Window on My Heart*, p. 184.
91. Jeal, *Baden-Powell*, p. 571.
92. Quoted in Jeal, *Baden-Powell*, p. 445.
93. J. A. Mangan, *The Games Ethic and Imperialism: Aspects of the Diffusion of an Ideal* (London: Frank Cass, 1998), p. 147.
94. Mark Girouard, *The Return to Camelot: Chivalry and the English Gentleman* (New Haven, CT: Yale University Press, 1981), p. 252.
95. Baden-Powell, *Scouting for Boys*, p. 11.
96. Ibid., p. 301.

97. Baden-Powell, *Rovering to Success*, pp. 108–30.
98. Ibid., pp. 71–73.
99. Ibid., p. 97.
100. F.W.W. Griffin, *The Quest of the Boy: A Study of the Psychology of Character Training* (London: Faith Press, 1927, 1930), p. ix.
101. Ibid., p. 103.
102. Ibid., p. 87.
103. Ibid., p. 69.
104. Ibid., p. 119.
105. Ibid., p. 113.
106. Ibid., p. 117.
107. Ibid., p. 124.
108. Robert Baden-Powell, *Scouting for Boys: A Handbook for Instruction in Good Citizenship*, ed. Elleke Boehmer (1908; Oxford, U.K.: Oxford University Press, 2004), p. 222.
109. Baden-Powell, *Rovering to Success*, pp. 24–25.
110. Ibid., p. 232.
111. Boy Scouts of America, *Boy Scouts Handbook, The First Edition, 1911* (Garden City, NY: Dover, 2005), pp. 245–46.
112. Ibid., p. 246.
113. Quoted in Jeffrey Richards, "'Passing the Love of Women': Manly Love and Victorian Society," in *Manliness and Morality*, ed. Mangan and Malvin, p. 93.
114. Girouard, *Return to Camelot*, p. 269.
115. Gathorne-Hardy, *Public School Phenomenon*, p. 272.
116. Ibid., p. 271.
117. Ibid., p. 266.
118. Quoted in Jeal, *Baden-Powell*, p. 637 n. 6.
119. David I. Macleod, *Building Character in the American Boy: The Boy Scouts, YMCA, and Their Forerunners, 1870–1920* (Madison: University of Wisconsin Press, 1983), p. 132.
120. Jeal, *Baden-Powell*, p. 470.
121. Agnes Baden-Powell and Robert Baden-Powell, *The Handbook for Girl Guides, or How Girls Can Help to Build the Empire* (London: Thomas Nelson, 1912; facsimile ed., London: Girl Guides Association, 1993), p. 22.
122. "Mother's letter," Jun. 11, 1909, in *Pamphlet B*, 1910, quoted in Jeal, *Baden-Powell*, p. 471.
123. A. and R. Baden-Powell, *Handbook for Girl Guides*, p. 83.
124. Ibid., p. 340.
125. Ibid., p. 376.
126. Baden-Powell, *Rovering to Success*, pp. 121, 122, 125–26.
127. "Character-building" entry, *Oxford English Dictionary*.
128. Rosenthal, *Character Factory*, p. 277.
129. Kenneth Roberts, Graham E. White, and Howard J. Parker, *The Character-Training Industry: Adventure-Training Schemes in Britain* (Newton Abbot, U.K.: David & Charles, 1974), p. 12.
130. Ibid., pp. 12–13.
131. Alfred Kazin, *A Walker in the City* (1946, 1951; Orlando, FL: Harcourt, 1979), p. 20, quoted in Jerome Karabel, *The Chosen: The Hidden History of Admission and Exclusion at Harvard, Yale, and Princeton* (Boston: Houghton Mifflin, 2005), p. 584 n. 103.

132. Alfred Kazin, *Alfred Kazin's Journals*, ed. Richard M. Cook (New Haven, CT: Yale University Press, 2011), entry for Jul. 25, 1963, p. 301.
133. Oliver Wendell Holmes, Jr., May 27, 1929, "Dissenting Opinion," *United States v. Schwimmer*, U.S. 644, p. 279.
134. The Henry Ford Museum. William H. McGuffey Papers, thehenryford.org /collections-and-research/digital-collections/archival-collections/182377. William H. McGuffey was an educator, a minister, an author, and a college president best known for creating the *McGuffey's Readers* textbooks. The collection contains correspondence, lectures, and photographs of McGuffey and his family.
135. L. Frank Baum, author's preface, *The Wonderful Wizard of Oz* (Chicago: George M. Hill, 1900).
136. Ibid.
137. The children's book writer Mo Willems addresses the question of "making believe" in one of his "Elephant and Piggie" books, *I'm a Frog*. Piggie, the ebullient, sociable, and optimistic pig, announces to her best friend, Gerald the Elephant, that she is a frog. Gerald, always a literalist, is puzzled: "I was sure you were a *pig*. You *look* like a pig. And your name *is* 'Piggie.'" When he asks her when she became a frog, and she answers "five minutes ago," Gerald is filled with the dread of metamorphosis: *he* doesn't want to turn into a frog, forced to hop all day and eat flies. Piggie takes pity on him, as always (she loves him), and explains that "It is okay. It is pretend." But Gerald doesn't know what "pretending" is, so she has to spell it out for him: "Pretending is when you act like something you are not." "Wow . . ." says Gerald, impressed. "And you can just *do* that?" "You can just go out and *pretend* to be something that you are not?" "Sure," answers Piggie. "Everyone pretends." "Even grown-up people?" Gerald wants to know, and she assures him of it: "All the time." Gerald is interested and willing to believe her, but he is still a bit nonplussed. "You really do learn something new every day," he says, looking right out at the reader as he says it. (Mo Willems, *I'm a Frog* [New York: Hyperion, 2013], pp. 12–42 passim.)
138. Noel Langley, Florence Ryerson, and Edgar Allan Woolf, *The Wizard of Oz: The Screenplay* (Monterey Park, CA: O.S.P. Publishing, 1994), p. 81.
139. Ibid.
140. Ibid., pp. 81–82.
141. Aljean Harmetz, *The Making of The Wizard of Oz* (Chicago: Chicago Review Press, 1977, 2013), p. 58.
142. Here he echoes, though there is no reason to think he knows it, Mopsa the shepherdess in Shakespeare's *The Winter's Tale*, another fantasy of wish fulfillment: "I love a ballad in print, alife, for then we are sure they are true" (4.4.265–66).
143. William Cummings, "Trump Proclaims 'National Character Counts Week,'" *USA Today*, Oct. 13, 2017.
144. For example, Steve Benen, "Trump's Awkward Declaration on 'Character Counts Week,'" *The MaddowBlog*, MSNBC.com, Oct. 21, 2019; Dana Milbank, "Impeachment Diary: The Day That Irony Died," *The Washington Post*, Oct. 22, 2019.
145. The writers may have had in mind the Values Clarification model of moral education.
146. See, for example, Sidney B. Simon and Howard Kirschenbaum, eds., *Readings in Values Clarification* (Minneapolis, MN: Winston Press, 1973); David Purpel

and Kevin Ryan, eds., *Moral Education . . . It Comes with the Territory* (Berkeley, CA: McCutchan, 1976), especially Sidney Simon, "Values Clarification v. Indoctrination."

147. Character Counts! Coalition (US), Josephson Institute of Ethics.
148. See whitehouse.gov/bebest, whitehouse.gov/presidential-actions. Tim Hill, "'Be Best': Does Melania Trump's Oddly Named Initiative Break the Laws of Grammar?" *The Guardian*, May 8, 2018.
149. Senate Joint Resolution 178, to proclaim the week of Oct. 16–Oct. 22, 1994, as "National Character Counts Week," congress-gov/bill/103rd-congress/senate-joint-resolution/text.
150. Bill Clinton, Proclamation 7141, Oct. 16, 1998.
151. Clinton, State of the Union, 1996.
152. Joseph Farah, "Bill Clinton and Character," *WorldNetDaily*, Oct. 22, 1998, wnd.com/1998/10/1233.
153. Barack Obama, Presidential Proclamation, National Character Counts Week, 2015, obamawhitehouse.archives.gov/the-press-office/2015/10/16/presidential-proclamation-national-character-counts-week-2015.
154. George H. W. Bush, speech to Republican National Convention, New Orleans, Aug. 18, 1988.
155. Nel Noddings, *Education and Democracy in the Twenty-First Century* (New York: Teachers' College Press, 2013), p. 117.
156. Alfie Kohn, "How Not to Teach Values: A Critical Look at Character Education," *Phi Delta Kappan* 78, no. 6 (1997): 428–39. Available at alfiekohn.org.
157. Ibid.
158. "What goes by the name of character education nowadays is, for the most part, a collection of exhortations and extrinsic inducements designed to make children work harder and do what they're told. Even when other values are also promoted—caring or fairness, say—the preferred method of instruction is tantamount to indoctrination. The point is to drill students in specific behaviors rather than to engage them in deep, critical reflection about certain ways of being. This is the impression one gets from reading articles and books by contemporary proponents of character education as well as the curriculum materials sold by the leading national programs." (Ibid.)
159. Common Core State Standards Initiative, "Myths vs. Facts," corestandards.org.
160. Angela Duckworth, "Grit: The Power of Passion and Perseverance," TED talk.
161. M. M. Credé, M. C. Tynan, and P. D. Harms, "Much Ado About Grit: A Meta-Analytic Synthesis of the Grit Literature," *Journal of Personality and Social Psychology*, 113 (no. 3): 492–511, Sept. 2017.
162. See, for example, a paper by Ethan Ris of Stanford University quoted in its entirety in Valerie Strauss, "The Problem with Teaching 'Grit' to Poor Kids? They Already Have It; Here's What They Really Need," *The Washington Post*, May 10, 2016; research of Todd Rose and Ogi Ogas at the Harvard Graduate School of Education, cited in Jeffrey J. Selingo, "Is 'Grit' Overrated in Explaining Student Success? Harvard Researchers Have a New Theory," *The Washington Post*, May 25, 2016.
163. John M. Doris, *Lack of Character: Personality and Moral Behavior* (Cambridge, U.K.: Cambridge University Press, 2002), p. 122.
164. Ibid., p. 126.
165. Ibid.
166. Ibid., p. 123.

167. Kohn, "How Not to Teach Values."
168. See Burton J. Bledstein, *The Culture of Professionalism* (New York: Norton, 1976).
169. James Burrill Angell, quoted in Shirley W. Smith, *James Burrill Angell: An American Influence* (Ann Arbor: University of Michigan Press, 1954), p. 30. See also Bledstein, *Culture of Professionalism*, p. 134.
170. Andrew Dickson White, *Autobiography of Andrew Dickson White* (New York: Century, 1905), vol. I, pp. 388–89. See also Bledstein, *Culture of Professionalism*, p. 151.
171. Charles Eliot, "Address to New Students," Oct. 1, 1906, *Harvard Graduates Magazine*, quoted in Ian A. M. Nicholson, *Inventing Personality: Gordon Allport and the Science of Selfhood* (Washington, D.C.: American Psychological Association, 2002), p. 29.
172. Jerome Karabel, *The Chosen: The Hidden History of Admission and Exclusion at Harvard, Yale, and Princeton* (Boston: Houghton Mifflin, 2005), pp. 131–32.
173. Langdon P. Marvin, letter to A. Lawrence Lowell, Jun. 9, 1922, quoted in Karabel, *Chosen*, pp. 132, 585 n.
174. See, for example, Karabel, *Chosen*, p. 582 n. 10: "Among those Yale administrators who referred to Jews as 'Hebrews' [was] the registrar A. K. Merritt (who also referred to them, not without irony, as 'the chosen race')."
175. Karabel, *Chosen*, p. 123.
176. James Angell, "Current Conditions at the University," *Yale Alumni Magazine*, 2 (Mar. 1923), quoted in Karabel, *Chosen*, p. 114.
177. Robert Nelson Corwin, "Memorandum on the Problems," and "Limitation of Numbers," Jan. 9, 1923, quoted in Karabel, *Chosen*, p. 112.
178. A. Lawrence Lowell, letter to Henry James, Nov. 3, 1925, quoted in Karabel, *Chosen*, p. 107.
179. Karabel, *Chosen*, p. 121.
180. For "intangible characteristics" in admissions criteria, see Karabel, *Chosen*, pp. 196, 199, 324–25, 484–85, 509–10.
181. Jeannie Suk Gersen, "The Uncomfortable Truth About Affirmative Action and Asian-Americans," *The New Yorker*, Aug. 10, 2017.
182. Drew Faust, letter to alumni and friends of Harvard University, Jun. 12, 2018.
183. Anemona Hartocollis, "Harvard Rated Asian-American Applicants Lower on Personality Traits, Lawsuit Says," *The New York Times*, Jun. 15, 2018.
184. "Character" entry, *Oxford English Dictionary*, 9a.
185. Anemona Hartocollis, "Harvard Does Not Discriminate Against Asian-Americans in Admissions, Judge Rules," *The New York Times*, Oct. 1, 2019.
186. Allison D. Burroughs, U.S. District Judge, United States District Court, District of Massachusetts, case 1:14-cv-14176-ADB, doc. 672, *Students for Fair Admissions, Inc. v. President and Fellows of Harvard College (Harvard Corporation)*, pp. 20–21.
187. Burroughs, *Students for Fair Admissions*, p. 25.
188. Ibid., pp. 63–64.

3. Claiming It

1. "Nationalism" entry, *Oxford English Dictionary*, 2.
2. For example, breitbart.com/clips/2018/08/19 and conservativeforce.com/2018/08.
3. "Warren Warns of Trump, Allies; Saying 'Fighting Back Matters,'" Associated Press, Jun. 16, 2017.
4. Paul Cartledge, introduction, Herodotus, *The Histories*, trans. Tom Holland, notes by Paul Cartledge (London: Penguin, 2013), p. xxi.

5. Benjamin Disraeli, *The Vindication of the English Constitution in a Letter to a Noble and Learned Lord* (London: Saunders and Otley, 1835), p. 16.
6. Max Weber, *The Protestant Ethic and the Spirit of Capitalism*, trans. Talcott Parsons (1904–5; New York: Scribner, 1958), p. 88.
7. Orrin G. Hatch, Republican of Utah, quoted in Michael D. Shear, Sheryl Gay Stolberg, and Thomas Kaplan, "G.O.P. Moves to End Trump's Family Separation Policy, but Can't Agree How," *The New York Times*, Jun. 19, 2018.
8. Quoted in ibid.
9. Frank Bruni, "Donald Trump's Small Hostages," *The New York Times*, Jun. 19, 2018.
10. Paul Krugman, "Fall of the American Empire," *The New York Times*, Jun. 18, 2018.
11. Andrew Roberts, "Brexit Will Be Good for the British National Character. It Will Introduce Risk-Taking and Self-Reliance," *The Times* (London), Jun. 19, 2016.
12. Quoted in Steven Erlanger, "European? British? These 'Brexit' Voters Identify as English," *The New York Times*, Jun. 17, 2016.
13. Clare Foges, quoted in ibid.
14. Fintan O'Toole, "Are the English Fit to Govern Themselves?," *The New York Times*, Jun. 16, 2017.
15. Adam Nossiter, "As France's Towns Wither, Fears of a Decline in 'Frenchness,'" *The New York Times*, Feb. 28, 2017. In French, this term is usually rendered as *francité* or *francitude*.
16. "France's Burkini Bigotry," editorial, *The New York Times*, Aug. 28, 2016.
17. "In Their Own Words: Marine Le Pen and Emmanuel Macron," *The New York Times*, May 5, 2017.
18. Quoted in ibid.
19. Frantz Fanon, *Black Skin, White Masks* (1952; New York: Grove Press, 2008), p. 18.
20. Romane Sarfati, quoted in Adam Nossiter, "Let Them Eat on Fancy Plates: Emmanuel Macron's New China," *The New York Times*, Jun. 14, 2018.
21. Josh Feldman, "Trump Rallygoer Who Assaulted Protester: Next Time We Might Have to Kill Him," *Inside Edition*, Mar. 10, 2016; Ashley Parker, "Black Protester Is Sucker-Punched by White Donald Trump Supporter at Rally," *The New York Times*, Mar. 10, 2016. The comments came in an interview with *Inside Edition* after the incident, when Mr. McGraw also said he liked "knocking the hell out of that big mouth."
22. Scott Conroy, "Donald Trump Says He Might Pay Legal Fees for Man Who Sucker-Punched a Protester," *Huffington Post*, Mar. 13, 2016.
23. Lindbergh, Sept. 11, 1941, Des Moines, Iowa, quoted in Wayne S. Cole, *America First: The Battle Against Intervention, 1940–41* (Madison: University of Wisconsin Press, 1953), p. 144.
24. Some of those interrogated "cooperated" with the committee, identifying (or confirming the names of) individuals who had once belonged to the Communist Party, or attended rallies, or otherwise could be thought of as "suspect." Those who "named names," like the film director Elia Kazan, the writer Budd Schulberg, and the choreographer and director Jerome Robbins, were "friendly witnesses," congratulated on their patriotism and rewarded by being permitted to continue their powerful careers. Others, who declined to do so, were blacklisted, including Lionel Stander, Abraham Polonsky, Judy Holliday, Zero Mostel, Ring Lardner, Jr., and the rest of the "Hollywood Ten."

25. Garry Wills, introduction, Lillian Hellman, *Scoundrel Time* (Boston: Little, Brown, 2000), pp. 18–19.
26. U.S. Congress, House Committee on Un-American Activities, "Investigation of the Unauthorized Use of U.S. Passports," 84th Cong., pt. 3, Jun. 12, 1956, quoted in *Thirty Years of Treason: Excerpts from Hearings Before the House Committee on Un-American Activities, 1938–1968*, ed. Eric Bentley (New York: Viking, 1971), p. 770.
27. Hellman, *Scoundrel Time*, pp. 93–94. See also Joseph Litvak, *The Un-Americans: Jews, the Blacklist, and Stoolpigeon Culture* (Durham, NC, and London: Duke University Press, 2009).
28. Ibid., pp. 96, 97.
29. *Congressional Record*, vol. 93, pt. 7 (Nov. 24, 1947), p. 10792.
30. Wills, introduction, *Scoundrel Time*, pp. 19–20.
31. Eric Hobsbawn, "Mass-Producing Traditions: Europe, 1870–1914," in Eric Hobsbawn and Terence Ranger, *The Invention of Tradition* (Cambridge, U.K.: Cambridge University Press, 1983; 24th printing, 2015), p. 280.
32. *Congressional Record*, Sept. 21, 1949, p. 13375.
33. Maarten Zwiers, entry for John Elliott Rankin, *The Mississippi Encyclopedia*, mississippiencyclopedia.org. Zwiers notes that "after calling radio commentator Walter Winchell a 'slime-mongering kike' during a congressional debate, Rankin was banned from the House floor for a day because of unparliamentary language."
34. *Congressional Record*, Apr. 23, 1953, p. 4320.
35. "Trump Accuses Democratic Congresswomen of Hating America, Says They Can Leave," *The New York Times*, Jul. 15, 2019; Michael Crowley, "At Rally, President Accuses Liberal Critics of Seeking the Nation's 'Destruction,'" *The New York Times*, Jul. 17, 2019.
36. Rep. Ilhan Omar (Democrat of Minnesota), tweet, quoted in "A Look at the 'Squad' Trump Targeted in Recent Tweets," *The New York Times*, Jul. 15, 2019.
37. Ted Lieu, "I Have Served in the Air Force and in Congress: People Still Tell Me to 'Go Back' to China," *The Washington Post*, Jul. 15, 2019.
38. Alexis de Tocqueville, *Democracy in America*, trans. Gerald Bevan (London: Penguin, 2003), pp. 525–26.
39. Ibid., p. 302.
40. Ibid., p. 301.
41. Albert Fried, *Communism in America: A History in Documents* (New York: Columbia University Press, 1997), pp. 7–8.
42. Donald Pease, "Exceptionalism," in *Keywords for American Cultural Studies*, ed. Bruce Burgett and Glenn Hendler, 2nd ed. (New York: New York University Press, 2014).
43. S. Mingulin, "The Crisis in the United States and the Problems of the Communist Party," *The Communist: A Magazine of the Theory and Practice of Marxism-Leninism*, Jun. 1930, pp. 500–18, quoted in Fried, *Communism in America*, p. 91.
44. Dick Cheney and Liz Cheney, *Exceptional: Why the World Needs a Powerful America* (New York: Simon and Schuster, 2015), p. 1.
45. Jonathan Martin and Ben Smith, "The New Battle: What It Means to Be American," *Politico*, Aug. 20, 2010.
46. Cheney and Cheney, *Exceptional*, p. 126.
47. William Shakespeare, *The Merchant of Venice*, 1.2.31–84 passim; 2.1.1–3; 2.7.79.
48. David Hume, "Of National Characters," in Hume, *Selected Essays*, ed. Stephen Copley and Andrew Edgar (Oxford, U.K.: Oxford World's Classics, 2008), p. 113.

49. Ibid.
50. Ibid., p. 115.
51. Ibid., p. 118.
52. Ibid.
53. Ibid., p. 119.
54. Peter Mandler, *The English National Character: The History of an Idea from Edmund Burke to Tony Blair* (New Haven, CT: Yale University Press, 2006), pp. 40–41.
55. John Stuart Mill, *A System of Logic, Ratiocinative and Inductive*, in Mill, *Collected Works*, vol. 8, ed. J. M. Robson (Indianapolis: Liberty Fund, 2006), p. 905.
56. Ralph Waldo Emerson, *English Traits* (1856; London: Tauris Parke, 2011), p. 76.
57. Ibid., p. 60.
58. Ibid., p. 62.
59. Ibid., p. 80.
60. Ibid., p. 77.
61. Ibid., p. 89.
62. Ibid., p. 83.
63. Ibid., p. 84.
64. My own experience of the Saturday Club, of which I was briefly a member, confirmed my sense that the art of table talk was indeed still alive and very well. If there was less talk of horses, diamonds, and pisciculture, there was, in compensation, a lively interchange about politics, literature, and art. I remember with particular fondness and admiration the participation of the club member affectionately called by the chairman "young Tony"—the eminent journalist Anthony Lewis, who must then have been in his sixties.
65. Oliver Wendell Holmes, "At the Saturday Club," 1884. *Complete Poetical Works of Oliver Wendell Holmes* (Boston: Houghton Mifflin, 1898).
66. Fanny Trollope, *Domestic Manners of the Americans*, ed. Pamela Neville-Sington (1832; London: Penguin, 1997), p. 168.
67. Ibid.
68. Ibid., p. 169.
69. Ibid., p. 20.
70. Ibid., p. 34.
71. Pamela Neville-Sington, introduction, ibid., p. xxxiii.
72. Marc Friedlander and L. H. Butterfield, eds., *Diary and Autobiography of John Quincy Adams* (Cambridge, MA: Harvard University Press, 1962), entry for May 8, 1832, vol. 4, p. 294, quoted in Richard Mullen, *Birds of Passage: Five Englishwomen in Search of America* (1994; London: Thistle, 2014), p. 263.
73. *Illinois Monthly Magazine*, 2 (1832), p. 505, quoted in Neville-Sington, introduction, Trollope, *Domestic Manners*, p. xxx.
74. *Edinburgh Review*, 55 (Jul. 1832), p. 481, quoted in Neville-Sington, introduction, Trollope, *Domestic Manners*, p. xxx.
75. Neville-Sington, introduction, Trollope, *Domestic Manners*, p. xxxvi.
76. In the introduction to *The Tocqueville Reader*, ed. Olivier Zunz and Alan S. Kahan (Oxford, U.K.: Blackwell, 2002), p. 30, the editors comment: "As the United States changed from a society committed to local forms of voluntary associations to one dominated by national organizations, *Democracy* [*in America*] lost much of its appeal. It was largely neglected by the reading public until American social scientists of the 1950s rediscovered the old idea of national character. They found inspiration in Tocqueville but appropriated his book for their own purposes, whether celebrating America as the only country born modern or exposing its mass society."

77. Vernon L. Parrington, introduction, *Main Currents in American Thought*, vol. 1 (New York: Harcourt Brace, 1927).
78. Isaac Kramnick, introduction, Alexis de Tocqueville, *Democracy in America and Two Essays on America*, trans. Gerald Bevan (London: Penguin, 2003), p. xliii.
79. Ibid., p. xlv.
80. Tocqueville, *Democracy in America*, p. 64.
81. Ibid., p. 532.
82. Kramnick, introduction, ibid., p. xxxiii.
83. Tocqueville, ibid., p. 302.
84. Ibid.
85. Ibid., p. 220.
86. Ibid., p. 277.
87. Ibid., p. 160.
88. Ibid., p. 571.
89. Ibid., p. 579.
90. Ibid., p. 550.
91. Ibid., p. 620.
92. Ibid., p. 722.
93. Ibid., p. 659.
94. Ibid., p. 658.
95. Tocqueville, "The Author's Note to the Second Volume," ibid., p. 489.
96. Tocqueville, letter to Ernest de Chabrol, Jun. 9, 1831, in *Tocqueville Reader*, ed. Zunz and Kahan, pp. 40–41.
97. Virginia Woolf, "Portraits of Places," *The Guardian*, Oct. 3, 1906. Reprinted in *The Essays of Virginia Woolf*, ed. Andrew McNeillie (New York: Harvest, 1986), 1:16–127. Several of the essays in *English Hours* (London: Heinemann, 1905) had been previously printed in *James's Portraits of Places* (London: Macmillan, 1883).
98. Pont was the cartoon signature of Graham Laidler (1908–1940). His pseudonym derived from Pontifex Maximus, a childhood nickname given to him after a visit to Rome.
99. Richard Hofstadter, "Prefatory Note" to *Anti-Intellectualism in American Life* (New York: Vintage, 1963), p. vii.
100. Richard Hofstadter, *The Paranoid Style in American Politics* (1965; New York: Vintage, 2008), p. 3.
101. John Randolph, *Texas Brags* (Houston, TX: Anson Jones, 1945), p. 36.
102. Ibid., p. 62.
103. Arthur Koestler, obituary notice for George Orwell (Eric Blair), *Observer*, Jan. 29, 1950, quoted in Bernard Crick, introduction, Orwell, *The Lion and the Unicorn: Socialism and the English Genius* (Harmondsworth, U.K.: Penguin, 1982), p. 7. Orwell's book was originally published in 1941 in the Searchlight Books series by Secker & Warburg, 1941.
104. Orwell, *Lion and Unicorn*, pp. 36–37.
105. Ibid., p. 38.
106. Ibid., p. 39.
107. Ibid., p. 38.
108. Ibid., p. 39.
109. Ibid., p. 36.
110. T. S. Eliot, *Notes Towards the Definition of Culture* (London: Faber and Faber, 1948), p. 31.

111. Kate Fox, *Watching the English: The Hidden Rules of English Behaviour* (2004; 2nd ed., London: Hodder and Stoughton, 2014), pp. 30–31.
112. Ruth Benedict, *Patterns of Culture* (1934; Boston: Houghton Mifflin, 1989), p. 46.
113. Margaret Mead, preface, ibid., p. xi.
114. Jean Stoetzel's *Without the Chrysanthemum and the Sword* (London: Heinemann, 1955), for example, claimed that postwar Japanese youth no longer held the views described in Benedict's book.
115. Mead, preface, Benedict, *Patterns of Culture*, p. xiv.
116. William O. Beeman, series preface, *The Study of Culture at a Distance, Volume I: The Study of Contemporary Western Cultures*, ed. Margaret Mead and Rhoda Métraux (1953; New York: Berghahn Books, 2000), p. xii.
117. Margaret Mead, *And Keep Your Powder Dry: An Anthropologist Looks at America*, expanded ed. (New York: William Morrow, 1971), p. 207.
118. Ibid., p. 24.
119. Geoffrey Gorer, "National Character: Theory and Practice," in *Study of Culture at a Distance*, ed. Mead and Métraux, p. 61.
120. Mead, *And Keep Your Powder Dry*, p. 17.
121. Ibid., p. 25.
122. Mead, "Preface from England—1943," in ibid., pp. xx–xxi.
123. Stoetzel, *Without the Chrysanthemum and the Sword*, p. 16.
124. Ian Buruma, foreword, Ruth Benedict, *The Chrysanthemum and the Sword* (1946; New York: Houghton Mifflin Harcourt, 2005), p. ix.
125. Beeman, series preface, *Study of Culture at a Distance*, ed. Mead and Métraux, pp. xvii–xxxi.
126. Alex Inkeles and D. J. Levinson, "National Character: The Study of Modal Personality and Sociocultural Systems," in *Handbook of Social Psychology*, vol. II, ed. G. Lindzey (Cambridge, MA: Addison Wesley, 1954), quoted in Inkeles, "National Character and Modern Political Systems," in *Psychological Anthropology: Approaches to Culture and Personality*, ed. Francis L. K. Hsu (Homewood, IL: Dorsey Press, 1961), p. 173.
127. Alex Inkeles, *National Character: A Psycho-Social Perspective* (New Brunswick, NJ: Transaction Publishers, 1997), p. 11.
128. Ibid.
129. Inkeles, "National Character and Modern Political Systems," p. 173.
130. Daniel Bell, blurb for Inkeles, *National Character*.
131. Inkeles, *National Character*, pp. 374–75.
132. Ibid., p. 376. The study he cites is Stephen Harding and David Philips, with Michael Fogarty, *Contrasting Values in Western Europe: Unity, Diversity and Change* (Basingstoke, U.K.: Macmillan, 1986).
133. Inkeles, *National Character*, pp. 378–79.
134. Ibid., pp. 379–80.
135. Seymour Martin Lipset, *American Exceptionalism: A Double-Edged Sword* (New York: Norton, 1996), p. 19.
136. G. K. Chesterton, *What I Saw in America* (London: Hodder and Stoughton, 1922), p. 7.
137. John McCain, "Why We Must Support Human Rights," *The New York Times*, May 8, 2017.
138. Swaha Pattanaik, "French Savers Are Likely to Reject Le Pen's Anti-Euro Message," *The New York Times*, May 3, 2017.
139. Ben Hubbard and Thomas Erdbrink, "In Saudi Arabia, Trump Reaches Out to Sunni Nations, at Iran's Expense," *The New York Times*, May 22, 2017.

140. Jochen Bittner, "Can the European Center Hold?," *The New York Times*, Mar. 24, 2016.
141. Herbert J. Gans, "Best Sellers by American Sociologists: An Exploratory Study," in *Required Reading: Sociology's Most Influential Books*, ed. Dan Clawson (Amherst: University of Massachusetts Press, 1998), pp. 19–27.
142. David Riesman, *The Lonely Crowd: A Study of the Changing American Character* (1961; New Haven, CT: Yale University Press, 2001), p. 4.
143. These powerful terms recur throughout *The Lonely Crowd*. Initial definitions, descriptions, and comparisons among them can be found in the first chapter, "Some Types of Character and Society," especially pp. 8–25.
144. Ibid., p. 165.
145. Ibid., p. 172.
146. John Maynard Keynes, *The Economic Consequences of the Peace* (1919; New York: Skyhorse Publishing, 2007), p. 29.
147. Sigmund Freud, "Group Psychology and the Analysis of the Ego," in *The Standard Edition of the Complete Psychological Works of Sigmund Freud*, trans. James Strachey et al. (London: Hogarth Press and Institute of Psychoanalysis, 1955; Vintage, 2001) [hereafter *SE*], vol. 18, p. 101.
148. Sigmund Freud, "Civilization and Its Discontents," in *SE*, vol. 21, p. 114.
149. Freud, "Moses and Monotheism" (1939), in *SE*, vol. 23, pp. 90–91.
150. Emerson, "Race," in *English Traits*, p. 26.
151. Emerson, "Religion," in *English Traits*, p. 166.
152. Ibid., p. 167.
153. G. K. Chesterton, "At the Sign of the World's End: The Jew and the Journalist," *New Witness*, Oct. 11, 1917, p. 562, quoted in Simon Mayers, *Chesterton's Jews* (self-pub., 2013), pp. 41–42.
154. G. K. Chesterton, *The New Jerusalem* (London: Hodder and Stoughton, 1920), p. 235.
155. Senator Gerald P. Nye, U.S. Congress, Senate, Interstate Commerce Committee, "Hearings on Moving-Picture and Radio Propaganda," Sept. 9, 1941, pp. 10–11, quoted in Neil Gabler, *An Empire of Their Own: How the Jews Invented Hollywood* (New York: Anchor, 1989), pp. 345–46. In response to his friend Nancy Mitford's book on the language and manners of the English aristocracy, *Noblesse Oblige*, published in 1956, Evelyn Waugh wrote an "open letter" of emphatic agreement, inviting her, by contrast, to "consider the cinema trade, the immigrant producers from God knows where who perhaps have never set foot on a private house in the kingdom. Their solecisms glare at us in blazing colour and shriek at us from amplifiers." ("An Open Letter to the Hon. Mrs. Peter Rodd (Nancy Mitford) on a Very Serious Subject," in *Noblesse Oblige: An Inquiry into the Identifiable Characteristics of the English Aristocracy*, ed. Nancy Mitford [1956; Harmondsworth, U.K.: Penguin, 1959], p. 61.)
156. Emily Apter, *Continental Drift: From National Characters to Virtual Subjects* (Chicago: University of Chicago Press, 1999), p. 18.
157. Gail Collins, "Wishing for a Tank-Free Fourth," *The New York Times*, Jul. 3, 2019.
158. Bruce Burgett and Glenn Hendler, eds., *Keywords for American Cultural Studies*, 2nd ed. (New York: New York University Press, 2014).
159. Will Wilkinson, "Conservatives Are Hiding Their 'Loathing' Behind Our Flag," *The New York Times*, Aug. 2, 2019.

4. Reading It

1. Donald Trump, news conference, Sept. 27, 2018. On Pillsbury's interview with Carlson, see, for example, Henry Knight, "Trump Brags About China's 'Total Respect' for His 'Very, Very Large Brain,'" shanghai.ist/2018/09/27/trump-brags-about-chinas-total-respect-for-his-very-very-large-brain, which includes a tweet from Pillsbury, saying that the Chinese think Trump is "brilliant," but denying that they said he has a "large brain."
2. Paul Broca, "Sur le volume et la forme du cerveau suivant less individus et suivant les races," *Bulletin Société d'Anthropologie Paris* 2 (1861), p. 139, quoted in Stephen Jay Gould, *The Mismeasure of Man*, rev. ed. (New York: W. W. Norton, 1996), p. 115.
3. Gould, *Mismeasure of Man*, p. 114.
4. R. C. Lewontin, Steven Rose, and Leon J. Kamin, *Not in Our Genes: Biology, Ideology, and Human Nature* (1984; 2nd ed., Chicago: Haymarket, 2017), p. 53.
5. Jeremy DeSilva, "Don't Brag About Your Large Brain, Pres. Trump," *Salon*, Oct. 7, 2018. Originally published at scientificamerican.com, Oct. 2, 2018.
6. Howard Gardner, *Frames of Mind: The Theory of Multiple Intelligences* (1983; New York: Basic Books, 2011), p. 14.
7. Gould, *Mismeasure of Man*, p. 22.
8. "To be phrenologized was a perfectly routine, even fashionable thing to do," noted the historian John Davies, in *Phrenology: Fad and Science* (New Haven, CT: Yale University Press, 1955), p. 37.
9. Charles E. Rosenberg, "The Bitter Fruit: Heredity, Disease, and Social Thought" (1974), reprinted in *No Other Gods: On Science and American Social Thought* (Baltimore: Johns Hopkins University Press, 1976, 1997), p. 41.
10. Colin Ford, *Julia Margaret Cameron: A Critical Biography* (London: National Portrait Gallery, 2003), p. 47. The "inventor of phrenology" here is Johann Caspar Lavater. Ford also cites the Lewis Carroll example, from Derek Hudson's biography of Carroll (1954; London: Constable, 1995), pp. 68–69.
11. Alexander Bain, *On the Study of Character, Including an Estimate of Phrenology* (London: Parker, Son, and Bourn, 1861), pp. b, 24, 29.
12. Alfred Russel Wallace, *The Wonderful Century* (New York: Dodd, Mead, 1899), p. 193.
13. R. R. Noel, "Reliques and Anecdotes of Dr. Gall," *Phrenological Journal, and Magazine of Moral Science*, 17 (1844), p. 155.
14. Nahum Capen, "Biography," in J. G. Spurzheim, *Phrenology, in Connexion with the Study of Physiognomy* (Boston: Marsh, Capen & Lyon, 1833), p. 108.
15. Pierpont, who also wrote a celebrated hymn, "The Pilgrim Fathers," later wrote the book *Phrenology and the Scriptures* (1850); his son James Lord Pierpont was the composer of "Jingle Bells."
16. Nahum Capen, *Reminiscences of Dr. Spurzheim and George Combe: And a Review of the Science of Phrenology, from the Period of Its Discovery by Dr. Gall, to the Time of the Visit of George Combe to the United States, 1838, 1840* (New York: Fowler & Wells; Boston: A. Williams & Co., 1881), p. 9.
17. *Edinburgh Review*, 25 (1815), pp. 250, 268.
18. George Combe, letter to J. G. Spurzheim, May 8, 1924, quoted in David Stack, *Queen Victoria's Skull: George Combe and the Mid-Victorian Mind* (London: Hambleton Continuum, 2008), p. 48.
19. Rosenberg, "Bitter Fruit," p. 255.

20. *Albany Evening Journal*, Jan. 14, 1840, quoted in Stack, *Queen Victoria's Skull*, p. 125.
21. Horace Mann, in *American Phrenological Journal and Miscellany*, 1848.
22. Julia Ward Howe, *Reminiscences, 1819–1899* (1899; New York: Negro Universities Press, 1969), p. 131.
23. Ibid., pp. 132–33.
24. George Combe, *A System of Phrenology* (Boston: Marsh, Capen, and Lyon, 1834), p. 264.
25. Quoted in *American Phrenological Journal*, 15 (1852), p. 42, quoted in Davies, *Phrenology*, p. 50.
26. Charlotte Brontë, *Jane Eyre* (1847; Ware, U.K.: Wordsworth Classics, 1999), p. 39.
27. Ibid., p. 115.
28. Ibid., p. 167.
29. "A Phrenological Estimate of the Talents and Dispositions of a Lady," in *The Letters of Charlotte Brontë, with a Selection of Letters by Family and Friends*, ed. Margaret Smith (Oxford, U.K.: Oxford University Press, 1995–2004), vol. 2, pp. 657–58.
30. Claire Harman, *Charlotte Brontë: A Life* (London: Penguin, 2015), pp. 308–9.
31. Charles Bray, *Phases of Opinion and Experience During a Long Life: An Autobiography* (London: Longmans, Green, 1885), p. 74.
32. Ibid.
33. Ibid., p. 75.
34. George Combe, *Journal*, Aug. 29–30, 1851, in Gordon S. Haight, *George Eliot: A Biography* (1968; London: Penguin, 1992), p. 101.
35. On Combe's response to Eliot's elopement, see Stack, *Queen Victoria's Skull*, pp. 208–11. See also G. H. Lewes, *The History of Philosophy: From Thales to Comte*, 2 vols. (London: Longmans, Green, 1867), vol. 2, pp. 435, 428–29 n.
36. Maurice L. Johnson, "George Eliot and George Combe," *Westminster Review*, 166 (1906), p. 568.
37. George Eliot, *Felix Holt: The Radical* (1866; London: Penguin, 1995), p. 67.
38. "I have found Veneration large in the head of the genuine Tory,—in him who really delights in contemplating kings and nobles, and regards them as invested with a degree of sanctity by a long line of descent, and the possession of hereditary authority," wrote Combe. "In the genuine Whig or republican, who see in kings and nobles only men liable to all the frailties of human nature, and requiring checks to prevent them from abusing power, Veneration is generally smaller." (Combe, *System of Phrenology*, pp. 264, 266.)
39. Lewes, *History of Philosophy*, vol. 2, p. 435.
40. Bray, *Phases of Opinion*, p. 22.
41. Ibid., p. 27.
42. Ibid., p. 28.
43. Ibid., p. 80.
44. Ibid., p. 24.
45. Ibid., p. 23.
46. George Combe, letter to Andrew Combe, Jul. 28, 1839, quoted in Stack, *Queen Victoria's Skull*, p. 134.
47. George Combe, letter to Andrew Combe, Oct. 5, 1839, quoted in Stack, *Queen Victoria's Skull*, p. 135.

48. George Combe, *Notes on the United States of North America, During a Phrenological Visit in 1838–1839* (Philadelphia: Carey & Hart, 1841), vol. 1, p. 126.
49. *United States Gazette* (Philadelphia), Feb. 5, 1839, quoted in Stack, *Queen Victoria's Skull*, p. 135.
50. *The Albion*, Dec. 1, 1938, quoted in Stack, *Queen Victoria's Skull*, p. 135.
51. New York *Evening Post*, Nov. 20, 1838, quoted in Stack, *Queen Victoria's Skull*, p. 135.
52. A. D. Spiegel, "The Role of Gender, Phenomenology, Discrimination and Nervous Prostration in Clara Barton's Career," *Journal of Community Health* 20, no. 6 (Dec. 1995), pp. 501–26; James Grant, *Bernard Baruch: The Adventures of a Wall Street Legend* (Mount Jackson, VA: Axios Press, 2012), p. 21; Davies, *Phrenology*, p. 38.
53. Davies, *Phrenology*, p. 47.
54. Quoted in ibid., p. 48.
55. Ross Lockridge, Jr., *Raintree County* (1948; Chicago: Chicago Review Press, 2007), p. 75.
56. Ibid., p. 77.
57. Ibid., p. 78.
58. Ibid., pp. 80–81.
59. Ibid., p. 80.
60. O. S. and L. N. Fowler, *The Illustrated Self-Instructor in Phrenology and Physiology* (New York: Fowler & Wells, 1851), pp. vii, 23ff, 57, 62. Section 1 is titled "Physiological Conditions as Affecting and Indicating Character"; Section 2, "Structure Corresponds with Character"; Section 3, "Shape Corresponds with Character"; Section 4, "Resemblance Between Human and Animal Physiognomy and Character"; and so on.
61. Ibid., p. 57.
62. Ibid., p. 62.
63. In *In Re Walt Whitman*, ed. Horace L. Traubel, Richard M. Bucke, and Thomas B. Harned (Philadelphia, 1893), p. 25 n.
64. Samuel R. Wells, *How to Read Character: A New Illustrated Hand-Book of Phrenology and Physiognomy for Students and Examiners* (New York: Fowler & Wells, 1868), p. 47.
65. Ibid., pp. 166–67.
66. Ibid., pp. 168, 169, 166.
67. Nahum Capen, biography of J. G. Spurzheim, in Spurzheim and Capen, *Phrenology in Connection with the Study of Physiognomy: To Which Is Prefixed a Biography of the Author* (Boston: Marsh, Capen, and Lyon, 1833), p. 77.
68. Ibid., pp. 74–75.
69. 6: *List, Schlauheit, Klugheit*, cunning; 7: *Eigenthhümsinn*, the sentiment of property; 8: *Stolz, Hochmuth, Herschsucht*, pride, self-esteem, haughtiness; 9: *Eitelkeit, Rhumsucht, Ehrgeitz*, vanity, ambition; 10: *Behuthsomkeit, Vorsicht, Vorsichtigkeit*, cautiousness, foresight, prudence; 11: *Sachgedächtniss, Erzichungs-fahigkest*, the memory of things, educability; 12: *Ortsum, Roumsinn*, local memory; 13: *Personnsinn*, memory of persons; 14: *Wortegedächniss*, verbal memory; 15: *Sprachforschungssinn*, memory for languages; 16: *Farbesinn*, colors; 17: *Tonsinn*, music; 18: *Zahlensinn*, number; 19: *Kunstsinn*, aptitude for the mechanical arts; 20: *Vergleichender, Scharfsinn*, comparative sagacity, aptitude for drawing comparisons; 21: *Metaphysischer Tiefsinn*, metaphysical depth of thought, aptitude for drawing conclusions; 22: *Witz*, wit; 23: *Dichtergeist*, poetry; 24: *Gemütlichkeit, Mitleiden*, good-nature; 25: *Darstellungsinn*, mimicry; 26: *Theosophie*, religion; 27: *Festigkeit*, firmness of character.

70. Wells, *How to Read Character*, pp. 55–56.
71. Sari Pekkala Kerr, William R. Kerr, and Tina Xu, "Personality Traits of Entrepreneurs: A Review of Recent Literature," working paper 18-047, Harvard Business School, 2017, p. 8. The Five-Factor model (also called the Big Five) is discussed in chapter 5, pp. 325ff.
72. Richard Dawkins, *The Selfish Gene* (New York: Oxford University Press, 1976).
73. E. O. Wilson, *Sociobiology: The New Synthesis* (1975; Cambridge, MA: Harvard University Press, 2000), p. 3.
74. Wells, *How to Read Character*, p. 64.
75. Ibid., p. 68.
76. Ibid., pp. 85–86.
77. Capen, *Reminiscences of Dr. Spurzheim and George Combe*, p. 157, quoted in Davies, *Phrenology*, p. 163.
78. Wells, *How to Read Character*, p. 97.
79. Ibid., p. 87.
80. L. Hamilton McCormick, *Characterology: An Exact Science, Embracing Physiognomy, Phrenology, and Pathognomy* (Chicago: Rand McNally, 1920), p. 523.
81. Edgar Allan Poe, in *Southern Literary Messenger*, 2 (1835–36), p. 286.
82. Edgar Allan Poe, "The Imp of the Perverse," in *The Collected Tales and Poems of Edgar Allan Poe* (London: Wordsworth, 2009), pp. 340–42.
83. Herman Melville, *Moby-Dick, or The Whale* (1851; London: Wordsworth Classics, 2002), chap. 80, "The Nut," pp. 289–90.
84. E. T. Craig, *Shakespeare's Portraits Phrenologically Considered* (1864; Philadelphia: printed for private circulation by J. Parker Norris, 1875), pp. 1–3, 6.
85. Stack, *Queen Victoria's Skull*, pp. 102–3. See all of his interesting chapter, "What the Actress Said to the Phrenologist," pp. 97–110.
86. Combe, *System of Phrenology*, p. 333.
87. Ibid., p. 334.
88. Ibid., p. 335.
89. *Phrenological Journal and Miscellany*, 1 (1823–24), p. 93.
90. "Shakespeare's Othello," *Phrenological Journal and Miscellany*, 1 (1823–24), pp. 514–15.
91. "Application of Phrenology to Criticism—Character of Macbeth," *Phrenological Journal and Miscellany*, 1 (1823–24), p. 96.
92. Ibid., p. 97.
93. Ibid., p. 94. See Henry Home, Lord Kames, *Elements of Criticism* (Edinburgh, U.K., 1762), vol. 2, p. 159, "the more natural language of Shakespeare."
94. "Shakespeare's Character of Iago," *Phrenological Journal and Miscellany*, 1 (1823–24), pp. 287–92.
95. McCormick, *Characterology*, p. 196.
96. Ibid., p. 249.
97. Ibid., p. 215; the analysis of "full lips" goes on for a further page.
98. David Buss, *The Evolution of Desire: Strategies of Human Mating* (New York: Basic Books, 1995).
99. McCormick, *Characterology*, pp. 43–46.
100. Ibid., p. 525.
101. Drs. Gall, Vimont, and Broussais, *On the Functions of the Cerebellum*, trans. George Combe (Edinburgh, U.K.: MacLachlan and Stewart, 1838), pp. 12–13; Combe, *System of Phrenology*, pp. 109–10.

102. McCormick, *Characterology*, p. 545.
103. Ibid.
104. Gordon Allport, *Personality: A Psychological Interpretation* (London: Constable, 1937), p. 52 n.
105. Ibid., p. 55.
106. Ibid., p. 52.
107. W. R. Henderson, "Henderson Bequest," reprinted in George Combe, *The Constitution of Man Considered in Relation to External Objects*, 6th ed. (Edinburgh, U.K.: John Anderson, Jr., 1836), n.p. Henderson instructed his trustees to "print and publish one or more editions of an 'Essay on the Constitution of Man Considered in Relation to External Objects,' by George Combe,—in a cheap form, so as to be easily purchased by the more intelligent individuals of the poorer classes, and of Mechanics' Institutions, &c."
108. Preface, George Combe, *The Constitution of Man in Relation to the Natural Laws* (London, Paris & Melbourne: Cassell, 1893), n.p.
109. Combe, *Constitution*, 6th ed., p. 341.
110. Preface, ibid., p. xi.
111. Kim Severson, "Tom Colicchio Changes His Restaurant's Racially Tinged Name," *The New York Times*, Aug. 22, 2017. Fowler's racial comments were both offensive and (needless to say) "unscientific." Many were based on previous racial assumptions for which phrenology was supposedly a "proof" ("Their large religious organs would produce those strong religious emotions and that disposition to worship, for which they are distinguished . . . Their large marvelousness accounts for their belief in ghosts and supernatural events so often manifested among them"). Others seem to have represented an attempt, however condescendingly such comments read today, to assess other qualities: "Their very large language, combined with their large perceptive organs generally, would create in them a desire to learn, and enable them to succeed in many things." Orson Squire Fowler, Samuel Kirkham, and Lorenzo Niles Fowler, *Phrenology Proved, Illustrated, and Applied* (New York: Fowler & Brevcort, 1836; 3rd ed. 1838), p. 32.
112. Preface, ibid., p. iii.
113. Gardner, *Frames of Mind*, p. 14.
114. Gould, *Mismeasure of Man*, p. 22.
115. R. A. Poldrack, "Mapping Mental Function to Brain Structure: How Can Cognitive Neuroimaging Succeed?," *Perspectives on Psychological Science* 5, no. 6 (2010), p. 753, quoted in Michael L. Anderson, *After Phrenology: Neural Reuse and the Interactive Brain* (Cambridge, MA: MIT Press, 2014), p. 130.
116. Anderson, *After Phrenology*, p. 131. Adapted from Poldrack, "Mapping Mental Function to Brain Structure," *Perspectives on Psychological Science*, pp. 753–61.
117. William R. Uttal, *The New Phrenology: The Limits of Localizing Cognitive Processes in the Brain* (Cambridge, MA: MIT Press, 2001).
118. Harriet Dempsey-Jones, "Neuroscientists Put the Dubious Theory of 'Phrenology' Through Rigorous Testing for the First Time," *The Conversation*, Jan. 22, 2018.
119. William James, *The Principles of Psychology* (London: Macmillan, 1890), vol. 1, p. 28.

5. Naming It

1. Jim Cullen, *The American Dream* (Oxford, U.K.: Oxford University Press, 2004), p. 177. "The American Dreams of Benjamin Franklin, Abraham Lincoln, and Andrew Carnegie rested on a sense of *character*; those of Douglas Fairbanks and Mary Pickford rested on *personality*. They were celebrities, people whose fame rested not on talent but on simply being famous."
2. A. A. Roback, *The Psychology of Character* (London: Kegan, Paul, Trench, Trubner, 1928), p. 6.
3. Ibid., pp. 159–60.
4. Morton Prince, *The Unconscious* (New York: Arno Press, 1973), p. 532.
5. Ian A. M. Nicholson, *Inventing Personality: Gordon Allport and the Science of Selfhood* (Washington, D.C.: American Psychological Association, 2003), p. 140.
6. Roback, *Psychology of Character*, p. ix.
7. Nicholson, *Inventing Personality*, p. 141. Nicholson cites as his source an unpublished 1991 doctoral dissertation by J. Parker, "In Search of the Person: The Historical Development of American Personality Psychology," York University, Toronto, Ontario.
8. William McDougall, *An Outline of Abnormal Psychology* (London: Methuen, 1926), p. 22.
9. Sigmund Freud, "Some Character-Types Met with in Psycho-Analytic Work" (1916), in *SE*, vol. 14, p. 315.
10. On *hamartia* in Aristotle, see Stephen Halliwell, *Aristotle's Poetics* (1986; Chicago: University of Chicago Press, 1998), pp. 213–30. Halliwell, discussing the difficulties of translating this crucial term, gives the equivalent as "tragic error, fallibility," in his index.
11. Sigmund Freud, "Explanations, Applications and Orientations," in "New Introductory Lectures on Psycho-Analysis" (1933), in *SE*, vol. 22, pp. 155–56.
12. Sigmund Freud, "Three Essays on the Theory of Sexuality" (1905), in *SE*, vol. 7, pp. 238–39.
13. Sigmund Freud, "Psychopathic Characters on the Stage" (1905/1906), in *SE*, vol. 7, p. 307.
14. Ibid., p. 306.
15. Ibid., p. 308.
16. Ibid., p. 309.
17. Ibid.
18. Ibid.
19. Ibid., p. 305 and n. 2.
20. Sigmund Freud, "Character and Anal Erotism" (1908), in *SE*, vol. 9, p. 175.
21. Sigmund Freud, "Moses and Monotheism," in *SE*, vol. 23, p. 75.
22. Sigmund Freud, "The Interpretation of Dreams" (1900), in *SE*, vol. 5, pp. 539–40.
23. Freud, "Moses and Monotheism," pp. 75–76.
24. Freud, "Character and Anal Erotism," pp. 169.
25. James Strachey, note, in ibid., p. 168.
26. Sigmund Freud, "On Transformations of Instinct as Exemplified in Anal Erotism" (1917), in *SE*, vol. 17, p. 127.
27. Quoted in Benedict Carey, "The Psychiatric Question: Is It Fair to Analyze Donald Trump from Afar?," *The New York Times*, Aug. 15, 2016.
28. Katherine Rosman, "The Property Brothers Are Fixing to Take Over the World," *The New York Times*, May 10, 2017.

29. Sigmund Freud, "The Dissection of the Psychical Personality," in "New Introductory Lectures on Psycho-Analysis," chap. 3, in *SE*, vol. 22, pp. 57–80. As James Strachey points out in an editorial note, most of the material in this lecture is derived from chaps. 1, 2, 3, and 5 of *The Ego and the Id* (1923).
30. Ibid., p. 73.
31. Ibid., p. 79.
32. Ibid., pp. 77–78.
33. Ibid., p. 64.
34. Sigmund Freud, "Notes Upon a Case of Obsessional Neurosis" (1908), in *SE*, vol. 10, p. 249.
35. Freud, "Interpretation of Dreams," (1900), p. 91.
36. Furneaux Jordan, *Character as Seen in Body and Parentage: With Notes on Education, Marriage, Change in Character and Morals* (London: Kegan, Paul, Trench, Trubner, 1896).
37. Ibid., p. 33. Jordan: "William Shakspere, who was not of extremely impassioned temperament, valued the success of the Globe Theatre more highly than the fame of being known as the author of Hamlet—a production which he never expected to be printed. The deeply impassioned Lloyd Garrison gladly hid himself from the public gaze after the downfall of slavery."
38. C. G. Jung, *Psychological Types*, trans. H. G. Baynes, rev. R.F.C. Hull (originally published in German, 1921; 1st English trans., 1923; Princeton, NJ: Princeton University Press, 1971; 9th printing, 1990), p. 159.
39. Ibid., pp. 464–65.
40. Ibid., p. 465.
41. Ibid., p. 467.
42. Wilhelm Reich, *Character Analysis*, trans. Vincent R. Carafagno (German ed., 1933; Eng. trans., New York: Farrar, Straus and Giroux, 1945; 3rd ed., 1990), p. 48. The German word translated as "character armor" is *Charakterpanzerung*, "the armor-plating of character."
43. Ibid., p. 52.
44. Anna Freud, *The Ego and the Mechanisms of Defence*, trans. Cecil Baines (German ed., 1936; Eng. trans., 1937; London: Karnac, 1993), p. 33.
45. Ibid., pp. 21–22.
46. A. A. Roback, *A Bibliography of Character and Personality* (Cambridge, MA: Sci-Art Publishers, 1927), p. 8.
47. Ibid., pp. 8–9.
48. Allport, *Personality*, p. 52.
49. Ibid., p. 48.
50. Ibid., p. 181 n.
51. Gordon Allport, *Pattern and Growth in Personality* (1961; London: Holt, Rinehart and Winston, 1963), p. 145.
52. Ibid., p. 163.
53. Ibid., p. 155.
54. Ibid., p. 30.
55. "Personality" (noun) entry, *Oxford English Dictionary*, I.4b.
56. William Dean Howells, *Literature and Life: Studies* (New York and London: Harper, 1902), p. 249.
57. Allport, *Pattern and Growth*, p. 28.
58. Ibid., p. 29.
59. Ibid., p. 32.
60. Ibid., p. 35.

61. Virginia Woolf, *Night and Day and Jacob's Room* (London: Wordsworth Editions, 2012), p. 56. *Night and Day* was originally published in 1919.
62. Sigmund Freud, "Libidinal Types" (1931), trans. Joan Riviere, in *SE*, vol. 21, p. 218.
63. womenrockproject.com/arianna-huffington-author-columnist-tv-personality-2.
64. Michael M. Grynbaum, "Ego Clashes Exposed in Leaked Emails from Democratic National Committee," *The New York Times*, Jul. 24, 2016.
65. Paul Krugman, "Lies, Lying Liars, and Donald Trump," *The New York Times*, Aug. 16, 2016.
66. Initially performed by the screen actress Dorothy Lamour in *Road to Utopia*, the song became a hit for Bing Crosby and then for Johnny Mercer.
67. On the history of FFM, see J. M. Digman, "Personality Structure: Emergence of the Five-Factor Model," *Annual Review of Psychology*, 41 (1990), pp. 417–40.
68. Lewis R. Goldberg, "The Structure of Phenotypic Personality Traits," *American Psychologist*, Jan. 1993, pp. 26–34.
69. Robert R. McCrae, James F. Gaines, and Marie A. Wellington, "The Five-Factor Model in Fact and Fiction," in *Handbook of Psychology, Personality and Social Psychology*, 2nd ed., vol. 5, ed. Irving B. Weiner, Howard A. Tennen, and Jerry M. Suls (Hoboken, NJ: Wiley, 2012), p. 68; Gordon Allport and Henry S. Odbert, *Trait-Names: A Psycho-Lexical Study* (Princeton, NJ: Psychological Review Company, 1936).
70. McCrae et al., "Five-Factor Model," pp. 65–91.
71. Ibid., p. 65.
72. Ibid., p. 74.
73. Ibid., p. 78.
74. Ibid., p. 82.
75. Freud, "Some Character-Types," pp. 324–41; Freud, "Psychopathic Characters on the Stage," p. 308; Marie Bonaparte, *The Life and Works of Edgar Allan Poe: A Psycho-Analytic Interpretation* (1933; English ed., 1949).
76. McCrae et al., "Five-Factor Model," p. 87.
77. Ibid., onlinelibrary.wiley.com/doi/10.1002/9781118133880.hop205004/full.
78. Goldberg, "Structure of Phenotypic Personality Traits," p. 27.
79. Sigmund Freud, "General Theory of the Neuroses," in "Introductory Lectures on Pyschoanalysis" (1917), in *SE*, vol. 16, p. 260.
80. *Desk Reference to the Diagnostic Criteria from DSM-5* (Arlington, VA: American Psychiatric Association, 2013), p. 321ff.
81. Freud, "New Introductory Lectures on Psychoanalysis," p. 156.
82. Otto F. Kernberg, *Severe Personality Disorders* (New Haven, CT: Yale University Press, 1984), p. 77.
83. Ibid.
84. Ibid.
85. "A high-level or neurotic type of character pathology including, predominantly, the hysterical, obsessive-compulsive, and depressive-masochistic personalities; an intermediate level of character pathology that includes the better functioning narcissistic personalities, some infantile personalities, and passive-aggressive personalities; and a 'lower-level' or 'borderline personality organization' that includes most cases of infantile and narcissistic personalities and practically all schizoid, paranoid, and hypomanic personalities, in addition to the 'as if' and all antisocial personalities." (Ibid., p. 93.) See also Otto F. Kernberg, *Object Relations Theory and Clinical Pyschoanalysis* (New York: Jason Aronson, 1976).

86. Quoted in Liam Stack, "Trump, Mika Brzezinski and Joe Scarborough: A Roller-Coaster Relationship," *The New York Times*, Jun. 29, 2017.
87. Peter Wehner, "Declaration of Disruption," *The New York Times*, Jul. 4, 2017.
88. "An Eminent Psychiatrist Demurs on Trump's Mental State," *The New York Times*, Feb. 14, 2017.
89. Bandy X. Lee, ed., *The Dangerous Case of Donald Trump: 27 Psychiatrists and Mental Health Experts Assess a President* (New York: Thomas Dunne Books, 2017). Bandy Lee, "Trump Is Now Dangerous—That Makes His Mental Health a Matter of Public Interest," *The Guardian*, Jan. 6, 2018.
90. Roger Cohen, "Trump 2020 Is No Joke," *The New York Times*, Jun. 23, 2017. See also Carey, "The Psychiatric Question."
91. Michael Schulman, "Fund Chief Capitalizes on China's 'Split Personality' Economy," *The New York Times*, Nov. 13, 2016.
92. Mona Charen, "Donald Trump Doesn't Have the Character to Be President," *National Review*, Mar. 21, 2016; Rick Ungar, "Donald Trump and the Decline of American Character—A Cautionary Tale," *Forbes*, Jul. 24, 2015; Richard North Patterson, "Trump's Character Is His Fate," *Huffington Post*, Oct. 8, 2015.
93. Michael J. Morrell, "I Ran the C.I.A.: Now I'm Endorsing Hillary Clinton," *The New York Times*, Aug. 5, 2016.
94. Jeremy Diamond, "Trump Escalates Attacks on Clinton's Character," CNN .com, Aug. 6, 2016.
95. E.g., "in one choleric tweetstorm, Trump managed to undercut" three claims about his travel ban (Dahlia Lithwick and Mark Joseph Stern, "Is Trump Trying to Lose?," *Slate*, Jun. 6, 2017).
96. "Warren Warns of Trump, Allies; Saying 'Fighting Back Matters,'" Associated Press, Jun. 16, 2017.
97. Edward Bernays, who organized the American publication of *Freud's Introductory Lectures on Psychoanalysis*, advised Calvin Coolidge, Herbert Hoover, the United States Information Agency, and the NAACP, and represented commercial products ranging from Lucky Strike cigarettes to Ivory soap, used ideas of group psychology derived in part from Wilfred Trotter and Gustave Le Bon.
98. Edward L. Bernays, *Propaganda* (New York: Horace Liveright, 1928).

6. Seeing It

1. Jessica Estepa, "Donald Trump on Carly Fiorina: 'Look at That Face!,'" *USA Today*, Sept. 10, 2015; Colin Campbell, "CNN's Chris Cuomo Confronts Donald Trump: 'Why Do You Talk About How Women Look?,'" *Business Insider*, Sept. 10, 2015.
2. John Caspar Lavater, *Essays on Physiognomy*, trans. Thomas Holcroft, 10th ed. (London: William Tegg, 1858).
3. Ernst Kris and E. H. Gombrich, "The Principles of Caricature," in Kris, *Psychoanalytic Explorations in Art* (New York: Schocken Books, 1952; paperback ed., 1964), p. 195. The idea was expressed "in a text attributed to Aristotle," and was widely believed in the late sixteenth and early seventeenth centuries.
4. Some of della Porta's woodcuts would be reprinted in Johann Caspar Lavater, *The Pocket Lavater; or, The Science of Physiognomy: To Which Is Added an Inquiry into the Analogy Existing Between Brute and Human Physiognomy, from the Italian of Porta* (Hartford, CT: Andrus & Judd, 1800), when Lavater's theories had become popular.
5. Charles Le Brun, *Méthode pour apprendre à dessiner les passions* (1698).

6. "Emotion" entry, *Oxford English Dictionary*, 1.
7. Susan James, *Passion and Action: The Emotions in Seventeenth-Century Philosophy* (Oxford, U.K.: Clarendon Press, 1997), p. 6; Gail Kern Paster, Katherine Rowe, and Mary Floyd-Wilson, eds., *Reading the Early Modern Passions: Essays in the Cultural History of Emotion* (Philadelphia: University of Pennsylvania Press, 2004), p. 16.
8. Lavater, *Essays on Physiognomy*, plate XXVIII, fig. 3; plate XIII, fig. 3.
9. Ibid., p. 12.
10. Ibid., p. 98.
11. Ibid., p. 99.
12. Ibid., pp. 106, 107.
13. Ibid., p. 107.
14. Ibid., pp. 108–9.
15. Ibid., pp. 464, 472. Others include: "Eyes which are large, open, and clearly transparent, and which sparkle with rapid motion under sharply-delineated eyelids—almost certainly denote five qualities:—

    Quick discernment.
    Elegance and taste.
    Irritability.
    Pride. And,
    Most violent love of women."

    and "A clear, thick, roof-shaped, over-shadowing eyebrow, which has no wild luxuriant bushiness, is always a certain sign of a sound, manly, mature understanding; seldom of original genius; never of volatile, aerial, amorous tenderness, and spirituality. Such eyebrows may indicate statesmen, counselors, framers of plans, experimentalists; but very seldom bold aspiring minds of the first magnitude." (Ibid., pp. 468, 470.)
16. Ibid., pp. 481–82.
17. Lavater, *Pocket Lavater*. For a consideration of pocket physiognomy in nineteenth-century Britain, see also Sharrona Pearl, *About Faces* (Cambridge, MA: Harvard University Press, 2017), pp. 26–56.
18. Lavater, *Essays on Physiognomy*, pp. 152–55.
19. Ibid., p. 339.
20. Quoted in ibid., p. 349.
21. Ibid., p. 427, plate LXVI, fig. 5.
22. Friedrich Nicolai, "Description of a Journey Through Germany and Switzerland in the Year 1781," in *Franz Xaver Messerschmidt*, ed. Maria Pötzl-Malikova and Guilhem Scherf (New York: Louvre Productions/Neue Galerie, 2011), p. 209. See also Antonia Boström, *Messerschmidt and Modernity* (Los Angeles: Getty Publications, 2012), p. 18.
23. Boström, *Messerchmidt and Modernity*, p. 1.
24. Ernst Kris, "A Psychotic Sculptor of the Eighteenth Century," in Kris, *Psychoanalytic Explorations in Art* (New York: Schocken Books, 1952; paperback ed., 1964), pp. 128–50.
25. Boström, *Messerschmidt and Modernity*, p. 55; Maria Pötzl-Malikova, *Franz Xaver Messerschmidt* (Vienna: Jugend und Volk, 1982), pp. 250–51.
26. Dorette Lau, "Tony Bevan and His Self-Portraits," *The Wall Street Journal*, Mar. 3, 2011, quoted in Boström, *Messerchmidt and Modernity*, p. 47.
27. Quoted in ibid., p. 50.
28. Kris and Gombrich, "Principles of Caricature," p. 198.
29. Ibid., p. 190.
30. Ibid., p. 198.

31. Ibid., p. 190.
32. Ibid., p. 196.
33. E. H. Gombrich, "The Experiment of Caricature," in *Art and Illusion: A Study in the Psychology of Pictorial Representation* (Princeton, NJ: Princeton University Press, 1960; 2nd ed., 1961; 2000), p. 343.
34. Ibid., p. 349.
35. Ibid., p. 350.
36. Henry Fielding, *Joseph Andrews and Shamela*, ed. Douglas Brooks-Davies (Oxford, U.K.: Oxford University Press, 1966), pp. 4, 5–6.
37. Jenny Uglow, *Hogarth: A Life and a World* (London: Faber and Faber, 1997), p. 368.
38. Ibid., p. 369.
39. William Hogarth, *The Analysis of Beauty*, ed. Ronald Paulson (1753; New Haven, CT: Yale University Press, 1997), p. 95.
40. William Hogarth, inscription to his engraving *The Bench*, 1758, in Uglow, *Hogarth*, pp. 339, 606–8.
41. Hogarth, *Analysis of Beauty*, p. 96.
42. Gombrich, "Experiment of Caricature," p. 336.
43. Ibid., p. 340.
44. Ibid., pp. 287–88.
45. Ibid., p. 299.
46. Ibid., p. 301.
47. Adam Begley, *The Great Nadar: The Man Behind the Camera* (New York: Tim Duggan, 2017), p. 46.
48. Ibid., p. 60.
49. Ibid., p. 81.
50. Philippe Burty, *Gazette des Beaux-Arts*, 1859, in ibid., p. 81.
51. Appeal to the legal tribunal concerning his brother Adrien's use of the name "Nadar jeune," 1856, quoted in Begley, *Great Nadar*, p. 100.
52. Félix Nadar, *When I Was a Photographer*, trans. Eduardo Cadava and Liana Theodoratou (Cambridge, MA: MIT Press, 2015), p. 101.
53. Ibid., p. 99.
54. Ibid., p. 97.
55. G.-B. Duchenne de Boulogne, *The Mechanism of Human Facial Expression*, ed. and trans. R. Andrew Cuthbertson (Cambridge, U.K.: Cambridge University Press, 1990), pp. 42–43.
56. Ibid., p. 2.
57. Ibid., p. 91.
58. R. Andrew Cuthbertson, "The Highly Original Dr. Duchenne," in Duchenne, *Mechanism of Human Facial Expression*, p. 235.
59. Duchenne, *Mechanism of Human Facial Expression*, p. 40.
60. Ibid., p. 43.
61. Ibid., p. 40.
62. Ibid., p. 4.
63. Ibid., p. 17.
64. Ibid., p. 101.
65. Cuthbertson, "Highly Original Dr. Duchenne," p. 231.
66. Duchenne, *Mechanism of Human Facial Expression*, p. 30.
67. Ibid., p. 102.
68. Ibid., p. 105.
69. Ibid., p. 114.
70. Ibid., p. 120.

71. Ibid., p. 122.
72. Ibid.
73. Verneuil, "Critique sur *Le Mécanisme de la physionomie humaine*," in *Gazette Hebdomadaire de Médecine et de Chirurgie*, no. 28, Jul. 11, 1862, in Cuthbertson, "Highly Original Dr. Duchenne," p. 235 n. 49.
74. Cuthbertson, "Highly Original Dr. Duchenne," p. 230 and n. 33.
75. Genevieve Stebbins, *Delsarte System of Expression* (New York: Edgar S. Werner, 1886), pp. 92–95.
76. Ibid., pp. 48–49, 107, 108.
77. Ibid., p. 123.
78. Ibid., p. 158.
79. Ibid., p. 131.
80. Ibid., pp. 135, 154, 159, 164.
81. Ibid., p. 73.
82. Ibid., p. 215.
83. Ibid., p. 28.
84. Jean Benedetti, *Stanislavski: His Life and Art* (London: Methuen, 1999), p. 169 n.
85. Charles Darwin, "Introduction to the First Edition," *The Expression of the Emotions in Man and Animals* (1872; London: HarperPerennial, 2009), p. 19.
86. Ibid., p. 247. Darwin notes that Charles Bell calls the muscles that uncover the canines the "snarling muscles." His etymological citation is from Hensleigh Wedgwood, *A Dictionary of English Etymology* (1865), vol. 3, pp. 240, 243.
87. Ibid.
88. Janet Browne, "Darwin and the Expression of the Emotions," in *The Darwinian Heritage*, ed. David Kohn (Princeton, NJ: Princeton University Press, 1985), p. 309.
89. Ibid., p. 312.
90. Darwin, *Expression*, p. 25.
91. Browne, "Darwin and the Expression," p. 317. See also Sander Gillman, "Darwin Sees the Insane," *Journal of the History of the Behavioral Sciences*, vol. 15 (1979), pp. 253–62.
92. Janet Browne, "Darwin and the Expression," p. 315.
93. Darwin, *Expression*, p. 236, plate V, figs. 2, 3.
94. Ibid., p. 242.
95. Ibid., p. 235 n.
96. Ibid., p. 220.
97. *Titus Andronicus*, II.5, in ibid., p. 297. Darwin, *Expression*, p. 239.
98. Ibid., pp. 80–81.
99. Ibid., p. 308 and n.
100. Ibid., p. 334.
101. Janet Browne, *Charles Darwin: The Power of Place* (Princeton, NJ: Princeton University Press, 2002), p. 59.
102. Darwin, *Expression*, p. 46.
103. Janet Browne, "Darwin and the Expression," p. 317.
104. Darwin, *Expression*, p. 310.
105. Ibid., pp. 308–9.
106. Christopher Ricks, *Keats and Embarrassment* (Oxford, U.K.: Clarendon Press, 1984), p. 4. As Ricks makes clear, Keats is arguably the great poet of the blush; in addition to his many glorious "Romantic" uses, we might especially consider, from a physiological or behaviorist view, this verse from a poem of 1818:

> There's a blush for want, and a blush for shan't,
> And a blush for having done it,
> There's a blush for thought, and a blush for naught
> And a blush for just begun it.

John Keats, verses included in a letter to John Hamilton Reynolds, Jan. 31, 1818, quoted in ibid., p. 200.

107. Thomas Henry Burgess, *The Physiology or Mechanism of Blushing* (London: John Churchill, 1839), p. 57.
108. Darwin, *Expression*, p. 186.
109. Eliot, "The Metaphysical Poets," in *Selected Essays 1917–1932* (New York: Harcourt, Brace, 1932), p. 250.
110. Darwin, *Expression*, p. 69.
111. Sigmund Freud, "Studies on Hysteria" (1893–1895), in *SE*, vol. 2, p 181.
112. Sigmund Freud, "General Theory of the Neuroses" (1916–1917), in *SE*, vol. 16, p. 399.
113. James Strachey, editor's introduction, Sigmund Freud, "Inhibitions, Symptoms, and Anxiety," in *SE*, vol. 2, p. 84.
114. Sigmund Freud, "The Interpretation of Dreams" (1900), in *SE*, vol. 4, p.264. This phrase, and the paragraph in which it appears, was first presented in a footnote, in the 1900 edition; from 1914 on, it was incorporated into the text.
115. E.g., his first principle, "When movements, associated through habit with certain states of mind, are partially repressed by the will, the strictly involuntary muscles, as well as those which are least under the separate control of the will, are liable still to act; and their action is often highly expressive" (Darwin, *Expression*, p. 56).
116. "Conscience (or more correctly, the anxiety which later becomes conscience) is indeed the cause of instinctual renunciation to begin with," Freud would suggest in *Civilization and Its Discontents*, but "later the relationship is reversed. Every renunciation of instinct now becomes a dynamic source of conscience, and every fresh renunciation increases the latter's severity and intolerance." Thus "in the beginning conscience arises through the suppression of an aggressive impulse," and "it is subsequently reinforced by fresh suppressions of the same kind." Ibid., p. 130.
117. Ibid., p. 134.
118. Ibid., p. 144.
119. Freud, "Interpretation of Dreams," p. 265.
120. Ibid., p. 608.
121. Darwin, *Expression*, p. 334.
122. Mary Gibson and Nicole Hahn Rafter, "Editors' Introduction" to Cesare Lombroso, *Criminal Man*, ed. and trans. Gibson and Rafter, (Durham, NC: Duke University Press, 2006), p. 23.
123. Mario Portigliatti Barbos, quoted in ibid., p. 23.
124. Giorgio Columbo, quoted in ibid.
125. Lombroso, *Criminal Man*, p. 53.
126. Ibid., p. 69. The editors note in their Introduction, "Lombroso's theory of atavism . . . equates white men with civilization and black, brown, and yellow men with 'primitive' or 'savage' societies" (p. 17).
127. Ibid., p. 235.
128. Ibid.

129. Ibid., pp. 378–79 n 30.
130. Cesare Lombroso and Guglielmo Ferrero, *Criminal Woman, the Prostitute and the Normal Woman* (1893), ed. and trans. Nicole Hahn Rafter and Mary Gibson (Durham, NC: Duke University Press, 2004), p. 83.
131. Ibid., p. 192.
132. Ibid., pp. 192, 188.
133. Lombroso, *Criminal Man*, pp. 60–61.
134. Ibid., p. 62.
135. Lombroso and Ferrero, *Criminal Woman*, pp. 154–55.
136. Ibid., p. 156 n.
137. Lombroso, *Criminal Man*, p. 241.
138. Ibid., pp. 111–13.
139. Ibid., pp. 118–19.
140. Sahil Chinoy, "The Racist History Behind Facial Recognition," *The New York Times*, Jul. 10, 2019. "Haunted data" is the phrase of Joy Buolamwini, a researcher at MIT, quoted in this article.
141. Ralph Waldo Emerson, *English Traits* (London: Tauris Parke, 2011) p. 36.
142. Norbert Glas, *Reading the Face: Understanding a Person's Character Through Physiognomy, A Spiritual-Scientific Study*, trans. Pauline Wehrle (Forest Park, U.K.: Temple Lodge, 2008), pp. 65–66.
143. Ibid., p. 11.
144. Ibid., p. 162.
145. Ibid., p. 163.
146. Ibid., p. 98.
147. Paul Ekman and Wallace V. Friesen, *Unmasking the Face: A Guide to Recognizing Emotions from Facial Clues* (Los Altos, CA: Malor Books, 2003), p. 3.
148. Ibid., pp. 4, 5.
149. Ibid., p. 5.
150. Ibid., p. 170.
151. See Paster, Rowe, and Floyd-Wilson, eds., *Reading the Early Modern Passions*, p. 7: "The result is not the photographic portrait of emotion, but the photographic portrait of acting—often bad acting."
152. Paul Ekman, *Emotions Revealed: Understanding Faces and Feelings* (London: Weidenfeld & Nicolson, 2003), pp. 210–11.
153. Ibid., p. 218.
154. Ibid., pp. 66–67.
155. Ibid., p. 246.
156. Paul Ekman, *Telling Lies: Clues to Deceit in the Marketplace, Politics, and Marriage* (New York: W. W. Norton, 1985; reissued with additions, 1992, 2001, 2009), p. 324.
157. Ibid., pp. 102–4; Ekman and Friesen, *Unmasking the Face*, pp. 12–13.
158. Daniel Dale, "'Sir' Alert: This One Word Is a Telltale Sign Trump Is Being Dishonest," Facts First, CNN.com, Jul. 17, 2019.
159. Barbara J. Sahakian and Julia Gottwald, *Sex, Lies, and Brain Scans: How fMRI Reveals What Really Goes On in Our Minds* (Oxford, U.K.: Oxford University Press, 2017), p. 61.
160. Ibid., p. 122.
161. William R. Uttal, *The New Phrenology: The Limits of Localizing Cognitive Processes in the Brain* (Cambridge, MA: MIT Press, 2001).
162. Sahakian and Gottwald, *Sex, Lies, and Brain Scans*, plate 5.
163. Ibid., p. 60.

164. G. Hein and R. T. Knight, "Superior Temporal Sulcus: It's My Area: or Is It?," *Journal of Cognitive Neuroscience*, 20 (2008), pp. 2125–36, quoted in Sahakian and Gottwald, *Sex, Lies, and Brain Scans*, p. 60.

7. Character Types

1. Most recent accounts of the development of the novel, if they mention it at all, refer for specifics to two scholarly studies: Benjamin Boyce, *The Theophrastan Character in England to 1642* (Cambridge, MA: Harvard University Press, 1947); J. W. Smeed, *The Theophrastan "Character": The History of a Literary Genre* (Oxford, U.K.: Clarendon Press, 1985).
2. Stephen Jay Gould, *Bully for Brontosaurus* (New York: Norton, 1991), p. 96.
3. Smeed, *Theophrastan "Character,"* p. 5.
4. G. S. Gordon, "Theophrastus and His Imitators," in *English Literature and the Classics*, ed. G. S. Gordon (Oxford, U.K.: Clarendon Press, 1912), p. 49.
5. Jeffrey Rusten, introduction, "Theophrastus, Characters," in *Theophrastus, Herodas, Cercidas and the Choliambic Poets*, ed. and trans. Jeffrey Rusten, J. C. Cunningham, and A. D. Knox, Loeb Classical Library (Cambridge, MA: Harvard University Press, 1993), pp. 11–13; Aristotle, *The Nicomachean Ethics*, trans. David Ross (Oxford, U.K.: Oxford World's Classics, 2009), books 2, 3, 4. Rusten provides a useful chart of Aristotle's "virtues and vices of character" organized under the headings "deficiency," "mean," and "excess"—where for Aristotle the "mean" is ordinarily the situation of virtue—commenting, "It is easy to imagine Theophrastus' work as inspired by his teacher's approach to vices." I transcribe it here using the English terms provided as translations for Aristotle's Greek:

   deficiency mean excess
   coward courage rash
   unable to feel temperance intemperance
   lack of generosity generosity profligacy
   niggardliness magnificence vulgarity
   pusillanimity magnanimity vanity
   unambitious ambitious-good ambitious-bad
   passivity gentleness irascibility
   self-deprecation truthfulness boastfulness
   boorishness wit buffoonery
   quarrelsomeness friendliness obsequious
   bad-tempered friendliness flatterer
   shameless polite bashful
   spitefulness righteous indignation enviousness

6. Aristotle, *Nicomachean Ethics*, 4.2.
7. Rusten, *Theophrastus*, pp. 18–23; Gordon, "Theophrastus and His Imitators," pp. 54–55; Smeed, *Theophrastan "Character,"* p. 3.
8. Gordon Allport, *Pattern and Growth in Personality* (London: Holt, Rinehart and Winston, 1963), p. 43.
9. Rusten, *Theophrastus*, p. 16; Gordon, "Theophrastus and His Imitators," p. 52.
10. Gordon, "Theophrastus and His Imitators," p. 52.
11. Ibid., p. 53.

12. Richard Aldington, compiler and translator, *A Book of Characters* (London: Routledge, 1929), p. iii. Aldington's text for Theophrastus was Octave Navarre, ed., *Théophraste, Caractères* (Paris: Association Guillaume Budé, 1920). A new translation by Pamela Mensch, published in 2018, gives the following list: The Dissembler, The Flatterer, The Talker, The Yokel, The Sycophant, The Senseless Man, The Babbler, The Newshound, The Shameless Man, The Miser, The Obnoxious Man, The Tactless Man, The Busybody, The Dullard, The Surly Man, The Superstitious Man, The Complainer, The Distrustful Man, The Slovenly Man, The Vulgar Man, The Social Climber, The Pinchpenny, The Charlatan, The Arrogant Man, The Coward, The Authoritarian, The Late Learner, The Slanderer, The Friend of Scoundrels, The Chiseler. In Theophrastus, *Characters: An Ancient Take on Bad Behavior* (New York: Callaway, 2018).
13. Amélie Oksenberg Rorty, "Literary Postscript: Characters, Persons, Selves, Individuals," in *The Identities of Persons*, ed. Amélie Oksenberg Rorty (Berkeley: University of California Press, 1976), p. 304.
14. Blurbs for *Characters: An Ancient Take on Bad Behavior*, trans. Pamela Mensch.
15. All quoted from Aldington, *Book of Characters*, pp. 30, 41, 36.
16. Smeed, *Theophrastan "Character,"* p. 4.
17. Ibid., p. 37.
18. R. G. Ussher, *The Characters of Theophrastus* (London: Macmillan, 1960), p. 5.
19. This is different from the list of dramatic roles, which in Jonson's play text, and typically in the period, is called "The Names of the Actors," although what it includes is not the personal names but the names of the performance roles. A list of what we would today call "the actors" is given in the second folio text, under the heading "The Principal Comedians."
20. Ben Jonson, *Every Man Out of His Humour*, ed. Helen Ostovich (Manchester, U.K.: Manchester University Press, 2001), pp. 101–10.
21. Ben Jonson, *Cynthia's Revels*, quoted in Aldington, *Book of Characters*, p. 335.
22. Ibid., pp. 336–38.
23. Ibid., p. 338.
24. Simon Callow, foreword, Antonio Fava, *The Comic Mask in the Commedia dell'Arte: Actor Training, Improvisation, and the Poetics of Survival* (Evanston, IL: Northwestern University Press, 2007), p. ix.
25. John Rudlin, *Commedia dell'Arte: An Actor's Handbook* (New York: Routledge, 1994), pp. 151–53.
26. Roger Cohen, "Goodbye to the Scaramouch," *The New York Times*, Aug. 1, 2017.
27. Callow, foreword, p. xi.
28. Smeed, *Theophrastan "Character,"* p. 6; Gordon, "Theophrastus and His Imitators," p. 68. The publication of Isaac Casaubon's Latin edition of Theophrastus in 1592 had attracted strong interest; Casaubon, a Frenchman, later moved to England at the invitation of King James. An early example of a "character" of the Covetous Man has been noted in Thomas Wilson's *Arte of Rhetorique* (1553), fifty years earlier than the explicit acknowledgment of Theophrastus as a model: "There is no such pinch peney on life as this good fellowe is. He will not lose the pairing of his nailes. His hair is never rounded for the sparing of money, one pair of shone serveth him a twelve moneth, he is shod with nailes like a Horse. He hath been knowne by his coate this thirtie winter." (Quoted in Gordon, "Theophrastus and His Imitators," p. 66.)

29. Including the noted playwright, poet, and philosopher Margaret Cavendish, Duchess of Newcastle, who produced witty accounts of "Fools" and of "A Puritan Dame," among other characters (Aldington, *Book of Characters*, pp. 387–88).
30. Earle's *Microcosmography* was described by G. S. Gordon as "the best of these early collections, and perhaps of all the collections of Characters in English" (Gordon, "Theophrastus and His Imitators," p. 69).
31. Edward Hyde (Lord Clarendon), *Characters of Eminent Men in the Reigns of Charles I and II* (London: R. Faulder, 1793), p. 194.
32. Earle, "Microcosmography," VI, LXXV, XXXVII, in Aldington, *Book of Characters*, pp. 13, 104, 55–56.
33. Overbury et al., "What a Character Is," in Aldington, *Book of Characters*, p. 167.
34. After Overbury's death, the works of other "gentlemen" were included in the collection—hence the clumsy but accurate "Overburian."
35. Henry Gally, *A Critical Essay on Characteristic-Writings* (1725; Lexington, KY: Hard Press, 2013), p. 13.
36. Ibid., p. 15.
37. Ibid., p. 12.
38. Ibid., p. 16.
39. There were 119 character essays in *The Genuine Remains in Verse and Prose of Mr Samuel Butler*, ed. R. Thyer (London: Tonson, 1759). The rest were found among Butler's papers in the British Museum and published for the first time in *Samuel Butler: Characters and Passages from Note-books*, ed. A. R. Weller (Cambridge, U.K.: Cambridge University Press, 1908).
40. Waller, *Samuel Butler*, p. 138.
41. Aldington, *Book of Characters*, p. 34; Waller, *Samuel Butler*, p. 126.
42. Smeed, *Theophrastan "Character,"* p. 66.
43. Deidre Shauna Lynch, *The Economy of Character: Novels, Market Culture, and the Business of Inner Meaning* (Chicago: University of Chicago Press, 1998), p. 55.
44. Smeed, *Theophrastan "Character,"* pp. 229–32. See his chapter "The 'Character' and the Novel," pp. 225–62, for further examples from English and German fiction.
45. "Podsnappery" entry, *Oxford English Dictionary*.
46. "Scholars have pointed out that La Bruyère's translation is slipshod and unoriginal, with frequent borrowings from the Latin version of Casaubon," says Jean Stewart, adding, "It was the accepted thing to have a Classical sponsor (as Boileau, for instance, had Horace)" (introduction, La Bruyère, *Characters*, trans. Jean Stewart [Harmondsworth, U.K.: Penguin, 1970], p. 12).
47. Jean de La Bruyère, "Characters," in Aldington, *Book of Characters*, pp. 499–501.
48. Allport, *Pattern and Growth*, p. 41.
49. Lytton Strachey, *Landmarks in French Literature* (1912; self-pub., 2017), p. 62.
50. Ibid., p. 62; La Bruyère, "Of Fashion" (13.2), in *Characters*, trans. Stewart, p. 250.
51. Lytton Strachey, "Lady Hester Stanhope," in *Books and Characters: French and English* (London: Chatto and Windus, 1922), p. 241.
52. Lytton Strachey, "John Aubrey," in *Portraits in Miniature and Other Essays* (London: Chatto and Windus, 1931), p. 28; and devastatingly shrewd estimates of "Six English Historians."

53. Virginia Woolf, *The Diary of Virginia Woolf*, vol. 4 (1931–1935), ed. Anne Olivier Bell (New York: Harvest, 1983), p. 26. Entry for May 19, 1931.
54. Roland Barthes, "La Bruyère," in *Critical Essays*, trans. Richard Howard (Evanston, IL: Northwestern University Press, 1972), p. 228.
55. Ibid., p. 233.
56. Ibid., p. 225.
57. La Bruyère, *Characters*, p. 91 (5.45).
58. Barthes, "La Bruyère," p. 226.
59. Ibid., p. 229.
60. Ibid., pp. 229–30.
61. Edmund Wilson, "Books of Etiquette and Emily Post," in *Classics and Commercials: A Literary Chronicle of the Forties* (New York: Farrar, Straus and Giroux, 1950), p. 374.
62. Ibid., p. 378.
63. Emily Post, *Etiquette* (1922; Jefferson Publication, 2015), pp. 189–90.
64. Emily Post, *Etiquette* (New York: Funk & Wagnalls, 1950), p. 51.
65. Aldington, *Book of Characters*, pp. 425–26.
66. Geoffrey Gorer and Ronald Searle, *Modern Types* (London: Cresset Press, 1955), pp. 96–97.
67. Ibid., pp. 79–82.
68. Ibid., p. 60.
69. George Eliot, "Impressions of Theophrastus Such," in *The Works of George Eliot* (Edinburgh, U.K.: William Blackwood, 1879), pp. 190, 232. Allardyce Nicoll, *Saturday Review of Literature*, XI (Apr. 20, 1935), p. 630.
70. Boyce, *Theophrastan Character in England to 1642*, p. 154.

8. The Difference Gender Makes

1. "Hussy" entry, *Oxford English Dictionary*.
2. See, for example, Michael Tackett, "From Annapolis to Congress? These Three Women Know Tough Missions," *The New York Times*, Jan. 29, 2018; Michael Tackett, "How Amy McGrath Went from Fighter Pilot to Victorious Democrat," *The New York Times*, May 23, 2018.
3. Matthew Haag, "Southwest Pilot of Flight 1380 is Navy Veteran Hailed for Her 'Nerves of Steel,'" *The New York Times*, Apr. 18, 2018.
4. Albert Henry Buck, *A Reference Handbook of the Medical Sciences* (New York: W. Wood, 1887), vol. 5, p. 162.
5. Tara Golshan, "65 Women Who Knew Brett Kavanaugh in High School Defend His Character," *Vox*, Sept. 14, 2018.
6. Patrick Leahy, "Newsmaker of the Day," *Democratic Weekly Address*, KVML, Sept. 18, 2018, printed in Mymotherlode.com.
7. E.g., "Brett Kavanaugh: Character Assassination by Democrats," National review.com, Sept. 2018; "Brett Kavanaugh Defies 'Grotesque Character Assassination,'" Breitbart.com, Sept. 24, 2018; Charlie Kirk, "The Character Assassination of Brett Kavanaugh," Townhall.com; "Feinstein vs. Kavanaugh: Anatomy of a Character Assassination," Foxnews.com.
8. 2,400+ Law Professors, "The Senate Should Not Confirm Kavanaugh," *The New York Times*, Oct. 3, 2018.
9. Adam Liptak, "Retired Justice John Paul Stevens Says Kavanaugh Is Not Fit for Supreme Court," *The New York Times*, Oct. 4, 2018.

10. Susan McFarland, "Trump Celebrates Kavanaugh Victory at Kansas Rally," United Press International, Oct. 6, 2018.
11. Tom McCarthy, "Trump Mocks Christine Blasey Ford at Mississippi Rally as Supporters Cheer," *The Guardian*, Oct. 2, 2018.
12. McFarland, "Trump Celebrates Kavanaugh Victory."
13. David Crary, "Kavanaugh-Ford Hearings: A Dramatic Lesson in Gender Roles," Associated Press, Sept. 28, 2018.
14. Randi Hutter Epstein, "Stop Calling Women Hormonal," *The New York Times*, Jun. 3, 2018.
15. Elaine Sciolino, "Madeleine Albright's Audition," *The New York Times*, Sept. 22, 1996.
16. See Karen Wolfers-Rapaport, "Eishet Chayil: A Pictorial View of the Woman of Valor," Chabad.org, n.d., chabad.org/theJewishWoman/article_cdo/aid/3270084/jewish/Eishet-Chayil-A-Pictorial-View-of-the-Woman-of-Valorhtm; Sara Esther Crispe, "Finding the Valor Within: Eshet Chayil (Part 2)," Dec. 5, 2014, interinclusion.org/inspirations/finding-the-valor-within-eshet-chayil-part-2; Shael Siegel, "Her Price Is Beyond Pearls," Mar. 3, 2007, shaelsiegel.blogspot.com/2007/03/her-price-is-beyond-pearls.html.
17. "What Is Real Jewish Beauty?," chabad.org/parshah/article_cdo/aid/4035875/jewish/What-Is-Real-Jewish-Beauty.htm.
18. Bari Weiss, "The Bikini Contest Is Over, but We Are Living Inside the Beauty Pageant," *The New York Times*, Jun. 5, 2018.
19. Philip Rucker, "Trump Says Fox's Megyn Kelly Had 'Blood Coming Out of Her Wherever,'" *The Washington Post*, Aug. 8, 2015.
20. Glenn Thrush and Maggie Haberman, "Trump Mocks Mika Brzezinski; Says She Was 'Bleeding Badly from a Face-Lift,'" *The New York Times*, Jun. 19, 2017.
21. Denise Grady, "Trump Takes the Hair-Growth Drug Propecia: How Does It Work?," *The New York Times*, Feb. 2, 1017.
22. "Ad hominem" entry, *Oxford English Dictionary*, B.
23. For a good sense of the early-modern context, see Mary Floyd-Wilson, "English Mettle," in *Reading the Early Modern Passions: Essays in the Cultural History of Emotion* (Philadelphia: University of Pennsylvania Press, 2004), pp. 130–46.
24. "Mettle" entry, *Oxford English Dictionary*, A3.
25. Virgil, *Georgics*, trans. John Dryden, vol. III, (1697), quoted in ibid.
26. A. Bronson Alcott, *Journals*, Mar. 31, 1938, quoted in "mettle" entry, A2b.
27. "Spunk" entry, *Oxford English Dictionary*, 5a, 5c.
28. Stephen Holden, "No Cartwheels (for Now), but Oodles of Spunk," *The New York Times*, Apr. 2, 2009.
29. Mike Hale, "Review: Thoroughly Modern 'Victoria,'" *The New York Times*, Jan. 13, 2017.
30. D. H. Lawrence, *Lady Chatterley's Lover* (1928; London: Penguin, 2006,), p. 66.
31. Tom Wolfe, *The Right Stuff* (1979; London: Vintage, 2018), p. 327.
32. Philip Dormer Stanhope, Earl of Chesterfield, *Characters* (London: Edward and Charles Dilly, 1778), pp. 59–60, 53.
33. Maynard Mack, *Alexander Pope: A Life* (New Haven, CT: Yale University Press, 1985), p. 631.
34. John Stuart Mill, "The Subjection of Women," in *On Liberty*, ed. Collini, pp. 132–33.
35. Ibid., p. 138.
36. "Manly" entry, *Oxford English Dictionary*, 2a.

37. Lady Bradshaigh, quoted in Jonathan Gathorne-Hardy, *The Public School Phenomenon* (Harmondsworth, U.K.: Penguin, 1977), p. 253.
38. Cecil Rhodes, codicil to his last will and testament, Oct. 11, 1901, quoted in Philip Ziegler, *Legacy: Cecil Rhodes, the Rhodes Trust and Rhodes Scholarships* (New Haven, CT: Yale University Press, 2008), p. 346.
39. Ibid., p. 33.
40. George Parkin, *The Rhodes Scholarships* (London: Constable, 1913), pp. 100–1.
41. Henry Newbolt, *The Book of the Happy Warrior* (London: Longmans, Green, 1918), p. 270.
42. William Plomer, *Cecil Rhodes* (1933; Capetown: Africasouth, 1984), p. 45.
43. Ibid., p. 46.
44. Ibid., p. 41.
45. Ibid., p. 168.
46. Lytton Strachey, *Eminent Victorians* (1918; London: Penguin, 1986), pp. 187–88.
47. Ziegler, *Legacy*, p. 34.
48. Anthony Kenny, *The History of the Rhodes Trust* (Oxford, U.K.: Oxford University Press, 2001), p. 59.
49. Ziegler, *Legacy*, p. 217.
50. Ziegler, *Legacy*, p. 364 n. 3.
51. Harvey C. Mansfield, *Manliness* (New Haven, CT: Yale University Press, 2006), p. 37.
52. Ibid., p. 91.
53. Ibid., p. 234.
54. Ibid., p. 204.
55. Ibid., p. 243.
56. Ibid., p. 234.
57. Ibid., p. 115.
58. Ibid., p. 244.
59. "Womanly" entry, *Oxford English Dictionary*, 1a.
60. All cited in ibid., 1b.
61. Barbara Stephen, *Girton College 1869–1932* (Cambridge, U.K.: Cambridge University Press, 1933), pp. 34–35.
62. Quoted in Sandra J. Peacock, *Jane Ellen Harrison: The Mask and the Self* (New Haven, CT: Yale University Press, 1988), pp. 31, 32.
63. Agnes Baden-Powell and Robert Baden-Powell, *The Handbook for Girl Guides, or How Girls Can Help to Build the Empire* (London: Thomas Nelson, 1912; facsimile ed., London: Girl Guides Association, 1993), p. 22.
64. Ibid., p. 24.
65. Baden-Powell, *Scouting for Boys*, p. 316.
66. A. and R. Baden-Powell, *Handbook for Girl Guides*, pp. vii–viii.
67. Joan Riviere, "Womanliness as a Masquerade," *International Journal of Psychoanalysis*, 10 (1929), reprinted in *Formations of Fantasy*, eds. Victor Burgin, James Donald, and Cora Kaplan (London: Methuen, 1986), pp. 35–44.
68. Ibid., p. 38.
69. Stephen Heath, "Joan Riviere and the Masquerade," in *Formations of Fantasy*, ed. Burgin et al., pp. 45–61. Some brilliant scholarly work has been done on this essay by theorists concerned with sexualities, with women in films, and with the fraught issue of "femininity" as it was described by Freud. In addition to Heath, see especially Judith Butler, *Gender Trouble* (1990; New York: Routledge,

2006), pp. 68–73; Mary Anne Doane, *The Desire to Desire: The Woman's Film of the 1940s* (Bloomington: University of Indiana Press, 1987); Gayatri Spivak, "Displacement and the Discourse of Woman," in *Displacement: Derrida and After*, ed. Mark Krupnick (Bloomington: University of Indiana Press, 1983).

70. Riviere's 1932 translation of "Female Sexuality" was reprinted, with minor revisions, in the standard edition of Freud, *SE*, vol. 21 pp. 223–43.
71. Dave Philipps, "New Rule of Transgender Troops: Stick to Your Birth Sex, or Leave," *The New York Times*, Mar. 13, 2019.
72. Marta Murray-Close and Misty L. Heggeness, census research report, quoted in Claire Cain Miller, "When Wives Earn More Than Husbands, Neither Partner Likes to Admit It," *The New York Times*, Jul. 17, 2018.
73. "Man up" entry, *Oxford English Dictionary*, "man," I.1 phrasal verbs, 1.

Afterword: The Character Effect

1. When, for example, President-elect Trump argued strongly (with threats of fines and tariffs) that American companies should manufacture their products in the United States rather than abroad, *The Washington Post* and the television talk-show host David Letterman produced evidence that Trump-branded clothing was being manufactured in China, Bangladesh, Honduras, and Vietnam. *The Huffington Post* headlined its report on this issue, "Trump to Companies: Do as I Say Not as I Do." (Ira Kalb, "Trump to Companies: Do as I Say Not as I Do," *Huffington Post*, Jan. 10, 2017.)
2. Timothy Johnson, "Brett Kavanaugh's Lack of Character, Credibility and Candor," *Media Matters*, Sept. 18, 2018.
3. Michelle Moons, "Trump on 'Historic Night' from Kansas," Breitbart.com, Oct. 6, 2018.
4. "Jets Rookie Herndon on DUI Arrest: 'This Is Not Who I Am,'" Associated Press, Jun. 5, 2018.
5. "Phlogiston" entry, *Oxford English Dictionary*, 1. Examples quoted from J. Hutton, 1794, and G. Wilson and A. Geikie, 1861.
6. Ibid. Examples quoted from Coleridge, *Miscellaneous Criticism* (1936), p. 279, and Arthur Young, *Travels Undertaken . . . with the View of Ascertaining the Cultivation . . . of the Kingdom of France* (1792).
7. Erving Goffman, *The Presentation of Self in Everyday Life* (1956; Garden City, NY: Doubleday Anchor, 1959), pp. 252–53.
8. James Mill, *Analysis of the Phenomena of the Human Mind*, ed. John Stuart Mill (London: Longmans, Green, Reader, and Dyer, 1859), vol. 2, p. 5.
9. Stephen Jay Gould, *The Mismeasure of Man*, rev. ed. (New York: Norton, 1981), pp. 350, 378. Under the heading of "the species problem" or "the species concept," this question has been much debated by biologists, including, among others, Ernst May and Theodore Dobzhansky.
10. Gayatri Chakravorty Spivak, translator's preface, in Jacques Derrida, *Of Grammatology* (Baltimore: Johns Hopkins University Press, 1997), p. xiv.

ACKNOWLEDGMENTS

In writing this book I have benefited from the assistance of many friends, old and new, whom it is a pleasure to acknowledge.

Eric Chinski and Julia Ringo, my editors at Farrar, Straus and Giroux, have been enormously generous with their time, advice, and professional skill. My agent, Bill Clegg, not only supported the book from the beginning, but also offered valuable notes on the text at an early and formative moment.

Bill Germano read the entire manuscript with characteristic care, wisdom, and deft expertise, and helped as well with key suggestions about titles, tone, and presentation. Throughout the writing process Bill Bennett was a consistently encouraging and responsive voice. Elizabeth Weckhurst dexterously located and obtained art permissions, and Kailey Bennett provided crucial assistance at the copyediting stage.

I am grateful to Simon Goldhill, the director of CRASSH (the Centre for Research in the Arts, Social Sciences and Humanities at the University of Cambridge), and to David Hillman of the Cambridge English faculty, for the opportunity to present some early thoughts on this topic at a works-in-progress seminar in the spring of 2016. The responses of seminar members were extremely helpful as the book began to take shape.

Funding from the Anne and Jim Rothenberg Fund for Humanities Research at Harvard University, the Harvard English Department's Hyder E. Rollins Fund, and the Tenured Faculty Publication Fund was essential in keeping the book on track. I appreciate the help of the English Department chair, Nicholas Watson, and the dean of Arts and Humanities, Robin Kelsey, in making such assistance possible.

My special thanks to Joanna Lipper, who has supported this project from first to last.

INDEX

Page numbers in *italics* refer to illustrations.

Académie Française, 139; Tocqueville and, 159
Access Hollywood tape, 40
acting: Callow and, 329–30; Delsarte System of, 298–300; Duchenne de Boulogne and, 291, 294; *Hamlet* and, 20; phrenology and, 226; politicians and character actors, 43–46; Trump and character actors, 43–44
Actor Prepares, An (Stanislavski), 300
Adams, John Quincy, 158
Addison, Joseph, 336
"Address to the Inhabitants of New Lanark" (Owen), 67, 69
admissions, 130; anti-Semitism and, 123–25, 397n174; Asian Americans and, 126–27; at Harvard, 123–29; personal rating and, 128–29
Aesthetic Gymnastics, 299
After Virtue (MacIntyre), 47
Albright, Madeleine, 352–53
Alcott, Bronson, 359
Aldington, Richard, 325–26
Alexander the Great, 17
Ali, Muhammad, 50
Allen, Danielle, 38
Allport, Gordon, 19; on characteristics, 257–58; Five Factor Model and, 260; on Freud, 255–56; Giton and, 339–40; *Pattern and Growth in Personality*, 255, 324; personality and, 232–33, 240, 242, 255, 257–58; *Personality*, 232–33, 255; Theophrastus and, 340
amativeness, 205, 212, 232, 235; age and, 218; Fowler, on, 214–16
American courtiers, 161
American Creed: Inkeles and, 178–79; Lipset and, 179–80
American Dream, 180, 241
American exceptionalism, 145; *Democracy in America* and, 164; Obama, B., and, 146; Wilson, W., and, 182–83
American President, The (film), 30
Americans, The (Gorer), 176
American Spectator, The, 32
Amyot, Jacques, 59
anal eroticism, 248–49
Analysis of Beauty, The (Hogarth), 283–84
Analysis of the Phenomena of the Human Mind (Mill, James), 381
Anderson, Michael, 237
And Keep Your Powder Dry (Mead), 175
Angell, James Burrill, 122
Angell, James Rowland, 124
anima, 252
anthropology: Beeman and, 177; Benedict and, 173–74, 176; culture-and-personality approach to, 174; in *Democracy in America*, 162–64; Gorer and, 175, 176; Mead and, 174–76

anti-Semitism, 186; admissions and, 123–25, 397*n*174; Hollywood and, 190
Aquinas, Thomas, 274
Aristotle, 4, 6, 121–22, 246, 412*n*4; *Ethics*, 64; *ēthos* and, 7; moral character and, 8; *Nicomachean Ethics*, 8, 9, 324; physiognomy and, 273; *Poetics*, 7; Rusten on, 418*n*5; Theophrastus and, 323–24
Arno, Peter, 167–68
Arnold, Thomas, 75–77
Arte of Rhetorique (Wilson), 419*n*28
Asian Americans, 126–27
athletes, 20–21; baseball, 47–48, 389*n*74; football players, 48–51; ice skating, 51–52; Wooden and, 50–51
Atlantic Monthly, The, 156–57
Austen, Jane, 16, 121, 217, 337

Baden-Powell, Agnes: Girl Guides and, 98–99; *The Handbook for Girl Guides*, 98, 99, 370–71; womanliness and, 371
Baden-Powell, Olave, 89, 99
Baden-Powell, Robert, 16, 79, 102, 392*n*63, 393*n*81; in army, 82; class mobility and, 88–89; drawings of, 84–86; *The Handbook for Girl Guides*, 98, 99, 370–71; *Lessons from the 'Varsity of Life*, 81; manliness and, 90–92, 364; McLaren and, 88; *Peter Pan* and, 89–90; "the Scoutmaster's conjuring trick," 84–85; as war hero, 87; on women and girls, 91–92, 97–98; *see also Scouting for Boys*
Bain, Alexander, 71, 198
Barrie, James, 89–90
Barthes, Roland: on La Bruyère, 341–43; metaphor and, 341–42
baseball: Baseball Hall of Fame, 47–48; Landis and, 389*n*74
Batton, Terry, 40
Baum, L. Frank, 106–108, 109
Beard, Mary, 326
Be Best (program), 113
Beeman, William, 177
behavioral modification, 101
Bell, Charles, 415*n*86
Bell, Daniel, 177
Benedict, Ruth, 173; *The Chrysanthemum and the Sword*, 174, 176
Bennett, William J., 120
Bernays, Edward L., 270; group psychology and, 412*n*97; *Propaganda*, 240
Bevan, Tony, 280
Biden, Joe, 270
Big Five, *see* Five Factor Model
biography: character education and, 61–62; character flaws and, 375; Smiles and, 61
Black Lives Matter, 49
Blake, William, 122
Blasey Ford, Christine, 350, 351; Trump mocking, 352
Blount, Martha, 360
Blow, Charles, 31, 36–37, 44
blushing, 307
Boehmer, Elleke, 86
Bonaparte, Marie, 263
Bonaparte, Napoleon, 316
Books and Characters (Strachey), 340, 419*n*12
Borges, Jorge Luis, 131
Boyce, Benjamin, 348
Boy Scouts, 15; name of, 82–83; Scout Laws of, 83, 84; *see also* Baden-Powell, Robert; *Scouting for Boys*
Bray, Charles, 205, 207–208
Brexit, 135–36
Broca, Paul, 196
Brontë, Charlotte: *Jane Eyre*, 203–204; phrenology and, 204; *Wuthering Heights*, 262
Brooks, David: on Cruz, 29–30; on Trump, 41–42
Browne, Janet, 302
Browning, Robert, 94
Bruni, Frank, 134; on politics and character, 28–29; on Trump, 28, 37–38
Building a Character (Stanislavski), 300
Burgess, Thomas Henry, 307
Burke, Johnny, 260

Burroughs, Allison D., 128
Burrows, Montagu, 369–70
Burton, Virginia Lee, 73
Buruma, Ian, 176–77
Bush, George H. W., 28, 35, 116–17
Bush, George W., 28, 45
Buss, David, 231
Butler, Samuel: *Characters*, 335; theory of humors and, 335–36

Cabot, Richard Clarke, 242
Caliban (Shakespeare), 18
Callow, Simon, 330–31
Campfire Girls, 97
Canterbury Tales, The (Chaucer), 363–64
Capen, Nahum, 200
Caractères, Les (La Bruyère), 337–38, 340, 341
Card, David, 129
caricature, 34; character heads as, 281; Gombrich and, 282, 283, 284; Hogarth and, 283, 284; Nadar and, 285–86; Philipon and, 282; Rowlandson and, 285; *see also* national caricature
Carlson, Tucker, 195–96
Carlyle, Thomas, 207
Carnegie, Dale, 16
Carracci, Annibale, 277
cartoonists: Arno, 167–68; Pont, 166
Casaubon, Isaac, 419*n*28
Cavendish, Margaret, 420*n*29
celebrities: character issues of, 53–54; Cosby, 55–56; Lauer, 53–54; moralizing, 54–55; Rose, 54–56; Weinstein, 35, 53
chabad.org, 353, 355
character, *see specific topics*
Character (Smiles), 12, 13–14
character, as changeable, 5, 64, 101
character, as fixed, 5, 101
"Character" (Emerson), 13–14
character actors: politicians and, 43–46; Trump and, 43–44
Character Analysis (Reich), 251
"Character and Anal Erotism" (Freud), 19
"Character and Success" (Roosevelt), 81
character armor, 253
character assassination, 350; Kavanaugh and, 351, 352
Character as Seen in Body and Parentage (Jordan), 251
character building, 79, 120, 372; habit and, 9; literature on, 99; national, 147; Owen and, 68, 102
Character Counts!, 113, 117
character disorders: Freud on, 245, 266; gender dysphoria as, 372; politicians and, 30–31
character education, 396*n*158; admissions and, 123–30, 397*n*174; biography and, 61–62; core values in, 117–18; educators, 105–106; *Ethics* and, 64; grit and, 119–20, 396*n*162; Kohn on, 117, 121; literature and, 121–22; moral lessons and, 120; Owen and, 65–70; religion-based, 117; university presidents on, 122–23, 124–25; women and, 62; *The Wonderful Wizard of Oz* and, 106–108, 109; *see also* National Character Counts Week
character evaluations, 64
character flaw, 4; biography and, 375; of Hillary Clinton, 31–32, 34; politicians and, 7, 31–32, 34; self-help industry and, 7–8; tragic flaw as, 7
character heads, 278–80, 297–98; as caricature, 281
character issue, 5, 24, 27, 28–29, 54; celebrities and, 53–54; football and, 49, 50; and Hillary Clinton, 31–32, 33–34; ice skating and, 51–52; Moore and, 39; "Thomas Jefferson and the Character Issue" and, 21–22
characteristic, 157–58
"Characteristic-Writings" (Gally), 335
characterology, 223, 256; evolutionary psychology and, 231
Characterology (McCormick), 230–31, 274
character.org, 117

character parts, 47
character pathology, 19–20, 266, 411*n*85
Characters (Butler), 335
Characters (Theophrastus), 9, 324, 326–28
Characters, or Witty Descriptions of the Properties of Sundry Persons (Overbury), 332–34
character test: politicians and, 24–25, 26–27; popular culture and, 25
character-training programs: habits and, 9; Outward Bound as, 100; *see also* Boy Scouts; Girl Guides
character trait: anal character as, 249; Freud, and, 19, 247–49, 265; psychoanalysts on, 18–20
character type, 5, 182, 348; Freud, and, 244–47
character witness, 350, 376–77
Charcot, Jean-Martin, 289
Chaucer, Geoffrey, 363–64
Cheney, Dick, 146
Cheney, Liz, 146
Chesterton, G. K., 180, 189–90
chivalry: in *Scouting for Boys*, 95–96, 370–71; in Victorian period, 63
Chosen, The (Karabel), 124, 125
Christianity, 180, 189; King James Bible, 353–55; self-help industry and, 15; Victorian period and, 125–26
Chrysanthemum and the Sword, The (Benedict), 174, 176
Churchill, Winston, 131
Cicero, 59; passions and, 274
citizen service, 114
Civilization and Its Discontents (Freud), 185, 309, 416*n*116
civil rights movement, 63
Classical Dictionary of the Vulgar Tongue (Grose), 359
Clifford, Craig, 21
Clinton, Bill, 24, 26, 192, 353; citizen service and, 114; impeachment of, 115; Lewinsky and, 114; National Character Counts Week and, 113, 114–15
Clinton, Hillary, 40; character flaw of, 31–32, 34; character issue and, 31–32, 33–34; Lady Macbeth and, 32; likability of, 353; Manafort on, 44; *The New York Times* endorsing, 33; temperament of, 269; Trump and, 268–69
Cloninger, Robert, 19
Cohen, Roger, 268, 331
Cold War, 190–91; *Democracy in America* and, 159–60; *see also* House Un-American Activities Committee
Coleridge, Samuel Taylor, 18, 379
Colicchio, Tom, 234
Collini, Stefan, 64
Collins, Gail, 192–93
Columbia University Research in Contemporary Culture, 174
Combe, George, 65, 200, 205–206, 208; *Essay on the Constitution of Man and Its Relation to External Objects*, 201, 233; lectures of, 201; on politicians, 405*n*38; practical phrenology and, 209; *System of Phrenology*, 226
Comey, James B., 41
commedia dell'arte, 330; psychology and, 332; Trump and, 331
Common Core, 118–19
commonplacing: character and, 11; *Hamlet* and, 10; Smiles and, 14
Conduct of Life, The (Emerson), 70
conformity, 121, 181
Coolidge, Calvin, 11
Core Standards, 118
Cosby, Bill, 55–56
Cragg, Tony, 280–81
Craig, E. T., 225–27
craniology, 199
craniometry, 195–96
Crichton-Browne, James, 301, 303, 306
Criminal Man (Lombroso), 310–12
criminals: Lombroso on, 309–315; Moore and, 39–40; tattoos marking, 312; women as, 311–13
Cruz, Ted: evangelicals and, 29–30; Trump and, 30
Cuba, 353–54

Cullen, Jim, 241
culture-and-personality approach to anthropology, 174
Cynthia's Revels (Jonson), 329–30

Dale, Daniel, 319
Darnton, Robert, 10–11
Darwin, Charles, 310; Bell, C., and, 415n86; Crichton-Browne and, 301, 303, 306; divine intervention and, 301–302; Duchenne de Boulogne and, 297, 301, 303; Eliot, T. S., and, 308; *The Expression of the Emotions in Man and Animals*, 301–309, 416n115; Freud, and, 308; *Studies on Hysteria* and, 308
Daumier, Honoré, 285
Davies, John, 210
Davis, Emily, 369
de Chabrol, Ernest, 164
decision, Foster and, 45–46
Deford, Frank, 20
della Porta, Giambattista, 273, 274
Delsarte System, 318–19; Aesthetic Gymnastics and, 299; dance and, 300; Stebbins and, 298–300
Delsarte System of Expression (Stebbins), 298–300
Democracy in America (Tocqueville), 143–44, 154; American exceptionalism and, 164; anthropology and sociology in, 162–64; Cold War and, 159–60; conservatism and, 160; psychology of democracy in, 162; wealth in, 161, 163
deontology, 64
Derrida, Jacques, 382
Deutsch, Donny, 267
Diagnostic and Statistical Manual of Mental Disorders, *see DSM-5*
Dickens, Charles, 207, 323; *Sketches Boz*, 336–37
Diderot, Denis, 20
disassociation, 376
Disraeli, Benjamin, 132–33; *Vindication of the English Constitution*, 14
Domenici, Pete, 114
Domestic Manners of the Americans (Trollope), 153–54, 157–59
Donne, John, 307
Doris, John, 120
Douthat, Ross, 38
Dowd, Maureen, 28, 195
Down and Out in Paris and London (Orwell), 322
Dreamers (illegal immigrants brought to the U.S. as children), 180–81
DSM-5 (*Diagnostic and Statistical Manual of Mental Disorders*), 19, 261, 264; personality disorder in, 265–66
Duchenne de Boulogne, Guillaume-Benjamin, *292*, 317; actors and, 291, 294; Darwin and, 297, 301, 303; Duchenne smile and, 294; *The Mechanism of Human Facial Expression*, 288–90; orthography and, 289, 291; women portrayed, *293*, 294–97
Duckworth, Angela, 119
duty, 64

Earle, John, 333–34
eccentricity, 5, 153, 155
Economic Consequences of the Peace, The (Keynes), 183–84
education: English public schools, 78–79, 80, 119; girls' schools, 96–97
Edwardian period, 88, 90, 96, 99
Egan, Timothy, 30–31
ego: Freud, on, 250–51, 259; poor, 250; *see also* id; super-ego
Ekman, Paul: *Emotions Revealed*, 317–18; *Telling Lies*, 318; *Unmasking the Face*, 316–17
Elgar, Sir Edward, 136
Eliot, George: *Felix Holt*, 206–207; *Impressions of Theophrastus*, 347–48; phrenology and, 205, 206, 207
Eliot, T. S.: Darwin and, 308; *Notes Towards the Definition of Culture*, 171–72; Orwell and, 172; *The Waste Land*, 350
Emerson, Ralph Waldo, 60; "Character," 13–14; *The Conduct of Life*, 70; eccentricity and, 155–56; *English Traits*, 153–56, 188; on Jews, 188–89; physiognomy and, 315;

Emerson, Ralph Waldo (*cont.*)
Saturday Club and, 156–57; Smiles and, 13–14; on steam power, 72–73
Eminent Victorians (Strachey), 366
emotion: hormones and, 352; Kavanaugh and, 351, 352; menstrual cycle and, 357
Emotions Revealed (Ekman), 317–18
England: Brexit, 135–36; eccentricity and, 155–56; *English Traits*, 153–56; Hume on, 152; national character in, 152–56, 165–66; public schools in, 78–79, 80, 119; singularity and, 153; Victorian period in, 47
English Hours (James), 165–66
"English National Character, The" (Mill, J. S.), 153
English Traits (Emerson), 153–56, 188
engraving, 6
Epaminondas, 59
"Epistle to a Lady" (Pope), 360–62
"Essay on Physiognomy" (Töpffer), 284
Essay on the Constitution of Man and Its Relation to External Objects (Combe), 201, 233
Essays on Physiognomy (Lavater), 275, 277
ethics, 5, 6, 54, 112, 120, 296, 319
Ethics (Aristotle), 64
ethology, 71, 153, 198
ēthos, 7
Etiquette (Post), 344–45
eugenics, 275–76
European Union, 135, 136, 180
evangelicals, 28, 38, 39–40; Cruz and, 29–30
Evans, Mary Ann [George Eliot], 205–206
Every Man Out (Jonson), 328–29
evolutionary psychology, 231, 318
Expression of the Emotions in Man and Animals, The (Darwin), 301–303, 309, 416*n*115; blushing in, 307; *Hamlet* in, 305; *Henry V* in, 304; self-attention in, 306–307; *Titus Andronicus* in, 305
extravert, 173, 251, 261, 262
Eysenck, Hans, 251, 263
face book, 271
faception, 271
facial recognition, 315
Facing History and Ourselves (program), 117
Fairbanks, Douglas, 241, 409*n*1
Faludi, Susan, 34
Fanon, Frantz, 137
Farrell, John A., 35
Faust, Drew, 127, 128
Fava, Antonio, 330–31
Feezell, Randolph M., 21
Felix Holt (Eliot), 206–207
feminism, 34; Mansfield on, 368
FFM, *see* Five Factor Model
Field, Sally, 353
Fielding, Henry, 283
Fiorina, Carly, 272
fitness, 355–58
Five Factor Model (FFM), 263–64; traits of, 260–61
"Five-Factor Model in Fact and Fiction, The" (Gaines, McCrae, and Wellington), 263–64
flaw, *see* character flaw
Fleiss, Wilhelm, 19
Flynn, Michael, 36
fMRI (functional magnetic resonance imaging), 272; color and, 320–21; morality and, 320; phrenology and, 236–37, 238, 319–20; Poldrack on, 236–37
Follen, Charles, 200
football, 49; protests and, 48, 50; sexual abuse and, 51
football character test, 25
Ford, Henry: Henry Ford Museum, 395*n*134; *The International Jew*, 189; *McGuffey's Readers* and, 106
Fors Clavigera (Ruskin), 322
Foster, John, 45–46
Fowler, Lorenzo, 87; on amativeness, 214–16; *The Illustrated Self-Instructor in Phrenology and Physiology*, 213–16; practical phrenology and, 209–211, 408*n*111
Fowler, Orson, 87; on amativeness, 214–16; *The Illustrated Self-Instructor in Phrenology and Physiology*, 213–16;

practical phrenology and, 209–210, 408*n*111
Fox, Kate, 173
Frames of Mind (Gardner), 236
France: nationalism and, 136–37
Frances, Allen, 267
free will, 64, 70–71, 117
Freud, Anna, 253–54
Freud, Sigmund, 94, 183, 289, 416*n*114; Allport on, 255–56; anal eroticism and, 248–49; "Character and Anal Erotism," 19; character disorders and, 245, 266; character trait and, 19, 247–49, 265; character type and, 244–47; *Civilization and Its Discontents*, 185, 309, 416*n*116; Darwin and, 308; ego and, 250–51, 259; group psychology and, 184–85; *Group Psychology and the Analysis of the Ego*, 184; heroism and, 247; id and, 249, 250, 259; *The Interpretation of Dreams*, 240; Jews and, 185–86; "Libidinal Types," 259; *Moses and Monotheism*, 186; narcissism of minor differences and, 184–85; Oedipus complex and, 263; personality and, 249–51; personality psychology and, 254–60; popularization of, 243–44; "Psychopathic Characters on the Stage," 19, 246; psychopathological drama and, 246; "Some Character-Types Met with in Psycho-Analytic Work," 244–45; *Studies on Hysteria*, 308–309; super-ego and, 249, 250, 259
Friedman, Thomas, 35
Friedrich Nicolai, 278–79
Friesen, Wallace V., 316–17
Froude, James A., 12
functional magnetic resonance imaging, *see* fMRI
Fuseli, Henry, 277, 278

Gaines, James F., 263–64
Galileo, 105
Gall, Franz Joseph, 197; craniology and, 199; multiple intelligences and, 236; phrenology and, 220–21, 232, 236, 237; Spurzheim and, 220–21
Gally, Henry, 335
Galton, Francis, 315
Gardner, Howard, 196; *Frames of Mind*, 236
Gathorne-Hardy, Jonathan, 78
gender, *see* women and gender
gender dysphoria, 372
Gerson, Michael, 35
Gianakaris, C. J., 59, 60
Girl Guides: Baden-Powell, A., and, 98–99; Baden-Powell, O., and, 89, 99; *The Handbook for Girl Guides*, 98, 99, 370–71; marriage and, 98, 99; masturbation and, 98
girls' schools: games at, 96; slang at, 96–97
Girouard, Mark, 91, 96
Girton, 369
Giton (La Bruyère), 338; Allport and, 339–40; Barthes on, 341, 342
Glas, Norbert, 315–16
Glasgow Literary and Commercial Society, 391*n*25
Goffman, Erving, 379–80
Goldwater, Barry, 249
Gombrich, E. H., 282, 283, 284
good character, 6, 26, 52, 53, 65, 378; decision and, 45; Doris on, 120; Kavanaugh and, 350; New Zealand and, 53–54
Goodwin, Doris Kearns, 23
Gordon, G. S., 324–25
Gorer, Geoffrey: *The Americans*, 176; *Modern Types*, 345–46; *The People of Great Russia*, 175
Gould, Stephen Jay, 196, 236, 323; *The Mismeasure of Man*, 381–82
Greeks, 7, 59, 96, 152, 202, 246; tragic heroes, 17; *see also specific topics*
Greeley, Horace, 203
Griffin, F.W.W., 93–94
grit, 119–20, 396*n*162; character education and, 119–20, 396*n*162; Trump and, 119
Grit (Duckworth), 119
Grose, Francis, 359
group psychology: Bernays and, 412*n*97; Freud, and, 184–85

Group Psychology and the Analysis of the Ego (Freud), 184
Guthrie, William, 18
Gynt, Peer (Ibsen), 44

Halliwell, Stephen, 7
Hamlet (Shakespeare), 11, 46, 309; commonplacing and, 10; *The Expression of the Emotions in Man and Animals* and, 305; performing character and, 20; as psychopathological drama, 246
Handbook for Girl Guides, The (Baden-Powell, A., and Baden-Powell, R.), 98, 99; womanliness in, 370–71
Harding, Tonya, 51–52
Hargreaves, Roger, 346; Theophrastan characters and, 347
Harvard University, 123; A. Lawrence Lowell, 124, 125; diversity at, 127; Drew Faust, 127, 128; lawsuit against, 126, 128–29
Hazlitt, William, 23
Heart of a Champion, The (Deford), 20
Heath, Stephen, 372, 423*n*69
Hegedus, Chris, 26
Heidegger, Martin, 382
Hellman, Lillian, 140
Henderson, W. R., 233, 234, 408*n*107
Henry Ford Museum, 395*n*134
Henry V (Shakespeare), 148; in *The Expression of the Emotions in Man and Animals*, 304; mettle in, 358; national caricature and, 147
heredity, 5, 175–76; Lavater on, 275
Heresy Hunt character test, 25
Herodotus, 132, 165
Hitler, Adolf, 100, 101, 171, 186, 190–91
Hobsbawn, Eric, 142
Hofstadter, Richard, 167
Hogarth, William, 277; *The Analysis of Beauty*, 283–84; caricature and, 283, 284; physiognomy and, 284
Holbein, 277, 316
Holmes, Oliver Wendell, 157
homosexuality, 84, 94
House of Representatives (U.S.), 179
House Un-American Activities Committee (HUAC): Hellman and, 140; Hollywood and, 138–39, 398*n*24; Jews and, 140–41; national character and, 138–39, 140–41; Rankin and, 140–41, 142–43
Howe, Julia Ward, 200–201
Howe, Samuel Gridley, 201–202
Howells, William Dean, 156–57, 257
How to Be an Alien (Mikes), 166
How to Read Character (Wells), 218
HUAC, *see* House Un-American Activities Committee
Huckabee, Mike, 146
Hughes, Thomas, 75–77, 80
Hume, David: on the English, 152; international character and, 151–52; Jews and, 188; national caricature and, 150–52; "Of National Characters," 188

Iago (Shakespeare), 227–30
Ibsen, Henrik, 244, 246, 262, 263
ice skating, 51–52
id, 249, 250, 259; *see also* ego; super-ego
Illustrated Self-Instructor in Phrenology and Physiology, The (Fowler), 213–15; Philoprogenitiveness in, 216
immigrants: Dreamers, 180–81; European Union, 192; un-Americanism and, 143
Immigration and Customs Enforcement (U.S.), 315
impeachment: of Clinton, B., 115; of Trump, 23, 112, 383
Impressions of Theophrastus (Eliot), 347–48
Industrial Revolution, 72
Inkeles, Alex: American Creed and, 178–79; *National Character*, 177–78
Innocents Abroad (Twain), 166–67
Institute for the Formation of Character, 65; adult education at, 67; classes at, 66
international character: Hume and, 151–52; "The Internationale" and, 191; Jews and, 187–90; national character and, 190–91

"Internationale, The," 191
International Jew, The, 189
Interpretation of Dreams, The (Freud), 240
introvert, 93, 251

James, Henry, 165–66
James, William, 195, 238
Jane Eyre (Brontë), 203–204
Japan: Benedict and, 173–74; Buruma and, 176–77
Jeal, Tim, 88, 89–90, 97
Jefferson, Thomas, 143
Jeffress, Robert, 40
Jenkins, Malcolm, 50
Jesus, Life Coach (Jones, L.), 21
Jews, 127, 152, 180, 397*n*174; anti-Semitism and, 123–25, 186, 190, 397*n*174; Chesterton and, 189–90; Emerson on, 188–89; Freud, on, 185–86; Hume and, 188; international character and, 187–90; *The International Jew*, 189; Lombroso on, 314; national character and, 140–41; wealth and, 188, 189
Jones, Laurie Beth, 21
Jones, Rakeem, 138
Jonson, Ben, 419*n*19; *Cynthia's Revels*, 329–30; *Every Man Out*, 328–29
Jordan, Furneaux, 251
Jordan, Jim, 43
Josephson Institute of Ethics, 112
Jowett, Benjamin, 11
Judge, Mark, 350, 376–77
Julius Caesar (Shakespeare), 356–57
Jung, Carl Gustav: anima and persona and, 252; *Psychological Types*, 251; social character and, 253; on soul, 251, 252

Kaepernick, Colin, 49; Trump and, 50
Kant, Immanuel, 19
Karabel, Jerome, 123; *The Chosen*, 124, 125
Kavanaugh, Brett M.: character assassination and, 351, 352; character witness for, 350, 376–77; confirmation hearing of, 351–52; emotion and, 351, 352; good character and, 350; Senate vote for, 351–52; "That is not who I am" and, 376–77; Trump and, 352, 376
Kazin, Alfred: greatness and, 104; on politicians, 103; *A Walker in the City*, 102–103
Keats, John, 415*n*106
Kelly, Megyn, 357
Kernberg, Otto, 266, 411*n*85
Kerrigan, Nancy, 51–52
Keynes, John Maynard, 183–84
King James Bible, 353–55
King, Martin Luther, Jr., 57, 63
Klein, Joe, 31–32
knights, 95–96
Knox, John, 369
Koestler, Arthur, 168
Kohn, Alfie, 117, 121
Kramnick, Isaac, 161
Kris, Ernst, 280, 281, 282
Krugman, Paul, 27–28, 36, 134

La Bruyère, Jean de: Barthes on, 341–43; *Les Caractères*, 337–38, 340, 341; Giton and, 338, 339–40, 341, 342; Phédon and, 338–39, 341; Theophrastus and, 343–44, 420*n*46
Lack of Character (Doris), 120
Lady Gaga, 32–33
Lady Macbeth (Shakespeare), 22, 227; Duchenne de Boulogne and, 32; Hillary Clinton and, 293, 295–97
Landis, Kenesaw Mountain, 389*n*74
Lauder, Ronald S., 280
Lauer, Matt, 53–54, 390*n*87
Lavater, Johann Caspar, 273, 316, 413*n*15; *Essays on Physiognomy*, 275, 277; eugenics and, 275–76; on heredity, 275; national physiognomy and, 277–78; "One Hundred Physiognomonical Rules", 276–77; on pathognomy, 275; physiognomy and, 275, 310; on women, 276–77
Lavoisier, Antoine, 379
Lawrence, D. H., 359

leadership, 16, 123, 366, 367; admissions and, 123, 126–27; presidential, 26, 28, 29
Leahy, Patrick, 350–51
leakage emblems, 318–19
Leaves of Grass (Whitman), 217
Le Brun, Charles: passions of, 273–74; pathognomy and, 277; physiognomy and, 274
Lee, Bandy, 268–69
Le Pen, Marine, 136–37
Lessons from the 'Varsity of Life (Baden-Powell), 81
Levinson, Daniel, 177
Lewes, George Henry, 70, 205–206, 207
Lewinsky, Monica, 114
Lewis, Anthony, 400*n*64
"Libidinal Types" (Freud), 259
Lichtenberg, Judith, 12
Lieu, Ted, 143
likability, 353
Lincoln, Abraham, 38–39
Lindbergh, Charles, 138
Lion and the Unicorn, The (Orwell), 168–71
Lippmann, Walter, 12
Lipset, Seymour Martin, 179–80
literary character: Allport and, 255; children's literature and, 74, 106–111, 346–48; Darwin and, 304–306; Duchenne and, 295–96; Five Factor Model and, 262–63; Freud and, 19, 244–45, 254, 265; national character and, 193; phrenology and, 223; "real" character and, 44–46, 76, 280; "Theophrastan character" and, 322–48 *passim*; *see also* Shakespeare, William; and *names of individual characters and works*
Little Engine That Could, The (Piper), 73, 74
Lives of the Noble Greeks and Romans (Plutarch), 59
Locke, John, 10
Lockridge, Ross, Jr., 211–12, 217
locus communis, 10
Lombroso, Cesare, 86; *Criminal Man*, 310–12; on criminals, 309–315; on Jews, 314
Lonely Crowd, The (Riesman), 181
Longfellow, Henry Wadsworth, 61
Lowell, A. Lawrence, 124–25
Lowell, Robert, 364
Lycurgus, 94–95, 96
Lynch, Deidre, 336

Macaulay, Thomas Babington, 11, 53
Macbeth (Shakespeare), 121, 244, 272, 359; Lady Macbeth, 22, 32, 227, *293*, 295–97
MacIntyre, Alasdair, 47
MacKaye, Steele, 298
Macron, Emmanuel, 137
Mahler, Jonathan, 48
Main Currents in American Thought (Parrington), 160
"Make America Great Again," 132
making believe, 106; *The Wizard of Oz* and, 108–110
Manafort, Paul, 44
Man and the Ram, The, 273
Manchester Literary and Philosophical Society, 391*n*25
Mandler, Peter, 153
Mangan, J. A., 91
manliness, 119; *The Canterbury Tales* and, 363–64; knights and, 95–96; manning up, 373; Mansfield on, 368–69; money and, 373; Rhodes and, 364, 365–67; Robert Baden-Powell on, 90–92, 364; Robert Lowell on, 364; in *Scouting for Boys*, 90–92, 95–96, 119, 370; self-control and, 90, 92; sensitive men and, 368, 374; Victorian period and, 91, 125–26, 364, 365–66; women and, 91–92
Manliness (Mansfield), 368–69
Mann, Horace, 201
Mansfield, Harvey C.: on feminism, 368; *Manliness*, 368–69
marriage: Girl Guides and, 98, 99; Rhodes Scholarships and, 367
Mary Poppins (fictional character), 63
masturbation: Girl Guides and, 98; Griffin and, 93; *Scouting for Boys* and, 90–91, 370

McCain, John, 375; Trump and, 389*n*81
McConnell, Mitch, 41
McCormick, Hamilton: *Characterology*, 230–31, 274; personality and, 232; on phrenology, 231–32
McCrae, Robert R., 263–64
McCullough, David, 23
McDougall, William, 243
McGraw, John Franklin, 138
McGuffey, William Holmes, 105–106
McGuffey's Readers, 395*n*134; Ford and, 106
McLaren, Kenneth, 88
Mead, Margaret, 174, 176; *And Keep Your Powder Dry*, 175
Measure for Measure (Shakespeare), 23
Mechanism of Human Facial Expression, The (Duchenne de Boulogne), 288–90
Melville, Herman, 224–25
Menander, 324–25; Theophrastus and, 328
Merchant of Venice, The (Shakespeare): national caricature and, 148–50; Portia in, 18, 148, 149–50
Messerschmidt, Franz Xaver, 278–81, 297–98
method acting, 20
#MeToo movement, 53
mettle, 360; in *Henry V*, 358; horses and, 358–59
Mike Mulligan and His Steam Shovel (Burton), 73–74
Mikes, George, 166
Miles, L., 224
Mill, James, 381
Mill, John Stuart, 3, 65–66, 69, 198, 380–82; "The English National Character," 153; ethology and, 71, 153, 198; on free will, 70; *On Liberty*, 71–72; *The Subjection of Women*, 74–75, 362–63; *System of Logic*, 71
Milton, John, 122, 262
Mismeasure of Man, The (Gould), 381–82
Moby-Dick (Melville), 224–25
Modern Types (Gorer), 345–46
Montagu, Mary Wortley, 369
Moore, Roy, 35, 41; alleged criminal actions of, 39–40
moral character, 8, 25–26, 154, 269; honor and, 361; politicians and, 38, 39–40
moral reasoning, 105, 120
More, Thomas, 105
Morris, Wesley, 55
Moses and Monotheism (Freud), 186
Much Ado About Nothing (Shakespeare), 349
Muslims, 180

Nadar, Félix: 285–87
narcissism, 184; Trump and, 37, 267
narcissism of minor differences, 184–85
Narcissus, 94
national caricature: *Henry V* and, 147; Hume and, 150–52; *The Merchant of Venice* and, 148–50
national character, 132, 195; American exceptionalism and, 145–46; Brexit and, 135–36; cartoonists and, 166–68; defining, 133; English, 152–56, 165–66; HUAC and, 138–39, 140–41; Hume on, 150–51; international character and, 190–91; Japanese, 173–74, 176–77; Jews and, 140–41; *The Lion and the Unicorn* and, 168–71; McCarthy era and, 135; populism and, 192, 193; residual observations of, 133–34; of Russia, 175; scholars and, 172–73; social sciences and, 173–84; Tocqueville and, 144–45, 157–59, 165, 400*n*76; Trump and, 134, 138; un-Americanism and, 138, 141–42; U.S., 134, 138, 157–59
National Character (Inkeles), 177–78
National Character Counts Week: Clinton, B., and, 114–15; irony and, 111–14; Josephson Institute of Ethics and, 112, 113; Obama, B., and, 116; Reagan and, 111; Trump and, 41, 56–57, 110–12, 119

nationalism, 132, 193; American Dream and, 180; France and, 136–37; internationalism and, 190–91; Ireland and English, 136
Native Americans, 157–58
Nazis, 100
nerve, 349–50
Neville-Sington, Pamela, 159
Newbolt, Henry, 80
New Phrenology, The (Uttal), 237–38
New York Times, The, 31–32, 38, 41, 192, 193; Cohen and, 268, 331; Dowd and, 195; endorsed Hillary Clinton, 33; faception in, 271; Harding and, 52; headlines of, 24; Krugman and, 27–28; "Overlooked No More" series in, 63; Trump in, 35, 36–37, 195, 267, 268
New Zealand, 53–54, 390*n*87
Nicholson, Ian, 243
Nicolson, Harold, 78, 80
Nicomachean Ethics (Aristotle), 324; mean in, 8, 9; virtues in, 9
Night and Day (Woolf), 259
Nixon, Richard, 11, 12, 24, 317; Trump and, 35–36
Noonan, Peggy, 23
Nordau, Max, 86
North, Thomas, 59
Notes Towards the Definition of Culture (Eliot, T. S.), 171–72
Nye, Gerald, 190

Obama, Barack, 27, 191; American exceptionalism and, 146; likability of, 353; National Character Counts Week and, 116
Obama, Michelle, 30
Oedipus, 6, 17, 343
"Of National Characters" (Hume), 188
"One Hundred Physiognomonical Rules" (Lavater), 276–77
On Liberty (Mill, J. S.), 71–72
orthography, 289, 291
Orwell, George, 78, 185; *Down and Out in Paris and London*, 322; Eliot, T. S., and, 172; *The Lion and the Unicorn*, 168–71
Othello (Shakespeare), 271; Iago in, 227–30
out of character, 5, 373, 375, 376, 377–78
Outward Bound, 100
Overbury, Thomas, 332–34
Owen, Robert: "Address to the Inhabitants of New Lanark," 67, 69; character building and, 68, 102; character education and, 65–70; Institute for the Formation of Character of, 65–67; "The Principle of the Formation of Human Character," 66

Packwood, Bob, 41
Page, William Tyler, 179
Paradox of the Actor (Diderot), 20
Paris Peace Conference, 183
Parks, Rosa, 105
Parrington, Vernon, 160
passions: Aquinas and, 274; Cicero and, 274; della Porta, 273, 274; Le Brun, 273–74; women and, 361–62
Pater, Walter, 78–79, 96
pathognomy, 274; character heads and, 278–81, 297–98; Lavater on, 275; Le Brun and, 277; *see also* Duchenne de Boulogne, Guillaume-Benjamin
Pattern and Growth in Personality (Allport), 255, 324
Pelham, H. S., 88
Pennebaker, D. A., 26
People of Great Russia, The (Gorer), 175
perfection, 42–43
persona, 272; Jung and, 252
personality: Allport and, 232–33, 240, 242, 255, 257–58; Bernays on, 240; of celebrities, 258–59; character and, 19, 44, 232–33, 241, 256–57; culture-and-personality approach to anthropology, 174; FFM and, 260–61, 263–64; Freud, and, 249–51; McCormick and, 232; models, 221; psychoanalysis and, 19; in psychology, 241, 242–43; Roback and, 243; as sexual appeal, 260; television, 267
Personality (Allport), 232–33, 255

"Personality" (song by Johnny Burke), 260
personality disorders, 19; in *DSM-5*, 265–66; Kernberg and, 266, 411*n*85; Trump and, 267–69
personality psychology, 173; Freud, and, 254–60; Theophrastus and, 340
Peter Pan (Barrie), 89–90
Phédon (La Bruyère), 338–39, 341
philanthropy, 109–110
Philipon, Charles, 282
Philoprogenitiveness, 216
phlogiston, 379
Phrenological Journal and Miscellany, The, 226–30
phrenology, 65, 87, 239, 274, 382; amativeness in, 205, 212, 214–15, 216, 218, 232, 235; Bain and, 198; Bray and, 205, 207; Brontë and, 204; categories of, 221–24; Colicchio and, 234; *The Edinburgh Review* and, 200–201; Eliot, G., and, 205, 206, 207; Evans and, 205–206; fMRI and, 236–37, 238, 319–20; Gall and, 220–21, 232, 236, 237; Gardner and, 236; Gould and, 196, 236, 323, 381–82; Henderson and, 233, 234, 408*n*107; Howe G., and, 201–202; *Jane Eyre* and, 203–204; McCormick on, 231–32; Melville and, 224–25; organs in, 221, 222, 223, 235; Poe and, 224; Poldrack on, 236–37; practical, 208–211; self-help and, 236; Shakespeare and, 225–30; temperaments and, 220; theater and, 226; in Victorian period, 198; Wells and, 209–210, 218, 221–24; Whitman and, 197, 217–20; *see also* Combe, George
physical appearance: 21, 25, 137, 255, 273, 278, 315; Baden-Powell, R., drawings and, 84–86; caricature and, 282; Darwin and, 303, 306–307; Delsarte and, 298–300; fitness and, 355–58; gender and, 356–58; La Bruyère and, 338–39; Lombroso's criminal man and criminal woman, 309–314; national character and, 137, 140; *see also* Duchenne de Boulogne, Guillaume-Benjamin
physiognomy, 274; Aristotle and, 273; character heads and, 278–81, 297–98; Emerson and, 315; Glas and, 315–16; Hogarth and, 284; Lavater and, 275, 310; national, 277–78; religion and, 315; Töpffer and, 284–85; *Unmasking the Face* and, 316–17; *see also* Duchenne de Boulogne, Guillaume-Benjamin
Pickford, Mary, 241, 409*n*1
Pierpont, John, 200
Pillsbury, Michael, 195–96
Piper, Watty, 73, 74
Plomer, William, 365
Plutarch, 61, 62; *Lives of the Noble Greeks and Romans*, 59; Weems and, 60
Poe, Edgar Allan, 262, 263; phrenology and, 224
Poetics (Aristotle), 7
Poldrack, Russell, 236–37
politicians, 5, 23; Bruni on, 28–29; character actors and, 43–46; character attacks and, 28; character disorder and, 30–31; character flaw and, 7, 31–32, 34; character test for, 24–25, 26–27; Combe on, 405*n*38; discounting character and, 41–43; Kazin on, 103; leadership of, 26, 28, 29; moral character and, 38, 39–40; re-election of, 162; *see also specific topics*
Polonius, 93
Pont (cartoonist), 166
Pope, Alexander, 3, 17; "Epistle to a Lady," 360–62
Portia (Shakespeare), 18, 148, 149–50
Portraits in Miniature (Strachey), 340–41
Post, Emily, 344–45
practical phrenology, 208, 217; Combe and, 209; Fowler, L., Fowler, O., and, 209–211, 408*n*111; *The Illustrated Self-Instructor in Phrenology and Physiology*, 213–16; Shawnessy and, 212–13, 219; Wells and, 209–210

Presentation of Self in Everyday Life, The (Goffman), 379–80
Prince, Morton, 242
Princeton University, 123, 124
"Principle of the Formation of Human Character, The" (Owen), 66
Promise Keepers, 51
Propaganda (Bernays), 240, 270
Prose, Francine, 326
Proverbs 31:10, 353–55
psychoanalysis, 241; Anna Freud and, 253–54; character traits and, 18–20; Jung and, 251–53; personality and, 19; Reich and, 251, 253–54; Theophrastan model and, 323; *see also* Allport, Gordon; Freud, Sigmund
Psychological Types (Jung), 251
psychology, 175, 176; *Analysis of the Phenomena of the Human Mind* and, 381; commedia dell'arte and, 332; of democracy, 162; evolutionary, 231, 318; extravert in, 173, 251, 261, 262; Inkeles and, 177–79; introvert in, 251; Levinson and, 177; personality in, 241, 242–43; Theophrastan model and, 323
Psychology of Character, The (Roback), 242
"Psychopathic Characters on the Stage" (Freud), 19, 246
Punch, 166
Pygmalion (Shaw), 349

Quest of the Boy, The (Griffin), 93–94

Raintree County (Lockridge), 211–12, 217
Raleigh, Walter, 165
Rankin, John, 140–41, 142–43, 399*n*33
Reading the Face (Glas), 315–16
Reagan, Ronald, 23, 317; National Character Counts Week and, 111
Reich, Wilhelm: character analysis and, 254; *Character Analysis*, 251; character armor and, 253
Rejlander, Oscar, 303–304
Rhodes, Cecil, 123; manliness and, 364, 365–67
Rhodes Scholarships, 123–24; manliness and, 364–65, 366–67; marriage and, 367
Richard III (Shakespeare), 46, 244, 377
Ricks, Christopher, 415*n*106
Riesman, David: anxiety and, 182; conformity and, 181; *The Lonely Crowd*, 181; shame and, 181–82; social character and, 181, 183–84
Riviere, Joan, 423*n*69; on womanliness, 371–72
Roback, A. A., 254; personality and, 243; *The Psychology of Character*, 242
Roberts, Andrew, 135
Robeson, Paul, 69, 143
Roller, Emma, 43–44
Romans, 59, 62, 152, 186, 357
Romney, Mitt, 26
Roosevelt, Theodore, 80; "Character and Success," 81
Rorschach test, 174, 177
Rorty, Amélie, 326
Rose, Charlie, 54–56
Rosenberg, Alyssa, 41
Rosenberg, Charles, 197, 201
Rosenthal, Michael, 88, 393*n*75, 393*n*81
Rowlandson, Thomas, 285
Rubin, Jennifer, 27
Rubio, Marco, 29
Rumsfeld, Donald, 45
Ruskin, John, 322
Russia, 175
Rusten, Jeffrey, 324, 418*n*5

Sandusky, Jerry, 51
Sandys, George, 369
Sanford, Mark, 27
Saturday Club, 156–57, 400*n*64
Scaramucci, Anthony, 331
Scarborough, Joe, 38–39
Schiff, Adam, 23, 383
Schumer, Charles, 132
Scott, Sir Walter, 135
Scouting for Boys (Baden-Powell), 82, 88; chivalry in, 95–96, 370–71; drawings in, 84–86; drinking in, 93; feminine skills in, 97; knights

in, 95–96; manliness in, 90–92, 95–96, 119, 370; masturbation and, 90–91, 370; self-abuse in, 83–84; as self-instructor, 87; Sparta in, 94–96; women in, 91–92, 97
Searle, Ronald, 345, 346
Selden, John, 375–76
self-control, 90, 92, 211
Self-Help (Smiles), 12–13, 61, 87; sales of, 73
self-help industry: audience for, 16; character flaw and, 7–8; Christianity and, 15; leadership and, 16; phrenology and, 236
selfishness, 94, 221–22, 229
Senior, Jennifer, 35
Seton, Ernest Thompson, 97
sexual abuse and harassment: Cosby and, 55–56; football and, 51; Kavanaugh and, 350–52, 376–77; Lauer and, 53–54; Rose and, 54–56; Weinstein and, 53
Shakespeare, William, 44–45, 62, 118–19; Caliban, 18; female characters of, 17–18; Globe Theatre and, 410*n*37; *Hamlet*, 10, 11, 20, 46, 246, 305, 309; *Henry V*, 147–48, 304, 358; human nature and, 17; *Julius Caesar*, 356–57; lying and, 377; *Macbeth*, 22, 32, 121, 227, 244, 272, 293, 295–97, 359; *Measure for Measure*, 23; *The Merchant of Venice*, 18, 148–50; *Much Ado About Nothing*, 349; *Othello*, 227–30, 271; phrenology and, 225–30; *Richard III*, 46, 244, 377; *The Tempest*, 69; *Titus Andronicus*, 305; *The Winter's Tale*, 395*n*142
Shakespeare's Portraits Phrenologically Considered (Craig), 225–27
Shaw, George Bernard, 61; *Pygmalion*, 349
Shawnessy, Johnny, 212–14, 219
Silliman, Benjamin, 200
Sketches Boz (Dickens), 336–37
slavery, 22, 67, 157, 165, 235
Smeed, J. W., 323, 336
Smiles, Samuel, 90, 269; biography and, 61; *Character*, 12, 13–14; commonplacing and, 14; Emerson and, 13–14; *Self-Help*, 12–13, 61, 73, 87; on women, 14–15
social character, 181, 183–84; Jung and, 253
social media, 24, 134
social science: anthropology, 162–64, 173–77; Riesman and, 181–84; sociology and, 162–64, 176–81; *see also* psychology
social type, 47
Society for the Diffusion of Useful Knowledge, 67
sociology, 176, 181; in *Democracy in America*, 162–64
"Some Character-Types Met with in Psycho-Analytic Work" (Freud), 244–45
soul, 60; Allen on, 38; human nature and, 5–6; Jung on, 251, 252
Southey, Robert, 67
Sparta, 94–96, 132
Spivak, Gayatri, 382
Sport and Character (Clifford and Feezell), 21
spunk, 359
Spurzheim, Johann Gaspar, 197, 219–20; funeral of, 199–200; Gall and, 220–21; love and, 200
Stalin, Joseph, 145–46
Stanislavski, Constantin, 300
steam engine, 72; *The Little Engine That Could*, 73, 74; *Mike Mulligan and His Steam Shovel* and, 73–74; television characters and, 73
Stebbins, Genevieve, 298–300
Steele, Richard, 345
Stephens, Bret, 38, 39
Stephenson, George, 73
Stevens, John Paul, 351
Stevenson, Robert Louis, 93
Strachey, James, 247
Strachey, Lytton, 131; *Books and Characters*, 340, 419*n*12; *Eminent Victorians*, 366; *Portraits in Miniature*, 340–41
Studies on Hysteria (Freud), 309; Darwin and, 308

Subjection of Women, The (Mill), 74–75, 362–63
Suk Gersen, Jeannie, 126
super-ego, 249, 250, 259; *see also* ego; id
System of Logic (Mill), 71
System of Phrenology (Combe), 226

Tacitus, 132
TED talk, 119, 259
television personality, 267
Telling Lies (Ekman), 318
temperament, 269
Tempest, The (Shakespeare), 69
Tennyson, Alfred, 101
Texas Brags, 167
"That is not who I am": Kavanaugh and, 376–77; as proof, 377
Theophrastan character, 322–23, 332, 336, 348; Aldington and, 325–26; Hargreaves and, 347
Theophrastus, 281, 325, 337; Allport and, 340; Aristotle and, 323–24; Casaubon and, 419*n*28; *Characters*, 9, 324, 326–28; La Bruyère and, 343–44, 420*n*46; Menander and, 328; personality psychology and, 340; psychoanalysis and, 323
theory of humors, 335
"This is not who *we* are," 124, 378–79
"Thomas Jefferson and the Character Issue" (Wilson, D.), 21–22
Thoreau, Henry David, 12
thrift, 95
Titus Andronicus (Shakespeare), 305
Tocqueville, Alexis de: Académie Française and, 159; de Chabrol and, 164; *Democracy in America*, 143–44, 154, 159; national character and, 144–45, 157–59, 165, 400*n*76; political events and, 159
Toles, Tom, 34
Tom Brown's School Days (Hughes), 75–77
Tombs, Robert, 136
Töpffer, Rodolphe, 284–85
tragic flaw, 7, 245
transgender individuals, 372, 373
Trevithick, Richard, 73
Trollope, Fanny: critics of, 158; *Domestic Manners of the Americans*, 153–54, 157–59; Native Americans and, 157–58; slavery and, 157
Trudeau, Garry, 167
Truman, Harry, 45; Kelly and, 357
Trump, Donald, 26, 27, 33, 39, 192, 322, 375; *Access Hollywood* tape of, 40; Blasey Ford and, 352; Brooks on, 41–42; Bruni on, 28, 37–38; as character actor, 43–44; commedia dell'arte and, 331; congresswomen of color and, 143; craniometry and, 195–96; Cruz and, 30; on Fiorina, 272; grit and, 119; Hillary Clinton and, 268–69; impeachment and, 23, 112, 383; irony and, 111–12, 113–14; Jim Jordan and, 43; Kaepernick and, 50; Kavanaugh and, 352, 376; leakage emblems and, 318–19; lying of, 36; "Make America Great Again" and, 132; McCain and, 389*n*81; narcissism and, 37, 267; national character and, 134, 138; National Character Counts Week and, 41, 56–57, 110–12, 119; *The New York Times* on, 35, 36–37, 195, 267, 268; Nixon and, 35–36; personality disorder and, 267–69; protester violence and, 138; psychiatrists on, 267–68; soul and, 38; on transgender individuals, 372; Trump-branded clothing, 424*n*1; vanity of, 358–59; victory and, 35, 38
Trump, Melania, 113
Turner, Frank, 63–64
Twain, Mark, 166–67
Twitter, 352, 380; characters and, 6

Udall, Mark, 26
"Ulysses" (Tennyson), 101
un-Americanism, 138, 141–42; immigrants and, 143
Unmasking the Face (Ekman and Friesen), 316–17
Uttal, William, 237–38

Values Clarification movement, 113
Victorian period, 48, 54, 64, 72, 88, 96, 216, 308; chivalry in, 63;

Christianity and, 125–26; in England, 47; manliness and, 91, 125–26, 364, 365–66; phrenology in, 198
Vindication of the English Constitution (Disraeli), 14
"Vitaï Lampada" (Newbolt), 80
von Bismarck, Otto, 11

Walker in the City, A (Kazin), 102–103
Wallace, George, 104–105
Warren, Elizabeth, 34, 132, 269–70
War Room, The (film), 26
Washington, Booker T., 12
Washington, George, 17; cherry tree and, 58–59
Washington Post, The, 34, 38–39, 41
Waste Land, The (Eliot, T. S.), 350
Watching the English (Fox), 173
Watt, James, 72
Watt, J. J., 49
Wattenberg, Daniel, 32
Waugh, Evelyn, 403*n*155
Weber, Max, 133
Weems, Mason L., "Parson Weems," 58–59, 62; Plutarch and, 60
Wehner, Peter, 38, 267
Weiner, Anthony, 35
Weinstein, Harvey, 35, 53
Weiss, Bari, 356
Wellington, Marie A., 263–64
Wells, Samuel R.: *How to Read Character*, 218; on murderers, 223; practical phrenology and, 209–210; terminology of, 221–24
When I Was a Photographer (Nadar), 286–87
White, Andrew Dickson, 122
Whitman, Walt: *Leaves of Grass*, 217; phrenology and, 197, 217–20
Wicker, Tom, 23
Wilkinson, Will, 193
Willems, Mo, 395*n*137
Williams, Edgar, 366–67
Williams, Raymond, 133–34, 141
Wills, Garry, 139
Wilson, Douglas L., 21–22
Wilson, Edmund, 61; on Emily Post, 344–45
Wilson, Thomas, 419*n*28
Wilson, Woodrow, 11; American exceptionalism and, 182–83; at Paris Peace Conference, 183
Winckelmann, J. J., 278
Winter's Tale, The (Shakespeare), 395*n*142
Wittgenstein, Ludwig, 280
Wizard of Oz, The (film), 108; philanthropy in, 109–110; *see also* Baum, *the Wonderful Wizard of Oz*
Wolfe, Tom, 360
womanliness: Agnes Baden-Powell and, 371; Burrows on, 369–70; as depreciative, 369; in *The Handbook for Girl Guides*, 370–71; money and, 373; Riviere on, 371–72
women and gender: bold, 349; character education and, 62; character of, 360–63; criminals and, 311–13; Duchenne de Boulogne and, *293*, 294–97; "Epistle to a Lady" (Pope), 360–62; fitness and, 355–58; Lavater on, 276–77; likability and, 353; manliness and, 91–92; menstrual cycle, 357; mettle and, 358–60; mother and, 14; with nerve, 349–50; passions of, 361–62; Proverbs 31:10 on, 353–55; Rhodes Scholarships and, 367; Robert Baden-Powell on, 91–92, 97–98; Smiles on, 14–15; *The Subjection of Women*, 74–75, 362–63; Trump and congresswomen of color, 143; *see also* Girl Guides
Wonderful Wizard of Oz, The (Baum), 106–108, 109
Wooden, John, 50–51
Woolf, Virginia, 3, 165–66, 369; *Night and Day*, 259
Wright, Frances, 158
Wuthering Heights (Brontë), 262

Young, Arthur, 379

Zeit, Die, 180
Ziegler, Philip, 365, 366, 367

A NOTE ABOUT THE AUTHOR

Marjorie Garber is the William R. Kenan, Jr., Professor of English and of Visual and Environmental Studies at Harvard University. She is the author of several books on Shakespeare, including *Shakespeare's Ghost Writers* and *Shakespeare After All*, and of books on cultural topics ranging from dogs and real estate to cross-dressing, bisexuality, the use and abuse of literature, and the place of the arts in academic life. The recipient of a Guggenheim Fellowship, she is a member of the American Philosophical Society.